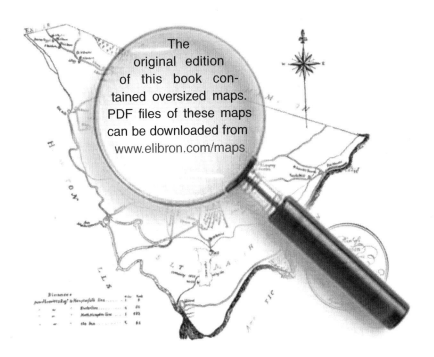

# SAMUEL SULLIVAN COX

# DIVERSIONS

## OF A

# DIPLOMAT IN TURKEY

Elibron Classics
www.elibron.com

# DIVERSIONS

OF A

# DIPLOMAT IN TURKEY.

BY

## SAMUEL S. COX,

*Late American Minister to Turkey.*

AUTHOR OF "BUCKEYE ABROAD," "EIGHT YEARS IN CONGRESS," "WIN-
TER SUNBEAMS," "WHY WE LAUGH," "FREE LAND AND FREE
TRADE," "ARCTIC SUNBEAMS," "ORIENT SUNBEAMS,"
"THREE DECADES OF FEDERAL LEGISLATION,"
"ISLES OF THE PRINCES; OR, THE PLEAS-
URES OF PRINKIPO," ETC.

---

"The wealth of shifting hues that lies
In Eastern Earth's unfathomed heart,
For every season's change supplies
A counterpart."

---

NEW YORK:
CHARLES L. WEBSTER & CO.
1893.

# PREFACE.

THE title of this volume indicates its scope and spirit. It has little to do with the art of Diplomacy. It is a Diversion because it turns aside from that esoteric art. Out of the channels of the diplomatic movements of Constantinople, and aloof from the cares and studies of the Author's ministrations in the East, it seeks to impart something of the relaxation, if not the amusement, which furnished the pastime of a sojourn of unequaled refreshment and entertainment.

The contrarieties of this experience furnish abundant sources of humor, to those who regard the essence of that subtle element as the inversion of human nature, in its outré and peculiar phases. How the observation of that human nature, under these strange conditions, affected the Author's own sense and associations, he has is these pages, assisted by the artist, essayed to portray. But it must be remembered that what would seem ludicrous, odd and funny to an American, might not seem so to an Ottoman, a Greek, an Armenian, a Bulgarian or any of the other Oriental peoples.

Constantinople is the capital of the Ottoman empire. It is an empire of vast dimensions. It is the seat of the central government. Its people are of every race and nationality. It has seventy odd dialects. It is composite beyond any other capital.

Upon these diverse races the Holy Ghost was outpoured at Pentecost. They were anciently governed by Roman and Byzantine rulers. This capital was, and is now, the genius of the Moslem faith, whose pulsations are potential in three continents. Even the distant regions now being opened in Africa, from Zanzibar to the mouths of the Congo, and from the Cape to the Atlas Mountains, feel the throbbing of this faith. It has affected and still affects the Hebrews in their wanderings and destiny. It has yet much to do with Christianity, as well by its rule over Palestine as by its control over the Churches of the empire. These wide relations give added interest to this remarkable city, its people and government.

Constantinople was the supreme seat of the ancient Christian councils, and the theatre of the most remarkable and wasting wars. Its changes are as startling as its sieges and romances. Its name recalls contests with the races of Greece and Central Asia, and with the chivalry which gave its glamour to the Crusades. Where is there a spot more vital with interest and glory?

Some of the chapters in this volume are dedicated to a description of the races which were once enlightened and the religion once expounded by Chrysostom, Gregory and Athanasius. Their candlesticks have fallen and their lights are extinguished. They need to be re-illumined. The efforts made by the Christian teacher and missionary will show how far this enlightenment may partake of its early splendor. The American missionary is foremost in this work. The West is supplying the East with the brightness of that torch which the East gave to the West many centuries ago. Along with the Living Word, which informs and inspires our better nature, is that subtle knowledge which the West is returning to the East concerning chemistry and other sciences. These elements of physical philosophy, which came out of the Orient, have a reflux, with ever-widening applications from the Occident, and are opening revelations beyond all the marvels of Arabic alchemy and astrology.

The first part of this volume concerns a sojourn of the Author among the diplomats of the Upper and Lower Bosporus, and his observations in and around the city.

The second part undertakes to deal with the ever-recurring Eastern question. Recent events in Asia, Africa and Europe, especially in Egypt, Armenia, Bulgaria and East Roumelia, give to this discussion an interest worthy of statesman-like study. I have eliminated from it all minor details, with a view to the general and permanent phases of the question as it affects the races and religions which have Constantinople as a centre and the horizon of the world as a circumference.

In a volume of this kind it is not intended to make either a diagnosis of the disease with which the Orient is said to be afflicted, or an analysis of the government which theoretically is almost perfect. The divisions of the empire for demonstrative purposes are, first, into vilayets, governed by a vizier. These are subdivided into sandjaks, each under the rule of a pasha. There are other subordinate divisions. There is much fluctuation in the political divisions of Turkey, but there is more of the old spirit of municipal freedom inherited from the ancient Arab, Greek and Roman rule than the political and speculative philosophy about Turkey recognizes. It is this spirit which gives permanency to government in the Orient.

While I am not prepared to say that the Turkish empire has been failing during the last three or four decades, yet if the reader will take the changes of two centuries, especially from the time when the Turkish power menaced Vienna, there has been a great declension. At the taking of Constantinople in A. D. 1453 the Ottoman empire had reached its acme. Those limits it can never reach again. Perhaps no country will ever boast, in our day, of such a quick and splendid conquest as the Ottoman made over the Orient, including the Balkans and the Danube.

Has the reader ever pondered upon what a wide jurisdiction the Sultan once exercised and what he still has ? It is upon the boundary line between three continents. Within its dominions are the most celebrated cities of classical and sacred history, or, at least, they have been comprised within this dominion. The sites of Carthage, Memphis, Nineveh, Tyre, Ephesus, Tarsus, Babylon and Palmyra; the cities of Alexandria, Jerusalem,

Damascus, Smyrna, Nicæa, Broussa, Athens, Philippi and Adrianople; and those other celebrated cities, Algiers, Cairo, Mecca, Medinah, Bassorah, Bagdad and Belgrade—all delivered their golden keys to the Sultan, as their Suzerain. The Mediterranean, the Sea of Marmora and the Black and Red seas saw the Turkish Crescent, and their waves were stilled before Turkish valor and seamanship. What mountains and ranges this empire comprehended! The Atlas and the Caucasus, Athos, Sinai, Ararat, Carmel, Taurus, Ida, Olympus, Ossa, Pelian and Haemus, and the Carpathian and Balkan ranges—these were, or are yet, a part of this remarkable realm. It embraced the most opulent and lovely regions of the world. It is full of historic memories, redolent of classical mythology and sacred to the memory of prophets and apostles who pursued their glorious paths through these vast dominions. And yet—and yet all bowed in the end before the nomadic Seljukian Turk, who came out of the recesses of Asia and elevated the Crescent and Star by his energetic zealotry in religion, his genius in polity, and his invincible force in war.

SAMUEL S. COX.

*New York, September 30, 1887.*

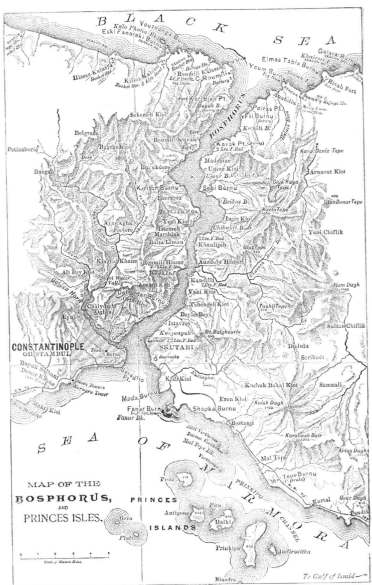

MAP OF THE
BOSPHORUS,
AND
PRINCES ISLES.

CITY OF CONSTANTINOPLE.

# DEDICATION

## PERMISSION.

To His Majesty Abdul Hamid II.,

*Emperor of the Ottomans, etc., etc.*

During nearly two years of sojourn at the capital of your empire I was not unobservant of its situation as a grand entrépôt of commerce as well as of its scenic enchantments. During that time, and while near Your Majesty as the American Minister, it was my special gratification to receive conspicuous marks of your friendship for my country, and I may add, if it please you, for my wife and myself. These evidences of your regard have followed me home and into another sphere of public life. Since my return to America I have often pondered over my reminiscences in the Orient. Among all their delights, none are more alluring than the recollection of the relation which I sustained at your capital.

I have observed the complex form of the government or governments of your empire, and admired the skill, vigilance and probity which you brought to bear in the reconciliation of all interests and the maintenance of your authority, not only as a civil ruler but as the head of the great Faith of the Orient.

In the following pages I have endeavored to do credit to my observation by never omitting to be just to your efforts for the maintenance of peace, and your forbearance and moderation in promoting harmony between other governments and your own.

I therefore have asked the privilege—so kindly accorded—of dedicating this volume to Your Majesty, as an evidence of the regard which I cherish, as well for your public virtues as for your private character.

I have the honor to be,

With the highest respect,

SAMUEL S. COX.

*New York City, September 30, 1887.*

Translation in Turkish

# CONTENTS.

|  | PAGE |
|---|---|
| PREFACE | v. |
| Dedication in English— } by permission— | vi. |
| Dedication in Turkish— } to the Sultan | vii. |

CHAPTER I.

Arrival at Constantinople ... 1–6

CHAPTER II.

Waiting for the Reception—Obsequies of General Grant—The Legation—Residence—The Salemlik Music ... 7–10

CHAPTER III.

Reception by the Sultan. ... 11–26

CHAPTER IV.

The Sultan at Prayers—Salemlik ... 27–35

CHAPTER V.

The Sultan in his Yildiz Kiosk—Presentation of American Books ... 36–45

CHAPTER VI.

Social Life at Constantinople—A State Dinner and Decorations ... 46–62

CHAPTER VII.

Diversion in America over Diplomacy in Turkey ... 63–75

CHAPTER VIII.

Compendium of Ottoman History ... 76–85

CHAPTER IX.

The Origin, Power and Fall of the Janizaries ... 86–95

CHAPTER X.

Salient Features in Ottoman Empire—French Influence ... 96–102

CHAPTER XI.

The last four Sultans—Incidents of their Reigns ... 103–111

CHAPTER XII.

The Latin Conquest of Constantinople........................ ...... 112–119

CHAPTER XIII.

The Capture of Constantinople by the Turks....................... 120–135

CHAPTER XIV.

The Upper Bosporus—Diversions at Therapia....................... 136–153

CHAPTER XV.

Possibilities and Actualities of Petroleum—American Interests........ 154–174

CHAPTER XVI.

Characteristics of Races and Classes in Turkey.................... 175–186

CHAPTER XVII.

The Jews of Turkey .......................................... ...... 187–207

CHAPTER XVIII.

Religions of the East—The Caliphate and its Consequences.......... 2c8–217

CHAPTER XIX.

Religions of the East—Moslem.................................... 218–231

CHAPTER XX.

The Orthodox Greek Church—Its Origin.......................... 232–255

CHAPTER XXI.

The Orthodox Greek Church—Its Architecture, Synods, Progress, Condition and Severance from Rome....................... .. 256–277

CHAPTER XXII.

The Latin Church—The Armenian-Catholic—The Armenian Gregorian Churches—Bulgarian and Other Churches............... 278–29ɔ

CHAPTER XXIII.

American Missions in Turkey—Their Magnitude—Obstacles and Rights 291–303

CHAPTER XXIV.

Turkish Language and Literature.............................. 304–314

CHAPTER XXV.

Turkish Wit and Humor........................................ 315–326

CHAPTER XXVI.

Stories of the East—Their Moralities............................... 327–347

CHAPTER XXVII.

Among the Cadis—Mahometan Justice—Humorous Illustrations..... 348–363

CHAPTER XXVIII.

The Dragoman's Story—"Which of the Two, the Bad or the Stupid Man?" ...................................................... 364–372

CHAPTER XXIX.

Diversions at the Legation...................................... 373–382

CHAPTER XXX.

The Lower Bosporus—The Cosmopolitan and Kaleidoscopic City— Scenes at the Bridge................................... ...... 383-401

CHAPTER XXXI.

The Caïques of the Bosporus.. ................................ 402–416

CHAPTER XXXII.

Dogs of Constantinople—A Canine Republic—Fights.............. 417–433

CHAPTER XXXIII.

Diversions in Pera............................................. 434–451

CHAPTER XXXIV.

Scenes and Diversions in Stamboul.......... ................... 452–472

CHAPTER XXXV.

Scenes and Diversions around the City of Stamboul............... 473–485

CHAPTER XXXVI.

Democratic-Republican Features in Turkey....................... 486–497

CHAPTER XXXVII.

Turkish Time—Fasting and Festal Days.......................... 498–511

CHAPTER XXXVIII.

The Harem—Innovations—Dresses and Incidents................. 512–529

CHAPTER XXXIX.

The Eunuch and other Incidents of the Harem.................... 530–540

CHAPTER XL.

Slavery—Its Conditions and Mitigations......................... 541–544

CHAPTER XLI.

L'enfant Terrible Turk—Education of Children................... 545–561

CHAPTER XLII.

Marriage of Moslems—Mahometan Marriages and Their Consequences 562–580

CHAPTER XLIII.

American Institutions in Turkey – Our Schools and Colleges......... 581–597

CHAPTER XLIV.

Contrariety of Opinion abo t the Fate of Turkey............ ...... 598–608

CHAPTER XLV.

Resources of Turkey—Taxation—Brigandage and Finances.... ..... 609–621

CHAPTER XLVI.

Is Reform possible in Turkey?—Railroads of the Empire in Existence
and Projected.............................................. 622–632

CHAPTER XLVII.

Oriental Problems—Prince Alexander and the Insurrection in Bulgaria 633–641

CHAPTER XLVIII.

Balkan Peninsula ; Roumania ; Servia—Preparations for fighting—
Greece—Its King and Queen................................ 642–657

CHAPTER XLIX.

Bulgaria and its Capital—Russia in the Conflict................. 658–666

CHAPTER L.

Fighting between Servia and Bulgaria—Prince Alexander.......... 667–675

CHAPTER LI.

Resignation as Minister—Return Home—Prince Ferdinand—Fresh
Events—Horoscope of the East—Conclusion....... ........ . 676–685

# LIST OF ILLUSTRATIONS.

Steel Portrait of Author...................................Frontispiece.
Map of the Bosporus............................................... ix
City of Constantinople............................................. x
Dedication to the Sultan in Turkish............................... xii
United States Summer Legation at Therapia......................... 5
Palace of Dolma-Bagtché........................................... 13
Gate of Dolma-Bagtché Palace...................................... 15
Sultan's Coachman ................................................ 16
Kiosk of Fhlamour ................................................ 17
Dwarfs of the Palace.............................................. 22
Garden and Palace of Yildiz....................................... 25
The Sultan's Favorite Steed "Ferhan".............................. 32
Hamal Carrying United States Census to Yildiz..................... 38
The Sultan's Kiosk at Yildiz ..................................... 40
A Moslem at Prayer................................................ 42
Cablakiai, or Food Carrier........................................ 51
Cuisinier, or Cook ............................................... 52
Legation Steam Launch *Sunset* off Prinkipo ...................... 65
Mehmet, The American Kavass ...................................... 69
A. A. Gargiulo, Dragoman of the United States Legation............ 71
The Minister's Four-Horse Act—an Ideal............................ 73
Girding on the Sword of Osman..................................... 79
Tombs of the Founders of the Turkish Empire, Osman and Orchan..... 81
Genealogical Tree of the Ottoman Rulers........................... 83
Aga, or Chief of the Janizaries .................................. 87
Commissary of the Janizaries ..................................... 88
Chief of the Janizary Chasseurs................................... 90
Arms of the Janizaries............................................ 92
Old Guns of the Janizaries ....................................... 94
Sultan Suleïman the Magnificent................................... 98
Roxolana, his best beloved Wife................................... 98
Sultan Abdul Medjid, Father of the Present Sultan... . ........... 108
Sultan Abdul Aziz, Brother of the Present Sultan.................. 109
Map of Constantinople at the Conquest............................. 112
Dandolo, Doge of Venice........................................... 117
Castle of Romoli-Hissar .......................................... 125
Bursting of Gun................................................... 130

Gypsies of the Bosporus .................................................... 144
Life-Saving Breeches.............................. ..................... . 149
Map of the Caspian Oil Region............................................ 155
Nymphs of Ancient and Modern Byzantium......... .................. ..... 160
The Hebrew Tinkering an American Petroleum Can.................... 162
A Bulgarian Woman................... ............................... 179
Albanian in Costume.................................................... 182
Circassians ..... ....... ............................... .......... 183
A Hebrew from Jerusalem............................................ 205
A Moslem Reading the Koran ....................................... 215
Dancing Dervishes .. ........ ..................................... 227
Fac-simile Signature of the Œcumenical Patriarch, Siméon I. A. D. 1474.. 254
Fac-simile Signature of Œcumenical Patriarch, Metrophanes III., A. D. 1567 258
Dionysius V., The Greek Patriarch—Recently Elected.. . ............. 271
The Armenian-Gregorian Patriarch—Monseigneur Vehabedian.......... 285
The Coat of Arms of the Washington Family.......................... 290
"Ghit!" With the Kavass........................................... 305
A Goose-Fight near Adrianople................. .. ............ 318
Scene from the Cadi, Chapter XXVII., Page 349...................... 318
King Solomon and the Queen of Sheba. ............................. 322
Pasha of Bagdad on a Spree........................................ 325
Hodja's Picture.............................. ...................... 334
Hodja Without his Latch-Key...................................... 335
The Hodja Sneezing in the Well................................... 339
The Hodja's Donkey on his Veracity ............................ 339
The Donkey's Ears and the Crazy Man............................. 346
A Modern Cadi ................................................... 348
Among the Cadis..... ....................... .................... 349
Turkish *Lex Talionis ;* or, Jumping on the Old Man ... ............. 355
The Donkey as a Detective.......................................... 359
The Worst Man in Turkey........................................... 366
The Stupidest Man in Turkey........................................ 368
The Sponge-Diver at the Legation................................... 375
Moussa Bey Buys a Bible .......................................... 379
Constantinople in A. D. 1632............... .... .................... 383
Four Separate Groups on the Sultana Validé Bridge of Different types, viz.:
*1st Group:* Tart-Seller;          *3d Group :* Zebeck from Interior;
         Arab from Mecca;                Circassian;
         Rug Pedler;                     Arab from Bagdad;
         Turcoman........... 391        Syrian Nomad...... 397
*2d  Group:* Turkish Woman from Mecca; *4th Group:* Ice-cream Seller;
         Armenian Family;                A Candy-Man;
         Woman and Slave from Saarit;    Water Pedler;
         Kurdish Woman from In-          Plate Merchant..... 399
         terior...........   . 393
The Mosque of Ortakeui and the Caïques. ........................... 407
Caïque at the "Sweet Waters" of Europe........................... 409
Ancient Galley.................................................... 415

Dogs in the Streets of Constantinople............................ 417
Donkey Riding in the Orient.................................... 425
A Dog Fight in Constantinople................................. 427
A Turcoman and his Bears..................................... 436
The Meat Seller and the Hungry Packs ......................... 447
The Burnt Column of Constantine.............................. 454
Bazaar Scene................................................ 460
The Turkish Cemetery at Scutari............................... 476
Tomb of Ali................................................. 479
"Sweet Waters" of Asia ...................................... 483
Group of Turkish Women at "The Sweet Waters."............... 484
Moon-Gazers Running for the Reward at Bairam................. 505
Interior Staircase of Dolma-Bagtché Palace..................... 507
A Turkish Lady of 1851....................................... 513
A Turkish Lady of 1887 ...................................... 516
Turkish Lady and Slave in the Harem........................... 518
The Muchoir Dance in the Harem .............................. 523
The Eunuch of 1887.......................................... 530
Turkish School Children....................................... 552
Turkish School Teachers....................................... 554
A Sum in Turkish Arithmetic.................................. 557
An Old Woman Looking for Brides in the Schoolroom............ 570
Dr. Cyrus Hamlin, First President of Robert College............. 584
The American Robert College.................................. 591
Turkey and the "Powers" Ready to Carve....................... 603
Bashi-Bazouks............................................... 617
The King and Queen of Greece................................. 655
Palace of Sophia—Bulgaria ................................... 661
Parliament Building at Sophia, Bulgaria ....................... 661
Prince Alexander of Battenberg, Prince Ferdinand of Coburg, the Czar
of Russia.................................................. 677

# CHAPTER I.

It is easier to do a thing again, than to do it the first time. This is a simple statement of a fact sometimes forgotten. Twice before my appointment as Envoy to Turkey, I had been to Constantinople. On the first occasion, in 1851, in life's morning, we, —*we*, I say—on a honeymoon—sailed thither in a French steamer up the Mediterranean. On the second occasion, thirty years afterwards, we traveled to Turkey from the land of the Midnight Sun. After visiting St. Petersburg, Moscow and Odessa, we crossed the Black Sea. We arrived in time to meet our then new Minister, General Lewis Wallace—of literary and military fame. Upon his staff, I temporarily served when the Minister was first presented to the Sultan.

Unlike our first voyage, the difficulty in reaching Constantinople in the year 1885 was at the start. There were strong bonds which attached us to our home and city, and myself to long-accustomed congressional life. Leaving the latter was a resignation more Christian than political. After the sumptuous Oriental banquet with which the people of New York honored me at the Hoffman House—a repast which had all the gravity of attraction and the levity of festivity—there arose other impediments. It was as difficult to leave the harbor as it was to obtain the consent of constituents. Then, in mid-ocean, among the icebergs of the banks of Newfoundland, the steamer of the Cunard line—the *Gallia*—broke her shaft, as if reluctant to bear us away. This incident may not be placed to the account of " Diversions." Our ocean voyage was nearly a score of days, when it should have been but half that time. Although we had not the full allowance of sea stores on board, we had the skill of mechanism, by which, after many days of anxiety, our shaft was patched up and the engine was again in motion.

The Fourth of July reached us when we were in sight of Ireland. That was a Diversion. Despite many sick days the writer had occasion to indulge his rhetorical jubilation. He endeavored to prove to his British cousins on board that our Revolutionary War was fought to assert the principles of the English constitution ; and that, in vindicating those principles, Great Britain was aggrandized by the magnificent secular growth of her successfully rebellious step-child.

Between Washington and Constantinople, forty days are allowed the Minister. Every one of these days was occupied, partly by the misadventure to the *Gallia*, and partly by reason of the earthly rest at London, Paris, Munich, Vienna and Buda-Pesth.

Many of the " Diversions " recorded in this volume were not simply produced by observation abroad, but by observations at home as to our movements. The cable seems to have been no unreluctant medium for remarkable stories. In this office it fulfilled one demand of humor, which may consist in retailing huge unveracities. For instance, the interesting intelligence was received in New York from London, that the United States Minister to Turkey left that city for Paris on his way to his new post in regal style, the railroad company having done him the exceptional honor of placing the royal salon at his disposal. Upon this announcement, the hundred-mouthed press made its commentaries: " Lo ! here is our President," said the journalist, "at Washington. Observe his habits. He rises from his shuck mattress at 4 o'clock in the morning. He works all day in his shirt-sleeves. He partakes of a frugal breakfast of mush and griddle-cakes. He lives so plainly that visitors cannot distinguish him from the janitor of the White House. Thus he sets a beautiful example of 'Jacksonian simplicity,' while this Minister to another Sardanapalus is speeding toward his post in a royal salon car, arrayed in purple and fine linen !"

Some journals called for immediate action. If such things continued, where would they stop ? The next thing would be that the Sultan would place, not only a royal salon, but a royal harem, at the disposal of this luxurious Minister of a Democratic Administration ! This pleasant prophecy was not fulfilled.

After a week's busy life in London, ten days in securing an outfit in Paris, two days at Munich looking at the breweries and foundries—which, in our callow conjecture, we took for palaces—three days at Vienna, where we saw the " Flying

Dutchman" of Wagner, and two days in Buda-Pesth, the superbly situated capital of Hungary—where an exposition was going on, of rare interest—and one day in Varna, on the inhospitable Euxine, and a night on the steamer from Varna—we arrive at Cavak, the fortified mouth of the Bosporus. It is a rough sea-journey, but when daylight dawns we see the house of our Consul, with our flag flying over it, at Therapia! We almost renew our former Turkish *kef* and say, "Well, at last, we are here to rest!"

No student, no man, can approach the city of Constantinople —the confines of Christendom—without peculiar sensations. These are not aroused merely by the novelty of the scenes and the strangeness of the costumes: the memories which are ever associated with the land upon which he enters invest the capital of the Orient with a mystic romance unknown to the Occident.

But a new and patriotic experience awaits us before we land. The captain of our Austrian Lloyds vessel raises the star-spangled flag, in honor of our country and the Envoy. Soon we sight the launch which Congress had voted. It flies the starry ensign.

The name of the Lloyds vessel is the *Uhland.* Its captain's name is John Mizzekinovnichvich. He is a Dalmatian of fair renown; and, like all Austrian subjects who take to the sea from the Adriatic, he has a magnificent physique. Besides, he speaks, as do all captains of the Lloyds, the English language. But who could or can speak his own sesquipedalian name in our tongue?

If I have made any mistake in giving our captain his proper name properly, it is because my orthography was not thoroughly cultured by my Dalmatian servant, Pedro.

Nothing eventful happened on our journey overland to the Black Sea. There were some embarrassments *en route* connected with the numerous boundaries and their Custom-houses. We were not on the overland train, which runs through in four days from Paris to Constantinople, although at first we intended to make that disposition of ourselves. Stopping at the cities named compelled us to undergo the experience of local travelers. In crossing the boundary line between Hungary and Roumania I was nonplussed, for I learned that our trunks were not on board. They were coming through by the express. In that baggage was my special passport, after which the officers of the customs were in quest before allowing us to go on. I had made a mistake in packing my carpet-bag. I took with me my commission as Envoy, signed " Grover Cleveland," and countersigned by " T. F. Bayard," instead of my passport. But what did it matter to a customs officer who could read neither passport nor commission ! I displayed my commission with its large eagle, its stars and its legend. Its text authorized me to perform all matters as to the office, and the said office to hold and exercise. To my surprise, the officer took the commission and bore it away. I never expected to see it again. How could I present myself to the Sultan ! It was my only credential. At length, to my relief, the officer returned with it. He had had it viséd by the stamp of the Roumanian agent, Ul Vamal. I had better luck on my return home through Roumania, when we stopped at its capital, Bucharest. There I had the good fortune to meet Sir William White, who had been my colleague at Constantinople during the Conferences. We remained at Bucharest a day. While there we received a pressing invitation to visit the King and Queen, the latter known as the accomplished Carmen Sylva, and the promise of hospitality and a dinner at Sanaii—their superb home in the Carpathian Mountains.

Without further passport incident or Custom-house Diversion we reached the mouth of the Bosporus at daylight. We had breakfasted, and were ready for *pratique.* Soon we pass through the gates—the supposititious gates—which keep all foreigners out of the Bosporus, unless with the consent of the Sultan. We reproduce the olden memories of our trip down the Bosporus six years before. After reaching the city, or, rather, the harbor, we embark upon our launch. After many greetings we steam back upon our course, some dozen miles, to Therapia.

We had already made arrangements with our lamented Consul, Mr. Heap, to unite the Legation with the Consulate at our Therapia home. Among the other friends who came to greet us was our former guide, the Greek Dionysius. Many of his wonderful stories had already produced their impression, and had vanished like writing in water.

The first week was passed in watching the wierd and witching water-way of this most wonderful Bosporus in its mid-summer robe, with its banks of verdure, its palaces of marble, and, above all, its luxurious ease and its relief from the discomforts of summer.

The day we landed, the Sultan's Foreign Minister, Assim Pasha, sent a messenger to tender us a cordial welcome. He prepared an audience with the Sultan, whose aide-de-camp came the day after our arrival, to greet us on behalf of His Majesty. Such greetings are compensation for the Diversion of

UNITED STATES SUMMER LEGATION AT THERAPIA.

those at home at our expense, and make up for the exile from old friends.

The home in which we are ensconced for the summer has one window looking out over terraces extending upward three hundred feet. This garden is leafy and green in the moist warmth from the waves below us. Its roses, magnolias, heliotropes, jessamine, Virginia and other creepers, make an exquisite picture. Out of another window there is a prospect of the hills of Buyukdere—one of the beautiful villages of the upper Bosporus, where my colleagues of many Legations reside. The *clappotage* of the waves against the stone quay almost under our window lulls one into a poetic swoon. Thus the first week passes by.

My predecessor, General Wallace, had to wait fifty days before his reception. Such occasions are frequently postponed, for reasons that appear strange to American etiquette, which soon admits to these diplomatic welcomes. My delay was not more than thirty days. The United States ship of war *Quinnebaug* happened to be in the Bosporus at that time, and its officers were anxious to be presented to the Sultan. As I had some experience in this business along with General Wallace, we made every arrangement for a good company, which should attend upon the Reception.

# CHAPTER II.

THE time spent in waiting for the reception by the Sultan is
passed in voyaging up and down the Bosporus, and in making the
diplomatic courtesies. We enjoy the courtesies, the Euxine
breezes and sights which belong to these extraordinary waters.

In the middle of August comes the sad news of the death of
General Grant. On the 16th of August the American colony
meet at the Consulate, together with a large attendance of ladies
and gentlemen of other nationalities. The officers and men of
the *Quinnebaug*, then undergoing repairs in the Golden Horn,
attend also. All pay such tribute to the memory of the ex-
President and soldier as was fitting his fame and virtues. The
occasion was the means of bringing the Minister near to many
with whom he was afterwards associated. The venerable Doctor
Wood presided. Many of the professors of Robert College were
there. Hobart Pasha, the Admiral of the Turkish fleet, and
whilom blockade-runner in our civil war, then in full life, added
his expressions of sympathy. Rustem Pasha, the present Turkish Minister at London, wrote to say how sincerely he associated
himself with the sentiments of grief felt by the American people
for the loss of their great citizen. The Minister was then called
on to do his first duty—alas! a melancholy one—in eulogy of
the deceased.

As General Grant was from my native State of Ohio—the home
of the Shermans, Sheridans, McPhersons and McCooks of our
conflict—it was my special pride to be known in Congress as his
devoted friend, perhaps next in that body to Mr. Washburn, of
Illinois. It was my privilege, just before the close of the war,
when Grant's army was before Petersburg and Richmond, to be
the General's guest; and just before leaving Congress I had the
honor to introduce the first bill to re-instate him in the army.

This relation gave me the privilege to speak with emphasis of the eventful life which had just closed, and in which cloud and sunshine so strangely alternated. May I be permitted to quote what I had occasion to say in that far-off country, concerning some personal reminiscences, as well as General Grant's public services?

"Does not our American pulse beat stronger, and our patriotic love grow warmer, by the contemplation of the character of such an American? If in life he was such a lever of power, in death his grave is the fulcrum of that reserved force which, in our future battles for law and liberty, will be felt as that of no other American, unless it be Washington and Lincoln!

"We read of the meetings of czars and emperors to determine questions of territory and state; we hear of the marriages of princes and princesses, and of efforts for the permanency of dynasties; but far more significant and illustrious is the departing splendor of this evening orb of the Western Hemisphere. Modest magnificence, unassuming pomp and sturdy strength—what qualities to allure other people to America as the cynosure of their hopes and happiness!

"Is it not fit, in this Oriental land, far from the sympathetic contact of our fellow-countrymen at home, that we, as Americans, should echo their sad refrain over the loss of our chiefest chieftain?

"The custodians of his fame are not only upon the Hudson and the Potomac: they are here also upon the Bosporus. His deeds belong no less to the North and South of our own land than to the remotest East and the farthest West of our planet. He belongs to all; and although with half-masted flag and mourning drapery, with muffled drums and wreaths of ivy and laurel, he is borne to his sepulchre upon the beautiful heights near our great metropolis, yet the heritage of his renown is not theirs nor ours only: it is the property of mankind. The East melts into the West and the West into the East before its brilliancy. It has no horizon. In every army, in every land, aye, among the hosts of the silent armies of our own land which have preceded him to the unseen bourne, there is a bivouac of the dead around his tomb, and a cordon of sentinels keeping eternal ward over his glory.

"The Epic Muse has sung of the heroes of these classic and romantic shores. Troy is within the jurisdiction of the Ottoman. Greece still peoples these lands. Jerusalem and its holy places are not unrealities to us. Here is the historic home of Homeric heroes. The Paynim and Christian, knightly Saladins and chivalric Geoffreys, and more recently captains of modern armies, have met in deadly encounter to aggrandize power, reconstruct boundaries, glorify patriotism, or vindicate faiths. Their deeds 'in majestic cadence rise and fall' to the music of lucent waters, under the bluest of skies and the most witching of associations. Nowhere else have there been sung sweeter lyrics or grander epics in honor of men of war and men of peace. Here the Iliad and the Odyssey rose to the swelling of the voiceful sea, but no strain of poetry, no burst of eloquence, has ever given to the holy air of the Orient a name more revered, a patriotism more exalted, and sacrifices more pure than those which are symbolized in the laurel wreath and civic crown upon the dismantled domestic altar of the soldier, statesman and man—Ulysses S. Grant!"

How soon one sad event follows another ! The year had not closed before, in a mournful procession, there was announced the deaths of General McClellan and Vice-President Hendricks, to both of whom I was personally attached from old associations. Then followed the death of General Hancock. It seemed as if, to the exile from home, there was added the poignancy of these fast-coming, regretful memories. And yet how soon such clouds are lifted, under a sky like that of the Bosporus ! Here, in the midst of *death*, we are in *life !* Many a vivid incident served to distract the mind from its bodings.

As the summer passes away, we fill its days; sometimes with excursions to the Giant's Mountain. Sometimes in our launch we cross to the Asiatic shore, or run up in our caïque where the " Sweet Waters " are situated. On Fridays we cross the Straits, and mingle with the throngs on the meadows near these " Sweet Waters," where thousands of Turkish women and children disport themselves, or enjoy their domestic picnics in groups under the shadows of the sycamores. The Bosporus is the same as of yore —renowned for more than two thousand years for its fish. We drop the line in its waters within a few feet of our own door. We catch the little shiners from the clear depths. They are both toothsome and beautiful. In our promenades, followed by our stately and obese Kavass, we pass up and down the quays, receiving the salutations of the soldiers of the barracks, or wander over the hills safe from all intrusion or fear. Everyone in the neighborhood of Therapia vies with each other in hospitality and courtesy.

The summers upon the Bosporus are prolonged late into the fall. Many of the Ministers and other residents upon the upper Straits never leave their country homes until the autumn winds sharpen in November. Then the walls of the gardens are festooned with vines tinted warm and red with the advancing season. They add a rich sheen to the beauty of departing summer.

We move to the city about the first of November. We had already organized the Legation under one roof. Our new quarters are comfortable. The rooms have such an unusual, sprightly and elegant aspect as to astonish the tourist and confound the economic State Department. The Legation rooms are near the Royal Hotel, where we lodge. Having taken a full suite on the second floor of the hotel, we have a splendid outlook, not only over the

Golden Horn, with its bridges and boats, and Stamboul, with its domes and minarets, but far beyond, over the Marmora Sea to the mountains of Asia, among which the Mysean Olympus shows conspicuous and pre-eminent.

From our rooms, every Friday noon, we are reminded of the Salemlik ; for passing up our rue—Petits-Champs—there marches a regiment with a band discoursing music, whose tones, half Oriental, mingle in strange symphony the wierd, barbaric wailings of the bagpipe with the round swelling bursts of more æsthetic instrumentation.

# CHAPTER III.

ALTHOUGH familiar with public life, its receptions and glamour, and although I had a peculiar opportunity as the extemporized attaché of General Wallace in 1881, when he was presented to the Sultan, still I experienced considerable tremor in relation to my own reception. After being advised by telegraph from Munir Pasha, the First Chamberlain, of the day fixed for the ceremony, and advised again of its postponement, and then, as is the custom, of another day being fixed, the anxieties were enhanced. Besides, had I not been informed by the initiated that I was expected to furnish my speech to His Majesty in advance, or, rather, through the Minister of Foreign Affairs, that it might be investigated, or, rather, read between the lines, so that nothing offensive should be said or suggested? According to the rule, the speech, in both the French and English text, is sent to the Foreign Minister. I need not say that it was short. It was the "greatest effort of my life," and laboriously I worked at it. The labor consisted in its abbreviation. Accustomed to the five-minute rule in Congress, I was cautioned that it would be wiser to make the speech even shorter than five minutes, if possible. I had more difficulty about the French than the English portion. For the benefit of callow diplomats, and as my colleague, Mr. Fearn, sought for it as a model at his audience with King George of Greece, I modestly transcribe it herein:

"YOUR MAJESTY:
"It is my special delectation to present from my Government the letters of the President of the United States which accredit me as their representative near your Majesty.
"Without indulging in any personal retrospect, in which are associated many early and recent memories of a charming sojourn in your superb capital, and of instructive travel in your historic country, and without indulging in any formal and unnecessary protestations as to the past and future relations between the Ottoman Empire and the States of the Federal Union, it is my pleasure to say, that, by inclination, interest, tradition, friendship and jus-

tice, there can be no other than relations of comity and kindness between the respective nations.    The United States would not, if they could, depart from the invariable policy which forbids all *entanglements* in foreign affairs, a policy which has signally marked our intercourse, and which has preserved from stress and severance, amidst all vicissitudes, our relations with other Powers.

"It is personally gratifying that I am enabled to follow a predecessor who has established satisfactory relations with your Majesty.    It will be my hope to be allowed to share in the good-will extended to my friend and predecessor.

"It is a delightful duty to assure your Majesty that it will be my endeavor to continue and increase (if possible) the cordiality of those ties by which the two great nations of the Orient and Occident are so happily imbound."

This speech caused me barrels of perspiration ; yet one word in the translation became almost a *casus belli*.    It was the word "entanglements."    I translated it *enchevêtrements*.    I had in my mind Washington's Farewell Address as to all foreign entangling alliances.    There is no synonym for the idea in French, except the word which, after much research, I had selected.    Nor is there in that polite tongue any compounding of syllables, as in the German.    My "entanglement" might be rendered as, for instance, a colt with a halter, a very interesting though by no means an exalting allusion.    When my French speech was scanned by the leading linguist in the Foreign Office in Stamboul, assisted by a cohort of polyglots, they lit upon the words *enchevêtrement*.    What could it mean?    Was it an American torpedo, or polysyllabic dynamite for the overthrow of the dynasty?    Whatever might have been their opinion of the explosive and perilous composition, I was satisfied, from intimations, that the delay of my reception for some days was occasioned by the confusion incident to this terrible six-footed word.    I felt, however, compensated for my linguistic pains, by laying the anxiety upon the altar of of my country, and kindling its patriotic flame with the "Farewell Address."

The speech was finally accepted in the sense in which it was intended, and thenceforth the respective countries never ceased to dwell together in diplomatic unity.    My apprehensions had been quickened when I remembered the august presence in which my personality was officially to appear ; for Turkey is, in a diplomatic way, among the most interesting of the Powers of the earth.

The past, present and future seemed to be concentrated in

the journey down the Bosporus, whose termination in the Reception was to be under such novel and happy circumstances.

As this volume is a record of personal reminiscence, it may not be accounted egotistic if I describe the subjectivity as wel. as the objectivity of the unusual situation.

I had but a few months before left a forum in which a quarter of a century of service had made a "property of easiness." After many wanderings between my native Ohio, my official home at Washington, and my adopted home—"no mean city"— New York, and after divers travels between America, Asia, Africa and Europe, I was about to become an official fixture

PALACE OF DOLMA-BAGTCHÉ.

amidst most romantic surroundings. I was about to meet, in most unrepublican fashion, the ruler of forty millions of people and the Caliph of two hundred millions. The Bosporus, the Seraglio Point, the silent gesture of the minarets, the marbled palaces, and the very uniforms and languages on every side, gave to the expected reception a bewildering delight. The bright blue of the summer skies, the rolling hills of the Asiatic shores, and the perpetual movements of the waters, with their strange craft, their restless birds, sportive dolphins, and peculiar people, added their thrilling sensations.

We start out from Therapia bravely. The white kerchiefs of

the ladies from the Legation balcony wave us their encouragement. The flag fairly snaps in the Euxine wind ; and the gilded eagle of the launch seems to protrude his beak, as if showing the anxiety and excitement of the hour. I am accompanied by the Consul-General, Mr. Heap—now no more—Professor Grosvenor, of the Robert College, and the officers of the Legation, including the Kavass.

We are to land at the marble quay of the Dolma-Bagtché palace —the incomparable structure of the world ! A description of it may not be uninteresting at this very point, for it is a part of the *mise en scene* of the performance : It is situated on the Bosporus. It is about two miles from the port of Constantinople. Its park is surrounded by a wall twenty feet high. Its gates are of white marble, and fit to open to the popes and rulers of the earth. They are superb in decorations of gilt and tracery of beauty.

This palace was built by Sultan Abdul Medjid. He was the father of the present Sultan, and a rare man and statesman. The road from Dolma-Bagtché to Yildiz follows the shore of the Bosporus, though one cannot see the stream through the village of Bechïktash. This name, when translated, means " stone cradle." All Turkish names of places mean something substantive. Here we turn to the left over a very well paved though steep and winding road. This road brings us, after much meandering, to the palace of Yildiz. The view from this high ground and palace is superb. Below us the rapid, blue Bosporus flows between the green and beautiful shores of Europe and Asia. It then washes the classic Seraglio Point, where so many of the Sultan's ancestor's wives and friends lived and died. The outlook over the rolling hills of Asia is entrancing, and this day we could plainly see Mount Olympus, in Asia, rising to the olden fame of its Greek namesake—as the superb guardian of Troy in her embattlements. But let me not anticipate.

We are received in cordial and courteous state, at the landing of this palace of Dolma-Bagtché, by the *Sous Introducteur des Ambassadeurs*—Ghelib Bey. He is in gay, gilt uniform. He speaks French with facile grace. We are then ushered by him into a waiting-room. There we find the commander of the United States steamship *Quinnebaug*, Captain Ludlow, who has with him seven of his staff, viz., Lieutenant Sperry, Lieuten-

ant Sturdy, Doctor Tryon, Lieutenant Fletcher, Lieutenant
Dickens, Chief Engineer Allen and his assistant. These officers
are in full uniform. They look brilliant beside the Minister in
his plain suit of black. Mr. Emmet, Chargé ; Mr. Gargiulo, the
interpreter ; Mr. Bigelow, the Marshal of the Consular Court;
and Mr. Demitriades, assistant to the Consul—these officers are
on hand in evening toilet. They are the Legation and Consular
officials. They have seen much service here at this venerable
capital.

GATE OF DOLMA-BAGTCHÉ PALACE.

After some talk, coffee and cigarettes we are driven,
slowly and majestically, as becomes those who are to be introduced into the presence of the Padishah of all the
Ottomans. Our vehicles are wonderful in their apparel of gilt
and satin, and superb in manufacture. They are the palace carriages. They are drawn by gigantic horses, and driven by solemn
Turks covered with gold lace, one of whom is pointed out as the
Sultan's coachman. I am happy in the possession of his portrait, which is here presented. On the way we pass in view the

beautiful kiosk of Fhlamour.  We are not now permitted to see
its interior; but if the interior be the counterpart of its exterior
grace and beauty, there cannot be found on our earth a structure
so elegant and attractive.  I make no apology for its presentation in the picture on the subsequent page.

Ten minutes, and we are at the gate of the small but beauti-
fully situated palace of Yildiz.  This favorite palace is built on
the summit of a high hill, in order, it is said, to prevent any

SULTAN'S COACHMAN.

sudden surprise from the foes of the Sultan.  But under present
auspices this is an unnecessary precaution.

The Bosporus in front of Yildiz is two miles broad.  It runs
about a mile below the palace.  There it melts into the Sea of
Marmora.  Yildiz in Turkish means "Star."  It is the star which
glitters between the horns of the Crescent.

Evidently we are expected.  All are on parade or guard.
America may be far away, but her abstinence from Eastern

KIOSK OF FHLAMOUR.

complications gives her a moral and near power.   Her modesty and remoteness make her all the more respected.

A guard of honor of 100 men is drawn up at the entrance to the palace.   The Minister leads the company in his carriage. He is followed by the others.   He is frequently saluted by soldiers along the route.   When he arrives at the palace he is met by Ibrahim Bey, who is one of the handsomest men of the Eastern type.   He escorts the Minister into a reception-room.   There we meet Osman Pasha, the hero of Plevna.   He is Minister of War, as well as Marshal of the Palace.   He talks with the Minister about General Grant, and anxiously asks after the children and widow of the General.   The Minister is met by Assim Pasha, Minister of Foreign Affairs, and by other officers of high rank and distinction.   The ovation evidently surprises the Minister. It is unusual and hearty.   Then again we have coffee and cigarettes.   The coffee is served in cups covered with diamonds. They are too beautiful to be discussed.   We are then waited upon with even more than Eastern courtesy.   Shortly after, we are shown up a broad stairway, over costly carpets which we have observed inside and outside.   The stairs are lined on either side by palace officials.   These dignitaries and officers are in strange contrast with the Minister and his suite.   Even the officers of the American man-of-war do not display in all their effulgence the elegance of the Pashas, chamberlains and other officials who meet us at the palace entrance.   We are conducted within, walking on Smyrna carpets of rare design.   We begin to look about us, as we feel more at home.   We take a mental inventory of the aspect of the Yildiz interior.

After crossing a spacious hall paved with marble, we are ushered into another reception-room.   A large divan is at one end, and chairs all round the walls.   The furniture is covered with red damask.   In the middle of the room is a marble table.   On this is placed a large silver candelabra for sixteen candles. Facing the divan is a pier-table supporting a large clock.   This clock is of silver.   Two magnificent Japanese vases are on each side.   The floor is covered with a priceless Smyrna carpet. Everywhere—in palace or in mosque—the carpet plays a principal part in Turkey and in the East.   Osman Pasha, Assim Pasha, Munir Pasha and other palace officials, who are not unknown to fame here and elsewhere, are in this enchanted chamber when we enter. Munir Pasha is an old friend of the American Minister. In fact, he chaperoned us when we were visitors in General Wallace's time. Munir leaves the room for a moment. He returns, announcing that His Imperial Majesty is waiting to receive the Minister. There is a rattling of *Quinnebaug* swords and a rise in gold lace. Then we proceed up a broad and elegant staircase in the following order : The American Minister is between the Minister of Foreign Affairs and the Grand Master of Ceremonies. Immediately following is the interpreter of the American Legation; then come the Legation staff and the officers of the *Quinnebaug*. On the first landing of the staircase we pause a little to observe a choice picture by the skillful brush of an artist signing himself "G. Washington." This was very pleasing to us Americans. It flattered our national pride. It also surprised us. No one knew that our *pater patræ*, was given to picture-work. We then enter a large hall. It is on the second story. On its walls hang four life-sized portraits of ancestors of the present ruler, to wit : On the right, on entering, is Sultan Mahmoud. He is the grandfather of the Sultan. He was a ruler of power, as the Janizaries found out. On the left, Sultan Aziz, His Majesty's uncle. This portrait faces the entrance on the right, where you see Sultan Medjid, father of His Majesty. He faces on the left Sultan Selim III., an ancestor of His Majesty. In the middle of this hall is a long table. The floor is parquet. We now enter the audience-room. It is very wide and long. Its floor is covered with a Turkish carpet. In the centre of the room is a long buhl table. There is a small table behind the Sultan, on which he leans while "audience" goes on. It gives him relief if the talks take too much dimension. The furniture in the room is not a prominent feature. Most of it is from Paris. The apartment receives light from three huge windows facing the east. On the walls hang superb oil paintings. The first on the Sultan's left represents a moonlight view of Stamboul and the Seraglio Point, one of the most notable, beautiful and commercial spots of the world. It is by the celebrated Russian artist Alvasowski. On the same side of the room is an exquisite night scene of the small Asiatic palace at the "Sweet Waters." It is by Ghickson. Who he is, connoisseurs know. On the other side of the room are three artistic paintings. The best of these represents the Midnight Sun in Norway. The other two are naval engagements.

The Sultan receives us, standing on a rug made of camel-hair felt, covered with embroidered flowers in different colored silk braid of Turkish work.

As we are ushered into the presence, we make three bows—one at the door on entering, the second half-way, and the last when we stop, a few feet from his person. We do not bow as low as the Turkish Ministers, but we do our best. The Sultan is standing at the far end of the room, in front of a table. As he is the conspicuous object of our attention, and a figure of great attraction, is it not proper to make a detailed description of this potentate of a great empire ?

The Sultan is middle-sized and of the Turkish type. He wears a full black beard, is of dark complexion, and has very expressive eyes. His forehead is large, indicative of intellectual power. He is very gracious in his manner, though at times seemingly a little embarrassed. He is dressed in the uniform of chief marshal of the army. He wears the following decorations: The Grand Cordon of the Osmanli, which is a green scarf worn across the breast; the first class of the Medjidie, in diamonds; the Nichan Imtiaz, an order instituted by his grandfather, Sultan Mahmoud, and the Nichan Iftihar. The insignia and medals are inlaid with precious stones. The green sash or scarf is of a rich color and texture. No person was ever decorated in more gorgeous array, and yet in his bearing and demeanor he is unostentatious. Notwithstanding the prejudice of the Ottoman against images, his photograph has been permitted. The frontispiece, which represents him as a cavalier, is a faithful likeness.

There is an etiquette which Turkish officials observe in the Sultan's presence. It has been much modified by time, and since the Crimean War greatly modified, like other old habits here, especially as they affect strangers. On approaching the Sultan the officials, when about ten yards distant, make a salaam. This consists in bending the body till the right hand touches the ground. The hand is then brought to the heart, the mouth, and then to the forehead. What does this mean ? Its idea is, that you take the earth from the ground as a symbol of lowliness. Then you carry the hand to your heart and head. The lips approve your regard. After the first salaam, you advance five or six yards and repeat. If you are an official, again and again you repeat until you are a yard and a half from the Sultan.

Then a third salaam is made. Then the person stops. He crosses his hands on the lower part of his stomach. This is said to be a relic of Persian usage. It has a meaning. It is intended to show that the servant has no concealed weapon in his hand. These officials never address the Sultan. Every time he looks toward them they repeat the salaam. After much genuflexion they are asked what their business is. They tell their story and bow lowly and bow out.

On this occasion the Sultan had on his right, and standing in single file, with their backs to the wall, about fifteen of his most distinguished aides-de-camp. The first of the line was Ghazi Osman Pasha. He is called Ghazi because he is a conqueror. Then came Ibrahim Dervish Pasha, Nuzret Pasha, Dreysse Pasha, Fouad Pasha, and others. As two of the Muchirs present at the audience have rather romantic histories, may I append a brief biography of them?

In 1867 Lieutenant Dreysse, of the French army, was stationed in Paris. He was a person of particularly engaging manners. He had a very distinguished presence. He was detailed as aide-de-camp to Prince Abdul-Hamid (the present Sultan), at that time a very obscure Prince in the suite of Sultan Abdul-Aziz. Dreysse made such an impression on the young Prince that when the latter came to the throne, his first thought was to have his old friend with him. However, having forgotten his name, considerable difficulty in finding his whereabouts was experienced at the French War Department. At last he was unearthed in a village on the Swiss frontier. He has since had every honor heaped upon him.

The other romance is that of Fouad Pasha. About a year ago a very serious conspiracy was discovered in the palace. Fouad Pasha was wrongfully supposed to be at the head of it. The regiment of Circassians which was involved in it was banished. It is said that Fouad disappeared for nine or ten months. His friends thought that he had been put out of the way. There are so many peculiarities of custom and condition here, that the ups and downs of life are not marvelous in such a land of wonders.

Upon this occasion, I looked in vain for the little dwarf whom I saw ride so fiercely an Arab steed at a former reception. I must be content with his photograph. I have also a picture of his predecessor, Abdur-Rahman. The latter Abdur was buffoon to the Sultan Abdul-Aziz, and at his master's death

DWARFS OF THE PALACE.

he entered the service of the Shah of Persia. He is a Turk, and still survives. He is about fifty-four years old, though scarcely three feet high. He is a bright-looking fellow, and, when dressed up in his Circassian General's uniform, as he used to be in the Palace of Dolma Bagtché, a most interesting little man.

At the presentation the officials—minus the dwarf—form in two lines on either side of the hall. The American Minister advances between the Foreign Minister and the First Chamberlain. The interpreter, Mr. Gargiulo, is near by. I do not make a very low obeisance, nor is it expected. I receive the proper intimation, present my credentials, and speak the speech as it was set down, and with appropriate decorum. The hush of the place conquers my rhetoric. The low tones in which everybody speaks naturally reduces the compass of the voice. The speech is hardly two minutes' long, but after it is finished I am relieved. The Sultan is pleased to respond most amiably. He is pleased to say that he is gratified with the selection made by the President. He has great satisfaction in knowing that I had been in the country before, and was familiar with its affairs and government. He makes the usual reference to the happy relations always existing between the two nations, and expresses the hope that they would continue. He is glad to extend the same friendship to me that he extended to my predecessor. After some pleasant and informal talk, he steps forward and shakes me warmly by the hand. Then the guests are severally introduced to the Sultan, who expresses his gratification at having made their acquaintance. We then leave the room, walking backward, making the three bows, as before. Muchir Munir Pasha, *Drogman du Divan Imperial*, stands during the audience on the left of the Sultan, and Assim Pasha, the Foreign Minister, on his right. Everything said to the Sultan is interpreted to him by Assim Pasha.

Before leaving, I thank His Majesty for allowing the *Quinnebaug* to be docked and repainted without charge, and for the compliment thus paid to the United States. After this a private audience is courteously accorded by the Sultan, at which some of the officers are present. It is regarded as an unusual courtesy. It lasts an hour. During its continuance much informal inquiry is made and answered. Among other matters, the Sultan asks:

"Have you been to Constantinople before?"

I respond: "Yes, your Majesty. I was here in 1851; thirty-four years ago."

This excites astonishment and interest, and I add:

"It was on our American great day—the Fourth of July. Then I saw your Majesty with your father. The occasion was the reception of the Cherif of Mecca. Your Majesty was then eleven years of age."

This led to much conversation about the changes since that time. After this private interview, the reception ended most happily; and we all returned to our homes with the same stateliness and style.

This was not my first meeting with the Sultan. I had been, as I have said, presented to His Majesty in 1881 with the staff of General Wallace. In my book, "Orient Sunbeams," the Yildiz palace is described by a few dashes of the pen. I have added much reminiscence to it since 1881. In that volume I indulged in a little general reflection upon this ruler of Turkey. I repeat it now as a first and lasting impression :

"He is a man of calm dignity and superior intelligence. Mahomed II., the grand progenitor of this line, who took the city from the effete Greeks, may have had more élan, as he had a larger army, but he had no more reserve in his eye than his descendant before us. Is not the present Sultan administering, amid troubles for which he is not responsible, a great empire of various nationalities and religions, and under manifold embarrassments? By his illustrious descent and inborn dignity, by his position as heir of the Othmans, Amuraths and Suleimans, he receives—as the Oriental chief should—that Occident which has never encroached upon his prerogative or domain, and has no inclination nor object in so doing."

I confess, before I had an idea of being here in any but a tourist's capacity, to an enthusiasm for this monarch. He is a king every inch, and without any dramatic ostentation. He deserves great regard for his rare ability. He is his own adviser. Amid his troubles and cares, and with the populations of divers religions and races, which he must reconcile to rule, he is not unworthy of the fame of Abdul Medjid, whose memory is to me a part of my earliest association with the city of Constantinople.

Before leaving New York, at our Oriental banquet, in June,

GARDEN AND PALACE OF YILDIZ.

1885, when called upon to respond to the kind wishes of friends, I pictured in my mind this reception as a climax of former experiences at this capital. I then indicated, with more lively rhetoric than would be appropriate at a court presentation, that to enjoy the Orient one should have thoughts impearled upon vestments of Oriental light, and imagery as enchanting as dreams of Cashmere. I had anticipated something of that bewildering exhilaration which one might indulge for a thousand and one nights and never surfeit. I spoke of the melody of the Eastern nightingale, who sings his love to the rose in the tender idyls of Hafiz. There was in my imagination all the rare emblems of the East, and I looked upon a residence in Turkey, to which this reception would invite, as the consummation of all poetic fancies. I was to give up for ever the old toilsome life of congressional wrangle. I was to watch calmly the progress of events in the Orient, with a view to seize every demonstration of war as an opportunity for commercial America. But ever and always, when I fancied myself amidst the changes and progressive liberalities flickering over and around the ancient and modern city of empire to which the President had accredited me, I could not help drawing contrasting pictures of the overshadowing grandeur of my own country.

Here, to day, at this reception, the poetry of these dreams is recalled in the traditions of empire and opulence. Was I not in the real presence of a race of men and rulers who made nations tremble with the shock of their arms, and who, at one time, bid fair to gain universal sway ! To what strange fancies such a thought gives birth, in the presence of the Caliph of all the Mahometans !

# CHAPTER IV.

ONE of the pleasant excursions which not only Ministers, but others who are strangers to Constantinople, and even the denizens of that city, care first and most to make is that on Fridays to the neighborhood of the mosque in which the Sultan offers his prayers. Most of the time while I was at the capital the Sultan was in the habit of saying his prayers at the mosque of Bechïktash. But there is in process of erection, and nearly completed, a new mosque, which is nearer his palace of Yildiz. It is on the summit of the hills above the Bosporus. It is called the mosque of Hamidiéa. It is named after one of the earlier and most devout Sultans. To this mosque he often goes.

This ceremony of attending mosque is never omitted, if the Sultan be alive. It matters not whether it hails or rains, whether there be an earthquake, a plague or a pestilence, or personal sickness—this observance is one of the scrupulous duties of the Sultan, who is at the same time the absolute Caliph of the Faith. The prayer which he offers cannot be said by any one else for him. It is a religious duty to be done by him in person. It is reckoned the most honorable of his functions and the greatest of all his privileges. To omit his appearance on that day would almost provoke a riot.

This custom came into use in the year A. D. 1361. Then the reigning Sultan, Murad I., having offered to give evidence before the Mufti in a case in which one of his favorites was concerned, his testimony was rejected on the ground that, according to the law of the Koran, no person can be admitted as a witness in a religious court of justice who has not joined in common prayer in the mosque. In acknowledgment of the justice of this decision, Murad proceeded, on the following Friday, in great state, to the mosque. He joined with the other worshippers, and performed his devotions as one of their own number. The custom has since been observed with the utmost strictness and regularity.

Sultan Mahmoud I., though very ill, insisted on going to the mosque, with the result that on his return to the palace he fell down dead at the entrance as he was dismounting from his horse. The same fatality happened to Sultan Osman II., who, heedless of the advice of his physicians, left his sick-bed in order to attend the usual Friday prayers. He returned safely to the palace, but expired on the following night.

The ceremony is not now attended with as much éclat as in the early days, when the Sultan's servitors were dressed in velvet and gold, and scattered handsful of gold and silver along his path as he passed on his way to the mosque of St. Sofia.

In those early days, when Turkish power was literally Sublime, the far-famed carpets of the East were spread over the ground, upon which pranced the Sultan's steed. The Oriental escort, with its flowing robes, immense turbans, military music and official retinue, has been more or less discarded by the fashions of the present day, and by the advancement of the Turk himself in European customs.

When the Sultan attends prayers at the mosque the time is fixed by the Turkish clock at 7. This means about 2 o'clock in the afternoon, European time. He generally comes in a large and elegant open carriage. He is accompanied by a trusted friend, the aged Namyk Pasha, who is the very pink of courtesy, and Osman Pasha, the hero of Plevna. From five to seven thousand troops usually keep the way on these occasions. They come in with bands of music from all parts of the city, bearing their sacred banners of green, inscribed with Koranic texts, and their own regimental flags. They are in line before the Sultan appears. Some of the battalions or regiments appear in fanciful uniform, such as the Albanian. I saw one regiment made up of the Nubians or Tunisians of Africa. They had a corps of stalwart sappers and miners, in leathern aprons and huge battle-axes. Every part of the dominion is represented by the troops. They are a strong body of soldiers—well officered. They have a variety of uniform. Their fine music and the *esprit du corps* of the escort give something more than a religious aspect to the occasion.

Those who would see the " Salemlik," or the Sultan, as he enters the mosque and comes from it, should take their stand about noon either at the guard-house or at the new quarters.

"In the multitude of the people is the King's honor." The population turns out *en masse* on these occasions. The black-tasselled, bright-red fez cap gives its color to the scene. The general tone of the uniform, however, is that of the Zouave, whose scarlet trousers reach to the knee. The soldiers are olive-colored, and bronzed with many a sun, and are of splendid physique. As the Sultan enters the mosque, he is surrounded by dozens of his officers, whose uniforms glitter with a profusion of gold lace and decorative orders. He is met by the Imam, or Moslem priest, at the door. There is no special order about the crowd, except that they are kept more or less in check by the soldiery. Carriages, horses and people mingle together in confusion. I never saw a drunken man nor any flagrant disorder occur during the ceremony. Many of the carriages contain the wives of the Sultan, his children, cousins and nieces, and his mother and aunt. Diamonds shine with unusual profusion upon the veiled beauties. Of course, there are many women present who are not Turkish, and, therefore, not dressed in the costume with which the reader will soon become familiar.

The Sultan enters the mosque. All is quietude without, until he has finished his prayers. Then is heard a bugle note ; a carpet is laid down, and the officers, who are his adjutants, Ministers and others, mount their horses. They are ready for the movement. The soldiers "present arms!" the iron gate opens, and the shout goes up—"Padisha! Chok Yàsha!"—The Sultan! Let him live forever! Sometimes the Sultan is mounted on a white steed, which is appareled for the occasion ; but generally, amid much salutation, he comes and returns in his carriage, takes the reins himself, and drives to and from the palace. His people close about him, and the spectacle is over.

You may ask how he is dressed. I have generally seen him in a blue-black frock coat, closely buttoned, edged with red cord. The present Sultan is a graceful rider, and when on horseback, like his fellow-countrymen, he shows to advantage. His title as Sultan does not signify all the power which he possesses as an absolute ruler, but yet it signifies much. Padisha signifies most. It is the chief and favorite title. It signifies Father of all the Sovereigns of the Earth. He has other titles, such as Imam-ul- Muslemin—Pontiff of Mussulmans; Alem Penah—Refuge of the World. Any more? Yes. Other titles are that of "Lord of

Two Continents and Two Seas, King of Kings, High and Mighty Lord, Servant of the Two Holy Cities, Shadow of God upon Earth; Hunkiar, or Man-Slayer." Any more ? Yes, more still. He is called Ali-Osman Padishahi—King of the Descendants of Osman ; Shahin Shahi Alem—King of the Sovereigns of the Universe ; Hudavendighar—Attached to God ; Shahin Shahi Movazem ve Hilloulah—High King of Kings and Shadow of God ; and, to illustrate the theocratic democracy which pervades the civil order and the Mahometan religion, he also bears the title of " The Son of a Slave." He thus combines with the highest human exaltation the lowliest humiliation. It is the law of the Koran. He is the son of a slave-mother, and, therefore, should he not be humble ? He is the Divine representative of Mahomet, and the father of his people, and, therefore, should he not be exalted ? His family line runs back with unbroken links to the middle of the thirteenth century, and though he may not be as great in war and as rugged in manner as Orchan or Sulieman, or as stately and tall as his brother, Abdul Aziz, or perhaps as kingly in theatric style as his father, Abdul Medjid, he has a splendid eye and a royal mien, becoming the lineage of Osman. His face is pale, and its general contour and features indicate a man who is amiable, shrewd, vigilant and able.

Perhaps the most sacred place in the neighborhood of Constantinople is the historical site of the mosque of Job, or Eyoub. It is situated at some distance from the northwest corner of the Stamboul triangle, a few yards from the Golden Horn. It is a hilly spot, selected for burial purposes. The mosque is never shown except to the faithful. It marks the burying-place of the great leader of the first Arab attempts upon the city, and therefore it has always been kept sacred from the foot of the infidel. Within the mosque is the green banner of the prophet, only used in great emergencies, as when Mahmoud II. carried it before his troops in their assault upon the Janizaries, when he destroyed them. Within it is treasured the sacred sword of Osman, with which the Sultan is girt when he is invested with power. It is the symbol of office and the pride of the Ottoman race. When poor Murad V. was called to the throne, after the tragic death of Abdul Aziz, in 1876, he was not allowed to assume this sword. He was *non compos.* Upon the last day of August, 1876, his brother, the present Sultan, Abdul Hamid II., after much sincere protest, took upon himself the Imperial duty with the sword of Osman. This ceremony is not witnessed by the outside world, and, therefore, I shall hereafter draw upon my pencil and fancy for a picturesque description of the scene.

Although the Sultan is thus exalted as the successor of Mahomet, it is permitted, after the Oriental method, to any one who approaches, to present a petition to him upon this occasion of prayer.

At the new mosque of Hamidiéa, where he occasionally worships, there is a lattice through which he can see his troops marching ; and, by the aid of a glass, he observes the guests who are assembled at the guard-house to do him honor. If he desires to confer with or to honor any of these guests, he charges one of his Chamberlains to convey to the personage his greetings. This occasion is seized upon to indicate his cordial good-will toward the foreign Ministers or distinguished people who may be sojourning in Constantinople. Oftentimes, these occasions are utilized to present colors to the new regiments, and sometimes speech-making is indulged in. Thereupon the flag is unfurled, and an aide-de-camp delivers, on behalf of the Sultan, a speech whose burden is not only patriotic, but religious and opulent of Oriental rhetoric. The responses are full of devotion to his Imperial person and the Holy Faith.

It is difficult to praise without undue encomium ; especially to praise those who have been unusually affable and kind to the eulogist. I feel this difficulty in regard to the Sultan, but I think everyone who has come in contact with the present sovereign of Turkey will allow me to express, with becoming earnestness, my opinion of his high merits and noble character. To ascertain these merits and appreciate his character, there must be some familiarity with his daily work and thought.

How does he administer his realm, with its multiform interests of mosque and state and its varieties of population and creed ?

In the first place, he is an early riser. After he leaves his seraglio and has partaken of a slight repast, his secretaries wait upon him with their portfolios. He peruses all the official correspondence and current reports. He gives up his time until noon to work of this character. Then his breakfast is served. After that, he makes a détour of his gardens and park,

THE SULTAN'S FAVORITE STEED, "FERHAN."

looks in upon his aviaries, perhaps stirs up his menagerie, makes an inspection of his two hundred horses in their fine stables, indulges his little daughters in a row upon the fairy lake which he has had constructed, and, it may be, attends a performance in the little theatre provided for his children in the palace.

At 5 o'clock in the afternoon, having accomplished most of his official work, he mounts his favorite horse for a ride in the park. This steed, as I have him pictured from the Sultan's own album, is a war-scarred veteran.

This park is very extensive, comprising many thousand acres. It is surrounded by high walls and protected by the soldiery. Oftentimes, being a fine shot, he tries his aim upon some of the wild fowl which are decoyed upon the waters of the park. He is at the palace for dinner at 7. He dines after the European method. It would be a task to make a catalogue of the gold and silver candelabra and massive épergnes which, with their flowers and fruits, decorate the table. Oftentimes he has company present. On such occasions his First Chamberlain, Munir Pasha, acts as interpreter, standing behind His Majesty's gold chair. He offers wine to his guests, but *he* indulges only in water. He observes the precepts of the Koran. The dinner is accompanied with music. A fine military band plays during this meal. The servants are dressed in scarlet, like the old English brigadiers, with gold epaulettes. You would think they were mutes, by the quiet way in which they serve. It is understood, of course, that the wives of the Sultan are never at the table. The wives of others are frequently invited, but on such occasions the Sultan does not preside. If the Sultan desires to converse with any one, there is a convenient room, where cigarettes and coffee assist the conversation. Humor is sometimes indulged in upon these occasions. There are the antics of the court dwarf and some tricks of the juggler or conjurer. But it is all over by 10 o'clock. The Imperial carriages are then at the door. The guests are attended to them by the Chamberlains. A troop of horse sometimes accompanies the carriages. After the guests depart the Sultan resumes his administrative work, which not only concerns the internal but the external affairs of his empire. He is one of the most industrious, painstaking, honest, conscientious and vigilant rulers of the world. He is amiable and just withal. His every word betokens a good heart and sagacious head.

The comment is often made in respect to the present Sultan, Abdul-Hamid, that he is timid; that he will not expose himself to the danger of assassination; and that he has withdrawn to the suburbs of the city on the European shore, where, protected by his soldiers, he lives in privacy and security. It is alleged that he resides in a fortress, although nominally a palace. I have yet to see in my observations of the Sultan and his actions any such evidence of fear. It might well be, considering the events which occurred when Abdul-Aziz was assassinated, and Murad, his brother was imprisoned, that the present Sultan would act with caution; but upon every Friday is he not seen? In these days of progressive science, if any one chooses to use the appliances of chemistry to destroy his life, is there not plenty of opportunity? When he appears at the mosque is there not always an immense crowd? His guard is more from custom and for pageantry than for protection. All Constantinople, and all the strangers within its gates, are on hand to see him drive his own team or ride his own steed. The multitude of both sexes throng upon the hills. The dignitaries of the empire and the Pashas, who are supposed to be jealous of his power, and who lose and gain offices with every change of the moon, are constantly near him. This proves that there is no dread of assassination quivering in the Sultan's heart. It is one of the fantasies of the ready writer of cablegrams.

The Salemlik of the Sultan, which I have endeavored to picture, has been well painted by a native artist, Hamdi Bey. It was painted for one of the citizens of New York, Mr. Elliot F. Shephard, who cultivates both art and religion. It presents His Majesty driving in an open carriage, accompanied by the venerable Namyk Pasha, of long and honorable service, and Osman Pasha, the hero of Plevna; but it cannot, and does not, represent the enthusiastic cheering with which he is received at the conclusion of his prayer, or the other proofs of the good-will of his people.

It is, I think, a favorite relief and pastime of the Sultan to show himself to the people in this *quasi* religious way. It matters not whether the Ministers who are waiting to see him are from Japan or Russia, China or America, Persia or Spain—he is always gracious with his courtesies. And what a splendid attraction it is for the populace of Constantinople! What a fête day, once every week! What variety in the uniforms of the soldiers!

What a changeable aspect the soldiers present from week to week ! to-day a regiment from the Soudan, to-morrow a battalion from Albania. Each Friday there is a new greeting to new people of strange and distant parts of the world. He is always ready, at this religious season, to bestow favors and to be pleased with the devotion of the Oriental people, and especially those of his own dominions.

# CHAPTER V.

DURING my sojourn at Constantinople, and while cultivating the graces which belong to the Envoy who, according to Lord Chesterfield, seeks the success of his mission, I found it was not only not at all improper, but thoroughly Oriental, to indulge in some gift making and taking. I do not speak of the little personal courtesies of this kind, but of those of an official quality. Indeed, as early as December 31, 1881, the Sultan desired to have sent to him from the United States, and at his own expense, an album with every description of fire-arms in photograph. There is nothing which he has inherited from his ancestors, to which he clings with such pertinacity, as the desire to examine all inventions pertaining to artillery, and the various armaments and explosives connected with warfare. To fulfill this expression of his wish was a part of my pleasure while serving near his court. A more superb photographic album of the arms and inventions from America could not have been desired. It was a recent collection up to date. Besides, he desired stereoscopic and other views of the scenes, objects and buildings which are considered the most interesting in the United States. These, also, it was my privilege, six years after his request, to present to His Majesty in the name of the President. The Sultan is also fond of trees of all kinds, as the cultivation of the grounds of Yildiz, amounting to several thousand acres, amply illustrates. He desired a collection of American fruit-bearing trees and shrubs, and also specimens of our various evergreen trees. The latter he desired packed in such a way as to preserve them for setting out in Turkey, with a likelihood of their growth. General Wallace thought there could be no difficulty in gratifying these requests of the Sultan. He suggested that our Government should bear the expense, and that they should be a present from the President to the Sultan, as a manifestation of good-will,

" at once delicate and happily expressive." I quote the language of the auther of "Ben-Hur."

Nothing was done in pursuance of these suggestions, although many promises were made to make an effort to comply with the wish of the Sultan. Surely it would be gross remissness, after the expression of the wish of the Sultan, if the sovereigns of the United States represented by our Government should not heed it. But it was not heeded for a long time. After the Sultan had paid for the docking and repairing of the United States ship of war *Quinnebaug*, I took the liberty in the fall of 1885 of recalling to the attention of the home authorities the request and promise in several missives. Mr. Bayard, the Secretary of State, at once gave a gracious and favorable reply. He did not stop there : he did better ; he proceeded to execute what had been promised.

In some meetings which I had with the Sultan, and in reply to his curiosity as to the miraculous growth of our own land in population and resources, I told him that the only way in which he could possibly understand our advancement would be to take the salient points out of our Census reports, and especially the Tenth Census (1880), have them suitably translated, and apply them to his own land. He would thus see what an advertisement a good census would be of the vast resources of his own empire. Having been Chairman of the Census Committee of the House of Representatives which reported the bill, and, I may say, engineered it through the House, by which our new system was inaugurated, I did not feel incompetent to talk with the Sultan on the subject. As a result of these communications, I was happy to report to my Government that two boxes containing photographic and stereoscopic views of scenery, edifices, etc., in the United States, together with a complete set of the Census reports, with the Census law and instructions and blanks, were received at Constantinople. Having informed the Sultan of my desire to present these articles in behalf of the President, His Majesty accorded me a reception in the afternoon of May 16, 1886. The boxes were borne from the Legation by a stalwart hamal to the palace, and there opened under the eyes of eager officials, who seemed to think that there was something in them—something strange and curious. The hamal of Constantinople is able to carry six hundred pounds weight of material. Had he known that he was bearing the ponderous statistics of over ten years of

HAMAL CARRYING UNITED STATES CENSUS TO YILDIZ.

American growth, he might have staggered under the heat and burden of the day. What a chance was here for the reporter of the American press, had he but known that the figures of our condition and advancement were laboring up the high hill of Yildiz for the instruction of an effete dynasty !

The boxes were opened on the first floor of the palace, in one of the side rooms, and their contents carried to a kiosk in the midst of the beautiful private garden of the Sultan, which is situated on the summit of Yildiz—the palace of the "Star." In this kiosk there was also a library. I present a picture of the kiosk, though I cannot, in the same connection, present a picture of the scene that followed. The volumes in the library are of the same red binding as the portfolios containing the photographs, so that at once the *entente cordiale* is established between the various volumes, there being harmony in their toilets.

In making the presentation, I had the honor to remark that no such representation could be had of any country as that which the President had thus presented. The natural scenery displayed what God had done for our land, and the views of edifices, bridges and other structures what man, under the conditions of our American life, had done in a century. The Census returns gave, in statistical, tabular and picturesque form, the grand results of our American policy and civilization.

The Sultan was delighted at the elegance, uniqueness and magnificence of the gift. After adjusting the stereoscope—on which was inscribed upon a silver plate : "From the President of the United States to His Imperial Majesty, the Sultan of Turkey"— he selected some of the views from the hundreds before him. They elicited expressions of delight and wonder. The photographs of the "Red Men" attracted his eager attention. He asked many questions as to their origin, their movements, and their present numbers, condition and government. I could see that he surmised them to be of that Mongol race— which in the cycles of history clustered in "Tartar tribes" on the territory between the Himalayas and the Mediterranean— out of which, as the most energetic, came the Seljukian Turks, who almost conquered Europe, as well as a large part of Asia and Africa. I endeavored to explain to him the relations of our Indians to the Federal Government—as wards—of whom it was

THE SULTAN'S KIOSK AT YILDIZ.

the guardian. He was anxious to know if they amounted to much, and how we provided for them. I explained, as well as I could, the effects of white raids, whisky and land-grabbing, as well as the "reservation" plan, and the probability that by intermingling with the white population, they would in time, and like our other races, be absorbed in our composite system of society. The towns and houses of the Zuni Indians attracted his attention, for they are counterparts of certain towns in Asia Minor, which I have just seen in photographs. Besides, are not the Indians themselves Tartaric in custom and costume, and have they not an Oriental veneration for the sun?

The Sultan asked curiously—pointing significantly to the minaret of the new mosque visible from the kiosk—if they believed in *one* God. I gave him a brief outline of the natural religion of these people, who have almost ceased to be interesting to ourselves except in romances, but who, as these photographs show, are a source of infinite interest to the ethnologist.

In thinking over these incidents, and the Sultan's query as to the religion of our Red men, I recalled the posture of Mahometan prayer, and the listening Moslem, his hand to his ears, in honor of the All-Audient Allah, together with the verse of Longfellow in his Hiawatha:

> "Gitche Manito the Mighty,
> He, the Master of Life, was painted
> As an egg, with points projecting
> To the four winds of the heavens.
> Everywhere is the Great Spirit,
> Was the meaning of this symbol."

Indeed, the Sultan not long since indicated his strange if not hereditary preference toward the tribes of other countries, who perhaps were more or less akin to the Mongolian or Tartaric tribe from which his ancestors were descended, by honoring an American who presented some Australian "Indians" for his observation and delight. Had I been in Constantinople at the time, I think I should have put in a *caveat* against them in behalf of the noble red men of America! An Australian, who is indigenous to the soil of that island, is always associated in my mind with the kangaroo, some of whose legs are inadequate. In some electioneering performances in the "wild West," when I

A MOSLEM AT PRAYER.

first ran for Congress, a company paraded on my own domain at a mass meeting. They were known as the Australian children, and were made to dance under the cowhide of the exhibitor, and under the delightful inspiration of gingerbread if they got through safely. I was asked by the proprietor of these Australian children to give a name to their chief. Without knowing the full significance of the meaning, I named him Cambyses. The Orient had even then its fascination for me, and the Australian, by some strange permutation, became its representative.

Nothing better could have been selected to interest the intelligent Orientalist than those rare portraits of the chiefs of our American Indians, whose origin Science may some day indubitably trace to the Mongolian "hive" of Central Asia. Nearly two hours of that beautiful May afternoon passed in thus reviewing the aborigines, scenes and resources of our country.

Not the less attractive to the Sultan were the Census volumes. Just before I went to Egypt, in February, I had a conversation with him as to the necessity of a census for his dominions. I was not unprepared to make the endeavor to explain somewhat the features of our system, and its results, as embodied in the fourteen books which the President had forwarded. The affluence of these returns—considered as an advertisement merely of our values and growth—evoked the Sultan's wonder. He specially examined the volumes on Forestry and Architecture, and made some notes for his own purposes. He referred to his love of trees, whereupon I expressed the hope that his wish as to the fruit bearing and evergreen trees from America might yet be gratified.

Each census volume was explained to him *seriatim*—agriculture, petroleum, minerals, manufactures, population, cotton, debts and taxation, &c., and so on to the last published. He marveled that with such abundant information as checks on human frailty, we should ever have peculations, spoliations, or maladministration. He concluded that, with such data for administrative policies, we could not be other than prosperous. He asked me if we had dishonesty in administration. I said that our civil war—like all other wars—had begotten frauds and corruption, which time and better administrations had abated. He congratulated himself fervently on his own recent policies of peace and forbearance, by which he had saved so much of taxation, grief and trouble to his people.

I had the honor, with much pride, thus to show the variety and completeness of the Tenth Census, with which, as statists of Germany, France and England have said, there is nothing comparable in the annals of other nations, and certainly nothing of the kind in Oriental countries. These volumes not only display the physical features of our country, by table and picture, but its rapid development and its political history, of which those features are a factor. The progress of settlements are here traced across mountains and valleys; the population with its variety of race and nativity ; its educational, benevolent and religious conditions ; its occupations and mortality; its industries, finance, commerce, wealth, debt, taxation, expenditure and revenues—all as data for social science and political order, and in such detail as to bewilder, if they were not so methodically arranged.

These elements pass in review before this autocratic ruler of forty millions of people, who, with intelligent grasp, comprehends their utility, and the need of their application to his own country. Then he reminds me of our conversation about a census for his own country, and said that he had directed his Grand Vizier, Kiamil Pasha, to organize a commission to begin the work. He was anxious as to its cost. I told him that ours was limited, by the first act, to three million dollars, or about seven hundred thousand pounds sterling, but that the publications nearly doubled this sum; and that for his purposes, and as the initiative, it was not necessary to spend a million of dollars to present a fair summary of the Turkish elements of population and wealth. He asked me if I would aid it by my advice, when the commission was formed. To which I responded that, consistent with my duties to my country and health, I would do so, if the President did not object. The law, the instructions to superintendents, enumerators, and blanks for returns, and the *modus operandi* of special experts, were fully detailed by the printed papers in the envelopes which were in the box. These envelopes he sealed with his own hand, and gave them direction at once. So that probably Turkey may, if peace prevail, have a census of her own.

Never was there such a *desideratum* for a country. For example : As to the population of Constantinople—no one can tell what it is, whether one or two million, much less of what elements it is composed. It is the greatest seat of commerce in the Eastern world. Its industries are manifold and various, and yet, there is no local data worth having, either for taxation or administration, nor statistical returns of any kind.

The afternoon passed away, with constant expressions from the Sultan of his obligations, and thanks for these remarkable gifts. I was charged to convey to the President His Majesty's high regard and esteem, and his thanks for this thoughtful and elegant present.

As an evidence of the delight which this peculiar present gave to the Sultan, he was pleased to direct his Chamberlain—Hadji-Ali-Bey—to show me about the grounds of his private park, whose beautiful arrangement of lake and fountain, mound, hill and vale, is only equalled by the prospect of the Bosporus below, and the Asiatic mountains beyond. To emphasize his delight still more, he was so courteous as to invite my wife and myself to dine with him at the palace. But this deserves a chapter by itself.

# CHAPTER VI.

IT is not very easy to define what society is. Perhaps the simplest definition is that it is social and friendly intercourse. If it be thought impossible to have such intercourse in Turkey, owing to the various races of its population, its many faiths and the seclusion of the Mahometan women, certainly I have not found it so. There is much visiting by the Turkish women among themselves, both in person and by proxy. They seek on every occasion to make visits of salutation, condolence and congratulation. They make visits when children are born, when people are married, and when people die. They visit much in the evening during the religious season, when in fact there is more freedom for the Turkish women than at other times. But as to the enjoyments of social life, as we regard them—where the amenities and delights of intercourse are elevating and instructive—these do not strictly belong to the Turks of the capital.

Can such a congeries of men and women, without the same nationality or creed, have that common interest which creates a social order ? In the other capitals of Europe where courts exist, there is always a grand centre. There is a big fly-wheel, as it were, by which the lesser machines of social order are regulated and moved. But owing to the reserve of the social system of Turkey this social centre is missing. Even the Sultan, notwithstanding his word is law, does not undertake to exercise any social power, except now and then by a dinner to the Cabinet, to an Ambassador, or to some of the officers of the palace. His life is passed as the slave of his people. It is a course of official drudgery from early rising to late retiring. He has no time for society. If it be said that he keeps aloof from social pleasures because of timidity or fear, I deny the statement. He is, as I have said, always seen publicly once a week. Very little care is

46

taken to protect him from the observation or the approach of the populace. He is always received with enthusiasm, and is easy and frank in responding to it. Passing between lines of troops, with crowds of military officers and Pashas, and ladies of the harem in their carriages, and amid the noise of the streets, drowned somewhat by martial music, he does not look a bit like the thin-faced, grizzly bearded, pale man, nervously fluttering his hand before his face by way of salute, hurrying into the mosque, and giving himself time only to throw a half-frightened glance around him, and soon lost to view before he can be well seen; yet it is the custom of European writers thus to represent him. He is not a grizzly bearded man, nor is his mien one of pale timidity. He is the head of a State, and is always caring for his people. Since he is not the head of society, so called, no other Turk can assume that position.

The truth is, the Turk is too quiet and reflective for the butterfly work of society. He is reproached by the "dudes" and popinjays who move in some of the Legations, because he likes old and kindly ways and because, instead of devoting himself to a club or to frivolity, he goes home and takes a contemplative smoke with his family, or invites some of his neighbors to come and smoke with him and listen to the stories told in the Salemlik. That society which New York, London, Paris, Vienna and St. Petersburg furnish, is not at all akin to this home sociality. The Turk goes to bed early—with the chickens. He rises early. His good old-fashioned ways are incompatible with the unprofitable social régime. Sometimes the Ministers and many State officials, including the Grand Vizier, attend the receptions given by the Foreign Ministers, but they seem to be more or less out of place. They are observant, never loquacious, and always reserved and self-contained. There can be no great social tendency in a democratic country like Turkey, where there is neither hereditary nor other nobility. Besides, riches take to themselves wings and fly away from Turk and Turkish homes more promptly than in other countries. Very few Turks there are who are very rich, or who keep their riches very long. There is no law of primogeniture ; so that families are not kept up in state and style from generation to generation, to lead society or to govern and grace it with their exceptional presence. When such a man as Hobart Pasha moved around in Turkish circles, or such an elegant gentleman as Rustem Pasha, the ex-Governor of the Lebanon, now Minister to England, used to leave his plain home, to spend an evening with a European friend, there was an occasional interest in Turkish circles of a social kind ; but Rustem Pasha was an Italian, though a faithful officer of His Majesty, and Hobart Pasha was an Englishman. The Greeks, Armenians and Levantines do not lead in the social order. Their wealth, which many of them have in abundance, has not much weight in the social hierarchy.

Is there any aristocracy of intellect or art in Constantinople ? There is one Turkish painter—Hamdi Bey. His pictures are greatly valued. There is now and then an editor, who, if his lucubrations are printed, and if he does not fall under the censorship, may be accounted a literary man, and this is all there is of it. There is an aristocracy of money, and yet not of society. A leading man in Pera, whose splendid home upon the Bosporus is only equalled by the elegant entertainments at his mansion in Pera, is the president of the Ottoman Bank—Mr. Foster. He represents a social coterie. It is gradually being merged with that of the dominant social people; I mean the Foreign Ministers.

It is not at all true, as is generally supposed, that there is much uncharitableness and jealousy between the different embassies—a German set here, a French set there, and an Austrian set yonder, or a special Russian set under the direction of the gifted Russian Ambassador. So far as I could observe, there were the kindest relations among all the Ministers; and yet they are a body by themselves. They enjoy one another's hospitality with great cordiality and unfailing iteration. It strikes me that, at present, the German element is in the lead; but how long will it remain so at a court where the Foreign Ministers are so transient that almost half of them have been changed since I arrived in Constantinople ?

There is a literary conclave here with an intellectual atmosphere, where poetry is recited and rare themes are discussed. This is outside of the routine of society. But the principal conversation among the various embassies and their attachés, concerns riding parties, lawn-tennis, dances, dogs, horses and flirtations. If you should undertake, while upon the cricket-ground or in the ballroom, to discuss any subject connected with art, science or literature, I doubt not you would be considered by the

bulk of the young English, French, German, Austrian, Russian,
Italian or Greek attachés, as *de trop*, or, in other words, a bore. It
seems that neither by position, money nor intelligence do embassies at Constantinople deserve the places which they assume as
the leaders of society. When it comes to carrying straws from place
to place they are active and vigilant; but when it comes to solid,
substantial ideas for the advancement and culture of those
who make Constantinople their home, they are not as important a factor as are the various religious societies, which
really form by themselves a social order of a self-sacrificing
and noble quality. And among these I would include the
American missionaries, both male and female, as well as the
Scotch, English, Dutch and German good folk who make
the Protestant churches and schools both attractive and instructive.

As early as A. D. 1837, when Miss Pardoe wrote her " City
of the Sultan," she remarked that there were three plagues
of Constantinople—fire, pestilence and dragomans. The dragomans still remain, but I find them a most reputable and indispensable class of public servants. The pestilence, notwithstanding the horrible condition of the streets, has not, of late years,
aroused anxiety. This may be owing to the good quarantine
established—under Fatalistic doctrine ! But the other plague—
fire—is not quenched. It is a perpetual scourge, for reasons
which are apparent in the wooden buildings of the city, and in
the careless mode in which the all-consuming pipe is used.
Besides this incendiary there is another. It is a sort of frame-
work over the hot coals in the brazier which is used for
warming the apartments. It is called the pandour. It is not
the "whiskered pandour" of poetry, but it is equally destructive. The family washing is hung upon it to dry. Of
course, after the clothes are dry a fire is likely to ensue. But the
fourth plague, which Miss Pardoe was inclined to think was
worse than all the other three, she designated as "politics."
She says : " The Faubourg of Pera always reminds me of
an ant-hill, with its diplomatic bustle and race for straws
and trifles, and its ceaseless, resistless struggle and its striving
to secure most inconsequent results." What she observed
forty years ago continues, not so much among the diplomats
as among the various civilians, who are jealous of each other,

and among the Greek, Armenian and other races, who are contentious among themselves.

One thing can be said in favor of the social life of the Turk. He seldom dines alone.   He is even more hospitable than the Arab with his salt.    If he is in his *konak*, or country house, every visitor is an invited guest to his table.   Let me make a picture of a real Turkish dinner:

The Pasha sits down, cross-legged, on a divan, and his eunuch, or aga, brings him a chased silver basin and ewer. After the Oriental method, water is poured upon the hands.   Another servant brings in a gold-embroidered napkin ; then drawing up a low table, which is becoming common now in our Western households as an article of bric-à-brac, being inlaid with mother-of-pearl, an attendant places upon this the waiter loaded with the repast.   There are many dishes, to suit a variety of tastes.   A favorite dish is a lamb roasted whole.   It is stuffed with rice, raisins, and the favorite pistachio nut.   This nut is sold upon the streets of Constantinople as commonly as the peanut in New York.   It is the pearl of good things.   Then comes a delicate dish of small fish, and there is no place equal to the Bosporus for this article.   Egg plant, if it be in season, appears fried in oil, and followed by boiled squashes stuffed with hash.   The Turkish hash is by no means to be derided, for it is neither second-hand nor equivocal.   The national dish is called *dolma*.   Hash is an element of that dish.   Hash and mutton is the *piece de résistance*.   Rice is served with it, as well as with rabbit, and both are cooked in vine leaves.   Then we have chicken breasts stewed in rose water, and cakes of flour and sugar, or dough sweetened and cooked.   Then come the jellies, the sherbet, the exquisite rose preserves and various "dulcet syrups, tinct with the cinnamon."   Nothing equals the rose preserves in the eye of the Oriental housewife; and here, by way of parenthesis, it is just to say that the housewifery of the Turkish matron cannot be overrated.   She has much to do, and does it well.   There are a number of side dishes in small saucers —most of them delicate and unfamiliar to us.   To crown the repast comes the *pilaf*.   This is a dish of rice, seasoned with butter and tomato juice, in accordance with an invariable custom at every meal.

Is not this *menu* a sign of advanced civilization ?   Is not this a

CABLAKIAI, OR FOOD-CARRIER.

51

CUISINIER, OR COOK.

feast fit for Lucullus? One of these Eastern dishes has as much patriotic flavor as the roast beef of Old England, the frogs of France, the *olla* of Spain, or the hog and hominy of America. It is the plenteous *pilaf*, the national dish. It is worthy of all acceptation. It is sometimes spelled *pillau*, but generally pronounced p'laf. It is on every Turkish table. It may be made in various ways, but its very soul consists in the essences and sauces which belong to the stewed meats, over which plain boiled rice is poured. The rice is as white as the unbolted snow of Boreas. To a Turkish or Arab peasant or soldier a dish of *pilaf* is a feast of the gods, and as prepared here in the East it would adorn a Delmonico dinner.

I am not aware that the Roman gourmand ever ate with his fingers, nor have I ever seen any classic announcement of the number of tines to his fork ; but it will be many decades before the Turk gives up the habit of eating with his fingers, or regarding the knife, fork and spoon as otherwise than unhandy tableware—wasteful and ridiculous.

Are there any liquids on the table? No. No bottles, no pitchers? No ; only a large glass of water for each guest at the end of the entertainment.

The meals for the palace, and frequently for the *konaks*, are brought from a distance. You will notice their carrier in the picture. He is called the "*Cablákiai.*" The other personage is the cook. These are orginal sketches—not commonplace photographs.

The trays are carried from Dolma-Bagtché to Yildiz, nearly a third of a mile distant—and up-hill. The meats are contained in copper dishes, so that they can be heated on a charcoal fire after their arrival at Yildiz. There is, however, a kitchen for the Imperial family connected with the palace of Yildiz. Their dinners do not travel that distance, but the tray is in service at all the dinners.

An American friend asked me, on my describing these twenty-odd dishes, whether the Turk " waded " through all this variety with his fingers. If the Turk had asked the question of a New Yorker whether he " waded " through all the dishes of the Hoffman House *menu* with a lot of cutlery, the answer in each case would have been an equation—" why, certainly !"

A story is told of the Shah of Persia, during his visit to Europe, which was exceedingly amusing to some Turks to whom it was mentioned. It was, that after dinner, forgetting temporarily Western customs—having used his fingers in dining—he wiped his hands on the lace curtain, which was conveniently near him. This was after dining with the Emperor of Austria. He thought the curtains were hung up for his special service.

These remarks are prefatory to a description of the best possible dinner—at the palace itself. But it could hardly be termed a Turkish meal. It happened in the spring of 1886, after our return from Egypt. It is unnecessary to say how much of the preliminary preparation seemed to us dispensable. The calling of the landeau, and the liveried coachman with his simple gold band, and the capture of the dragoman *en route* to the palace, were not the least indispensable requisites for such an occasion.

We had been informed that the German Ambassador and his wife were to be our companions at the feast, and that the famous violinist Wilhelmj was to be present. He was to have the honor of playing for the Sultan, and as a German, he was under the patronage of the German Ambassador.

It is the custom of the Sultan—and for some reasons which are more or less connected, as it is humorously said, with astrology —always to postpone an engagement, especially when it involves an interview, or a dinner with the representative of a foreign power. The dinner at Yildiz, to which reference has been made, was twice postponed. The same thing happened to Herr Rado-witz, the German Minister ; but at last, the invitation was fixed for Saturday evening, the 29th of May. Luckily, owing to my perusal of history on that day, I found this date to be the anniversary of the entrance of the Ottoman emperor into Constantinople. According to Chesterfield's canon of diplomatic grace, I incidentally mentioned to the Sultan this pleasing fortui-tousness. I think he had forgotten it, for he seemed to regard me with a smile of amazement that an alien should be so ready in Ottoman annals.

Many distinguished gentlemen and officials were invited to meet us. The details of the dinner were published the next day in the papers, in many languages. All that it becomes me to say is that it was throughout, especially in its conclusion, a remarkable proof of the friendship of the Porte for the German and American nations.

When we arrive at the gate of Yildiz, the Kavass dismounts. He is no longer wanted, and he retires to the Legation. The soldiers on guard escort us up the drive, and the coachman, conscious of the presence of royalty, lashes his horses into a gallop.

"Are we late?" I ask, tremulously.

"About five minutes," responds the dragoman. We breathe freely.

In the gloaming of the evening I only notice that the garden wall is a mass of Bankshire roses and the palace a wilderness of lights. The carriage stops. We alight. We are met at the vestibule by a grand Pasha in uniform and decorations. We walk upon carpets, ascend and descend steps into the marble entrance, and there are invited to take off our wraps. We are ushered into a small side room, and find M. and Mme. Radowitz, together with other invited guests, among them Dr. Mavroyéni, the Sultan's physican, whose son is now the Turkish Minister to America. The German Ambassadress is dressed in elegant white satin, with a gold and silk embroidered train. It is unnecessary to state how the American Minister's wife is dressed. In some nebulous way, I know that pink satin and point lace figured on the occasion. The gentlemen greet us, and remain standing. In a few minutes the master of ceremonies leads the way to the upper salon. He is followed by the Ministers and the rest of the company. Each is presented in turn to the Sultan. Mme. Radowitz, with a grace beyond all expression, sinks to the floor in her salaam. The American Minister's wife, from her Democratic manner of courtesy, is not expected to make quite such a display; and she does not. We are in the presence of the Sultan. If I were to give the opinion of the female portion of the company, I should say that he has large fine eyes and a most gracious manner. The latter is illustrated by his cordial shaking of the hand with all. On his motioning to the ladies they are seated on the divan. He then calls up the three princes; his son, who is seventeen years old, and his two nephews. These youths wear military suits, epaulettes, spurs and swords. They are each presented in their turn. How the company is disposed, with the view to a movement towards the dining saloon and table, it is unnecessary to state; except this, that the Sultan accompanies his guests to the door of the grand salon, with a parting salutation and remark that he will continue the reception after dinner.

The table is a picture. It is wide and long, with a gorgeous display of flowers fruits, lights and crystal shades. We enter at the end of the room and are tendered our respective seats. Our little ministerial family are placed among the Princes. One of the nephews, Tewfik, is about ten years of age. He is a meek, quiet, subdued-looking child. He speaks Turkish only. The Sultan's son and nephew speak some French. When the dinner begins, although they do not drink wine, there is much geniality. We happen to have other genial companions at the table. They are acquainted with some of our Turkish-Egyptian friends. Some of them served in the wars together. Meanwhile the Sultan's band plays rare music from the adjoining room, and the dinner goes on very much like a French or Russian dinner. I find that the Princes are anxious about geography. They inquire about Egypt. They ask about America. We explain much of the recondite history of Egypt, including incidental remarks about the mummies, temples and tombs. Although they only drink water, we drink their health, and they enjoy it. Asking after their amusements, we do not receive much information. I imagine that the Princes are more or less restricted by their exalted position. The *menu* is tempting. The wines are good. The service, in silver at first, and then in gold, winds up with the finest crystal for finger-bowls. Dainty little gold shells hold the ices. Ten servants in gold-trimmed uniforms and fez caps serve the table.

The dinner is not tedious, for it is not long. The *bon-bons* are passed about, the princes being always first served. Each takes one, and passes it to my wife with a quaint courtesy. After arising from the table, we march down the line of Pashas, aides and servants, all of whom bow, after the Oriental method. Then passing through a corridor, we enter a polished green and black tiled coffee-room, which has a dais railed off at one end. How rare and beautiful are the Turkish carpets and divans here! How tempting for a siesta, after dinner! How exquisite the chairs and the malachite tables!

After being seated, the dragoman surprises my wife and the company. He approaches her with a box.

" I have something to show you, Madam," he says.

" Yes," she responds. " It is lovely outside. What is in it ?"
He opens it, remarking, " Shall I put it on you ?"
" What do you mean ?" she inquires.
" I have the pleasure of decorating you, at the Sultan's wish,
with the Grand Order of the Chefekat."

Thereupon he throws the Cordon over her head, and, with the
aid of the German Ambassadress, who is familiar with the decoration, it is decorously arranged.    It is a surprise as well as an
honor, coming as it does almost within one year of our service
with the American Legation.    It is a star in brown, gold and
green enamel, with diamond brilliants.    It has five points, and
twenty-six diamonds on each point.    Surely no woman of good
training would refuse such a gift !    It is fastened upon the
front of the corsage, and, with the Cordon, it serves as an ornament to the dress.    The Pashas, the aides and the officers
make their felicitations on the happy event.

My wife told me confidentially afterwards that she thought
for a brief, ineffable moment that she was a bride again.

This decoration is a jeweled ornament which is generally bestowed upon the wives of such Ministers here as are *personæ
gratæ*.    It originated with the present Sultan, or his father, in
order to honor Lady Layard for her services in the hospitals
during the Crimean War.    It is called the " Order of Good Works."
The presentation was made with much exquisite tact.    My wife
received it amid general congratulations before she was aware
that a question might be raised as to the propriety of its reception by the other member of her family.    However, I raised no
such question.    The Constitution in no way inhibits a man's wife
from receiving presents ; and if it did there is no special penalty
in connection with a gift of this nature.    The ostensible reason
for this presentation, as its name signifies—being charitable benefaction—could not well be contested by the Minister after the
fact was accomplished by the consent of the wife, " without any
coercion on the part of her said husband."

Whatever may be said of the matter, these courtesies do not
loosen the friendship of the two nations.    They have no tendency
toward demoralization.    That I can understand ; for they do
not lead me to be partial to aristocratic institutions or monarchical governments.

There has been much interchange of kindly regard between

the Sultan and Shah. The Sultan frequently wears the Grand Cordon of the Persian Order of the Lion and Sun, and he is prompt to confer decorations on those who represent his co-religionists. These occasions make very pronounced the religious relations btween the two countries ; not merely by cordons of honor, for the Sultan is more practical. He has invited many of the Persian youth to avail themselves of the advantages of his schools, within the domain of Turkey. This accords with the benevolence which is authorized and enjoined by the Koran.

Whenever there are sufferers from fire and earthquake upon the islands and lands which belong to the Turkish empire, there is always a relief commission, of which the Sultan is the chief patron. When he tenders relief to refugees from Turkey in Europe, going to new homes in Asia, there is much contention and anxiety on the part of his Ministers and friends to show àn interest in the charity. A house is burned down at Bechïktash, and a child in consequence loses its life and its mother her reason. It happens near the palace of Yildiz. The·Sultan hears of it. He exempts the owner of the house, by force of his autocratic power, from any government tax, and presents him with a sum of money as a token of sympathy for his misfortunes.

Presents of value are by no means uncommon in the East. They play a great part in diplomatic and social life. They are not limited to those of the same faith. They are often given by the Sultan to the Greek and Armenian patriarchs and the Hebrew chief rabbi ; and often the present is in money.

These gifts are seldom bestowed to dignify those with whom the Sultan comes in contact beyond their meed, but they always produce the proper fruit and give encouragement to those kindly relations out of which the charities and tolerations of this Eastern life spring. Why should this not be ? If His Holiness the Pope can confer the insignia of the Order of Pius IX., on the Grand Vizier, and upon other Turkish officials, why may not there be a reciprocity in that regard ? So the Sultan sends to the Pope, through the Catholic Armenian Patriarch, a rich ring, to bind in harmony their respective religious efforts.

Benevolence in the East is by no means limited. It is catching. It extends to the Legations. If the Sultan may give gratuities to the Grand Rabbi, or to the Patriarch of the Greek Church, or a ring to the Pope, and exercise other elegant amenities, why should not there be a calico-dance in mid-Lent, under English auspices for sweet charity's sake? Why should not the German Ambassadress, to help the kindergarten, institute a bazaar for that purpose?

Among the presents fabricated for Pope Pius IX., was one from the Sultan Abdul-Medjid in the year 1853. It is an Oriental saddle. Its cloth and leather, except, of course, the seat, were encrusted with jewels, mostly diamonds. It may not be known, but it is nevertheless true, that among the Turks there is no present which is so appreciated as that of a horse or saddle. Although the Popes are not in the habit of riding on horseback, at least since the time when one of them was thrown from his horse in the Forum, the saddle was a very beautiful specimen of a gift, and well intended by the father of the present Sultan. The precious stones in the saddle, however, have been removed since it was first hung upon a peg in the Vatican. They now decorate a chalice presented by the ex-Queen of Spain to the Pope.

Considering the unusual circumstances of the evening, this digression may be pardonable.

After the presentation of the decoration to my wife, on this occasion, and after other courtesies, the ladies enter the carriage. They are driven toward but not to the harem. They are not invited to see the domesticities. The gentlemen follow upon foot. The beautiful lights in the gardens and from the windows make the scene like one from the Arabian Nights. The plashing fountains and the fragrance of the air produce the impression of something magical and marvelous.

Then we enter a grand salon, with a parqueted floor covered with rugs, divans, chairs and tables, where a rare library, a white porcelain stove and numerous secretaries fill the side walls, from which depend red satin hangings. Here the Sultan receives us again. A beautiful table occupies the centre. Upon it are some American photographs. It happened on that very morning that another box of American photographs was received through the Porte, and not through myself as Minister. His Majesty sits in an arm-chair at the head of this table, dressed, as usual, in his dark-blue frock coat, suit, sword and fez cap. His black whiskers and large eyes produce a picturesque effect. He seems more at ease than any of his company. He chats with each and all, and always on appropriate subjects, and with musical, subdued tones and fluent language. Every sentence is received by the interpreter with a profound bow, carrying his right hand from near the floor to his heart and head. The sentences are passed through our own dragoman to the ministerial ear with equal grace. To the German Ambassadress the Sultan apologizes for not seeing and entertaining her before at his dinner-table. It is because of the Greek troubles. He points to the photographs of the Emperor and Empress of Germany on a side table. He cherishes them as friends. To the American Minister he expresses regret at the delay in seeing him, and the delight which he experiences at receiving some new pictures from the President.

These courtesies ending, the violinist Wilhelmj is ushered in. He has a large forehead, and the air of a man of genius. He makes a graceful bow at the door, and seems relieved when he reaches the piano stool, where an accomplished Pasha awaits and afterwards accompanies him in some rare and rich music. The national air of Germany is given, on the rendering of which the Sultan and all of us rise. Then, as a tribute to Germany, or to the unseen goddess of Metaphysics, he asks each of us to smoke. The ladies, of course, decline, but the American Minister is not in that mood. The Sultan lights his own cigarette from a silver match-box, and pointing to it says:

"Tell my friend Mr. Hewitt that I keep his gift by me, as a pleasant souvenir."

When we retire to the library, the Sultan shows his guests the elegant specimens of American art and scenery which he had received in the morning. He had selected a few from the new lot. He also shows me a letter in Turkish from his Minister, which informs him of the arrival of the package. He states that he has directed the Minister to telegraph the President his grateful regard and thanks for these interesting gifts. He also requests me to send a similar message.

The tea is then served in gold cups and saucers. The music is concluded. Thanks are sent to the musician, along with a pretty decoration. Then the Sultan rises, takes little Tewfik, his nephew, by the hand and leads him to the piano, saying, apologetically:

"The boy will give us some music, although he has only learned by the ear."

The quiet little Prince plays a spirited march. It is a national air. Then he plays from "Norma." After that he leaves the piano and stands in his place meekly, till the Sultan indicates for him to sit. The Sultan kindly explains that he is a child of one of his brothers, who had died when Tewfik was but a few months old, and that he was educating him as well as his other nephew as companions to his son.

The Sultan now arises. He will detain us no longer. It is etiquette at the palace to remain until the Sultan gives the signal to leave. This he generally does by a glance at his watch, saying :

" I fear you will be late ;" or, " Perhaps I am detaining you."

He shakes hands with the ladies first; and then the gentlemen, with their best grace, back out. The bouquets are distributed to the ladies. A little remark of mine, which was caught as I left the room, caused the Sultan to recall the Minister and the dragoman. I had mentioned that our President was about to be married. He suggests to the dragoman to ask the Minister whether the Ottoman ruler could not in some way honor the expected bride of the President. Of this, perhaps, hereafter, with proper reserve, as it became a diplomatic Diversion.

As we retire, after many kindly greetings, we look in vain for lattice and curtain to indicate the harem. Every window opens into a beautiful garden, and every garden is filled with flowers and sparkling fountains. It is a fairy scene ; but no houri. We enter our carriages at the park gate, take our venerable Kavass along, and, with a cavalry escort behind, we move toward Pera; and thus this Oriental entertainment is ended !

The tales which have been told concerning the life of Abdul Medjid, and his brother, Abdul Aziz, and of their enormous, capricious personal expenditures and luxuries, should be taken as we take the Oriental tale about the jewels and precious minerals of the earth seen in some cave opened by some magic influence. In the matter of display, ornamentation, luxury, retinue of officers—military, civil and ecclesiastical—there is much demonstrative Orientalism even yet, for the gratification of the people and sojourners upon the Bosporus ; but in this regard there has been great advancement on the line of simplicity. This palatial dinner illustrates this line of advancement.

The palaces have their alabaster bathrooms, and gates of

green and gold of marvelous beauty—places for dreams—pleasure-houses for rare festivities like those of Kubla-Khan or Yildiz, but they also have their offices for the labors of statesmanship. They may have treasure halls, where rubies, sapphires, emeralds, diamonds and pearls of rare loveliness and immense size are so numerous and wonderful as to stud the very walls of embroidered satin and the very rugs beneath your feet with costly jewels ; but after all, our feast at the "Palace of the Star" signalizes its memory more by the amiability of the Sultan than by the decorations which we observed or which he bestowed. All the jewels of his palaces and treasury could not make the balm of its recollection more fragrant and sweet.

If any of my Democratic-Republican constituents should be so curious about this representation at this royal palace and feast, I ask the question that was asked about John the Baptist, "What went ye out for to see?" I could not truthfully respond that I saw a man shaken like a reed with the wind—as the Sultan is often represented—but I could say that I saw "a man clothed in soft raiment," and that I beheld those which are "gorgeously appareled and live delicately in the King's courts."

# CHAPTER VII.

THE name by which I have christened this volume indicates that its pages are not entirely serious. The volume is intended to record Diversions. The word has a comprehensive meaning. It means that which draws the mind from care or study, and thus relaxes and amuses. It is not only an entertainment, but a recreation. I will not say that I was limited in my recreation or amusement to that which was immediately around me. I found much delight in perusing the American newspaper, with its numerous and comic caricatures, and its marvelous but humorous interviews between His Majesty and the American Minister. I have made a collection of these remarkable drawings ; some of which make "old wrinkles come" with mirth and laughter. Here is one before me :

The Minister is sitting, capped with a red and tasselled fez, in baggy breeches, upon a scarlet cushion. He holds an improbable pipe of impossible size. Its amber is between his lips, while an odalisque fairy is tendering him Oriental sherbet. Another picture represents the Minister done in little, sitting on a foot-stool at the feet of a gigantic Sultan with a tremendous turban that would have done honor to the Janizaries in the time of Selim I. The Sultan has a drawn cimeter, the like of which cannot be found in the treasury within the Porte or in any armory on earth. A chibouque of immensity is connected with an endless snaky convolution; while occasionally the Sultan ceases to smoke in order to roar "like all Tattersalls," at some fancied joke of the Minister. Another represents the Minister, with crushed hat and spike-tail coat, bowing before the Sultan, who sits cross-legged—which is not his position on any except such picturesque occasions—while out from behind the arras peep numberless "lights of the harem" curious to observe the ceremony.

Most of these arrangements of diplomatic jocoseness, are from the pen and pencil of the American press. They are strangely anachronous and exaggerative. The American humor revels in exaggeration ; and why may not the absent enjoy it as well as those who are at home !

Even the most sedate papers in America had cable despatches which stated that the Minister was presented with a set of valuable Turkish jewelry by the Sultan. They proceeded to read section 1751 of the Revised Statutes, which forbids any diplomatic or consular officer asking or accepting any present for himself or any other person. Many compliments were heaped upon the Minister because he had been made the recipient of Turkish jewelry ; and one of our papers playfully remarked that the only gift the Minister could make in return would be some jokes of questionable age and of impossible comprehension, but which might form a brilliant parure for the Moslem festive board.

This story of the jewels started from a pleasant incident. It happened during my first interview with His Majesty. The present Mayor of New York, Mr. Hewitt, and the Sultan are great friends, having met each other in Constantinople some years ago. Their friendship had been cemented by a library of books of rare interest sent by the Sultan to the Mayor. Mr. Hewitt entrusted the Minister with a return gift. It was very handsome ; the very best sample of Tiffany's workmanship. It was a covered vase of graceful shape, intended as a receptacle for keeping sweet the Sultan's smoking tobacco, albeit of American growth, which Mr. Hewitt furnishes the Sultan from time to time. The vase was of beaten metal of various shades, in which silver was blended with gold in such a manner as to produce a most harmonious effect in colors. The chasing was in Arabesque design, with two shields appearing on opposite sides of the vase, one bearing an imperial monogram and the other the emblems of Turkish sovereignty. Along with the vase was a match-box, in the shape of a cigar. This opened very mysteriously. These articles had been transmitted to the Sultan the day before the Reception ; and at the private interview granted, much was said about the friendship which existed as well between the United States and Turkey, as between Abdul Hamid and Abram S. Hewitt. The cable, from some mangling of this incident, gave rise to these fables about a present to the Minister. Indeed, a poet from Ohio went so far as to attribute

LEGATION STEAM LAUNCH "SUNSET," OFF PRINKIPO.

to the Sultan this lyric gush as to Turkish generosity and impecuniosity :

> " Please accept this jeweled casket,
> For I, Abdul Hamid ask it.
> The bill is unpaid, I know, sir,
> But the head of him I owe, sir,
> Is now rolling in the basket !

Other papers not given to the jocose had exquisite etchings of the Minister, in a swallow-tailed coat, making his obeisance before the Sultan. It described the ministerial hair as oily, like that of a Chatham Street barber, while a small rose nestled in the button-hole of his coat, to which an odalisque nightingale sang its song. A half-dozen richly dressed eunuchs salaamed before the enamored Envoy. It was said that the Sultan had gotten himself up to receive the Envoy regardless of expense ; and that he had even gone so far as to have his shoes polished—a most unusual honor to be paid a foreigner. Although the two eminent personages could not understand each other—so ran the story—they managed to carry on quite a conversation. The Sultan at length invites the Minister to visit the harem. That gentleman puts on his killing smile and acquiesces ; but by a strange break in the concatenation of the wire in the Black Sea, the Sultan is led to keep a watch on the Bosporus, owing to a remark about Civil Service Reform, a senseless subject to discuss under such sensuous circumstances.

The picture which illustrates this wonderful account has several odalisques gazing from behind an embroidered screen. As they are the special lights of the harem, a terrific-looking Nubian, in a voluminous turban, with a drawn cimeter, and a meteoric crescent above his forehead, is placed on guard, expecting momentarily the order of the Sultan to decapitate the Minister.

All this indicates not only the free and easy way in which the sovereigns of America speak of a brother sovereign in another sphere, but it also shows the great progress which has been made in the reception of Envoys since the time when the grandfather of the present Sultan, seated behind the curtains upon his throne in the Bagdad kiosk on Seraglio Point, simply opened the hangings for the purpose of passing out his hand to be kissed by the Ambassadors.

But it is when the American journalist is in his funniest mood that he records as something pleasant the somewhat musty anecdote, common in America, which plays on the word Bosporus (Bos-for-us!), and adds to its playfulness the remark that the point of the pun, as perpetrated by the Minister, did not penetrate his Majesty's intellect for some time, but that when it did he celebrated the event by sending the Minister a handsome glass pipe, formerly used by the females of the harem.

It will be noticed that most of these sportive accounts do not refrain from allusions to the domesticities of the palace.

Is it not one of the liberties of the American people that its independent citizen may take a lively interest in the discussion of the domestic affairs of everybody? Therefore, it was not at all unexpected to find in American journals the statement that the new Minister was, in this regard, Extraordinary in many senses besides that of Envoy. May I not be pardoned, therefore, in reproducing for Oriental surprise—for it cannot be indignation—a few samples of this marvelous and hyperbolical literature?

In one of these journals the Minister is represented as arrayed in his insignia of office and knocking at the door of the harem, just as "His Majesty is putting on his Turkish rug and tying his Daghestan around his high standing collar!" What follows is none the less unexpected from the newspaper: The door is opened by an ebony Ethiopian, as innocent of raiment as if there had never been an apple in the Garden of Eden.

"Well, Mungo," says the Minister, "is the Son of the Moon up yet?"

"Walla, walla!" is his only response.

The Sultan, seeing the Ethiopian embarrassed, has him recalled. By a wave of his hand he summons the Minister into his presence.

"Mr. Porte, I believe?" says the Minister, who is also embarrassed.

"That is my name. Take an ottoman?" replies the Sultan, motioning to a small foot-stool at his side.

"Thanks," says the Minister. Thereupon the interview proceeds.

"I have come, my Lord High and Mighty, to let you know that my nation isn't afraid of the 'unspeakable' Turk any more than it is of any other furren' bird."

The Sultan, not understanding this American *argot,* makes a salaam.   Whereupon the Minister offers to wager even ducats that if he was dressed in the loose fashion of the Sultan himself, he (the Minister) could touch his toes without bending his knees, as many times in an hour as the Porte himself.

" Do you smoke ? " inquires the Sultan, ignoring the challenge and the wager.

The Minister avoids smoking, but remarks :

" I am powerful thirsty, High and Most Mighty Lord of the Horizon!   If you will give me a drink of that lighted concoction of yours I will be obliged," says the Minister, pointing to the chibouque at the Sultan's side, thinking it to be a demijohn of *rakee,* from Trebisonde.

The Sultan tolerates this unwonted familiarity.   He gathers his family around him.

" These ladies here are your daughters, I presume," remarks the Minister.

" You have a sublime father, young ladies ! "

" Please confine your attentions to business," remarks the Sultan, flushing to the roots of his fez.

" Well, I do mean business !   What's the matter with your daughters, anyhow?   Peek-a-boo !   Ah, there !   I see you "— sings out the festive Envoy to a beautiful Circassian, who wears the customary mosquito-proof cloak over her shoulders and a fluffy band of tulle over the lower part of her face.

" Look you ! " says the Sultan, " Child of the Setting Sun ! Look you, Sir-r-h !   I will order a bastinado for you !"

" Two of them," suggests the Minister—" on toast !"

" You are rushing business, young man," says Abdul, without quailing, and reaching for his cimeter.

" Put up your cheese knife ! " says the Minister.   " It doesn't scare.   The sooner you simmer with your cimeter the better it will be for all hands—and heads," stroking his black beard composedly.

Evidently the Minister has the advantage, for he exclaims defiantly, while waving an imaginary star-spangled flag above the star and crescent :

" Sew me up, and drop me in the Bosporus, if you can ! Hah !   Hah !   You tremble !   Ta-ta ! "

Before the Sultan could have the Minister throttled—for so

writes the American journal—the Envoy goes singing down the
palatial carpets to the front door :

Porté, Porté,
Fat, fair and forté.
Don't try on me your manners horté."

The Minister then salaamed the door.

One of our poetasters, in singing of the disaster to the steam-

MEHMET, THE AMERICAN KAVASS.

ship *Gallia*, which brought us across the ocean, attributed the
breaking of the shaft to some joke of the Minister, and the engineer begged him not to joke again. The shaft of the ship broke,
and could not, or would not, again make any stroke; and all, said
the facetious journalist, as the sad result of a joke.

These home felicities anent the head of the Legation might
have been withstood ; but the iconoclastic journalist dared to lay
his mace, like the second Mahmoud, upon the person of the Kavass
—our guide, Janizary and friend ! What is a Kavass, and who

is he?  He has a history of hundreds of years ; and ours at the Porte is none other than Mehmet, who has served the American Legation for thirty years.

Every personage of old Turkey, except the Janizary, is represented in the mosaic of different people and races at Constantinople.  The Janizary is represented by the Kavass. This official goes ahead of the Envoy when afoot, or with him on the launch or ferry, to protect him from the Moslem.  He is an antique repetition of the old guard, chosen from the Janizary *corps* to guard the Giaour or Christian from the insults of the Mahometan.  He comes down from the olden time, and is as much out of place as an old flint-lock musket in modern battles.

Such an odd, old, obsolete genius of antiquity is our Kavass Mehmet.  He is the picture of goodness.  His photograph I found in the establishment here of Abdullah Frères.  He accompanies the Minister and family, when they take their walks abroad along the stony paths of the shores of the Bosporus, or when the launch lands them at an Asiatic palace across the Straits ; or when the Minister makes his calls at the Porte on the Ministers of State, or upon the Foreign Ministers upon the upper Bosporus ; or when they go a-shopping in the Greek shops of Pera or in the bazaars of Stamboul.  On these occasions the Kavass is sure to be the accompaniment.  The American Kavass weighs 350 pounds.  He wears a blue frock coat braided in black, a golden belt, a sword in a silver sheath, and pistols of portentous size and antiquity.  He orders all the urchins, donkies, arabis and beggars out of the ministerial path.  He has his uses in the narrow streets.

It was this valuable adjunct of our diplomatic Diversions whom the caricaturist represented quite otherwise than he appears in the picture herein presented.  That he is heavy, grave and gorgeous in full attire, is easily observed.  That he is handsome, is true, if to be so, be to be good and honest.  I vindicate him by this faithful portraiture.

It was hardly a "Diversion," but still it is worth mentioning as one of the encouraging features of our system of diplomacy, that almost the moment I brought our Legation out of a dirty side-alley in Constantinople and fixed it in a respectable quarter and in nice chambers, at less expense, my attention was called by the home authorities, to a most unusual contingent ex-

A. A. GARGIULO,

DRAGOMAN OF THE UNITED STATES LEGATION.

pense. It was not peculiar to Turkey. It was said to be incurred by our Ministers in "non-Christian countries." By way of illustration, these authorities cited some charges in the accounts of Mr. Emmet, our able Secretary of Legation, and the Chargé before my advent in Turkey. They likewise hauled Mr. Benjamin, late Minister to Persia, over hot coals. The object of all this was, to learn whether the needs of this kind of service in these distant lands absolutely required these expenses. At once many of these expenses were discontinued by the Department, after a full investigation by myself of every item connected with the Legation. Among these items, which for fifty years had existed, was an allowance of four horses to the Minister and one to the dragoman. These were disallowed promptly; although they had existed from the time of Commodore Porter's ministry in 1830. Each horse was accounted to consume sixteen dollars a quarter. These were allowances, as commutation for the extra expense of traversing the narrow and horrid streets, where carriages were impossible, and which both Minister and dragoman were compelled to traverse, every day, either to the palace or to the Porte. This commutation of horse was an economical convenience to the Minister and dragoman. My attempts in Congress for economy, and my report on the subject to the Department, seemed to arouse all the exquisite fun and dainty deviltry belonging to the Mephistophelian press of my native land. With the aid of some clerks in the State Department or the Treasury, the public press was enabled to enlighten my fellow-citizens about certain sudden changes from a stingy Congressman to an extravagant Minister ! I was represented, both by word and caricature, as riding on four splendid Arab steeds bare-back—I mean the steeds bare-back. Of what use was it to deny this unbridled luxury ! Need I say that at that time I was lying upon an ottoman well racked with the sciatica ? But the Jeffersonian simplicity of the Administration was demolished by these fantastic and fancied Oriental pictures of a ministerial circus performance over the horrible pavements of the capital of Constantine !

The most hyperbolical of these exaggerations of American humor had reference to the reception described in a preceding chapter. Even alliteration's artful aid was called in, and the sobriquet of the Minister was used to indicate the scintillation which "Sunset" and the Sultan invariably produced in their

THE ACTUAL CONDITION ON AN OTTOMAN

THE MINISTER'S FOUR-HORSE ACT—AN IDEAL.

séances. My meeting with the Sultan is thus described by one of our humorous papers ; I need not mention its name, but it girdles the earth in forty minutes:

They—Sultan and Minister—meet on the shore of the Golden Horn. The Sultan advances a few paces and says :

"Gracious Son of the Mighty and Glorious West, I salute thee. Star of my Soul and Apple of my Eye, welcome to the Sublime Porte. I hail thee as a bubbling fountain of delectation, dearer to my sight than the rose to the nightingale, more precious than the shade of the date-palm to the weary traveler on the desert. Thrice welcome to these classic shores."

Then the Minister responds :

"O High and Mighty Sultan, Child of the East, Playmate of the Evening Star, Companion of the Vagrant Zephyr, Old Chum of the Red, Red Rose, I salute thee and thank thee. I greatly rejoice in the decision of my master at home, who hath sent me to these classic and legendary shores. May our communion and companionship overflow with joy and pleasantness, without a fleeting shadow to darken the sunshine of our content. Again I thank thee, and connect the kiss of international good-will with the flower-garden of thy Eastern cheek, O Vermilion Rose-Tint of the Fading Twilight, Soft Liniment of My Weary Frame, and Precious Pad of My Liver."

We are led to exclaim, in the language of *Puck's* own motto, " What fools these mortals be." But we must remember that our American extravaganzas come out of the Orient through the Celtic medium ; and, as these chapters will prove, the Orient is of this quality of humor, " all compact."

The very nature of the East—physical and human—speaks of " skies full of splendid moons and shooting stars, and spouting exhalations—diamond fires." If in pursuing the behest of the religion of the East, we make the West tributary to Oriental doctrine and contemplation, may we not be excused for modeling our Brobdingnagian phrases on the spire-steeple style ? Especially when these phrases are so neatly turned as in the verses of an Ohio poet :

> I am very glad to meet you, Mr. Cox ;
> With a royal shake, I greet you, Mr. Cox ;
>   Just seat yourself at ease, sir,
>   And take some snuff and sneeze, sir ,
> I would like to sleep and eat you, Mr. Cox.
>
> Oh America, I love it, Mr. Cox ;
> I am great, but not above it, Mr. Cox ;
>   I hear the climate's healthy,
> And the country's very wealthy —
> Oh, that gold, I'd like some of it, Mr. Cox.

> You shall take the place of Wallace, Mr. Cox ;
> By familiar name shall call us, Mr. Cox ;
>   We will have our fun together,
>   And we'll never mind the weather,
> For we'll have a hack to haul us, Mr. Cox.

More especially, may we not be pardoned when we regard the splendid empire which this Emperor still controls ; and likening, as I often do, its primary elements to those of our own country— with its diversity in unity—turn from these flippant and harmless pleasantries of our jolly journalists, to the solid forces of rule and character which the Emperor displays in the midst of all attempts to despoil him of his territory or derogate from his good name.

Properly to dignify this Ruler and Caliph of the great Eastern country, and to correct the errors which too much frivolity may have created in reference to his character, let me in the next chapter make a compendious statement of these historic realms.

# CHAPTER VIII.

## COMPENDIUM OF OTTOMAN HISTORY.

TURKEY is not what she was; but she is yet an empire, politically and otherwise. Her possessions in Europe are peopled with 8,650,000 folks of divers races. This number includes Roumelia, which is nearly autonomous, and Bosnia, Herzegovina and Bulgaria. The latter is, as yet, a tributary principality. Outside of Europe lies the real Ottoman power. Counting Egypt, Tripoli and some of the Grecian isles, and not counting the sacred rule in Asia and Africa, the Sultan, Abdul-Hamid, is the Emperor of at least 36,000,000 of people, and, as the Mahometan father, of nearly two hundred millions of the faithful.

This does not count Tunis, which France has. It does not count other realms, as India, Borneo—aye, even to Congo, Liberia and Guinea—which have devotees of the Islam faith.

Constantinople alone has over seven hundred thousand people. Reckoning the people along the Bosporus, it is double that number. They live mostly at or about the old point, the ancient Byzantium. They have a grand dépôt of commerce and intercourse. But their harbor really runs from Kavak, or, rather, from Fanaraki and Fener, near the mouth of the Black Sea, to the Dardanelles. There these clear, deep and flowing waters connect with the tideless Mediterranean.

Counting Bulgaria, Bosnia, Herzegovina, Roumelia, Servia, Wallachia and Moldavia—Turkey in Europe is roughly estimated at an area of one million eight hundred square miles. Deduct about one-fourth of this territory for the recent changes since the Berlin treaty, and you will have a reasonable estimate of her European domain.

A Turkish historian remarks that, as in gazing at the sun the eye becomes dazzled, so the mind becomes confused when it attempts to regard the brilliancy of the career of this illustrious Turkish race. It is not difficult, however, to trace this race to one of the five nomadic tribes which comprise the Turanian family. They have been called Tartars. These tribes gave such populousness as Central Asia had in the early centuries—even beyond the Caspian. It is supposed that the name Turk is derived from the Chinese appellation *Tu-kiu.* The Turks were an imperial race, who lived west of China two hundred years and more before the Christian era. The historic pen becomes more or less confused, as it undertakes to separate the Huns, Tartars and Mongols, who, under their respective chiefs, ravaged from time to time the Asiatic and a large part of the European world. But out of seeming confusion, and after many dispersions, it is tolerably sure that the Turks became more or less subservient to a great Khan in the gold mountains of Altai. There they became forgers of iron and makers of weapons. From these men the Turks of to-day claim their origin. The iron-working nations —including the large family of Smiths, whose ancestor was Tubal-Cain—have ever held the world in thrall. The Turks, with their iron weapons of that early day, cast off the yoke which pressed upon them, and established a royal camp in the gold mountains. They became nomadic on the Asiatic plateau.

What religion they had before their conversion to Mahometan-ism is rather nebulous. They worshipped the elements. They made sacrifices to the Supreme Being. They were more or less controlled by the doctrines of Zoroaster. Their criminal code was strict. Theft was punished by tenfold restitution, and other crimes more heinous, with death. To show their soldierly origin and aptitude, no chastisement was considered too severe for the coward. Of course they met many rivals in arms before they crossed into Europe. They fought the Persians, but still they moved on, eddying hither and thither, adding to their strength by their warlike energies. Sometimes they united with others; oftentimes they had Greeks for allies as well as enemies. The Romans sometimes sought alliance with them, to strengthen the wings of their advancing eagles.

When Mahomet appeared in the middle of the seventh cent-ury, his religion gave unity and zealotry to the Turkish tribes Thereafter, out of these traditions, half fact and half fancy per-haps, the history of Turkey takes authentic shape. While many Turkish princes ruled in Palestine, Syria and Egypt, the one great tribe of Seljuk, known as Turkoman, inhabited the district of Bokara. From this tribe descended the victorious Turks who carried the banner of the Prophet under the walls of Vienna only two hundred years ago, and who, defying augury, remain a power in Europe until this day.

After one of their great victories, these Seljukians assembled to elect a king. The question naturally arose, among so many splendid warriors, Who shall be chosen? The mode adopted for its solution is singular. A number of arrows are inscribed, each with the name of a tribe, family and candidate. The arrows are tied in a bundle. A child draws out the lucky one. Togrul Beg, the grandson of Seljuk, and a lineal descendant of the Turanian emperor, thus becomes the first Sultan elect. His kingdom, through division, falls into decay. Out of it springs a clansman of the same tribe. His name is Soliman. He is with the first of the Turkish hordes that land in Europe. He becomes an ally of one of the Greek contestants for the Byzantine throne, and finally the guest of the successful rival, by whom he is royally entertained at Scutari, on the Bosporus, with his two thousand cavalry.

From this time on the Turkish power rapidly develops, especially in Asia Minor. It continues to increase until the thirteenth century, when it meets the Tartar wave of conquest, led by the genius of Genghis-Khan, of their own stock. Before it, falls this Seljukian dynasty; but only temporarily. When the great Mogul, Ghengis-Khan, loses his conquests by too much extension, the Turks recover from their disasters. They renew their war against the Greeks. They are joined by their brethren who had emigrated from their Asiatic home in Khorassan. It so happens—perhaps the Turks would call it destiny—that Ertoghral, the leader of these kinsmen of the Turks, in his movement westward from Khorassan finds himself and his four hundred families in the presence of two contending armies. He takes sides at once. He is chivalrous: he sides with the weaker. It turns out that the weaker side wins. It also turns out that it was the side of the Sultan Alladin himself. Ertoghral becomes an Emir on the shores of the Black Sea. He continues the Turkish war against the Greeks.

By this time we approach solid historic ground. It is the last year but one of the thirteenth century. Now arises a military genius. He gives prestige and name to the proudest of the Turkish race. His name is Osman, or Othman. He is a states-

GIRDING ON THE SWORD OF OSMAN.

man as well as a soldier. His is the physical arm which strikes, and the dauntless courage which inspires his soldiers. In his reign the arts of peace as well as of war are cultivated. These include the erection of mosques and the education of children, the proper tenure of land and its cultivation, and religious toleration to the Christians whom they conquer. It was in this Osmanli statesmanship that the many liberalities known as the Capitulations of Turkey had their origin. It is said that Othman ruled even after his death ; so great was the influence of both the civil and the military organizations which he had created. It is the sword of Othman—to which I have adverted in a former chapter—which every successive Sultan must wear at the coronation. That ceremony is not complete until the act of girding it upon each successive Sultan is enacted. He is then the Emperor of the Ottomans. Othman's counsels are a royal testament to the Turk. It is his line which, in direct descent, rules in Constantinople to-day.

His son Orchan improves the inheritance which he receives from his father. He increases the army and extends his sway to the Bosporus. The arts and sciences are encouraged. The basis of Turkish naval power is laid. Of course the Turks are more or less belligerent all the time. The weakness of the Greek empire leads to a call upon Orchan for aid. He unites his forces, and even his family, with the Emperor at Byzantium.

A son of Orchan succeeds. He bears the banner of the Crescent into Thrace across the Dardanelles. Then Amurath, as his successor, advances that banner over Thrace, and fixes his capital at Adrianople. His conquests north of the Balkans make him its grand suzerain. Servia, Bosnia, Bulgaria and Albania bow beneath his sceptre.

If you should visit Broussa, you would see with interest the capital and the tombs of the founders of the Turkish empire. There are the mortuary chapels of the Sultans Osman and Orchan. They stand on the site of the ancient Greek cathedral dedicated to St. Elias. Osman died soon after the conquest of the city by his son Orkhan, and was, by his own desire, interred in the building, which was converted into a mausoleum. The large drum of Osman—one of the emblems of royalty, given to him by Alladin, Sultan of Iconium—was suspended over the head of the tomb, whence the name of Daoul Monastir (the Monastery of the

TOMBS OF THE FOUNDERS OF THE TURKISH EMPIRE, OSMAN AND ORCHAN.

Drum), by which the building was subsequently known. The chapel was completely shattered by the earthquake of 1855. The modern buildings now covering the remains of the founders of the Ottoman dynasty preserve no trace of the architectural beauty of the old church of St. Elias. The mausoleum of Sultan Orkhan, in the same enclosure, contains many family tombs, but that of his first wife, the virtuous and beneficent Christian, Princess Niloufer, finds no place there : she was interred near the wall of the enclosure. The sketch herein represents the condition of these famous tombs.

A more elaborate statement of the rise of the Moslem power and its progress will be found in the subsequent chapter upon the Caliphate. The advancement of the Turkish secular empire runs hand in hand with the growth of the Caliphate and its extension over three continents.

The number of sovereigns who have successively occupied the throne raised by Osman, including its founder and His present Majesty, is thirty-three. It may be interesting, as each was an unquestioned Caliph, as well as a Padishah, to give their names in chronological order, viz.:

1. The Sultan Osman, or Othman, surnamed Ghazi, or the Conqueror. He began his reign in the year A. D. 1299. He reigned 27 years.

2. Sultan Orchan; proclaimed A. D. 1326. He reigned 34 years.

3. Sultan Amurath I. (Murad); proclaimed A. D. 1360. He reigned 22 years.

4. Sultan Bajazét, the Thunderer; proclaimed A. D. 1389. He reigned 13 years. The Interregnum of Suleïman and Moussa then began. It lasted 11 years.

5. Mohamet I., the Gentleman; proclaimed A. D. 1413. He reigned 8 years.

6. Amurath II. (Murad); proclaimed A. D. 1421. He reigned 30 years.

7. Mohamed II., the Conqueror of Constantinople ; proclaimed A. D. 1451, and reigned 30 years.

8. Bajazet II.; proclaimed A. D. 1481. He reigned 30 years.

9. Selim I.; proclaimed A. D. 1512. He reigned 8 years.

10. Suleïman I., the Grand and Lawgiver; proclaimed A. D. 1520. He reigned 46 years.

GENEALOGICAL TREE OF THE OTTOMAN RULERS.

11. Selim II.; proclaimed A. D. 1566.   He reigned 8 years.

12. Amurath III. (Murad); proclaimed A. D. 1574.   He reigned 21 years.

13. Mohamed III.; proclaimed A. D. 1595.  He reigned 8 years.

14. Ahmet I.; proclaimed A. D. 1603.   He reigned 14 years.

15. Mustapha I.; proclaimed A. D. 1617.   He reigned 1 year and was deposed.

16. Osman II.; proclaimed A. D. 1618.   He reigned 4 years. Mustapha was then proclaimed the second time, A. D. 1622. He reigned 1 year.

17. Amurath IV. (Murad); proclaimed A. D. 1623. He reigned 17 years.

18. Ibrahim I.; proclaimed A. D. 1640.   He reigned 8 years.

19. Mohamed IV.; proclaimed A. D. 1648.   He reigned 39 years.

20. Suleïman II.; proclaimed A. D. 1687.   He reigned 4 years.

21. Ahmet II.; proclaimed A. D. 1691.   He reigned 4 years.

22. Mustapha II.; proclaimed A. D. 1695.  He reigned 8 years.

23. Ahmet III.; proclaimed A. D. 1703.  He reigned 27 years.

24. Mahmoud I.; proclaimed A. D. 1730.  He reigned 24 years.

25. Osman III.; proclaimed A. D. 1754.   He reigned 3 years.

26. Mustapha III.; proclaimed A. D. 1757.   He reigned 17 years.

27. Abd-ul-Hamit I.; proclaimed A. D. 1774.   He reigned 15 years.

28. Selim III.; proclaimed A. D. 1789.   He reigned 18 years.

29. Mustapha IV.; proclaimed A. D. 1807.  He reigned 1 year.

30. Mahmoud II.; proclaimed A. D. 1808.   He reigned 31 years.

31. Abd-ul-Medjid; proclaimed A. D. 1839.   He reigned 22 years.

32. Abd-ul-Aziz; proclaimed A. D. 1861.   He reigned 14 years, and was deposed.   Murat V. was then proclaimed, but not crowned.   He reigned only a few months.   He was deposed for alleged insanity.   He is still living, in close confinement.

33. Abd-ul-Hamid II.   He was proclaimed A. D. 1875.   He was born on the 22d of September, 1842.   He is the thirty-fourth sovereign of the Ottoman dynasty, and the second son of Abdul Medjid, who died on the 25th of June, 1861.   He has four sons. It was the eldest, Mehmet Selim, born on the 1st of January, 1871,

with whom we dined at the palace, but he does not inherit the throne. Two others are respectively about nine years old, one being born in February, 1878, and the other in the next month. He has a daughter, Zekihe, born in 1871, and another, Naïme, born in August, 1876. His brothers are of great consequence in a dynastic point of view. He has five brothers, one older than himself—Murad, who is not competent to rule. The youngest is sixteen years of age. He has three sisters, the eldest about his own age. Besides an aunt, he has nine cousins. The brother next in the order of succession under the Ottoman law is Mehmet Reshad. He is now about forty-three years of age. These relatives are often seen driving or riding about the city, and not infrequently at the " Sweet Waters " of Europe, where every class of people congregate. They are of distinguished appearance, dressed in Frank costume, except that each and all wear the inevitable fez.

# CHAPTER IX.

ONE of the determinative factors in the history of Turkey ought not to be omitted from this compendium. For a time, more important than Sultans, more potential than the Crescent, and almost rivaling the religious element of the Ottoman empire, was the organization known as the Janizaries. They were a body of men who had their origin in the reign of Amurath, the son of Orchan. They were born Christians, but in their education they became Moslem. They were fearfully destructive of the Christian people. As the ally of the Turk, they held Europe in terror for many hundred years.

It may be asked : How could such a body of Christian men become such zealots in the Mahometan faith and in the Turkish army ?

By the Mahometan law the Sultan is entitled to one-fifth of the spoils taken in battle. Amurath applied this law by the selection of the best captive Christian youths. These he trained in the Islam religion and in the use of arms. They were called *Yengi-cheri*, or new soldiers. Their faces, like their costumes, were white, which was interpreted to mean, shining and cheerful. They became the flower of the Turkish army. The same body was afterwards recruited from the Christian youths whose parents were Turkish subjects.

No man can be compelled to serve in the Turkish army, even yet, who is not a Mahometan. The strain for war material upon the Mahometan population was very great, but it was relieved by the education of these Christian youths in the Moslem faith. What battles these troops gained, how they were handled at the final taking of Constantinople, and how at last they were utterly destroyed by Sultan Mahmoud II., after nearly five hundred years of existence, is a conspicuous part of Turkish history.

This *corps* of Janizaries was the first example of a regular

AGA, OR CHIEF OF THE JANIZARIES.

COMMISSARY OF THE JANIZARIES.

standing army upon our planet. They were a sort of body-guard. Like the Roman pretorians, which, under Vitellius, numbered sixteen thousand, they controlled the State. They made and unmade the Turkish Cæsars. They became the instruments of despotic rule, and that rule was their own. Their force supplanted the patriarchal form, which always had mitigating circumstances amidst the worst surroundings. Their excesses went far in the time of Mustapha the Fourth, who came to the throne in 1807. When they could not use him as their tool, so as to repeal the reforms of his predecessor, they deposed him from power. They murdered the Sultan Selim, and endeavored to assassinate his brother, Mahmoud.

When these Janizaries chose to rebel, it was, in one sense, a rebellion of the stomach. They turned their kettles bottom up, as a symbol of their disregard. They thus refused their food, like spoiled children, and would not be dependent upon the Sultan, who would not grant all their caprices.

The Janizaries were not all destroyed by Sultan Mahmoud the Second. They have sometimes reappeared in certain neighborhoods in the same uniform, but not with the same intense and active organization. Mahmoud the Second broke their power. He was the son of the first Abdul Hamid, and the father of Abdul Medjid and Abdul Aziz, and therefore the grandfather of the present Sultan.

It would be impossible to make even a brief sketch of this remarkable *corps*, without giving some idea of the picturesqueness of their white uniform and of their arms. I have been fortunate enough to find in Constantinople a volume which bears evidence of being printed both in that city and Paris in 1882. It is a rare album. It contains the figures, uniform, arms and equipage—the whole paraphernalia, in fact—of this remarkable *corps*. It is an authentic album. It is compiled by one Ahmed Djèvad. He was a colonel in the Turkish army and a member of the Government. It contains the engravings of over forty of the Janizaries—officers, soldiers and servitors. It is impossible to describe the uniqueness and picturesqueness of the costumes of these soldiers. The head-dress has no parallel, except, perhaps, among the original effigies in the Museum of the Elbecci-Attica, at Constantinople, where are preserved, in all their splendid attire and gaudy color, the costumes of the officers

CHIEF OF THE JANIZARY CHASSEURS.

of the Sultan, and of this *corps*—from the chiefs of the Black and White Eunuchs, with their wands of silver, to the cook, with his manifold involutions of turban and sash. I present some of these heads, to represent not so much the costumes of the Janizaries, as the wonderful serenity which seems to reign upon their countenances, beneath the enormous plumes which cap their head-gear. I would specially call attention to the "Ousta du 32 Orta de Chasseurs." He has no rival in costumes, unless it may be among the warriors of central Asia or interior Africa.

This album contains engravings showing every species of gun, spear and arrow. It has pictures of arrows with torpedo heads. The variety of the guns, including breech-loaders, is wonderful. Many arms of which modern invention has vaunted itself may be seen among the ancient weapons in the Museum of the capital. Thanks to Colonel Djèvad, we have a good representation of them. Their authenticity no one can dispute.

I insert herein a sketch of a couple of javelins which I find in the book. Does the smoke that comes from the point indicate some tendency toward conflagration? With the new element of dynamite, and other explosives which have been introduced into modern warfare, why may not some inventive American make a similar torpedo, not simply to be fired by a gun, but by hand! It certainly would be a safe mode of procedure, as there would be less danger to the man who throws it or to the vessel from which it is fired.

When Mahmoud the Second came to the throne, in 1808, the institutions of Turkey depended upon the Janizaries. When the Grand Vizier of this Sultan undertook to reinstitute the liberal measures for which the Sultan's uncle had died, the Janizaries revolted. They successfully attacked the regular troops. They compelled the Grand Vizier to take refuge in a building, where he perished. They attacked the seraglio. They compelled the Sultan to revoke his liberal measures. But this was the last display of Janizary arrogance. Their insolence hastened their destruction. They had been used, through many vicissitudes, by the factions of the empire, and had become a standing menace to its existence. It became a question as to their existence or that of the empire. The Sultan resolved to break them up. He issued a decree for this purpose. They rebelled against it.

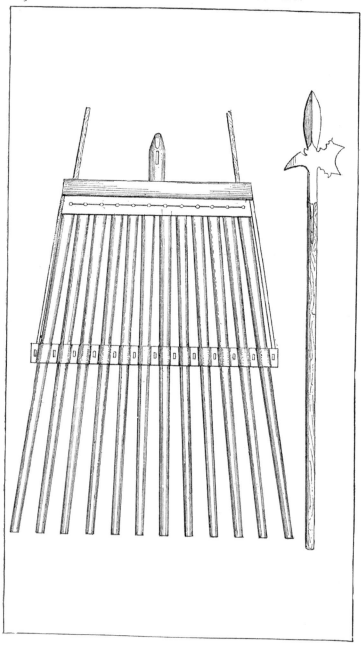

ARMS OF THE JANIZARIES.

Twenty-five thousand of them sprang to arms. The Sultan was prepared for this. They were exterminated by a massacre, horrible in detail ; but it was indispensable, if the efforts which Mahmoud was making for the regeneration of his people were to succeed.

It was not without the exercise of firmness and courage that Mahmoud was enabled to suppress this *corps*. It was an issue of life or death with him. History repeats itself. It is the pretorian of Rome or the strelitz of Russia over again. The matter approaches a crisis. That crisis grows out of a very insignificant affair. The indignant Janizaries espouse the cause of a comrade who has been struck by an Egyptian. They show their reversed sign of the camp-kettles. They threaten to fire the city, and assemble in front of the palace of their aga, or leader. We present his picture among the rest. They demand the heads of the Grand Vizier and the Mufti, who favor reform.

The Sultan hears of the insurrection. He hastens across the Bosporus, assembles his faithful troops, invokes the religious orders, takes from the mosque of Achmed the sacred standard, and summons the Mussulmans, as if for a holy war. The rebels entrench themselves at Etmedam, near their barracks. The regular troops occupy all the streets. Their cannon are so planted as to command the open space. The Sultan risks his life, in demanding the dispersion of the insurgents. A brave officer precipitates the contest by firing his pistol upon the priming of a cannon. Then the artillery begins its sanguinary thunder. It is not an action; it is a massacre. There is no quarter. The Janizaries seek to enter the barracks and entrench themselves; but the barracks are fired. Those who escape the sword, perish by the fire ! The bodies that are not consumed by the fire are thrown into the sea. There is an inhibition against eating fish for some time afterward. The rebellion is suppressed and the Janizaries are annihilated !

The traveler will notice, as he goes through the various cemeteries where the Janizaries are buried, that certain monuments are decapitated; that many carved turbans of marble are not there. Vengeance pursued them even after death. The power of the state was not weakened by the destruction of this *corps*. It has often been likened to the destruction of the Mamelukes by

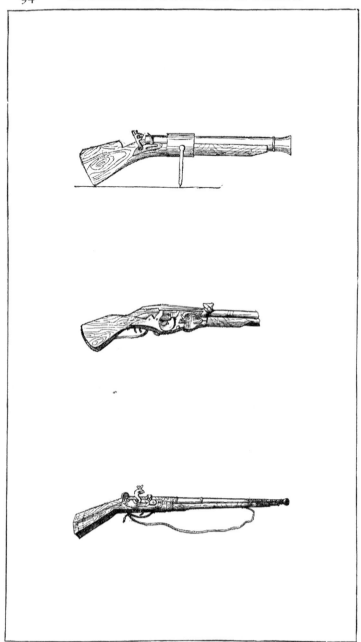

OLD GUNS OF THE JANIZARIES.

Mehemet Ali in 1811, and such doubtless it was, both in its horrible detail, and in its beneficial results to the Moslem power. The Janizaries had borne the brunt of many a battle; in fact, of most of the battles that led to the victorious advancement of the Crescent. They fell by their ambition and insubordination.

# CHAPTER X.

FOLLOWING Amurath—who besieged Constantinople A. D. 1422, before his successor captured it — are many Sultans who extended their conquests in Asia Minor and Europe. Many of these conquests remain until this day as the possessions of Turkey. Macedonia, Thessaly and parts of Greece, as well as portions of the Balkan Peninsula, indicate how high the Turkish tide arose in those days ; and a reconstructed map of Turkey in Europe to-day shows how far that tide has subsided.

Constantinople, however, existed long under Greek dominion, notwithstanding the weakness of its rulers and the feebleness of its defense. It had succumbed, at the time of the Fourth Crusade, to the Latins—a most cruel conquest, making an execrable page of human history. But anterior to the fall of Constantinople before the Turkish arms, a second Tartar wave under Timour swept over the same ground marked out by his Tartar predecessor. The Ottoman Sultan, Bajazet, at the battle of Angora fell before this Tartar inroad. The schemes of Timour were too great for his execution. He thought to conquer the world, but in retiring backward upon China he was killed, and his conquests were dissolved by his death.

One of the singular incidents of the war of 1877-78 in the Balkans, between Russia and Turkey, is the fact that a major-general in the Czar's suite was none other than Genghis Khan, a descendant of the famous conqueror, Genghis Khan, the " Scourge of God." He is described by an American pen as a great, burly, good-natured soldier, with high cheek-bones and black hair and beard, the perfect type of a Tartar, as depicted in any child's geography. Thus the fourteenth century and its Scourge is reproduced upon the olden plains of Thrace.

After the death of the Asiatic conquerer, Timour, there was nothing to stop the Turk from making sure of his conquests in Europe, or gaining the much - coveted capital of the three seas and two continents near the shores of the Bosporus. But the Byzantine rule was not yet to succumb, although it was honey-combed with corruption and only defended by mercenaries.

The Timour and Tamerlane Tartars, who overran the world, were of the same race as the Turk, but not of the same moral quality The Turk, when he accepted the Arab civilization along with the Koran, accepted the best refinement and exaltation of each. It is said that Genghis Khan slew between five and six millions of the human race. Empires built upon education and advancement fell before him. How proud these Tartars were, to be accounted the " Scourges of God " ! They were indeed the irony of Nature; for where their standard was raised, no grass ever grew again. At least, that was their boast. Not so with the Turks.

It has been already stated that the Turkish race had its origin in the fastnesses of a gold mountain range. Out of this range came these Scourges. It is not so celebrated in geography as the Alps, Himalayas, or the Rockies of America. The invading Turkomans adopted a creed which had hardly been consolidated or understood among those who adhered to it. They became inspired with a fanaticism which intensified their native courage. Out of their emergencies came a progress unequalled in the romances on our star. No such stories have ever been told in the life of any other nation.

Behold this horde of nomads on their first emerging from the Asiatic mountains ! After many wanderings and fightings, they make conquest of the richest provinces of Asia. They overthrow the Byzantine empire, displace the Christians in the very land where Christ was born, and, crossing continental waterways, seize upon the fruitful lands between the historic seas of ancient Greece. Almost by a single dash, unequalled in the campaigns of Cæsar, or even Alexander, and with the aid of new inventions in gunnery—inventions of their own Tartar race—they command a proud position in the family of nations.

At the time of the accession of Suleïman the Magnificent, in 1520, the Ottoman power was most dominant. The Turks then held all the Slavic country as far as the capital of Hungary. They held many tributary states along the Danube. They held the Crimea and the shores of the sea of Azof, almost completing the circuit of the Euxine. Fifty millions of people

SULTAN SULEÏMAN, THE MAGNIFICENT.

ROXOLANA, HIS BEST BELOVED WIFE.

regarded the Sultan as their sovereign. He received tribute from the House of Hapsburg. His fleets, under Barbarossa, controlled the Mediterranean. Turkey was then not only a great Power, but the first among the Powers of Europe.

Roxolana was the wife of Suleïman the Magnificent. She is supposed to be of French descent, but was really a Russian slave. The magnificent Sultan made her *Khorum-Sultana.* He thus legitimated her and her son. She was a seductive and accomplished woman, and for nearly a score of years shared with Suleïman the throne. What her character was, how wicked she was, and how she strove for her own son, to perpetuate her own blood upon the throne of Islam, is well recorded in contemporaneous history.

It seems that the Sultan, Suleïman the Magnificent, had an heir to the throne. Mustapha was his name. He was a son by an earlier marriage. Roxolana was his step-mother. Throughout her reign, she conspired with others to inflame her old husband to deeds of cruelty. Among these deeds was the destruction of the legitimate heir, Mustapha. It is a long history, but it is to the everlasting degradation of the race that the Emperor who had given so much glory to his reign should have succumbed to such a woman—even though she be described, in the history of those days, as " ever so fair, yet full of hateful thoughts, most finely masked."

I call attention to the portraits of these personages. I present Suleïman in all his magnificence and Roxolana in all her head-gear. These pictures are taken from an old and rare volume, called the History of the Ottomans, published in London in 1610, and which was kindly presented to me by Senator Wagstaff, of New York, to whom it descended as an heir-loom.

What events in Europe may have helped this remarkable people to a continuance of their power, are not wholly recorded in the pages of Gibbon. In this connection a chapter might be written upon the advent of Napoleon Bonaparte, whose Oriental ambition and invasion of Egypt greatly changed the relations of the Osmanli to the outside world. The situation of the Turkish capital had also much to do with these events. The struggle for supremacy and commerce in the East has been going on for many centuries. The Italians at one time seemed to be dominant in this regard.

But it is to France that the Christian world has been indebted for the "Capitulations," or treaties by which the alien population of the Ottoman dominions have been protected in their rights of trading, residence, conscience and other personal liberties.

During the long centuries of this struggle the French monarchs have had varying emotions and policies about the Orient. Sometimes they have been chivalric and Christian, and sometimes the reverse. When it concerned commerce, all the subterfuges which belong to diplomacy were resorted to by the "grand monarchs" of France, for their own aggrandizement. Notwithstanding all this, France has been, and is, less mercenary in her Eastern relations than any other nation. She was early known for her devotion to the Holy Places. She is still the guardian of the Christian subjects in the East, and especially those of the Latin Church. Of course, her guardianship does not include American and English Protestantism, which in the last fifty years has become not only an educator but a power in the East. In her early days, France led the fight of Christendom against the Moslem. Was it the elder Disraeli who spoke of the events of history which did not happen, by which the whole course of empire might have been changed? So a like condition in the East might have changed empires and creeds. It is said that Charlemagne was anxious to wed the Empress Irene, who, after her dethronement, made the island of Prinkipo, her first home in exile. Charlemagne was willing to overlook her infamies, in order to reunite the Latin and Greek races and churches under one empire and head, and thus to rescue Christianity and its Holy Land and places from the followers of Mahomet. Irene lost her throne, and the great Charles did not win his bride. The result is known. If the marriage had been solemnized, what then?

When Napoleon thought to strike the world by some grand military effort, he marched on the East. There he dealt the blow. His Minister at the court of the Sultan at the summit of his greatness and power, when France antagonized Russia, was a Corsican, General Sebastiani. It may be pardoned to one who has voyaged somewhat around the world, and visited the island of Corsica, if I state that in 1868, while at Ajaccio, the birthplace of Napoleon, I naturally sought for all the local mementoes belonging to that hero; but I did not dream of seeing there Napoleon's great general who had ravaged Spain, and so ably represented him at Constantinople.

One day, while wandering about the suburbs of Ajaccio, I was directed to a cave where it was said Napoleon had studied geometry. In going thither, I passed through a lemon-orchard. It was the very garden which Napoleon had planted. Whom should I see in the garden but a tall, military-looking old gentleman of some ninety years of age. He was bowed by years. He was walking slowly under a yellow umbrella. The guide pointed him out as that illustrious, daring and obstinate illustration of Corsican character, General Sebastiani.

At the beginning of this century, or, rather, before Napoleon became a great power, Sebastiani was selected by him for the mission to Constantinople. At that time the contest for supremacy was between France and Russia; England then, as now, taking a prominent hand. Sebastiani was a true Corsican. He had rare strength of mind. He made himself the controller of the destinies of Turkey, as it seemed then, according to the Napoleonic idea. He was the strategist of those movements by which the Orient was rescued from Russia, and by which France—unlike her present subordinate relation of neutral or ally of Russia— became for the time paramount. He it was who had the Bosporus closed to Russian ships. He it was who gave the prestige to the French army in Dalmatia, which enabled it to maintain the integrity of the Ottoman empire. He it was who ruled Selim III. with as much power as the Grand Vizier himself. He it was who dictated those policies upon the Danube, which have become traditional, and which so long preserved its principalities to the Turkish rule. It was this same Sebastiani whom, after three score years, I saw as an old man, under a yellow umbrella, watching his oranges and lemons, at the very spot where the young Napoleon used to play in Corsica. What memories could he not have divulged as to those early struggles in the Orient in which he was chief actor! In 1808, however, he was compelled to make a precipitate retreat from Turkey. In his hurry he destroyed his instructions, his correspondence, and other papers of importance. By some mistake he burned his own marriage contract. Madame Sebastiani, then expecting her accouchement, was unable to retreat with him from the Bosporus. She was protected by the Austrian Minister under most romantic circumstances.

How far the policy of Napoleon, which originated in the brain of his wily Corsican confederate Sebastiani, influenced the complications of the Eastern question may never be known. Strange as it may appear, France, during part of this time at least, was an ally, though a secret one, of Russia—as she is to-day. The alliance was then directed against the Porte. It transpired to the amazement of its rulers. I refer to the treaty of Tilsit, by which all the provinces of the Ottoman empire in Europe—Constantinople and Roumelia alone excepted—were, in the language of that day, to be " withdrawn from the yoke and vexations of the Turks." The correspondence of Napoleon with Sebastiani revealed the fact that a partition of Turkey was then agreed upon, which would give to France, Bosnia, Albania, Epirus, Greece, Thessaly and Macedonia; to Austria, Servia; and to Russia, Wallachia, Moldavia, Bulgaria and a part of Thrace. The little remnant of Turkey in Europe would have been almost as meagre as that possessed by the Greeks when their empire fell before Mahomed the Second in 1453. What a high-handed example this treaty affords to the landless—who are not kings or emperors !

It has frequently occurred to me that I missed an opportunity in Corsica when I saw this tall and grand old diplomat and soldier. Had I imagined that I should ever sojourn near the Sultan in the city in which he—Sebastiani—exercised his early diplomatic acumen, I certainly would have taken some risk, if not pains, to draw from him the incidents of his Eastern career. Since his day, or, rather, since the day of the great Napoleon, French power has waned in the Orient, so that France may now be considered a secondary influence at the court where she once held the primacy.

# CHAPTER XI.

SINCE the Conquest there have been twenty-eight Sultans, including Mahomed the Second, the Conqueror, who died in 1481, and the present Sultan, Abdul Hamid, who was crowned in 1876. These remarkable men — the Mahomeds, Bajazids, Selims, Suleïmans, Osmans, Murads and Abdul Medjids—form a direct line of sovereign descent from conquering stock, and are unequalled in history for the genius of their statesmanship and the valor of their armies.

As the Turks move to their conquests from Asia to Europe, they find the land which they subdue peopled with numerous races of different religions, customs and interests—Armenians, Kurds, Druses, Maronites, Arabs, Jews, Wallachians, Gypsies— all in intrigue one against the other, and all clamoring to be recognized as superior in the curriculum of political life and domination.

Some historian says that if we would have a proper idea of the difficulties of government in Turkey, we should consider what the British House of Commons would have to do if it were called upon to legislate for nineteen Irelands instead of one. And yet this Seljukian nomad from the interior of Asia, by his forbearance, genius, skill and equability, brought under discipline and control all the various phases of human nature which are illustrated within Turkish borders, and gave peace, protection and prosperity to all. The rule was continued by energy, decision, toleration, justice and chivalry.

This historian is somewhat at fault in his illustration. The Turk did legislate for and not against his subjects, of whatever race or creed. From the first it was, and is to-day, Turkish policy to give Home Rule its largest and best operation ; and to sacrifice no section of its subject-races for the betterment of any other race under its sway. It will strike the impartial reader that the British House of Commons might, even at this late day, learn something of the true principles of legislation from Turkish municipal policy.

The grandfather of the present Sultan, Mahmoud II., knew that he had alien hostility, worse than domestic broils, to overcome. This hostility was fomented, if not created, principally by one of the European powers. Hence he never could institute stable government for Turkey while the Janizaries existed. Although they were forty thousand in number, he wiped them out in a single day ! Their horrible deeds no longer became the reproach of Turkey. Their destruction was the decapitation of forty thousand murderers at one stroke of the royal cimeter. This was the beginning of new Turkey. The Janizaries were not, however, the only menace to the power of the Ottoman Sultans. Mahmoud the Second was almost overthrown by one of his own subjects—the great Viceroy of Egypt. Under Mehemet Ali, and by the aid of his grand captain, Ibrahim Pasha and a skillful Frenchman, known afterwards as Suleïman Pasha, the Egyptian armies became masters of the Holy Land and of Syria. In 1832 Ibrahim, with an army of thirty thousand men, defeated sixty thousand of the Sultan's Turks at Koniah. Ibrahim was moving on Constantinople, when his march was stopped by the interference of European diplomacy. The Porte did not recover Syria by military force, although it made efforts in that direction as late as June 24, 1839. The Great Powers had to combine to restore the wasted provinces of Syria to the Porte. A fleet menaced the shores of the Holy Land, and finally Ibrahim evacuated Syria and retired to Egypt. After this he made a grand tour of Europe, and was recognized as late as 1846–47–48 as a man almost as remarkable as Mehemet Ali.

Out of the conflict between Turkey and Egypt, and the stress put upon the former by the Powers, came the reforms, which have been failures only in the eye of those who expected more than was possible

Many reforms upon the Turkish body, both politic and social, have been started within the last four decades. It is hard to tell just when they began. Was it when the Sultan Mahmoud II. began to circulate portraits of himself, to foster music, and to establish military bands of his own outside the Janizary *corps ?* A representation of the human form and the use of music were forbidden by the Koran, and the Janizary had become quite a permanent order.

Since the time of Mahmoud the Second there has been no more drowning in sacks of wives and odalisques, no decapitation of officials, and no strangulation of deposed Sultans or of the brothers of reigning Sultans. With the death of Mahmoud, such cruelties—which had the sanction of legality in Greek and Roman custom—ceased. Mahmoud was a great student. He studied such material changes of his country as could be tolerated. He endeavored to better the condition of the Christians. Notwithstanding the conflicts of his time, and the discontent of the old Moslem at his innovations, he struggled for thirty years to ameliorate the condition of his people of all races and creeds, until death ended his splendid career. The present Sultan has allowed not one human life to be taken since his accession to the throne. Of what other monarch of his time can the like be said?

Abdul Medjid was a boy when he came to the throne of his father, Mahmoud the Second, but he did what he could to carry out the reforms of his father. The famous Hatt-i-humayoun, or "august writing," announced a new order as to taxation and justice in the empire. The Berlin treaty of 1878 confirmed this advanced movement. Many monopolies were overthrown, education was elevated and energized; and in spite of all opposition—even that of religious fanaticism—it is due to truth to state that the Turkish Government met the crisis with as much firmness as was possible, in the midst of such troubles and trials as few nations ever encountered.

The Crimean War had closed with the treaty of Paris in 1856. Neither the war nor the treaty pleased Russia. For neither, could Turkey be justly blamed. Every time that Russia struck at Turkey, Turkey seemed weaker than before; but Turkey did not and has not succumbed, although she has copied some of the worst elements of European nations. What has transpired in the Balkan Peninsula since the Treaty of Paris, and what reforms have taken place for the good of the country—these are well summed up by an English Consul when he says: "If we compare Turkey as she is with what she was twenty-five years ago, the change is marvelous." Lord Palmerston said in 1856 that Turkey had made greater progress than any other nation in Europe. Was this because she had a greater field for reform? At all events, she reformed. The present condition of Turkey at least proves that much.    Ever since the death of Abdul Medjid, in 1861, and at the present time—despite great expenditures and demands upon her exchequer, and even after the perils following the suicide of his brother, Abdul Aziz, and the imbecility of another brother, the Sultan Murad, who was deposed promptly—there is evidence of an anxiety for reform, backed with much executive energy.

Abdul Medjid had a storm-tossed administration.    It lasted long.    He was among the best of the Sultans.    Among the conspicuous and illustrious embodiments connected with his reign of advanced thought, was the renewal of the bill of right and freedom of worship to all equally with Mahometans.    Of course this could not be fully carried into effect except at the capital    As to other places, it was a dead letter.    He did all that was possible by his government for liberality.    There were reforms in connection with taxation, so as to defeat the cupidity of the tax-gatherer.    But restless Russia would not keep within her limits.    With these evident signs of improvement in Turkey the Czar became more aggressive than ever.    The revolution by which Austria and Hungary were in collision—in fact, the cataclysm of Europe in 1848—disturbed somewhat the Turkish realm; and in 1853, two years after my first visit to Constantinople, I was not too young to observe that the general peace of Europe, which had remained undisturbed since 1815, was trembling before a fresh disturbance of the Eastern question.    The Crimean War grew out of a wrangle about the Holy Places.    It was a question of privilege.    The Greek Church, through Russia, demanded one thing; France, as the protector of the Latin Church, another. Russia had some pretext for her demand, growing out of an old treaty of 1774.    The Turks were perplexed.    What was Greek or Latin to Turkey?    Was she to be a mere cat's-paw to drag the Christian chestnuts out of the fire?    The matter came to a head; the Russian demands were denied ; war came.    We know the result, for the Crimean struggle is not yet forgotten.    The siege of Sebastopol still retains its pre-eminence in the history of military strategy and engineering skill.

Now we    come close to the time when Abdul Aziz, breaking loose from the best thoughts of his early reign, fouled the attempts of reform.    What came to him personally from his resistance to the onward march of events, is told to every passen-

ger who goes up and down the Bosporus. There is pointed out
a certain mark of broken masonry in the palace of Tchiragan:
it indicates an improvised breach in the wall where the dead body
of the Sultan was carried out after his suicidal bath.

It is not for me to repeat the oft-told tales which connect the
Sultans, even of our latter days, with self-indulgence in luxurious
excesses; nor do I give heed to the thousand-tongued rumor of
the taking off of Abdul Aziz, or, as a consequence, of the
aberrations in the mind of his brother Murad. It is said, however, and related on the authority of one of his seraglio, that,
just before his death, the unfortunate Sultan, Abdul Aziz, on
entering his prison in the palace, traced on the dust that covered
the table this verse in Arabic :

> "Man's destiny is Allah's will,
> Sceptres and power are His alone;
> My fate is written on my brow,
> Lowly I bend before His throne ! "

On looking out of the window of his palace, and seeing that
his iron-clads had been placed in front of his prison, with the
guns pointed toward him, he was appalled by the sight, and
exclaimed, with emotion, to his mother, who was present: " See
to what use the force I have created for my empire is applied ! "

When Murad was approached by those who had dethroned
Abdul Aziz he turned deathly pale, and exclaimed : " What is my
offense, that I should be doomed to an untimely death ?" He did
not then know of the conspiracy by which he had been elevated.
He had a short reign. He soon became *distrait*, for what reason
no one knows, and few care to know. It is said that he is still
confined in one of the marble palaces upon the Bosporus. His
feeble body and mind, aggravated by excesses, led, as it is
alleged, to his deposition on the last day of August, A. D. 1876.

There is, however, two sides to his story. He owned a
fine estate on the island of Prinkipo. There he was happy.
There he spent his summers. There he lived more like
a private gentleman than a prince. In this he was not
singular. The unpretending style of the Turkish gentleman is quite in contrast with the splendor of the royal palace.
Murad visited his neighbors, Christians and all. He was
fond of music, and he practiced his music with them. His

SULTAN ABDUL MEDJID, FATHER OF THE PRESENT SULTAN.

SULTAN ABDUL AZIZ, BROTHER OF THE PRESENT SULTAN.

manners were distinguished and affable. The condition of a Sultan in prospective is worse than that of the poorest hamal. Murad passed his time under an espionage which was in itself an imprisonment, and which gave him—even while enjoying the pleasures of the Princes Isles—many unhappy days. When he was fixed upon as the successor of Abdul Aziz, he had to change this island life. He could no longer read his Dante, nor play Rossini's music. When he came to the throne he was utterly cut off from his old companions.

The bloody incidents of that insurrection overthrew Murad's reason, and before he could be invested with the sword of Osman, which conferred royalty, his mind was a blank. He was removed from power and consigned to one corner of the palace of Tchiragan, which is also pointed out to the traveler on the Bosporus.

He was succeeded by his brother, the present Sultan, who very reluctantly assumed the grave office which he has filled so well. Thus the present Sultan was raised to the throne as the thirty-fourth ruler of the house of Othman. His character had not then been fixed or known. He strongly resisted the importunities of his friends to place him in such a perilous position, but there was no other man possible. By the decrees of state and the order of succession, he, as the next brother, became the representative of the Turkish faith and state. Who could better represent his people, or with more moderation, affability, fidelity and probity? Aye, or with more humanity?

Properly to introduce Abdul Hamid the Second upon the later stage of Oriental affairs, the origin of the Ottoman race and dynasty should be traced—as I have endeavored—to its springs in Central Asia. Besides, the reader should consult, not merely Gibbon, but the history of that remarkable rule in Turkey which has had its vicissitudes of order and anarchy from its beginning up to the present time. Its pages tell us that when the Sultans became apathetic and debauched, the Janizaries dominated over all. Whenever avarice and lust, often provoked and assisted by the Christian subjects of the Porte, left their sinister mark upon the empire, a foreign element came ever menacingly to the front. That element was inspired by the greed of dominion. It began actively with the reign of Peter the Great. It was organized in steadfast intrigue. It sought the dismemberment of Turkey with a view to its own aggrandizement. It never failed to obstruct the path of Turkish progress. It has attempted its work in Bulgaria. It has succeeded in northeastern Turkey in Asia. It began to exhibit itself before the Ottoman occupation of Constantinople, and it is prosecuted to this very day by the accomplished Russian Minister, Nellidoff, as the agent of the Czar in Constantinople. It is the Muscovite policy.

Since the accession of the present Sultan, it is apparent that his rule has permeated the empire with a wise and honest sovereignty. To-day he reigns triumphant under the old banner of One God—and Mahomet as the Prophet—not as some irreverent writer has interpreted, "One God—and Backsheesh as the Prophet." This interpretation comes too close to the reproach on us for our "Almighty Dollar." I therefore reject it all the more readily. I have observed, heedfully, much of the progress of Turkey within the last three decades, and from what I have seen of it I believe that the Turk is to-day the only man who can give Turkey the proper impulse to overcome the *vis inertia* of her laggard progress, so as to bring her forth into the light and liberty of a new civilization. If you question the ability of this people for such advancement, look for the inspiration of their remarkable race and rule, and you will find an answer in those rare qualities which Gibbon catalogued when he said that they were distinguished for their patience, discipline, sobriety, bravery, honesty and modesty. It is because of these solid characteristics, and in spite of the harem, in spite of autocratic power, in spite of the Janizary and seraglio, that this race and rule remain potential in the Orient. It is a good omen that the head of the Turkish Government to-day is a man of honest intentions and clear intellect, and that he gives unremittingly his time to the service of his people. He is not merely an amiable and humane Prince, but wisely versed in statesmanship. His heart is touched by suffering, and his views lean strongly to that toleration of the various races and religions of his realm, which other and more boastful nations would do well to imitate.

# CHAPTER XII.

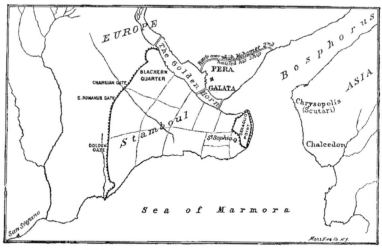

MAP OF CONSTANTINOPLE AT THE CONQUEST.

It is impossible to recapitulate or picture all the strange vicissitudes through which the capital of the Oriental empire has passed. How often it has been besieged—how it was held by Greece, Rome and Persia—how it was attacked by Arabs, who were driven back by the strength of its walls and the chemistry of the Greek fire—how again and again the Moslem forces undertook its siege—how the great Slavonic power, Russia, in the ninth, tenth and eleventh centuries, attempted to make this its objective point and centre of operations. All this would require volumes. The scope is too large for the " Diversions " to which this book is devoted. It might be a matter of interest, however, to consider, in passing, the graphic and wonderful conquest of the city under Baldwin of Flanders, and Dandolo, the aged Doge of Venice, in A. D., 1203-04. It was Dandolo's remarkable power which set up the house of Flanders in the palace of the

Comneni. The Greeks recovered their capital in A. D. 1261. After that the second Amurath besieged it. But it was not until A. D. 1453 that Mahomet the Second made good the prophesies of the Prophet, by capturing the city.

A city like Constantinople, which has been besieged twenty-four times and taken six times, must have a history worth repeating, even though it be in a meagre way.

The country around the capital is instinct with thrilling memories: every mountain and valley, and, but for its mobility, every drop of water, has its history. The great strength of the city was not in the Divine Wisdom, after which its principal church was named, but in the walls which, shortly after the Christian era, were built to strengthen it against invasion. The invasion did not always come from the Turk when the Greek held the city. And when the Christian manned her walls, the Crusader was sometimes the invader. So it was at the Latin Conquest.

In the Month of May, 1097, Godfrey of Bouillon, with an army of some three hundred thousand men, having the Holy Land for its objective point, came crusading in this direction. His army was composed of a different class of men, and under conditions quite unlike those of the first Crusade that followed wildly Peter the Hermit. The Crusaders under Godfrey, when they encamped, to resist the attacks of the enemy, made breastworks out of the innumerable bones of the Crusaders who had preceded them. What a sacrilegious horde these later Crusaders must have been, to make such a resurrection of the Paladins !

The first fall of Constantinople must not be confounded with that of the Turkish capture of the city. The first fall was in 1203. It occurred at a time when Innocent III. was the Pope of Rome, when the Fourth Crusade was under way, and when the greatest of the Venetian Doges, Henrico Dandolo, wielded the trident in the eastern Mediterranean. The history of the expedition has been well written, for there is abundant material. The crusade left Corfu on the 23d of May. Along with it was young Alexis, who aspired to be emperor of the Greeks. Why it was deflected from Egypt is a part of the mystery of its attack on Constantinople. The wily Venetian, Dandolo, had been paid to leave Egypt alone. Besides, he had the animus of an old grudge against Constantinople. Had he not been blinded by its emperor? Although ninety odd years of age, he was following his Nemesis.

The imperial journey of young Alexis was that of a conquering hero. On the 23d of June the fleet anchored off San Stefano, which is on the European side of the Sea of Marmora, some twelve miles southwest of Constantinople. The sight of the city was an incentive to the Crusaders. Its walls and towers, its palaces and churches, made the enterprise a magnificent romance. Dandolo was the genius of the undertaking. Leaving San Stefano, the fleet harbored at the Princes Islands. These islands may become familiar to the reader from my account of a summer's residence on Prinkipo, the chief isle of the group.* From these islands it was but a few hours' sail for the fleet into the Bosporus. The traveler will observe upon the Asiatic side of the shore, off Chalcedon, a cemetery crowded with monuments, in strange contrast to the Turkish cemeteries around, with their cypresses and turbaned tombs. It is only a mile from Constantinople, and here the army disembarked. Here they gathered in the crops which had just been harvested. It was but a short move from Chalcedon to Scutari. Scutari is well known to the American colony, for upon its heights is situated the most interesting school under American auspices in the Orient. Nine days the Crusaders waited, with an occasional skirmish to whet their appetites for plunder. It is unnecessary to picture the consternation of the city, the negotiations which were begun, and the suspicions that were engendered.

The walls of Constantinople remain to-day as they were then. They form a triangle. Two sides of the triangle bring them down to the water's edge. The waters are deep enough to float the iron-clads of the Turks, as they then floated the galleys of the Venetians. A display was made upon the galleys, by the barons and knights, with Dandolo at their head, of the person of the young pretender to the throne. Proclamation was at the same time made before the crowds upon the walls, from the galleys of the Venetians, of his right to the heirship. The Greeks who garrisoned the walls laughed at the proclamation. Then the business of the siege began. It was inspired by the rich booty in prospect. Religious services alternated with military display. At the end of ten days an attack was made upon the walls. The tourist will observe, upon the heights of the European side of the Bos-

---

* "Isles of the Princes ; or, the Pleasures of Prinkipo." By S. S. Cox. Putnam's Sons. New York, 1887.

porus a conspicuous Genoese tower, upon which the Turkish flag flies every fête day and every Turkish Sabbath—Friday. It is known as the tower of Galata. It confronts the old city of Stamboul. Two bridges of boats now connect Galata with Stamboul. It was under the shadow of this tower, at the point known as Tophane, now used as a Custom house, where the troops landed. It is near the mouth of the Golden Horn. It is now a large open space, which at the present time, or at least when the writer left Constantinople, is crowded with many of the armaments which the genius of modern invention has produced. At the time of the siege there was a chain boom across the Golden Horn from Galata to Stamboul. It was protected by the tower of Galata Behind, the hills slope, and upon this slope lived the Hebrews of the city. It is still the most thickly populated portion of the European part of the great city—known as Pera. How to possess the tower of Galata, in order to reach the European end of the chain, is the question. The castle is captured. The chain is now in the control of the invaders. The fleet enters the Golden Horn. Victory ensues upon the sea against the Grecian galleys.

Here then is the scene and the order of battle: The attack is to be made by sea as well as by land. The ships are to be brought close up to the wall on the north side of the city. Ladders are to be thrown out from the ships to the walls, on the part of the navy, manned by the Venetians, while the Crusaders are to attack on the west side through the landward walls. A bridge has to be made across the Golden Horn, or an old bridge of stone repaired. On the 5th day after the capture of the harbor the army of the Crusaders is in position near the Golden Horn, and almost opposite the Imperial Palace of Blachern. From the camp of the Greeks there is a splendid prospect. All the waters which make Constantinople the capital of commerce in the Orient are within view. St. Sophia towers above all. There are triple walls to guard the city. Machines are ready to hurl the vast round stones, that are still seen piled up upon the quays of Constantinople—relics of the siege. This camping-place is historic. Hosts of Moslems had before attacked the city from this point. Travelers who have visited the mosque of Job, or Eyoub, have no difficulty in locating the place.

The attack is made with varying success, but it fails on the landward side. On the northern side it is more successful. Dandolo, then nearly a hundred years old, and blind, directs the attack from his own galley. The Greek fire is at this time the most conspicuous element of warfare in the East. Dandolo has anticipated the day of iron-clads: his ships are shielded with raw-hides to resist this fire. From the cross-trees of the ships to the walls is the order of battle, as the vessels are moored close to the shore. In spite of the stones which are thrown in immense quanti-ties, and reckless of the cross-bows of the besieged, the fight is hand to hand on the scaling-ladders thrown out from the ships' tops to the walls. The Gonfalon of St. Mark is borne on shore by the old Doge, who leads his followers into the conflict. At last the Gonfalon is seen floating from one of the towers of the walls. Twenty-five of these towers are captured in succession. In vain the Greeks try to rally. Even the mercenaries, or auxiliaries, made up of the hired Norsemen and Englishmen, and Warings and Pisans, endeavor in vain to recapture the towers.

The result of this fighting is a great conflagration in the city, and the repulsion of the invaders. It is not necessary to recount in detail the consequences of this attack: how the Emperor Alexis fled; how the aged Isaac was restored to the palace; how a revolution broke out in the city; what resulted from a deputation of the invaders who entered the city; what differences broke out within the army of invasion ; the intrigues which were incident to the rule of the city; the terrific fire which broke out a second time ; in fine, the confusion, dissensions and anxieties on both sides and in both armies, which resulted in the deposition of the old and the proclamation of a new emperor. These facts form chapters in this magnificent romance.

Even before the fall of the city there were many divisions made, in anticipation of the spoils and the Government. As Mr. Pears, in his History, says : " The bear-skin having been thus divided, it only remained to capture the bear." The Crusade had been forgotten. The lust of plunder and of power alone inspired the invading host.

No one at this day, when munitions of war can be improvised so readily, can realize the genius and industry which prepared the machines for hurling stones, the battering-rams, the ballista, the mangonels and the enginery for war of that time. The prepara-tions were completed by the 8th of April, A. D. 1203, for another as-

DANDOLO, DOGE OF VENICE.

sault. One line of battle was formed upon land. That line stretched from the Blachern Palace, at the northwest corner of the wall, to the Petrion. The Petrion I am familiar with. It is a very unwholesome quarter of the city. It is almost impossible to pass through it now, for its stench and filth. It runs parallel with the Golden Horn for about one-third of the length of the harbor walls, eastward from Blachern.

The attack was made, as before, by the navy from the cross-trees of the ships to the walls. The walls meanwhile had been heightened. The feat of conquest had thus been made more difficult. The assault again failed.

Another assault is made. A tremendous fire rages throughout the city. At length the city is entered through one of the gates upon the land side, after the Venetians obtain a foothold in the towers. It is late in the evening when the Crusaders enter the city.

Then begins the carnival of plunder. Never was there such a systematic, shameless and terrible sacking. These soldiers of Christ, as the historian says—sworn to chastity, pledged before God not to shed Christian blood, bearing upon their own breasts the emblem of the Prince of Peace, under vows to redeem the tomb of Christ from the Moslem, bring down upon themselves the reprobation of the great and good Pope and the indignation of the world for their brutality. Such scandalous orgies and barbaric cruelties, such sacrilegious robberies of churches, palaces and homes, had never before been equalled in the history of mankind. The plunder by Mahomed, with his Turks, in A. D. 1453, is a summer-holiday excursion compared with this Christian capture and sacking. Nothing is spared—neither the works of art, nor the sacred vestments, images or vessels of the churches. Exclusive of what was stolen and what was paid to the Venetians, money to the value of eight hundred thousand pounds sterling was distributed among the army. It was the richest prize of all the ages. Sismondi estimates the wealth of the city—in specie and property—before the capture, at twenty-four millions of pounds sterling.

Such a capture could not fail to result in quarrels among the captors. For generations after this, the Latin Conquest continued to be a byword and a reproach. Like the conquests of Alexander, when they fell under the control of his generals, they faded away, because of the lack of that skill in governing which alone can make domination lasting.

Dandolo, the genius of the Conquest, died A. D. 1208. I have seen the stone in St. Sophia which marks his sepulchre, or which did mark it, for the stone is a part of the pavement in the women's gallery of the great Church of St. Chrysostom. It is worn and dusty. It was by an accident that I happen to see it. Our dragoman, Mr. Garguilo, who is of Italian descent, was along with me, on a summer evening—as we are wandering through the upper corridors of the Church of the Divine Wisdom—when I observe some dim letters on the pave beneath my feet. At once I am on my knees dusting the stone with a handkerchief. I read : DANDO—! This, and nothing more. Where is his body ? The dragoman promises to investigate the problem.

# CHAPTER XIII.

WHAT wonderful attractions this city of Constantine had before its fall! Owing to the resistless state of the provinces, it allured everyone who had means to live within its walls. Those who honored art and studied the sciences were here gathered.

Above all, this city was the seat of intellect, of theological intellect; for here, or in its vicinity, were settled for the coming centuries the tenets of the Christian faith. And beyond that, there was codified and almost developed in this new Rome a body of jurisprudence, known as the Justinian Code. It contained the principles of the Roman Civil Law. Edwin Pears, one of the eminent lawyers of Constantinople, has said of this law, "that for precision, subtlety, grasp of principles, and wonderful adjustments, it has made a powerful impression upon the world." When we remember that it was from here we received the authenticated dogmas of Christendom, and the principles of the Roman law, which have been followed in continental Europe almost since the time of early empire, and which have become the law of the whole civilized world, except where the common law of England is regarded as paramount—it may be truthfully said that this wonderful capital ranks second only to Rome itself in her influence for civilization, religion and progress. This city is not alone a place for ethical memories; for nowhere can we find in the highways and byways of our planet, more splendors of wealth, luxury and refinement than she once possessed. Gibbon, in closing his seventeenth chapter, generalizes about her commerce in the following sentence :

"Whatever rude commodities were collected in the forests of Germany and Scythia, and far as the sources of the Tanais and the Borysthenes; whatsoever was manufactured by the skill of Europe or Asia; the corn of Egypt and the gems and spices of the farthest India—were brought by the varying winds, into the port of Constantinople, which for many ages attracted the commerce of the ancient world."

At the present day there is no spot so specially central for commerce, or which is within reach of so many fruitful and populous countries as Constantinople. Looking at the map and glancing at the Black Sea, we find a passage of eighteen miles open to the Sea of Marmora, which is a lake under the shadows of the domes and minarets of Stamboui, as capable of being defended as the outlet of the Dardanelles.

Constantinople has always had a liberal policy as to commerce. Her trade concessions have increased her wealth and power. Her situation is so favorable that there never was, nor can there be, without some strange convulsion of nature, a mart for the collection and distribution of merchantable products between the hemispheres, equal to this entrépôt on the Bosporus. What a shame it is that only lately have the Powers of the East and the economies of the West been invoked for the encouragement of her trade, the building of railroads, and the extension into the opulent interior of all the best and fleetest modes of transportation. Much is yet to be done before the khan and caravan of the ancient merchant shall be transmuted, by the magic of trade, into the dépôt of the railroad !

May I be allowed, in this connection, to copy from a singularly attractive work, called " The Captain of the Janizaries," by Mr. James M. Ludlow, of New Jersey, a short colloquy, which indicates just what the relation was between Constantinople and the Powers of the earth at the time she was about to fall into the hands of the Turk ? His book has reference to the times of Scanderbeg, and the contest which preceded the arrival of Mahomet the Second upon the Ottoman throne. The attempt was then made to arouse the Christian power of Constantinople against the Turk, while the Italian and other elements were striking him in Europe. It was an attempt to put some new life into the old Greek empire. Constantine, the sixteenth of that name, was then the emperor—the last of the emperors. He danced attendance upon Italian dukes and other influences of the West. He sought an agreement with the Pope, in a creed which was irreconcilable with that of the Latins. At the same time he was demoralizing his reign with his uncurtained harem, and shamed the very Turk himself; yet, when the crisis of fate came, he alone seemed to be worthy of the ancient Greek prowess. He fought and died—the last of the stock which had over a thousand years of empire.

The incidents of the capture of the city by the Turks are more romantic and attractive than those of any other capture or siege in history. One of these incidents is the navigation overland of the Ottoman vessels. Much ridicule has been expended upon the Eads mode of ship-transportation by rail. Why is it so strange? Only last year a screw steamer—the *Duke*—was transported over Florida fifty miles or more, by the Pensacola and Atlantic Railroad. The vessel did not show a sign of steam. Reading the history of the capture of Constantinople, I was somewhat amazed that any one should be surprised that mechanism in our day should not easily harness its forces to transport ships by rail. There seems to be nothing novel or difficult in the feat. The principle is as simple as the A B C of science. The difficulty, if any there is, with the Eads scheme, is not mechanical, but merely economical. Its accomplishment has depended on the doubts of those who do not believe in associating government or its administration with mere " business." When a scheme depends on the loan of government credit, or the issuance of government bonds, there is only one view of the case presented. This view should not blind us to the utility or virtue of the plan or invention of the ship railway. Doubtless, in ancient times, in Egypt and elsewhere—and even in Central America, near the proposed Eads railway—immense masses of matter were moved by means of railways, tramways, or similar devices. Evidences remain, in the solid rock, of such facile contrivances. Mr. Eads, with that practical sagacity for which he was distinguished as an engineer, may have had his inventive faculties aroused by pondering upon these marvelous mechanical results of the early epochs. It is not my purpose to discuss the feasibility of the Eads project, nor to compare it with any other plan for inter-oceanic transit. This has been done elaborately by engineers. Admiral Ammen, in a tractate, has considered the various disadvantages of "taking a laden ship out of water at Tehuantepec, and whisking her over a distance of 140 miles or more, and over an elevation of 738 feet, making a broad cut of seventeen feet."

As a legislator, I would give great weight to his opinion. I would not tamely allow the American eagle to be caged on any isthmus, nor take another bird, domestic or aquatic, as emblematic of our abandonment of the Monroe Doctrine, in order that the bird might be plucked. But as a question of physics, I would like to hear an amicable discussion on the feasibility of taking up and whisking the laden ship over a railroad. John Roach, who is now dead, but who was acquainted with such matters, stated that the performance would endanger the hull. In this view William H. Webb concurs. Harlan & Hollingsworth say that if the foundations of the railroad, having six tracks, could be made substantial, so as not to yield under the immense weight of a loaded ship, they believe a cradle could be constructed to receive it, and transport it the distance named without injury. They are doubtful about the ordinary wooden vessel venturing upon such a journey. They doubt whether underwriters would take the risk of damage. Other experts in shipbuilding expressed similar opinions. But they are all iron-workers, and wooden ships seem to be passing out of commerce. These opinions had reference somewhat to the material of the ships. The Pusey & Jones Company, of Wilmington, Del., thought that a good iron ship might endure this transportation without damage, but still it would be a risk. As to wooden ships, or thin-plated iron ships, they thought it would be simple destruction. They regard the dynamic effect of the load, and of the boilers and machinery, as an extraordinary peril. In short, in their opinion, a ship railway would always encounter grave and scarcely surmountable difficulties. Mr. Rowland, of the Continental Works, has some notions as to the best method of moving heavy bodies on wheels. He draws his argument from the condition of vessels and the injury which they sustain by being dry-docked. Mr. Nathaniel McKay, who is a practical man in relation to such matters, holds the opinion that Captain Eads's proposition is a delusion. As the builder of some one hundred ships, some of them among the largest sailing-ships in the world, he says the greatest care which shipbuilders are compelled to exercise is in laying the keels and seeing that the foundations for the launching-ways have the best possible bearing that can be devised, so that the vessels may be launched with safety, without injury to the hull, when sliding a distance of only one and a half times its own length. Mr. Delamater does not believe in the scheme, although he admits that such a feat could be done. It was for him a question of expense ; the expense would be too great for private capital. Our New York Mayor, Mr. Hewitt, with whom I talked on this topic, is familiar with forces, mechanical as well as political. He inclined to the opinion that the plan would only be practical if an immense tank were made and filled with water, and the ship were floated therein *en route.*

These opinions represent one side of the question from a practical standpoint. Properly, to offset them, the results which history furnishes, and especially the siege of Constantinople, should have reference to vessels such as are now in use; otherwise the analogy fails. It is well known that the Venetians transported some of their large galleys from the River Adige to the Lake of Garda. A similar feat had been accomplished by Augustus after the battle of Actium. It was attempted by Hannibal at the siege of Tarentum. But in size, even the largest Venetian war galley, or the triremes that were accustomed to plow the Mediterranean, not to speak of the vessels which were used by the Turks at the siege of Constantinople in 1453, were but as children's toys, compared with the sailing and metallic vessels of the present day. On the other hand, it may be truthfully urged that there is no comparison between the physical forces which are now developed and the forces employed in ancient times or in the Middle Ages. I stopped in a hotel in Chicago more than twenty years ago, which was quietly lifted two stories higher by the aid of six thousand jack-screws, without my being sensible of the motion. And why may not a ship be lifted and carried, with the remarkable mechanical appliances of to-day, irrespective of its weight or its load ?

But the reader may perhaps ask, What has the Eads ship railway or Chicago hotels to do with the fall of Constantinople? Only this: that had the Greeks given as much attention to applying the mechanic forces to resist as their invaders did to capture the city, there might still be a Greek empire in the East, and no Eastern question to vex diplomats or to give cause for large standing armies in Europe.

The history of the defense of Constantinople in A. D. 1453 reveals a redeeming picture of the heroism of one man, the Emperor Constantine, and the few thousand Greeks and auxiliaries who were with him during the siege. So many attempts had been made upon the city before the time of Mahomed II., and so

CASTLE OF ROMOLI-HISSAR.

staunch had been its defenses, that the Greeks relied upon its
traditionary strength, instead of the improvements in mechanism
and armature which the Turks were sedulously studying and using.

The Latins held the city for sixty years; the Greeks,
after incessant warfare, again obtained possession of their
capital.    They did not hold it long.    The Turks were
eager to seize the prize.    Amurath the Great had made the
attempt.    It was reserved, however, for his persistent son,
Mahomed II., to consummate the work.    This Sultan omitted
no effort in its prosecution.    The Turks were then—about the middle of the thirteenth century—the most accomplished artillerists
of the world; almost the only ones.    They knew that the city of
Stamboul could not be taken from the land side of the triangle.
They did not attempt to take it from the Marmora Sea side of
the triangle; and as they were cut off by chains and other barriers from coming down the Bosporus into the Golden Horn,
what did they do ?    They copied Augustus and Hannibal, and
anticipated Captain Eads.    The story is worth retelling, in the
light of six hundred and thirty odd years of progress in maritime warfare, transportation, gunnery and mechanism.

Mahomed II. was one of the greatest of the Turkish Sultans.
He was of that manly mold and stamp that conquers obstacles.
He was not discouraged by them, although they had impeded all
the efforts of his predecessors.    It was this Sultan who resolved
to starve this great city into capitulation.    His plan was to cut it
off from the Euxine entirely.    To this end he built, at the narrowest part of the Bosporus, which is midway of its length, the
stronghold called *Boghazkesen*, which, being interpreted, means
the "Cut-Throat."    This is upon the European side of the Straits,
and opposite the Asiatic fortress which Mahomed I had built.
This part of the Bosporus, with the surrounding scenery, is one of
the most picturesque spots of the world.    Three thousand men
worked for three months, under the protection of his army, to
build their great fortress of Romoli-Hissar.    Every vessel that
sailed by was compelled to pay tribute.

No pleading nor diplomacy could divert the coming storm
from the city.    In vain the Greek Emperor, Constantine, entreated
that the crops around the city might at least be spared for food.
Mahomed's only answer was:

"I will feed my horses therewithal."

Notwithstanding this shortening of supplies, Mahomed found that it was no easy task to take Constantinople. It had been called, in the edicts of emperors, " *The Well-Defended.*" Its enormous walls and towers still remain to attest their formidable strength. Artillery had not then risen to the fine art that it is to-day; but even then Greek Gatlings, Hungarian Armstrongs and Wallachian Krupps were at work perfecting cannon of enormous calibre. Out of these were projected granite balls, some of which weighed twelve quintals, or 1,200 pounds. Some of these monstrous balls are still arrayed in harmless pyramids outside the castle of Romoli-Hissar. Orban, the Wallachian iron-founder, made the gigantic machine which threw such balls. It required 700 men to serve it. It threw a shot a mile, covered the horizon with a canopy of smoke, and filled the air with its thunder.

While the Turkish preparations were going on for the taking of the city, its gates were closed and the garrison were upon their vigilance. Alas! on mustering them there were only 4,973 efficient men within the walls. To these were added 2,000 foreigners, among them 500 Genoese. The latter came by way of the Mediterranean. They were commanded by one Justiniani. Only a few ships were at the call of the beleaguered Greeks— fourteen in all—and even these were pressed from the foreign shipping in the port. The walls, strong as they were, had not been repaired for years. Some repairs were hurriedly made. Physical forces were sought from Christian Europe, but in vain. As a last resort the Emperor endeavored to close the schism between the Catholic and Greek churches. No army came, however, to reinforce the proposed ecclesiastical unity, out of which might have come a tremendous energy of defense. On the 12th of December, A. D. 1452, the Roman Catholic Legate celebrated mass in honor of this unity of Christendom ; but the Greek priests regarded it as sacrilege. They cried out :

"Give us the Turk's turban rather than a Cardinal's hat !"

Christendom, therefore, kept aloof from the contest. It saw with indifference the Ottoman wind his powerful folds around this last barrier of the Greek Christian, and not with much regret, for the Greek orthodoxy had not infrequently been the champion and abettor of Moslem aggression.

The month of April, A. D. 1453, saw more than 200,000 Turkish soldiers encamped upon the land side of the city. This was not the first, nor second, nor third, but the twelfth time that the Moslem had invested this magnificent city. Mahomed's Kismet had told him that the city was fated to be Mahometan. Mahomet, his prophet, had promised it hundreds of years before. It was a part of the faith. During this very investment one of the grand Sheiks had discovered the bier of Eyoub (which is Arabic for Job), the sacred leader of the third siege. A mosque now marks the spot where this bier was discovered. This discovery gave exaltation to the *esprit* of the Mahometan troops. It was as if the green banner of the Prophet himself had been newly found and unfurled.

The Greeks fought on the walls with intrepidity. They were led by the Emperor. The Italians did their work well. It was no easy task to fill up at night the breaches which the day had made, and to deepen the ditches so as to aid the defense. The Turks did not have the Greek fire. It has long been obsolete. What it was no one now knows; but in spite of the shields of triple hide to guard the wooden towers and the draw-bridges of the Turkish invader, his machines were burnt by the Greek fire, which the Greeks alone had. There was, therefore, no way on the land side to approach the walls. At the end of April a sea fight took place outside the harbor. The Ottoman fleet were thrown into confusion by the chemical missiles of the enemy, while reinforcements from Italy, in ships, entered the harbor. These ships, in spite of the numbers against them, sailed through the Turkish fleet. The chains were let down to admit them, and were drawn up again behind them.

This disastrous sea fight led the Turks to ruminate over a new plan. The Greeks were in the full possession of the Golden Horn, and held it along with the Marmora Sea. The Turkish vessels were in the Bosporus, more than a mile above, but below the fortresses of Asia and Europe. Since the Turkish ships could not enter the Golden Horn by water, Mahomed and his engineers conceived the daring thought of entering the Golden Horn with his ships *by land!* As the old chain and the strong walls and fortifications protected both city and harbor, Mahomed undertook to transport his boats overland and launch them in the Golden Horn. The canals of Grant and Butler, in our civil war, had a similar strategy for their object, but the Turks were the more successful engineers. Mr. Pears, in his "Fall of Constantinople," says that Mahomed transported his boats over the neck of land between the modern Tophane and the valley now known as Cassim Pasha. Galata itself at that time was a walled city, and of course the boats of the Turk were transported to the northwest of the walls.

The Turkish fleet sealed the Straits at the spot then, as now, known as Bechïktash. It is on the European side of the Bosporus—just above the superb imperial marble palace of Dolma-Bagtché. The palace of Yildiz, amidst its grounds of pleasance and beauty, is situated just above Bechïktash, on a height which overlooks the blue Bosporus and the azure mountains of Asia beyond. It was from Bechïktash on the 20th of May, 1886, that I witnessed the sacred camels cross the Bosporus laden with the Holy Carpet for Mecca—amidst the prayers of the devout believers, and a throng of one hundred thousand Moslems of both sexes and all ages. More than three hundred years before, the most singular work of engineering which war had up to that time called forth, had here its experiment and success—not without religious awe and ceremony, and not upon "ships of the desert," but with real ships, energized by the same religious *esprit*.

It is not my purpose to refer to the political or dynastic complications which led up to the siege, nor to the consequences to Italy, and especially to Venice and Genoa, nor to the Greek people or to the Western Powers, by reason of the fall of the city. For two centuries, including the latter half of the thirteenth century, there had been a rapid decay of the Greek empire. The country round about the city had been desolated. The merchant princes of Venice and Genoa had rifled palace, church and temple, and carried away the marble columns and exquisite mosaics. On the other hand, the Turks had been trained under the rule of their Great Sultan, Amurath, who taught them honesty and valor by his own noble example. When the son of that Amurath—Mahomed II—succeeded his father, he was a young man. He was only twenty-one years old. Young as he was, he made cool preparations for the taking of the city. It was, to him, the fulfillment of prophesy. Gibbon depreciates him somewhat. He says: "He was doubtless a soldier, and possibly a general." But the growth of his empire and the fall of the great capital are evidences of his persistent genius for war and conquest. Be-

BURSTING OF THE BIG GUN AT THE TURKISH CAPTURE.

sides, at that time he had, in addition to his immense army—which was variously estimated at from one hundred thousand to four hundred thousand men—before the city the famous Janizary corps. They were twelve thousand in number. They were of the selectest blood of the Christians who had been taken in battle and been trained in the Mahometan faith. When the siege began, the Janizaries were placed midway on the land side of the walled city before the gate of St. Romanus. Perhaps the most salient feature of this remarkable siege was the blending of the methods of ancient and modern warfare in its operations. The catapult and the ballista of the Greeks and Romans were on hand, hurling their showers of darts and stones. But just as the present Sultan utilizes every valuable invention that comes to the Bosporus, so his ancestor utilized the newest means of destruction then known to the world of invention and engineering. As now, so then—the Sultan resorted to the foreigner for the most refined and efficient means. He established a gun foundry at Adrianople, and employed the Krupp of that day, Orban of Wallachia, as its superintendent.

On the 6th of April, A. D. 1453, the siege began with the firing of the big guns. The very big gun was brought from Adrianople. It was planted, and fired. Other guns were fired with 600-pound balls against the gates. It was all in vain. The very big gun burst, and the engineer was hoist with his own petard. He was killed by his own "arm."

The first assault was resultless. In spite of the navy, the big cannon and the portable turrets, and even the valor of the Janizaries, the city defied its assaults. The attempts on the land side had failed.

Then came the inspiration and the attempt—which is the *gravamen* of this chapter—to convey some of the Turkish vessels overland and launch them within the harbor of the Golden Horn. Some sixty of the Turkish vessels were in the Bosporus, anchored between the great towers in Europe and Asia and the place where the Palace of Dolma Bagtché now stands. The distance between the last-named place and the available point on the Golden Horn for the launching of the overland ships is some five miles. The traveler will notice a high ridge overlooking the Golden Horn, upon which is situated the City of Pera, now a European city inhabited by the Ambassadors, dragomans and dogs. There is a long, sloping declivity from Pera to the waters of the Golden Horn. This slope is now occupied by an old neglected Turkish cemetery, whose tombstones lie around in the utmost confusion, amid old cypress-trees. The space to be traversed by the ships was then not only hilly but wooded. A passage was cut over the hills and through the valleys, and laid with planks which had been well greased for the occasion with the fat of sheep and oxen. All the flotilla, armed cap-à-pie, sailing through the woods and down the hilly slopes into the Golden Horn, was the first object which met the Greek sentinels upon the towers of the city. The work of transportation was done by oxen and men, an innumerable host, and the fleet and the army were thus brought in unison within the inner recess of the harbor, whence the city was most assailable !

There is some contrariety of opinion as to the route which the ships pursued overland, in order to reach the Golden Horn from the Bosporus, but the route indicated by the map on the first page of the previous chapter is generally considered the one then taken. The surface of the land between Bechiktash and the Golden Horn is quite hilly and rugged even yet. It is probable that it was more so at the time of the Ottoman conquest. The splendid palace of Dolma-Bagtché had not then been erected, and the various streets and avenues in its rear were certainly not laid out at that time as they are to-day. A deep valley intervenes between that palace and the Military School and Arsenal, which are prominent objects of observation at this time from the Bosporus. It was, therefore, no ordinary physical work to overcome the acclivities between the two points over which the ships were hauled. Besides, it was at a time when the utmost vigilance in the camps of the Italians, Greeks and Turks was observed.

The contest for Constantinople might well be called one of the pivotal struggles of the world. It was stupendous in its preparation and in its consequences. After the Turkish fleet was launched in this way, a bridge was built, and artillery was placed upon it, the garrison quietly looking on. The siege then began on the land side, and at the end of forty days the gate of St. Romanus was in ruins, its towers were razed and the Turks were ready to assault the city. Such a scene was never observed before, or since, on those classic shores. The Moslem still holds his rule at the Palace of Yildiz, above the very point on the Bosporus from which the movement of his ships by land began.

There are many stories—many of them apocryphal—about the entrance of Mahmoud within the church of St. Sophia. It is said that he reined his steed under the mighty dome, and made that imprint of his bloody hand which is still pointed out to the credulous tourist by the patriotic Greek *valet-de-place*. It is further said, that this *sign-manual* is the prototype of the *toughra*, or cypher, wherewith the Sultan signs all edicts of state. This *toughra* appears in the frontispiece, beneath the picture of the Sultan Abdul Hamid II. It has an involuted look quite diplomatic.

The Turks, after their method, bathe themselves and fast, and perform other religious ceremonies, preparatory either for death and the delights of Paradise, or victory and the spoils of the rich city. The cry arises from the Moslem, "God is God, and Mahomet is his Prophet!" Then the Turkish infantry advance to the attack. Not even the valor of the faithful friends of the Emperor of the Greeks—the last of a line of a thousand years—can withstand the fury of this assault. Under the eye of the Sultan himself, the Janizaries pioneer the way. A giant of that famous corps, Hassan by name, leads the host to victory. The Greek emperor falls, a hero amidst a cohort of cowards. On the 29th of May, A. D. 1453, after a siege of fifty-three days, the besieged people rush, as with one accord, toward the Church of St. Sophia, hoping for the descent of the Saint from heaven to save them from the enemy. It is otherwise decreed. Not the Saint but the Star and Crescent descend on St. Sophia and the city.

The complications which have confused the dynasties of Europe and the political philosophers and diplomats of the world then began. It still goes on. Whatever may be said of the rule of the Ottoman in the old city of Byzantium, one beneficial result was accomplished by its fall in A.D. 1453: the literary treasures heaped on heap within the libraries and crypts of the monasteries and churches of the city and its environs were scattered throughout Europe; scholarship received a new impulse in the revival of its learning, and the world, instead of merely marking time, began a march toward a higher civilization than the Rome of Augustus or the city of Constantine had ever attained. How much of this progress was due to the Arabic science, which Mahomed the Second brought into the Golden Horn, we shall probably never know.

Strictly speaking, there was no Greek empire of the East when the Turks took the city.  It had crumbled away centuries before.  The Saracens had cut off many of the Asiatic provinces which owed allegiance to Byzantium.  The kingdom of Jerusalem and other important places of the East had nearly all been rescued from the crusading Christians.  Until the accession of the first of the Basils, in the year A. D. 867, the empire was usually regarded as an eastern branch of the Roman empire.  After that, it became in fact the Eastern or the Byzantine empire.  Let there be no confusion; for if " Byzantine " be the designation, it must not be forgotten that the empire was also Roman.  It was called Roumania.  It was new Rome.  It was thus distinguished from the Old Rome.  The nomads only knew Constantinople as the capital of Roman territory.  " Romaic " is still the designation of the Greek-speaking population of that empire.  The city of Erze-*roum* and the province of Roumelia are a nomenclatural acknowledgment of the potentiality of Old Rome.  The Patriarch of the Orthodox Greek Church is described as a bishop of New Rome.  Greek, however, was the language of the Eastern empire, as it was also of the educated classes of Rome herself.  It was the language of elegance and refinement.  The Latin had its place, and helped to strengthen or modify the Greek.  Naturally enough the sturdy old Roman fathers despised the Greek tongue as thoroughly as the English Saxon despised the French; and for the same unreasonable pretense ; for had not the Greeks, like the French, an elegance and refinement that seemed unmanly to the ruder races ?

Call the Eastern empire by what name we will, it was a tremendous power.  It was an empire.  It lasted with miraculous pertinacity.  To what is this permanancy attributable?  Municipality !  During all the changes in the capital and in the provinces, and until the empire finally fell before force, the forms of municipality, Grecian and Roman, remained.  The very Essnafs, with their artisan and trade-unions, had their share in the rule of the city.  Absolutism never entirely undermined the spirit of Home Rule.  The citizen was one thing and the soldier another.  The foreign mercenary was oftentimes called in to suppress the citizen. This municipal system was the opposite of centralization, which seems to have its analogy to-day in Russia, where the Emperor is looked upon as the father of his people, and is hedged about with a divinity. His acts are only questioned by the Agnostic and Nihilist. Still, even the Czar, like the old Byzantine emperor, is surrounded by local municipal authority—a municipal commune, the *Zemstro* —which the steam-engine and the telegraph have not altogether dissipated in this nineteenth century. But Russian peasant municipality is not even a shadow of the old Roman and Greek municipality.

However much the Greek may have worshipped his emperor; however much he may have been absorbed by trade; how muchsoever the people may have been separated, one from the other, —by mountains upon the mainland and islands upon the sea—the old municipal spirit survived. The merchant princes of the elder empire, like the merchant princes of the Grecian race to-day, had a power of their own which never deferred to absolutism.

The spirit of municipal freedom was a part of the condition of the Conquest by the Turk. It is one element of his permanency both in Europe and in Asia. It was nothing new to him. It descended to him as it did to the Greeks and Romans, from Patriarchal rule in tribal groups. It is the *patria potesta*, at once the law of Nature and the old civil law, which gave power to Rome—old Rome and new Rome—and which inspire the refinements of modern polity.

## CHAPTER XIV.

THESE Bosporus banks, by general consent, are considered the most beautiful for scenery, convenient for commerce, salubrious for health, and interesting for association on the globe.

When we came here in 1885 we took up our residence at the upper end of these remarkable Straits, at Therapia. It is in sight of the Black Sea. That sea, purified of the dirt of the Danube, Dnieper and Don, runs through the Bosporus into the Sea of Marmora, and thence into the Mediterranean. So clear are these waters, so breezeful in their motion and so useful to trade, that at no hour of the cool days of summer can one fail to see an Austrian, Russian, French, German, Italian or Turkish steamer making a snowy wake over their blue, very blue, very deep blue surface; not to speak of the hundred sail and caïques (or row-boats) which make the Bosporus picturesque and attractive.

There is a great similarity between the waters of Constantinople and those of New York. This, tourists often remark. The East River connects Long Island Sound with New York Harbor just as the Bosporus connects the Black Sea with the Sea of Marmora ; and the Golden Horn not inaptly represents the Hudson River, except in this, that the Golden Horn nearly divides the city of Constantinople. Perhaps the East River better represents the Golden Horn, as it separates New York from Brooklyn. Stamboul, the old city, is situated on a peninsula, and is very like New York City. The other part of the city, which is called Pera, would represent Brooklyn; while Scutari, across the wide river, which is always attractive by the Florence Nightingale Hospital, might be said to represent Jersey City.

It is a question, however, whether New York, Naples or Constantinople possesses the rarest harbor in the world. With all my partiality for New York—and perhaps because I know its defects from taking an active part in remedial legislation—I am inclined to give the palm to the harbor of the city of the Sultan, and in this connection to express a preference for the comfort upon the vessels which navigate the latter waters, and for the gorgeous panorama they unfold.

In going to and fro on the Bosporus, especially on the larger steamers which navigate the Black Sea or cross the Marmora, the passengers are made up of every race, order and color of people, from the venerable Pasha, whose family is hid behind the curtains, to the poor government clerk, who depends upon the Pasha's bounty. If you take a long journey to any of the ports of the Black Sea in the large steamers of Russia or Austria, you will find the same Pasha, traveling with his family and dining with the passengers, while his wives, too often, browse outside on the deck without a murmur. The deck-passengers on such steamers are a motley mixture: lazy, black eunuchs, servants, business men, and women and children of every nationality massed together in heterogeneous confusion.

Therapia and Buyukdere have always had a quarrel. It is probably a sanitary quarrel. The burning question is, Which enjoys the milder climate? I have never tried the latter, but I have the former. The former is always fresh and cool in mid-summer, while Buyukdere is reported to be otherwise. Therapia has the advantage of the breeze of the Black Sea. From our home in Therapia we could always look into its mouth. Buyuk-dere appears like a town shut in, as if it were situated on an inland sea, but its improvements have surpassed those of Thera-pia. When the ten thousand led by Xenophon had completed their retreat, they stood upon the summit of Mt. Teches. Their joy was greater than that of Moses and his Israelites when they beheld the Promised Land, for Xenophon and his host sighted the Pontus Euxinus and its realities, which I have the pleasure of seeing from my home at Therapia, under its wondrous sheen of beauty, every day of summer, and in comparison with which the land of Jordan and its environment are tame and uninteresting.

Philologically and mythologically, the name of the Strait has received considerable discussion. It is generally agreed that it means the " Harbor of the Ox." Webster's " latest " says that Bosporus is the more correct orthography. It is the English way, but this mode depends on etymology. Without regard to this, it is the spot where the goddess Io crossed on the back of that animal. The schoolboy will remember the legend of that lady, who traveled over all the world, with Juno closely following after her, because Io was too well beloved by Jupiter. She was put to great straits in the pursuit—in fact, compelled to cross the Straits which separated the Old from the New World. Our learned men, like Lord Bacon, who find so much recondite wisdom in the classics, say that her crossing the Straits indicates the progress of agriculture ! I suppose this comes from ploughing the sea with an ox. The more learned idea is that agriculture came from the East to the West—hence the myth of the Ox, which was the animal first used in farming, and therefore typical of the noblest pursuit by which man lives.

Notwithstanding this legend, the Bosporus was more cele-brated for its fish than its oxen. It was called the " Fishy Bosporus "—thus uniting piscatorial and agricultural occupa-tions. According to the earliest accounts, the early Byzantines drove a rich trade in fish. Shoals of fish, and especially of a fish called pelamys, a sort of tunny, were accustomed to come down from the Black Sea, attracted into the harbor by the fresh water which flowed into its upper end. What was in the water to attract these finny creatures, whether marine insects, or whether they were attracted by the growth of seaweed, which served as pasture, has not been cleared up. Doubtless the stream lured the fish along, as running water always does, and its currency made the early fortunes of Byzantium. It was to fish that the name " Golden Horn " is to be attributed. It was derived from the " net " earnings which poured out of this cornucopia !

Within the radius of no other point, unless it be Thebes or Athens, are there so many classical associations as those which have the Bosporus for a nucleus. Here, unless we except Noah and his ark, was the first naval exhibition on record, and upon this spot, fixed with certainty by pundits, the Argonauts landed and erected altars and offered sacrifices. Here were the several temples erected by the Greeks, but unhappily destroyed by the Persians, Turks and other invaders. The names signify the sites of old renown. The home of the Gauls is Galata; ancient Metopon is Tophane, so familiar to our launch and to our foot, and where the guns of Krupp and Armstrong stand in belligerent array. The temples of Venus and Diana afterwards became

churches of the Saviour and the Saints. The burning rocks
furnish the tomb of Barbarossa. The old Rhodian port is now
known as Bechïktash. It was once honored by a temple to Apollo.
All the places which confuse the mind with their Greek and
Turkish names, from Cavak to San Stefano, give to this
renowned current, with its impetuosity and mystery, a history
which the reign of the Ottoman has not destroyed, and which no
power can entirely destroy.

It may be difficult to revive many of the associations connected
with this history, for, like the Straits, the history often runs contrariwise. Elsewhere I have spoken of the classic rocks at the entrance
of the Bosporus; of Richard the Lion-Hearted and his prison
here; of the castles of Europe and Asia; of the Giant's Mountain; of the old Genoese castle celebrated for the siege of Haroun
Al Raschid, with two hundred thousand men, and of Godfrey
de Bouillon and his army, which was encamped along these
waters. And yet these figures of classic and crusading history
seem but dreams in this age of reality. The sooty emanations
of the Shirket ferry, as it goes up and down the Straits, speak of
new motors and a new element of civilization. No one can
enjoy a visit to Constantinople and its environments like those
who tinge the realities of the present with the visions of the past.

With the aid of the launch, we were enabled to visit, as a
special Diversion, a scene which has both a classic and a geologic
association of intense interest. An hour from Therapia will take
you into the Black Sea. A half-hour more will take you to the
Cyanian rocks, or Symplegades, outside of the Bosporus stream—
rocks famous in Grecian lore. They used to be movable, and
opened to engulf, like icebergs, the sailors and vessels venturing
near. Captain Jason, the skipper of the *Argo*, went through
them safely. He left an altar upon their top, which remains to
tell of his scrupulous piety and of Medea's parental devotion.

In one of my rambles along the Asiatic shore I picked up
under a hospitable roof—once a Turkish harem, now a home
where Armenian and Turkish girls embroider the rare fabrics in
gold, silk and silver for the refugee fund of the East—a rare
volume of poetry. It is entitled, "The Life and Death of Jason,"
by William Morris. It starts with Jason in Thessaly, beside the
tumbling sea, "where once dwelt a folk men called the Minyae."
It follows the princely hero in his roving, after the demand for his

kingdom, and after the promise for its loyal reconstruction, if he would only find the golden fleece of that ram that had carried Phryxus to Colchis, where the fleece was located. It follows the ship to the Bosporus.

How does the vessel pass the Symplegades? To answer this question requires a description of the rocks. These I visited one Sunday. There was a smooth sea and a clear sky for that visit. Hardly a ripple struck their rocky sides, and not one of the old tumultuous waves splashed and roared through their dark caverns. How unlike the rocks of Mr. Morris's poem! He locates them at the narrow ending of the sea. So far, good. That means the Bosporean mouth. But the shifting winds and the flapping sail there and then, which confused all seamanship, we did not experience. The Jason mariners heard the pounding of the rocks and saw the steaming clouds of spray. The "polished bases" of the rocks were hidden from them by these clouds of spray, except when the sun cast its glittering eye into the churning waves and moving caves. The clamor and the movement scared the Grecian crew, but not their intrepid captain. Juno stood by him. He was ambitious, and his arm had the strength of seven men. His voice was stentorian, and when he saw his danger, he cried out to the gods to know if the quest for the fleece was to end thus ignobly.

The *Argo* is driven toward "the clashers." Jason takes the helm. He begs of the gods to let him through the gates. A dove comes to the rescue. It is so nice, in poems and when at sea, to have a dove handy. By its flight the open place in the rocks is shown, and in the very nick of time, after a big blow had spent itself. Jason clutches the tiller tighter; his sailors grasp the oars with mighty force, and the ship is driven

> "Unto the rocks, until, with blinded eyes,
> They blink one moment at those mysteries,
> Unseen before—the next, they feel the sun
> Full on their backs, and know their deed is done!"

The Bosporus is by no means always a placid or a safe stream. Horace describes it in four words:

> "Novita Bosporum Pœnus perhorrescit."

There is beneath the tranquil waters of the Bosporus a constant collision of currents. This is a danger to navigation, as the writer has had ocular demonstration. It has been ascertained, beyond doubt, that while the upper current will bear you on its surface from the Black Sea to the Marmora, the under current runs exactly in the contrary direction. This was proved in early days by the fishermen, who, in dropping their nets to a certain depth, found which way they swung. Besides, it is recorded in the early writers who discussed the navigation of the Bosporus.

I have read Herodotus. He is called the father of history, and sometimes the father of liars. In his lifetime his reputation was good, in his own community, for truth and veracity. He is therefore competent as a witness in any court of law. He does not disdain to speak of the Symplegades. It must have been an old story even in his time. He was a good story-teller, for he tells us how Darius ascended these rocks for a view of the Black Sea. It must be true, for I have done the same myself. There is nothing in the fact to boast of. I did it with a sprained ankle. There was much vaunting among the earlier Greek explorers. How they magnify every obstruction to navigation! Evidently, since the day when the veracious Herodotus wrote, there must have been many structural changes in and around the mouth of the Bosporus. He says that the Ionian fleet which accompanied the Scythian expedition of Darius sailed through these rocks. This is impossible; unless there was some special seismic or volcanic arrangement made for his Persians. Moreover, he says that on one of the islands there was built a temple; but I am a living witness that there is now little room on the top of the largest island for anything but an altar, which still remains. It is likely—since Herodotus cannot be gainsaid—that a larger island existed. It must have been the great obstacle at the mouth of the Bosporus to the navigation of the Euxine.

Different causes have been given for the opposite currents of the Bosporus. Maury attributes it to the specific gravity between the surface and under water. This is a very learned view and weighty. It strikes even the unlearned. The water at the bottom is more impregnated with salt, therefore heavier than the water at the top, and there is an effort of the two to find their proper level. Another explanation is: That there is an underground communication between the Caspian and Black seas ; the surface of the Caspian being lower than that of the Black Sea, it is thought that the water is sucked from below through this underground channel, thus creating an undercurrent to the north and to the Caspian. This is rather a recondite explanation ; but it would not be inconsistent with hydrostatics. Once upon a time, it is said, by geologists and others, that the Black Sea, the Sea of Azof and the Caspian were one. This great inland body of water was on a higher plane than the Mediterranean and the Marmora. It was held in by the Symplegades, which plugged the mouth of the Bosporus. About fifteen hundred and thirty years before Christ a volcanic eruption broke down this barrier and flooded all the Mediterranean, deluging the lower countries on the south. The thirty years is put in for exactness. Ancient writers refer to this deluge. Dr. Washburn, of Robert College, confirms this view, but is not positive as to the date. He offered to furnish me with some geological matter of his own in confirmation; but I never received it, to my regret.

From all these data there can be no doubt in the mind of the reader that some great seismic movement once tore down the gates at the mouth of the Bosporus, and the pent-up waters found their level in the Mediterranean, even to the flooding of the countries in northern Africa. I have to admit, however, with all my own and my borrowed hydrostatics, that it has taken a long time for the two seas to find a common level—for the Euxine is still running out. Perhaps the most obvious cause of these transverse currents is a difference of temperature. A test for this is as simple as the one for salt. I confess that I have never made either.

It is a matter of ancient record that the Bosporus has been frozen over twice. Unless the seasons have very much changed since the early days, this would seem to be very doubtful—even if recorded by Herodotus—especially a freezing over the " Devil's current," which is swifter than a mill-race, with the hydrostatic power of a sea behind it. But with all its geological and seismical riddles, no Strait is so famous in history, and no locality presents such a combination of picturesque loveliness and sublimity as the Bosporus. And in this remark I do not depend for vindication upon the grand works of man—the domes and minarets which give their romance and charm to old Stamboul and the Seraglio Point —nor upon the crafts, impelled by steam, oar and sail, which everywhere ply upon the bosom of the water, but upon the shores, which are as lovely as the heavens which bend over them.

It is difficult to describe the subtle charm of the landscape of the Bosporus. As well try to picture with words the idiosyncrasy of a human face of which you are enamored. Wherein consists the peculiarity of this landscape? What makes the light of its atmosphere?

No answer to these queries could indicate the ineffable charm.

Aside from all associations around the Bosporus, such as the great strife by which Islam was here enthroned upon the ruins of the Eastern Church ; aside from the fact that this strife is still being waged upon these shores, a strife which takes hold upon the viewless world to come—there is a fascination in its past, present and future which fires the imagination like the new scenes of the Yellowstone or the Yosemite, and radiates it with the influence of poetry and the affluence of color and imagery. Even a traveler accustomed to the balm and beauty of the skies of southern Italy may here find its counterpart in the soft balminess and delightful beauty of earth and sea and sky.

Still the Bosporus might be improved. It has some *un*-fragrances. Going up and down a good deal in our launch, we meet with many a nuisance. The horses that die are thrown into the stream. It is expected that they will be carried off by the current, bnt the current is eccentric. When it goes down seemingly, it may go up really, and when it appears to go up or down, it may swirl off into an eddy. The bodies that are thrown into the Straits often rise to the surface, and are floated into a corner. There they lie and rot until assisted by some boatmen to drift again into the current. There are a great many unused caïque-holes, called *caik-hanes*. Many of them have no gates. They are, therefore, sinks of putrefaction. They are nauseating, with their bad odors. Animals are sucked in to taint the house which is above the hole. It is not unusual to see dead horses, dogs, calves and porpoises on both sides of the Bosporus.

Another drawback to the beauty of the stream may be mentioned. In the Orient, where there are seldom any fireplaces in the buildings, you will see in the winter the beauty and architecture of the houses destroyed by long sheet-iron pipes protruding from the windows. In the better houses—palaces, even—the only warming apparatus, as in the palace of the

Vatican, is a large iron or brass basin, called a *mangal*. This mangal contains glowing coals, free from unpleasant gas. It is sometimes richly chased. I have seen exquisite work of this kind in the palace of Yildiz. Its elegance does not compensate, in inclement weather, for the absence of a stove or so in the roomy houses. Hence the ungainly stove-pipes.

GYPSIES OF THE BOSPORUS.

One trip ought not to be omitted in the summer season. I shall never forget it, as it led to the locality of a strange race who have the Orient for their origin —I mean the Gypsies of the valley of Buyukdere. Buyukdere means, in the Turkish, "the forty trees." On the beautiful tented fields spread out around these trees I have seen in mid-summer these Gypsies. They are as ready to shoe your horse as to tell your fortune. These wanderers are disliked by all the inhabitants of Turkey. Does this come from fear of the mysterious ? We found nothing but kindness in visiting their tents, and a tender of food and hospitality. Call them Zingari, Tartar, Gigonza, Gitanna, or Rom (man), as they call themselves, or as we call them, Gypsies; whether they came from India, fleeing before Tamerlane, or elsewhere—they lead here, as in other places, a most remarkable, itinerant life. This is not their worst condition. Despised by the Turk, and without commiseration from the Christian, they are the pariahs of the land ; and yet to me, constantly observing them, both in the field and in the city, I could not make out that they were worse than the ordinary people, except in their vagabondage. Over the Galata bridge their little girls, in their picturesque raven hair, brown complexion, splendid eyes and white teeth, in tatters and rags, dash after and beg from every carriage. The mothers carry their babes in slings, sometimes on the back and sometimes at the breast. The stalwart men carry poultry or calves under their arms; but they all betray a remediless condition of abject poverty. The Christians call them " children of the Evil One ; " but they have ever shown, when I have met them, only the common importunity for alms, and that plentiful humor and good temper which is in happy contrast with their condition.

In a former chapter the Gypsies were referred to with as much charity as our vagrant human nature demands. We are all Gypsies, in the sense of trade and locomotion. The difference between the Gypsies of the Old World and those whom we see vagabondizing, telling stories, trading or stealing horses, and occasionally kidnapping a child, is the difference between one class of vagabonds and another.

The evidence from the language traces the origin of this race to India. In the fifth century a Persian king received from an Indian king a pretty gift of 12,000 musicians of both sexes. They were *luris*. It is Persian for Gypsy. They are known in Arabia as the Zott people; in Turkey as *zigeuner*, or musicians; and among themselves as *Rom*, or man. Sometimes they became so predatory that an army was called in to subdue them; but since A. D. 855, when they came into the Byzantine empire, they have not caused any turbulence in the composite social order of either the Greek or Ottoman empires.

Another trip worth making in mid-summer is to Kilios, the life-saving station near the Symplegades. It is not necessary to say why I made this trip.

It was no slight adventure which took us over the bosom of the Black Sea in our frail " mouche," to visit Kilios. When we arrived at that point we were amply repaid for the trip by the kindness of Captain Palmer's officers, for the captain was then absent, and by the practice with the rocket and other apparatus.

Since my visit to this wild and wonderful point on the Euxine, I have studied the service at these posts. It is sustained by a tax on the tonnage, levied under Turkish authority. The tax is not much, but it is enough, although it is said one can never have enough of a good thing. The gentleman here most interested in this service is Mr. William H. Wrench, the British Consul at Constantinople. He is the " European Delegate on the Adminis-tration of the Black Sea Life-Saving Service." He is vigilant and active in his duty. It is a delight to have such a humane, practical hobby. That I know from nearly twenty years' expe-rience at home as to the same benignant service.

The service here within the last four years has guarded a coast line of thirty miles on each side of the Bosporus. There are eight stations on the European coast, two of which possess lifeboats. These boats are in good order, and are manned by seventy men and four officers. There are seven stations on the Asiatic coast. Two of them have lifeboats, with seventy-two men. These men are nearly if not all Turks, and, as my observation shows, they are sober, active and brave men. Work is still going on for the improvement of these stations.

Captain Samuel Palmer, the hero of the incident I shall relate, superintends the European stations. When on a visit to his station, there was shown me, with much sensibility, the photograph of his father, who was drowned in 1878 near Kilios, in assisting to rescue the passengers of a stranded Turkish transport. He looked, as his son looks, the incarnation of dauntless pluck, cool caution and commanding qualities.

The Asiatic stations are commanded by Matthew Summers. He is also English, and is known in England for his honorable association with the rocket service. The crews here do not use the howitzer to throw the line, as we do, but the rocket. The relative value of the two methods has been tested. The advantage is with the gun.

The incident I meant to relate concerns a Russian vessel—the *Emperor Alexander II.*, a mail-boat of the Russian Steam Navigation Company. This vessel was making for Constantinople from Odessa, when she stranded on the 18th of February, 1886, between 1 and 2 o'clock in the morning. She struck ground about eighteen miles west of the Bosporus entrance. The patrol saw her strike, and gave the rocket signal. Within an hour fifteen men from the two rocket stations of Ak-Bownad and Agatchli were on hand with their rocket apparatus. Before the danger became imminent, whi-r-r! whizz! went a rocket over the vessel. The *entente* was at once established between ship and shore, between peril and safety. Kilios was twelve miles off. Captain Palmer was there. A messenger was sent for him. He was reached at 4 A. M. The messenger traveled his twelve miles in loose sand. Our life-savers know what that means. There was a heavy sea. The captain, however, launched his lifeboat. He had a hard time in getting her through the surf. The current was against him. In two hours he made only four miles. He put his boat about and went back with the current to Kilios. The waves increased. At the entrance to Kilios harbor—a most romantic, wild and desolate place—his boat was imperilled. A comber, such as whelmed a Barnegat boat off our New Jersey coast not long since, took his boat abeam, after it was knocked over by a heavy sea. The boat filled. It escaped by a few feet from a wild dash against a sunken rock, for the shore is rocky, as all know who have entered the Bosporus. But the gallant captain beached his boat. Then, like King Richard, he called for a horse, and reached the scene of the disaster at 10 in the forenoon.

What had happened while the captain and his men were thus struggling? The Russian captain had sent a bottle ashore by the buoy. It contained only the name of the vessel. When Captain Palmer appears, a man in the ship is placed in the buoy and is hauled ashore. He is a Turkish shepherd—in charge of two hundred and fifty sheep aboard. Following him in the buoy are the passengers, numbering about one hundred. They land in quick succession and are sent to the nearest station, where hot tea, brandy and dry clothing are ready. The large number saved require extra provision, and other stations are summoned, with their hands for the whip line and their comforts for the rescued. The laborers on the Government farm near, and some charcoal burners, also come to the rescue. By 4 in the afternoon ninety-six persons, among them thirty-one women, are saved. They are all, except two, Russian peasant-pilgrims bound for Jerusalem.

This curious shipload of pilgrims was brought down to Constantinople, where they were cared for. The Sultan sent them a large purse for their comfort, and the Russian Embassy gave them every attention.

When I started on my Egyptian journey in February, 1886, upon the Russian steamer *Cæsarovitch* I had a close look at about one hundred of this class of sheepskin-clad pilgrims. They are of the Greek Church, and believe that if they can only reach the Holy City their calling and election are sure. They go in droves to the Old Jerusalem, with an eye on the " New." Far away, upon the shores of the Volga, Don and Dnieper, they live and worship with a faith that makes religion a romance. With only funds enough to reach Jerusalem, they venture forth under the guidance of some leading man or woman, who directs and cheers them on their way with recitations and prayers that shame the *soi-disant* Christian folk of other lands. When they arrive at Jerusalem the great Russian convent buildings receive and care for them till their eyes are gladdened with glimpses of the golden pavements and alabaster walls, and then, if alive, they return to their Russian homes.

The marvel of the saving grace of the life service, as illustrated above, on the Black Sea is in the number of lives saved, and at the rate of one in every three minutes of the time employed. There are in our incomparable service but few incidents like this. I recall the rescue of the *Amérique* passengers, near Long Branch, as one of these incidents.

I will conclude this incident by a description of the *modus operandi* by which this marvel was effected. Both Captains Palmer and Summers are inventive men, and have endeavored to improve their paraphernalia. I made a little sketch of the " rigging " of Captain Palmer. The reader will see that instead of employing one traveler-block, Palmer uses two, the one attached to the breeches buoy and running on the hawser in the usual manner, but the other, which is called the " leading traveler," runs on

the hawser about four feet in-shore of its companion when the
hawser is set up from the shores to the wreck. It is kept at this
distance by a clove-hitch in the whip line, which thus passes from
one traveler to the other, exerting its force on the "leading
traveler" in bringing the breeches buoy from the vessel to the
shore, and on the traveler in taking the buoy to the vessel. From
the "leading traveler" to the breeches buoy two slings descend,
which are attached to the points at which the two in-shore slings of
the buoy itself are made fast. By this arrangement, so says
Palmer, not only is the breeches buoy kept level on the water the
same way as by "Summers's method," but the hawser is not

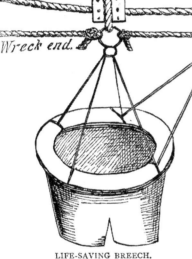

*Wreck end.*        *Shore end.*

depressed into the V-like
shape it assumes when all
the weight of the man in
the buoy falls on one traveler alone; and as the hawser is not so depressed, the
drag for the men hauling
on the whip line is from
one-third to one-half less
heavy.

LIFE-SAVING BREECH.

Captain Palmer was not
forgotten by the Russian
Government, for his efforts in saving the passengers of the ship *Alexander II.* The Czar sent him a splendid testimonial, and the company to which the ship belonged, gave him a more substantial
reward in a silver service, in recognition of his courage and skill.

Speaking of the Life-Saving Service, in which our own country
takes so much pride, I have had occasion to know of another
heroic act. It was achieved by a common Turk. His name was
Mustapha. I here recount it: A ship is wrecked off a high bluff
in the night; cries of distress near the bluff are heard. Mustapha
is let down the bluff over a hundred feet by a rope secured
around his body. Being a seaman, he struggles with the waves
which dash violently against the bluff. He seizes the imperiled

man, but is himself dashed senseless by the waves. He loses his grip on the man. He is drawn up. Then having been brought to by his friends, he goes down again, and a third time. Finally, he brings up the sailor, or, rather, the dead body of the sailor. This hero is the much decried Mussulman, yet the Mussulman certainly attested his faith by his works. He is but one among thousands of the same race. Whether it is brave because it believes in Fate or not, certainly his Allah has "made him just and right, sufficient tc have stood, though free to fall."

Most of the officers of the Turkish Government live outside the city in summer. They have palaces or *konaks*—country villas—upon the banks of the upper Bosporus or upon the hills round about. On the upper waters of the Bosporus, Therapia and Buyukdere are approachable by the Shirket, or ferry, which lands every quarter of an hour. These ferries are crowded with people; for no people are more fond of movement out-doors than the Levantine and Turkish population. Some hours' ride above the city, at Buyukdere and Therapia, on the European shore of the Upper Bosporus are situated the palaces of the Ambassadors of the great Powers. Here are the Russian, English, Austrian, German, French, Persian, Italian, American and Greek Ministers. Most of them live in grand style. Their resources are seemingly unlimited. They are visited by the Pashas, Beys, Effendis, Agas, and other notables and officials of the Ottoman empire. When convened under various auspices—as, for example, at the Russian Legation, under the rockets' glare and pyrotechnic display outside, and music, flowers and festivities within—the scene is quite dramatic. These embassies are in perpetual motion, toward and from one another. By *stationnaires*, i. e., large naval vessels, or by steam launches, or by ten-oared caïques, they move up and down the Straits, and zigzag across to Asia and back, as if in perpetual unrest. This is diplomacy.

When the conferences were in session during the summer of 1885, this movement was accelerated ; for the Bulgarian and the Egyptian questions were very prominent among the Pashas and the Ministry, as well as among the Ambassadors of the great Powers. Sir Drummond Wolf, the English special Ambassador, was here, doing his *devoirs*, among the other Envoys, at the Porte in Stamboul, and at the Sultan's palace of Yildiz. I met him frequently on the quay at Therapia, where, as old Parliamentarians, we talked of the battles we had fought in legislative capacities.

These Ministers, with whom I mingled much in the summer of 1885, are not distinctively national. They are selected for their cosmopolitan manners, tact and ideas. The then English Minister was Sir William A. White. He was followed by Sir Edward Thornton, whom I knew in Washington. But since that time Sir Edward has retired. He is followed again by Sir William. This latter gentleman has been abroad almost all his life. He was recently in Roumania, where he acted as Minister. He knows many languages, and he is perhaps more accomplished in the Danubian questions than any one connected with any embassy. Among the others whom it is pleasant to recall, is the Baron de Calice, the Austrian Ambassador. He tendered to us our first dinner, and made up by his courtesy, and that of his charming wife, for that which our Department of State seemed to find lacking at the Austrian court in the reception of the Minister whom we tendered to Vienna. He is a man of varied accomplishments. He has made treaties in the farthest East, in Japan, and early won consular laurels at Liverpool. The Italian Minister is Count Corti, who is well known in America, having represented his country at Washington for many years. He has been transferred to London. The French Minister at that time, Count de Noailles, was called away by the death of his father. M. Nellidoff, the Russian Ambassador, is a man of great experience, *finesse*, and skill in diplomatic arts. He was chosen for this capital, to aggrandize his country's interests. He is well seconded by the Chancellor, M. Onou. M. Radowitz, the German Minister, left his grand palace upon the heights of the Bosporus, near the city, for his home on the Upper Bosporus, where Germany is now building another palace for her Legation. He seemed to be the least troubled of any of the Ambassadors about the impending questions. The American Legation, where we spend the summer, is situated above the English Legation in Therapia. Our flag is always flying upon Sunday and on fête days, within fifty feet of the clear, plashing waters of the Bosporus, midway between the quay and the hill-top, and in sight of the mouth of the Black Sea. The residence is surrounded by a beautiful garden, in which the magnolia-trees are conspicuous.

Its terraces reach to the top of the mounta.n, ana are covered with flowers, shrubs and creepers. The frequency with which the steam launch of the American Legation moves about during the summer of 1885 shows that Mr. Heap, the Consul-General, and the Minister himself, who reside together, are keeping up their part in this Oriental movement. What a curious life it is ! It is called rest by some of my friends at home. I should call it restive.

This life has its comic phases. One of them consists in the strange commingling of various nationalities, united under an order established by the wisdom and foresight of the early Sultans.

"Foresight," I say, for it was here, upon the shore of these waters which flow to the old Propontis, that Suleïman, the son of Orchan, and grandson of Othman, saw the crescent of the moon rise before him ! It was the emblem of his race, and in its sign he entered the continent of Europe, and conquered. Temples and palaces floated up out of the great deep, and mysterious voices blended with the sound of the sea, exciting in his heart a yearning for enterprise and a sense of supernatural mystery. This is the story told by the German historian. It is often quoted as an inspiration. Out of it the earlier Turks forwarded their schemes of conquest and advancement.

There is no parallel to the climate of the upper Bosporus. In the summer, the proximity of the seas creates a current of wind which mitigates the hot weather ; but the same influences do not obtain in winter. In summer the air is so deliciously pure that it is tonic to the body and exhilaration to the spirit. Some one has said that Constantinople, in its best season and estate, drives away all care, and makes existence a beatitude ; or, to use the exaggeration of another, "Here you could almost be willing to lose your dearest friends, and rejoice at their departure." The climate had not this Lethean effect on me.

The winter upon the Bosporus does not, as I have said, begin until late, so that its rigors, which are experienced in February, have no counterpart in December. We therefore make it our pleasure and duty to seek a softer clime.

The President having given a sixty-day leave in February, we spend the remainder of the winter in Egypt and Greece. Such an excursion, I venture to say, no man ever enjoyed more than the writer. At the time I left Constantinople the Egyptian question was under full headway in Egypt. Ghazi Mouktar Pasha had been sent as the special high commissioner of the Sultan to that bedevilled country. Our arrival at Alexandria, and subsequent sojourn and Nile trip, under the telegraphic au spices of the Sultan to his commissioner, if they were recounted, would make an episode quite as diverting as any of our Ottoman experiences.

# CHAPTER XV.

To enhance the American influence in the Ottoman empire requires something besides our American teachers and preachers. Trade is the forerunner of civilizing influences as well as its concomitant. Our trade with Turkey is insignificant. Our flag is never seen on the Bosporus, except upon our launch. Such trade as we have is the importation of petroleum and the exportation of rugs and carpets. The petroleum trade is of the largest amount and interest. From recent developments, it would seem as if the crust of the ultra-American earth was in competition with our own crust, in spouting its petroleum. How can I take a universal view of this growing question? Europe, Asia, Africa and America are engaged in giving light and force out of the bowels of the earth. Since magic belongs to the East, I must evoke some supernatural or sub-natural enginery. I will visit the Sultan, and borrow from him the celebrated " cap of Fortunatus," which tradition intrusts to that ruler. It is not generally known that this wonder of our boyhood was in the custody of the Sultans ; but every one knows that whoever puts this cap on his head, and wishes to be in any part of the world, will find himself there in a moment. I am graciously favored by His Majesty with the loan—for this chapter only—of this invisible head-dress. I can now do more than Madame Blavatschi, or the other theosophites. I can not only fly, myself, to the uttermost and innermost parts of the earth, but I can take you, my reader, with me.

" I wish to be in America." Presto ! Here we are ! " Give us a peep at petroleum." " Where are we ?" " One moment in New York, the next in Pittsburg !" " What is this infernal noise ?" We are in the " Petroleum Exchange." Hear the growling of the Bears and the bellowing of the Bulls ! It is not war between England and Russia. No: it is the roaring of gas and the eruption of oil. Whenever a disturbing shock comes from some oil-well which spouts lively or dries up speedily, what an uproar ensues ! A is carrying bundles of this stock, and B disposes of his load. Values change, and stocks break with every new discovery or disaster. Bankruptcy depends on so many more barrels *per* day from West Virginia, and affluence from so many less *per* day from Pennsylvania. In one day, on the Pittsburg

MAP OF THE CASPIAN OIL REGION.

Board, the transactions include 13,000,000 barrels, and with all the chances of *rouge et noir* at Monaco. This beats the feats of the old enchanters.

In all these vicissitudes little account is taken of the 14,000 square miles in this Russian territory, in and around Baku, whither we can " wish" ourselves in the twinkling of an eye. Little is thought, in this desperate gambling, of the strata which we see with enchanted eye : starting from the Crimea, underlying Caucasia—the land of our ancestral race and language—and the Caspian Sea, to the vicinage of Baku, where the soil absorbs the oil as if it were a huge sponge to be squeezed, and where 20,000 acres alone of petroleum land have furnished 1,000,-000 tons of oil annually. Here we are in the " Black California," as the Russians call it, which furnishes fuel for locomotive and steamer, and kerosene for Central Asia and Europe. The wells are elevated, so that gravity can run the crude article into Baku for refinement and export.

One fountain at Droojba, in September, 1883, spouted two million gallons per day into the air 300 feet, from a depth of 574 feet, while the adjacent wells pursued their usual avocations undisturbed. The immensity of this product does not give you an idea of the reserve in the Caucasus. I mention these instances, as a fact and a warning, to account for the inrush of this oil into markets where once our own petroleum prevailed. No wonder the oil sells cheaper at its source and in the neighboring countries! There is a large margin for profit, because of its cheapness. No wonder the market in the Turkish empire, which was once all ours, is now divided between Russia and America!

A dissertation upon Oriental petroleum would be wanting in the poetic and pietistic elements, if we should forget Lalla Rookh and the Fire Worshippers. Were not the magi located at Baku ? Was it not here that the sacred fire of Zoroaster, guarded by the magi, burned for thousands of years ? It was only once extinguished—at least so say the learned Mahometans— in the month of April, A. D. 569. What happened then ? Amina, the beautiful wife of Abdallah, for whom, when he married her, two hundred virgins of the tribe of Koreish died of broken hearts— then gave birth to Mahomet ! Without a pang of travail, but with many portents, the prophet enters the world ! A celestial light glorifies the Oriental heavens ! Lakes become dry ; the Tigris overflows ; the palace of Persia shakes, and its towers topple. And more: all the idols of the world fall down ; the angels pitch the devil into the deep sea, and the fires of Baku and the Parsees are extinguished !

The Mahometan yet calls the enemy of his faith Giaour ; from an Arab word, Guebir, signifying a fire-worshipper. We might infer that the Mahometan world would not be partial to the Baku oil, in preference to the American.

Observe, as we pass up and down the Bosporus, at the narrowest gateway flanked by the grand towers of Roumeli-Hissar on the one side, and Anatoli-Hissar on the other, that row of small houses on the Asiatic side, of uniform shape. What are they? Nothing, in a romantic way. It is not here that Darius crossed on his bridge of boats. It is not here that Richard the Lion-Hearted was imprisoned. These are unhistoric, practical petroleum depositories ! They are, I assure you, the architectural results of much diplomacy and some selfishness.

By the regulations of Constantinople, all vessels loaded with petroleum arriving from any quarter must anchor at this storage dépôt at Pacha Bagtché, which is midway between the Black Sea and the Sea of Marmora. This dépôt was originally established by the Ottoman government as a measure of safety. It was intended to prevent the accumulation of large quantities of petroleum in the city and suburbs.

Petroleum from the United States comes mostly in Italian sailing-vessels carrying from 12,000 to 30,000 cases. The article from Batoum, intended for local consumption, is frequently conveyed in small sailing-vessels carrying 500 to 1,000 cases, or a proportionate quantity in barrels. They anchor at this dépôt, and are allowed to sell their cargoes from the deck, paying no warehouse charges. If ships coming from the United States wish to avail themselves of this privilege, they have the right to do so ; but it would be a manifest disadvantage for them to pay demurrage for the long period it would require to dispose of their large cargoes.

No vessels of any nationality loaded with petroleum are allowed to discharge at the wharves of Constantinople; all, without distinction, being obliged to go to the dépôts at Pacha Bagtché for this purpose. These stores were, in the first instance, built by the government, and offered few conveniences for the rapid discharge of ships and the delivery of the petroleum for consumption. Subsequently, a concession was given to Samni Bey and his consorts to build larger and safer stores, and a wharf where vessels could lie and discharge much more rapidly, and without the expense of lighterage. For these additional facilities and economy in time and money, the tariff for storage was increased, which led to much discussion and correspondence. It was finally reduced to the rate which the American Legation and the Russian

Embassy were of opinion would be just and sufficient  So it has
remained, but not with any formal consent on their part.

Boats carrying fifty cases, or fifteen barrels, convey the
petroleum to the city.   Many of these boats belong to the importers.   They are of uniform build and size.   They are colored blue, and assist to make the water scenery of the beautiful strait, with its Shirket ferries, poetic caïques, antique Norse
*yechts* of graceful prow, and enormous Austrian and Russian
steamers a picture in both oil and water !   These azure boats
are built of iron.   Only a limited quantity of petroleum is allowed
to be received in the stores in town.   The capital of the land of
Kismet—where it might be supposed that predestination was a
prevalent doctrine—takes many precautions for human safety,
irrespective of the fateful genii of the Koran.

We are glad to know that there is no discrimination in Turkey against American petroleum, whether at the dépôt or elsewhere ; at least by the Ottoman government.   If any facilities
have been granted to the Russian trade which have not been
equally extended to ours, no complaint has been made at the
Consulate or Legation.   Importers of the American article are sufficiently awake to their own interests to promptly protest against
discrimination. .

The greatest local obstacles of our trade in Turkey and in the
islands of the archipelago, are the frauds connected with the sale
of the American petroleum.   The " Danaos," whom Virgil feared,
when bearing gifts, are generally the cunning culprits.   They substitute the poorer Russian article in our American boxes and
cans, and sell it for the better American.   But such impositions
cannot last long.   They soon find their remedy.

What a useful utensil for every purpose, here in the East, culinary and otherwise, is the square American tin can in which the
oil is imported!   You see it where that house is building; it holds
the water to mix the mortar.   You see it in the vineyard up there
on the hill ; with it the vine-grower waters his plants.   You see
it on the hillside, on the rocks, and in the meadows ; at the
" Sweet Waters " of Asia and Europe, where those gay *hanoums*
congregate, arrayed in their many-hued silk *feridjïes*, to coquet
and gossip.   It holds the water from which their sherbet is made.
On isle and mainland, in city and country, wherever we " wish "
ourselves, the American tin can passes current, taking the place

of wooden and tin buckets. I have even seen it, in its debased,
oxidized condition, used to repair fences upon the hilly turnpike,
on the road to the Sultan's palace at Yildiz. A few days ago I
saw a dozen watermen, upon the isle of Prinkipo, using it to fill
the casks upon their donkeys.

It is being used—this uncanny can—to revolutionize the taste
of the Orient, thus :

Throughout Constantinople and Turkey, the principle of life,
water, is everywhere recognized as a part of the religion of the
people. Fountains of exquisite beauty display, in gold letters on
an azure ground, along with their clear lymph, the legend of the
Koran, " By water everything lives." There are public fountains established by individual piety, street fountains for miscel-
laneous drinking, and fountains in the mosque courts for puri-
fication before prayer. Some of these—as the elaborate one at
the seraglio gate—are of marble. They are finely decorated;
some are carved and colored, and some are gilded. The roof is
a series of domes. They are of all forms and sizes. They are
called " Well of Paradise," Sacred " Fountain of Mecca," or
some other poetic name. They are visited by women—who bear
the amphora of the antique world? Oh! no. The Ottoman
*hanoum* of Stamboul bears to the fountain the American petroleum can ! She is in strange contrast with the graceful Greek
nymph of our classic fancy.

If the women of other countries would observe the mode, or
pursue the practice, of walking over rough and hilly ground, with
jars or buckets of water neatly balanced on their heads, there
would result quite an æsthetic development. More graces would
hover around their forms. The superb carriage of the Spanish,
Greek and Egyptian—I may say Oriental—women, is due to the
long-continued habitude of going, like Rachel, to the well. I
have seen such living pictures of the Nubian women as would
shame the ramshackle, stunted, awkward woman in more civilized
societies.

Our artist has endeavored to make the contrast between the
ancient nymph and the modern female of the fountain. There is
not so much grace in the costume of the modern as in that of the
ancient. This is owing to the clumsy *feridjie.* Still, she is
erect and stately, and until she begins to carry her can by
a handle, and not upon her head, her pose will not be demoral-

WITH AMERICAN PETROLEUM CAN,

NYMPHS OF ANCIENT AND MODERN BYZANTIUM.

WITH GREEK AMPHORA.

ized. But this change in our can has begun. The descendants of Jacob, forgetting how Rachel looked when she was wooed
and won at the well, have begun to tinker with the can. The
sketch which I present is from an oil-painting which I found
in General Cluseret's room, near Constantinople. The General,
after fighting all over the world for freedom, and after the
death of the Commune—whose history he has just published in
Paris—was exiled from France. He then took part with the
Turk. When the big wars were over here, he turned to the easel.
The sketch of the Hebrew soldering the American can is one
of the children of his art.

Meanwhile, the world demands more light. The lamp holds
out to burn in realms that never knew aught but natural illumination—a farthing dip or a little wick in a small vessel of grease. It
demands cheap illumination, which means cheap transportation ;
and if the Orient can furnish her own oil, the day is not distant when
the American article will have a limited territory for its market.

Still, as the competition grows sharp, new sources spring from
our own earth, and along with them the remarkable natural gas
which Ohio and other localities are using for every emergency of
mechanical energy and domestic life.

The figures which show the magnitude of our oil and gas
business are majestic " columns " of grandeur and pride :

Statistics show that 53,000 wells have been drilled in Pennsylvania and New York since the discovery of petroleum, at a
cost of $200,000,000. These wells have produced 310,000,000
barrels of oil, which were sold at the wells for $500,000,000.
This represented a profit to the producer of $300,000,000.
The amount of oil exported is placed at 6,231,102,923 gallons.
In the pool in one county in western Pennsylvania alone,
$3,200,000 has been expended in machinery and drilling. This
does not include the many millions that are represented there
in the natural gas industry. Independent of the oil business,
there is about $50,000,000 in natural gas plants in that State.
What this and other States may show when the eleventh census is taken, confounds anticipation, and distances the Caspian
and its wonders.

To what uses, besides that of light, may not this element be
dedicated ! It is already taking the place of coal. Twelve barrels of oil in a tank on the tender ran a Pennsylvania locomotive

THE HEBREW TINKERING AN AMERICAN PETROLEUM CAN.

116 miles. The residuum of petroleum, as a substitute for coal, is just coming into use in America. In this we are copying the carriers of Baku. Three years ago, on the Russian railroads in Asia, oil was used as fuel; then, a year later, its residuum; then it fired up the 300 steamboats on the Caspian and the Volga. The use extended to Swedish and Egyptian railroads and factories, at a great saving.

The refineries of Baku and the factories of Odessa gave up English coal for the cheaper fuel. One ton of it was equal to two of coal. The North Caucasus Railway to Novorossisk has opened new outlets for the marvelous factor among the forces, and from a new field upon the Black Sea. This oil residuum has been used upon our Pacific coast by the Central Pacific Railroad. It saves forty per cent. The saving on the Swedish railroads is from twenty-five to fifty per cent. This new element has hitherto been wasted. Now, it is selling at Baku for ten cents a ton, and it is produced there at the rate of a million tons a year. What will the world of navigation say when, by burning it, the steamship which wrestles with the ocean displaces 2,500 tons of coal with 1,000 tons of residuum, while the latter only occupies the space of 600 tons of coal? Will it not revolutionize the navigation of the seas?

In view of such eventualities it may not be out of place to detail some particulars of this trade and its regulation, together with such facts as bear upon this industry in the countries of the East. While it may not be an entertaining Diversion, it may interest the utilitarian American.

The Russian petroleum has proximity to the Turkish markets. That is an advantage which no tariff can affect or ameliorate. Transportation is protection *pro tanto*, and sometimes prohibition. It has not yet reached the latter stage here, as against our American product. The Baku oil is not as rich as the American. So it is said by our American traders, though vehemently disputed by the Russians. Once, when I was spouting a little jet of rhetoric at the Commencement of the American (Robert) College, I happened to say :

"As the olive-trees of the academy furnished their purest oil for the victors of the Grecian festivals, so this institution furnishes no crude article, like that from Baku, wherewith to strengthen the wrestlers in the intellectual arena of these elder lands. Under the direction of your energetic president, Dr. Washburne, and his American associates, your lamps are filled, and burning with the white light of the refined American article!" My wife was sitting in the audience, next to Mme. Onou, the accomplished wife of the Russian Chancellor of the Legation. She quickly said, in a quick, crispy whisper :

" Ah, madame, your husband is making figures of speech, not figures of statistics! Russia is ahead on quality, and by nearness on quantity, and will have the market !"

"How did Mrs. Cox reply ?" In French, of course. Is it not the language of diplomacy? "But what did she say ?" She passed it off *lightly*, as became the subject and the occasion.

Madame Onou to the contrary, notwithstanding, I think that the Baku article contains only. thirty-five per cent. to our sixty-five or seventy. Therefore, if I am correct, the Russian will be used mostly for lubricating purposes.. But there is room for doubt, because its low price, its unlimited quantity, its cheapness of transportation, and its new refining processes, now being adapted from the American, are attracting attention from the enterprising capital of Sweden, Germany and Russia.

The magnitude of the business at Baku may glut these Turkish markets, if not others ; and unless the " Standard " and other companies either risk and make losses to " hold their own," or buy out Baku physically, from the nadir, whence comes the oil, to the zenith toward which it spouts, America may have to open fresh wells of petroleum, seek new fields for her business, or go into liquidation.

A London journal has a correspondent at St. Petersburg, who places the total quantity of raw naphtha pumped or received from the Baku wells at 2,000,000 tons for 1885—that is 400,-000,000 gallons. Of this, 500,000 tons of kerosene have been distilled, and sent from Baku alone. Two-thirds of this goes into the many-mouthed Volga, at Astrakhan, upon flotillas, which are fed and propelled by the oil that they carry in their tanks. Although the Volga is shallow, the boats are made to suit the navigation. Passing the shoals, they run to their dépôts at Tzaritzin, Kazan, Nijni, and Reybinsk. The Volga, at the first-named place, is not far from the Don. By many highways and byways, by rail and cistern-wagons, the product is distributed to all parts of Russia, to the Baltic ports, and thence to other lands. Hamburg is already a grand dépôt for the Russian petroleum, with refineries at Riga and elsewhere. This is a rival of no mean proportions. It would be vain to ignore it. The oil is sent in bulk. No casks are used except to foreign ports. It is thought that cistern-vessels will soon be used to run the oil across seas. One-third of this Baku product goes through Batoum—a free port no more. It goes by rail to the Black Sea, thence it reaches the Danube. It finds welcome at Odessa, Constantinople and Marseilles; and, *via* the Suez Canal, it is on its way to the extremest East.

The petroleum people at Baku cannot expect to be above the peril of bankruptcy, until they complete the construction of their pipe-line from the Caspian to the Black Sea. This they will do in time. Nevertheless, the exportation from Baku is increasing. The improved methods of carriage and refining have enlarged the importation from one hundred and sixty millions of gallons in 1885, to three hundred and seventy-seven million gallons in 1886. Since 1883 it has increased fivefold.

"Naphtha is a great desideratum among people where the forests above ground have been destroyed, and where the forests which have been carbonized for millions of years beneath ground have not yet been developed."

Yes, I thoroughly agree with the statement. Italy and other countries are studying closely the Russian naphtha industry. I should not be surprised to see the Italian Navy, as a consequence of the reports from Baku, substitute naphtha for coal. But this will not be done until the pipe-line has been constructed and the burning of the article becomes less dangerous.

Would my reader know how much petroleum comes to this port of Constantinople and the Mediterranean from Baku? I have here a statement from the 1st of January to the 30th of September, 1885. It is as follows: In Italian vessels, 6,334 tons; in Austrian vessels, 3,747 tons; and in Greek vessels, 3,173 tons—being a total of 13,254 tons.

Upon the application of our Consul-General here, Mr. Heap, the Russian Consul-General did not consider it expedient to inform him of the quantity of oil exported under their flag from Batoum during that period, so that the statement given is incomplete. It would be safe to add at least 33 per cent. to the amount furnished by the other three Consulates—Italian, Austrian and

Greek. Most of the petroleum arriving here from Batoum in Russian vessels is intended for consumption in this market. That exported in Italian, Austrian and Greek vessels is about equally divided between this and Mediterranean ports. There were 256,-870 cases of petroleum imported from the United States in 1885. The wholesale price of American petroleum is generally from 3 to 4 piastres (13 to 18 cents) per case higher than the Russian.

"When and where was petroleum first discovered? What is its antiquity and history?"

Petroleum is not by any means peculiar to our time or to America. It is as old as the earth, and its development antedates the "Cities of the Plain." That it should be found in Asia was not a surprise. That it should be found in such quantities and so easy of transit on the Caspian and Black seas was surprising to our speculators. That it was recently found on the Red Sea in Egypt ought not to have surprised anyone. The wells near Jebel Zeit, on that coast, 170 miles south of Suez, were reported upon by M. Petit, a French civil engineer, at the request of Nubar Pasha, the Prime Minister, as early as 1883, with specimens and analysis. Much money was then spent to develop the sulphur and oil enterprises at this point, under the Bassano concession. It had a steamer and a syndicate, but it failed: first, because of the intolerable climate; second, for lack of water, and, third, because of remoteness of provisions. In other words, even the cheap Arab labor of those parts could not overcome the local and climatic disadvantages. In September, 1884, a Belgian mining engineer, M. Debay, was sent there to report. He gave favorable accounts. Under his direction, thirty skilled Belgian workmen were sent to the place. Finding neither vegetation, habitation nor water, his little colony had a harsh time. He, however, bored away until February, 1885, just before his contract expired. Then suddenly the oil rose two metres, or more than seventy-nine and one-half inches above the sea-level. This led to the latest exploration, in which Egypt speculated largely in connection with her debts and resources.

Now it is thought that the new appliances for pumping and the better organization of the industry may overcome the former obstacles. When I was in Egypt, in March, 1886, rumors were rife of the extraordinary yield from these Jebel wells; but they have not been realized, or, if realized, published. There seems to be a lull in the *bruit* by which they were heralded. The son of the premier, Nubar Pasha, together with other engineers, including an American friend, Mr. Mitchell, a geologist, whom I met at Cairo, returned from an expedition to the " suspected " spots on the 22d of March. They reported that petroleum undoubtedly exists ; that the geological formation of the country is favorable to the existence of larger quantities at lower depths ; that the store of oil is generally distributed over a large area in the neighborhood ; that under existing unfavorable conditions a single source yields about two tons daily ; that the specific gravity is 88, and that the spot is easily accessible from the coast, where there is good anchorage.

There are many other evidences in the East of the existence of petroleum. The late engineer of the government works at Cairo, Mr. Garwood, in a letter which I have seen, suggested to those who are interested in Egyptian petroleum to make a diligent search in the neighborhood of the Helouan sulphur baths. They are about twenty miles from Cairo, or in the wady, or valley, near the petrified forest, about the same distance from Cairo. Oil may be struck, and then worked at a far more remunerative figure than it ever will be from Jebel Zeit.

" Was it from some long since disused source at Helouan that the mummy-cloths, saturated with petroleum, were prepared for those who found a last resting-place in the necropolis of Memphis, which is not a great distance from Helouan?"

This query indicates that preparation of the dead for their immortalization on earth must have called into ancient use petroleum in some of its forms for this pious purpose.

What possibilities or probabilities there may be in the Orient for the production of petroleum are not yet fully ascertained. They are in the region of conjecture. An intelligent writer from the northeast corner of the Mediterranean, pictured in a Stamboul journal the other day the opulence of that district of Cilicia, as well in mines of coal, silver, copper, iron and galena as, probably, in petroleum. A railroad has been in part made to Mersina, the port of Tarsus—Paul's old city of education. The rivers on that coast I have visited. The coast on the south shore and west of the Gulf of Iskanderoon, as I bear witness, is low, with lakes and rivers where lighters or boats can be used. Here was once the garden of the world, which had in its circuit such cities as Aleppo, Antioch and Tarsus. It is surrounded by splendid mountain ranges. It produces wool, madder, gums, skins, berries and wheat. These seek, even over bad roads, by donkeys, camels and carts, exportation to the ports of Europe and Turkey. Nor is it marvelous that signs of petroleum should here exist. Perhaps these are surer signs than those of Jebel Zeit, on the Red Sea. Time will tell. There is near by Tarsus a stream of mineral water flowing from the cavity of a limestone rock. It is rank with the smell of bitumen. The soil over which it passes is dark. It is called "Itch water," for the natives who have that disease cover themselves with the black muck and get cured in a brief time. This system is commended for use on the Argyle estate.

This stream is only three hours' ride from Tarsus. Who knows that Tarsus may not again come to the front, dropping the scales from its sightless eyes, and under a new light and less itching give some trouble to our Pennsylvania, Ohio and West Virginia proprietors, if not to those of Jebel Zeit or Baku !

For the present Baku holds the lead in the East. It is springing into immense importance, like its sister city Batoum, under oily and Slavonic auspices. Although the sacred fire is not now worshipped there, oil is. It permeates all social and physical life. Even the rubles are greasy. The dry streets are dampened with the naphtha. You shake a man by the hand ; your grip slips before the cordiality is expressed. Oil is talked day and night— at the hearth where it cooks the meal, and at the coffee-house where it is wagered. The steppes about the city are arid, but under them lie countless millions in the sunless lakes. The city is improving under these lubricities. Gardens and parks are supplanting the blackness with which the town was painted by the subtle element. The old palace of the Khan, and the winding, narrow streets, the strange Persian Moslem women and men, and other features of old Baku, no longer attract the tourist. He goes to see oil spout. It is oil, oil everywhere.

Baku is situated on a little bay upon the west coast of the Caspian. It has already 75,000 people ; for its growth is unrivaled in the East. Its railroad crosses a mountain 3,200 feet high, called Songame. This trans-Caucasian railway is 561½ miles long. It runs by way of the superb city of Tiflis, and affords the tourist a view of the grand scenery of that mountain-

land of our earliest progenitors. Its western terminus is at Batoum. Batoum is therefore the entrepôt of the great trade of the
Caucasus, and much of the trade of the Caspian and beyond
The waters of the Volga, which have their confluents almost
from Arctic regions and empty at Astrakhan, with the Caspian
for their outlet, the Don and Dnieper, the ancient Tanais and
Borysthenes, as well as the Danube—all are by the railroad connection made to swell the importance, commercial and strategical,
of Baku, this new-born Oil City of Asia.

Eastward the star of empire takes its way. It follows the
rails *en route* to India. This iron way has a greater function than
carrying oil for Russia or for English traffic to and from India.
Although it is, when made, to have a longer reach—say 1,122
miles to Libi, the first railroad station in India—still it is the old
route described by Pliny, from Cabul to India. It overleaps the
Hindoo-Koosh, extends westwardly to the Oxus, near Balkh, and
thence down the Oxus to the Caspian. Once on the Caspian, the
traffic which enters at Baku, as things are ordered, will, at
Batoum, be under Russian control. Not far from Baku, on the
trans-Caucasian railroad, the river Aras joins the Kour. From
this point—say at Adji-Cabul junction—the future railroad will
proceed to Teheran via Resht. The country is rich in petroleum
and in soil. Altogether it will not be more than 550 miles from
Adji to Teheran. This would bring Persia into the world.
These routes have been surveyed, and have undergone much
discussion. The Russians contemplate a great central Asian
railroad. It is to connect their commercial and especially their
military communications. The Standard oil agent, who was here
on the way to and from Baku, told me that it was impossible for
the outside world to know the grandeur of the scale by which
Russia is pushing her military power into the heart of Asia.
Troops he saw by the thousands, of which no journal or correspondent takes notice. They are on the constant advance. The
Caucasian railway was built for troops and their transportation.
The railroad now building from the Caspian to Tashkend will
run 1,100 miles farther toward sunrise. It points unmistakably
to the sealed wonderland of Thibet, toward which the English
are pushing their so-called peaceful embassy (*à la* Burmah, I
suppose) under Macaulay and his commercial travelers.

To make these connections profitable the Russian government

subsidizes. She is making a new Caspian port at Mikhailoffsky, to overcome the shallowness of the present harbor and give access to vessels of large tonnage, and to economize in the cost of reshipment. Money and time are lavished for the magnificence and munificence of Russia in aggrandizing her interests, martial and commercial, on the Caspian. In all probability Persia will become a mere dependency, soon to be bound hand and foot to the car of the autocrat, whose splendid visions of an almost universal empire are fast being realized in these seats and lands of ancient renown.

"But what connection has this with petroleum?" Quite as much as to-day has with to-morrow. It is the prelude of great events. To-morrow—"new style," the 17th of July, or "old style," the 4th of July—Batoum ceases to be a free port. After that date all merchandise arriving there pays the usual duties levied in all Russian ports.

"Well, what of this? What is its meaning? What is it to us?"

The Fourth of July is not a good day to place restraints on freedom, even in Russian "style." This restraint is not merely an economic measure. It is not intended altogether to check smuggling or to collect revenue. Nor is it, as Russia says, an advantage to the naphtha trade merely, or to the merchants of Baku and its vicinity. It is a deliberate act of Russia in derogation of the fifty-ninth article of the Berlin treaty. This article was made on the urgency of Bismarck and Disraeli to avert war. Although insignificant in itself, it may be the cloud, "no bigger than a man's hand," charged with electricity to set not only diplomacy to buzzing, but Krupp to booming. On the horizon it seems like summer lightning; but it may be charged with a thunderbolt. What, after all, and in view of recent developments, is the Berlin treaty to Russia, or to the Powers? An elastic string to be stretched by the strongest!

When I was first in the Orient, Batoum was known as a petty port, and safe in the wintry weather for quite a number of ships. It had a bazaar, it had some coffee-houses, a khan, or tavern, some few private houses, and a mosque, all built of wood. It was then in Turkish territory, but near the boundary. Its people belonged to the Georgian branch of the Caucaso-Thibetan race. It was coveted by Russia; but it was nobly defended against her. It was, however, acquired by Russia in 1878, not by conquest, but by treaty, and on certain conditions. It is near the ancient seats of Grecian and Roman, and later, of Genoese adventure and commerce. It is the readiest point of communication with Persia, Georgia and Armenia. Although it can never be the rival of Erzeroum, with its half-million of souls and immense traffic, yet with the railroad terminus and the oil trade it bids fair to be quite a rival, not only in Eastern trade, but in our own petroleum business. Under Russian auspices, in some measure, it is already the rival of Samsoun, a southern Turkish port, and of Trebizond, a southeastern Turkish port on the Black Sea.

By the Berlin treaty of 1878 Russia acquired Batoum. It is not a sanitarium, for fevers are there. But, notwithstanding, Russia quietly went to work to fortify it as soon as she acquired it. She fortified without protest. Turkey was not in a condition to protest. The other Powers were oblivious or careless. The fortification was accomplished. It was a part of the plan of resurrecting the old Russian naval power on the Black Sea.

It was followed by a defiant destruction of a clause of the Berlin treaty. That clause, the 59th, made the cession of Batoum to Russia dependent on its being a free port. Russia declares, upon her own responsibility, without deigning to consult the other six " signatories ' to the treaty, that Batoum must change its commercial character, and be a Russian city, under Russian tariffs and exactions. It is due to truth to say that the Russian government does not pretend to justify its notification about the free port of Batoum on the ground of the faith of treaties ; she places the matter on the ground of commercial convenience and interest.

The railway over the Caucasus, and the trade between England and Persia, she contends, have altered the circumstances, and, therefore, she no longer uses Batoum as her emporium. Besides, the oil interest demands that Batoum should no longer be free. But will the oil men relish an edict which adds to their burdens a customs tax on their machinery ?

Suppose that this does not affect Turkish trade ; suppose France, Austria and Germany, and even Italy, do stand indifferent, saying that this is too small a thing about which to risk a quarrel ; suppose England is left without an ally among the " signatories," and that the fortification is complete—what does Russia care for English or possible Italian protests ? Nearly all of the trade of

Batoum that is not Italian and Turkish is English.   If England can afford to lose this trifling traffic and stand the manifestation of Russian bad humor, and observe with serenity the exaltation of the Slavonic element, can she sit still while Russia is seeking to flank and outmanœuvre her in Asia ?

Should these Russian demonstrations in the Black Sea, as at the Crimea and Batoum, be more than a mere *coup de théâtre*, the Black Sea will become a Russian lake.   If this new movement be only a matter of trade or chagrin, the next time Russia makes war on Turkey, the latter will find a chain of naval stations and forts from Odessa all around to Batoum.   In that case, before the English or allied fleets could enter the Dardanelles another Russian army *corps* might dictate near Constantinople a new and more permanent treaty than that of San Stefano. Constantinople might then see the Cross over St. Sophia.

One feature of the negotiations on this head is, that if the reasons for declaring Batoum free no longer exist, and if the fortifications are to remain at Batoum, why may not other clauses of the Berlin treaty be abrogated by other parties ?   Why may not Bulgaria become independent and annex East Roumelia, irrespective of treaties ?   Why may not England and other Powers be relieved of their obligation, conditioned on this cession of Batoum to Russia, and enter the Straits at their will and pleasure?

If I should say that the prominent question of the East is one of grammar ; that it concerns the power of expression in the Anglo-Saxon language ; that the thesaurus of our language and the history of philology have had their scientific interest in the question, and their sources of verbal manufacture in and around the lands of which this new contest is the focus—the answer would be challenged as rather remote.   But if we must go to Rome and Greece for the origin of our language, this discussion takes us still farther East.   It takes us to the *fons et origo* of the Teutonic tongues.   It takes us to the Caspian, and gives an idea of the antiquity and mosiac qualities of our wonderful language.

The contest for Batoum and its connections takes us by rail to Baku, and from Baku to the inner sanctuary of our language.   If we go to Armenia, in fancy, for the Garden of Eden, we may more surely go to the Caucasus and the Caspian for the ancestral consanguinity of our own tongue and its relatives.   Grammarians have in the last analysis divided the languages of our earth into three great tribes. The most important to us of these three is what is known as the Indo-European, or Indo-Germanic. This includes many stocks, and among them the Saxon and Celt, who gently lie down together in linguistic love. How is this proven? By the words common to the various tongues. The words most familiar to our own tongue belong to a mountainous country, a cold climate and a tideless sea.

These terms fulfill the conditions which point to the vicinity of the Caspian and the Caucasus. Philosophy, history, philology and tradition here agree. Besides, these tongues of the Indo-European stock have no original words which signify their genesis in a different country. It is ascertained beyond a doubt that there are affinities between our own language and the languages of this interesting Caucasian land and Caspian Sea. The oldest dialects once spoken there are akin to our own. For instance, the Zend is the oldest in use; then comes the Pehlvi, and then the modern Persian. It is shown, in examining certain roots of our own words, that 57 Zend, 43 Pehlvi, and 162 modern Persian are allied to Saxon roots.

Is it not one of the eccentricities of this reflux wave of language and civilization, that the Indo-European people are pushing their adventures for knowledge and business into these early centres of historic interest?

"Old Persia! New Persia!" exclaims Marvin, summing up the situation. "What visions they conjure up of the extension of the White Czar's dominions toward the British empire! Persia, a mere khanate, dependent for its existence upon the nod of the empire of Russia! If the rocks at Baku could speak, what tales they could tell the slovenly slippered Persians loafing about the bazaars, under the eye of the bearded, heavy-booted Russian policeman, of the great creed and great empire of their ancestors! Once upon a time these Persians of the elder time resorted to the Surakhani altars to thank the great fire god—Petroleum—that they were not as other people; poor, cowardly, oppressed creatures now, but once warriors and statesmen, from Delhi to Constantinople."

Persia will be nothing between the upper mill-stone of Russia and the lower one of Great Britain!

> Yon waste where roaming lions howl,
> Yon aisle where moans the gray-eyed owl,
> Was once the proud Persian's great abode.

Thus anathematizing Russia for her aggrandizement, Great Britain for her tame acquiescence, and Persia for its rotten-ripe condition, Marvin preaches a sermon and makes a prophecy from the oleaginous rocks of Baku. These are the rocks upon which English power in the East will split.

The Russians will be the element in the great Caspian region; "while," as Marvin prophesies, "a mere handful of white faces will be all that will represent English suzerainty at Benares and Allahabad; Merv will be a busy Russian mart, another Kazan or Orenborg; and Baku, with a population of half a million or more of Russians, the all-powerful metropolis of the Caspian."

While I am not aware that these dynastic and imperial prophecies concern us Americans greatly, still, their fulfillment, in a business point of view, does affect us in an article which is the fourth in values in the catalogue of our imports. It is in vain, therefore, for us to seem indifferent to these ratiocinations and revelations as to the Caspian future. True, they were made by a journalist three years ago; but to-day, the world of diplomacy here and elsewhere is ringing its wild changes and charges upon one remarkable transformation scene on the Black and Caspian seas. Russia deliberately, before the eyes of Europe, tears up the Berlin treaty. After her staunch defense of it in the East Roumelian imbroglio, from one motive or another she gives formal notice to the signatory powers that Batoum shall be no longer free but Russian! As these strange shadows are cast by this old Light of Asia into the dreams of empire and the paths of commerce, I turn down my argand lamp, and bid my readers "Good Night."

# CHAPTER XVI.

## CHARACTERISTICS OF RACES AND CLASSES IN TURKEY.

THE costume of the Turk has changed very much in what I may call my own time—since 1851—especially the head-gear. So have his characteristics. The Turks, and all subjects of Turkey who are not Mussulmans, wear a red fez with a black silk tassel. It is shaped like an ordinary tumbler. It is never removed except on going to bed. Then the old-fashioned white cotton cap takes its place. Some of the subjects of the Porte wear a black fez. There are grades of color in the red fez. But from the Sultan down to the mendicant in the street, the red fez is a sign of a *rayah*, or subject. It is not so much a sign of his religion as the turban is. The turban covers the old conservative, the iron-clad, the moss-back, dyed-in-the-wool Mussulman ; and the larger the turban the tougher and more venerable the devotee. The fez is sometimes called a *tarbouche*, especially in Egypt. It is customary for the old-fashioned Mussulman to wrap several yards of muslin around the fez, and the more voluminous the head-gear the more pious its wearer.

It was not without an effort that the two or three preceding Sultans were enabled to change the street dress of the people, and substitute the fez for the turban, or the shoe for the slipper or baboosh. It was a long time before other ancient Moslem ways were eliminated. Even yet, a walk through Stamboul proper shows that the blood of the ancient Ottoman still stirs beneath its European investment.

The Turks have no very marked vices ; no catalogue can be made of them. The worst they do is hidden from the other people who reside among them. The Koran forbids them to play cards for money, and they observe the Koran. It commands them not to quarrel and fight, and they are scarcely ever arrested, like the burly Englishman, for contesting with fist or foot in the street.  They never blaspheme.  There are few cases of murder among them.  They are too honest to be thieves.  They do not regard poverty as a reproach, much less as a crime.

It is the custom of those who pretend to be the censors of morals, to speak of the lack of progressive sagacity of the Ottomans.  They are called barbaric ; and every dastardly act or crime committed by the Christians of the Orient—I mean the Greeks, the Italians, the foreigners who reside in the Turkish dominion—is attributed to the Turk.  But I assert that those nations who imagine themselves to be very high in the scale of advancement have much of democratic-republican liberty to learn from a nation which gives every one a fair field of enterprise, and opens to the humblest bootblack the office of the Grand Vizier.  Moreover, when it is said that the courts of administration tend to cruel oppression, especially upon the peasantry, it will be found that in the main this is not true ; and where cases of wrong do occur, they can generally be traced directly to the ill-conduct of the Governors, who are often of another race than the Turkish.

It has always been the case in the East, that there has been an immense amount of corruption.  It is not necessary to apologize for it ; and those countries whose criminal calendars are choked with vile murders and burglaries and wife-beatings, and marital infelicities and infidelities, and whose language is brutal and whose insults are coarse, are not the nations who should throw stones at the Turkish people.  The divorce courts of Berlin, Paris and London give us revelations which the worst that we can imagine of the harem cannot equal in sickening detail.

A French writer, in comparing the Turkish with other peoples, praises their justice, impartiality and religious tolerance, and commends the simplicity of their organization, the rapidity of their executive work, the facility of their resources, the absence of "red-tape," and the informalities of their prompt action.

There is much habitual simplicity in the Orient.  Out of this habit springs their hospitality, which is unbounded ; and hospitality is but another name for unworldliness.  Some years ago, in one of the remote Arabian provinces of the empire, there was some gold coinage put into circulation.  The people had never seen it before.  They did not like it.  They preferred the old white shekels of the fathers ; and a Yankee captain who came along that coast, drove a thriving business by trading off old silver coin for gold coins of equal size.

Judging by the thousands of soldiers whom I saw after the *emeute* in Bulgaria in 1885, and by the physique and robustness of those who, every Friday, pass our Legation on their way to the Salemlik, I think that the average Turk is in a contented and healthy state. He shows an equable temper and a regular life. His religious observances and grave countenance give to his habitual reserve, not merely the outward sign, but the inward kindness joined with an easy manner. Suppose he has the love of ease ; suppose he is deficient in our ethics and education ; suppose his mental faculties are not fully developed and sophisticated ; suppose he does loll upon a divan and pass the time with his guests in talking of indifferent things ; suppose he is content with his chibouque and coffee, his mosque, bath and repetitious prayers, his game of chess or backgammon ; suppose he is eager to listen to the old tales, proverbs and parables, or revels in the enjoyment of his astrologies and his pilaf—it may be said of him, that when he comes down to work as a mechanic or merchant, he is honest and fair in his labor and dealings. As a farmer he serenely plows his fields and reaps his harvests, amid the vicissitudes of his lot and his trials with the tax-gatherer. At home he is a model of domestic tenderness toward his family, and loyal to his sovereign and religion. In summing up his character, the qualities of patience, candor, contentment and resignation are conspicuous beyond those of any other race upon the footstool. If the religion of the Koran pervades every act of his life, and mixes with his every occupation ; if his prayer, by its frequent dropping wears away the stoniness of his heart, still he preserves the refinement and hospitality that belong to the Orient. He will give to his guests all that he has—" eggs, fruit, coffee, bread, fish, honey with Scio wine, and all for love, not money."

While here as Minister, I received letters frcm many parts of the United States, inquiring whether Turkey has not set an example in regard to the " prohibition " of ardent spirits. The answer is : that the Turk, under the law of Mahomet, does not drink himself nor sell spirituous liquors. I do not accept the report that there is a taste for drink spreading among the Turks,. or even among the Arabs. I do not believe in the existence of the dissipated Mahometan, as a rule. The rakee-bibbing Turk is not a character to be suppressed by statute, because he does not exist. Perhaps a little spirituous liquor discreetly imbibed might stir the Turk into more activity. This might be tolerated, even if the beads on the beaker's brim brought him into more frequent conversation with the bibulous Christian. It might elucidate things hidden in connection with Eastern faith, or those hidden caves of wealth which require only a bottle of rosoglio to inspire the magic words, " Open sesame ! " The lamp of Aladdin, in the absence of American or Baku naphtha, might burn brighter if fed with a little alcohol. It is something to the credit of the Turk, and certainly to the discredit of other races in Turkey, that when one of their own kith, or a Greek or Armenian, gets drunk and goes staggering around at the festivities, he is, in the Eastern phraseology, considered drunk, *à la Franka.*

The Turk is not the same in personal appearance as his ancestors in Central Asia. The Parthians who antagonized the Romans, and the Kurds who harassed Xenophon and his ten thousand Greeks, have descendants who are still ferocious ; but the Turk corresponds more nearly with the European than with the Asiatic type, because of his inheritance of Caucasian blood from the maternal line of Georgia or Circassia—which is the bluest of the European stock.

One of the offices performed by the head of a Turkish household is the bringing on his return home, every evening, an offering to his family. You pass in the streets of Pera and Stamboul, toward the going down of the sun, at every turn, a Turk going to his house, but always full-handed. He carries a gift, no matter how trifling : it may be a cluster of grapes, a box of sweetmeats or fig paste, or a fish, or some fruit or vegetable. This offering is always made to his penates. If for a day he should omit it without explanation, the females of the harem would be apt to infer that a divorce was impending. There is something very beautiful about this custom. It is not limited to the household. When we left Egypt to return to Constantinople, the wife of the Turkish High Commissioner, Ghazi Moukhtar Pasha, sent us a present of rare fruit, including pineapples. They were not only done up in a shining white napkin, but the napkin itself was covered with a rare purple silk handkerchief. The latter still remains as a souvenir of the signal courtesy of this estimable family into whose harem my wife had the pleasure of an entrée. Notwithstanding the lapse of time, the fragrance of that pineapple still hangs around the elegant fabric in which the fruit was ensconced.

Among other qualities to be mentioned, is the unselfish kindliness with which the Turks treat their superiors and inferiors. They illustrate, in their daily observance, what Sir Thomas More has said so pithily: " To be humble to superiors is duty; to equals, is courtesy ; to inferiors, nobleness ; and to all, safety." This is

A BULGARIAN WOMAN.

both gentle and wise. Therefore the Golden Rule is not considered a mere form by them : it is practically illustrated. The richest defers to the poorest. Women and children and the weak receive protection in every emergency. Parents are reverenced by sons, and all the agreeable elements which belong to hospitality find abundant illustration.

When the traveled Turk returns from a Western trip, he still retains, or expects to retain, his pride as to the nature and situation of his own people and their splendid capital. This is not surprising to me. The morals of Western civilization appear loose to the austere followers of Mahometanism. They cannot understand how our women can be good mothers and faithful wives. They think vanity is at the bottom of all their display, and that the desire of pleasing others than their own, is the inspiration of their desire to shine in unveiled social life.

Certainly a people like the Turks cannot be far aloof from the best instincts and moralities of our nature. They love rural scenery. They seek beautiful spots for the festival and home. They like commanding points in a landscape. Their kiosks, vineyards and flower-beds are in the favored nooks. They love to drink in the balmy air and bright prospect. Their happiness consists greatly in that natural joyance which is the essence of country life.

These are some of the salient features of this race, which once horrified mankind, and which occasionally still startles them, under fierce provocation. Like the pirates and vikings of Norseland, they have been much modified by time and circumstance.

They are surrounded by other races and peculiar classes, some of whom deserve a photographic script. These are the Greeks, Armenians, Franks, Kurds, Persians, Bulgarians, Circassians and the Slavs, including the Montenegrin, and the Albanian, or Croat. The Jews deserve a separate chapter. They are "chosen" for that purpose.

I have often been struck with the fact that while the men of these various races are shrewd, money-getting merchants—active in all the various phases of life—they pay little attention either to literature or science. There is but one artist known among the Turks, and he gives his time mostly to the Museum near the Porte. It is very difficult, in such a community, to keep up an interest, either in the theatre or the opera. Our conclusion is, that the land of the Greek, the land of the Garden of Paradise, which fancy locates in Armenia, the land of Assyrian, Judean and classic interest, has not so many of those active and gentle amenities which add to the social life of the West many of its alluring, elevating, comforting and instructive features.

The Greeks have one vulnerable spot. Otherwise they might conquer the Orient, as they did in earlier days. They are, in this, like Achilles ; but the spot is in the heart, not in the heel. It is infidelity toward each other. They are jealous of one another. They are perpetually quarreling about ascendancy.

Social ties and individual friendships give way before their quarrels. Even at Fanar, where their religion seems to be con-
centred, there seems to be more or less of discontent.

I have said that there is little of what we call social life in
Turkey. The Turks encourage none ; for no outsider can visit
them at their homes. The various Christian churches and sects
are often in collision, and at the best the sympathy which should
belong to such institutions does not exist to a great extent. The
Christian population, which is mostly Greek, are not particularly
attached to one another, for they are, many of them, "shoddy"
people. There are among them many millionaires. They have
made their money quickly, either in cotton or on the Bourse.
They are looked down upon by the old Phanariot Greek families,
who are blue-blooded, and petted by their Turkish rulers, in
whose service most of them are proud to be engaged.

It is often very difficult to distinguish a Jew, an Armenian, a
Turk or a Greek, one from the other. To do so you must be very
observant. You want to know the man first. The genteel
haughtiness of the Turk will soon enable you to tell that the man
whom you are addressing has not the cunning subtleness of the
Greek. His manner distinguishes him from the Albanian, Jew
or Arab.

The Armenians are the sharpest people in the world.
They are the Yankees of the Orient, with much additional acute-
ness. They are divided, also ; some, as will appear, lean to the
Catholic faith, and some to their own Church ; and both away
from the Greek orthodoxy.

The Levantines—the descendants of the French, Italian, German and other settlers of European origin—are also among the
shrewdest of people. They are a class by themselves, and mingle
very little with the Greeks or the Armenians.

It is a mooted question as to which race is paramount for
sharpness, or, as we call it, smartness. I will not attempt to de-
bate that question. Certainly, the Turkish is not the one, although
it is the ruling power. The Frank or Levantine is not the one ;
nor the Greek, nor the Jew It is a common saying, and likely
has some basis of fact : that it takes the wit of four Turks to
over-reach one Frank ; two Franks to cheat one Greek ; two
Greeks to cheat one Jew ; and six Jews to cheat one Armenian ;
but when the Persian, the Kurd and the Croat, the Dervish,

the Gypsy, the Eunuch and *hamal*, which we have endeavored to
photograph, come into view, the Armenian will take the prize.
Whether it is from lack of conscience, or because he has more enterprise, or because he has been thrown, like the Hebrew, on his
own resources in his wanderings from his native land—it is certain that wherever he is, whether as the Prime Minister of Egypt,
or Secretary of the Treasury in America—I mean Governor
Thomas Corwin, of Ohio, of Armenian-Hungarian descent—the
shrewdness of this race gives them grace, humor, eloquence,

ALBANIAN IN COSTUME.

genius, and above all, intrepidity in self-seeking, or, in one word,
smartness.   The Armenians have never been intimidated by
threats, and therefore they are successful.

The *hamal* is generally an Armenian.   To see him moving
with dignified Samsonian strength and stride, amidst the various
pen-venders, sugar-mongers and obscure menders of things,
who howl all the day about their wares or trades, is one of
the interesting sights—if not sounds—of the Metropolis. He wears
a loose gray jacket with white sleeves, gray gaiters and red belt.

He carries fabulous loads upon his shoulders. I have seen him carry pianos, and even carriages, up-hill on his back. One needs to observe a *hamal* going up the hill of Pera, to understand what the Bible means in its Oriental metaphor, when it says, "Bear ye one another's burdens." When his fête day comes along, a high and festive time results. He makes strange music with an old pipe, and dances along the streets of Pera as an elephant amidst crockery.

The great body of the Jews are wily, and very difficult to catch

CIRCASSIANS.

in a trade. The Greeks are always more or less timid. The Levantine is anything you please, for he has no nation. The lessons of the Korán seem to have made the Turk the best of the populations which he governs and by which he is surrounded. What he would be if he belonged to a subjugated people under Christian despotism, is another and, to be hoped, improbable question.

The Bulgarian is generally described as an honest, hard working, but rather slow and stupid laborer or peasant. The ferocity attributed to his character is denied—it can be justly denied of late years—but according to history in the Middle Ages, nothing was comparable to the outrages of which the Bulgarian was capable. Now, he is considered too tame—by some, too domestic and sober. He is the demure head of a family, which enjoys its dance on the common ; or a peasant faithful to his work in the fields, or joyous at the rose harvest beneath the Balkans. He has not, as a rule, been subject to much instruction. His demonstrative faculty is feeble. It is of the peasant I speak, not the upper classes.

Recent events have demonstrated that the Bulgarian has much conservatism to the square inch. The whole people are possessed of a patience in their enthusiasm, not to be compared with any other nation which has struggled, or is struggling, to be free. Those who are not prejudiced, and who have visited Bulgaria, say that a more uninviting race on casual acquaintance than its peasantry hardly exists. What better could be expected of a subjugated people ? Centuries of oppression, extortion, misrule and injustice will go far to deaden, in any race, the sense of manly independence and courage, and to replace these virtues with cunning and duplicity.

The Bulgarian is, as a race, gifted with honesty, sincerity and economy. He is quiet and peaceful, not caring much for the dogmas of the Church, but independent enough to separate both from the Greek Church in Russia and the Greek Patriarch in Constantinople. Our American College on the Bosporus has vindicated his intellectual stamina, for, in its curriculum, the Bulgarian generally carries off the highest prizes. It is not unknown that the leaders in the movement for Bulgarian independence are graduates from the Robert College, where their minds have been developed, permeated, disciplined and elevated by American teaching and tenets.

The Circassians, when the Russians thrust them forth after the long wars in which Schamyl was their heroic leader, were kindly invited to Turkey by the Sultan. Many of them are yet to be seen around Constantinople, and not a few in their peculiar array. They have a dignified and military carriage ; their faces are tanned ; they are mostly clad, somewhat after the Russian method, in long gray, close-buttoned coats, which are girded with the sash. The head is wrapped in a sort of handkerchief. Their arms are a sword by their side and pistols in their belt; and the cartridges are carried in semi-circular rows upon the breast of their coat. The engraving from a photograph herein, shows the peculiarity of their attire. When I first saw this cartridge arrangement, I thought it was a musical instrument for the lips, and perhaps it sometimes does make music. When under proper restraint, the Circassians may be good soldiers and officers; but those with whom I had some diplomatic " Diversion " in Asia Minor, and who robbed and committed outrages which it is not best to mention, are the Circassians now resident there. They formerly lived in the district around Adrianople, but their accumulation of cattle and sheep, without labor or care, since they have enjoyed the hospitality of Turkey, looked suspicious. The truth is, that their accumulations were stolen from the more industrious Bulgarians or Turks, and, as a consequence, the male Circassian is not now in good odor in Turkey. If it were a female Circassian, I would not be so sweeping in my remark, but qualify it by saying that, outside of the harem, the Circassian is not admired.

I have read, in the accounts of Montenegro, descriptions of the brave mountaineers who people that wild country of the Black Mountain. I have seen many of them upon the Bosporus, and in the isle of Prinkipo, where we summered in 1886. They are gardeners and farm-hands. I have seen some of the same race who dress as if they were princes. The truth is, that their wives at home do most of the work. They prepare the toilets of the men with exquisite skill, work in the fields, and embroider or fashion the clothes of their grandiose husbands. Once I saw in the procession going to the Salemlik, a cavalier whose equine accoutrements seemed golden; and the surtout which covered his dress was, in fact, worked with gold chains on an elaborate Plutocratic pattern. No doubt he spelled his name with a " Vitch," as representative of the Prince of Montenegro. If I had been possessed of an instantaneous photographic apparatus I should have risked his yataghan to capture his habiliments.

Among the peculiar costumes which one sees upon the Galata bridge are those of the Croats. They belong to the same Græco-Slavonic race as the Albanian. They wear long white robes fastened with a broad belt, out of which many ferocious weapons peep, but are seldom drawn.

The Persian merchants are by no means undistinguished for politeness, cunning and trickery. In these accomplishments there is no class in Persia or in Turkey that excels them, except the Armenian. What has been said of the Armenian, Persian and Hebrew in Turkey, may be also said of the same races in Mesopotamia and the provinces. But in Asiatic Turkey, between the Tigris and the Euphrates, the merchant who does most of the dealing is an Arab, the Turk being there either as a civil functionary or an army officer. Europeans are rarely found in that country now. In 1885 Bassorah had only fifteen Europeans, and Bagdad but fifty-one. I learn that whenever trouble arises there affecting the European, if the English, French and Russian Consuls are derelict, he had better call in a Mahometan priest, as then he will be more likely to have a satisfactory result.

The Kurd is a warrior and spoilsman. It was the Kurd that fought Xenophon, over the numerous parasangs which we traveled in callow classical days. The Kurd harassed the Greeks in their retreat. He was a formidable enemy of the Roman legion. The Crusaders opposed him in vain ; and to-day he is the most incorrigible of the subjects of Turkey. To hold him, when caught, is like attempting to hold water in a cullender ; and to catch him is indeed like catching a Tartar. He gives to the government and to diplomacy more trouble than our aborigines give to the Federal Government.

# CHAPTER XVII.

## THE JEWS OF TURKEY.

It was my especial good fortune, when trouble and trial seemed to be renewed in the persecution of the Jews of Russia, Roumania, Morocco and other lands, to make such public remonstrance in Congress as, I think, eventuated in some restraint, if not altogether in the cessation, of such persecution. More recently, while acting as Minister to Turkey, I have had the opportunity of observing, within my own bailiwick, the condition of the Hebrews in their ancient land. As Judæa and other parts of the Orient are still the home of thousands of that race, and as they will seek, even unto death, or, rather, as they near the fatal goal, for "thy palaces, oh Jerusalem !" to brighten their dying eye and to illumine their latest hope, it is not without interest, as well as emotion, that I have observed the political, social and religious relation which the Jews hold to the dominant rulers of the Orient.

There is no authentic census of this empire ; so that the information which I give, although meagre, has been obtained from the rabbins of Constantinople and Jerusalem, who have interested themselves in furnishing it.

The Jews of Constantinople are descendants from those who were once expelled from Spain. They returned upon their Eastern track in the sixteenth century. The language spoken by them is a mixture of bad Spanish, worse Greek and infamous Turkish. Ever since these Jews were banished from Spain by the bigoted King Philip II. they have had little fair play in the arena of mankind. But Constantinople cannot compare with some other cities of the East for its Hebrew population.

Salonica has 35,000 Jews. It is a commercial place with a future. It is a paradise for Jews. When you are rowed ashore there, your boatman is an Israelite masquerading in Turkish fez and trousers. On landing, you are hustled by porters in turbans and red shoes ; but they are Jews. You enter the Custom-house: the mob of officers, with their continuous gabble, are Jews. Jews in turbans and Jews out of turbans; Jews as builders of houses and Jews as barbers—the children of Israel are everywhere, in every kind of work. They are dealers in metals, in old clothes, and in almost every object that belongs to the city where Paul, the Apostle of the Gentiles, preached to the Thessalonians nearly 2,000 years ago.

It is a matter of doubt how this element ever reached Macedonia. Did they come from the East with Alexander the Great, on his return from conquest ? When the Jews were dispersed, would they not naturally go to the nearest islands, and thence to the mainlands of Greece ? The New Testament makes mention of them in early days at Thessalonica. It was some 250 years B. C. that the Jewish mercantile tendencies were noticeably developed. In these early days the cities of Macedonia were enriched by synagogues in great numbers. It is said that some of the Jews in Salonica are ostensibly Mahometan, but privately—otherwise.

There is no occasion in Turkey at the present day for any such reproach of hypocrisy, as the Jews are partial to the Sultan, and the Sultan has been tolerant of them. They have no hierarchy. They are Congregationalists. Each congregation is independent. It is ruled by its own chief-rabbi. The Hebrew representative head is at Constantinople. He is called the *Khakambashi*. He is the chief of the Israelite nation of the empire. He is a part of that system by which, in this country of divers religions, the rule of the Ottoman is enforced through ecclesiastical heads. There is a civil council also, connected with the chief rabbinate, whose functions will be explained hereafter. In order to arrive at a decision in religious and civil cases in a Jewish community, judgments are expected from those most learned in the sacred books. These are followed by the Turkish administration—just as our United States courts in the several States follow the local laws. Could there be a better system of home rule ? It is carried almost within the family, in order to reconcile domestic litigation and to prevent intolerance. The head of the Hebrews is next in rank after the Greek and Armenian Patriarchs.

There has been great effort in the Orient to convert the Jews to Christianity. It has had little or no success. The Jews are

reserved. They are impervious to the intrigues of the Greek and
Slav. There is no section of the subjects of the Sultan that
gives him so little trouble. Jew and Mahometan get on admirably together. This is often disputed by the transient tourist, but
I know to the contrary. Yet between the Jew and the Greek
there is always an antagonism. It was so in the time of Christ
and "the Fathers."

The Jewish population in the Ottoman empire, which includes
Egypt, is only about 350,000. Of those, 90,000 live in Turkey
in Europe, the remainder in Asia and Africa. Bulgaria, where
the contest is for self-government against the pressure of Russia,
contains 18,000 ; Roumelia, which is a part now of Bulgaria, has
7,000 ; the rest of Turkey in Europe, known as Old Thrace in
classic history, 18,000; and Macedonia, immediately north of
Greece, but still under the Turkish empire, 45,000. The principal cities of the Ottoman empire which contain the greatest
Jewish population are Constantinople, which has 45,000 ; Bagdad,
well known to the reader of "Thousand and One Nights,"
30,000 ; Smyrna, a city of great commercial importance, 25,000 ;
Aleppo, in Syria, 10,000, and Jerusalem, not 20,000, as is represented, but fully 22,000. The English Bishop, in a recent letter
asking for aid for his Protestant church at Jerusalem, states that
during the past few years the number of Jews in Palestine has
increased from 15,000 to 42,000. This is an accurate statement.
It is confirmed by my informants.

So far as commercial transactions go, I do not know that the
habits of the Jewish people could be improved by any Christian-
izing conversion. They are as good, if not better, than the Greek
and Armenian merchants. Stories are told of Jewish merchants
greatly to their credit. For instance: A Salonica merchant
receives a large order from foreign merchants for prunes. The
part of the country from which he expects these prunes lies two
hundred miles away. What does he do? There are no postal
communications, no telegraphs; he simply hands over money
enough for the purchase to a Jew. This commercial traveler goes
off to the interior with the money. He may not return for some
months; but the business is done faithfully. Baker in his book
on Turkey says that he met a merchant who had twenty-seven
thousand pounds sterling (nearly $150,000) out in this way, and
no goods in his store to show for it. His only security was the

honesty of the Jewish commercial traveler; yet the purchases came safely to the store in due time. Now that the United States has sent a Hebrew as Minister to Turkey, perhaps we will have more authentic accounts of his race and their progress. One thing I think my successor will find, that the Jews, under the guidance of the chief of the Israelitish nation in the empire, are free to resolve against the intrigues of either Armenian, Greek or Slav.

Why should not the Jew and the Mahometan do well together? Did not Mahomet draw largely upon Moses? Let the reader of the Koran, or of the history of its Prophet, recall its pages of teaching out of the Pentateuch. Let him go along with the young Mahomet and his caravan to Syria. Let him observe the prophet meeting with the remnants of the lost tribes near the Red Sea, and draw from them the lessons of the Divine judgment against idolatry. Like Abraham when he came from Chaldea, Mahomet had a mysterious reverence for Syria. Was it not here that the angel of God spread his wings over the patriarch? Was it not here that the idea of the Unity of God first dawned on Mahomet? The religion of Mahomet is not behind that of the Jew and Christian in reverence for the Wise King and his valiant father. Their tombs in Jerusalem are guarded by the Turk with vestal vigilance. Why should not the Moslem and the Hebrew live in accord with such revelations?

The thrift, care and trading skill of the Hebrews have not been the result of recent events. The fact that they made out of so small a territory as Judæa such a wonderful nation, indicates a natural superiority which has not yet been sufficiently rated. They always were a staunch people, ready to do battle for their own. Even in the time of Moses they numbered half a million fighting men. They must have numbered two millions of people when they revolted against the Romans. Galilee alone furnished one hundred thousand fighting men. In the time of Solomon his kingdom was greatly enlarged. It extended as far as the Euphrates; and what is better, like the wise ruler that he was, he had peace with it all

It is very hard to estimate the immense wealth of the Jews in the time of Solomon. The Bible shows what it cost to construct the temple and other buildings, and this perhaps is a standard by which to judge the power and wealth of the nation at that time.

The Jew is always ready for the march. From the time he evacuated Jerusalem he has ever since been evacuating other countries under the pressure of persecution. Hence in eastern Europe he still divides his property into three parts; one of floating capital, another in jewelry, and the third in the money of the country. So that the ecclesiastical persecution, which drove him from land to land, always finds him ready to depart with portable property.

The Jews and Jewesses of the East are said to have less of that crafty look belonging to trade which centuries have more or less engrafted upon their features. There are Jews whom I have seen around Jerusalem and Constantinople, and especially among the old men, who remind one of the very best pictures of the best artist's representatives of the great prophets of Israel. There are the dark, oblong eye and the prominent nose still visible. But the Jews of the East have been noted as having high foreheads, a noble mein, and a spiritual beauty set in features made pure by contemplation of those things that make the glory of Jerusalem and of Jehovah.

The Jews of Constantinople inhabit that quarter which lies between the Fanar, where the Greek Patriarch lives, and the mosque of Eyoub, outside of the walls, which is so sacred that Christians are prohibited from entering it. Many Jews, also, live on the Pera side of the Golden Horn. I cannot say that the body of them are well-to-do. They are poor. I cannot say that they lack avariciousness, for they have that in common with other races in the Orient. Those who trade with you in the bazaars are as apt as others to impress you with their probity, or its lack, though I have yet to know, personally, of any bad faith on their part.

It is an interesting spectacle to observe the Jewish quarter. A walk or ride on a Saturday from Fanar to Eyoub will show you three Jewesses to every Jew. The Jews are perhaps off on some peripatetic or pedling journey, for they are pedlers as well as artisans and merchants. But the Jewesses, ah, the Jewesses! Many of them have rare beauty. They sit in coveys, like partridges, but with gayer plumage. They sit where they can be seen ; all of a family in one room. They are exclusive, like their race.

The Jews have been so loyal to the Sultan and his government that his charity has been bestowed upon them freely. He often makes the chief rabbi the almoner of his bounty. In some of the Turkish cities outside of Constantinople the Jews make a better worldly showing than in Constantinople. In Broussa the brilliancy of the windows of the Hebrew houses are an index of the cleanliness within. The women who look out from these windows have head-dresses of exquisite beauty, rich in gauze or painted handkerchiefs and ornamentation of flowers and jewelry.

The rich Jews of Constantinople are seen promenading on the quays or through the streets upon Saturdays, dressed in their fur gaberdines. Their women—like those in northern Africa whom I have seen—when attired in full dress, rival the gala-toilets of their Turkish sisters. I have before me a picture of one of these Jewish ladies. She is in a full dress of white silk. It is confined above the hips by a broad girdle of wrought-gold, clasped with gems. Above this robe she wears a pelisse, which is of dove-colored cashmere. Costly sables overlay this robe. The sleeves are loose, and fall back to reveal the bracelets and the rings that flash upon her fingers, for, in this respect, the Jewess is not unlike the Turkish, Armenian or Greek lady—in fact, she is like her sex. If she cannot compare with the picture which Isaiah in his third chapter paints of the luxurious and jewel-bedizened and feet-tinkling angels of his time, it is because her poverty will not allow the extravagance. The more costly the gems of her head and robe, the more important and glorious she appears. Her turban is of enormous size. It is formed of the pointed muslin of the country. It is also covered with jewels of rare quality. Beneath it are pearls and emeralds, as to the size and value of which, as they gleam over her brow, down on each side of her face, and even upon her shoulders, no estimate of mine can do justice.

It has been said by those professing to be familiar with the condition of the Hebrews of Constantinople, that they wear a subdued and spiritless expression. The same old picture of crouching humiliation, with the stealthy glance of mercenariness, is attributed to the poor Jew of Turkey. While he may feel the constraint which his condition imposes, and while within the last two generations he has been the subject of outrage—not he alone, but those of his household and of the gentler sex—still there has been much reform in this direction. Formerly, it was a custom when the Turks and Greeks passed the Jews, even upon the water, for the former—the superior beings, who do not disdain to worship the Nazarine—to raise one hand, and, with outstretched finger, to count the number of the Jews upon the boat. This enumeration was thought to bring heavy misfortune on the numbered party. The Jews, like most Orientalists, have faith in such spells. They never fail to retort so that the curse should fall back upon the Turk or Greek. Thus was the bitterness renewed from time to time by this mirth of the tormentor and the sufferings of the tormented. But this custom has happily gone to the rear. As an illustration of this progress in other respects, as well as with reference to the Jew, may I not relate a story?

The Sultan, Mahmoud the Second, renews an old order—which was defied by Sir Stratford Canning, the British Minister—by which Christians on horseback, as well as Turks, should dismount in riding past his palace. One day a man passes on horseback before the palace, without dismounting. The zaptieh, or policeman, on duty calls a halt. He explains to the horseman that the order is general.

" It applies to all—Christians and Turks equally."

" But," says the horseman, to the consternation of the policeman, "I am not a Christian."

The zaptieh responds : " But you are a Turk, are you not ? "

" No," said he, " I am a Jew ; and therefore neither a Turk nor a Christian."

He was allowed to pass ; it was a proof, not of the persecution of, but of the indifference toward, the Jews in the East.

It must be said for them, as a class, that the Hebrews spend their Sabbath religiously. They are most conscientious in their ceremonies. While they may be accused of extortion and avarice, they never fail in caring for the poorer portion of their own people. This charity inspires them with the hope of terminating their lives at Jerusalem, to which they look forward, but with a better prospect beyond this life, which has been to them a sorrowing pilgrimage.

The same hostile feeling toward the Jews which reigns among Germans, Russians and Roumanians, exists to some extent in Turkey. Foolish charges about kidnapping children, and accusations about their stringency in business, are not uncommon here, as in Europe, but in spite of all that may be said of the Hebrews, they are not as bad as some of their neighbors. They are very rich when rich at all, and very poor when poor at all. They have a greater liking for the Moslem than for the Christian. Is this a parodox? No. The Moslem may sneer at the Jew, but he has more charity toward him than he has toward the Christian. The Jew will always take the Moslem's side against the Christian; and the wealthy Israelite, as the late imbroglio about Bulgaria attests, always assists the government.

The Jew when poor is limited in his industries to a few trades, generally those practiced by the laboring classes. The coarsest and dirtiest work of the town is performed by him, but he does it with patience. He is the chimney-sweep, tinker and the boot-black, but he still holds aloft the oracles of Jehovah and looks forward to the beautiful city of his Love as the resting-place for his weary foot and aching heart.

It is to the Sultan of Turkey and to the institutions of that country that the enjoyment of Jewish liberty and citizenship is due. Hebrews of Constantinople have told me that they have nothing to complain of in connection with the rule of Turkey. Whatever may be their social condition, their political condition has been that of a race which has been treated with clemency and equality. As to citizenship, the Hebrews enjoy the same rights as the Ottoman himself. Besides, they are exempted from military service, from which no Mahometan is excepted.

From the earliest times many of the high offices in Turkey have been filled by Jews. I wish I could say that their worldly condition is equal to their political privileges and opportunities, but it is not. Perhaps that section of them who are most advanced in material goods are the Jews of Salonica. That city contains very many rich Jews. Some of them are millionaires. In Bagdad the Jews have a large business, and are the traders with the East Indies, while in Smyrna they are honorable and extensive merchants. It is in Constantinople that the population shows a painful contrast. There are men among them who are worth a million of dollars. But the general cause of this impoverishment can be traced to the fact that they have not turned their attention, as in other places, to commerce and other kindred adventures. In Beirut and Damascus, like Smyrna, they are the exporting merchants, and their work shows immense fruit in the accumulation of wealth.

In many parts of the Orient different races are set apart one from the other. Certain quarters are given to certain races, as well as to certain trades and professions. This has not, however, been the case with the Jews in Constantinople. Notwithstanding there is no compulsion upon them in this regard, the Jews in Constantinople seem to preserve this custom; they live as neighbors with one another fraternally in special quarters. For instance: Haskeüi has a population of twenty-one thousand inhabitants, who are nearly all Israelites; Balat, ten thousand ; and Kouskoundjouk, five thousand. These are suburbs of Constantinople. The Jewish houses are generally clean, though many families dwell in the same habitation. As in New York, so in Constantinople, the families are extensive, the children numerous —and they bid fair some day to overflow outside of Constantinople to those other places in Syria and Judæa which are so well known to the reader of the Bible, and which are sacred beyond all other associations to the Hebrew and Christian.

The Jews in Turkey are orthodox. There is scarcely any schism among them. They observe what is known as the Spanish rites. The Chief of their religion is the Grand-Rabbi. His jurisdiction extends to all parts of the Ottoman empire. As already stated, he is consulted by the Ottoman government and the Sultan on all matters pertaining to the Hebrew faith and community. Each community has its own Grand-Rabbi, who depends on the Chief, who is a perpetual resident at Constantinople. The Consistory of the Grand-Rabbi, or Hahem Bashi, is administered under an organic law. This law is considered as a sort of by-law of the empire. It is an *imperium in imperio.* It is a copy, in fact, of the old system from the earliest days of history in the Greek and Roman empires, whereby the ecclesiastical and civic functions of certain races and religions were reserved to those races and to their synods and councils respectively.

The Jews are called "the people of the Book." When it is remembered that so much of the Moslem religion embodied in the Koran is derived from the Hebrew Bible, and that many of the rites and ceremonies connected with birth, marriage and

death, which we see every day performed in the mosques and in
the cemeteries of the Moslem, were taken by Mahomet from the
Hebrews of the East, who sojourned among the deserts of
Arabia, it will be readily believed that the Hebrew faith and the
great Hebrew teachers, prophets and psalmists are equally
venerated by the Moslem, both in the literature of his religion
and in the ceremonies of his faith.

The Moslem prays to an all-audient God. Although he turns
in the direction of Mecca to make his prayer, as the Jew did
toward Jerusalem, and as Mahomet himself at one time did, he
looks to every point of the compass in recognition of the ever-
during, invisible and ineffable presence of Jehovah. As a consequence of this similarity between the Mahometan and the
Hebrew faith, it follows that no imagery is worshipped, that
idolatry is not permitted, that even the pictures of prophets and
saints, which adorn and give beauty to the churches of the
Greeks and other religions of the East, have no more place in
the mosque than in the synagogue.

Polygamy is absolutely forbidden to the Israelites in Turkey.
Although I have been told that there are some in Bagdad who
are allowed to marry under the Moslem law, still they
are limited to four wives. The nuptial ceremony is that which
Solomon depicted in his fascinating picture of the bridal canopy,
with its wood of cedar, its pillows of silver, its bottom of gold,
its covering of purple, and in the midst thereof it was paved with
gold for the fair daughter of Jerusalem.

There are no mixed marriages among the Hebrews in Turkey. Divorce is acknowledged, as it is always acknowledged among
the Moslems. Govermental authority may be called upon to
execute the sentence of the Jewish tribunals on matters connected
with marriage and divorce. As a general rule, the Jews marry
when they are twenty or twenty-two years old.

One thing struck me as peculiar in connection with the aspirations of the Jews in Europe and in the Orient. While the Jews in
Austria, Germany, France, Hungary and other parts of Europe
have filled offices of great trust, have become bankers, editors,
musicians, orators, legislators and artists, distinguishing themselves before those of other races in the refinement and skill with
which they have elevated learning, art and science, yet in Turkey
they seem to have little or no aspiration for and association

with statecraft and other elevating pursuits. At least, they interest themselves very little in politics.

They like the liberal ways of the government, which are in great contrast to the treatment of Hebrews in Russia, Roumania and Germany. And though they may be persecuted in a social way in remote places in Turkey, where the central government does not reach, still they are devoted to the government of the country. They are prompt to recognize the kindness of the Sultan, and to show their loyalty to him. I will not say that the Jews of Turkey are the equal or the inferiors of the Jews of other parts of Europe. There is a reason for this, and a sad one. They have partaken of the general stagnancy which belongs to the Orient, owing to the everlasting Eastern question, which, by its unrest, has forbidden men to reach out for those higher aims in life that are the result of stable civilization.

During the last two centuries there have been no conspicuous literary movements among the Ottoman Israelites, but since the Israelitish Alliance has begun to found schools and interest itself in the Hebrews of the East, there is a marked advancement, not only from year to year, but from week to week. This is apparent in Jerusalem, as I shall show.

The Turkish language, or the language of the country, is not the common language of the Jews. Those who inhabit Syria talk Arabic, and those in Macedonia modern Greek. Among the three hundred and fifty thousand Jews in Turkey, more than two hundred thousand talk a Spanish idiom. It is a dialect that has been much corrupted. But the great body of the Jewish traders in Constantinople and elsewhere speak French. The truth is, that nearly all the people of the Levant, including Turks themselves, who are perhaps more reserved on this head, speak many languages. They speak them with facility. They are taught tongues almost before they learn anything else. It is one of the marvels in the East that it is almost a matter of inheritance that even the vocal organs of the Levantine seem to be polyglot.

There are about six Hebrew newspapers published in Turkey. Two of these appear in Hebrew. One is the *Habazeleth*, the other *Hatsevi*. The others are Spanish, but with Hebraic characters. The other four are called *El Telegraph* and *El Tiempo*, of Constantinople, *La Burna Esperanza*, of Smyrna, and *La Epoca*, of Salonica. Much of my information in relation to the Hebrew people comes from the editor of the *Telegraph* at Constantinople. That journal takes quite an interest in political affairs, and though under the censorship of the government, it has fallen under no objurgation, as have other newspapers in that city.

I need not say to the Hebrew reader that the customs of their race in and around the Turkish capital are still patriarchal. Indeed, most of the Oriental customs connected with the family are of that quality. The family life is always exemplary. The members of the family are respectable, and rarely, perhaps never, is there to be found the Jewish-Spanish woman of bad fame. They cling with great fidelity to the religion of their ancestors. They strictly observe all Jewish ceremonies, and yet in doing honor to their wonderful ancestral code, it is to be hoped that they will not become, in adhesion to their belief, either bigoted or fanatical.

The Jews of Constantinople, not being blest in worldly goods, cannot make those offerings for the poor of their own class, or those of other parts of the empire, which the European and American Jews have made with such charitable abundance, but still they do their part in providing for the needy and the afflicted.

I have said that there were few schisms, if any, in the Jewish race of Turkey. I may modify this by stating that the Karaites are protesting Jews. They do not agree with the Talmud. There are few families of them ; hardly seventy-five in Haskeüi. They live in special quarters by themselves. They are not in communication with other Jews. They are not, perhaps, as brilliant intellectually as other Jews, for they have not the same opportunities nor advantages for education and philanthropy. In fact, they are disappearing, from one cause or another, while the orthodox Jew, who believes in the Talmud, seems to be improving with the lapse of time. In Egypt, however, the Karaites are improving with wonderful advancement. There are some five hundred families who are residents of Cairo.

But whatever may be the differences of opinion in this remarkable faith, one may stand at the capital of the Turkish empire, where for thousands of years commerce has made its centre, and dynasties and policies have had their nucleus, and observe with an interest only next to marvelous, the survival, even in the midst of dire persecution, of this race of men. The Hebrews are associated with the prophets and law-givers and poets and heroes of a history which has no peer in the annals of mankind. They are a race which, transplanted under new skies to a new hemisphere, under institutions of liberality and toleration which they have rarely known in their wanderings throughout the earth, have elevated their scale of being. Their sons and daughters have attained an intellectual superiority and primal beauty which belong to the chosen people of God.

If I should select the one special trait for my admiration and exaltation in connection with the Hebrews whom I have observed in the Orient, I should say it was their grand sentiment of love and profound veneration for the sacred city of Jerusalem. Although scattered throughout the empire and among a composite people who speak even seventy-two languages, from Mt. Sinai and Bagdad to far Albania and Bulgaria—wherever they are and whatever they do, their harps are still hung upon the willows of exile, and they still sing of Jerusalem as the Psalmist sung : "If I forget thee, Jerusalem, may my hand forget its cunning and my tongue cleave to the root of my mouth."

They cannot sing the Lord's song in a strange land, but whenever their circumstances allow, they move, as if by some strange, divine magnetism, toward their Holy City, animated by a strong and ardent desire to spend upon the mountains round about, or within its walls, the serene evening of their lives, with the hope of a grand immortality beyond the grave.

The interest in the Jews of the East does not centre in Constantinople, but in Jerusalem. They number about forty-two thousand in Palestine. More than half that number are in Jerusalem. The rest are in Hebron, Jaffa, Saffed, Tiberius, Haifa, Akka and the rest scattered throughout the country. In A. D. 1824, there were only thirty-two Jewish families in all Jerusalem, and but three thousand in all Palestine. This increase has come in the last twenty years. This gain has been in spite of interdictions by the Turkish government, for I think that that government has had an apprehension lest there should be Hebrew colonies formed in their old beloved land. Four-sevenths of these Jews are Askenazim. They are of the class to which the Jews of Russia, Germany, Austria and the Danubian provinces belong. The rest are, like the Jews from Constantinople, of Spanish descent from Spain, Morocco, Algiers and

Tripoli. It has always been known that a large settlement of Jews has existed in the southwest of Arabia. Doubtless from these Mahomet learned most of the incidents and doctrines which he taught in the Koran. These Jews from the desert have been isolated. They were of the tribe of Gad, and until recently have had no communication with other Jews. From the time of their expulsion from their tribal lands east of the Jordan, more than seven hundred years before Christ, they have lived like the Arabs of the desert. They seem to have been impelled toward Jerusalem, by a belief that the time of the Messiah had come, and that it was the will of Jehovah that they should be among the first to appear at their national restoration. They are distinguished from many of the Jews of Palestine by peculiar traditions and traits, which point with certainty to their early Hebraic origin and seclusion. They are said to be a simple race and to have a chastened bearing.

There is a small community in Jerusalem known as Caraim. They are called " the partisans of the text." They deny the authority of the Talmud. Their little synagogue is underground. It is of great antiquity, and one of the most interesting places of worship in Jerusalem, having much of the interest which clings about the antique form of worship that belongs to the early monks who lived in caves. The body of the Jews of Palestine, however, are called orthodox. They defer to the Talmud and other traditional teachings. They are opposed to change, and are distinguished from those known as reformed Jews, who have become so prominent, rich and influential in America and Europe. The Askenazim cling to the old Jewish customs. They do not fall in naturally with the people among whom they dwell, as do other Jews. They differ from other Jews regarding the Mosaic law as well as the Talmud. Being thrown in close association with the Sephardim, these peculiarities of custom and taste are more noticeable.

To be sure, all these classes are Hebrews, and they all look for the approaching jubilee, when their country will be restored to them and a Messiah will appear. Another class of Jews are those who study what is called the Kabala. They are mystics. It is not uncommon in the East, where the sky is deep and the stars have a magical influence, and contemplation creates devotion—the realm from which all the religions of the world have emanated—

that the strange mysteries of creation and of the spiritual nature should have a secret fascination. The language of the Bible is interpreted by them somewhat after the Swedenborgian method, with hidden meanings between the lines. Miracles are wrought, or supposed to be wrought, in vindication of their strange tenets.

The Askenazim Hebrew speaks a language known as a sort of German tongue. It is a compound of the German, Hebrew, Russian and other languages. Its written dialect is a medium of communication for nine-tenths of the Jews of Europe. That spoken by the Sephardim is Spanish. It has the music, purity and dignified flow of that graceful tongue. The Jews from Arabia speak Arabic, and nearly all the Palestine Jews have some knowledge of Hebrew, and many of them speak it with great facility. The largest portion of the Jews of Palestine are Turkish subjects. Many of them, however, register at the Consulates of their native land and preserve their foreign citizenship. It is within my knowledge that this custom, however, is changing. They are enrolling themselves as Turkish subjects. This custom tends to propitiate the Turk, who has always feared the social regeneration and building up of a state within his dominion. I think that it helps the Hebrew to be more self-respecting as well as more respected. It would seem as if they believed that they had come to stay in their old land without the *animus revertendi.*

In former days the Jew came to Jerusalem when he was in old age. He came to secure the special blessings which should follow a burial in the Holy Land. Now young men are coming, and women; in fact, families. They emigrate as our emigrants go West. They come to build up permanent homes for themselves and their children. Three-fourths of the Jews of Palestine are well off. They live upon the proceeds of invested funds or business pursuits. Wealthy Jews are going there. The remaining fourth consists of old persons. They are supported by the benevolence of their co-religionists. As in the East it is especially the custom and tradition from the earliest days that beggars should be allowed, as an incentive to charity, so the Hebrew people are not an exception to this rule. Many of them are found living in hovels wretchedly poor and pitiable. Much money has been raised in Europe and northern Africa to assist the poor. It is called the Chalouka. These funds were not exactly as charity, for they were a means to a higher end than the sustenance of the physical body. They were intended to encourage learning, and the beneficiaries were men who devoted their lives to Talmudic and other theological studies. This charity is not favorably regarded by many of the Jews themselves. I have been told that it stimulated a spirit of scholastic pride and gave rise to discussion and contention. The Jews of Europe, while extending these benefactions to their co-religionists, have given it another direction. Agricultural colonies and the industrial schools are the main objects of these gifts. The most encouraging results are expected from this change in the dispensation.

I have said before that there is an *imperium in imperio* within the Turkish realm. This has existed for many centuries. There are Jewish judicial tribunals in Judea, and these have power to punish, by penalty and excommunication from the synagogues, for breaches of the Jewish law. The Turkish government, especially in respect to the domestic relations and the distribution of property and estates, assists the Jewish ecclesiastical tribunals by the execution of their judgments and by other penalties.

I have heard it said in America that the Jews are fond of litigation. In my early days I was the lawyer of a large number of Jews in Cincinnati, but I never observed this attribute. There is, however, but little litigation among Jews in the East. They settle their difficulties before the Rabbins. In fact, the Rabbins have much to do with the internal government of the Jews in Palestine.

The sects which I have described have among them six hundred Rabbins. The chief Rabbi of Jerusalem belongs to the Sephardim. The Rabbins engage in no direct business. They are assisted from abroad. Many of them have official incomes and private resources. They are also teachers, readers, judges, and for these services they are paid. They receive money for prayers offered on anniversaries of deaths and for the sick. Many of these ecclesiastics visit northern Africa, Asia, Europe and America, to collect the charity to which I have referred.

Charity in another sense, however, belongs to Jerusalem. There are two hospitals with forty beds. The Rothschilds' Hospital is to be enlarged. It is situated without the walls. There are other associations in Palestine for assisting Jewish women and the poor and aged Jews, for educational purposes and orphanage, as well as for the loan of money without interest to those who are needy and enterprising. The Israelitish Alliance is endeavoring to enlarge the sphere of these operations, which are oftentimes limited to the sects to which I have referred. In time, through its influence and its schools, and through agencies now growing immensely in influence in the East, many of these differences growing out of sectarianism will vanish.

As to education, it has generally been conducted upon the Turkish standard, which is almost altogether limited to a knowledge of the Koran. So the education of the Jewish children was formerly confined to instruction in the law and the Talmud. The divergence from the old modes consists in branches of general study, including foreign languages, which includes the Arabic. There are six primary schools in Jerusalem, with seven hundred pupils. There are nearly one hundred professors of Talmudic literature, who teach in private houses classes numbering from five to ten scholars each. As a consequence there are advanced schools, like our own high schools.

The Rabbins have opposed that general system of elementary education of which America has been the champion. But it has secured a foothold in Jerusalem, and is approved by the people. The principal school of this elementary character was established in A. D. 1882. It is under the auspices of the Israelitish Alliance. That Alliance is reaching everywhere around the world, although its centre and direction is in Paris. After much opposition in Jerusalem, this school numbers 150 scholars. It is thought that it will soon increase tenfold. It could be thus increased if the resources would allow. In addition to elementary study, the pupils are taught Hebrew, Arabic, English and French. The latter is the principal language taught. Workshops have been established to assist the pupils in various grades. Many go out from the school and earn good wages as the result of their apprenticeship. The school is fast outgrowing its present limitations. Its cost during the year A. D. 1883, up to the 1st of September was $7,200. Never was there a more splendid opening for a race whose children have no equal in all that makes up memory, reasoning, imagination and judgment. There is an agricultural school near Jaffa. It was established by the Alliance in A. D. 1869. It has 737 pupils. It gives a general education, like our primary schools. It makes practical farmers. It has a great future. Its expenses for the last year were $9,800, while its receipts were $5,300. It will soon become self-paying. There is another school of the Alliance at Haifa, with 100 scholars, which was founded in 1881. I cannot too highly praise the Israelitish Alliance, not merely because I am partial for its kind words toward myself, a stranger, after I had undertaken to expose the persecution of the Hebrews in Russia, but for its benevolent objects. Never since the children of Israel have been dispersed over the world has there been a more vigilant, enterprising and useful institution. It was established under the auspices of the great lawyer, once Minister of Justice in Paris, M. Cremieux. I found its friends and officers in correspondence in Damascus when I was there several years ago. Men of standing and wealth gave it their help, morally, physically and pecuniarily. The Hebrews of New York know how beneficent and far reaching are its benefactions. From its current contributions and its invested funds, which for the six months ending December 1, 1885, amounted to $47,000, schools have arisen and workshops for technical instruction throughout the Orient and northern Africa.

The Alliance endeavors to expunge the lines which divide the Jews into sects, reconciling their jarrings and bettering their condition among the nations wherein they have been dispersed.

Perhaps no more difficult task could be undertaken than that which endeavors to reconcile the Jews at Jerusalem among themselves, and with the new conditions of human advancement.

As I write this paragraph, in the summer of 1887, I am advised that the two journals of Jerusalem, the *Habazeleth* and the *Hatzevi*, have been burned by the Rabbis of the Sephardim. Why were the black candles lit, the cornet blown, and the journalists accursed? For alleged slander. This consisted in calling for an account of the donations and their disbursement. The Hebrews of other lands, including America, are laughing at the ceremony of ostracism and the childish anger of the Rabbis. The ban has been tried before, on Sir Moses Montefiore, but without cutting him short in his length of days. Amsterdam once tried the ban against Spinosa, but it was a vain bull against a comet of rare brilliancy. Recently Baron Edmond de Rothschild has been visiting Palestine. He and his rich family have been bountiful to the Jews of Jerusalem, but when the

the Baron proposed to endow a school where something besides
the Bible and the Talmud could be taught, he was opposed by
the unprogressive Rabbins. They succeeded in their efforts, for
the school closed for want of pupils, as the Rabbins petitioned
the Sultan to avert this attempt to wrest Palestine from his rule,
in the interest of France !

What has eclipsed the Hebrew race? Why do such things excite our special wonder? Surely they need at Jerusalem a Pres-

A HEBREW FROM JERUSALEM.

byter Omnium Judæorum—with undisputed authority, such as
the great Sasportas, the eloquent De Silva, the learned Abendana,
or the accomplished David Nieto—who, while looking to the select
radiance of the past of Judaism, could inspire the scattered tribes
with the glory of a better day for Jerusalem and their race.

The Alliance may, in time, liberalize this Rabbinical mass at
Jerusalem. The Jews outside of Judæa believe in its methods.
To show the kindness of the people toward the Israelitish Alli-

ance, I may be permitted to state that at the municipal theatre of the Petits-Champs in Constantinople, under the patronage of the French Ambassador, Count Montebello, a charity ball was given for the " children " of Israel. Perhaps it would surprise some of the children to know that among those present as a committee, there were Elias-Pasha and Isaac-Bey, and others of the Hebraic type. Some of these are thoroughly interested in the vindication of their race.

The reader will remember the Russian and other persecutions, and the necessity which fell upon the Jewish race throughout the world of providing for the refugees. Then it was that the Alliance became useful, not merely in turning the tide toward Palestine— to reach which there were many obstacles, as I am personally a witness, but to our own country. It was thought by many to be impracticable to send these Jews to Palestine and to pro- vide for the refugees at that point. It is thought by many devout Jews that this dispersion among the nations of the earth is a posi- tive blessing.

One thing is observable to a traveler in Judæa, and it is per- haps the most significant and interesting fact connected with the Jewish re-occupation. I refer to the agricultural colonies, of which there are eight at present. These are prosperous. I have seen the two which are distant from Jaffa some two and a half hours. They were established about ten years ago. They were pioneer colonies. They now number five hundred and fifty souls, princi- pally Russians. They have a farm of about twenty-eight hun- dred acres. They have fifteen thousand vines, thirteen thousand olive-trees, and bid fair to make that land once more blossom as the rose.

It is eighteen hundred years since the new dispensation. Dur- ing that time most remarkable changes have taken place in Pales- tine and among the Jews. History records the humiliation and per- secution of this wonderful people. They have been thought by some to be an unseen and an unknown quantity among the nations of the earth. Quietly and without ostentation, by some supernal influence, Jerusalem at last is becoming through its new population, a Jewish city. A majority of its population are Jews. Its trade is Jewish. It will own the soil of Palestine in time. This prosperity has inspired many with the hope that the re- demption of Israel and the restoration of their old country is drawing nigh. Leaving their traffic behind them, they come with their own handiwork to redeem the waste places of Zion. It would almost seem beyond belief, but considering our age of physical progress, with the factors of electricity and steam, it does not seem improbable that the prophesy will be fulfilled which declares that in the last days " Zion shall be filled with judgment and righteousness, and that Jerusalem shall dwell safely, and that there shall be power upon the house of David, and upon the inhabitants of Jerusalem the spirit of grace and supplications. No lion shall be there, nor any ravenous beast shall go up thereon ; it shall not be found there. But the redeemed shall walk there ; and the ransomed of the Lord shall return, and come to Zion with songs, and everlasting joy upon their heads. They obtain joy and gladness, and sorrow and sighing shall flee away. And I will plant them upon their land which I have given them, saith the Lord my God."

Great changes are taking place in the Orient. The Muscovite is ever ready to move down upon the Bosporus. The great land animal challenges the great colonial empire of England in Asia. The various Powers of the earth are moving for the aggrandizement of their dynasties and boundaries. And shall Judæa be left alone ? Shall the six millions of the Hebrew race, which have given so much to civilization, to poetry, to finance and to religion, be alone exempt from the onward movements of our time ? Shall there be no manifestation of the great powers of the earth which are revolutionizing mankind at the centre of our earlier theology ?

There is a majestic meaning in the events which are taking place in the world. They point with no unmistakable finger toward the beautiful walls of Jerusalem. If it be the purpose of Jehovah to return the Jews to Palestine, why may not the ravening wolves, which have driven Israel almost to despair, and which have used the force of brutes against her, be balked in their endeavor; so that the hope of the Hebrew shall have realization even in our time ? All is possible with Jehovah. Seek Him that maketh the Pleiades and Orion and turneth the shadow of death into morning.

But until that day doth come, America seems a chosen land for a chosen people. Here, under our Constitution, is their vine and fig-tree.

# CHAPTER XVIII.

By the word Caliphate, or, more correctly, Halifate, is implied the supreme and combined political and religious authority of the Ottoman ruler. The title of Caliph signifies heir or successor. It was given by the Prophet to his disciples or successors. These followers started from one end of Arabia and advanced in armed bodies, with irresistible force, as far as Bagdad. They proclaimed the sacred law of the Koran and propagated the Mohammedan religion.

The first Caliph to gain distinction was the Arab leader, Omer Ipni Hatab. In A. D. 637, the sixteenth of the Hegira, he stormed Jerusalem. Afterwards, on the site occupied by Solomon's temple, he built the mosque bearing his name. It still remains, in an excellent state of preservation.

At first there were several Caliphs. The title was arbitrarily assumed by the chiefs of the most powerful tribes in Africa and Asia. These tribes, though they became united by the bonds of one common religion, were still constantly waging war against one another. The strife often ended in the almost total extermination of the weaker side. This was the fate of the tribe of the Fatimiés. They were in the course of time exterminated by the Devlet Eyoupié tribe, of which Yousouf Salahedin, Sultan of Egypt, is said to have been the founder. This latter tribe fell a prey to the superior strength of the Mamelukes. These in their turn were vanquished by the Circassians. These in their turn were finally subdued by the Sultan Selim, of Turkey. In A. D. 1517 the Sultan Selim conquered and became master of the whole of Egypt. He was officially acknowledged by the Cherif of Mecca as protector of the two holy cities of Islam, viz.: Mecca, where the Prophet lies buried, and Medina, where he was born. The Turks having thus subdued the Arab tribes, the title of Caliph came to be the exclusive hereditary right of the Sultan, who is also styled "Commander of the Faithful." His right to this exalted title there is none to dispute, since the fall of the Mahdi and other pretenders.

The present Turkish dynasty, as we have seen, was founded in the thirteenth century by Osman, or Othman. The father of Osman was Erthogrul, which in English means "Straightfor-ward." The tradition goes, among Turks, that while out on a journey he was hospitably entertained at the house of an Arab, This Arab was greatly venerated among his countrymen for his learning and piety. One night during his sojourn with this personage Erthogrul had a wierd dream. The greatness and glory in store for his descendants were thus revealed to him. Before retiring to rest he had noticed his host taking out a large volume from a bookcase and reverentially placing it on a high shelf in the chamber where the guest was to sleep. Erthogrul inquired of his host about the book. He was informed that it was the Koran, the Sacred Word of God revealed to the prophet Mahomet. Erthogrul, as soon as his host had withdrawn, took down the book. He spent the entire night reading it. He remained standing up all the time in a most respectful attitude. When in the early morning he went to bed and fell asleep he heard a voice which said to him:

"For that thou hast done reverence to my everlasting word, thy sons and the sons of their sons shall receive honor upon honor, and shall be glorified in all ages to come."

This promise began to be redeemed in the person of Osman, the eldest son of Erthogrul. Osman embraced a military career. He showed such extraordinary military talent and performed so many unprecedented feats of personal valor that he soon became the idol of his followers. He gradually succeeded in organizing them into a regular and irresistible army. He was thus enabled to conquer and acquire for himself a large extent of territory. This included the fortified town of Karadja Seher and other Byzantine strongholds in Asia. He also lent his aid in defeating the enemies of Aladdin, the Sultan of Iconium. In recognition of this service Osman received from the latter the title of Emir and the insignia of princely rank, consisting of a standard, a drum, the tail of a horse and a sabre. These insignia are still preserved with other sacred relics in the Imperial Treasury at Constantinople.

After these conquests Osman became Sultan of the Turks, or Osmanlis, as they preferred to be called in honor of their leader. At this juncture further warfare is suspended, in order to give himself and his soldiers rest. He attends to the internal organization of his newly acquired kingdom. He begins a vigorous reform by transforming the Christian churches in the town of Karadja-Hissar into mosques. He appoints Imams, or priests, to perform the services, and a Molla, or religious judge. He orders Friday to be kept as a day of rest and prayer. He strikes the first Turkish coins with his superscription. He builds Yeni-Seher, or New-town. Here he makes his capital. He appoints his father-in-law, the Sheik Edepali, as Mufti.

Osman reigns for twenty-seven years. On his death he is succeeded by his second son, the Sultan Orchan. The elder brother, Aladdin, conscious of his own inexperience and diffidence in military matters, makes over the right of succession, being content to occupy the subordinate post of Vizier. This office was specially created for Aladdin. The word Vizier in Arabic means a carrier. In this instance it signifies the carrier of the charges of the State.

Orchan, unlike his brother, was like his father. He was an intrepid warrior. While his father was still living he made several successful campaigns. In the course of one of these he took Broussa. He largely added to his dominions. He was the founder of the *Yéni-tcharis*, i. e., Janizaries. The strength of this corps was at first limited to one thousand men. In after years it gradually increased to forty thousand warriors. Besides the *Yéni-tcharis*, the Turkish army consisted originally of a number of battalions of regular infantry. These are called, in Turkish, *piadés*. Their regular infantry went by the name of *azap*. The *spahids* are regular cavalry and the *akindjis* are irregular horsemen.

The prophet Mahomet was born in Medina, in central Arabia. He died in Mecca, where his tomb still exists. It is in the custody of the Cherif or High Priest of Mecca. The office of Cherif of Mecca has been hereditary in the same family for ages. The Sultan's approval of the appointment of a new Cherif is a matter of form.

Mahomet was a driver of camels. While following this avocation he made the acquaintance of a monk from the Monastery of St. Catherine on Mount Sinai. The monk, it is said, foretold to Mahomet the great eminence to which he would attain. In consequeuce of the revelation, he asked, in advance, for Mahomet's indulgence in favor of the Christian community and certain privileges for the monastery of St. Catherine on Mount Sinai. Mahomet gave the promises.

According to the Turkish tradition, Mahomet, acting under a sacred inspiration, abandoned his trade of camel-driver. He retired to a secluded hostelry. There he spent his time in prayer, religious meditation and fasting. It was while thus engaged that an angel appeared to him one night, and delivered to him the Koran. Mahomet, in his turn, communicated its precepts to his disciples, whom he named *Houlifaï.* These followers, in a very short time, swelled in numbers to such an extent that they soon constituted a powerful and well-disciplined, if not properly organized, army. At the head of this army Mahomet started on his religious expedition, proclaiming the new faith. This comprised a belief in one God, and in Mahomet as the prophet and emissary of that God.

In the course of his conquests and triumphal march through Arabia and Syria, Mahomet came to Mount Sinai ; there he again met his old friend the monk of the monastery of St. Catherine. Having reminded Mahomet of his former promise, the monk obtained from him an "*actinamen,*" or official act. This conferred upon the monastery in question the promised privileges, and upon the Christians in general the free exercise of their religion. The *actinamen* was dictated by Mahomet himself. It was taken down by one of his followers, Ali Amboudalip. As Mahomet could not write, he made his mark on the document. He dipped his hand in the ink and brought it down on the paper, leaving thereon the impression of his five fingers. This incident is commemorated in the "*toughra*" or Imperial ensign, which may be seen on every Turkish official document and coin up to the present day. There is another origin given in a former chapter for the *toughra*, but this is as veritable as the other. It appears in the signature of the Sultan in the frontispiece. It is literally a sign-manual, with a slight difference for each Sultan or Caliph The present Sultan has a design below the signature.

The document was kept at St. Catherine's monastery in Mount Sinai until A. D. 1517. Then the Sultan, Selim I., took it into his own possession as a sacred relic. He gave in exchange for it an authenticated copy, certified by himself. This is still preserved. It bears the following heading:

" This paper has been written by Mahomet, the son of Abdullah, and Emissary of God, the Guardian and Preserver of the Universe, to all of his nation and religion, to be a true and sacred grant for the race of the Christians and the offering of the Nazerites." Is not this the fountain and origin of the " Capitulations " and toleration toward the Christian and other sects ?

The Koran, as proclaimed by Mahomet and his disciples, was subsequently collated and expounded by two Imams named Azam and Safi. Those of the Mussulmans who faithfully follow the teachings of these two holy men are styled Soonites ; that is, the orthodox or true believers. All those who have adopted the theories of other expounders of the Sacred Book go by the names Mehzembis or Kiaffir; that is, heretics and unbelievers. The Persians who follow the doctrines of Ali, son-in-law of Mahomet, and some of the Mussulman sects in the East Indies, are of the latter class. The Turks, and especially the descendants of Osman, pride themselves on being the only true believers. A sect among the Turks bears the name of Fatimié. It is so named after Mahomet's daughter Fatima, who is held in great respect among Mussulmans. It is related that as Mahomet was lying at the point of death in his harem, the most prominent of his lieutenants assembled outside. They were anxious to hear his last instructions. Fatima came out to them bearing the Prophet's standard. She handed it to them, saying :

" This is Mahomet's last wish. Take this standard and march forward !"

This standard is still preserved in a golden case in the Imperial treasury at Constantinople. It is of a green color. It is torn to shreds and attached to a kind of bayonet. It is never brought out except on occasions of great emergency, when a sacred war is declared. Then every true Mussulman is expected to take his place in the ranks and fight for his religion. The last time it was displayed was when the Sultan, Mahmoud II., destroyed the Janizaries.

The Mussulman religion accepts and acknowledges the authenticity and truth of the Holy Scriptures. It recognizes Christ as a prophet sent by God. It altogether rejects the history of his Crucifixion and Resurrection. Islam has borrowed many religious usages from the Old Testament; such as the circumcision, ablution before prayer, and others. A true Mussulman must make his ablution and perform his devotions five times a day. The washing before prayer is called in Turkish *apti*, and the prayer itself *namaz*. The five daily prayers are styled: *Sabah namaz*, morning prayer; *Oïli namaz*, noon prayer ; *Kenti namaz*, afternoon prayer; *Axam namaz*, evening prayer ; and *Guedjé namaz*, night prayer. At the time fixed for each service the Hodja, or priest, ascends to the minaret of the mosque and calls the faithful to prayer. If prevented from going to the mosque, a Mussulman performs his devotions wherever he happens to be at the moment the Hodja's call is heard. In his house, in his shop, or even in the public street, he is wholly indifferent to the curious sight he may present to passing strangers. Boatmen, with passengers on board, will often, on hearing the call to prayer, leave their oars and go through their devotions. They will do this quite regardless of the inconvenience of passengers or the danger from passing steamboats.

Ablution must inevitably precede prayer. The hands must be washed first; then the arms up to the elbows; then the face, the ears, the mouth, the top of the head and the feet. If boots difficult to take off are worn, then the boots must be washed. Where there is no water, as, for instance, in the desert, the ablutions may be performed with fine sand. This washing before prayer is a religious rite. He that washes is cleansed from sin. He is thus rendered worthy to address himself in prayer to God.

The Mussulmans keep Friday as a day of rest. As stated, this was ordained by the Sultan, Osman I., the founder of the present dynasty. Of other religious festivals, the most important are the Baïram, which is as nearly as possible an equivalent for our Easter. It is preceded by a whole month of fasting, called Ramazan, or sacred month. This fasting is observed only in the daytime, say from 4 A. M. to 8 P. M. At the latter hour, every day during Ramazan, a cannon announces its end. The daily fast is generally broken at sunset with an olive and a cigarette. Then follows a rich repast. This is succeeded by another at 2 o'clock in the morning. At 4 o'clock in the morning another gun is fired to warn the faithful to cease eating. Then the day's fast begins.

The fast is made obligatory by law. The law prohibits not only eating, but drinking, even of water. Smoking is also forbidden. Under such conditions, it can be understood that little or no work is done during this month. The government offices are open, but business is practically suspended. On the 15th day of Ramazan occurs the ceremonial of the Hirkaï Sherif, or Worshipping of the Sacred Mantle of the Prophet. On the morning of that day, the Sultan, according to immemorial custom, proceeds in great state to the palace of Top Capou in Stamboul. He is followed by the royal cortège, the procession being lined on either side by troops. The palace is the ancient residence of the Byzantine emperors. The sacred relics and treasures of the empire are kept here. Here, in a special apartment, enveloped in precious covers and safely locked in a magnificent coffer of ebony, is preserved what is believed to be a mantle worn by the Prophet on state occasions. On his progress to the palace, the Sultan is accompanied by the Imperial princes and the dignitaries and officers of state. He is conducted to this sacred apartment. Here, after the recitation by the Imams of the prayers appropriate to the occasion, the Padishah, in his quality of Caliph, proceeds to open with his own hands the coffer containing the mantle. He takes it out from its many covers. He presses the sacred relic to his lips. He then steps aside, while all his followers, including the Grand Vizier, the ministers, the members of the Imperial household, the superior military and naval officers, and the civil employees up to a certain rank, go in turn and according to the order of their rank, through the ceremony of kissing the mantle. When the Sultan retires, the faithful, if they desire, are admitted to make their devotions to the sacred relic. It is kept exposed for this purpose fifteen days.

The Ottoman code, with the exception of certain concessions made in recent years regarding judicial cases between Ottoman subjects and foreigners, is based entirely on the religious law or precepts of the *Cheri*. Jurisdiction in all strictly religious matters is in the hands of the *Sheik-Ul-Islam*, who is the Primate of Turkey, and of his subordinates. Among the latter are the *Muftis*, or bishops ; the *Imams*, or priests ; and the *Hodjas*, teachers or professors of theology. The administration of civil and penal law is entrusted to the body of Ulemas. These are men learned in the law. From among them are chosen the Mollahs, or religious judges ; the Mudirs, or mayors ; and the Kaimakams, who are prefects or sheriffs. To the religious order belongs a body called *Hafouz*. These learn the Koran by heart. They are considered as the guardians of the Sacred Book. As in the Christian Church, so also in the Mussulman religion there are several orders of monks ; they are called *dervishes.* Their monasteries are called *tékés* in Turkish. Unlike the Christians, who seek the most secluded spots whereon to build their monasteries, the dervishes prefer to erect their houses in the very centres of the large towns. There is also an order of wandering dervishes.

A MOSLEM READING THE KORAN.

These have no fixed place of residence. They go about barefooted and bareheaded; they never comb their hair or beard ; they live mostly on alms, which are freely bestowed upon them by the faithful.

The mosques are neither built by the state nor by subscription. For the most part, they are built by the Sultans or the Validé Sultanas; that is, the mothers of the reigning Sultan. This Sultana is venerated as the veritable Queen.   The Padishah's consorts are only secondary to her.

Mosques, of smaller size and less imposing, are often built by private individuals.   There is said to be a mosque in some part of Turkey (I forget the name of the locality) called *Sankim Yédim Djami.*   It is called " The mosque of the-same-as-if-I-had-eaten-it."   This curious appellation the mosque owes to the fact of its having been built by a thrifty individual, who confined his expenses to the most absolute necessaries of life.   Whenever his eye caught anything that tickled his palate, but which he considered that he could well do without, he would go up to the vender of the article, and bargain hard until he obtained his own price, then he would walk away home.   There, taking out the money he would have had to pay had he bought the article, he put it in a separate box saying, " Just-the-same-as-if-I-had-eaten-the-thing !"   By this method he economized in ten years sufficient money to build a mosque of fair size and structure.

What came from this strange race of soldier-nomads and zealous religionists, or, rather, from the creed of Islam established by the camel-driver, of which they were the champions; what came through that "pure religion revealed by God to Abraham"— may be observed more in detail as we particularize in the next chapter.   How far the adoption of Monotheism—with an authoritative prophet, from whom there was no appeal—alienated the faith of the East from the Law of Moses and the teaching of the Nazarine, will appear in the sequel.   If we should judge of a faith by its successes, it has a wonderful virtue.   When the Prophet began his sacred war in A. D. 623 by rallying 314 followers against double that number of Meccans, who could have dreamed that in the beginning of the eighth century his disciple, Abderrahman, would rally a force of 400,000 men upon the plains of distant France; or that in the middle of the fifteenth century another devotee should conquer the finest physical and commercial centre and political and religious capital of the world !   Who could have believed then that this faith, under successive Caliphs, would refine the nations of Europe by the introduction of mathematics and chemistry, chivalry and art, and dominate over at least 160,000,000 people of our earth !   True, this faith may have allured, by its persuasive and sensuous appeals, and glowing and extatic visions of the unknown world, and it may enchant the pagans of Central Asia and interior Africa, but was it less potent amidst the culture, gallantry and intellect of Europe in its mediæval centuries? Now, what do we perceive on the horizon of its future? In the regions of the Soudan, Borneo, Ghana, Tookroor, Boosa, Berissa, Wawa and Kiama, even unto Timbuctoo, it is the established religion. It encroaches upon the domains of European powers in western Africa. Its schools and mosques light the pathway of the De Brassas and Stanleys through undiscovered countries. Fresh tribes flock to the standard of the Prophet, whose religion to them is better than—none.

If this faith is failing in Europe, if Algiers and Tunis succumb to France, if Persia should yield to Russia, Egypt to England, Morocco to Spain, Zanzibar to Portugal, and Abyssinia to Italy, the Mahometan still holds the sacred cities of Jerusalem and Mecca, and the water-ways of the Bosporus and the Euphrates. He predominates in Asiatic Turkey, Afghanistan, Beloochistan, Arabia, a great part of India, and bids fair to control what there may be of religious faith in Africa. Surely this is a spiritual realm, extensive enough for one Father of the Faithful.

The Sultan, rather in his capacity of Caliph, once asked the author :

"Are there no Mahometans in America? Could I build a mosque for them in your country?"

My response was rather nebulous and diplomatic. I replied :

"I am not aware of any Mahometan body of people sufficient to constitute a mosque. If there be any, I should find them in—in—in—San Francisco. Your Majesty, under our institutions, would find no impediment to building a mosque, for our code allows the exercise of any religion. It tolerates even the atheist. In this regard it is based on the liberalities of Your Majesty's 'Capitulations,' which forbid any constraint from the state upon the conscience and soul."

Thereupon I mentioned to the Sultan that I had read some accounts of the bad treatment of the Moslems in the south of Africa, from the bigoted incursions of the Dutch or English. He made a memorandum of the incident, as a faithful Caliph of an extensively accredited faith.

# CHAPTER XIX.

It will not do for the Puritan, the Calvanist, or the Catholic—Anglican or Roman—or any one who boasts of the simplicity of his Christian faith, to criticise too harshly the faith of the Mahometan. The Calvinist will find much to encourage him by the study of the Koran. So with any one who believes in the unity of God and discards the Trinity. The mind which accepts the idea that God gave tables of commandments unto Moses, at the time of the destruction of the golden calf, cannot well deny that there was something sublime in the divine rage of the iconoclastic Moslem when, with cimeter and battle-axe, he destroyed the splendid effigies of Greek art and the colored pictures of the Egyptian tombs and temples.

Without preface, let me give the main prescripts of the code of Mahomet. The Rev. Dr. Hamlin's book, "Among the Turks," has a fair summary. If the code be not worthy of a God, it is worthy of a prophet. It is as follows :

The first article asserts the fundamental principles and sources of knowledge, and the creation of the world ; and the second, that the Creator of the world is God, Allah ; that He is one and eternal, that He lives, is all-powerful, knows all things, fills all space, sees all things, is endowed with will and action ; that He has in Himself neither form, nor figure, nor bounds, nor limits, nor number, nor parts, nor multiplications, nor divisions, since He is neither body nor matter ; that He exists of Himself, without generation, dwelling-place or habitation ; outside of the empire of time ; incomparable in His nature as in His attributes, which without being exterior to His essence, do not constitute it. Thus God is endowed with wisdom, power, life, force, understanding, regard, will, action, creation, and the gift of speech. This speech, eternal in its essence, is without letters, without characters, without sounds, and its nature is opposed to silence.

These teachings of the Koran—its angels and genii, its peris and fates, its heaven and hell, its predestination, death and resurrection, and the duties of its devotees to spread the doctrine of Islam, with its pious practices, such as prayer, ablution, fasting, pilgrimages, abstinence from unclean meats and from intoxicating liquors—these elevate, almost as much as the promised sensual enjoyments depress, the Mahometan religionists. Is it owing to some infirmity of our nature that the body of mankind are predisposed to the enjoyment of sensuous ideas? These ideas, in a large measure, control their action, and give to it impulsive force. When, therefore, Mahomet charged his devotees to pursue the infidel even unto death, with force and arms, he gave them roseate promises. While these promises have done much to promote the temporal power of his religion, they have done more to forward its dissolution. The inquiry has often been made, "What part of the Koran promises paradise to the triumphant Mahometan?" I make the best quotation possible as an answer:

"The whole earth will be as one loaf of bread, which God will reach to them like a cake; for meat they will have the ox, Balâm, and the fish, Nûn, the lobes of whose livers will suffice 70,000 men. Every believer will have 80,000 servants and seventy-two girls of paradise, besides his own former wives, if he should wish for them, and a large tent of pearls, jacinths and emeralds; 300 dishes of gold shall be set before each guest at once, and the last morsel shall be as grateful as the first. Wine will be permitted, and will flow copiously, without inebriating. The righteous will be clothed in the most precious silks and gold, and will be crowned with crowns of the most resplendent pearls and jewels. If they desire children, they shall beget them, and see them grow up within an hour. Besides the ravishing songs of the angel Israfil, and the daughters of paradise, the very trees will, by the rustling of their boughs, the clanging of bells suspended from them, and the clashing of their fruits, which are pearls and emeralds, make sweetest music."

To the sensuous races of the East there are here promised, perhaps, more of the delights of a paradise than are afforded by sitting on a cloud tuning a golden harp. Besides, it has a subjective humor that can be appreciated by those whose domestic felicity is not all that could be wished for in this world.

Although the religion of the Turks has many strange features, it is a mistake to suppose that it is very distinct from that of other civilized nations. Whatever we may think of its founder ; however unacceptable may be some of his doctrines ; how much soever he may have drawn from the Mosaic and the Christian writings, in matters pertaining to the Unseen World ; yet, as a scheme of religion, influencing as many if not more millions of people than Christianity, is it not worthy of being considered by other peoples than those immediately in the neighborhood of Turkey ?

The ordinances of the Mahometan faith are strictly observed wherever the Prophet is accepted. A Mahometan, when the time arrives for his prayer, has no business with worldly affairs until his prayer is ended. To him no earthly business can compare with the duty of prayer.

The tourist does not see Mahometanism unless he passes over the Galata Bridge, into old Stamboul. There, in and around the mosques, if not in the latticed houses upon the Sea of Marmora, he will meet the old Turk, who retains his ancient dress and ideas. His head still swells with an immense turban, and, what is most striking, it is uniformly of a green color. Those who wear a turban of this color are Emirs. They are the descendants of Fatima, the daughter of the Prophet, who was the wife of Ali, his disciple. In one respect these green-turbaned Moslems are like the ancient Egyptians—they carry the certificate of their descent upon their persons. Nearly every Mahometan in thirty is an Emir. He is entitled to respect. He may enter exalted callings. Any career is open to the Emir. The Emirs have a chief. He has sovereign authority. He decrees punishments. As the Janizaries kept alive the military enthusiasm of the Turk, so the Emirs arouse the religious spirit of Islamism.

This simple faith believes in the angels and in the Scriptures. It teaches immortality, resurrection and judgment. It shakes hands across the abyss with John Calvin. It is fatalistic to the extent only of holding fast to God's absolute decrees and predetermination both of good and evil. Mahomet did not split hairs, like Calvin ; so he accepted the predestination of evil as well as of good. He was logical. Leaving dogma, his logic believes in good works and religious observances. Its first test of belief is prayer. Mahomet called prayer "the pillar of religion and the key of paradise." In this view wherein does he differ from the Christian ? He would accept no submission without that "key." Prayer may be silent, except on great occasions in the mosque, when it is repeated aloud. It is no new thing to pray toward some particular sacred spot. Before the Christian era religion had its points of the compass, and before the veiling of women, and their exclusion from the mosque, or, at least, their isolation behind the lattices in the mosque, other and Christian churches shut the women as closely behind their jalousies as the Turk shuts his behind those of the harem. The Mahometan idea is that the presence of women in the mosque during worship is incompatible with prayer, as their presence might inspire a different kind of devotion than that which belongs to the faith.

The first chapter of the Koran is a prayer. It is a prayer which is held in great veneration by the Mahometans. It is considered the quintessence of the Koran. It is often repeated. It is the Lord's Prayer of the Moslem. There has been much discussion as to its recondite meaning, for, be it known that there have been many contentious theologians in the Orient ever since the time of the early fathers. The fathers defined closely the true meaning of certain words and phrases upon which an eternity of happiness or misery depended. This prayer to which I refer is a sample of the very best meaning of this wonderful Mahomet:

"Praise be to God, the Lord of all creatures! The most merciful, the King of the Day of Judgment! Thee do we worship, and of Thee do we beg assistance. Direct us in the right way, in the way of those to whom Thou hast been gracious, not of those against whom Thou art incensed nor of those who go astray."

The foregoing are the words of the Moslem common prayer, without any of its wearisome repetitions, which protract it to a great length. Some portions are repeated three, six and even nine times at each course. The same repetitions are to be found in our Christian Litanies.

This prayer will remind the reader of the Psalms of David :

"O God most high, there is no God but God. Praises belong unto God. Let thy name be exalted, O great God. I sanctify thy name, O my God. I praise thee; thy name is blessed, thy grandeur is exalted, there is no other God but thee. I flee to Thee against the stoned demon, in the name of God clement and merciful. Praise belongs to God, most clement and merciful. He is sovereign of the Day of Judgment. We adore thee, Lord, and we implore thy assistance. Direct us in the path of salvation, in the path of those whom thou loadest with thy favors, of those who have not deserved thine anger, and who are not of those who go astray. O God, hear him who praises thee. O God, praises wait for thee. O God, bestow thy salutation of peace upon Mahomet and the race of Mahomet, as thou didst upon Ibrahim and the race of Ibrahim, and bless Mahomet and the race of Mahomet, as thou didst bless Ibrahim and the race of Ibrahim. Praise, grandeur and exaltation are in thee and to thee."

While praying, the pious Mahometan uses his chaplet of beads. This habit was, no doubt, derived from the Buddhist or Christian ceremony. It is an aid and ally in devotional exercises. Edwin Arnold, in addition to his exquisite "Light of Asia," has written a book of poetry containing ninety-nine lyrics, strange in form and wierd in spirit. Each one is garnished with a quotation from the Koran, and each one of the ninety-nine beads on the chaplet, or string, which the devout Mahometan carries, recalls one of the divine attributes and names of Allah. These chaplets are sometimes made of pearls, coral and amber. Sometimes fragrant wood constitutes their material.

The most solemn sight connected with any religious ceremony that I have ever witnessed was the one upon which I looked from the gallery of St. Sophia. Below me were thousands of human beings in regular lines, all looking toward Mecca while they prayed. Not a single suppliant connected with this devotion failed to bow his head to the floor, as by one impulse, when the shrill chant of the priests died away among the pillars and in the dome of the vast temple. Occasionally there was a pause, as between the summons and the judgment.

Sometimes I have wished that the Greek and Turkish priests were more harmonious in their chanting. Their wild, shrill, delirious outcries seem to have been inherited from some ancient pagan orgies and not from the gentle religions of later times, which voicelessly enthrall, by their subtle effect, the spiritual nature.

The Turk has at least an outward show of piety. If he be a good Moslem, his life is regulated by his faith. He moves with a humility which belongs to a reflective mind. He may be rich and live in luxury within his *konak* or palace, but when he enters the mosque there is for him no worldly pomp. He is in the presence of the unseen God. He prays without ceasing, aligned with others, some of whom may be beggars, water-carriers or charcoal venders. Here he feels that he is but one of the atoms among the many which make up a remarkable and infinite congregation of souls. Certainly such humility is in strange contrast with the complacent luxury of Western churches, with their richly cushioned pews, their carved pulpits, their gilt-edged hymn-books and their sometimes pompous clergy.

The call to prayer is a picturesque feature of this remarkable faith. Morning, noon and night that shrill cry echoes over these wonderful cities and waters:

" Most High! There is no God but the one God! Mahomet is the Prophet of God! Come to prayer! Come to the Temple of Life!"

This speaks of a devotion which must have its response from the other world. It is the daily, almost hourly, recognition of God by a whole people who acknowledge his Everlasting Name and their dependence on his Providence. No need here for " putting God in the Constitution," for the One God is as much their king as he was to the Jews in the days of their theocracy.

It is a singular phase of the Oriental life in the " Land of the Sun" that the day begins when the sun goes down. Then it is the first time of prayer; the second is two hours after sunset, and the third is at the dawn. Each time the chanting of the muezzin from the minaret calls the faithful to prayer. The most important time of prayer is at noon. The Sultan recognizes this when he comes out to the mosque on Fridays. The fifth and last prayer is about 3 o'clock in the afternoon. It is determined when away from human reckoning, as in the desert, by the length of the shadow either of a stick, a dromedary, or other object. The shadow must be of the right length; that is, of its own height upon the ground.

Alms-giving is a chief part of this faith. It is a part of all the religions coming from the Orient. It is not peculiar to Mahometanism. Begging is a passport to every place, from the Sultan's palace to the seventh heaven of paradise.

Fasting also is an observance of the Mahometan. His Lent,

from one moon to the other, is kept with religious regard while the sun is above the horizon. How often have I looked over and seen the wonderful beauty of Stamboul in that Ramazan season, when the mosques are burning their countless lamps, and from minaret to minaret there is a profusion of brilliant lights ! It is during this month that the worship of the Prophet is celebrated with a splendor only limited by Moslem skill in illumination. When the electric light shall appear in the East, to penetrate the dark places of Stamboul and shed its refulgence through St. Sophia, Suleiman, and the other grand mosques and structures of the capital—with their immense interiors filled with surging and kneeling forms and bowing foreheads—the splendors of the Roman ritual in St. Peter's, and the glories of Westminster Abbey and St. Isaacs, will be eclipsed before those of Islam.

I will not now undertake to compare with others the festal days and rites of the Turkish religion, nor the obligation of pilgrimages, nor the ablutions with water, nor other fundamental practices of this faith ; nor can I augur as to the abstinence from wine and strong liquors, and the other restrictions which Mahomet evidently copied, if he did not improve, from the Levitical law ; but I think it will not be unprofitable to allude to one of the gentlest features of Moslem life—it is kindness to the brute creation. This seems an institution of the East. It is derived, doubtless, from the Egyptian or Hindoo ideas of metampsychosis. Every bird that washes its wing in the Bosporus, every donkey which with sorrowing step, works up the hill of Pera, loaded to the earth ; the cooing ring-doves of the mosque, which feed freely from the open grain boats of the Straits; the horse with thunder in his neck and gentleness in his eye; and the ox which treadeth out the corn in the provinces—all would, if they could, speak of Moslem kindness toward the brute creation, which becomes mutual, blessing as it is blest.

The usury which is practised by the Armenians and others, and eating the flesh of swine, or of any animal that has died a natural death, are as severely avoided by the Mahometan as they were by the ancient Hebrews. Gaming too, is not in vogue. They have their dice and their backgammon, and many other games for amusement, but not one for gain.

When the adherents of the Greek orthodox Church make complaints of the Mahometan, because he does not love art, and because he will not have pictures, only mottoes from the Koran, in the mosque, it would be well to ask the orthodox people as to the quality of the painted and smoked pictures in the Greek churches, as well as their vaunted miraculous qualities. If it be a question of superstition, let the miracles of their holy springs and wells be analyzed, with the chemistry of the water. It would be well also to ask them, when they come to the remarkable attributes of the priesthood, why relics still perform such cures as are attributed to them. I have been myself at a witching monastery, in a lovely grove near the castle of the Seven Towers in Constantinople, where the Greeks pass certain holidays in dancing and praying. I have seen the miraculous fish in its fountain. It is an old and trite story about the last Emperor Constantine and the broiled fish which leaped out of the pan and swam about in the water, in order to fulfill a prophecy about the fall of the city.

It is impossible to give a very minute description of the Mahometan rite of circumcision. It is more sedulously regarded in the Moslem economy than in the Hebrew, from which it was taken. The ceremony calls for grand preparations at the *konak*, or house, of the family. All the Faithful within the range of the family acquaintance are invited to the feast which accompanies the ceremony. The sons of the poor families of the vicinage are collected to undergo the rite, on the same occasion with the rich man's sons. Was it not Montesquieu's father who made a beggar the god-father of his famous son, to remind him all his life that the poor were his kith and kin? The incident has an Oriental tinge.

Only one sex ventures into the salon where the circumcision is to take place ; the other is excluded *pro tempore*. Behind bars and curtains, and with a superfluity of rich dresses, jewelry and confectionary, the ceremony begins. Upon the little mattress coverlets are laid down, stiff with golden embroidery; then the silk or satin pillows are strewn about profusely ; toys, oranges and presents of all kinds, including fruit and flowers, artificial and real, are brought to attract or distract the attention of the children. Wild Arab music appeals to the ear, for the same purpose. The cymbals clash, the tambourines rattle, and the drum adds its thumping unmelodiousness. One after another the young children, aged from five to ten, are borne into the appointed chamber. A company of actors or mountebanks, in fantastic array, with musical instruments, fill up the swelling scene. All this happens before the dinner, which is served at sunset. The dinner does not differ from the general Turkish dinner, such as I have described, where no knives and forks appear ; but there is more than the usual richness and abundance of viands, whose climateric is the famous *pilaf.*

When the spectacular ceremony begins, various modes are improvised by both women and men to peep into the sacred chamber. While it is going on, the buffoonery, jugglery and jesting proceed, together with the performance of a Turkish band, which adds to the clatter and distraction.

Strange people, strange religion, and strange ceremony ! yet there is, doubtless, a sanitary value in the practice; although it may be also a strictly religious rite.

The contest of Mahomet for supremacy in Arabia and the East, considering his environment, was lofty and sublime. It matters not whence he received his dogmas ; he certainly embraced the salient points of Theism, Judaism and Christianity. Whatever may be believed of his revelation to-day, it has a theological sublimity. What though his doctrines inspired his followers with predatory impulses ! They were promised a paradise, if they fell battling under the banner of the Prophet. How could it be otherwise, than that the Crescent should wax over a church militant, and the symbols of another religion wane in the Semitic East? The decree announced by Mahomet for the promulgation of his faith, to slay all those who refused to accept it, has long since passed away from the Mahometan mind, as it has from that of the Christian. The student may read Hallam's History of the Middle Ages. He may ponder upon the revolutions which followed the Ishmaelitish religion. He may analyze the passions and temper of the Arabic race ; but one thing cannot be ignored, and that is : that the " People of the Book," as they were termed in the Koran—the four uni-theistic sects, the Christians, Jews, Magii and Sabeans—were recognized everywhere by the Mahometan with toleration. Can it be said that all these sects tolerate the Mahometan ? Would any of them draw the sword against him, because of his creed ?

There is more toleration among the Turks than we have been accustomed to believe existed. They tolerate many sects in their own creed. There are several orders of Dervishes. These are distinguished one from the other by the canons of their faith. There is a sect that is materialistic. There is another that worships the Virgin Mary ; and still another that believes in the Saviour and the twelve apostles. Each of the various orders has some peculiar characteristics, but all are tolerated. Some are known as howling and some as dancing Dervishes. It is impossible with the pen to represent the former, but the pencil does something in the sketch to give an idea of the latter. Of course there is more or less of superstition in connection with the

DANCING DERVISHES.

Dervishes. They pretend to cure diseases. So far as I could see, with my fallible sight, they succeed in the mind cure. I have seen long rows of patients lying horizontal—babies and soldiers among them—and the Dervish walking upon their bodies. They arise—well. Is it faith that cures, or what ? These Dervishes are versed in astrology. They have quiet, and perhaps I might say cunning, manners. They are skillful enough never to be enmeshed in the intrigues of the court or the cabals. How rarely have I read of any scandals connected with the Mahometan religion ! Our own journals are full of scandals in the Church, both in America and elsewhere. Only one such Moslem instance can I recall : at Broussa, in a certain quarter, there was a Tekké. This is a name for a *quasi* mosque. Its Imam yielded to certain temptations of the flesh and the devil, and made his place the resort of Bacchanals and worse. It was not long before he was removed, for such practices cannot exist in a Mahometan country.

The Turk has always admired intellectuality, or the "Men of the Book." One of the most celebrated of the Mussulman saints had a tender attachment for a Christian monk. At the request of the Mussulman, they were buried together. Their twin-tomb still exists at Iconium. The Christian head of the Iconium monastery possesses a privilege superior to that of all the Ottomans, viz., the girding on the sword of Osman, the Conqueror, upon the Sultan, in the mosque of Eyoub, upon his accession to the throne. There are evidences in history of Christian nuns asking and receiving the kindly regard of the Moslem ; and, at times, for some adornments in the shape of carpets for their chapels. A few months ago, there were reciprocities, presents and assurances of friendship between the Sultan and the Pope.

Those who inveigh so strenuously against the alleged bad faith of the Moslem, must remember that there are always two sides to a question, and more especially when it is one of a religious quality. In the year A. D. 1444, after the sword had been flashing over the Balkans, and through Greece and Asia Minor and along the Bosporus and the Danube, it was agreed that it should be sheathed and have an absolute rest for ten years. The Hungarians, through their leaders, among whom their grand champion, Hunyades, was prominent, gave the sanction of soldierly honor to this truce. Cardinal Julian also confirmed it, by the rites of the religion of which he was an exalted representative. It was signalized by oath upon the Gospels—the most sacred oath possible to a Christian. On the part of the Turks, the Sultan Amurath, in the presence of his civil and ecclesiastical servants, swore to the pact upon the Koran. This peace was strictly observed by the Turk. How was it observed by the Christians ? As they never intended to keep it, they broke it. Its breach was made on the plea that there was no faith to be kept with the Infidel. In disregard of its sanctity, the Christian Powers move upon the East. It seems as if the Ottoman would be swept out of Europe. But what is the result? The Moslem starts the old war-cry. He has the *morale* of the issue. In every mosque there are solemn appeals to Allah. The Sultan leads the hosts of the Faithful against the invaders at Varna; and at the head of the Janizaries, on a truce and in a field between the two armies, he reads aloud the violated treaty. It is held aloft upon a lance-head within sight of the Christian armies, and with a thunderous voice the Sultan utters this most singular invocation :

" Oh, Thou insulted Jesu ! avenge the wrong done unto Thy good name, and show Thy power upon Thy perjured people."

It is not necessary to say upon whose banner victory alights. The perjured are routed. The Turk is dominant over the field. The Moslem faith has, by this victory, a new lease of power and a larger dominion ; and that too, through the intercession, as believed at the time, of the Jesus Christ to whom the Moslems appealed.

The Mahometans have always reverenced our Saviour as a great judge and prophet. Even at the great mosque in Damascus, which I have seen, there is a minaret dedicated to the name of Jesus Christ.

As one among many examples of the toleration of the Sultan toward those who do not accept the Mahometan religion, I may state that, in the Ministerial changes recently effected, Agop Pasha, a non-Mussulman, became Minister of Finance. He was chosen for his merit as a financial administrator, which had been well attested, by the orderly methods of his books, as a man of business, and his clear conception of the fiscal future of Turkey.

To what extent are the Turks fatalists ? I might answer this question by saying : Not to any greater extent than our own Calvinists. I might illustrate this by many examples of their mode of making their calling and election sure. They have a wild invocation in battle. It is this : " Heaven is before you ; hell behind you ; fight bravely, and you will secure the one ; fly, and you will fall into the other ! " There is not much fatalism in this, for if the soldier be destined for Hades, then, according to Calvin, not all his heroism can save him from perdition.

I recall another instance—not without some shuddering. I made a visit one Friday to the howling Devishes. A company of this sect was established below the hills of Pera on the northwest. To reach the spot we had to pass through the neighborhood of Kassim Pasha. It is the home of pestilence. It is known by the unpleasant and malodorous name of the Cloaca Maxima. It was such places that made the plague and the cholera a scourge in earlier days. Since leaving Constantinople I have heard that the authorities are taking drastic measures in regard to filling up this terrible drain. The enlightened Turk, like the enlightened predestinarian believes in " using means " to work out the decrees, and to give them the most favorable turn he can. Another example of this kind is their life-saving service and their quarantine.

Sad indeed are the accounts which passengers, anxious to reach Constantinople, give of the quarantine at Cavak, at the head of the Bosporus. They are compelled, without distinction, to pass their time on the vessel at this station, in sight of all the wonders of the Bosporean waters and shores, upon which they are forbidden to land. The Sultan makes no discrimination between those who are his own Ministers or those who are foreign Ministers, and the ordinary traveler. All alike are placed in the common jail-bounds of the ship, waiting for the lapse of the four days of confinement. Sometimes our launch used to ply around the quarantined vessels with our healthy flag flaunting, and many were the anxious inquiries from American tourists, to which we responded as best we might, when we could not go on board to welcome our countrymen. Indeed, these vessels were in one sense prisons—without, however, the meagreness of prison fare, or the healthy labor of the galley-slave. I have heard some wails about the way the precepts of Vatel, if not those of Soyer, were disregarded. The question of quarantine is really neither a culinary nor an international question. It is a question of " Kismet." One of these prisoners once said to me :

" I can understand how a noble murderer at the gibbet should feel a pride in the moral example which his death would afford, but the imprisoned victim of a quarantine has no such consolation. Its hindrance vindicates no principle ; it affords no example ; it can have no pretense to any prophylactic character."

Yet, Mahometan quarantine defies Fate. It laughs at Kismet. It scowls at Calvin and the Koran. The Turk undertakes by this imprisonment, more strict than that of any other port of Europe, to make provision for the future of this life, at least. He does not trust to fate, nor practice on the precept, " what is writ, is writ."

Could the author of this religion be the gross impostor he has been often represented? Did he fabricate his faith for purposes of ambition and universal conquest? A wealthy merchant, he drops into a bankrupt; and leaving Mecca a ruined man, he has but one thought, and that is to build a little mosque in which to harrangue his hearers. He has rare dashing spirits to aid his career. When most exalted by his conquests and power, he is most simple and humble. He dies poor.

"He left," says Irving, "neither a golden divan nor a silver dirham, neither a slave nor a slave girl, nor anything but his gray mule, Daldal, his arms, and the ground which he bestowed on his wives, his children and the poor."

Here is self-abnegation without alloy. At the death of a beloved child, he is resignation itself. In the article of his own death he proclaims his hope of salvation through the compassion of Allah and his trust in His mercy. Does he bow before his Destiny as if it were written in the everlasting decree? Yes. Not a word escapes him in derogation of his uniform teaching and his inviolable faith. In summing up his character, I adopt the language of our countryman, Washington Irving, who made the life of this strange, prophetic man a study for his gifted pen :

"It is difficult to reconcile such ardent, persevering piety with an incessant system of blasphemous imposture, nor such pure and elevated and benignant precepts as are contained in the Koran, with a mind haunted by ignoble passions and devoted to the groveling interests of mere mortality; and we find no other satisfactory mode of solving the enigna of his character and conduct than by supposing that the ray of mental hallucination which flashed upon his enthusiastic spirit during his religious ecstasies in the midnight cavern of Mount Hara continued more or less to bewilder him with a species of monomania to the end of his career, and that he died in the delusive belief of his mission as a prophet."

# CHAPTER XX.

ADHERENTS of the orthodox dogma consider their Church as the great trunk from which the other branches of the Christian faith have sprung. To ascertain how far this belief is sustainable, it is necessary to cast a short retrospective glance into the history of Christianity from the time of its foundation, A. D. 33. In that year the first church was established in Jerusalem by the apostles. Two years later came the persecution against Stephen and his followers. The apostles were then obliged to quit Palestine and betake themselves to the adjacent countries. Philip the Deacon went into Samaria proclaiming Christ and the gospel. Peter, having traveled through Judea, made a vast number of converts, and among others the Roman Cornelius and his family. In A. D. 36–40 the first church was founded in Antioch. There for the first time believers in Christ were called Christians.

The work begun by the apostles was steadily continued by their successors. As far back as A. D. 170, Christianity had already spread over a large portion of Asia. It included Persia, Armenia and Arabia. In the latter country the gospel was interpreted by Origen and Pantenos, the great teachers of the School of Catechism of the new faith founded in Alexandria. Much success was obtained in Neo-Cesaræa by Gregory the miracle-worker. His last words before dying were to express satisfaction at leaving only as many infidels (17) as he had found believers on his coming into the country. In Africa, and especially in Alexandria, Christianity was largely taught. Here it found many converts. But the firmest hold obtained by the new faith was in Europe. There the apostle Paul taught with much success.

It is most painful to read of the fearful persecutions to which the apostles and their successors were subjected while carrying on their great work of preaching the gospel. The Jews were the first to rise against them. They were irritated to the highest degree by the teachings of our Saviour developing so rapidly through the exertions of the apostles into a regularly established faith. Of the persecutions inflicted on the apostles, prominent are the cruel imprisonment of Peter and John, the stoning of Stephen, the Protomartyr, the butchering of Jacob, the son of Zebedee, and the throwing of Jacob from the height of the temple.

Other cruelties were perpetrated on the rest of the apostles and their followers. These continued until the taking of Jerusalem in A. D. 70, when the Jewish power and influence seemed to be effectually destroyed. For a time the Jews were obliged to cease their persecution of converts to Christianity. They had their own misfortunes. The respite, however, was but very short, for their inveterate zealotry again found vent, and in a yet more cruel manner, on the occasion of the Jewish insurrection in A. D. 132. The revolt was headed by the false messiah Varhova. On his defeat by the Roman Emperor Adrian the Jews ceased to exist as a nation.

To these persecutions of the primitive Christians succeeded those by the pagans. In every country into which Christianity was introduced its converts were subjected to every imaginable species of cruel treatment. Their houses and property were pillaged, and themselves put to death after suffering the most agonizing tortures. Many Christian communities with their elders were obliged to abandon their homes and seek refuge in caverns in the desert and in woods. Even there they were exposed to hunger, thirst, cold and to being devoured by wild beasts. The fiercest of these pagan persecutions were during the reigns of the Emperors Nero and Domitian. Traïanus, who succeeded the last-named emperor in A. D. 98, issued an edict against all secret societies. This was aimed against the Christian religion mainly, which at the time had to be practised in secret. The Christians having thus come under the ban of the law, their persecution became even more oppressive and systematic than before. Yet under sufferings the most terrible, those early converts to the Christian faith displayed a heaven-born courage and perseverance of which it would be impossible in this short sketch to convey any accurate idea.

Rome had then the whole world under her rule. As emperor succeeded emperor, each one appeared anxious to surpass his predecessor in the excesses inflicted against Christians in every part of the empire. The most violent of these persecutions took place in the reign of the Emperor Diocletian, A. D. 284–305. Instigated by his brother-in-law Galerius, Diocletian issued in A. D. 303 a decree ordering all Christian churches to be pulled down and the Holy Scriptures to be destroyed. This was followed in A. D. 304 by another edict, to the effect that all Christians who refused to worship and sacrifice to idols should be forthwith put to death. The consequences attending this latter order were fearful. In Asia Minor alone 15,000 Christians were massacred in one single month. In Egypt 140,000 were put to death. It is computed that 700,000 died in prison. These massacres continued until the year A. D. 310, when Galerius, being attacked with an incurable disease, issued in A. D. 311 a decree ordering all further persecutions of the Christians to be stopped, and desiring them to pray to their God for the salvation of his soul.

This was the condition of the Christians until A. D. 311. Constantine the Great was then proclaimed emperor in Brittany. He succeeded his father Constantine Chloros. In A. D. 312, the new emperor declared war against the Roman Maxentius. The latter was a bitter enemy of the Christians. His power was utterly crushed by Constantine, who thus became sole emperor and absolute monarch of the West. From the moment he mounted his father's throne he showed a marked leaning toward the Christian religion. Upon taking the reins of the government of the East and West into his hands his first care was to give the Church of Christ his powerful protection. He suppressed with a strong hand the evils to which it had for three whole centuries been subjected. He extended to it every possible support that, under the circumstances, the state could then afford.

In A. D. 323, after his victory against Licinius, Constantine himself embraced the Christian faith. Consequently it became the state religion throughout the Roman empire. The property that had been confiscated was returned to the churches. He also, by special decree, dedicated Sunday to the worship of God. He ordered that day to be kept as a day of rest. Later on Constantine removed his seat of government from Rome to Constantinople, or Byzantium, as it was then called. He rebuilt the city and adorned it with many exquisite works of art and a large number of magnificent churches.

Upon this adoption of Christianity as the religion of the Roman empire, it became incumbent upon the state to establish rules for the government of the Church. Reforms were introduced in quick succession. These tended to constitute the Church a distinctly separate establishment, having no direct communion or relations with the state. The latter, however, undertook to make all necessary provision for the proper maintenance of the religious communities. Livings were appropriated to the use of the churches. It was made lawful for churches to accept legacies. Church property was made inalienable, and the clergy were freed from taxation. Legislation upon ecclesiastical matters, both temporal and spiritual, was made over to the local, or in cases of supreme importance, to Œcumenical synods, or assemblies of the superior clergy. The resolutions of these bodies were invariably submitted to. They received the sanction of the Emperor. They thus became invested with the authority of law. Finally, the right of trying the clergy, whether for religious or criminal offences, was invested, in the bishops, and ecclesiastical courts were established for the purpose.

The hierarchy, or graduating offices in the Church, were allowed to remain at this time as originally ordered by the apostles. The clergy were elected. This appears from their name in Greek, meaning " vote." All ecclesiastics before receiving ordination were chosen by vote. They were divided into three ranks : First—the bishops, who were and are still considered as the immediate successors of the apostles, and who were also styled shepherds, vicars, popes and patriarchs, according to the different countries in which they resided. Second—the elders, or priests ; and Third, the deacons.

Originally all the bishops ranked equally. But as each circle from the centre of which the Christian faith was being propagated began rapidly to widen, it was found that the bishops who occupied those few centres did not suffice for the wants of the daily increasing communities. Consequently power was given them to appoint, each in his own radius, other bishops, acting under them. This arrangement rendered it necessary that some distinctive title should be given to the bishops at great centres, to distinguish them from their subordinate bishops. They were accordingly at first styled Proti. This title was subsequently —on the occasion of the first Œcumenical synod held in Nicæa

—changed to Metropolitan. The latter title came from the centres from which the other Christian communities had received admittance to Christ's church. The Metropolitan Church was looked up to by their communities. It was held in estimation as that of a mother of their own churches. The first to receive the title of Metropolitan were the bishops of Jerusalem, Antioch, Alexandria, Ephesus, Corinth and Rome.

These Episcopal sees were also styled apostolic thrones, as having the gospel direct from the apostles. The most prominent among these Metropolitan or Episcopal sees were those of Antioch, Alexandria and Rome. To the latter see all the Churches of western Europe were subjected. The Bishop of Constantinople—the capital of the great Roman empire—received by courtesy the title of Patriarch. At the time, however, he did not actually rank higher than the other Metropolitans. Then the latter only recognized as their Master and the Head of the whole Church, the Saviour Jesus Christ.

It is maintained by the orthodox that the first symptoms of a desire for supremacy came from Rome. It was vehemently resented by the other prelates, and especially the successive Patriarchs of Constantinople. It culminated in the separation of the Western Church from the Eastern. All the Christian communities dependent upon the Metropolitan see of Rome were then collectively styled the Western, in distinction from the Eastern Church. This separation, or schism, took place in the year A. D. 1054. The Papal see of Rome was at the time held by Leo IX., and the patriarchal throne at Constantinople by Michael Kiroularius. The latter had been for some time most vehemently protesting against the innovations, as he regarded them, which were being daily introduced into the Western Church by the Popes. He considered them as in direct violation of the ecclesiastical laws laid down by the apostles and the successive synods. He denounced the manner in which the observations addressed on this subject to the Popes, by himself and the other Metropolitans, were received. Being apprised of a new " violation " of the precepts of the Church on the part of Rome, he sent by the Bishop of Bulgaria a letter to John, Archbishop of Trania, in Italy, in which he bitterly complained of and condemned the Pope's conduct as schismatical.

When the bearer of this letter reached Trania he found there an envoy of the Pope, Cardinal Humbert. The envoy, having read the Patriarch's letter, sent a translation of it to Pope Leo. The latter, in reply, wrote a long missive to the Patriarch. He denied the right of the Patriarch to question or condemn the conduct of the Church of Rome, "whose actions could be judged by no mortal." The Pope ended his letter by calling upon the Patriarch to hasten to repent and beg forgiveness for his sin, " lest he be incorporated in the tail of the dragon who had swallowed up the third part of the orbs shining in the heavens." Notwithstanding the tone of this letter, both the Patriarch and the emperor replied in very conciliatory terms. The former urged the necessity of a perfect accord among the churches ; the latter directed that the Pope should send an embassy to Constantinople, to discuss the different questions with the local synod.

In compliance with this request the Pope sent an embassy, with Cardinal Humbert at its head. Immediately on its arrival in Constantinople the embassy was admitted to audience of the Emperor, to whom Cardinal Humbert handed a letter from the Pope. This contained many bitter complaints. The foremost was that the Patriarch should have presumed to adopt the title of Œcumenical Patriarch. On leaving the Emperor, Cardinal Humbert paid an official visit to the Patriarch. He omitted to give the Patriarch the usual brotherly salutation or greeting. With a stiff bow he handed him a copy of the letter he had already delivered to the Emperor. The Patriarch, after attentively perusing the letter and examining the seals attached thereto, began to entertain a suspicion. It was to a certain extent confirmed by the inconsistent utterances of some of the members of the embassy. He suspected that the letter was a forgery, and that Humbert had no special powers from the Pope. He concluded that the envoy was simply the organ of a conspiracy concocted by a Byzantine duke by the name of Argyros, who had settled in Italy. He thought the object was to derive political advantages from a separation of the Churches. He therefore refused to hold further parley or communion with Humbert and his followers. In revenge, Humbert, on July 16, A. D. 1054, went to the Church of St. Sophia and placed on the communion table an aphorism excommunicating the Patriarch, the bishops and the communicants collectively of the Eastern Church.

The Patriarch, on being apprised of this extraordinary proceeding, called immediately a meeting of bishops.   It was then and there resolved that a petition should be addressed to the Emperor denouncing Cardinal Humbert and his suite as impostors, and demanding their expulsion from Constantinople.   The petition was duly presented to the Emperor.   He replied in writing, stating that, having gone carefully into the matter, he was himself inclined to believe that there was some intrigue at the bottom of the affair.   But, having no positive proofs, he felt bound to treat Cardinal Humbert with the respect due to a person invested with the office of ambassador.   Consequently, he would not consent to the Patriarch's demand for the expulsion of the mission.   On receipt of this reply of the Emperor, the Patriarch Kiroularius again called together the synod of bishops present in Constantinople at the time.   A minute was drawn up in condemnation of the proceedings of the embassy.   The synod, by way of retort, placed under anathema both the proceedings and all those who might approve or adhere to them.   This minute was afterward signed by all the other prelates of the Eastern Church.   This served to consummate the complete separation of the Church of Rome from the Church of Constantinople.

Besides this struggle for supremacy, the primary causes which led to the separation were certain alleged reforms introduced into the original doctrines of the Church by the Popes of Rome. These reforms the churches in the East refused to admit.   The Eastern Church condemned them, as being opposed to the teachings of Christ and the apostles.   The principal among these reforms, introduced long before the severance between the churches became accomplished *de facto*, were:

The insertion of the word "filioque" in the Nicæan Creed.

The substitution of unleavened for leavened bread in the celebration of the Lord's Supper.

The belief in the existence of the "purgatorium" as a half-way house between earth and heaven, or hell; and

The infallibility of the Pope.

These are still the essential points of difference between the Church of Rome and the orthodox Greek Church.   The latter regards herself as remaining firm to all the traditions of the Church originally established by the apostles, down to the most minute particulars. Its doctrines are to be found in a number of articles of faith. These comprise:

The Nicæan Creed, so called from its having been drawn up by the first Œcumenical synod held at Nicæa in A. D. 325.

The Creed of St. Athanasius, which establishes two different but inseparable dogmas—that relating to the Holy Trinity, and that explaining the mystery of the Incarnation of the Son of God.

The Holy Catechism of the orthodox Church, as taught in their schools.

The other dogmatic teachings contained in the canons of the ten topical synods; and

The canonical epistles of the elders of the Church, which were fully discussed and confirmed by the Sixth Œcumenical Synod.

Moreover, a full exposition of the doctrines of the Eastern orthodox Church is to be found in the Patriarchal epistle, which was approved as a true confession of the orthodox faith at the synod held at Jerusalem in A. D. 1672. A copy of this, bearing the signatures of all the orthodox prelates, was sent in A. D. 1723 to England, by way of reply to the overtures made by the Protestant clergy for a closer intimacy with the Eastern Church.

The spiritual government of the Eastern orthodox Church is in the hands of the Œcumenical Patriarch, assisted by a synod of twelve bishops, chosen on the demand of the different sees subject to the throne of Constantinople. The title of Patriarch comes, of course, from the Old Testament. It was originally conferred on some of the most eminent only of the prelates of the Church. It is a token that they were worthy to be held in the same kind of respect as the ancient Patriarchs mentioned in the Scriptures. The first prelate to receive the title of Patriarch was the Bishop of Antioch, in Syria. It was subsequently conferred in succession on the Bishops of Rome, Alexandria, Jerusalem and Constantinople.

The bishops of Rome and Alexandria, before they received this title, were styled Popes. On the separation of the Churches they retained only that of Pope.

Before the separation of the Eastern and Western Churches there were, therefore, five prelates of the whole Catholic Church bearing the title of Patriarch. The right to bear this title was duly confirmed to each of these five prelates at the first and second Œcumenical synods. The following is the order of precedence then settled:   Rome first, styled "first among equals;" Constantinople second ; and then Alexandria, Antioch and Jerusalem.

These five Patriarchs were likened by some of the Byzantine theologians to the five senses of the body. This may be seen from a letter addressed by Peter, Patriarch of Antioch, to the Bishop of Venice, in which he says :

"It is nowhere written, and consequently inadmissible, that the Bishop of Venice shall be styled by the title of Patriarch, for we only know of five Patriarchs in the whole world : those of Rome, Constantinople, Alexandria, Antioch and Jerusalem. For, as our body is governed by five senses, so the body of Christ, our Holy Church, is governed, like unto the five senses, by the five patriarchal thrones."

After the severance of the Churches, when the Bishops of Rome dropped the title of Patriarch, they went back to the original title of Pope. The Patriarchs, after this, numbered only four, until the sixteenth century. Then Russia, under the Emperor Vladimir, having entered the fold of the Eastern Church, the number was raised to five by the consecration of a Russian prelate, with the title of Patriarch. He was to govern the Church of Russia and rank fifth in the order of Patriarchs, i. e., after the Patriarch of Jerusalem. This Russian patriarchate continued until the year A. D. 1700. Then the tenth Patriarch, Adrian by name, having died, Peter the Great suppressed the patriarchal office. He appointed instead, a synod of bishops to govern the Russian Church. This change was effected with the full consent of the Patriarch of Constantinople, in whom, after the separation from the Church of Rome, the supreme power of the Eastern Church had become vested.

The Church of Constantinople, or Byzantium, was established by the apostle Andrew. He built the first house of worship there, in the place then known as Argyropolis. It is now called Foondooklo; or, literally, hazelnut village. It is situated on the European shore of the Bosporus, and is the third village on the west bank, and next to Tophane, which, as an artillery factory and dépôt, is in contrast with this peaceful association of its neighbor. In A. D. 36 the same apostle constituted Byzantium an Episcopate. He appointed his disciple, Stachis, as first bishop. Of him mention is made by the apostle Paul in his Epistle to the Romans.

Paul consecrated him with his own hands. Stachis governed the Church of Byzantium for sixteen years. He was suceeded by Onissimos, who died in A. D. 53. From this period up to the building of Constantinople by Constantine the Great, there were eighteen successive bishops of Byzantium. Simultaneously with, or, rather, in consequence of, the removal of the capital of the Roman empire to the shores of the Bosporus, the Bishops of Constantinople assumed the title of Patriarch. The first to do so was Metrophanes I. Two years before, he had succeeded Bishop Trovos in the Episcopal see of Byzantium. The patriarchate of Metrophanes I. was marked by the holding of the first Œcumenical synod. It was, by order of the Emperor Constantine, assembled at Nicæa in A. D. 318 to pronounce judgment on the heretical teachings of Arios. Arios was a native of Libya and a distinguished mathematician. Before this he had gone to Alexandria, which was still at that period a great seat of learning. There he was ordained a bishop by Peter, the Holy Martyr, Bishop of Alexandria, and was deemed a very important acquisition to the Church. Soon after his ordination, however, he most painfully surprised and alarmed his friends by attacking, both by word and writing, the Church in its most fundamental doctrines. He caused it to shake to its very foundations.

In the midst of the prevailing enthusiasm for the sublime religion of Christ, which had now spread over the whole of the civilized and even over a great part of the uncivilized world, Arios came forward to cast a gloom over the Christian world by denying the divinity of Christ. He stamped upon the doctrine relating to the Holy Trinity. For these teachings, then regarded as blasphemous, Arios was excommunicated by Peter, Bishop of Alexandria. But soon after he received absolution, and was again admitted to the Church by Achillas, the successor of Peter in the bishopric of Alexandria. Achillas also ordained Arios as High Priest of Alexandria, and made him a professor of sciences.

During the Episcopate of Achillas, Arios remained perfectly quiet. He showed a sincere repentance for his former transgression. No sooner, however, was Achillas dead than he again commenced his heretical teachings, and this time with such force and argumentative persuasion that he soon began to draw to his side many converts, even among the higher clergy. Seeing this, and fearing the evil might take still larger dimensions, the new bishop of Alexandria convoked a synod of bishops from different parts of Egypt and Libya. They solemnly excommunicated Arios and his followers. Meanwhile the dissensions in the Church arising out of this proceeding on the one hand, and the anti-Christian teachings of Arios on the other, came to the knowledge of the Emperor Constantine. He first despatched the Bishop of Controuva, Osios by name, to Alexandria with a mission to effect a conciliation with Arios. This mission was a failure. The Emperor, unwilling to resort to extreme measures against the Arionites, in his quality of "summus pontifex" of the Church, sent word, according to the historian Photius, to every town and country, over the whole world, for all the bishops and elders of the Church to assemble in a sacred synod in the fortified town of Nicæa. The purpose was to hear the arguments brought forth by Arios, and to pronounce sentence accordingly.

The synod was held in A. D. 318, and, either by a noteworthy coincidence or by premeditated arrangement, this was also exactly the number of clergy who took part in the deliberations. Among the prelates present were the Pope Sylvester of Rome, Alexander, Patriarch of Alexandria, together with St. Athanasius, Eustace, Patriarch of Jerusalem, St. Spiridion, Bishop of Treithuntos, St. Nicolas, the miracle-worker, and Paul, Bishop of Neo-Cæsarea. The latter attended in a dreadfully mutilated condition. His lower limbs had been burnt a few years previously by order of the Emperor Licinius. Many others of those present also bore marks of the martyrdom to which they had been subjected in the reigns of the emperors immediately preceding Constantine the Great.

The Patriarch of Constantinople, Metrophanes I., was unable to attend the synod, owing to his old age. He was at the time over one hundred years old. He was represented by one of his suffragans.

The convocation was presided over by the Emperor in person. The deliberations lasted about a month. The most noted speakers on the side of Greek orthodoxy were Eustace, Patriarch of Antioch, and Osios, Bishop of Controuva. On the side of Arios were ranged Eusebius, Metropolitan of Nicomedia, Paulinus, Bishop of Tyrus, the Metropolitan of Cæsarea, and others. Both parties contended with zeal and ability in support of their respective doctrines. Ultimately the result of the discussion was to deprive Arios of many of his late supporters.    The august assembly, with only a few dissentient voices, solemnly confirmed the sentence of excommunication already passed upon him and his followers.    As the only and very simple answer to the teachings of Arios, the synod drew up the creed of the Christian religion, known as the Nicæan Creed.    The synod, before dissolving, determined also the manner of fixing Easter Sunday in each year.    They passed other resolutions having reference to the temporal and spiritual government of the Church.

Notwithstanding the sentence of excommunication passed by the synod, and other subsequent endeavors for its suppression, Arianism, while yet in its cradle, took deep root.    Some years later it had grown so much that in A. D. 371 the Arionites, favored by the then Emperor, Oualentus, obtained by a large majority the election of one of their own sect as Patriarch of Constantinople. They then proceeded to drive the orthodox clergy out of all the offices of the Church, and even out of their principal places of worship.    This state of things, however, only lasted a few years. Upon his accession to the Byzantine throne in A. D. 378, the Emperor Theodosius the Great took up the cause of orthodoxy with a strong hand.    He succeeded in stamping out the Arionites.    He thus put an end to the dissensions in the Church in respect to their doctrines.

In this difficult work the Emperor was very ably assisted by two of the most brilliant luminaries of the Eastern Church, St. Athanasius, some time Bishop of Alexandria, and Gregory, the theologian.    The latter, on the dismissal of the Arionite Patriarch elected in A. D. 371, was appointed to the patriarchal see of Constantinople.    This appointment was conferred by the Emperor without regard to the law concerning the election of Patriarchs and other prelates of the Church.    It was characterized by some of the bishops as anti-canonical.    Theodosius therefore called together, in the year A. D. 381, in Constantinople, a convocation of bishops, which received the name of the Second Œcumenical Synod.    This assembly confirmed the nomination of Gregory to the patriarchal throne.    It afterward occupied itself with re-asserting the doctrines laid down by the first synod.    It affirmed the triumph of orthodoxy against Arionism and other teachings regarded as heretical.

Though the nomination of Gregory was confirmed by the synod with only a few dissentient voices, the dissenters, towards the close of the sitting, received large reinforcements. They ultimately developed into so strong an opposition that the Patriarch found it necessary to tender his resignation. This was accepted. Then the synod, at the request of the Emperor, submitted a list of names for the office to the Emperor. The latter had reserved to himself the right of choosing from them the new Patriarch. How the successor to Gregory obtained the patriarchate is an incident worth relating.

It had been arranged that each member of the synod should send in the name of the prelate in whose favor he wished to vote. Thereupon a list was to be drawn up of those who had obtained the largest number of votes. This list was to be submitted to the Emperor. The list being in due course presented, the Emperor's choice fell on a person named Nectarius. This was a surprise to all. The Emperor's attention was attracted to Nectarius because his name appeared last on the list. He was altogether unknown to the Emperor.

When the name of the Patriarch-elect was communicated to the members of the synod, they began to inquire among themselves as to the identity of Nectarius. It then came out that not only was he not a member of the synod, but neither a priest nor yet a member of the Church. He had not even been baptized ! He was, in fact, a native of Tarsus. He had held for some time the office of prætor, or prefect, in Constantinople. Being anxious to return to his own country he had called, previous to his departure, upon the Bishop of Tarsus. His object was merely to ask for letters of introduction, which would help him on his way back. The Bishop had been for some time pondering as to whom he should give his vote for the patriarchate. The venerable aspect of Nectarius so impressed the Bishop that he at once determined to vote for him. Tarsus, being on terms of intimate friendship with the Patriarch of Antioch, prevailed upon that prelate, who at first laughed at the idea, to place Nectarius's name on the list. When, however, it came out that the nominee was not even a true Christian, there was great commotion among the clergy. Notwithstanding this, the Emperor remained firm to his choice, and ultimately Nectarius was baptized, consecrated, and unanimously elected Patriarch of Constantinople in the month of May, A. D. 381.

Nectarius remained at the head of the Church of Constantinople for sixteen years. He was succeeded on his death by John the Chrysostom, or Golden-mouthed. Chrysostom, while yet vicar of the see of Antioch, had obtained a world-wide fame as an eminent preacher and writer. He was called to the patriarchal throne by the Emperor Arcadius in A. D. 398, on the recommendation of the all-powerful eunuch Eutropius. John, by his eloquence and exemplary life, soon drew to himself in Constantinople, as he had done in Antioch, the entire sympathies of the great multitude. From the court itself he for some time continued to receive many tokens of the honor and respect in which he was held. His gift of persuasion, and the influence he had acquired over both the people and their rulers, was particularly demonstrated on the occasion of the disgrace of Eutropius. Sentence of death had been pronounced by the Emperor upon this eunuch. John succeeded in saving his life. Eutropius, hearing of his condemnation, sought refuge in the cathedral church of St. Sophia. Here the guards were sent to arrest him. The eunuch was anything but a favorite of the people. They were ready to drag him from the sacred edifice. They were about to do this, when they were suddenly stopped by the Patriarch. The latter, mounting the pulpit, and pointing with outstretched hand toward the late powerful Minister of State, who lay cowering and trembling at the foot of the great altar, preached extempore, and in the best Greek style, that famous sermon beginning with the words "Vanitas vanitatum et omnia vanitas." The Patriarch ended with an appeal to those in power and to the people not to violate the sanctuary of the Church. He warned them to lay no violent hands on the sinner who had sought refuge therein. His pleading had the desired effect. Eutropius was allowed to go free.

John's frequent allusions in his sermons, in condemnation of the immorality and extravagance prevailing at that time among the higher classes and those about the court, at length brought about his downfall. His preaching became so irksome to those against whom his strictures were addressed, and even to the court itself, that gradually a strong party was formed against him. This consisted of those high in office. Nearly the whole of the nobility were arrayed against the Patriarch. They determined to obtain his removal from the patriarchal throne and from Constantinople. In this they succeeded ; but how? By abusing him to the Empress Eudoxia. They charged him with having in one of his sermons spoken in disrespectful terms of her vanity. It is the old story. The woman, more than the empress, resented the affront. She immediately began a correspondence with the Patriarch of Alexandria, Theophilus, as to the necessary steps to be taken for the deposition of John. There was danger of arousing the indignation of the people and those of the clergy who were devoted to the Patriarch.

By Theophilus's advice, in answer to the Empress's appeal, a meeting of bishops was called. These were chosen entirely from among those who had grievances against John. The meeting was held in the year A. D. 403, under the presidency of the Patriarch of Alexandria at Chalcedon. John was summoned to attend, to hear the charges and to defend himself against them. John refused to obey a summons proceeding from an ecclesiastical court which had been convoked without his knowledge. He was thereupon deposed from the patriarchal office for disobedience.

The imperial sanction was obtained to this sentence, through the influence of the Empress. She exercised absolute sway over her husband, the weak-minded Arcadius. The execution of the sentence was entrusted to a palace functionary. This officer broke by night into the Patriarch's palace and arrested him. The latter was conducted with all speed over the Bosporus to the Asiatic shore of the Black Sea. Here a further journey inland was stopped. On the morrow, when the news of what had taken place became known among the people, they rose up in a body and demanded the instant recall of John. The army itself took the side of the people.

The Empress and those about her at first refuse to entertain the demand of the multitude. The Empress sends a body of sailors, whom the Patriarch of Alexandria had brought with him, to quell the insurrection. The people, however, fight with determination. They soon obtain the advantage over the armed force sent against them. They march against the palace, with the intention of breaking into it. The Empress takes fright. She asks Arcadius to order the recall of John. This happy news quickly spreads among the people. There is a general rush to the shore. The Bosporus is rapidly filled with hundreds of ships. Boats full of people go to meet their beloved Patriarch. And thus John of the Golden-mouth is brought back in triumph and placed on the patriarchal throne in the midst of general rejoicing.

After this the Patriarch John occupied the see of Constantinople for another year. Again he afforded matter of displeasure to the court. This was in the year A. D. 404. This time he was definitively deposed. His enemies had prepared for this. They had employed foreign troops to frustrate any action of the people in his favor. John was first exiled to Concousos, in Armenia, and thence he was sent farther inland to Pityus. It was on the journey to the latter place that he died, November 14, A. D. 407, at the age of sixty.

Four hundred and fifty of this Patriarch's sermons have been preserved. They are convincing proofs of the deep knowledge and the shining rhetorical powers possessed by this eminent prelate of the Greek Church. John, along with his two contemporaries, Gregory the theologian, and Basil the Great, Bishop of Cæsarea, are honored as saints by that Church. It has bestowed upon them the distinguished appellation of the three great luminaries of the Church.

I once asked a professor of Greek in the East:

"What is the distinguishing feature of Chrysostom's eloquence? Why does he come down to us as the ecclesiastical Cicero?"

The reply was:

"His descriptions of the grandeur of the soul, and its quality of permanence and immortality; these furnish most frequently the theme which, like molten gold, came glowing from his eloquent lips. And, with it all, his earnestness and honesty gave emphasis to his terrible phillipics and his lofty ideas."

It is hard for any one—scholar or churchman—in the West to recognize how this Patriarch is still revered by the orthodox devotees and scholars of the East.

John, the Golden-mouthed, was succeeded on the patriarchal throne of Constantinople by Arsakius, the brother of the Patriarch Nectarius. He was highly respected, both for his many virtues and his very old age. He died a year after his election. Atticus was elected in his place. The only distinguishing characteristic of his patriarchate is that he continued uninterruptedly to occupy the throne for twenty consecutive years. This is the longest term on record. Next after Atticus came Sisinius I. He

died two years after his election.    He was succeeded in A. D. 428
by Nestorius.  The latter was surnamed " The Heretic," because of
his adoption of a new doctrine closely allied to that put forward
by Arios.    According to this doctrine, known as the Nestorian
Creed, there is a clear distinction between the human and divine
nature of Christ.    It admits that the Virgin Mary is to be revered ;
but only as the mother of Christ.  It repudiates any claim of sanctity for her as having given birth to God himself or the Son of God.
The reason given for this is, that the human nature adopted by
Christ on his coming into the world was only the outer garment
or temple within which his divine nature was enclosed.    In plainer
terms, the impression it was intended to convey by this doctrine
was that Christ was only human.    It admits that he was endowed
with supernatural gifts and power.    Still, he was only human, and
not co-substantial with the Father.

The gradual propagation of this doctrine naturally caused a
violent commotion among those anxious to uphold the precepts of
orthodoxy as originally laid down by the two Œcumenical synods.
A division ensued in the Church.  The greater part of the clergy
of Constantinople, the Patriarch of Antioch, and the Emperor
himself, Theodosius the Less—so called in contrast to his grandfather, Theodosius the Great—openly avowed this creed and sided
with Nestorius.    In defense of the orthodox dogmas were ranged
the Patriarch of Alexandria, Kyrillos, with his chapter, and the
entire Church of the West.    The latter succeeded in enlisting to
their side the sister of the Emperor, Pulcheria.    During her
brother's minority she had been acting as regent.    She still continued to exercise great influence in the conduct of state affairs.
Though only a very young woman, she had, during her regency,
displayed a wonderful talent for government.    She had given
many proofs of very sound judgment.    Her efforts in this instance
to persuade the Emperor to withdraw his support from the Nestorians proved unavailing.    She pleaded that at least a synod of
ecclesiastics from all parts of the world might be summoned to
consider the question at issue.    This, she said, would put an end to
the existing anarchy in the Church.    Her plea was successful.    On
November 19, A. D. 430, an imperial edict was issued summoning
all the bishops in every part of the world to assemble at Ephesus
in the week before Pentecost of the following year.    The convocation is known as the Third Œcumenical Synod.    It met on the

22d of June, A. D. 431. There were present about two hundred bishops from different parts of the East, including Egypt. The Pope of Rome, Celestin, was unable to attend personally. He sent three exarchs to represent himself and the other prelates of the West.

The presidency of this synod was given to the Patriarch of Alexandria, Kyrillos, who, as already stated, was at the head of the orthodox faction. The debates lasted only a few days. They ended in a resolution, carried by an overwhelming majority, condemning the new doctrine as heretical, and Nestorius and his followers were placed under anathema. In pursuance of this resolution and anathema, Nestorius was shortly afterward deposed. He was exiled to an African oasis, where he died.

Hardly, however, had the commotion to which this eventful occurrence had given rise subsided when another heresiarch, Archimandrite Eutychius, appears on the scene. His doctrine is even more pronounced than that of Nestorius in opposition to the canonical precepts of the Christian religion. He enlarges upon the idea of Nestorius as to the two different natures of Christ. He declares that the divine nature of Christ had undergone a complete change through the process of incarnation.

To condemn in an authoritative manner this new doctrine, it became necessary to have another convention. Accordingly the Fourth Œcumenical Synod was convened by the Emperor Marcianus, the husband of Pulcheria, the Emperor Theodosius the Less having died the year before, in A. D. 450. This synod assembled at Chalcedon, now known as Kadikeui, on October 8, A. D. 451. It is on the point almost opposite Stamboul, on the Asiatic side. The synod was attended by 630 bishops, or, according to some writers, by 520. The Eastern Church attaches great importance to this synod. It was the most largely attended council in the history of the Church. Weighty resolutions were passed by it. The doctrine of Eutychius was unanimously condemned as heretical and blasphemous. The synod then proceeded to deal with other important matters. It passed a resolution intended to suppress abuses of the monkish orders, by forbidding them to take any active part in matters ecclesiastical or political. It passed a measure confirmatory of that already adopted by the Second Œcumenical Synod, conferring on the Patriarch of Constantinople the right to rank second after the Pope of Rome in the hierarchical order of the Church. The reason for this is stated in Article 28 of the Acts of the Fourth Synod, as follows :

"Constantinople being the second capital, the new Rome, of the empire, it behooves that the bishop of this city should have the place of honor next after the Pope, to whom the first place belongs by right of Rome being the place of residence of the Kings."

This latter part of the wording of the resolution was at the time opposed by the clergy of the West present in the synod. They objected to it as laying down the rule that the first place of honor was given to the Pope, not by any special ecclesiastical right, but simply because Rome happened to be the capital of the empire. It followed that if at any time Rome were to be deprived of this honor—which actually did take place when the Eastern and Western empires were united some time after—the precedency of the Popes would become extinct and precedence be given to the bishop of the new capital.

It is essentially this article that gave rise to the dissensions between the Churches of the East and the West. These culminated in the schism, or separation, to which reference has already been made.

The synod in question granted to the Patriarch of Constantinople full jurisdiction over the churches of the whole of Asia, Thrace and the Black Sea. This jurisdiction is maintained up to the present time. It should here be stated that the bishopric of Constantinople was originally a mere dependency of the Metropolitan see of Heraclea. It was in A. D. 318 that Constantine the Great removed his throne to Constantinople, and then the patriarchate was constituted into an independent see. The right, however, was reserved to the Archbishop of Heraclea of ordaining each newly appointed Patriarch. Up to the present day the Patriarchs are, as a general rule, chosen among the Metropolitan and bishops of the Church. This dispenses with the necessity of ordination. But it is still the custom, as a memorial of his former office, for the Metropolitan of Heraclea to hand the patriarchal crozier to the Patriarch-elect on his enthronement. Heraclea is now a little station for steamers on the southern coast of the Black Sea, about 120 miles from the Bosporus. There are 300 Turkish and but seventy Greek houses. It hardly rivals Nicæa as a place for hunting snipe, and certainly not Chalcedon for Christian culture, and these—with Constantinople—are the eminent seats of early ecclesiastical renown and power.

Though enfranchised from his subjugation to the see of Heraclea in A. D. 318 the Bishop of Constantinople enjoyed no special privileges. According to strict ecclesiastical canons, he did not rank any higher than the other bishops of the East or of the West. The title of Patriarch and his right to the second place after the Pope in the hierarchical order was hitherto accorded to him by courtesy merely. It was a courtesy in compliment to the court by whom he was, as a rule, appointed.

The Fourth Œcumenical Synod, however, raised at once the dignity of the patriarchal throne of Constantinople into one of great eminence. It brought under the patriarchal sway all the churches in the East, with the exception of those of Alexandria, Antioch and Jerusalem. These only were allowed to preserve their independence. Furthermore, the synod confirmed to the Bishop of Constantinople his right to the title of Patriarch. It also conferred the same title on the three other independent sees mentioned.

The annex of Œcumenical to the title of Patriarch was unknown at this time. It was for the first time adopted by the Patriarch, John II., on his election to the see of Constantinople in A. D. 517. The annex was confirmed by a local synod ; that is, a convocation of the Bishops subject to the patriarchal throne. This was in the patriarchate of John IV., in A. D. 582. This proceeding gave rise to vehement protestations on the part of Rome. It greatly conduced to widen the gulf between the Churches of the East and the West.

The Pope contested the right of the Patriarch to the annex of Œcumenical. He did this on the ground that this annex conveyed an idea of predominance over all the other prelates of the Church. He was naturally anxious to preserve the title to himself. It had been duly accorded to him by previous synods. The Patriarch, on the other hand, and the whole of the clergy of the East, regarded the annex as bearing a different meaning from that attributed to it by the Pope. According to them the term Œcumenical, as employed by the early Church, was synonymous with that of Christian. This view was on the theory that Christianity was destined to extend over the whole of the inhabited earth. The Greek, word οἰκουμενιός, the root of which means a *house*, could, in this sense of the inhabited world, only mean Christianity. It was in this sense that it had been assumed by the Patriarch of Constantinople. In support of this interpretation they referred to Basil the Great, John the Golden-mouthed, and Gregory, the theologian, to whom successively in former times the title of Œcumenical, i. e., Christian teacher, had been given.

The Greeks insist, and they are supported by several European writers, that it was merely in this sense that the annex in question was assumed, and continued to be held until the final rupture with Rome. This interpretation was adhered to by the Greeks up to the time Constantinople fell into the hands of the Turks. Then it was that the Patriarch became the supreme head of the Christian community in the East. The title Œcumenical came thenceforth to be regarded as carrying with it the interpretation objected to by the Popes of Rome. It was then regarded as expressing a real predominance over all the other clergy of the orthodox Church.

While on the subject of titles, it may be interesting to give the full titles—or encomiums, as they are styled in Greek—of the different Patriarchs. These are read in church when any one of the Patriarchs is officiating in person. The titles are announced by one of the deacons, just before the reading of the Epistle for the day. They are chanted by the two choirs successively. The ceremony is quite scenic and impressive. The Patriarch is in full canonicals, with mitre and crosier. He is surrounded by the bishops and the clergy who are taking part in the service with him. He stands on a throne by the Communion table and blesses the congregation. The encomium appropriate to the Œcumenical Patriarch is very simple and short, running thus :

" Of . . . . . . . (the name of the Patriarch), the most holy and Œcumenical Patriarch, God have mercy and grant long life."

That of the Patriarch of Jerusalem is as follows :

" Of . . . . . . . (the name), the most blessed Patriarch, of the Holy City of Jerusalem and of the whole of Palestine, Syria, Arabia, beyond the Jordan, Cana of Galilee, and of the Holy Sion, God have mercy and grant long life."

The Patriarch of Antioch is prayed for thus :

" Of . . . . . . (the name), the most blessed and holy Patriarch of the great city of God, Antioch, of the entire East, our Lord and Master, God have mercy and grant long life."

But the most curious piece of composition is the encomium given to the Patriarch of Alexandria. The following is a literal translation:

" Of . . . . . . . (the name), our most holy and blessed father and shepherd, Pope and Patriarch of the great city of Alexandria, Libya, Pentapolis, Ethiopia, and of all the land of Egypt, father of fathers, shepherd of shepherds, high priest of high priests, thirteenth of the apostles and judge of the earth, God have mercy and grant long life."

How ceremonious are these grand officials of the Eastern Church, and how tenacious of their titles, and especially that of Œcumenical, may be seen by their signatures. The signatures of two of these Patriarchs I present in *fac-simile.* One is that of "Simeon, by the mercy of God Archbishop of Constantinople, New Rome, and Œcumenical Patriarch." He was the Patriarch in A. D. 1474, before Columbus discovered America. The other is that of " Metrophanes, by the mercy," etc. He was of the year A. D. 1567. The necessities of this volume require these signatures to be diminished in size. They are mammoth in extent in the original—in fact, two or three feet long—and the cabalistic letters measure an inch each. The features of the Patriarchs—for I have seen two of them—are as imposing and classic as the *sign-manual* is grand and gigantic.

The Patriarchs of the Greek Church, like the Pope of Rome, are elected ; but the Patriarch for five years only. They are chosen by the clergy in common with the laity. Joachim IV., the recent Patriarch, was a man of splendid presence and scholarship. I have seen him going up and down the Bosporus in his caïque, the admired of all admirers. Much dissension seemed imminent, pending the election of his successor, but it was successfully accomplished with the aid of the—Moslem and the Sultan! The election took place on the 12th, or, in the new style, the 24th, of January, 1887. The delegates had been elected amid much contention. About the virtues and faculties of Monseigneur Dionysius the Fifth, late Metropolitan of Adrianople, who was elected, I shall speak in the next chapter.

If the question be asked, What to us in America is Joachim, or Dionysius ? I would answer, Are Gibbon and the history of the great Greek Church obsolete with our people ? Have we forgot-

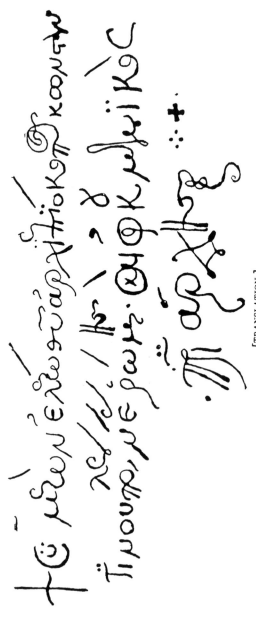

[TRANSLATION.]

Simeon, by the mercy of God, Archbishop of Constantinople, New Rome, and the Œcumenical Patriarch

In modum Buck

† Συμἰων Ἐλὶω Θεοῦ ἈρχιΘεπίσκοπος Κωνσταντινουπόλεως, Νἰας Ῥώμης καἰ Οἰκουμενικὸς Πατριάρχης

FAC-SIMILE SIGNATURE OF THE ŒCUMENICAL PATRIARCH, SIMEON I., A. D. 1474.

ten the grand history of this Church, which has given so much of the fatherhood of the Church to our own era?

Its personnel may not attract our Western world, but its relation to the early eras of Christianity should give to each organ of its wonderful polity a reflected and splendid effulgence.

Preliminary to the election of the Patriarch is the issuing of the *Bouyourouldon*. It would require the assistance of the Grand Logothete, Aristarchi Bey, the younger brother of the former Turkish Minister to the United States—who is the translator for the Greek Patriarch—to render this word into English. It signifies a document to be read before the holy synod. When this document is read, the Monseigneur replies in that synod in Turkish, for his majesty, the Sultan and his Ministers. Then a meeting of the synod and the council is held at Phanar, to arrange for the election of a new Patriarch. In doing this they pursue the old patriarchal method coming down from the ancient times, as fixed by the councils which once met in this patriarchate.

Is it not strange, in the light of Paul's Epistles, to read the names of the diocesans to which the *Bouyourouldon* is addressed —under the sanction of the Caliph and ruler of Islam? How pregnant it is with ecclesiastical wrangles, canons, synods, conventions and history! Here are some of the names:

Cæsarea, Ephesus, Cyzicus, Nicomedia, Nicæa, Chalcedon, Dercos, Salonica, Adrianople, Amasia, Janina, Broussa, Bosnia, Crete, Trebizond, Phillipopolis, Smyrna, Mytilene, Varna, Scio and Uskub. Here, in these localities, the Gospel of Christ was first preached. Here his churches were first organized. Here, through the centuries down from the beginning of our era, remained unquenched the candles of the Eastern Church, that claims to be the only orthodox expounder of the Gospel of the New Dispensation.

# CHAPTER XXI.

IN the preceding chapter the writer has given an outline of the history of the Eastern Church from its foundation up to the early part of the sixth century, and especially of its councils and controversies.

Passing over minor incidents, the next important event in the history of the Eastern Church of which we have record, is the building, or, more properly speaking, the restoration, of the church of St. Sophia. This was done by the Emperor Justinian in A. D. 532. The church was first built by the Emperor Constantine the Great, in A. D. 326.' He dedicated it to the supreme Wisdom, *Logia*, of God, Jesus Christ. It is from this that the church derives its name of St. Sophia. In A. D. 358, either because it was found too small or had suffered by earthquakes, the church of St. Sophia was rebuilt on a larger scale by the Emperor Constantine. In A. D. 404 it was set on fire by the people in revenge for the exile of the Patriarch, John the Golden-mouthed. The roof and part of the chancel were then destroyed. It is stated that the throne of this Patriarch and his pulpit were saved from that fire. They are still preserved in the present patriarchal church at Constantinople. St. Sophia was again restored by the Emperor Theodosius in A. D. 415. It was again set on fire and entirely destroyed at the time of the revolt of " Vinca," in A. D. 531. This was in the reign of the Emperor Justinian. On the suppression of that revolt and the re-establishment of order in his capital, Justinian decided to restore the church of St. Sophia. To him is due the exquisite style in which we see it at the present day. The work of restoration was confided by the Emperor to two architects, Anthemius Tralliainus and Ysidore the Melisian. This unparalleled production of their genius speaks, and will continue to speak, their fame for ages. While these architects and engineers were drawing up their plans and discussing the various scientific questions connected with the work, the Emperor, with that energy and activity which formed the principal traits of his character, was busily occupied in getting together the necessary material and having the space cleared for the erection of the wonderful edifice. It is related that immense sums had to be paid as compensation to owners of the property that had to be pulled down. As an instance, we are told that a widow of the name of Anne had a piece of property valued at eighty-five litres of gold—equal to about twenty thousand dollars. This she persistently refused to give up for less than five hundred litres of gold, or one hundred and twenty-five thousand dollars. The matter was reported to the Emperor. He arose at once and proceeded in person to the widow's house, with the object of persuading her to reduce her demand. When the woman heard of Justinian's approach she ran out to meet him. She fell at his feet. She there and then made a free grant of her property, on one condition only. It was this: that at her death she should be buried beneath the entrance to the new church.

Meanwhile messengers were despatched in different directions by the Emperor to procure the finest colored marble and other valuable material. All the museums and treasuries of the state were ransacked for works of art and treasures of every description with which to adorn the church. It was intended to be a lasting monument of Christianity and of Byzantine architectural taste and art. Everything having been got ready, the foundation-stone of the new edifice was laid by the Emperor on the 23d of February, A. D. 532. The work was completed in about six years. The expense amounted to three thousand Roman quintals of gold, or about seventy million dollars.

Pure gold and precious stones were, so to speak, strewn about in every part of the interior. The edifice presented such an imposing and magnificent aspect that the Emperor Justinian, when entering it on the day of its consecration, gave vent to the exultation he felt in these words:

"I have surpassed thee, O Solomon!"

The resolutions passed by the four Œcumenical synods and the efforts of the emperors of the eastern portion of the Roman empire to suppress heresies in the orthodox Church were not entirely successful. The opinions propagated by Nestorius, and afterward by the Archimandrite Eutychius, had taken root in

*Metrophanês, by the mercy of God, Archbishop of Constantinople, New Rome, and Œcumenical Patriarch.*

In modum Graek

+ Μητροφανης, ἐλέῳ Θεοῦ Ἀρχιεπίσκοπος Κωνσταντινουπόλεως, Νέας Ρώμης καὶ Οἰκουμενικος Πατριάρχης...

FAC-SIMILE SIGNATURE OF ŒCUMENICAL PATRIARCH, METROPHANÈS III., A. D. 1567.

several parts of the empire. This was principally in Syria and Egypt. In these countries the faction that had embraced the teachings of Eutychius was daily increasing in number. They were known by the name of Monophysites. As the word implies, they were believers only in one (the human) nature of Christ. They were also called Jacobites, after one of their principal reformers, Jacob Baradæus.

In the larger towns of Syria and Egypt, however, which were under the immediate influence of the Byzantine monarchy through its political and ecclesiastical representatives, orthodoxy still reigned supreme. It was principally in the more distant provinces that these heresies found the larger number of converts. Imperial and patriarchal edicts, which it would take too long to enumerate, were made to induce these dissenters to return to orthodoxy. Certain concessions were offered on the part of the Established Church. These attempts, and the efforts of the Fifth Œcumenical Synod, convoked in Constantinople by the Emperor Justinian in A. D. 553 for a similar purpose, proved abortive. Syria and Egypt were lost to the Byzantine monarchy and taken by the Arabs in A. D. 640. Thereafter, all attempts at conciliation having been considered useless or unnecessary, these dissenters were left to establish a Church of their own. This Church is still existing. It constitutes the only non-conformist community of the orthodox Church.

The attempts made, up to the time of the Arab conquest, to bring back the Monophysites to the orthodox creed had the opposite effect. They largely contributed in producing a new doctrine. This carried away many of the orthodox who had shown a willingness to make a concession to the Nestorians. They were willing to acknowledge that Christ, though endowed with two different natures, had only one will. These concessionists received the name of Monothelites. This name distinguishes them from the Monophysites on the one hand, and the staunch orthodox on the other, who were opposed to any concession. This doctrine of the Monothelites first made its appearance in A. D. 639. It did not begin to attract any attention until the year A. D. 678, in the reign of Constantine Pogonatos. This emperor determined to root it out effectually. After taking the opinion of the Pope of Rome in the matter, he called together the Sixth Œcumenical Synod. It was held in Constantinople in A. D. 680. There were present at this synod 289 prelates, including the Patriarchs of Constantinople and Antioch, and representatives of the Pope, of all the Bishops of the West, and of the Patriarch of Jerusalem. The synod passed a solemn resolution to the effect that the orthodox had always acknowledged, and would continue to acknowledge, Christ as endowed with two different natures, united, but not to be confounded. These two different wills the council held to be distinct from but never opposed to each other.

The Emperor sanctioned this resolution. He issued an edict forbidding all further discussion on the subject, upon pain of degradation as regarded men in Holy Orders, and confiscatory of their property and exile as regarded laymen.

After this the slight bonds which still existed between the orthodox Church and the dissenting communities in Syria, Egypt, Armenia and Persia were entirely broken asunder. Orthodoxy then became strictly confined to the Greek nation. There it continued for several ages afterward, until it was propagated among the neighboring Slavonic race.

The Sixth Synod, like its predecessor, the Fifth Œcumenical Synod, had occupied itself exclusively with the discussion of dogmatical questions. These were the most pressing and ostensibly the only object for which it was called together. But there were at the time other matters of no less importance that required attention. There was especially need of certain reforms. These were in regard to ecclesiastical discipline and the private life of the clergy. The laxity in both became sadly felt by the Church itself. Accordingly the reformers prevailed upon the Emperor to call another synod. This was done in A. D. 691, in order to complete the work of the last two convocations. This synod goes by the name of the Trullus or Arched Chamber Synod. The chamber in which it was held had an arched roof. The synod voted 102 canons. Six of these the Roman Church subsequently refused to acknowledge. Two among these six resolutions deserve special mention. They afterward exercised great influence in the relations between the Eastern and Western Churches. These two are the 13th and 86th canons. By the first, marriage was made permissible to the clergy; by the second, it was determined that thereafter the bishops of Rome and Constantinople should enjoy equal rank in Church hierarchy.

These two resolutions subsequently became very important factors in consummating the entire severance of the two Churches. They have always been most resolutely upheld by the Greek and denied by the Latin Church. Nearly ten centuries after the Trullian synod, these two resolutions were the first to be inscribed on the standard raised by the founders of the Protestant religion.

For some time after this synod the Eastern Church may be said to have enjoyed comparative tranquillity. In the year A. D. 754 the question of the worship of the images and pictures of the saints was suddenly started. It culminated in a resolution passed by a synod called by the Emperor Constantine V. This resolution required that all such images and pictures be removed from the different churches, monasteries, public places and private houses. It not only forbid their worship, but rendered it an offense to make an image or paint a picture of Christ, the Virgin Mary, or any of the saints.

This resolution was sanctioned by the Emperor. It gave rise to repeated disturbances. It was afterward canceled by the Seventh Œcumenical Synod. This synod assembled at Nicæa A. D. 787, in the reign of the Empress Irene. It was under the presidency of the Patriarch of Constantinople, Tarasius. By the decision of this synod the pictures of saints were restored to the churches, " as contributing," according to the words of the decision, " to a more appropriate adornment of the places of worship, and as lasting memorials of the martyrs of the Church, from whose lives the people might derive profitable lessons." The synod further determined that, though it was right to bestow a certain veneration on such pictures, worship was due to God alone.

This was the last of the Œcumenical synods that are acknowledged by the Greek Church.

The writer has referred to the Œcumenical synods at some length. This he has done in chronological order, while entering into most of the details which preceded and followed them. Upon their decision actually rests, up to the present day, the whole edifice of the Eastern orthodox Church, both as regards its doctrines and its government in general.

Having submitted my manuscript on this head to those learned in the ecclesiastical lore of the Greek Church, it has received approbation as a just and temperate disquisition upon one of the most important movements of the human mind, in its search after spiritual truth and salvation.

The severance of the Church of the East from that of the West was *de facto* accomplished in A. D. 1054. Among various causes which, the orthodox allege, were instrumental in bringing this about, there was one principal cause, namely : the persistent striving, from the earliest times, of the Popes to obtain absolute dominion over the whole Christian Church.

In the West the Popes scarcely met with any obstacles in effecting their purpose. By the ninth century all the Churches in Europe, formerly independent or otherwise, except that of Ireland, had already acknowledged the supremacy of Rome. The different Churches in the East, however, held firmly to their ancient traditions. They opposed at all times a determined resistance to the efforts made to subrogate them to the Papacy. The Popes naturally seized every possible opportunity to assert their position. They denounced the Eastern prelates as disobedient churchmen.

It was for this reason that the relations between the two Churches were never of a very friendly nature. But up to the ninth or tenth century amicable relations were at no time actually interrupted.

In A. D. 857 the Patriarch of Constantinople, Ignatius, was deposed by the Emperor, Michael III. The Patriarch had been in great disfavor at the court. This was owing to some violent language that he had been using concerning the prevalent immorality. The Emperor, to make up to the clergy and the people for this arbitrary measure, offered the patriarchal throne to Photius, a layman. The latter had great renown and universal respect, because of his learning, his eminent qualities and his aristocratic descent. Photius at first declined the offer. At last he was obliged to accept. The clergy and the people loudly clamored in his favor. He was duly promoted, in the space of a few days, through the different ecclesiastical grades. He was ultimately ordained a bishop and raised to the patriarchal office. This was not the first instance of a layman having been at once raised to the highest dignity in the Church. There was no special law to the contrary at that time. This practice had to be resorted to on certain special occasions. On this occasion there was a faction comprising the friends of the ex-Patriarch. They declared the election unlawful. Furthermore, the disturbances resulting from the two respective decisions relating to the worship of images had not yet entirely disappeared.

Under these circumstances Photius and the Emperor Michael agreed to convene a synod to discuss Church matters in general Among the prelates invited to attend was, as usual, the Pope of Rome. Nicholas was then Pope. He took this opportunity to assert his claim to supremacy. He replied to the invitation by letters addressed to Photius and the Emperor. He expressed in lofty terms his disapproval of the arbitrary deposition of Ignatius, and of the uncanonical election of Photius. He did not, however, refuse to send representatives to the synod. This synod assembled in Constantinople in A. D. 861. It declared, by a large majority, the election of Photius to be perfectly valid. This decision exasperated the Pope to such an extent that he called immediately a synod of his own bishops at Rome, and obtained from them a decision placing Photius under the ban of excommunication. Photius retaliated in A. D. 867 by convoking another synod. This, in its turn, pronounced excommunication against the Pope Nicholas and his adherents. At this point, Basil, the Macedonian, usurped the empire by the murder of the Emperor Michael III. Basil deposed Photius and recalled the Patriarch Ignatius. The latter, in revenge for the humiliation he had been made to suffer, called a synod in Constantinople in A. D. 869. Under the pressure brought to bear upon it by Ignatius and the numerous representatives of the Pope, the synod decided in favor of the right of the latter to exercise absolute rule over the whole Christian Church. This synod is recognized by the Roman Catholic Church as the Eighth Œcumenical Synod. Its action was, however, denounced ten years later, when Photius was reinstated in the patriarchal dignity. This was done by another synod, very numerously attended. It also ratified the acts of the synod convoked in A. D. 867 by Photius. Thus the severance of the Churches, or schism, as it is called, was brought about. Thenceforward, the relations between the Churches of the East and the West became practically, though not yet officially, interrupted. They were broken off entirely in A. D. 1054 under the circumstances already related.

Subsequently, attempts to effect a reconciliation were made at different times by some of the Byzantine emperors. Being hardly pressed by barbarous incursions from Asia, they thought that by conciliating the Pope they might succeed in obtaining assistance against these enemies from some of the European states. These attempts were opposed by the orthodox. To secure the aid of the Pope would involve a sacrifice of the independence of the Eastern Church and its traditions. The clergy and people of the East raised such a cry of indignation that all further attempts of this nature had to be abandoned. The last of these attempts for reconciliation was made by the Emperor John Palæologos VII. This was in the middle of the fifteenth century, at a time when the Emperor was very hardly pressed by the Turks. The latter had already conquered the greater part of the Byzantine empire. At this time they were threatening the capital itself. The Emperor in this emergency went, A. D. 1439, to Florence, with the avowed purpose of effecting a reconciliation of the Churches. With him were the Patriarch of Constantinople, the Bishop of Ephesus and other noted prelates of the Eastern Church. The Greek dignitaries expected to discuss freely all questions and settle all differences Instead of this they were, it is said, compelled to sign an agreement acknowledging the rule of the Pope and the doctrines of the Roman Church. When the news of this capitulation reached Constantinople there arose a fearful clamor among the clergy and people. They loudly protested against union upon such terms, or any union at all.

Two synods were then called, one in Jerusalem in A. D. 1443, and the other in Constantinople in A. D. 1451. Both synods stoutly denounced the agreement in question. It was declared null and void, on the ground that it had been forcibly extracted from the prelates who accompanied the Emperor to Italy. This action aided the Turkish capture of the city.

From its establishment, up to the time to which we have arrived in this short sketch, the Eastern orthodox Church had always been governed strictly in accordance with the rules laid down by its various synods and its principal law-givers. The interference of the Byzantine emperors in questions both dogmatical and administrative, was considered proper. It was in imitation of the like privilege enjoyed by the kings of Israel. Following their example, the emperors on taking possession of the throne were solemnly anointed. They thus considered themselves as becoming invested with a certain sacred character. Hence the Emperor, as we have seen, called together the synods. He sanctioned the election of the Patriarchs. He reserved to himself the undisputed right, on certain occasions, of deposing them and appointing others of his own choice. When the Patriarch happened to be in favor at court he became all-powerful.

In the mean time the extent of the jurisdiction of the Patriarchs of Constantinople was daily increasing. Especially was this the case after the neighboring Slav nations, and notably the Bulgarians and Russians, had embraced Christianity and had become members of the orthodox Church. On the other hand, the jurisdiction of the Patriarchs of the East became sadly curtailed after Egypt, Syria and Palestine fell into the hands of the Arabs. The patriarchates of Jerusalem and Antioch were subjected to considerable oppression on the part of the Crusaders. The latter drove out the Patriarchs and appointed Latins in their stead.

Although efforts had been made in former times to turn the Slavonic races to Christianity, little was accomplished until the ninth and tenth centuries. The Bulgarians were converted by two monks from Salonica, named Methodius and Kyrillos. This was during the patriarchate of Photius. He largely contributed to their conversion. The monk Methodius persuaded the barbarian king of the Bulgarians, Bogore, to embrace the Christian religion. In order to convert the king, this monk displayed before him a picture representing in striking colors the Day of Judgment. It also portrayed the felicity of the just in paradise, and the tortures to which the wicked were to be subjected in the future state. The king, it is related, was so impressed with the picture and so frightened at the sight of the tortures, that he forthwith consented to be baptized. His example was followed by the whole of his people.

The Russians were admitted to Christianity about one hundred years after the Bulgarians. This was in the reign of the Empress Olga. She came expressly to Constantinople in A. D. 955, to be baptized. It is related of Vladimir, her grandson, that he sent a mission, consisting of a number of Russian nobles, to different countries to study the different religions. The members of this mission, after visiting other parts, came to Constantinople. Here they were wonderstruck with the splendor and impressiveness of the Greek worship. On their return to Russia they recommended the orthodox faith to their emperor, as the most preferable. The king accordingly hastened to adopt it. Vladimir received baptism in A. D. 988.   He at once compelled all his subjects to be baptized.   They were baptized in groups in the river Dnieper.

For several years the successive Metropolitan bishops of Russia were Greeks.   They came from and were ordained in Constantinople.   At first they made Kieff their cathedral town.   Afterward they removed to Moscow.   The Russian Church remained under the immediate control of the patriarchate of Constantinople until the sixteenth century.   About this time the Patriarch Jeremiah II. happened to go to Russia in order to collect subscriptions in aid of the poverty-stricken churches under Turkish rule.   At the urgent request of the Czar and the Russian clergy, the Patriarch conferred upon the Metropolitan of Moscow the title of Patriarch of Russia.   Notwithstanding this, the Church of Russia still continued dependent upon the Œcumenical throne of Constantinople. We have already related how Peter the Great suppressed the patriarchal office in Russia in A. D. 1722.   He then appointed a synod of bishops.   It has since been governing the Church of Russia.

We now come to a new, and the last, period in the history of the Greek orthodox Church.   In A. D. 1453 Constantinople was taken by the Turks.   The Greek Church had hitherto enjoyed all the privileges of a state religion.   Now it suddenly found itself in the power of foreign rulers of a widely different creed.   But the conqueror, Mahomed II., was as clever as a politician as he was dauntless as a warrior.   He carefully considered and fully understood the truth of the axiom, " Parcere subjectos et debellare superbos.' He was anxious to quiet the fears and stop the further exodus of the panic-stricken citizens, who were flying in every direction.   He immediately turned his attention to the Church.   Being apprised that the patriarchal throne was vacant in consequence of the death of its late occupant, this Sultan orders the election of a new Patriarch.   He directs the election to be carried out in strict accordance with the forms hitherto observed on such occasions.   Under the Byzantine emperors it was the custom to install the Patriarch-elect with imposing ceremony.   After his election in the Patriarchal Church by a conclave of the higher clergy and representatives of the people, the Patriarch proceeds in state to the palace.   There he is received by the Emperor surrounded by his court.   The Emperor presents him with a golden staff.   It is ornamented with precious stones.   He receives a high-bred gray horse out of the imperial stables, richly caparisoned. On leaving the palace, after his audience with the Emperor, the Patriarch mounts this steed and, attended by a numerous suite, proceeds in great state to the Cathedral Church. Here his enthronement takes place.

Mahomed the Conqueror determines to follow the example of the Byzantine emperors in this respect. The election of the new Patriarch, Gennadius by name, is announced. The Sultan then requests the Patriarch to come, in the usual manner, to the palace. Upon his arrival at the palace the Sultan receives him with great honors. He invites the Patriarch to luncheon. When the Patriarch rises to depart, the Sultan presents him with the usual golden staff. He accompanies him, notwithstanding the Patriarch's protestations, down to the outer court of the palace. Here a magnificent steed is waiting. The Sultan actually aids the Patriarch to mount. He orders all the court officials and a large body-guard to accompany him to the Patriarchal Church of the Holy Apostles. Here his enthronement takes place, with all the former pomp and ceremony. Here was indeed a clever conqueror. He knew how to hold, by gentleness, what he had won by force !

This custom of the Sultan's reception of the Patriarch-elect continues to be observed until the year A. D. 1657. It is then interrupted, and the ceremonial is confined to a visit of the Patriarch-elect, accompanied by twelve bishops, to the Sublime Porte. At this place they are received by the Grand Vizier. This lasts until A. D. 1840. Then the former custom is revived by the Sultan, Abdul Medjid, father of the present Sultan. This custom still continues to be practised on the election of a new Patriarch. Now, an aide-de-camp of the Sultan attends upon the Patriarch-elect, and accompanies him in court-carriages to the palace. There he is received in solemn audience by the Sultan. Instead of the former golden staff, the Patriarch-elect is invested with the Grand Cordon of the Imperial Order of the Medjidié. On leaving the palace, the Patriarch and his suite proceed in state to the Sublime Porte. Here he pays official visits to the Grand Vizier and the Minister of Public Worship. Thence, in the same state, he proceeds to the Patriarchal Church at the Fanar. There the usual ceremony of the enthronement takes place. The Patriarch is received at the entrance of the church by the Metropolitan of Heraclea, who hands him the patriarchal pastoral staff.

Besides these honors, Mahomed the Conqueror conferred upon the first Patriarch elected after the taking of Constantinople, by letters patent, the dignity of Ethnarch, or head of the Orthodox Community under Turkish rule. He also granted him judicial powers in all matters coming under the jurisdiction of the Church. The Patriarch and the archbishops and bishops under him were further exempted from the payment of all tribute and taxes. By this means the Conqueror succeeds in securing the sympathies of the conquered people. The conquered Greeks thus preserved their religion intact, and, through that religion, as they fondly deem, their national character and their present social position in the world.

The privileges thus conferred upon the Church and its head, and especially the new dignity of Head of the Orthodox Community, carried with them weighty responsibilities. The effects of these were not long in being felt in the most acute manner. As head of the Orthodox Community, the Patriarch was held responsible for the acts of that community in every part of the Ottoman empire. The Church of the East and its dignitaries had often thereafter to atone for acts opprobrious to the state committed by the Greek subjects of the Porte. The execution of the Patriarch Gregory V. and of the members of his synod, in A. D. 1821, for their collusion with the Greek revolution, affords one of many instances. The Patriarch Gregory was dragged forth by emissaries of the Porte from the Patriarchal Church at the Fanar. This was during the service on Easter Sunday in that year. He was hanged by the neck to one of the gates of the Patriarchate. This gate has remained closed ever since. His body was left hanging till night set in. It was then cut down and thrown into the sea. Next day it was picked up by the captain of a Greek merchant vessel, and carried to Odessa. There, by order of the Czar, it was buried with regal honors. In A. D. 1871 the remains were claimed by the Hellenic government. They were given up and conveyed in a Greek man-of-war to Athens. They are buried in the church of the classic Metropolis. This act of the hanging of Gregory and his synod was the last of the kind committed by the Turks; but there are two sides to this Oriental question.

The orthodox Patriarchate of Constantinople is styled now the Great Church. This name it simply derives from the Church of St. Sophia, in consequence of its size. St. Sophia was called, in the Byzantine period, " the large church." After the taking of Constantinople, when St. Sophia was transformed into a mosque, and the Patriarch removed his seat to another church, the name was preserved to the Patriarchate. This was done as an indication of supremacy over the other sees of the East. The patriarchate was at first removed to its former locality—the Church of the Apostles. The Patriarch Gennadius was soon obliged to abandon it, owing to its distance from the Christian quarters of the town. He betook him to another church, dedicated to the Virgin Mary. The Church of the Apostles was then pulled down by order of the Sultan. Upon its site was erected the magnificent mosque known to this day, after its founder, as the Mosque of Sultan Mehmed. In A. D. 1607 the church which then served as the Patriarchate was occupied by the Turks. They transformed it into a mosque, under the name of Fetié Djami, that is, " The Temple of Victory." The Patriarchate was then removed to the Church of St. George, at the Fanar, on the Golden Horn. Here it remains installed up to the present time.

The Œcumenical Patriarch, in his administration of the affairs of the Church, was, up to the year A. D. 1860, assisted by a synod of twelve bishops. In that year a number of reforms were introduced. One of these provided for the formation of a representative council. It consisted of a certain number of clerical and lay members. The former were to be nominated by the Patriarch, and the latter to be returned by ballot from the different parishes of the capital. This council still exists. There are now, therefore, two different bodies sitting at the Patriarchate—the synod of twelve bishops, and the mixed council. The synod occupies itself exclusively with spiritual matters. The discussion of administration and financial questions is reserved for the council. The Patriarch presides *ex officio* over the sittings of both these assemblies. The Churches of Russia, Greece, Servia, Roumania and Bulgaria were formerly both administratively and spiritually under the immediate jurisdiction of the Patriarchate of Constantinople. Now they are self-governed, but with a due regard to the decisions of the Patriarch in all spiritual matters.

The list of bishops and Patriarchs who, from the time of the apostle Andrew up to the present, have occupied in succession the episcopal throne of Constantinople, comprises in all about two hundred and fifty names.  Its present occupant, Dionysius V., just elected, is reputed to be a man of sound learning and excellent administrative qualities.  He was elected in February, 1887, on the resignation of Joachim IV., who has since died.

The ritual, or form of worship of the Greek orthodox Church, has ever remained intact.  Under the Turks, owing to the diminution of the means of existence, the ritual has been divested of some of the imposing splendor with which the services were conducted in the Byzantine period.  The service comprises a number of hymns and psalms appropriate to the various festivals and the liturgy.  During the service, the Eucharist is conducted with imposing devotion by the officiating priest.

Prominent among the doctrines of the Greek orthodox Church is the belief in the transubstantiation or the transformation of the bread and wine into the body and blood of Christ.  This is attributed to the invisible co-operation of the Holy Ghost.  The Greek Church is said to possess one great advantage over the other Christian communities.  It is this: the Gospel is read in its places of worship in the Greek language, in which, it is generally admitted, it was originally written.

Baptism, according to the rites of the Greek Church, involves complete immersion in the water.  The immersion is repeated thrice, "In the name of the Father, of the Son and of the Holy Ghost."  After the third immersion the child is anointed with the Holy Chrism.  This ointment is specially prepared by the clergy and blessed by the Patriarch.  This form of the rite conforms to the philological meaning of the word $Βαπτίζο$, and is often adverted to by the great body of the Protestant Baptists in confirmation of their creed.

Confession forms one of the sacred rites of the Greek Church.  It is not inculcated in the sense or the form in which it is exercised by Roman Catholics.  Confession, according to the orthodox ideas, takes simply the shape of a conference between the member of a congregation and the minister.  Of course, this is an attenuation of the Catholic confession.  The subject of the conference is as to the former's competency to partake of the Holy Communion.  Confession must always precede this rite.

Besides the festivals common with all the other Christian Churches, such as Easter Sunday, Christmas Day and Epiphany, the Greek Church has only one other festival particularly its own.

DIONYSIUS V., THE GREEK PATRIARCH—RECENTLY ELECTED.

That is the festival of Orthodoxy. It is observed on the first Sunday in Lent. It is in commemoration of the restoration of the pictures of the saints to the churches.

There are fixed days in the year on which the Patriarch officiates in person. These are Christmas Day, Epiphany, Good Friday, Easter Sunday, the festival of Orthodoxy and the feast of St. Andrew, the founder of the Church of Constantinople. The service as performed by the Patriarch is most imposing. Twelve bishops, six priests and six deacons, all in full canonicals made of rich stuffs, take part with him in the celebration.

The Greek Church dictates but does not now actually impose, except on the clergy, the observation of a limited number of fasts. Of these the principal are, one of forty days' duration preceding Christmas Day, and another extending over the seven weeks in Lent.

There are no monkish orders in the Greek Church, as they are understood and organized by the Roman Catholics. During the Byzantine era there was a large contingent of men in Holy Orders who chose to live in seclusion. A great number of monasteries were gradually established by these devotees. They were richly endowed by the state and private individuals. Most of these monasteries were destroyed at the Turkish conquest. Their property was confiscated. Since then the number of orthodox monks has greatly decreased. At the present day it has dwindled to only a few hundred. They are concentrated at Mount Athos. This has always been the great and is now the only centre of orthodox monastic life. From this circumstance it is largely known among the Greeks as the Holy Mountain.

The first monastery at Athos was founded in the ninth century, in the reign of the Emperor Basil, the Macedonian. There are now about forty monasteries on the Holy Mountain. Each has its own separative organization. They constitute one great and united federation. The monasteries existing in different parts of the empire in the Byzantine period, and especially those within the precincts of the capital, are found, on close examination, to have been nothing more than great seats of learning. At these the orthodox clergy were mostly educated. They were thus enabled to rank high in the world of culture and science. After the Conquest, these monasteries, or academies, were suppressed. Soon after, learning became almost extinct among the Christians in the

East. The greater part of the inferior orthodox clergy continued for many years, as they are now, to be immersed in crass ignorance.

Commencing with the present century, however, and more especially since the granting, after the Crimean War, of the charter in favor of the Christian population of the Ottoman empire, the condition of the clergy has improved. The larger portion are now attaining to the eminent position occupied in the Byzantine period.

As attempts were made, both before and after the final rupture in A. D. 1054, to effect a reconciliation between the orthodox and the Roman Catholic Churches, so also attempts have, at different times, been made to draw nearer the Greek orthodox and the Protestant Churches. The barriers are much less insurmountable than those separating the Protestant Churches from that of Rome. Hitherto these attempts have proved futile. This is owing to the stern refusal of the orthodox Church to agree to any concessions which, even indirectly, might affect its own doctrine or its ancient traditions. Not only the Church, but the Greek nation itself, holds firmly to the doctrines and traditions of the Church. This strict adherence has preserved the national character and language. It has enabled the Church and nation to hold their own through many centuries of foreign rule. The Greek race regard the orthodox Church in a double sense : it is an anchor of salvation, in a religious and a national point of view. It has harbored them safely, as a Christian people and as a nation, amidst all the tempestuosities of revolution.

The extent of the civil authority exercised by Christian religious communities in Turkey, through the graces of governmental toleration, is remarkable. I have seen myself—so as to verify the statement—that there is a prison connected with the Greek patriarchate. I will not vouch, as some have done, that minors who have attempted to turn Mussulmans are here confined for their apostacy. I believe the statement to be true to some extent. While the Turks threaten or banish those who discard the Mahometan religion, they allow the Greek Church the like privilege. Out of this toleration comes much of the trouble to the Protestant teachers from America. They are striving nobly to elevate the races of European and Asiatic Turkey, and that too despite the bigotry, not of the Moslem, but of so-called Christians.

We have seen that under the decree of Constantine the Great, Christianity became the state religion of the whole Roman empire in A. D. 323. Then was established the see of Constantinople, with its Metropolitan bishop, equal in dignity with the Metropolitan bishops of Jerusalem, Antioch, Alexandria, Ephesus, Corinth and Rome. At the present day much remains of the formula, ceremony and organization which the orthodox Greek Church perfected and perpetuated through the centuries following this foundation.

At the end of last year, His Holiness, Monseigneur Joachim the Fourth, owing to ill health, asked leave to resign his office as the Patriarch of the Greek Church. The Ottoman government was asked, according to prescriptive regulations, to confirm the resignation. His Holiness desired to retire to the island of Scio, his former home. The requests were granted. The Metropolitan of Cæsarea was made the *locum tenens* of the patriarchal throne.

Joachim IV. always received much attention and kindness from the Sultan. He was elected in 1879. He was only fifty-eight years of age when he retired from the patriarchate. He built the grand school at Fanar, on the banks of the Bosporus.

The Porte once attempted to restrict the rights of the Patriarch Joachim, who was suspected of doubtful loyalty to the Porte and of having too much Greek patriotism. This was inconsistent with the loyalty due to the Turk. It was some time before the jealousies were settled and the relations of the Porte and the Church reconciled. Joachim protested, and then tendered his resignation. As he represented five millions of Greeks in the empire, to say nothing of the Greeks outside of it, and as the Church of Russia was a cognate religion, the moderation and good sense of the present Sultan prevailed. The matter was satisfactorily settled. The ancient rights, recognized and confirmed by Mahmoud the Conqueror of Constantinople, were restored to the Greeks.

The Sultan is potential in these matters of ecclesiastical control, even when it does not affect his own religion. Questions preliminary and otherwise, as to the recent election of a Patriarch, had been mooted at the meetings of the subordinate councils. These concerned the delegates to the Supreme Council  An appeal was made, as in the olden time, unto Cæsar. The question was submitted to the Porte and the Council of State for decision. Thus, at the present day, Mahomet controls the Greek Church in the last appeal, as to its ecclesiastical personages and polity.

In the last interview which Joachim had with his sovereign, an additional fifteen thousand piastres were given him to defray the expense of the voyage to the Grecian islands. On his departure from the Sultan he was given the special honors of the palace. Honors were again heaped upon the ex-Patriarch on his retiring to seek health among the islands and at the Broussa Spas; notwithstanding this, the election of his successor had already taken place, and all the salutations consequent thereupon had been exchanged. Surely this is an example of toleration not unworthy of the attention of some Christian sects and countries.

In these modern days, the hierarchy of the Greek Church is divided into three classes. These are the patriarchs, the archbishops and the bishops, who cannot be married, and are chosen from the monastic orders. Next follow the parochial clergy, who must be married men. Then the monks, who, as stated, are not allowed to marry.

There are many divisions of monks. Some are ascetic. The latter live apart in cottages. They approach the condition of Anchorites. Some are Cenobites. The latter are more social in their retirement. The communities have various governments. In some the government resembles a commonwealth. A monetary consideration is sometimes given on entering a fraternity. Then the admitted monk becomes part proprietor of the possessions. Many of the monks do their own work. In the monastery of Mount Sinai the brethren have serfs. These are taken from the Arab tribes. Most of the monasteries are in a state of decay. None of them are what they used to be in the former times of monastic power.

In a little volume called the " Isles of the Princes," published contemporaneously with this volume, by the Putnams, the author has endeavored to picture the life and habits, as well as the structures and localities, of these institutions.

It may be that the modern orthodox Greek is thoroughly pious. If his phraseology, in some parts of Turkey, is competent evidence in his behalf, it will be hard to prove that he is not always thinking of his Maker. When you bid him good by, he says :

"In the name of God, Farewell."

If you ask for water at dinner, an orthodox gentleman will reply :

" By God! I will give it to you, for God's sake."

If some one should ask whether the cook has boiled the vegetables sufficiently, the probable answer is :

"In the name of God, he has not."

This is not pure profanity. It emanates from the habit of orthodox veneration. Still, it grates on Occidental ears.

The devotion to the Greek Church of the peasant, especially if he be a Slav, is something astounding to Western Christians. If the banner of their Father, the Czar, were to be raised to-morrow against the Turk, there would be another Crusade, with all the Middle Age fanaticism. The number of pilgrims who passed through Odessa in the year A. D. 1886 for Jerusalem, Mount Athos, and other sacred places was five thousand. These were mostly of the agricultural class.

Yet sometimes this Church, even in the midst of the Greeks, has its little drawbacks. In the spring of A. D. 1887 a strike was going on in the island of Scio—Homer's own island. It was a strange strike. The people did not promptly pay their tithes to the Church. The priests refused to exercise their office. The priests appealed to the Bishop. He tried to help his clergy by putting the excited parishes under his interdict. The ecclesiastical interdict was a new thing at this time. It was familiar enough in the Middle Ages. When it occurs, the clergy must abstain from the exercise of their ministry. There is no baptism, no marriage, no masses and no burying of the dead with the rites of the Church. In this dire extremity some of the laity perform the most pressing offices, such as burying the dead. Still, the departed are buried without ecclesiastical aid or ceremony. It is not a satisfactory burial for the corpse or its friends. The people become more or less restless and confused. The women are unhappy. What do they do? They request the secular governor, a Turk, to make the Christian priests who are on a strike, return to their duty ! The governor asks the Porte for directions. Thus it is again, that even in a quarrel between a Christian priest and his flock, redress rests in the hand of the Caliph of Mahomet !

It is very hard, however, to be rid of ritual. It is a part of that symbolism, art and commemoration which sways all souls that look to a future world; for there will ever be a class of minds which require architecture, music or ceremony, even at the grave, to lead them up through and despite of the contaminated reason of man to a higher world, whose peace passeth all understanding.

It is owing as much to its ritual as to its fixedness, that the Greek Church has become so powerful and permanent. Its obedience is more passive than that of the Latin Church. It is less restless than that Church. In Russia it claims immortality because of its immobility. When the Latin Church was contending in politics and fighting evils in the moral realm, the Greek was contending over frivolous questions, such as, "Did the Saviour ascend in his robes, or naked?"

But for its logomachy, it might have held Constantinople to-day, by a generous unity with Rome.

# CHAPTER XXII.

THE LATIN CHURCH—THE ARMENIAN-CATHOLIC—THE ARMENIAN
GREGORIAN CHURCHES—BULGARIAN AND OTHER CHURCHES.

To the general reader, in America and Europe, it is unnecessary to give either an analysis or a history of the Catholic Church. Its tenets and annals are discussed in the Occident with fullness and freedom. Its life in the East, where it is known as the Latin Church, as distinguished from the Greek Church, it is not a part of these Diversions to portray. Originally championed by France, inspired by the Crusades, the companion of the commercial enterprise of France, Spain, and especially Italy, it has left an indelible impression on the land of its early apostles. The conflicts between the Greek and Latin Churches for supremacy and for the guardianship of the Holy Places, and other subordinate contests, mark the importance and strength of the Latin Church and the dominancy of the Holy Father at Rome over the Latin religionists of the East. It requires no prolonged residence in Constantinople, Jerusalem, Smyrna, Alexandria or the other prominent cities in the Turkish dominion, to ascertain that the good and learned men and the unselfish and devoted women of the Latin Church have a field for their exertions in the East which every tolling bell and melodious vesper, from its every church and convent, echo with solemn, sweet vibrations.

The present Pope has followed the plan of his predecessors in reference to those Eastern communions which had been alienated from the Church of Rome. The heresy of Nestorius, which is as old as the fifth century, gave to Christ two natures, one divine and the other human, and which held it to be an abomination to call Mary the Mother of God; and that of Eutyches, the contemporary of Nestorius, which denied this double nature of Christ, holding that he was entirely God previous to the Incarnation, and entirely man during the Incarnation—these, together with the schism of Photius, gave to an earlier Leo—viz., Leo III.—infinite concern. He began the work of reconciliation, and he succeeded. The Holy See was thus strengthened in the East. But it was attacked by the Russians or its Greek co-religionists. This was as late as A. D. 1871–72–73 and '74. The vengeful Cossack whip was used to scourge the Catholic devotee. That failing, fines were tried. In A. D. 1875, as will be seen in Father O'Reilly's "Life of Leo XIII.," page 382, fifty thousand persons and twenty-six priests were forced to abjure the Catholic communion and join the orthodox Greek Church. These facts are authentic. They were plainly told to the Czar Nicholas when he visited Rome, and by the Pope himself, with great excitation. During the Turko-Russian War of A. D. 1877–78 some mollification of this persecution was made by the Czar; but it was made out of politic motives. After the war ended, the road to Siberia was again thronged with Catholic martyrs, and the vengeful Cossack whip began to scourge anew.

How did this treatment of Catholics by Russia affect Turkish Catholics? In this way: The Czar is the father of the Slavonic orthodox Church. Many of its members reside in the Turkish dominions. Pilgrims from Turkey go to Rome and lay at the feet of the Holy Father their devotion. These signs of sympathy led to practical measures to unite the Slavonic Catholics closer to the Papal see. The hierarchy was established in Bosnia and Herzegovina.

A college founded at Rome in A. D. 1577, known as the College of St. Athanasius, is a nursery for Greek students. Therein is taught the Catholic liturgy and the Catholic chant in Greek, together with the graces of Greek oratory. Through this medium the Greek colonies and isles, and other places along the Mediterranean where the Greeks reside or their language is spoken, are furnished with Catholic teachers, and its churches are inspired with the ritual of St. Peter.

Catholic churches farther east, even to the borders of Persia, have been in great straits. It is to these venerable churches that special attention has lately been given by Pope Leo XIII. The Chaldean Church had been widowed by the death of a Patriarch. He had been contumacious in his allegiance to the pontificate. But he returned to his duty. After his decease a new Patriarch of "Babylon of the Chaldeans," Monsigneur Abolionan, was elected. The Sultan confirmed his election. The Porte ratified what St. Peter had done. It was a guaranty of protection and toleration. Thus old Mesopotamia was reinstated in its early Christian allegiance, the Moslem consenting.

It would seem, from the history of Catholicism in the East, that the dogma of infallibility had created division there, as it had in Bavaria. The Armenians led in this dissent. This schism left some heart-burning and scars. An attempt was made, with measurable success for a time, to enlist the Sultan on the side of the schismatics. The prudent course of the present Pope has not only healed up the old wounds, but has enfolded, through the aid of the Sultan, those who had been recusant.

It was a great gratification to the Catholics of Turkey when, on the 11th of December, 1880, the Pope rewarded Monseigneur Hassun, who had received much ecclesiastical buffeting, by bestowing upon him the Roman purple. After four centuries the Orient secured another cardinal. The Sultan was honored by the choice. He acknowledges this tribute to his Armenian subject. The Sultans have never lacked in the hospitalities of the Orient.

In furtherance of his plan, the Pope has instituted an Armenian college in Rome. Education is progressing amidst the Armenians and Chaldeans. The Dominicans have a college at Mossoul, on the Tigris. Where Abraham was born, where Babylon rose and fell, where empire came and went in luxury and conquest, and in these domains where the past predominates—the living word, according to the Catholic faith, is being taught to the descendants of these historic people.

It is not this Latin Church to which this chapter is assigned. There is a branch of the Latin Church peculiarly Oriental, which is in close association with the Papal authority at Rome. It is of the Armenian branch that I propose to speak. But this Armenian Catholic Church is itself an offshoot of the Armenian Church proper ; and therefore it is that I begin with a full statement of the system and history of the latter. This statement may have its interest enhanced by the bold attempt of the Russian White Father—the Czar—to capture the land of Armenia, as well by force of arms and steam locomotion as by educational influences and religious propagandism. It is the belief of the writer that Russia would be willing to forego her entrance into Constantinople, and would be content with seeing the Crescent float for many years yet over St. Sophia, provided she could absorb the land about Erzeroum and Trebizond. Nay, Russia would not question the title of the fresh prince of Bulgaria, or the control of that country by its own Sobranjé, or its own autonomy, provided she controls the lofty plateau whence the "four great rivers" pour down their waters in various directions. Then she would have and hold the nucleus of the mountain system of Western Asia, and thus be fortified for the great struggle for which she is preparing, against all comers who challenge her magnificent Asiatic career of conquest.

The fact that the brightest of the Armenian race is being instructed in Robert College and in the United States, and return to the Armenian people as teachers in theology and morality, is significant of that future when the question shall be raised, "Shall it be Cossack or republican?"

The Armenians are a very ancient race. Before their conversion to Christianity they were Fire Worshippers, like many of the other Asiatic nationalities. The Christian faith was introduced into Armenia by the apostle Andrew, toward the end of the third century. This was in the reign of King Tiridatis. From him the new religion received all the patronage and support in his power. Tiridatis subsequently sent Gregory, an Armenian of staunch religious principles and much learning, to Leontius, the Greek Bishop of Cæsarea. The king requested that Leontius would ordain Gregory as a bishop. This request was complied with. Gregory on his return to Armenia baptized the King. The King then ordered the entire population to be baptized in the river Euphrates.

Besides the Armenians, Gregory baptized a large number of Persians, Medes and Assyrians. History gives the number as about four million persons. He founded several churches, and appointed a number of bishops to administer the affairs. Arostanes, a son of Gregory, had been ordained by his father Archbishop Catholicos of the whole of Armenia. Arostanes accompanied King Tiridatis to Nicæa at the time of the assembling of the First Œcumenical Synod. In this synod the Archbishop took a leading part. During their stay in Nicæa, he and King Tiridatis were entertained with special honor by the Emperor Constantine the Great.

In after years the Armenian Church was exposed to severe

trials and tribulations at the hands of the kings of Persia, to whom Armenia had become a tributary. The worst persecutions of the Christians in that part of the world were in the reign of the Persian King Savor. By his orders ten thousand persons were put to death. Men, women and young girls suffered the most horrible tortures. Neither this nor subsequent measures, however, were effectual in suppressing the passionate attachment of the Armenian and Persian Christians to their faith. This attachment to it was so strong that they voluntarily submitted to a royal edict that was issued, ordering every one who acknowledged the Christian religion to be forthwith put to death. The poor Armenian devotees came before the authorities, of their own accord, to declare their faith in Christ. They feared that by remaining silent they should appear to deny Him. At last the Emperor Constantine the Great was apprised of their sufferings. He wrote a strong letter on the subject to Savor. This had the effect of persuading that monarch to cease his tyrannical oppression of the Christians in his dominions.

The doctrines, ritual, and general organization of the Armenian Church were borrowed originally from the Eastern Church. The Armenian Church grew up under the see of Cæsarea. It remained under the partial jurisdiction of that see for nearly a century. The successive Catholicos, or Archbishops, of Armenia were invariably appointed and ordained during that time by the Metropolitans of Cæsarea. Afterward, the Catholicos solicited and obtained his franchise from that see. The Armenian Church then became practically independent. It continued to be in direct communion with the Eastern Church until the assembling of the Fourth Œcumenical Synod. This synod was held in Chalcedon in A. D. 451. The Armenians were unable to attend it, owing to an invasion of the Persians under their king, Toudigerd. This king laid waste the whole country. He carried off the Catholicos and a large number of the Armenian clergy to Persia. They refused to worship the Sacred Fire, and he put them to death. The Armenians, owing to the narrowness of their tongue, did not appreciate the precise meaning of the doctrine of the Incarnation as established by that synod. They imagined that the synod had admitted the Nestorian theory on the subject. This theory, they knew, had been already condemned as heretical. They therefore rejected the decisions of the synod, and broke off all further intercourse with the other Christian Churches. Subsequently, however, they received satisfactory explanations from a mission sent expressly from Constantinople. They then agreed to reconsider the matter. A grand conclave of the Armenian clergy was, accordingly, held in Erzeroum, in the year A. D. 628. The question at issue was carefully considered. Ultimately they decided to withdraw their previous rejection of the decisions of the Fourth Œcumenical Synod. Thus the Armenians recognized the validity of that synod and accepted the precepts laid down by it. But these proceedings do not appear to have met with general approval in Armenia. Shortly afterward a faction headed by a theologian named John Vartabet called another convocation. This assembly unanimously denounced both the Armenian synod, held at Erzeroum, and the Fourth Œcumenical Synod. They refused to accept the decisions of either. The Armenians thus became divided among themselves into two factions.

The strife between these factions lasted for a considerable time. At length the Catholicos Narsès—a man of great administrative ability, with a strong leaning toward the decisive union of the Armenian with the Eastern Church—wrote on the subject to the Emperor of Constantinople, Manuel Comnenus, in A. D. 1170. He requested the Emperor to send some noted theological scholar to Armenia, to discuss the matter and find a means of bringing about the desired union. The object was to put an end to the internal dissensions of the Armenian Church. The Emperor, desiring this, promptly responded to the request of the Catholicos. He sent Lucian Theorianus, a distinguished professor of theology. Narsès went to meet him at Roum-Kalé, a small town on the Black Sea. For several days the two learned men were engaged in discussing the different points on which the Greek and Armenian Churches were at variance. Theorianus argued that the difference had arisen out of erroneous interpretation, on the part of the Armenians, of some of the decisions of the synods and of certain passages of the Scriptures. Narsès was deeply anxious for the removal of the difference. He therefore admitted the arguments of the Greek. On the latter taking his departure, Narsès entrusted him with letters to the Emperor and the Patriarch of Constantinople. These letters admitted his entire acceptance of the precepts of the Eastern Church. He expressed his ardent desire to see the bonds which formerly united the two Churches drawn closely together. He promised to call, at an early day, a general synod of the Armenian bishops. This was for the purpose of arranging the return of their Church to communion with the Eastern Church.

Before this promise could be carried out Narsès died. At first his successor, Gregory IV., showed an eager disposition to follow the course pursued by Narsès on the question at issue. The taking of Constantinople by the Crusaders at this juncture caused a break in the negotiations. A turbulent state of affairs in the East followed this event. The Catholicos changed his views or policy. He approached the Armenians with offers of a tempting nature. He persuaded them to agree to a union with the Roman Church. This proposal was first brought forward at a Synod of the Armenian clergy, held at Adana in A. D. 1314. Subsequently it was discussed more fully at another convocation which assembled at Sis, the capital of the Armenian regency in Cilicia, in A. D. 1367. The union was finally decided upon at a grand synod, held in A. D. 1370 at Erzeroum. At this convention the Armenian Church adopted the doctrine and, to a certain extent, the ritual of the Latin Church. It at the same time placed itself under the jurisdiction and protection of Rome. But this deference to Rome does not appear to have been based upon very strong foundations. Shortly afterward the great body of the Armenians returned to their own persuasion. They re-affirmed their ecclesiastical independence. A small number, however, remained faithful to Rome. This offshoot still survives. Its adherents are known as Armenian Catholics, to distinguish them from the Gregorians. The latter are the followers of Gregory, the first bishop of Armenia. He was the founder of the Armenian Church.

The supreme authority of the Gregorian Church is still, as in former years, in the hands of the Catholicos. He resides in the monastery of Achmiadjin, near Erivan, in Russian Armenia. This monastery covers a large area. It contains three magnificent churches, built close together in the form of a triangle. Next in dignity after the Catholicos comes the Armenian Patriarch of Constantinople. He has a palace at Coum-Capon, in Stamboul. He is acknowledged by the Turkish authorities as chief of the Armenian community. On state occasions he is allowed to take rank

THE ARMENIAN-GREGORIAN PATRIARCH, MONSEIGNEUR VEHABEDIAN.

next after the orthodox Greek Œcumenical Patriarch. The present incumbent is Monseigneur Vehabedian. He is a man of most imposing appearance. I am happy in securing a most superb picture of this prelate. It is presented herein. His features, character and function cannot but interest the American readers, who, if not attracted by the history of the remarkable race of which he is a type, are interested in the progress of that race in the Christian faith, evidenced by so many of their number now sojourning for education in the United States.

Politically, the Armenians ceased to exist as a self-governed nation, as far back as A. D. 223. Armenia was invaded by Alexander the Great. Afterward it was invaded by the Roman legions, under Vespasian. It was subsequently annexed to Persia. It remained thus until A. D. 852. Then it was conquered by the Arabs. In A. D. 1079 it passed into the possession of the Byzantine emperors. It was taken from them in A. D. 1357 by the Mamelukes. Finally, in A. D. 1402, it became a part of the Ottoman empire. It is now dismembered and apportioned between Turkey, Persia and Russia.

The Gregorian-Armenians number 3,725,000 persons. Of these 2,325,000 live in Turkey, 1,000,000 in Russia and 400,000 in Persia. The Catholic Armenians number 80,000 persons. They are mostly in Constantinople and in the larger towns of Turkey. This small community comprises the wealthiest and most respectable families among the Armenians. It is the remnant of that portion of the Church which broke off and remained faithful to Rome when the great body of Armenians denounced the convention signed at Erzeroum and re-asserted the independence of their Church.

Although the Armenian Catholics acknowledge the supremacy of the Church of Rome, they preserve much of the Gregorian form of worship. Their Church is administered quite independently of Rome. Originally, they had but one spiritual chief, bearing the title of Patriarch. He had his seat in the town of Bagarsabat. Then he removed to Sis, in Cilicia. He now resides in the monastery of Vzomar, on Mount Lebanon. But until A. D. 1832 neither this chief nor the community itself were officially recognized as a separate religious institution by the Turkish authorities. It was through the intercession of the French Ambassador in Constantinople that they then obtained permission from the

Sublime Porte to perform openly and freely their religious duties. After this time they had churches of their own. This was a privilege which had before then been denied them. Until this privilege was allowed them, it was necessary for them to have recourse to the Gregorian-Armenian priests for the performance of the rites of baptism, marriage and interment. Their divine service had also to be conducted in the Roman Catholic churches. Upon their official recognition by the state, as a distinct religious community, they obtained the right of electing a second spiritual chief, entirely independent of the one at Mount Lebanon. This is the chief who has his residence at Constantinople, bearing the title of Patriarch. He is described in Turkish, in the Imperial Firman, as Millet Bashi Ermeni Catolic. This title is conferred upon him on his election as chief of the Armeno-Catholic community. The present holder of this office is Monseigneur Azarian. He is a highly distinguished prelate. He belongs to one of the most noted Armenian families. Recently he was the bearer of a superb ring from the Sultan to the Pope. The other spiritual chief of the Armenian Catholic community, who resides on Mount Lebanon, holds, in addition to his other title, that of "Peter." This was conferred by Pope Benedict XIV. On Sundays and great fête days the French flag floats over the Armenian Catholic churches. This is done as a sign of the protection afforded to them by the government of France.

The well-known convent of St. Lazare, in Venice, belongs to the Armenian Catholic community. It is inhabited by the order of Mectarist monks. It is thus called after its founder, Mectar, who died in A. D. 1740. From this convent missionaries used formerly to be sent into Armenia to make proselytes. Their efforts met with such determined resistance, on the part of the Gregorians, that the movement had to be given up. Since that time the Mectarist monks have turned their whole attention to the development of Armenian literature. They have published many useful and very ably written works relating to their national history.

It is not the object of the writer to dilate in this volume upon the religious aspects and divisions of the various Churches of the East, or to express any opinion upon their dissensions. It may be permissible, however, to express the hope that a closer affiliation and unity may soon take into its embrace the whole Church of Christ.

Bulgaria has become prominent in the Oriental question. Her Church is only identical with the Greek Church in doctrine and ritual. It is not now in communication with that Church. It long since rejected the Church of Rome. A quarter of a century ago it ceased to harmonize with the Greek Church. After a controversy extending over twenty years it illustrated its independence by severing its relation with the Patriarch of Constantinople. The Bulgarian Church has now its own Exarch. He is the spiritual head of the Church. Like the other Patriarchs, he resides at Constantinople. His name is Monseigneur Josif. His independence of spirit was shown even against Midhat Pasha at the time the latter was paramount in the councils of the Notables and Reformers. It is one of the strange things connected with the career of Midhat, that he persecuted and was about to imprison the Exarch and his friends up to the very last moment of his power. Midhat was dismissed from the sovereign favor of the Sultan. It is a part of the history and treatment of the Exarch of Bulgaria, that he was banished to a fortress, because he declined to sign a statement that the Christians were opposed to their deliverance from the Turks by the Russians.

The service of this Bulgarian Church is conducted in the Slavonic tongue, which is regarded by the Bulgarians as a sort of religious language. It is the same language that is used in Russia and other Slavonic countries.

Greek Christianity is not the only religion in Bulgaria. Much religious dissent has appeared recently in that country. This is attributable to the spirit of investigation which comes from education and freedom of speech. In fact, there is a reformation growing out of the relations which Robert College has for several years sustained with Bulgaria. This is the only case of American intervention in the East that has come under my notice. One thing is certain: the Bulgarian Christians have been more or less influenced by the large roundabout liberalities and learning of Robert College. I should signalize the grand work of Doctor Long, of that College. He has translated the Bible into the Bulgarian language. He is an American, from West Virginia. He is one of a class of men of rare scholarly minds. He does not allow his devotion to the medical profession and his love of physical science to detract from the earnestness of his faith or his reverence for the Deity. In the future history of the reformation in Bulgaria, much of its impulse will be traced to Robert College and to this distinguished American. Upon this phase of Eastern life it will be my pleasure and privilege to enlarge hereafter.

There is one romance connecting America with the Orient, and religion with patriotism, which should be recorded. It involves the " Star Spangled Banner." I warn my reader that with this sedate subject of religion I am about to associate a patriotic incident.

The Washington family has been traced back to the time of the Norman Conquest, and to the north of the Humber. The princely see of Durham had a prelate who was a feudatory of the Conqueror. He was a warrior-priest, and had many feudatories under him. Among the rest was the knightly William De Hertburn, who, in exchanging his village of Hertburn for the Manor of Wessynton, gave not only the first recorded link in the family, but the immortal name of Washington, "further West."

The Ottoman dynasty had risen to a formidable power ; and Richard the Lion Hearted had pawned his patrimony for a Crusade, and had been imprisoned on the shores of the Bosporus ; the story of the Plantagenets had been played before the world ; stately and warlike scenes in the West and East had come and gone ; and the name of De Wessynton, after illustrating many heroic qualities, had died out from the chivalric rolls of Durham; but it was preserved in the cloister by a doughty abbot. The stock was divided into various branches. It was scattered over England. About the time the great-grandson of the Conqueror of Constantinople—Suleïman the Magnificent—had raised his realm to its acme of fame, one of the Washingtons, Laurence, was practising law at Gray's Inn. When the Sultan Ibrahim was trying to foil the intrigues of the Eunuchs, Colonel Henry Washington was defending the city of Worcester for King Charles against Cromwell. Happily for America, England became uncomfortable for the Cavaliers who had fought for the Stuarts, and the brothers John and Andrew Washington emigrated to loyal old Virginia. John settled near the Potomac. His grandson Augustine was there born. There he lived, married and died. Of his sons, George was the eldest. But, as the genealogy shows, although he was out of the direct line, he had inherited the stamina of the stock.

What of all this, now and here? There is another George Washington living at Constantinople. He is the chaplain of the

British Legation, and by no means mute, if not so glorious as his American namesake. He is in the direct line from the De Wessyntons of the Conquest. In his keeping is the crest of the family. What is the romance to which I have adverted? Nothing less than the incomparable growth of a great Western nation, directed, moderated, energized and inspired by a descendant of the martial and priestly family whose stock is traced in the stalwart folk of Northumberland, and whose branches are as widely apart as the Bosporus and the Potomac.

The Rev. George Washington is an accomplished gentleman and scholar. He is quite friendly to Americans, as, of course, he should be. I cannot refrain from inserting here a little note which he sent to my wife. It contained his own card, and, doubtless, the arms on that card, as has been often surmised, if not proven, gave the first idea of the American "Star Spangled Banner."

" PERA, January 19, 1886.

" DEAR MRS. COX: It might interest Mr. Cox to see these quarterings, of which I was speaking to you the other evening. You see the 'Stars and Stripes' are there. I have always heard that the story I mentioned to you was correct, viz.: that, casting about for a flag when independence had been declared, the Americans thought that they could not do better than take their General's family quarterings as a foundation.

" Hence the Stars and Stripes!

" With kind regards, believe me,

" Yours, very truly,<br>" GEORGE WASHINGTON."

# CHAPTER XXIII.

## AMERICAN MISSIONS IN TURKEY—THEIR MAGNITUDE, OBSTACLES AND RIGHTS.

THE long continuance of the Ottoman empire is a more difficult problem than its decadence. I have attributed this continuance to "liberal institutions and laws." If the decadence has set in, it is because the Ottoman is beginning to repent of these liberalities, and to resort to a system of persecution quite alien to his earlier modes and "Capitulations."

There is a class of citizens in Turkey called "rayahs." They are Christians of various races—Armenian, Greek and Bulgarian. When Constantinople was taken by Mahomed the Conqueror, he did not commit one tithe of the outrages or illustrate one-thousandth part of the wrath of the Christian princes who broke down the Greek empire in A. D. 1203. He elevated the Christians and Jews. He created an *imperium in imperio* of ecclesiastical dignitaries and functions. He gave Greek and Armenian patriarchs for Greeks and Armenians, and a Jewish chief-rabbi for the Hebrews. The Sultan himself invested them. They were civil chiefs as well, and they remain as such. To-day there is nominally a head for the Catholic or Latin Church, and one also for the Protestants. The office of the latter is vacant. As one sign of the times, the vacancy remains unfilled, despite protests.

These respective heads of the religious sects tend to make Christians and Hebrews free in their consciences and souls. Imperial iradés confirm these grants. Education is also guaranteed. In the division of the municipal authority, the Christians are not omitted. Most of these grants were called "Capitulations," not because they indicate a capitulation on the part of the Porte after conquest, to Christians and Jews, but because they are embodied in a code of "Chapters," or "Heads," from "caput."

Recently the Porte has endeavored to get rid of some of these "Chapters;" but they remain, like our bills of rights or the

Spanish fueros.   If not executed, they remain as codes, to which
appeal may be made when persuasion fails and force is near.
These Capitulations were of special service to the American missionaries.   These men began their life work as early as A. D. 1831.
When Messrs. Goodell, Dwight, Shauffler and Holmes came here,
they did not meet opposition so much from the Turk as from
their fellow Christians.   Dr. Hamlin began in 1837 as an agent
of the American Board.   He took charge of a school which was
located at Candilli.   In time, through the aid of Mr. Robert and
other Americans, it became the Robert College.   It now dominates
the European side of the Bosporus, half-way between Constantinople and the upper mouth of the Straits.   The vicissitudes of these
early American missionary heroes were, and are, those of a peaceful crusade, full of Christian effort, and, at all times, of danger.
Commodore Porter, the naval hero, father of our Admiral, was
then United States minister, and the great Englishman, Sir Stratford Canning, was then potential at the Porte.   The Sultan
Mahmoud, who destroyed the Janizaries at one sanguinary *coup*,
had just died when Dr. Hamlin began his work.   Abdul Medjid, a
youth of sixteen, came to a tottering throne.   Mehemet Ali, the
all-powerful Viceroy of Egypt, had been stopped in his career in
Syria.   Reschid Pasha, who died in exile in Arabia a few years
ago, was the foreign minister.   He gave impulse to civil and
religious freedom.   Shortly after Abdul Medjid's accession the
prescript was issued known as Hatti-Cherif of Gul-Hane.   Like a
bombshell it fell among the *muftis*.   It is called Hatti-Cherif
because it is an "illustrious writing," and called Gul-Hane, or
Rose Garden, after the usage of the East, where names are given
with significant associations.   The Rose Garden was the name
of the place within the walls of the old Seraglio Point, where this
happy augury of Christian progress and protection was proclaimed.
That garden is now a government printing-office.   Where once
the houri of the padishah were cribbed, the type-setters and
pressmen fabricate journals and volumes.   Standing at the
case, or distributing type, may be seen a hundred printers, with
deft fingers, having the hand of "little employment, and therefore the daintier sense."

Eheu ! Postume ! Postume—labunter anni—how the years
have glided since, as a tourist, on my honeymoon, I visited this
garden, then blooming with roses.   It was in A. D. 1851—five

years before the Magna Charta for rayah and Christian—that I saw Constantinople for the first time. I can say of the Seraglio and the Rose Garden, as Burke said of Marie Antoinette, "Never upon this orb appeared so beauteous a vision." Its beauty is fadeless, though it is only a memory.

The garden of roses which I was then allowed to see is no more. My memory of it was that of an Eden, luxuriant in tree and shrub. The cypresses waved, ever green and fresh, the vine clung to the wall, whose bare face it decorated with green tendrils. Tender-eyed gazelles peeped out of leafy coverts, like odalisques of large sad eyes. Arches and pyramids of green foliage bent and rose in every vista. There was then a mimic lake occupying the centre of this garden of pleasure. It is now only a lake in a garden of pleasant memory, for a railroad makes its practical curve around the seraglio site. There were isles, and rustic bridges, and shell walks, margined with roses which the nightingales wooed. Orange bowers were pendant with golden fruitage. Fragrance filled the air from rare shrubbery, whether imported or exotic I then never cared to know. It was in life's dawn. The garniture of nature screened each charming bower.

I did not surmise then that this garden of roses would ever give to the long-suffering rayah and Christian, guarantees of justice and freedom. Yet from this Rose Garden came the "thought of the public good," and the recitations of trust in Allah that the subjects of the Sultan should be ensured "perfect security for life, honor and property, fair taxes and honest methods in their collection, and deliverance from the scourge of monopolies." Hear ye this, oh America! No venal concessions, no soldiering to destroy agricultural industry, fair trial of the accused, no death secretly or publicly, by poison or by any other form; in fine, a council of justice. In the presence of the relics of the Prophet and of all the Ulema and grandees of the empire, the Sultan took an oath to observe these grants to the people, with a penalty for their violation. And the roses, in their sweetest *attar*, effloresced an "Amen!"

This was a splendid tribute to the genius and order of Turkey in the afternoon of its existence.

Was this Magna Charta regarded? Is it obsolete now? Yes, and no. It accomplished much to elevate and advance the public service and popular well-being. In spite of "old Turkey" there was opened the path to schools, to printing, to reparation of wrong and the vindication of right, and, above all, to the relegation of all religious thought to a Higher Power than the state.

That which the Christians had struggled for, and against native prejudice and intolerance, had come to pass. The Koran had recognized a lofty place in its theological history of Jesus, son of Mary, born at " Beyth'ul Cahhm "—cattle market—of a virgin by the breath of the Archangel Gabriel, on the 25th of December, 5584, under the reign of Herod, Rauhh Ullah—"Spirit of God." This recognition, once a part of the Moslem faith, was renewed in a practical canon of liberal polity, amidst obloquy, and with prayerful thanksgiving.

Following this second recognition of the Saviour, Jesus Christ, was the repeal of the Mohammedan law as to apostates. A Mussulman was formerly condemned to death for apostasy. A Moslem woman was condemned to be beaten at prayer-time, five times a day, for the same crime. All that was changed.

The progress of physical science, with its practical advancement, struck Turkey as well as other lands. The Turk was not impervious, especially to mechanical inventions. No better artisans ever lived than those who made, and yet make, Damascus and other Eastern cities famous for steel, textiles, leather, iron and wood. I have not been unobservant of the attention of the juvenile Turks, who, when the American launch in which I steamed stopped at the quay, would regard, not the persons on the boat, but the movement of the engine in the hold, and of the screw in the clear water. The child was father to the man.

The Crimean War came not merely to stop Russia's aggrandizement or kill off the canines of Constantinople: it stirred the sediments of the empire. Its boil and bubble brought much scum to the top. It was not unlike our own war in the United States, which brought the essentials of life and liberty. It gave added impulse to the schools and churches, Bible-house and colporteurage. After the Crimean War Robert College became not only possible ; it became a tangible force. There it stands, a cynosure of all eyes, above the Bosporus, with its towers of pride and power. What influences enabled the Americans to obtain this superb site, and the building permits, and to begin the structure, are not unknown to diplomacy. Mr. Robert, a New York merchant, furnished most of the money, $200,000, and the name. Mr. Seward and Edward Joy Morris, formerly the Minister here, and John P. Brown, dragoman, inspired, along with occasional help from tourists like General Grant and Admiral Farragut, the impetus to consummate the work. The dedication of the College was a polyglotical arrangement, for English, French, Turk, American and Bulgarian, each and all, gave their tongue and tone to the celebration of the enterprise.

Whatever may be the codes which have prevailed during the reigns of the thirty-seven Sultans ; whether from the Koran or from the "six revered books," the Fetvas, or from the report of decisions of the head of Islam, or from the fifty-five volumes of Ibrahim Haleby, called the "Confluence of the Seas," because it was such a multitudinous and tumultuous concourse of the jurisprudence of the empire, containing everything civil, criminal, religious, military, economic, judicial, sumptuary and agrarian—one thing remains : a sober, industrious, kindly and forbearing mass of people, whose influences may be on the wane because of a domestic canker, and whose rulers may be too tardy in accepting the new conditions of an advanced era.

In spite of this improgressiveness as compared with Western progress, the Scriptures have been translated, and the Bible-house stands eminent in Stamboul, with its accumulations and printing establishments. Schools, churches and literature proceed. No one need live or die in Turkey without education or such light as to the unseen existence as the Word of God gives. The Catholic and Protestant missions have permeated and leavened the social and domestic order. Fundamental changes and new laws have come, along with the steam ferries, tunnels and street-cars. The Christians and Jews have better hopes of the temporary future and less fear as to their faith in eternal life.

As an evidence of this remarkable progress, and from an American standpoint, let me make a résumé of the monied, moral and religious interests here invested. They are the facts in this great Oriental programme. They are the results of the American missions in Turkey.

The societies or other chartered organizations in the United States which carry on missionary or educational operations in the Turkish empire are the following :

1. The American Board of Missions (Boston), occupying

European Turkey, including the part of Bulgaria south of the Balkans, and Asiatic Turkey except Syria.

2. The Presbyterian Board of Foreign Missions (New York), occupying Syria.

3. The United Presbyterian Mission Board (New York), occupying Egypt.

4. The Board of Missions of the Methodist Episcopal Church (New York), occupying Bulgaria, excepting the portion which lies south of the Balkans.

5. The Foreign Mission Board of the Reformed Presbyterian Church (New York), occupying the territory of the tribe of Nusariyeh pagans in north Syria.

6. The American Bible Society (New York), furnishing the greater part of the Scriptures used in the fields of the above Society.

7. The trustees of the Constantinople Bible House (New York), controlling the buildings used by several of the above Societies at Constantinople.

8. The trustees of the Syrian Protestant College of Beyrout (New York).

9. The Trustees of Robert College at Constantinople (New York).

10. The Baptist Publication Society (New York), supporting a missionary and his wife in Constantinople.

11. The Church of the Disciples, supporting a missionary and his wife in Constantinople.

Here are some statistics of the operations of these Societies and associations within the Turkish empire :

| | |
|---|---:|
| Cities, towns and villages occupied .................................. | 394 |
| American citizens, men and women, engaged in the work of the Societies................................................ | 254 |
| Turkish subjects employed as assistants or agents in various departments ................................................ | 1,049 |
| Number of high schools and colleges.............................. | 35 |
| Number of girls' boarding-schools................................ | 27 |
| Number of common schools.. ..  .............................. | 508 |
| Pupils under instruction in the educational institutions of these Societies | 25,171 |

Of these, 13,750 pupils are in the schools of the American Board in European and Asiatic Turkey, 6,075 in those of the Presbyterian board in Syria, and 5,106 in the schools of the United Presbyterian Board in Egypt.................................................

Preaching places (about)...  .....  ....  .......  .................  400
Average aggregate attendance at each Sabbath service..............  50,000
Organized churches...  .........................  ..............  138
Number of church members .................................. ...  10,776
Average sale of Scriptures and parts of Scriptures, per annum (copies)..  50,000
Average sale per annum of religious books, tracts, school-books, etc.,
    about (copies)................ .....  ......  ................  100,000
Number of newspapers or other periodicals published by the Societies..  13

Some of these figures are under the actual numbers. The increase in the missions of the American Board in Turkey has been 39 per cent. in number of pupils, and 47 per cent. in number of church members in the last eight years.

The property and business interests of these Societies in the Turkish empire are as follows : The value of real estate, book-manufacturing machinery and material, book stock on sale, school apparatus, etc., which belongs to these different Societies is about $1,000,000 in various parts of the empire.

The annual expenditure of the Societies within the Turkish empire for the support of schools and colleges, for rents and repairs of buildings, for taxes on real estate, for manufacture of books and newspapers, and for the salaries of the 1,303 persons employed as above stated in the various operations of the Societies, is $360,000.

This sum, annually sent from America to Turkey, may be regarded as the proceeds of 3 per cent. of American capital set apart for the purposes of these Societies, and amounting to $12,000,000 !

These devoted Americans, while they feel it to be their duty to preach evangelical Christianity to all who choose to listen, and to sell books to all who will buy, do not seek to gain adherents to a sect. They would arouse our kind to conform their lives to good and Scriptural principles. They are not proselyting agents in any other sense than that which is implied by the simple education of youth and the public declaration of Christian truth to the consciences of men.

It is to be regretted that there are any divisive movements among the Protestants who are ameliorating the condition of the Turkish empire. Although there may be a multiplicity of sects and a variety of councils, it is not altogether certain whether this multiplicity and variety tend to utility and strength. The Baptists and Campbellites have as much right in Turkey to make their own movement, and to make baptism a capital question, as the Presbyterian, the Methodist, or any of the other American foreign missions have to propagate their own peculiar doctrines with their own means. That will not be disputed. But it is certainly to be regarded as a portion of the past strength of the Protestant movement in Turkey that there has been so much unity among the brethren; and when the annual May meeting at Constantinople brings forth the active and intelligent missionaries, it is to be regretted that all Protestants are not in one phalanx to meet the combined attacks of the Greeks and Armenians, who, more than the Moslem, controvert their faith and persecute their followers. This persecution, especially by the Greek Church, or its bishops, is one of the anomalies of Christian warfare. In many regions, notably in the Trebizond field, there was an attempt made to collect the episcopal dues of such Greeks as became Protestants. When the protesting folk refused to pay, they were imprisoned. This led to discussion in assemblies. The Protestants were charged with being children of the Devil; and their New Testament was denounced as apocryphal. Out of these controversies grew the old spirit of inquiry. It is this spirit which not only gathers into the Protestant fold many Greeks and Armenians, but attracts the attention of the intelligent Turk. Whenever there is a probable increase in the Protestant flock, an Armenian is found to hint to the Turkish government that there is a lurking conspiracy. Then, as in the aforetime, the conspirators are driven to private houses. Then the proprietor is imprisoned. And so out of persecution, as of old, comes the power which energizes this new Protestant crusade of the East. One result is that in the collisions between the so-called Christian sects of the East and the American Protestants, the Turks gain information and prejudice dies out. In some portions of Turkey the missionary is preferred in the Armenian-Gregorian churches, for the old Armenian has his picture of the saint, the same as the Greek. He kisses the picture, but the protesting disciple in his Church refuses. That drives him to the Protestant. The Turk, who does not believe in pictures, takes note of the nearness of the relation between his unseen God and that of the Protestant who is also an Iconoclast.

Now and then we read of a few Mahometans who are baptized in the Protestant faith. But it is a truth that very few Turks have ever gone into that association. There are many discouragements connected with these missions. They grow out of differences and divisions. They are attended by the withdrawal of members. It has gone out that in the matter of spiritual life the cities, and especially Constantinople, though set on hills, are not a shining light. If I were to be asked what is the chief utility and strength of the Protestant missions of Turkey, which are fed by American money, I should say the educational institutions. They are not evangelizing, but they are elevating. They have no trouble in filling their halls and churches with patient and attentive auditors, and doubtless the streams are well watered at these sources. The effect of these missions is seen especially in the schoolrooms of the lower class of people, and in the readiness with which the native girls sympathize with educational movements. The educational work in Turkey has for its thinking head and active members Robert College and the Home School for girls at Scutari. Of these I shall speak in another chapter, giving an account of their Commencements in 1886.

To be more precise, let me say that the American Foreign Missions for Turkey are divided into four departments. The European-Turkey Mission has as its head the venerable Dr. Elias Riggs, with many assistants. It is a sample of many others. It has its stations, out-stations, churches, missionaries, physicians, female assistants, pastors, preachers, teachers, church members, Sabbath-schools and pupils. During the Bulgarian excitement of last year, the cloud of that war which, though impending, was fringed with much luminous beauty by the ministrations of these American missionaries to awaken new life among the Bulgarians in their struggle for national unity. At Constantinople Monastir, Phillopopolis and Samokov, our American missionary heroes and heroines, notwithstanding the political prejudices of the Greeks and others, fought the good fight of their faith. The Western Turkey Mission, which has its headquarters at Constantinople, and its presiding director, Dr. Pettibone, assisted by Dr. Henry O. Dwight and Henry S. Barnum, has been incessantly at work. Nor should I fail to mention Dr. and Mrs. Wood, who have retired after fifteen years of service at Constantinople, and fifty years of honorable work as missionaries, followed by the grateful recollection of friends in Turkey and America. They, like Dr. and Mrs. Bliss, are seeking a rest after the burden and heat of their service. In the Western Turkey Mission, which comprehends Broussa, Cæsarea, Constantinople, Marsovan, Nicomedia, Sivas, Smyrna and Trebizond, the American forces are well marshaled by those who give spirit and health, activity and success. Their labors may be found recounted in the reports made to the American Board in every recurring year. Without going into detail, I may say that the publications in this department are simply enormous. There were twenty-one issued in the past year in the Armenian language, amounting to 2,362,900 pages ; the same number in Armeno-Turkish, 3,817,600 pages ; three in Arabo-Turkish, 1,539,000 pages ; twelve in Græco-Turkish, 975,200—in all, fifty-five publications, 8,694,500 pages, making an aggregate from the beginning of 394,556,712 pages.

In an old country like that of Turkey, where old forms of religious faith exert such an influence, it requires an intense exertion, such as only these types illustrate, to gain the trust and confidence necessary to direct the pupil and the neophyte within the path marked out for their deliverance.

Another department is the Central Turkey Mission. It comprehends Marash and Pantab, where Dr. Trowbridge is the superior. This is a most interesting mission. It is gaining in influence. Its professors were educated in the United States. It has only one limitation on its influence—its accommodations. Its seminaries and hospitals give aid to the work ; yet with all these gentle and humanizing influences, and amid the Armenian community (so-called Christian), the priests of the Armenian religion were not slow to see that the Protestant gospel, according to the American tenet, was sapping the foundation of their authority. Upon the plain of Isis, near the very altars of Alexander the Great, from which Cicero dated his letter to Atticus, near the remains of the two walls, which in the time of Xenophon constituted the gates of Syria and Cilicia, upon the very point where archæology locates the trophies of Alexander, after the battle of Isis—here mobs of men and boys led by fanatics, club in hand, beat the American people unmercifully, and despoiled them of their goods. Where could they look for protection ? There were no American Consuls near. The Minister was remote—at the capital. When the little flock of pastor Hatcher and his family were dispersed, they found refuge in the house of a Moslem

Aga. Thither the Armenian rabble drove them for asylum. This happened in the very region where St. Paul was born, and where the hope of Protestant success was most sanguine.

And last, the Eastern Turkey Mission : The farther we go from the seat of power on the Bosporus, the more difficulties are encountered. Such missionaries as make Erzeroum, Harpoot, Mardin, Van and Bitlis fortresses of the Protestant crusade, have to struggle against poverty, native Christian hate, and sometimes Mahometan persecution, inspired by Greek and Armenian, only equaled in bitterness in the early days of the Church.

Taking the religion of the Saviour as their standard, it would naturally occur to the Christian men of Constantinople of diverse creeds, that they should unite in some evangelical union. This has been done. Many congregations up and down the Bosporus have united. The Dutch Legation seems to be one of the nuclei of this unity, and its chapel is often used for evangelical purposes.

Recognizing the fact that the institutions which they establish can only be of permanent importance so far as their roots are planted in the soil of Turkey, the missionaries aim to make every church and every school self-supporting and independent of foreign funds. Where they expend funds upon existing churches and schools, it is as an aid to the pastor's salary, or for the construction of buildings, or such auxiliary purposes.

As a rule, the missionaries fully recognize the delicacy of the work in which they are engaged. They endeavor, by the use of discretion and tact, to avoid offending the religious susceptibilities of the people among whom they live. During a period of nearly sixty years since the first of these missions was opened in Turkey, the Turkish government has never, it is believed, presented a single specific charge against American missionaries or their employees for illegal or offensive conduct. If any such charge has ever been made, it has never been sustained. Their relations with the Turkish government have sometimes been severely strained, but never broken.

The expenditure of a large sum annually within the Turkish empire by these societies is naturally an indirect advantage to the Imperial treasury. Moreover, the missions pay annually a considerable sum directly into the treasury, in the way of taxes on real estate and customs duties on material for use in book manufacture, and other imports. Furthermore, high officials of government have repeatedly borne testimony to the services to civilization rendered by these various Societies. Nevertheless, the missionaries are not always treated with due regard to their rights, as engaged in lawful occupations and as the citizens of a republic friendly to the Sultan. In such cases they are forced to appeal to the representative of the United States near the Sublime Porte.

The direction on which the protection of the United States government is most frequently sought is the book trade. The Societies engaged in this business conform to the law of the land. No book is published or offered for sale without authorization of the Board of Censors at the Department of Public Instruction. Nevertheless, officials of the government sometimes arrest the agents, seize the books, or impose whimsical restrictions upon the right to sell what the central government has distinctly authorized to be sold. Such illegal interferences with the trade of American citizens are vexatious, costly and very difficult to redress.

Another line on which the protection of the United States government is sometimes required, is in case of attempts on the part of Turkish officials to close the schools of these Societies. Most of the existing schools were established before the existing school law, and have continued for many years with the knowledge and tacit consent of the local officials. In some places officials have demanded the suspension of the schools, because they have not the formal authorization required by the new law When such authorization has been applied for, great reluctance has been shown in granting it, and once or twice the application has been made an excuse for summarily closing the school. The missionaries are perfectly willing to submit their schools to government inspection, but they are unwilling to submit the question of the existence of long-established schools to the caprice of an official who may prefer, without valid reason, to withhold the required permit.

It is hoped that the United States government will defend the missionaries in their claim. According to all precedent, these schools have acquired the right to exist, and the large investments of capital, made in good faith under former laws of the empire, should not be put in jeopardy by the interpretation given to more recent decrees.

The missionaries are occasionally obliged to seek aid from the Legation, as in cases of robbery and personal violence. Of course, those whose business requires them to travel do it at their own risk. But the Turkish government becomes responsible when it uses its power to protect the robbers who have attacked American citizens on the highway, or when it permits its provincial officials to release such criminals without punishment, or to refuse to make the attempt to recover stolen property when its whereabouts is known. Cases of such negligence or bad administration on the part of provincial officials have so often occurred that it is not difficult to understand how the robbers are forming an impression that Americans can be robbed without risk.

In concluding this brief outline of this department of American interests in Turkey, it is hardly necessary to say that the "missionary interest" thus described has a warm hold upon the hearts of Americans in all parts of the United States. The sum of $360,000, contributed annually for these institutions in Turkey by thousands of American citizens, north, south, east and west, and of every political party, represents the popular vote of a great constituency which has studied the work of these Societies and believes in their benefactions. The influence of the various Societies acting together, therefore, is not small, and will be sure to come to the support of the Minister of the United States, who is charged with the protection of the legal rights of the Societies in the Turkish empire in any crisis in which he may desire such influence to be exerted at Washington or at the Porte.

Protection, thus far, has not been stinted. The recent troubles in the Turkish empire, by withdrawing soldiers from Syria and Asia Minor, have lessened the protection to life and property; and *Puck* well pictures the hopeless impotence of the United States, without a navy, in these remote complications involving her citizens. But a better day is dawning. The "Alliance" of Protestants is coming to the aid of the Foreign Ministers, who, like the British, Swedish, Dutch and American, have immense and growing evangelical interests under their aegis.

# CHAPTER XXIV.

THE Turkish language is not a difficult one to learn. Its system of orthography and pronunciation is by no means complicated. It has ten vowel sounds. It does not employ combinations of two or three consonants to represent a single sound, as in other languages. The written language is not subject to any standing rule as to accent. Accent and quantity are not to be confounded in the Turkish. Linguists praise the beautiful characteristics of this tongue for its melody and euphony. Its rules are a guide to the tones of all the subordinate and inflectional parts of words. In its etymology there is no definite or indefinite article. Its noun knows no gender. It has singular and plural numbers, but not properly any inflections of case. It has, however, a declination of nouns. It has a preposition which follows the noun, and which should be called a *post*-position.

No one, in a few paragraphs like these, can give an idea of the Turkish grammar. Its adjectives, like the English, are invariable, whether they qualify a noun, singular or plural. They precede the noun. Even for the degrees of comparison there is no change of termination. An adverb signifying "*more*" is placed before the adjective to make the comparative, and another, "*most*," for the superlative. An adverb, *chok*, signifies *much*. It is always upon the Turkish lip. We have, probably, the same word for the same idea when we say *chock*-full; it means much-full. The Irishman from Waterford appreciated the word when he said that the Celt of that country never drank anything, for he was "always chock-full."

No nation or race which has asserted itself so prominently as the Seljukian Turk could avoid the egotism of the personal pronoun. This they have in various forms, as well as the demonstrative, interrogative, relative and indefinite pronouns.

It is the verb which indicates the refinement of language.

"GHIT!" WITH THE KAVASS.

In Turkish it is simple and regular in its formation and in the modification of its meanings. Generally, every verb is formed as regularly as the ramifications of a tree. The system has thirty-six verbs, twelve being affirmative, twelve negative, and twelve impotential. Six of the twelve are active, and six passive. Of these three are simple, and three causative; and one of each three is determinate, one indeterminate and one reciprocal. The original verb has something like the Greek root. It is the stalk upon which all the other verbs grow. The moods, tenses, numbers and persons are generally formed by the regular addition of special letters or syllables. The adjective even plays the part of the adverb. It qualifies both verbs and nouns. All adverbs of place and time are merely the nouns used with or without a preposition affixed. The conjunctions and interjections are quite unlike the English.

There are many conveniences in the Turkish language; as, for instance, the addition of the syllable "*ji*," which indicates an employer, a workman, or a man engaged in a peculiar work; as in the case of the word *shèkèr*, which means sugar; the dealer in sugar is simply a *shèkèrji*. The word *yàlàm* means a lie; but *yàlànji* is a liar. By a curious turn of speech the interrogative *nè*, which means *what?* when it is *neji* means what trade or occupation of the person. Sometimes *t* is changed into *d;* as, for instance, the word *ghit* means " go," and the word *ghidiji* means " a goer." There is no more useful word to a man in Turkey than " Git." It is useful in America also. It is generally used with " Haidi, git." Literally, " Git up and git ! " Take this sentence: Al, kùzum ; ish-ta Hamal inyèngizi ; ushàkala bèràbèr GHIT—! Being translated, it means, " Here, good fellow, take your porterage and go with the servant." But, generally speaking, the word *ghit* has a meaning which trips on the American tongue in Turkey with homely vehemence. In a city which seems to be abandoned to trade, and where there is no way of compelling cleanly habits, and which is only saved from cholera by a strict quarantine, Euxine breezes, and running water, and within whose narrow and illy paved streets you are liable at every step to tumble over a tawny cur, and where refuse heaps and foul spots make no impression upon the custodians of public health and locomotion, you are often, in such surroundings, saluted by beggars—able-bodied beggars—who ought to be forced to sweep the city from one end to the other. These filthy beggars are allowed to touch and even pull your garments, calling a halt on your promenade. But for the protection of the Kavass, all strangers and the Ministers are oftentimes at the mercy of these vagabonds. Indeed, as I have shown in another place, there is a chartered fraternity of mendicants, who, the more pestilential they look the more audacious they are. A licensed beggarly ruffian levies a tribute of a piastre upon a pedestrian. What can the pedestrian do? He can only be ransomed from contagion by prompt payment. In these cases the word *"Ghit!"* has a sanitary and solacing signification. Even in the wide streets of Pera, where tramway cars are drawn up in the middle of the streets, and while the *hamal* deposits his load on the narrow pavement, and itinerant passengers are comparing notes in the midst of these impediments—and the confusion is increased by a dozen pack-horses laden with sacks of charcoal—in such an emergency, what is the poor pedestrian to do? He cannot use a revolver. He cannot use a cane. His only resource is the Turkish word, "Ghit." It is effectual, if backed by the sword of the Kavass and the obsolete pistols in his sash; for the Turkish and other denizens of the capital respect authority, even when backed by the weakest sign of means to enforce it.

The Turkish language is said to be identical with the Arabic in its alphabet. It has, however, some additional letters. Like most languages it has many foreign words. The wonder is that it has not more, since Constantinople is polyglot. It is easy to speak, but difficult to read it. The reason for the former is that it is expressive, soft and musical. The reason for the latter is that the vowels are generally omitted in writing or printing, and there are no marks of punctuation. This is a Semitic peculiarity, I believe, as to the vowels. Thirty-five years ago, when I was in Constantinople, there were many scribes sitting cross-legged around on the corners of the streets who did writing for the passers-by. These professional characters are now rare. Almost every one here can write and read now. In writing, the characters run from the right to the left, and rather diagonally. They run up more obliquely toward the end of the line.

The Turk when he writes takes a small piece of paper in his hand; and then, with a little stick of reed, sharpened at the end, he makes his characters with great fluency. There is no slit in this reed. He does not move the hand in writing; he moves the paper.

There are various kinds of handwriting in Turkey, as there was in Egypt in early days.   One kind is applied to sacred literature, another to official documents, and a third to the ordinary correspondence.

The Arab is not a musical, though it be a scientific, romantic, eloquent and poetic language.   It has harsh, inharmonious sounds.   It is high-pitched and guttural, as compared with the euphony of the Turkish tongue.   In fact, the Turk has been called a gentlemanly man because he speaks with a softened and hushed enunciation, but this is by no means his only title to that designation.

It is a historic indictment that the Mahometan Turk and Saracen was a destroyer of literature, and that the great library of Alexandria, with its works of inestimable value, was burned by order of the Mussulman army.   Is it not well to ask whether the tale thus circulated be really true ?   The Moslem writers are unanimous in denying it.   The unsophisticated remark attributed to Omar the Caliph, when appealed to concerning the Alexandrian library, is often quoted to show the vandalic quality of the Mahometan.   It was this:

" The contents of the books are either in conformity with the Koran, or they are not.   If they are, the Koran is sufficient of itself.   If they are not, they are pernicious.   Let them burn!"

Perhaps the hugest lying ever written to throw obloquy upon a race or a religion, is the allegation that the baths and furnaces of Alexandria were for months fed with the books of this library.   Without proof of this charge it must fail.   It would be enough to say that the Mahometan always respected the "Men of the Book," meaning at the same time, among others, the men of letters.

The American student has not to venture far within the arcana of Oriental science and mystery, in order to learn what the Arabic mind has done for civilization and advancement.   Dr. John William Draper has collected and analyzed the learning on this subject.   Although he may have variated, as some consider it, the modes of thought by which the Arabian mind treated the accumulations of fact, without the essential generalizations which make philosophy and science; still, in regard to astronomy he shows us who first discovered the motions of the sun's apogee, and who demonstrated the third irregularity of our satellite. Their names are lost in the rushing crowds who fill the observatory and laboratory of science and the niches of the temple of fame. There are names like El Hazen, Wefa and El Batini, that are worthy of being classed in the same category with Copernicus, Newton, Priestly and Lavoisier. It has been said that the Arabian philosophy merely copied after the Greek masters, Plato and Aristotle. If this be true, is it not all the more creditable in the Arabians? Indeed, without the aid of Plato and Aristotle, the splendid commentaries of the Western mind in philosophy, science and religion would be but shining dross and useless inaptitudes.

It is said that the Arabians have no literature of their own, that they gave their mental as well as physical energies to the conquest of sea and land, and that they have been destroyers and not restorers. To offset this charge, it must be confessed that they have a wonderful place in the world's history, by means of a genius for government, if not a taste for art and literature. Why is the Turkish pen a stubbed stick without a split? It must be understood that the reed makes a tolerable pen. Besides, it is cheaper than our wooden-holder pen, in a country where the forests have been eaten off by the goats and destroyed by the peasantry. Although the pen of the Turk has not been as mighty as his cimeter, it must be taken into account that with such a poor stick of a pen he has done wonderfully well.

To any one who has read Sir Walter Scott's " Robert of Paris," the grandiose style of chronicling the events of the Greek empire will provoke a smile ; and yet, long before his day, such chronicles were the only source of knowledge as to these border lands between the Occident and the Orient. There was much nebulous light burning over the Danube, the Euxine and the Bosporus. They were faint, flickering beacons, to which the Western Powers looked, and by which they were guided in giving encouragement and help to the East in the struggles of the Greek and the " Barbarian." When the Turkish conquest came, there had been little of literature and less of art cultivated by their predecessors. The Turk added nothing to the advancement of those years, except the art of war, and something from the fragmentary poems of the Arab and Persian. The Turk was a peasant and a soldier ; and, I may add, a ruler. Before the conquest, Greek history was an alternation of palatial assassination or monastic retiracy, and a mass of demoniac intrigue. The literary light which, like an aureole, surrounded the Arab brow at Bagdad, and as far west as Cordova and Granada, and as far east as Delhi, never irradiated the conquerors of Constantinople. Many of the Sultans were conspicuously grand in their thoughts and deeds of conquest. They planted the foundations of the empire. Their successors gave it permanence through education, literature and the arts. But most of the amenities were limited, and almost lost in the contamination of a sensuous faith.

Suleïman the Magnificent stands first among the Ottoman rulers ; but in balancing the probabilities as to the advancement of our race, there is not very much connected with the Turkish supremacy to show that even he gave to it any great impulse, like that gained from the Arabian invasions along the Mediterranean.

The Turkish tongue is enriched by many Arabic and some Persian words. These came into the language along with the religious dogma. Besides, the terms of luxury and art that belong to the Orient, and which were unknown to the Tartar ancestry of the Turk, have their place in the Turkish language. You can hear them dropping like bubbling honey from the mouths of the Turkish ladies who are shopping in the bazaars, or in the smooth words of the shopkeeper who responds. The old tongue of the Turk is not unknown to many uncivilized people, who roam over the plains of northern Asia, just as the language of the border of Scotland is heard among the Norse descendants of Scandinavia.

It is said that the language is similar to that of the Latin. In its softness, yes ; but in its copiousness, no.

The Turk in his litigations has no " advocate." He is his own attorney and speaker. He tries his own case. He does his own work with his own tongue. He practices rules and arts of rhetoric with grace and skill. His *crescendo*, toward the climax, complies with the rules of Quintilian and the practice of Cicero.

You may not know the object of a Turk's speech from his proem. It is the end that clinches the discourse. His conclusion is the key to his meaning. To listen to him in the bazaar, as he expands upon the glories of his broadcloth and silks, you are at a loss which to admire most, the exquisite broidery of his phrases and praises, or the elegant texture of his fabrics. Yet there is not so much of the advocate as the judge in his manner. He does nothing, not even in the sale of a chibouque, without dignity. His frequent response of "Yok," which means " No," advises you that his mind is determinately made up.

In balancing these merits and demerits of the Turk, I am endeavoring to separate him from his Arabic friends and co-religionists, and to be discreet in laudation. Nevertheless, it is true that the Turkish people have adopted many of the finer elements of the Arabic character, if not the literature. It is within my own personal knowledge that many of them, in a half-monastic way, take to themselves, as other less cultured Turks take a harem, the rare volumes of Arabic literature, to read, cherish and love. There is such a scholar, with a rare library, upon the eminence near the American college. He is devoted to his rare old volumes. Many of his treasures are manuscripts which record the scientific triumphs of the Arabian people.

Out of all this has already come a respectable literature in the Turkish language. Some of it is from other languages, but much of it is original. A part is poetical, as nearly all Oriental literature must be. It is historical, because there are no such fields for history as the Balkan and Asia Minor peninsulas, Mesopotamia, Syria and Judea. As a general thing, letters, although appreciated, are not cultivated in Turkey to-day. The body of the Turkish people are not highly educated, but they are not uninstructed. The ordinary Turk, however, is free from vices, and the Turk who seeks promotion in the state invariably seeks an education outside of Turkey. To a limited extent, those who would expound the Koran, or who would seek government employment, disdain to be entirely ignorant of or aloof from the elegant life of lettered ease which is led by some of the diplomatic and other people in and around the Porte. The Turkish colleges and schools have large funds for their endowment. In fact, there is a minister specially dedicated to look after all the "foundations" of education. It is to be regretted that his duty is mostly connected with the foundations of the mosque. The studies are under the guidance of the ulemas. I do not think the literature taught by the ulemas is practical. It is rather the result of metaphysical subtlety. It comes out of the old school, of which Aristotle was the best teacher, and of which Scotus himself was the best scholar. The rhetoric and logic which the Arab drew out of the Greek manuscripts in their crypts have been applied to philosophical questions of a most simple and insignificant character. It has struck others than myself that the physical science, with its enginery, its telescope and microscope, and its machines for the transmission of sound and words by electricity, are regarded by the average Turk either as miracles or as toys for childish curiosity. When Dr. Hamlin, of Robert College, first introduced into the palace the magnetic telegraph, and demonstrated how intelligently words could be transmitted to a distance without talking, the scene was very diverting, but not more so than the wonder over new discoveries in our own home. The curiosity of the Turks was childlike, but it was the curiosity of those who desired to learn; and they have learned. In Turkey to-day the telegraph is in constant requisition among all classes of the people, and at a cost infinitely less than that of any other country in the world. The government controls it. The effect of this control is not in the direction of centralization of power.

There are among Oriental, and especially Armenian, tales, a collection from the East Indies, called the " Five Books," as well as the " Arabian Nights," with which we are familiar. They defy scientific analysis. They are stories of Oriental Cinderellas, about the Snake Child, and the Brahmin's Enchanted Son, and others. There are stories from Albania, in which physical and animated nature is personified, like those of the Danish Andersen. These make up abundantly a literature of the lower classes within the dominion of Turkey, irrespective of race.

In the comparative absence of books and newspapers in Turkey in earlier times, the tombstone was considered a vehicle for the communication of sentiment. This consists with the gravity of Ottoman character. As the cemetery was often sought by promenaders, picnic parties, condoling acquaintances and friends of the deceased, there is much obituary literature worked in upon the stones. In the great burial-ground of Eyoub, on the tomb of an infant, it is said:

" This is a flower that has scarcely bloomed. It is prematurely torn from its stem. It is removed to those bowers whose roses never languish. Its parents' tears will supply refreshing moisture."

Again, this is written of a young lady:

" The chilling blast of fate caused this nightingale to wing its course to heaven."

Of a lady who dies in child-birth it is said:

"Tree and fruit are both transported to the gardens of paradise."

On a child's tomb:

"Here below is but a frail rosebud ; the bitter wind of destiny blew upon its stem."

Here is a mother's lament for her daughter:

"The bird of my heart has flown from my soul for the gardens of paradise."

On a mother's tomb we read:

"Traveler, I ask of thee a prayer; if to-day it is needed for myself, to-morrow it will be required for you."

The following epitaph is a remarkable specimen of literature, *al fresco:*

"Here lies the man who eats no onions."

Was he a Lazarus or a Dives? Onions were the food of the opulent.

One might write a chapter about the newspaper press of this capital, but it could not be written with much satisfaction by those who believe in John Milton's "Plea for Unlicensed Printing." The newspaper in Constantinople began nearly half a century ago. Oscanyan Effendi, ex-Consul-General Ottoman at New York, now a member of the Press Club of that city, and a rare linguist, was its progenitor. It was called the *Byzantine Advertiser.* It had a native name, *Aztarur Bizàntian.* It struggled manfully for existence, but it could not long survive the inclemency of the government and the indifference of the people. While the Turkish newspaper press still lacks the freedom which the American, French and English press enjoy, yet it has grown into a power, as the number and variety of its issues indicate. There are a score of dailies and as many weeklies in this capital. Even the resident Persians have a *Star Aktar.* These papers copy the French methods. They are all compelled to be reticent on news as well as on public questions. The newspapers of Constantinople which circulate most among the English, German, Italian and Levantine population are printed in English and French ; such as the *Levant Herald* and the *Oriental Advertiser.* There is a French *Journal de Constantinople.* The authoritative paper is the *Tarik.* The latter is the organ of the Turkish government. There is a Greek paper, the *Neologos*—well named. There is an Armenian and a Hebrew paper; but the most independent paper of them all is, perhaps, the *Levant Herald.* The sign of its vitality is that of its constant overhauling by the censor. I am inclined to believe, from my knowledge of this censorial performance, that much of the work is superserviceably and ignorantly done. The portion expunged by the censor is generally that which is the least obnoxious to the government of the Porte. Frequently, my friend Mr. Edgar Whitaker, of the *Levant Herald,* has had his best lucubrations cut in whole or in part. On such occasions this little item appears:

*Notre article politique d'aujourd'hui reste, sur la demande de la censure, en portefeuille.*

No one can rely upon any of these papers for fresh news. During the time the Conferences were held in Constantinople, and of the short war between Servia and Bulgaria, we were indebted to the London papers for the only particulars. As to any news from America, it was like angels' visits, few and far between.

# CHAPTER XXV.

It is commonly thought that the Turk has no humor. To be as cross as a Turk is an apothegm. The Turk is always supposed to be as solemn as Pythagoras, and as sedate as a Scotch Presbyterian. If he be allowed to have any humor, it is regarded as that of a grim sort, which is more akin to North Albion than to Attica. There is some injustice done the Turk in this matter. He can fit his fancies for humorous ideas, and give them racy application on occasions fit, but, unlike the Frenchman, he is not given to the manufacture of *jeux d' esprit.* Turkish humor is generally free from the coarseness which belongs to the isolated Englishman. The national characteristics of gravity and reflection are too strong to admit of the irrelevant hilarity in which the Greeks and Italians indulge ; but the Turk is never backward in being forward when the least sparkle of humor is illustrated. Especially does he exercise his quiet and sedate quality of fun at the expense of foreigners.

Of course, the Turk indulges somewhat in masquerade while moving through the mazes of diplomacy at Pera ; but when he is by himself, he is really fond of pleasantries. He can play off the weaknesses of others. He makes prey of unsophisticated foreigners, with all the soberness of a Rocky Mountain stage-driver expatiating to a " tenderfoot " from the States. His advantage consists in a droll exaggerative quality, which, if it do not evoke a guffaw, tickles like a feather. These exaggerations have expression in tropes and figures, and frequently in piquant and pertinent stories.

But the Orient is rich in something else besides humor; it abounds in abundant metaphor, and which is akin to fun. The Turk is never stinted in phrases of a superlative character. The metaphorical exaggeration of the Orient reaches its climax in a burst of enthusiastic gratitude, when one of the new Pashas acknowledges an honor conferred upon him by the Sultan.    One of these favored Pashas exclaims :

"Your sublime favor has been as a southern sun-breeze, even to the remote corner of my insignificance !   Had I all the various voices of the universe for pens, and the condensed stars of heaven for a page whereon to describe your bounties, I should still lack both space and means to record them."

The exaggerated expressions of the Orient are to be accepted with much allowance.   There is no malice in the big stories, and no intention to pervert the truth ; but from the very constitution of the language itself there are, from the Arabic, Hebrew and other languages, roots, from which grow luxuriant amplification and ramification.

The Turkish or Oriental mind has not that intense, condensed and expressive sense which French and Americans regard as wit. Occasionally in public places, you may meet a company of players and singers, who, in addition to other performances, indulge in buffoonery.   Sometimes this is grotesque, but it is not funny to us, or witty to any race.   It is often a caricature upon the prevalent manners.

The subject of a favorite performance, for instance, is a mysterious beauty—a princess.   Her charms, like all Oriental charms, are enhanced by the veil.   The play in which she is the heroine is a sort of *al fresco* festivity.   It is played as Thespis played—in the "open."   There are no scenic aids except a tent, which represents a harem.   The spectacle is upon an area of beaten ground under the shade of trees.   The ground is covered with a carpet, upon which sit cross-legged spectators.   There is an open shed for the female portion of the audience. The humorous characterization consists of some young person smothered in a veil inside of the tent, or harem, whose door is open.   Through the open door the lady is seen, affecting the languishing attitude and duck-like waddling habitual to the ladies of the East.   The mimicry is well done.   It produces a piastre's worth of hilarity.   Inside of the tent, the heroine sits entranced, while her lovers play, beneath her supposed lattice-window, the *gusle*—a sort of goose-neck banjo.   The suitors are as numerous as those who wooed Penelope.   The coy beauty is superbly rouged upon the cheek, and charcoal gives additional darkness to her eyebrows.   She cannot be wooed by any goose music; Oh, no!

Her slaves come forth and pummel the suitors with cudgels. This "brings down the house." In the next scene, a funny old man enters disguised. He it is who is behind the canvas, personating the adorable beauty! He sings in falsetto the most tender airs, which delight the audience. Shades of Gilbert and Sullivan! They never struck notes like these in their most comic operas; for of all the music which can be caricatured on a high pitch with a shrill whining, the airs of the Orient furnish the climax. This mummy of an old man, with his tender trills and squeaky treble, is, to the suitors, an houri; and his song and melody that of paradise. The audience know all the time that the beauty is that discordant, ugly old man. In that lies the raciness of the performance. To the Turk, contrast is the essence of dramatic vivacity; hence the old man's amative words and high pitch of admiration produce tumbling oceanic swells of fun.

It may not be generally understood, but it is a fact, of which I have had some diplomatic experience, that the Turkish language is extremely susceptible of conundrums, puns and double entendres. A little shade here, or a little more color there, and the whole sense of a word or sentence becomes changed with surprising facility. It is therefore easy to be comical in Turkish, since the comic is defined to mean a sudden jerk of the understanding from one extreme to another. The player is not backward in taking advantage of this trait of the language in the *al fresco* performances.

When acting the parts of lovers—as in the play to which I have referred—they get into all sorts of strange positions. Some swing their bodies, and others caper about with fantastic exclamations that remind one of the opera bouffé. The lover has a lantern on the end of a pole; this, in his amorous agony and awkwardness, he pokes into all sorts of faces and places. The result is, a whack here, and a kick there, and a tumble all around the stage. At last the *dénouement* takes place. The conquering hero, who is always the tenor, appears. To him the beauty yields, with blushes. Her veil drops, and she responds in a deep bass voice! Then the chorus becomes excited. Beauty surrenders to the Beast, and the play ends. The whole performance is very much like a conflict among ducks and geese.

In fact, such ornithological fights are not unknown in the East. They furnish sportive recreation. I have often been struck

A GOOSE-FIGHT NEAR ADRIANOPLE.

SCENE FROM THE CADI.   CHAPTER XXVII., PAGE 349.

with the prominent part which the goose plays in Oriental countries. In Montenegro it used to be common for the nobility to
play upon the banjo already referred to—the *gusle*. It is so
called from the Slavic word *gusj*—a goose. It comes from the
same root as our English word. The instrument is so called
from the goose-like neck. The Montenegrins play a variety of
tunes on this rude violin, although there is but one string drawn
over the bridge. It is played with a bow, and by pressing the
strings with the left hand. When thus evoked it has, for one
string, a wonderful number of notes and variations of sounds.
Its expression is not exactly artistic, but it is truly pathetic in
its monotony in ordinary hands.

The most conspicuous part which the goose plays in the Orient
is in a fight! In some parts of Turkey in Europe the bird is
trained for fighting, and a goose-fight is looked upon with more
interest than any cock fight ever was in Cuba or New Orleans.
The goose that has the longest and strongest neck wins in the
duel. The fighting is done by twisting one neck round the other.
A goose *main*, therefore, depends for its victory on the main
strength of the neck.

The Ottoman or Mahometan literature, whether it be written
or oral, often takes the form of story or parable with a *moral*.
In fact, local names are associated more or less with some phase
of morality. Midway between Therapia and Buyukdere there is
a beautiful terrace overlooking some stones, against which the sea,
surging in from the entrance to the Bosporus, beats violently.
I often visited these stones, and endeavored to draw a sermon
from them. One of them was formerly called Dikæa, which
means the "Just Stone." It has its legend. Two merchants
agree, before a journey over the Euxine, to place what gold they
have beneath this rock. They swear that should one return before
the other, he who first arrives will await for the return of the
other before taking possession of the money. One of them is
intent upon breaking the engagement. What is the result?
The very stone prevents the perfidy. On looking for the gold
the first who returns can find the gold nowhere. When the
partner returns, he is informed of the loss of the money, when
lo! the gold appears in the very spot on which it had been deposited. Here is proof, upon a rocky foundation, of a fidelity beyond
that of ordinary brick and mortar bank-vaults.

If it be true that maxims, stories, fables and parables are typical of the characteristics of a race, there can be no doubt of the honesty of the Turkish character; for all through their legends and traditions, the honesty and justice of the Ottoman is celebrated.

Oriental stories have endless variety. They are often used by our Occidental *littèrateurs* and poets to give grace to their numbers and elevation to their ideas. I glance into an American magazine; I find a story in six verses. It is Oriental, for it is about a dervish. It points the moral in the first verse—it is the virtue of fasting. But this enables the devout to come only half-way to God. The second verse indicates prayer; but this is not sufficient ; neither are pilgrimages; for God does not come to the devotee who is only prayerful or a pilgrim. The third verse suggests alms-giving, but this of itself is not sufficient. The dervish becomes discouraged. He toils along the road with his one coarse loaf. In the fifth verse he meets a crippled beggar; the cripple craves charity of the dervish; the loaf is given—in God's name. Then—then, the Mighty Splendor fills the desolate air. A light divine overflows from a heavenly place, and he knows that it is the light of Allah's face!

Take another analogue. It is also about beggary. A cripple sits in the city's gate. The grand folk pass through it, seeking a sacred shrine in the forest near by. They deny the beggar alms. His need is sore. " We seek to find out God," is their answer to his petition, as they pass on to the shrine. The beggar dies ; he realizes the prayer. He alone has found out God!

A diligent searcher after the folk-lore of Turkey could bring forth many odd, not to say funny, superstitions. Some of them have fun for us, but not for the Turks. The stories have their roots in old legends of infinite interest, as coming from the Orient and associated with our Scriptures. Let me mention a few:

Many are connected with the Evil Eye, and the attempt to exorcise it or prevent it. Children are especially guarded against the Evil Eye. A word from the Koran is a sufficient defense, or some beads, or a little garlic, or an herb of some kind. Incense is often used as a precaution against this terrible Evil Eye. The Weelees of Egypt and the Ghinns of Bagdad, and other evil spirits, are still as active as they were during the Thousand and One Nights in forming many of the qualities of the lower classes of Turkey. Many people use what is called dog-bread as a charm. It is thus named simply because little bits tied up in a handkerchief passed over the head of the child are afterwards given to the dogs. Again, many designs in a dress or coverlet are slightly irregular or imperfect. They are made so for a purpose. It is thus intended to show that nothing but Allah can be perfect. Sometimes you will notice persons spitting very much while in conversation with you. This is a superstitious mode of cultivating the salivary glands to protect the expectorator against the Evil Eye. The donkeys in the island of Prinkipo are always decorated with blue beads, and so with the horses and oxen; and even the ugly buffaloes have similar decoration. These adornments are supposed to divert, by their attraction, the evil looks of the envious.

A superstition among the Turks is that nothing should be wasted that might be used as food for dogs or fish. Another is that no paper should be left lying around loose; for *non constat*, but that it may bear the name of Allah. Oftentimes a piece of paper with Allah on it, is swallowed in water by the sick. These are Oriental customs; and there are a thousand more that might be picked up. In Moslem lands these customs have a religious aspect. The visitor must beware not to enter the house for the first time with the right foot. He must use certain days that are not unlucky. The Sultan, as we have seen, observes this custom in giving or postponing his dinners. The proper time for his hospitalities depends on astrological calculations; hence, the first day set may turn out to be an unlucky one. We may smile at these superstitions, but the Turk does not. Sometimes they are quite as inconvenient to him as to others. It is said that the office of Muned-gim Bashi, or astrologer to His Majesty, exists, and that it is filled by an intelligent and eminent man. It is his duty to calculate the propitiousness of times and seasons: when should the hair be cut or the nails be pared; when be doctored or go on a trip; or when is it best to rest. All these are ciphered out by the official Zadkiel. It is hinted that Sir Drummond Wolfe's mission about Egypt failed because the times selected for the negotiations were unlucky. Whatever truth there may be in these asseverations about astrology—and doubtless they are exaggerated—there is a sobriety regarding them which, to the irreverent American mind, is related to the

KING SOLOMON AND THE QUEEN OF SHEBA.

humorous. These superstitions have been carefully collated by authentic writers, and if we should add to them others which come down traditionally, it would only amplify what is already well known, and that is, that the Orient, the land of religions, is the land of strange and weird fancies about Evil, and of remedies supposed to be salutary and potential against its influences. But most of all, and related to these traditions, are the "moralities" which are their companions.

One of the odd things of the East is the devotion paid to certain vegetables and certain trades. For instance, the onion, which is not held in high esteem by Western nations, is called by the Kurd, "Your Excellency." To dine on the inside core of the onion is considered evidence of high dignity and immense opulence.

One of the strangest of all the Turkish stories is one current about Solomon and the Queen of Sheba. The Turks have no nebulous or indefinite *dramatis personæ.* They personify them as well as other creatures by both name and trade. The Queen of Sheba's name is Balkiss. She is the twenty-second queen of Yeman, which is a seaport on the Red Sea When she calls on Solomon, she has a wonderful reputation for beauty, but there is one defect for which nothing can compensate. It is more than hinted to Solomon that Her Majesty's nether limbs are covered with hair like unto that of a she-ass. What did this wisest of men do in order to settle this question? Why, he arranges, with the aid of a mirror, and running water under it, to find out whether, as reputed, her ankles are hirsute. When Queen Balkiss steps into the room where the great King Solomon is sitting in state, she raises her robe to avoid the water. The plan is a success.

Queens did not wear stockings until Elizabeth of England set the fashion. Sheba's secret was thus revealed. But, like most Oriental troubles, a magical paste was manufactured by the king's apothecary, so that the feet as well as the legs of the fair Balkiss become as downy as the cheek of a new-born infant.

There are a great many singular, if not witty, mottoes in the Turkish tongue. Sometimes they are written, as I have shown, upon old gravestones, and sometimes upon the tablets of the baths. In the latter place there is one which says, appositely:

"Do not be quite so shy of taking off your clothes; for

what is life if not a place where each one must drop the robe
of flesh ! ''

\*    \*    \*    \*    \*    \*    \*

Here is another:

" Send provisions to be placed in your tomb, for no one will
take you in after you are dead.''

In the old cemetery below our hotel in Constantinople, there
is a tomb of a man who had been buried by the falling of a house.
He makes his own epitaph:

" I was walking leisurely, when, good Lord ! what evil befell
me! I was reduced to ashes, and beneath this stone you will
find them.''

\*    \*    \*    \*    \*    \*    \*

There is a wine, almost a syrup, made by the Arab from the
date.   It is a favorite drink of the Bagdad gourmand.   A story is
told of it:

A famous Caliph loves this brew.   In one of his wanderings,
he enters the cabin of a peasant.   The peasant is so pleased with
the Caliph that he produces, not merely milk, but a bottle of the
date-wine.   The Caliph takes a drink, and says to the peasant:

" Do you know who I am ? ''

" No," replies the peasant.

" I am a eunuch of the court," says the Mahdi, or Caliph.

" Allah! bless you !'' replies the peasant.

Then the Caliph takes another pull at the magic bottle.   After
a slight hesitation he again asks:

" Do you know who I am ? ''

" Yes," responds the peasant, " you are the guardian of the
harem.''

" No," says the Caliph, " I am one of the Mahdi's generals.''

The peasant is duly respectful.   The Caliph takes a third
draught with a delicate hurrah.

" Do you know who I am now?   I am the Commander of the
Faithful," says he, with a magnificent Oriental hiccough.

The peasant makes no remark at this third drink.   He takes
the bottle away.   The Caliph demands it back.

" Not a drop!" says the peasant.  " When you first drank, you
were a eunuch at ceurt; when you drank next, you were a general; and at the third drink you were the Commander of the

PASHA OF BAGDAD ON A SPREE.

Faithful! One more drink, old fellow! and you will be the Prophet himself."

He drew the line on Mahomet.

Beyond all doubt, the triple walls of Constantinople, with their towers and massiveness, are the most interesting of her monuments. They are in excellent preservation, especially on the two sides of the triangle bordering the Sea of Marmora and the Golden Horn. Upon the land side of the triangle, running five miles across, from the Seven Towers on the Sea to the port of Haidanhaissar, the walls are a perpetual scene of wonder. They are majestic. They are everywhere overspread with luxuriant and wandering foliage. In the old dry moat there are gardens and trees, the terebinth, cypress, sycamore and other species. You want to walk thither and ponder, properly to investigate these walls. You should read up their remarkable defensive history. It is not my purpose now to describe them, or to dwell upon them, except to recall one little story which has all the moral fragrance of the Orient:

One day, in the year A. D. 549, Justinian, the emperor, is making progress across the city. He loses from his crown its most splendid jewel. It is a diamond of twenty-five carats. It is a great loss. No search discovers it until after nine hundred years of remarkable vicissitudes. Then the diamond again gives its light to the sun. It is found amid the rubbish of the wall by a little shepherd-boy while attending his goats. He uses it in some game with his playmates. The boy's father sees it. He observes its beauty. He obtains a hearing from the Sultan, Mahomed II., the Conqueror. The father is made Chief Shepherd in return for the imperial jewel. The story runs that the child is brought up and educated at the expense of the Sultan. The diamond is known as the shepherd's stone. It is among the rare gems of the treasury in the-Porte. It has another fatality not so felicitous:

In the time of another Sultan this gem is sent to a jeweler to be reset. The jeweler is an Armenian of great skill. He is exceedingly solicitous, too careful perhaps, in his work. His hand is tremulous, and it slips! Voilà! he observes a crack in the jewel! He falls back and dies, for he has not sufficient sight to see that it is only a hair from his eyebrow which has fallen upon the diamond.

# CHAPTER XXVI.

## STORIES OF THE EAST—THEIR MORALITIES.

THERE is a moral flavor and natural justice pervading most of the Eastern tales. Endeavoring to collect such of them as have not hitherto seen print, I place, as among the best, the following :

The story is told of a Sultan—whether in Egypt or Turkey, I cannot tell—who, calling all his Ministers together, directed that each one should come fully robed. They came, clad in their richest Persian and cashmere shawls and garments. When this cabinet meeting was over, the Ministers retired in the order of their rank. As each guest retired, he was conducted to a chamber and stripped of his magnificent robe of state. The despoiled garments were ultimately returned to the Ministers—for a consideration. This was one of the ancient modes of replenishing an exhausted exchequer. No doubt some of the ministerial wealth had been acquired by a stripping process from the people. The Sultan's mode was retributive. It tended to a decrease of vanity, and it was a tax on luxuries.

Turkey is not without its reformers, but even the best of them, Midhat Pasha, was the hero of the following narrative :

When he was Governor at Rustchuk, on the Danube, he made many enemies. A band of these engaged in a conspiracy to assassinate him. They went to Rustchuk, and were followed by one of Midhat's Wallachian spies. This spy informed the Pasha of the plot. When the assassins arrive at Rustchuk they are arrested. Being brought before the Pasha, they at first deny, but at length admit, that they have been commissioned to kill him. He asks them :

" How much were you to be paid ? "

They answer : " Twenty-five thousand piastres."

" What !" replied Midhat, " is my life held so cheap ? If you will kill the man who sent you, I will give you double that sum."

The would-be assassins willingly consent to the more liberal offer. They are paid twenty-five thousand piastres down. They are requested to return for the balance as soon as they should despatch their former employer. They soon after return, with sufficient evidence that they had performed their contract. They demand the other twenty-five thousand piastres. They are asked :

" Have you indeed killed your first employer ? "

They admit the deed, and produce the evidence of it.

" Then," says the noble reformer to his retainers, " these men have committed murder. Hang them ! "

Both assassins are at once strangled.

It seems, from this story, that Midhat was engaged in the strangling business before the fall of Abdul Aziz.

\*　　\*　　\*　　\*　　\*　　\*　　\*

Many stories are told of Turkish generals who manage bodies of men with great cunning, as well as cruelty. One is told of a Bey, whose underlings revolt at his cruelty. He cajoles them with promises, and they return to his palace, bringing with them their purses. Around him are the officers and Kavasses, whom self-interest has attached to him. The moneys which he had taken from the revolters are conveniently near his grasp from the divan on which he is seated. He tells them :

" If you will divide yourselves into two parties and fight against each other, I will graciously pardon the victorious party and present them with all the moneys and permit them to depart; but if you do not agree to this proposal I will kill you all."

They consent to these conditions, since they can do nothing else. It is Hobson's choice. Half their number are soon weltering in blood. Then the conquerors claim the reward. But the Bey has his loyal officers around him. He commands them again to divide, and to fight against each other. They know their fate in case they fail to fight. Being in the power of the Bey, they fight until only one of their number remains. The Bey kindly orders him to approach, commends his valor, tenders the promised gold, and with a grim smile makes a sign. The head of the young man rolls at the tyrant's feet. This is one of the dramatic stories which used to be told, by which a reputation of cruelty was established for the Turk throughout Europe two hundred years ago.

\*　　\*　　\*　　\*　　\*　　\*　　\*

In former times, more than at present, the Sultans of Turkey had in their court, dwarfs and buffoons. These were allowed more liberty than any one else in the empire. Sultan Ahmet the Second had a buffoon who had a wide reputation for his skill in repartee. The Sultan and his officials endeavored in vain to embarrass him with intricate questions. He was always on his guard, however. He smiled whenever they tried to confound him.

One day the Sultan said to this buffoon :

" I want you to commit an offense, and find a reason to excuse it that will be more reprehensible than the offense itself."

" Very well, your Majesty," said he, " I will serve you rightly."

Two hours later the Sultan went into his garden to take a walk. He was accompanied by his followers, the buffoon being of the number. After many turns in the garden, the buffoon found occasion to be near the Sultan, and, all at once, gave His Majesty a severe pinch on his side. The Sultan turned upon him and said :

"You wretched creature ! You deserve to be hanged. You shall swing for this presently."

He calls for the executioner. The buffoon, without losing his presence of mind, says :

" Just as it pleases your Majesty. I am your slave; dispose of me at any time ; but the act which you resent so much is a mistake. I pinched you, thinking it was the Sultana—your wife."

The Sultan thereupon recollects his curious proposition. He acknowledges that the excuse for the offense is far worse than the offense itself. He countermands his order to the executioner, and resolves to make no more foolish propositions to the buffoon.

There is always a moral, in the form of a maxim, to these stories. In this latter case it is this : " *If you care to have peace in this world, do not give confidence to ignoramuses or idiots. Either from their hand or from their tongue, some evil never fails to come !*"

\*    \*    \*    \*    \*    \*    \*

The reports, generally oral, of cases before the Oriental judges, or cadis, have a quaint sense of humor.

I have the record of an old trial before a cadi : It is the exceptional case of a hot-headed young Turk who was found intoxicated. After the case had been heard by the cadi, a compromise was proposed and accepted. Everybody is relieved. The foreign parties present are not a little astonished at the mode which the released Turk took to show his delight. Selecting with care, a particular hair in the whiskers of his adversary, who had prosecuted the case, he gives it a sudden jerk, drags it out, and assures his opponent that he is his best friend ! The prosecutor—a Frank—rubs his cheek, accepts the comical compromise, and is rejoiced afterward to learn that the peculiarity of the action is considered in Turkey as a mark of great condescension and amity.

The moral is—*that upon a hair compromises depend. Maxima é minimis suspendens.*

\*     \*     \*     \*     \*     \*     \*

While on a diversion, two friends, Mustapha and Shemsi, become tipsy. They start for home. As they are going through the streets of Pera, ready for any adventure, Mustapha notices a big Janizary going along, who wears an enormous turban like some of those pictured in this volume. The Janizary has a wide, fat neck. It is all exposed. Mustapha takes a fancy to him, and says to his boon companion:

"I have a good mind to slap, with the flat of my hand, the nape of the neck of that jolly old Janizary."

All the efforts of Shemsi to prevent him from so doing are useless. Shemsi reasons with Mustapha:

"You are going to do a very risky thing. The least that may happen to you will be endless trouble."

"No," said Mustapha, "I feel like doing it. How can I resist my feeling?"

Then he runs after the Janizary and gives him an immense resounding slap on the neck. The Janizary is astounded and indignant. He is terrified, too, all at once. He hesitates, not knowing what course to take to resent the indignity to his person and office. He is especially puzzled, as Mustapha keeps on laughing like a fool. One moment of reflection is sufficient, however, for the Janizary. He draws out his yataghan and pursues the tipsy fellow. Shemsi intervenes. He begs the Janizary to spare his friend, He pleads first the irresistible impulse, and next that Mustapha is insane. Finally he succeeds in persuading the Janizary to refer the matter to the court of the cadi.

They all go together to the cadi. The defendant confesses the assault. The cadi takes down his code, and after a long, solemn search he pronounces a decision. It is this:

That the defendant shall pay to the Janizary two paras (about fifty cents), in full reparation for the insult and injury.

The Janizary feels his blood running up to his eyes. He addresses the cadi:

" Is this the law, your honor? Are you not mistaken?"

" No," says the cadi, "there is no doubt of it."

" But," says the Janizary, "read it again. There must be some mistake."

" Know ye not, sir," says the cadi, "that whatever comes out of the cadi's mouth is undebatable; because the law I am giving you is the law of Allah!"

" Yes," replies the Janizary; "but, O cadi! I hear that the least finger-cut done in accordance with the sacred law does not ache ; while in this case my neck doth ache, and I would like to see the law."

" Here is the law," remarks the cadi, showing the book.

While the cadi is bending over his volume to show the law to the Janizary, the latter, under the pretext of reading it, approaches the cadi. He administers to the learned judge a sound whack on the nape of his neck.

" What do you mean by this?" shrieks the cadi.

" It means," says the Janizary, "that, it being the sacred law—the will of Allah—I want you to be the recipient, according to law, of the two paras in which you mulct my assailant."

The cadi has no more to say. He is estopped. He abides by his own construction of the law.

*       *       *       *       *       *       *

I can hardly call it a Diversion ; but a singular adventure happened at the Legation during one day in mid-summer. The Legation building is situated on the *Rue Petit Champs*. While looking over some despatches one morning, a card is sent up, in the latest style of pasteboard. On it was the name of a Turkish gentleman. I cannot recall his name, but he was an Effendi, if not a Bey. He enters with a distinguished air. He is invited to be seated. He is admirably dressed. His toilette has an elegance that shames the *personnel* of the Legation, and the ordinary or even the extraordinary Turk who affects the European costume. He desires to know from me, in French, if I speak Turkish. I tell him that I do not. He then begins in French with the greatest calmness ; but the glazed and wild eye, or something, leads me to suspect before he talks long that he is *distrait*. I send to the chamber of the dragoman ; I ask him to translate for me from the Turkish into the English in a quick way. I remark to the visitor with much suavity :

"You desire to see the American Minister?"

He replies : " Yes, Excellency "—the common appellation of all Ministers, whether " excellent " or not

" I have been to the English Legation; I craved its protection, but I have failed. I now desire the protection of the great republic of America, which never fails to be just to the unfortunate."

I bow politely to the compliment. He resumes :

"I am a man of property, unmarried, and have been living at the Hotel d'Angleterre, but for the summer I have moved from that hotel to the Hotel Bellevue, at Buyukdere. While at the Hotel d'Angleterre, I was constantly pursued by persons who desired to take my property and my life."

His eyes shine with a wild, demoniacal lustre, so that I look about me anxiously for the Kavass, with his unloaded silver-handled pistols, and the capoujü, with his big spoon. They are looking in on the scene with Ottomanic gravity.

"When I went to the Hotel Bellevue," resumes the visitor. " I was still pursued, and by the same parties ! I am pursued for another reason than simply to get my property ; I am the son of the highest personage in the Ottoman empire. I am the next inheritor of the throne of Suleïman and other Sultans. I am a descendant lineally of the race of Mahomet. I am the Caliph of the Mussulmans and the Ruler of the people ! "

He did not become violent. He was singularly and tremulously apprehensive of death from the pursuit of his enemies. The dragoman was disposed, at first, as I thought, to smile ironically ; but I gave him the hint, and we both commiserated, in two or three languages, the unfortunate situation of this heir to the throne. We lamented the impotency of the United States to protect a Turkish subject, even though that subject had royal blood in his veins. We remitted him to that palpable law of the Koran, which shields the faithful in all the emergencies of this present life and makes his future beatific.

The Mahometan generally respects the beard. This man had none. His face was smoothly shaven. His eyes had an unnatural brightness in them. His cheeks were ruddy with health, and he seemed in every respect sane. After the interview ended, he thanked us politely for our sympathy and departed. He never returned.

It is nothing new for our citizens abroad to become crazed about some apparent lack of sympathetic action on the part of their Government. I read the other day of an American making a raid with a pistol through the State Department at Washington, because our Consul at Lisbon had received his salary as a circus performer. As he was unable to collect his salary from the circus manager, he had appealed to the Consul, who had received it. This lunatical incident has been accounted for. Owing to the peculiarity of his performance in the circus, which consisted in placing a paving-stone on his head, while another gentleman struck it with a sledge hammer, the claimant had become embarrassed. Perhaps the other gentleman, in one of his blows, struck too low!

If such incidents occur in the Legations of the Occident, how much more frequently are they likely to happen in the Orient, whither the stragglers of all lands venture!

I cast the veil of reticence over many of these cases. It is a wise provision of the Turkish Foreign Office to have a mute act as messenger. It was a comfort to me, on one occasion, to know that no one but a mute could see, not hear or talk of, my embarrassments in the anteroom of the Porte. A little *backsheesh* makes of him a silent and cautious friend. At one particular time, when much depended upon my entrance to the chamber of the Minister of Foreign Affairs, the mute in charge of the ante-room came out to see me. With wild, acrobatic gestures, and such inarticulate noises as Dr. Johnson made over his tea, this silent servant of the Porte indicated that I was expected. He did more. He made his salutations—not as a Giaour or Parsee, to the rising sun—but to the western orb of day. This, to me, was a puzzle until the Dragoman, Mr. Gargiulo, explained its meaning. How this mute knew me and my *nom de plume*, I never could learn. He had a sign for all the Ministers. The English Minister he indicated by a motion over his cheek— plainly signifying mutton-chop whiskers; the Russian Minister, by a shake, as if the Russian bear and Arctic frost had chilled him. When he referred to the American Minister, he pointed to the glorious West—evidently meaning "Sunset"—my pet name, and that of our launch.

It seemed to me at first, upon going abroad, that diplomacy

ought to be a happy and peaceful means of furthering all the gentle interests of mankind. Was it not the guardian of commerce, the pioneer of science, the messenger of peace, the destroyer of discord, the instructor of nations, and the angel of good-will to men? In many ways, the well-being of mankind might be more or less enhanced by an honest and vigilant diplomatic service. But perhaps the most feather-headed and callow geniuses whom we love to weep over upon our star are those diplomats who, with a small range of intellect and a limited rank in the service, undertake to direct the world in its career of advancement.

HODJA'S PICTURE.

(*This likeness is taken from a Turkish journal.*)

A curious history might be written of the frivolous quarrels of diplomats, both of ambassadors and ambassadresses,. who have had their Diversions abroad. I must reserve that history for another occasion.

I cannot refrain from publishing to the Western world a few Turkish fables. They introduce the famous Narr-ed-din Hodja. He is an imaginary person; not a Sawney or a Joe Miller, but the embodiment of that Turkish humanity which suits the humorous Ottoman sensibility. He holds the same rank with the Turks as Æsop with the Greeks. It is a fictitious name, under which a large number of anecdotes have been collected and compiled.

Narr-ed-din Hodja, as the title (Hodja) implies, is supposed to be a man learned in religion. He is the representative and exemplar of Turkish humor, pure and simple. He is represented as living at Bagdad. All the surroundings attached to his anecdotes are Turkish. He is not supposed, like Æsop, to have written them himself, but he is simply connected, supposititiously, with humorous sayings and doings. He is the Mrs. Harris of

HODJA WITHOUT HIS LATCH-KEY.

the Ottoman Sarah Gamp. He is clever, homely and deep; but more often he is the victim, as will be seen from the following :

One night, before retiring to rest, Narr-ed-din says to his wife:

"If it rain to-morrow, I shall go to my field. If it do not rain, I shall go to my vineyard."

"Say, if it please God, Hodja," suggests his wife.

"Whether it please God or not," replies the Hodja, "I shall go to one or the other."

"Hodja," says his wife, "say, if it please God."

"Nothing of the kind," says Narr-ed-din; "I shall go."

Next day it is not raining, and the Hodja starts to go to his vineyard. He has not gone far, however, before he is stopped by the king's troopers. They compel him to work all day, to repair the roads. It is quite late at night when he is set free. By the time he arrives at his house, every one is fast asleep. He knocks at the door. His wife, putting her head out of the window, asks who it is.

"Wife," replied Narr-ed-din Hodja, "if it please God, it is I."

*The moral which this tale teaches is exquisite for its suggestiveness of the necessity of dependence upon the Divine and not upon the selfish human will.*

\*      \*      \*      \*      \*      \*      \*

When the Hodja made up his mind to marry, his neighbors came to him and told him that if he married, his "wife would turn his house upside down."

"Very well," says he, "I will take care of that."

A few days after, he began building his house. Instead of beginning at the foundation, he surprises his neighbors by preparing the tiles for the roof. The neighbors come again and inquire of the Hodja :

"What are you doing?"

"I am building my house," he responds.

"But," they reply, "you cannot build a house, starting from the roof."

"Yes," says the Hodja, "but did I not tell you I am going to marry?"

"What then," say the anxious neighbors, fearing he had gone clean daft.

"What then? Did you not tell me that if I married, my wife would turn my house upside down? Now, I build it so that when she turns it upside down, it will be right-side up. If what you say to me be true, I advise you to follow my plan toward your wives. As they never agree with you, give them the opposite of what you wish, and you will always have your own will."

The moral whereof is : *that often by indirection and tacking we bring the ship into port.*

\*    \*    \*    \*    \*    \*    \*

The Hodja having built his house to his own satisfaction and that of everybody else—offers it for sale. He makes a bargain, but asks of the purchaser, as a favor, to be allowed to drive a nail on the wall of one of the rooms ; the nail to be his own property. This is granted.

The buyer is soon established in the house. Shortly after midnight, the owner hears a knock at his outer door. He descends to inquire :

"Who is there?"

"It is I," says the Hodja; "I wish to tie a string on my nail." Two or three days pass, when again the knock is heard about the same hour. Again the demand is made :

"What is wanting?"

The answer comes, "I pray you, good friend, I should like to untie that string from my property." This performance being repeated several times, compels the purchaser to abandon his purchase for a song.

The moral of which is : *to make sure of the character of the vender, when you become the vendee.*

\*    \*    \*    \*    \*    \*    \*

The Hodja was considered the most learned man in his town. Every one called on him for information and advice. One day a number of people called, and demanded of him a reply to this question :

"When, O Hodja! will be the end of the world?"

"Oh!" says he, "ask me something difficult. That is very easy to answer. When my wife dies, it will be the end of half of the world ; when I die, then the whole world will end."

Moral by Sir Boyle Roche : *Single misfortunes never come alone, and the greatest possible misfortune is followed by one greater.*

\*    \*    \*    \*    \*    \*    \*

Another story is told of the Hodja : He used to teach in the parish school. He had taught his pupils that, whenever he happened to sneeze, they should all stand up, and, clapping their hands together, should cry out :

"God grant you long life, Hodja !"

This the pupils regularly did whenever the Hodja sneezed. One day the bucket gets loose and falls into the well of the schoolhouse. As the pupils are afraid to go down into the well to fetch up the bucket, Narr-ed-din Hodja undertakes the task.

He accordingly strips, and tying a rope round his waist, asks his pupils to lower him carefully into the well, and pull him up again when he gives the signal. The Hodja goes down, and having caught the bucket, shouts out to his pupils to pull him up again. This they do. The Hodja is nearly out of the well, when he suddenly sneezes ! Upon this, his pupils immediately let go the rope, begin to knock their hands together, and shout down the well :

"God grant you long life, Hodja !"

But the poor Hodja tumbles down to the bottom of the well with a tremendous crash, breaking his head and several of his bones.

The moral of this story is—*too neat for explication.*

\*　　\*　　\*　　\*　　\*　　\*　　\*

One day Narr-ed-din Hodja is too lazy to preach his usual sermon at the mosque. He simply addresses himself to his congregation, saying :

"Of course ye know, oh, faithful Musslumans, what I am going to say to you?"

As the Hodja stops, evidently waiting for an answer, the congregation cry out with one voice :

"No, Hodja Effendi, we do not know."

"Then, if you do not know, I have nothing to say to you," replies the Hodja, and immediately leaves the pulpit.

Next day he again addresses his congregation, saying :

"Know ye, oh, faithful Mussulmans, what I am going to say to you ?"

Fearing that if, as on the previous day, they say "No," the Hodja would leave them again without a sermon, the congregation this time, replies :

"Yes, Hodja, we do know."

"Then if you do know what I am going to say," quietly says

THE HODJA SNEEZING IN THE WELL.

THE HODJA'S DONKEY ON HIS VERACITY.

the Hodja, " of course, there is no need of my saying it. He again steps down from the pulpit, to the consternation of the congregation.

On the third day, the Hodja again puts the question :

" Know ye, oh faithful Mussulmans, what I am going to say to you ? "

The congregation, determined not to be disappointed again, take counsel among themselves on the question. Accordingly some of them reply :

" No, Hodja, we do not know," while others cry :

" Yes, Hodja, we do know."

" Very well, then," says the Hodja, " as there are some of you who do know, and others who do not know, what I was going to say, let those who do know, tell it to those that do not know;" and he quickly descends from the pulpit.

The moral of this story is not always in the mind of the clergy. It is this :

*If you can find nothing worth saying, do not trespass on the congregation by trying to say it.*

*     *     *     *     *     *     *

The Hodja borrows from a friend a large copper vessel, in which to do his washing. A few days afterward, the vessel is returned clean, washed and polished. Inside of it is another but much smaller copper vessel.

" What is this, Hodja ? " asks his friend; " I lend you one vessel and you bring me back two ! "

" It is very curious," says the Hodja. " It appears that your vessel is with child when you lend it to me. While in my possession it must have given birth to this baby vessel. Of course both belong equally to you."

" Oh ! thank you, good Hodja," says the man, laughing, and without more parley agrees to receive back both vessels.

Some time after this, the Hodja again applies for the loan of the large vessel—the mother vessel, as he describes it. The demand is readily granted. Before leaving, the Hodja inquires after the health of the " baby vessel." He expresses his pleasure at hearing that it is doing extremely well.

A week, then a month elapses, but no Hodja appears to bring back the borrowed vessel. The proprietor at length, losing patience, goes himself to obtain it.

"Very sorry," says the Hodja, "but your copper vessel is dead."

"Dead, Hodja!" cries the other in surprise; "what do you mean?"

"Just what I say," replies Narr-ed-din Hodja; "your vessel is dead."

"Nonsense, Hodja!" says the man—irritated at the Hodja's quiet manner; "how can a copper vessel die?"

"Read up your natural history, my good friend," answers the imperturbable Hodja," puffing quietly at his long pipe, "and you will see that everything that gives birth to a child must inevitably succumb in due course to the fate of all mortals. You were willing enough to believe that your vessel had given birth to a 'baby vessel;' I do not see, therefore, why you should now doubt my word as to its being dead."

Although the Hodja could prevaricate in speech, and appropriate to himself his neighbor's chattels, he nevertheless teaches in this fable that it is not wise to take unfair advantage of your neighbor.

*The biter will sometimes get bitten.*

\*       \*       \*       \*       \*       \*       \*

A mendicant knocks at the Hodja's door.

"What do you want, my friend?" asks the Hodja, putting his head out of an upper floor window.

"Come down, Hodja Effendi, and I will tell you," replies the mendicant.

The Hodja obeys, and coming down to the door, asks again of the man what is wanted.

"Alms," is the answer.

"Oh! very well," said the Hodja, "come with me up-stairs."

Leading the way, the Hodja conducts the man to the topmost floor of his house. Arrived there, he turns round and remarks:

"I am very much distressed, my good friend, but I have no alms to give you."

"Why did you not say so down below?" inquires the man angrily.

"Why did you not tell me what you wanted when I asked you from the window? Did you not make me come down to the door?" retorts the Hodja.

The moral whereof is :
*Be polite and considerate when you beg favors.*

\*       \*       \*       \*       \*       \*       \*

A friend calls on Narr-ed-din Hodja to borrow his donkey.

"Very sorry," says the Hodja, who does not want to lend the animal, "but the donkey is not here ; I have hired him out for the day."

Unfortunately, just at that moment the donkey begins to bray loudly, thus giving the direct lie to the Hodja.

"How is this, Hodja ?" says his friend; "you say the donkey is away, and here he is braying in the stable !"

The Hodja, nothing daunted, replies in a grave manner :

"My dear sir, please do not demean yourself so low as to believe the donkey rather than myself—a fellow-man and a venerable Hodja with a long gray beard."

The moral of the last fable some people never will perceive. It is this:

*An ass will always reveal himself by some inappropriate remark. Asses should be seldom seen, and never heard. The wise man hideth his ass when the borrower cometh around.*

\*       \*       \*       \*       \*       \*       \*

The story-tellers of the East are a literary guild of their own. Their practice is as old as Homer. Most of their tales, as I have shown, have a moral. In the early training of the child, by its nurse or tutor, wonderful stories are told to the children. Some of these tales are at the root of that education which is necessary to form the character of a true believer. As an instance, the child is taught not to be afraid of death ; not to be astonished at anything, no matter how wonderful; and not to say in conversation anything but what is necessary to promote its own interest. All this is given to the children in allegoric stories. I will undertake to give here some of these stories.

We have often been told of the justice of Solomon, as to the two babies who were brought before him. There is a better case of that before a cadi in Egypt. A pair of women come before him. They complain that one of his Kavasses had seized a cup of milk without payment, and had swallowed it. The man is recognized. When the cadi is through with the case, he adjudges that the accused shall be ripped open. The moral is in the ripping :

*Per curiam: If milk be found in the stomach of the Kavass the plaintiffs shall receive their five paras, the price of the milk; but if there be no milk, they shall be ripped up in turn, for accusing one of the household unjustly."*

The Kavass is ripped; a little milk is found in him, and the women receive their money.

I desire to place upon record the fact that at no time in the history of the American Legation was my Kavass ever so wanting in milk as to cheat the milk-woman. He is a Moslem, and has been trained in the moralities of the story.

\*　　\*　　\*　　\*　　\*　　\*　　\*

There was a man who, in despair on account of his poverty, decides to commit suicide. He procures a rope ,and goes to the top of a mountain to hang himself on a tree. When he is near the tree he finds the Devil waiting for him. The Devil asks :

"Why do you want to die ?"

The man, whose name is Ezek, answers:

" I have nothing to live upon; I am tired of life."

"Why?" says the Devil; " do not do anything of the kind; I will give you the means of making money."

"What means ?" answered Ezek.

" Now look here," says the Devil ; " I am going to transform myself into a donkey. You will mount the donkey and go to the city. You will pass through the main street. When you get near the house of Ahmed Bey, you will make your donkey go as fast as possible. Ahmed is a great amateur of fast-running donkeys. He will call you in ; but do not stop ! Go on ! Larrup your donkey. Be sure Ahmed will find you, and then, make your bargain."

Ezek mounts the donkey. When he comes near the house of Ahmed, he lets the bridle loose. The donkey starts with a dash. Ahmed, seeing the donkey, knocks on the glass of the window. He opens the window and shouts to Ezek. It is of no use. Ezek will not stop. Then, in a great hurry, Ahmed calls for his servants. He orders them to rush after Ezek, and bring him forthwith, with his donkey. The servants give chase, and with the greatest effort Ezek is brought back. He is asked :

" Will you part with your donkey ?"

He replies : " I do not want to sell the donkey."

Ahmed then treats him more graciously, and asks him what he would sell his donkey for.

Ezek says : " I have no intention of selling."

Ahmed offers him $300. Ezek refuses.    $500 ; he says " Yok !" $1,000 ; still no.    Finally, the bargain is concluded for $2,000.    Ezek receives his money and delivers the donkey.

One may imagine the care that the Bey would take of such a precious donkey, which cost him such a price.  He arranges a separate place in his stable for the donkey.  He buys a new saddle and bridle, and as there is in the courtyard of his house a fountain, he himself insists upon taking the donkey every day to the fountain.  He does so for several days, opening the spout, filling the basin, and allowing the donkey to drink freely.  One day, Ahmed is holding the bridle in front of the fountain and the donkey is drinking,  All at once, the donkey slips into the spout, leaving Ahmed Bey with the bridle in his hands.  At first, Ahmed is astounded.

" Can I believe my senses !" he exclaims.  Yes ; the donkey shows him his two ears sticking out from the spout !  The ears are in motion. The poor Bey would call for help, but he is voiceless.  After many efforts he screams out ; the servants appear.  He relates what has happened.  While he is telling his story, the donkey still wags its ears, but only to the Bey.

" Why, master," say the servants, " it must be a mistake. How can a donkey go through such a small spout as this ?"

" Why," says the Bey, " there it is, moving its ears ; look ! look ! look ! "

" Oh, what a pity ! " say the servants.  " Our master is crazy."

Then they take the Bey into the house, hoping to quiet him. It is useless.  He tells his story to everybody, and in the most emphatic way.  Finally, it is decided to place him in an insane asylum.

When he is taken out of his house he has to pass before the fountain.  He looks on the spout.  He notices the ears of the donkey.  They are still moving.  He cannot resist.  He screams out :

" There it is, still !  I see its ears ! "

When he is at the asylum, his friends go to see him.  They

ask for his story. This he repeats. Then the friends conclude that he is still crazy.

But after a few days Ahmed thinks about his condition. He makes up his mind to get out of the asylum. So he changes his policy, and when a friend asks him:

"How did that donkey manage to slip through the spout," he answers:

"Now, my friend, how can you imagine such nonsense! Can a donkey go through a fountain spout?"

By giving this answer he is freed. He goes home; but as soon as he enters the court of his house, lo! the donkey shows its ears again. Ahmed sighs, but is careful not to say anything. Had he spoken, he would have been returned to the asylum.

There is a moral to this, as to all Oriental tales. It shows that when a man makes a statement which may militate against him, he must afterward change it, with such skill as to turn it in his favor.

As the analogue, fable or parable is a favorite mode of teaching in the East, I relate the foregoing; but truth is still a better teacher. A true story, therefore, I will now deliver:

For some twenty-five years the Turkish government has been doing its best to have roads built in Asia Minor, and, although the people in the interior have been at work all this time, not one road has been completed. There was a Governor-General of Castamouni some fourteen years ago. He was a good Turkish scholar. As soon as he reached Tueboli, a seaport on the Black Sea, he forwarded a telegram to Constantinople as follows:

"The roads from Castamouni to Tueboli are finished. I have come over them with my carriage."

The Governor-General comes from the latter town in his carriage. There is general praise in the papers and in official quarters. Has he not finished the road? When he arrives at Constantinople he is received with great honor. Some time later it is found that there is no road between the two places except the original pathway. In examining carefully the telegram, it is found that the expressions used in it meant *with* his carriage, not necessarily *in* his carriage. The Pasha did not lie. Those who read the telegram did not understand it; that was all.

There is a way of writing in the Turkish language which is very elastic. The Turks are masters of this style. Their children

THE DONKEY'S EARS AND THE CRAZY MAN.

are taught in this style early. There are a great many Turkish scholars among the Christians. Some of these manage the language quite well, but never better than the Turks. Any document written by a Christian, no matter how well written, the Turk detects its source immediately. It lacks the Ottoman elasticity. And yet there are few nations who seem to give out really fewer ambiguous voices than the Ottoman.

# CHAPTER XXVII.

AMONG THE CADIS—MAHOMETAN JUSTICE—HUMOROUS ILLUSTRA-
TIONS.

A MODERN CADI.

THE police administration of the present day in Constantinople is very unlike that of the past. Look upon the picture of the ancient cadi, and compare him with the judicial personages in the

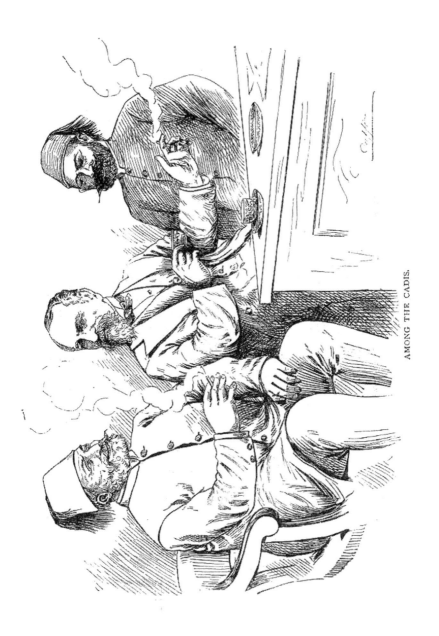

AMONG THE CADIS.

companion sketch.    The difference in costume is not greater than in the code that they administer.

No longer in Pera or in Stamboul does the judge sit turbaned and cross-legged to administer to offenders his own will as the law. The police business is modeled upon that of Paris, and the tribunals have the same mode of procedure.    Barring the red fez cap which the police justices wear, and an occasional cigarette and cup of coffee, their courts are the same as those of the Occident.    The *Tribunal Correctionel de Pera* takes care of the police matters of this suburb.    Important cases, involving felonies of high degree, are sent to the higher tribunals in Stamboul.    In such cases the tribunal at Pera is only an examining and committing court.

Taking along our dragoman, I make a call at the Court House in Pera.    It is in the centre of the thronging population on the Grand Rue.    When we enter, the court has not convened, but the Chief Judge, Hilmi Effendi, is upon the bench reading papers.    He is a Turk.    He has had great judicial and police experience in the interior before he came here.    He is noted for his shrewd knowledge of the kind of characters who come before him—a veritable Judge Dowling of the Tombs of twenty years ago.    He speaks French, but not English.

We are invited to a seat by his side, and pass the time in talking about modes and codes of criminal practice in various countries.    We agreed that it was a cruel fate to be imprisoned simply because one happens to be an observer of a crime.    In fact, we agree that it is one of the ridiculous eccentricities of human order thus to punish the innocent, that society might have security.

One thing leads to another, until our talk takes the direction of the whims of the elder day of the old cadis, who, like our Western squires in America, substituted their own sense of equity as the rule of right.    Between cigarettes and coffee I relate a story of a Hungarian justice, doubtless of Oriental origin :

\*        \*        \*        \*        \*        \*        \*

In the interior of Hungary a Turkish agent is sent to buy cavalry horses to recruit for the then probable war with Bulgaria and Greece.    While there the agent desires that the proprietor of a village, with whom he was contracting, should show him a specimen of the Hungarian mode of proceeding.

"Wait a few moments," says the proprietor, who is also a magistrate, "and I will see who is in the town jail."

Calling his constable, he is informed by that officer that a goose thief had been apprehended during the night, and is in confinement. He sends for the criminal.

"Are there any witnesses?" asks the judge.

"Two," is the answer; "the man who owns the goose and a man who saw the theft."

After hearing the evidence, the judge, in his fierce and harsh Hungarian-Finnish-Tartaric tongue, calls up the culprit and says:

"You have been found guilty, and I fine you ten kreutzers and ten days' imprisonment for stealing the goose!"

Thereupon the judge summons the owner of the bird:

"I fine you ten kreutzers and ten days' imprisonment for allowing your goose to be stolen!"

Having thus disposed of the parties, the judge, turning to the witness, says:

"Sirrah! I fine you ten kreutzers and ten days' imprisonment for not minding your own business!"

\* \* \* \* \* \* \*

Hilmi Effendi listens with interest to this story of Slavonic justice, and remarks that almost as odd a case recently came before one of the courts of Stamboul.

A creditor comes to the judge to have a note sued. It is for 1,500 piastres, and not due until three years after the complaint is made. The judge entertains the suit, and condemns the creditor to confinement for three years.

"For," said his honor: "How do I know where you will be three years hence, so as to pay you the piastres, unless I hold you?"

We agree that this is an improvement on the American custom of the imprisonment of witnesses in criminal cases.

\* \* \* \* \* \* \*

In Egypt, long before the Turkish rule in that region, there were struggles between the Mamelukes and the Circassians. A Circassian chief, through the advice of a servant, who, though ignorant, was naturally astute, happened by accident to discover the weak points of the ruling government in Egypt. Upon these points, as upon the rounds of a ladder, he ascended to the throne.

Formerly the Circassian had promised the servant that if ever he obtained that eminence, the servant should receive the appointment of Chief Judge. The servant's name was Caracoush, meaning "black bird." So, as soon as the chief was enthroned, he gave Caracoush the promised post. Among the many cases that came before him was the following petition:

"Being a burglar by profession, and compelled by want to rob a house, I select that of a tailor. To enter it I must make my way through the courtyard. This is surrounded by a high wall. In jumping from this wall I am caught on the spikes the tailor had fixed in the wall to suspend ropes for the washing. The result is, I lose an eye. I now demand that my eye be restored, and that the fellow who drove the spike shall be punished."

The judge reads the petition, and concludes that justice is due the petitioner. He summons the tailor, to whom the matter is explained. The tailor argues that the thief has no business to jump into his yard in the night, so that if he lost an eye, it is his own fault. But the judge remarks:

"The thief is only practising his profession, and the law only punishes robbers."

"If," he says to the tailor, "you had not driven the spikes in the walls, the thief would not have lost his eye ; therefore your eye must pay the forfeit."

The poor tailor begs and cries in vain. The verdict is pronounced. It must be executed. After a long struggle, the tailor seizes the knees of the judge, kisses them vigorously, and with tears in his eyes exclaims:

"Oh ! mighty judge. Your decision is sound, but consider. Am I not supporting a large family—my old mother, my wife, and my seven young children ? They all depend on me, and I myself depend on my two eyes. Am I not a tailor ? Do I not need my two eyes ? If I lose one, how can I pass the thread into the needle's eye ? How can I do my fine sewing ? My reputation will suffer and all of us starve !"

Seeing some sign of relenting in the judicial countenance, the tailor is encouraged. He resumes, brightening :

"I have a neighbor who is a sportsman. When he aims at the game he shuts one eye. Why, great judge, his two eyes are an embarrassment for him ! Had he but one, it would save him the trouble of shutting the other. Moreover, what difference does it make to this robber? All he wants is an eye pulled out. Whether it be mine or that of the sportsman's, what matter? It is all one to him."

The argument sounds plausible. The judge considers a moment, and then sends for the sportsman. In spite of protests he decrees the loss of the sportsman's superfluous eye. The verdict is carried into execution, and judicial logic is vindicated !

\*     \*     \*     \*     \*     \*     \*

After this recital, coffee and cigarettes are brought into the court and placed before us on the bench, and we resume our good-natured confabulation. We are joined by one of the associates of the court, Sabit Effendi.

Finding my hearers interested, I entreat them to listen to one more of my Egyptian stories, illustrative of Arab justice. I had heard it from a story-teller in Cairo in my recent rambles in Egypt:

I had been trudging about with our Kavass, Hassan-Hassan, when I note a crowd in front of an Arab coffee-house listening to an Arab story-teller. Hassan is good in Arabic, and seeing me much interested, he translates the story faithfully. It interests me the more, as it had some incidents quite familiar to the readers of Shakespeare. It was all about a poor Arab soldier, who had a young and pretty wife, whom he loved passing well. An old and wealthy Jew becomes suddenly enamored of her. The soldier, being out of employment, is in great need and distress, and his wife almost starving. She proposes a plan for work. He is to buy a hatchet and ropes, and repair to the forest. There he is to cut wood and sell it, while she takes to needlework. He goes to the Jew for a loan to set up in business. The Jew sees his opportunity, and, after the usual haggling, loans the money on a bond. The penalty of the bond is the same old " pound of flesh." It is the Shylock story with some variations. The soldier risks the penalty, but fails on pay-day. The parties are summoned before the judge. Half the penalty of the bond is tendered.

" Produce all the cash, or prepare to die ! " cries the Jew.

A scuffle—not set down in Shakespeare—ensues. The soldier vanishes, and the Jew and the officers start in pursuit. Here Shakespeare fails again, and the Orient comes to the fore. In running away, the soldier tumbles over a woman in the street. She is in an interesting situation. Trouble unmentionable ensues.  Her husband joins in the pursuit.  A little farther, the soldier runs against a horseman and a horse.  He strikes the horse to clear the way.  It is a valuable horse, and the blow puts out one of its eyes.  The horseman then pursues the fugitive. The soldier escapes out of the city, and seeing a stone quarry, prepares to hide by leaping into it.

"Bismillah!" he cries, and tumbles in.  He falls on a shed, under which an old man is lying.  The rafters give way.  The old man is killed, and the old man's son seizes the runaway, ties him, and brings him before the cadi.

The soldier is of an observing turn of mind.  As he is dragged along to court he notices an old man staggering and drunk. Further on he observes a shrieking man tied on a bier *en route* to the tomb to be buried alive.  These observations terrify the soldier.  When he reaches the judicial presence he trembles and perspires at every pore.  The witnesses for the state are called— Jew, husband, horse owner, and the son of the old man.  The reporters take down the evidence, and the lawyers argue ; and thus *per curiam :*

To the Jew :  "Bring out your scales, sirrah !  Sharpen your knife !  Cut off the pound of flesh !  It is a foolish bond, but the soldier must pay the forfeit.  But, mind you, no bone, no skin, shall be touched.  One cut only.  No additional torture by more than one cut.  Neither"—and here comes in our own Shakespeare—"neither exceed nor come short of the exact one pound ! If you do, the Koran hath a retribution in its law."

The Jew gives up his claim, and is fined five silver pieces for unreasonable prosecution.

To the relative of the disabled woman :  "Let the woman be made over to the defendant and restored to her health and her previous condition, and then to her injured husband.

The relative is shocked, and especially so when the family is fined ten pieces for taking up the time of the court.

To the horseman :  "Send for some sawyers !  Divide the horse longitudinally, from the middle part of his head to the end of his tail.  You, complainant, take the sound half.  The other part to the defendant, who must pay 100 pieces for the loss."

As this sum would not be equal to the loss of the animal, the horseman is allowed to withdraw on paying twenty pieces.

To the son of the old man who was killed :  "Let the offender be dragged to the stone quarry, placed on the spot where the old man lay, and let the son jump down on him."

The young man thereupon modifies his original statement, and says : " On second thought, the affair was an accident."

On this phase of the case, the son is fined forty pieces for bringing the suit before the learned tribunal.

The story-teller does not stop here. With all the marvelous

TURKISH *lex talionis*, OR JUMPING
ON THE OLD MAN.

sequences and imitations of one of the thousand and one tales, he holds his audience eager to know the rest. One of the excited auditors cries out in Arabic, while a murmur thrills through the crowd :

"What of the drunken man ? What of the burying of the live man ? What has that to do with it ?"

"Well," resumes the story-teller, "well, the soldier-prisoner being reluctant to leave so good a judge, and seeming anxious to say something, the judge asks him to talk.

"' Oh ! learned judge,' he says, ' you are so wise that I wonder at seeing in your bailiwick forbidden liquor and a drunken old sot.'

"' Thank you,' says the judge. ' The law is, that forbidden things are lawful in cases of necessity. I appointed that venerable man to test the spirits brought here for sale. It disguised him in his lawful duty.   Therefore I now know its poisonous adulteration.   As to the burying case, the burial was ordered by the court, for know that six years ago that man's wife was married to another man according to the statute, two witnesses having sworn that the husband had died at Bagdad.   The first husband appears, claims that he is not dead, and advances a claim for the restoration of his wife.   I send for the two witnesses. They stand to it that they attended the funeral and saw the man buried.   Therefore this is not a real man, only his image or ghost.   There must be an end of trouble and litigation.' "

The soldier has some misgivings, but dissembles them.   He praises the cadi's equity and retires.

\*     \*     \*     \*     \*     \*     \*

The justices seem to suppress with difficulty considerable hilarity over this story.   After resuming our cigarettes and refilling our dainty coffee-cups, the chief, Hilmi Effendi, remarks that these Arabic precedents are often quoted in the interior—meaning Asia Minor—and that he would call on me some time and take up the Egyptian thread, and follow the clue until its labyrinth led us to the sacred precincts of Mecca.

Our dragoman, Mr. Garguilo, who is well versed in the Koran and familiar with the courts here, breaks the reserve in which he had indulged.   After a few whiffs of his cigarette and a twinkle in his big Levantine eye, he gravely remarks that not only is the administration of justice conducted with a curious and humorous turn in the East, but the detection of criminals often displays a cunning that a Vidocq might envy, or a Gaboriau long to describe. In illustration, he says :

\*     \*     \*     \*     \*     \*     \*

" Let me give, not a romantic incident, but a veritable narrative—as it was told to me some years ago, when I was trying a case at Kharpoot."

As the police court is not to convene for a hour, the patience of the Ottoman is called to the front, and the dragoman begins his recital, as follows :

" A few years ago," said he, " on the occasion of the anniversary of Queen Victoria's accession to the throne, Mr. J. H. Skene, English Consul at Aleppo, gives a dinner.   He holds an evening reception, where the *crême* of the society at Aleppo is gathered. A large number of guests are invited to the Consul's table. Great pains are taken to make the dinner as pleasant as possible. In Aleppo nothing speaks so eloquently as display. Flowers in profusion decorate the table and the apartments. Every piece of silverware is brought out to add to the splendor of the festivity. The table service is of solid silver. The Kavasses of the Consulate wear their gorgeous gold-trimmed clothes and bear their inlaid pistols and yataghans. After dinner the party leaves the dining-room.. They go into the salon, where a large number of guests are assembled. The party is a success.

" The servants of the house have been occupying themselves with serving the guests—passing coffee to one, tea to another, a narghilé to a third, and a chibouque to a fourth, and so on, so that everything in the dining-room is apparently trusted to the care of the Kavasses. But what is the surprise of the Consul when, on the day after the fête, he finds that the silverware has disappeared. Search is made in every part of the house. Not a single piece is discovered. There is general consternation, not so much on the part of the Consul himself as on the part of those in his service.' After mature reflection upon the mishap, the Consul calls the most intelligent of his Kavasses. He questions him. The Kavass insists that he did not steal the silver, and that he does not know who did.

"But the Consul is a good detective, and ready in his knowledge of men and things. He is also a cool-tempered man. He says to his Kavass :

" ' There is no use to swear. I am not going to change my opinion. I have good reasons to suspect you to be the thief, and I mean that you shall bring my silver to me within twenty-four hours, else you will be put in the hands of the authorities, and you will not get away until I find my property. There is no alternative.'

" ' Mr. Consul,' said the Kavass, ' I have already told you that I did not steal your silver.'

" The Kavass begs for two or three hours' time, and leaves. In an hour he returns, bringing with him by the bridle a little donkey. This he presents to the Consul, stating that the donkey would find the thief, if he would allow the animal to be placed in one of the rooms and the window shutters to be closed, so as to darken the room.

" ' Do so!' said the Consul, who is curious to see what would result.

" After the donkey is placed in the dark room, the Kavass asks the Consul to call everybody in the house—masters, employees, Kavasses and servants. They come. They are placed in front of the door of the room where the donkey is.

" When all are present, the Kavass says :

" ' Now we are to enter this room one by one, and as soon as we get in, we are to take a pull at the donkey's tail. The donkey will make no sign. It will say nothing unless the robber is among us. Then you may depend on it he will bray, and indicate who has stolen your goods. Oh, do not laugh. I have had occasion to make use of that remedy. It never fails.

" ' Now,' says he to the Consul, ' you go in first and pull the tail. We will all follow you, one by one.

" The singular procession begins, the Consul in the lead. Every one enters the room and pulls at the donkey's tail, but the donkey does not bray. After the performance is over and all come out, the Consul asks if all of them have really pulled at the tail. All respond emphatically, ' Yes.'

" ' How strange it is,' said he, ' that the donkey did not bray ! It seems that the thief is not to be found among us. I cannot explain it otherwise.'

" He then forms them in a circle around him.

" ' Now, gentlemen,' he says, ' hands up, please.'

" Every one obeys.

" ' Here is your man, Mr. Consul,' says he, all at once, pointing at one of the party—a servant. ' You see, every one who entered the room pulled at the tail, and thus got his or her hands blackened, while this man did not pull on the tail, as he was sure the donkey would bray. Consequently his hands are clean.'

\*　　\*　　\*　　\*　　\*　　\*　　\*

" The fact is," said our dragoman in conclusion, " there is so much superstition among the common people of the East that such devices are sure to make an almost supernatural impression. However, the man confessed, and the silver was returned."

We generally concurred in the opinion that such modes of detection would not operate successfully in London, Paris, New York or Constantinople, where no such childish ruses would produce the required results ; but the simple Arab of the

THE DONKEY AS A DETECTIVE.

interior shrank from the *experimentum crucis,* as if it were not a
donkey's tail powdered with charcoal, but an ordeal of fire, under
the judgment of Allah.

What is the principle lying at the foundation of these simple
proceedings and strange rulings of the old Oriental officers and
cadis ? Some general thought must be their base. This question
we agreed to reserve.

We bade our judicial friends good by, and carried with us the
memory of a happy hour, amusing and instructive.

May I attempt a commentary as the conclusion of my string
of anecdotes ?

From the time of Solomon's decision as to the proprietorship
of the disputed baby, to the case of the bad Manhattan husband,
who was paroled in charge of his wife by Justice Power, there
have been many rare touches of this homely equity, after which
law is said to limp. The Orient is the *fons et origo* of these wise
tests, which are applied by sagacious judges to the affairs of men.
The idea which lies nearest to the corner-stone of Mahometan
power is the idea of justice, honestly administered, without technical hindrances. An incident in the history of this capital city
will serve to test this remark.

After Mahomed II. had conquered Constantinople, he was
told that the fall of the Greek empire had been predicted by two
Greek priests two years before, and that these priests were still
in the city. Mahomed sent for them. He asks :

"How did you know that I would besiege and take Constantinople ? "

They respond :

"It was not a guess, nor a prophecy, your Majesty ! It was
by close observation of the lack of administration, and especially
of justice, by which we formed our opinions."

"How long is my power over this country going to last ?"
asks Mahomed.

"We cannot tell now," respond the priests. "We must have
three months' time in which to make investigations as to the
administration of justice, and for that we require a firman from
your Majesty, so that we may be allowed to visit the courts, and
also 5,000 piastres for our traveling expenses."

The Sultan grants all they ask, and they leave.

During their tour they find themselves in a village where a

certain Mehemed had bought a horse from a man of the name of Osman. He paid for it three hundred piastres ; that is, one hundred cash and two hundred on time, to be paid two or three days later. Mehemed took the horse home, but, to his surprise, it refused all food. The animal was sick. In the morning Mehemed took the horse back to Osman, protesting against the bargain. He had intended to buy a sound horse. This one was sick. He wished Osman to take it back and return the one hundred piastres paid. Osman answered that he had sold a sound horse, and declined to take a sick one back. He insisted on the payment of the balance due. The neighbors interposed in vain, and the two parties concluded to apply to the court. Mehemed and Osman start for the chief town to see the judge. When arrived at the court they find the judge absent—gone to his bath. As the hour is late they decide to return home and come back in the morning, bringing the horse with them. Unfortunately, during the night the horse dies in the hands of Mehemed.

The second day they go to see the judge again. Both sides state the case. Osman insists that he can produce witnesses to testify that the horse was sound. Mehemed asserts that the best evidence of the horse being sick is that he died the previous night.

"Oh," said the judge, hoping to find a clue on which to found a decision, "when did the horse die ? "

" The second day after it was taken by Mehemed."

" Why, then, did you not come while the horse was alive ?' asks the judge.

" We came, but you were at the bath.''

" Now I see," rejoins the judge, and, turning to his servant, orders him to bring a box wherein his documents and moneys are kept. The box is brought and opened.

" What is your claim, Mehemed ?" he asks.

" The restitution of the hundred piastres.''

The judge, taking the sum from the box, hands it to Mehemed. He then asks Osman:

"What is your claim ?''

The payment of the two hundred piastres, the balance of the price for the horse.''

Taking from his box this sum, it is paid over to Osman.

On being asked, " What does all this mean ?" the judge replies :

"Had I not been absent when the two men came the first time, I would have been able to decide justly, in accordance with the sacred law; but my absence from the bench, at the bath, postponed the trial, and meanwhile the horse dies. I cannot give any decision. It is my fault, and that is why I pay these sums."

The two priests return to Constantinople. They state what they had seen.

"Well,' said Mahomed, "what is your opinion now as to the durability of my power?"

"Your Majesty," said the priests, "as long as justice continues to be administered as we have witnessed it, your reign here will be everlasting!"

If one should look for the idea of Oriental justice underlying the stories I have narrated, it would be found in the reality or *simulacrum* of that rule which is written in the Mosiac code—the *lex talionis*.

Kind, hospitable and trusting as are the Orientals, they have ideas of revenge not based on passion or malignity. It is a part of their system. There is a story at the end of the "Thousand and One Nights," which illustrates in a whimsical way this law of retaliation. The story is thought by some annotators to apply to Moses; but it has a varied application in literature. It is found in a certain form in Parnell's "Hermit," but its true source is in the Koran, or, rather, in the Pentateuch, from which so much of the Koran is derived. Here is the story abbreviated:

A prophet goes into a mountain, beneath which is a spring of water. During the day he sits on the summit, and the people who come to the spring see him not. He sees them. One day he perceives a horseman dismount at the spring. He puts down his leathern bag, rests, drinks, and retires. He leaves the bag behind him. It is full of gold pieces. Another man comes, drinks and departs. He takes away the bag. Then there comes a third man. He is a wood-cutter. He rests and drinks, when lo! the first man dashes in, distressed for the loss of his bag of gold pieces.

"Where," he exclaims, "is my leathern bag of gold pieces?"

The wood-cutter replies: "Truly, I know nothing of it."

The horseman draws his sword and slays the wood-cutter. He searches his clothes, but finds nothing, and departs.

The prophet upon the mountain observes these incidents. He

addresses Allah to resolve the mystification of his mind about the divine justice of these proceedings. Allah says to him:

" Occupy thyself with thy devotion ! One thing is thine ; another is mine. You are limited in your knowledge. You see but in part,. and hence you fail to reason. The father of this horseman had forcibly taken a thousand pieces of gold from the property of the father of the supposed robber. I only put the son in possession of his own. The wood-cutter had slain the father of the horseman. Wherefore—the retaliation !"

Then the prophet exclaims: " Extolled be Thy perfection ! There is no Deity but Thee, Keeper of genealogies and All-wise Dispenser of justice !"

After all, are not most of the codes, East and West, to say nothing of human conduct, founded upon this natural law of Moses and Mahomet—the law of retaliation ? Were this not an element in human action and jurisprudence, would we not lack many serious and humorous illustrations of the better side of that nature ?

Thus philosophizing, we return to the Golden Horn. There we take our launch for the isle of Prinkipo, where we are passing our second summer in the East.

# CHAPTER XXVIII.

THE DRAGOMAN'S STORY—"WHICH OF THE TWO, THE BAD OR THE STUPID MAN?"

SEVERAL years ago the dragoman of our American Legation at Constantinople was asked to act as arbitrator in a dispute between a foreigner and an old Turkish doctor in law and theology. After several meetings with them, the dragoman concluded that the doctor was an ill-natured and unmanageable person. The latter had served for some years as cadi of the Civil Court at Smyrna. The dragoman related a story for his instruction. The story as to its place was in old Stamboul. As to its time, it does not matter much. Its moral is for every place and for all time. But it took place at the end of the sixteenth century, when the Turkish power was well established and growing. In other words, it was during the reign of Amurath III., the sixth emperor of the Ottomans, and grandson of Suleïman the Magnificent. This Sultan was not, as the sequel of the story shows, the worst of the Ottoman emperors. He was a tall, manly man, rather fat and quite pale, with a thin long beard. His face was not of a fierce aspect, like other Sultans. He was no rioter or reveler. He punished drunkards, and as for himself he indulged only in wormwood wine. His people knew that he loved justice, and although, according to an old chronicle, he caused his brothers to be strangled, "at which so tragicall a sight that he let some teares fall, as not delighting in such barbarous crueltie, but that the state and manner of his gouernment so required," still, he was, as the time was, a good prince.

But to the dragoman's story. Its moral had its uses, as the sequel reveals. This is the story, as it was told in one of the leisure hours at the Legation last summer:

"There was a man, Mustapha by name, who lived near the Golden Gate. He was well off, and when about to die, he called his son to him and said:

"'My dear boy, I am dying. Before I go, I want to give you

my last will. Here are one hundred pounds. You will give it to the worst man you can find. Here are one hundred pounds more. This you will give to the stupidest man you can discover.'

" A few days after, the father died. The son began to search for the bad man. Several men were pointed out, but he was not satisfied that they were the worst of men. Finally he hired a horse and went up to Yosgat, in Asia Minor. There the population unanimously pointed out their cadi as the worst man to be found anywhere. This information satisfied the son. He called on the cadi. He told the story of the will, and added:

" 'As I am desirous that the will of my father be accomplished, I beg you to receive these hundred pounds.'

" Said the cadi, ' How do you know that I am so bad as I am represented?'

" 'It is the testimony of the whole town,' said the son.

" 'I must tell you, young man,' said the cadi, 'that it is contrary to my principles to accept any bribe or present. If I ever receive money, it is only for a con-sid-er-a-tion. Unless I give you the counter-value of your money, I cannot accept it.'

" This reply of the cadi seemed just. It puzzled the young man. However, as he desired to fulfill his father's will, he continued to urge the cadi:

" 'Mr. Judge,' said he, ' if you sell me something, could not the will of my father be fulfilled?'

" 'Let me see,' said the cadi, looking around to find out what on earth he could sell to the youth, without destroying the spirit of the will. He reflected for a long time. Then all at once he was struck with a bright idea. Seeing that the courtyard of his house was filled with snow, about two feet deep, he said to the youth :

" 'I will sell you yonder snow. Do you accept the bargain?'

" 'Yes,' said the youth, seeing that there was nothing of value in the snow.

" The cadi then executed a regular deed, the fees of which were paid, of course, by the purchaser. The son then paid the hundred pounds for the snow.

" The boy went home; but he was not quite certain that he had strictly fulfilled the will of his father; for, after all, the cadi did not appear to him to be so very bad. Had he not decidedly refused to accept the money without a legal consideration?

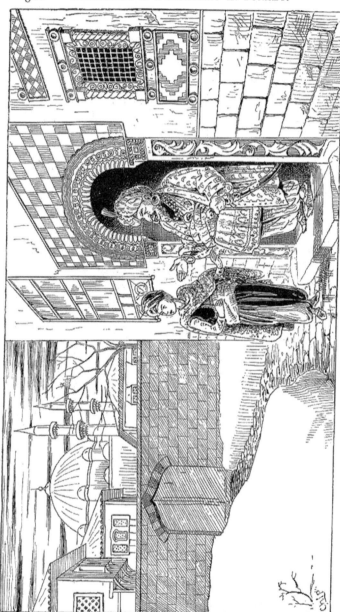

THE WORST MAN IN TURKEY.

" His perplexity was of short duration.

" The second day, early in the morning, the scribe of the cadi called on the youth and told him that the cadi wished to see him.

" 'Well, I will go,' said the youth.

" 'No,' said the scribe; 'I am ordered to take you there.'

" The youth resisted, and the scribe insisted. Finally the youth was compelled to submit, and went.

" 'What do you want of me, Cadi Effendi,' said the boy.

" 'Ah! you are welcome,' responded the cadi; 'I wanted you to come, because you have some snow in the courtyard which bothers me a great deal. The authorities cannot shoulder such a responsibility. Is not the deposit exposed? Can it be put under lock like other property? Besides, does it not occupy the road to which the people have the right of easement? What follows? The result is, that your snow will be trampled or stolen, or it will melt, and then all the responsibility will rest on me. I am not prepared to assume it. I request you to carry away your snow.'

" 'But, Cadi Effendi,' said the boy, 'I do not care. Let it melt; let it be stolen; let it be trampled on; I will make no claim for its value.'

" 'Nothing of the kind,' said the cadi. 'You have no right to close the public way in that manner. Unless you take away your snow, I will confine you in prison, and make you answer for the nuisance, and for the decay of the property, which may be claimed by your heirs at some future time.'

" 'Let it be swept out,' said the youth; 'I will defray the expense.'

" 'Nonsense!' indignantly responded the cadi. 'Am I your servant? Besides, will it not take a great deal of money to have the snow swept out?'

" 'I will pay the expense, whatever it is,' said the youth.

" 'Well, it requires twenty pounds,' said the cadi.

" 'I will pay that sum,' said the youth.

" Thus the cadi squeezed out twenty pounds more from the son of the deceased.

" The youth is, however, content. He is glad to find in this cadi a man of the meanness so indispensable to the fulfillment of the will of his father.

\*     \*     \*     \*     \*     \*     \*

THE STUPIDEST MAN IN TURKEY.

"After this experience the youth goes in search of the stupid man. He must filially fulfill the second clause of the will.

"While engaged in this search for stupidity, the son limits his efforts to his own fair city of Stamboul. He is on the street leading up to the Sublime Porte. He hears a band of music. It is moving toward the Sublime Porte. He is curious to know what it all means. He walks toward the music. When at a short distance he discovers a grand procession, with a display of soldiers. He notices a comparatively old man riding a white Arabian horse. He is dressed in a magnificent uniform. His breast is covered with decorations of every size, color and description. The trappings of the horse are covered with gold embroideries. The old man is surrounded by a dozen high officials of the government of Amurath III. They, too, are dressed finely; they have recently returned from the Caucasus laden with riches, and they display their grand robes and jewels. They have gorgeously embroidered uniforms and ride splendid horses. They are followed by an immense crowd. All Galata, as well as Stamboul, is afoot to see the sight. Murmurs in three-score dialects rise on the sunny air. The son of Mustapha follows the crowd. He asks a pedestrian in a green turban, who sits by the fountain :

"'What is the procession about?'

"He is informed that the old man is the newly appointed Grand Vizier of Amurath. The Vizier is going to take possession of his post. He is thus escorted with the usual solemnity.

"When the procession arrives at the gate of the Sublime Porte, the Grand Vizier dismounts on the foot-stone in front of the entrance, and, strange to say, there on that very foot-stone is a big tray; and on the tray, a human head freshly decapitated.

"The sight is blood-curdling. The youth is struck dumb with horror. Then, recovering his senses, he finds out the meaning of the usage. He is told that the bloody head is that of the preceding Grand Vizier, who had acted wrongfully, and was therefore beheaded.

"'Will his successor succeed him in the tray also?' asks the youth, of a zaptieh who was standing near to police the procession.

"'Nowadays, it is difficult to escape it,' is the answer of the policeman.

"After this answer, the youth makes immediate inquiries.

He discovers the 'Kiahaja' of the new Grand Vizier, for every Grand Vizier has a *factotum*. He goes to the Kiahaja and requests him to deliver to the Grand Vizier the hundred pounds which his father had willed. The Kiahaja, after inquiring the name of the youth and his whereabouts, receives the money. Later on, he takes the hundred pounds to the Grand Vizier. This high official is puzzled.

"'Who,' he inquires, 'is the friend that left the money to me, and why?'

"He calls for the youth. The youth comes. The Grand Vizier asks him about his father. The boy replies:

"'His name was Mustapha. He lived near the Golden Gate; but you did not know him, my lord!'

"'But he knew me?'

"'No, my lord, he did not.'

"'Then why this bequest to me?'

"The youth then gives the Grand Vizier the story, and adds that he could not expect to find a more stupid man or a greater idiot than the Grand Vizier; therefore, he concludes that the hundred pounds are due to that official, under his father's will.

"This puzzles the Grand Vizier, who says:

"'How do you know that I am a stupid man? Neither you nor your father knew me.'

"'Your acceptance of the position of Grand Vizier,' says the youth, 'in the presence of the dead head of your predecessor, speaks for itself. It needs no explanation.'

"The Grand Vizier can make no rational answer. He takes hold of his beard, strokes it, and considers for a minute.

"Then he says to the youth: 'Son of the good and wise Mustapha, will you not be my guest for to-night? To-morrow morning I must talk with you.' The boy accepts the invitation.

"In the morning the Grand Vizier calls the youth. He informs him that he is going to the palace of Amurath at the Seraglio Point. He desires the youth to accompany him. The boy objects. It is no use. The Grand Vizier compels him to go with him.

"They reach the palace. The Grand Vizier goes straightway to the Chief Eunuch, and thus addresses that beautiful Arabian:

"'Your Highness: I am aware that His Majesty, in bestowing on me the responsible and confidential position of Grand Vizier, did me the greatest honor a man can ever expect in this world. I am grateful to him for such a rare distinction. But, Highness, here is a young man who came to see me yesterday, and spoke to me in such a wonderful way that I feel bound to tender my resignation. After my conversation with him, I feel incapable of sustaining the dignity which His Majesty deserves.'

"The Eunuch is thunderstruck ! Up to that time no Grand Vizier had ever dared to resign. But the action of the Vizier seems so strange to the Eunuch, that the latter at once goes and reports it to the Sultan. The Sultan is amazed and indignant. He demands the presence of the Grand Vizier and the youth. When they appear they find that Amurath is not in one of his best moods. The Janizaries have been threatening him. His wife, sister and mother, on whom he relies for comfort in his poor health and mental distress, have in vain endeavored to placate and pacify him. His pale face grows scarlet with anger. He hotly addresses the Grand Vizier:

" ' How is it, sirrah ! that you presume to dare to tender your resignation ?

" ' Your Majesty,' says the Grand Vizier, 'I know that I am doing a bold act ; but it is this boy,' pointing out the simple youth, ' who compels me to do it. If your Highness wants to know the reasons, the boy will give them to you. I am sure that after hearing them you will acknowledge that, as I am considered the most stupid man in your empire, it is not becoming to your dignity to retain me as your immediate representative.'

"The boy is then called. He gives his story. The Sultan smiles. His innate sense of justice returns. He issues an iradé that henceforth no Grand Vizier shall be beheaded."

    \*      \*      \*      \*      \*      \*      \*

Thus ends the dragoman's story. He has recited it for a moral purpose. At its conclusion he addresses the old doctor of Moslem divinity and law, as follows:

"Now, my dear Mollah, you do not wish me to see in you the bad cadi of Yozgat. I shall feel exceedingly sorry if you compel me thus to designate you. I have known you twenty-five years. I have always held you in great esteem. Let me continue this esteem, if possible."

"As to your opponent," resumed the dragoman's arbitrator, "I am willing to place him in the situation of the Grand Vizier;

because he has stupidly placed himself within your claws. I will then take the position of the youth who, by his courage and frankness, succeeded in extirpating a usage which worked to the disadvantage of the Sultan's government and our country."

\*        \*        \*        \*        \*        \*        \*

The dragoman having thus concluded his tale, the Mollah changes color; from crimson to blue, from blue to yellow, and from yellow to green. He tries to smile. He desires to go away; but as the dragoman expects this movement, coffee had been ordered.

In the Orient no breach of etiquette is so indecorous as that of declining a hospitable cup of Mocha.

The coffee is brought in. It is swallowed, and two or three cigarettes are smoked. The Mollah is cooled down. Finally he accepts reasonable terms in the dispute.

On this, as on other occasions, an amicable understanding is arrived at by the application of a timely story with an Eastern moral. The moral is this:

*How useful are, sometimes, these odd incidents of life, discreetly narrated, which, when you hear them, seem to amount to little, but which, when you know how to use them at the proper time, are a great relief and a positive benefaction.*

# CHAPTER XXIX.

THE word "diplomacy" appears first upon the tapis at the end of the eighteenth century. It is derived from the Greek word "diploma." It may be defined, according to the law of nations, in an extended sense, as signifying everything connected with the administration and negotiation of foreign affairs.

I never had occasion to use what diplomats call the inter-territoriality, which is vouchsafed by the law of nations. It is laid down that a foreign ambassador is entitled to demand a special guard to assure his safety. This is usually done, say the writers, by the representatives of the Christian Powers in the East, and in the Barbary states.

Other officials besides the Kavass are associated with the American Legation. Their personalities are a constant diversion, whether in or outside our chambers. One of our officials is a little *caffeji*. He was promoted from the position of coffee vender in the alley below our rooms, where he lived in harmony with the dogs which were born beneath the escutcheon of the United States. He was kind to the dumb brutes, and it was through his ministrations that a dozen of them lived from puppy-hood to maturity. He is promoted to be *capouji*, or door-keeper, when the messenger and Kavass are absent. He is a good Moslem. His salary is equal to seven dollars a month, but that was cut off by our ever-vigilant First Comptroller and Department of State, yet we had not the heart to discharge him. He desired to be married—again; to add a younger lady to his home. He came to me in distress for a couple of *lira turque*, to aid his marital desires. This was bestowed. The Legation, however, is not responsible as a *particeps criminis* in polygamy. Besides, presents are made to him. Does he not assist Mehmet the Kavass to sustain the American dignity? When assaulted by unjust, crazy or importunate folk who call on us, doth not his eyes snap

fire, while his coffee cools, as if anxious to take a hand in vindication of the magnificent American inter-territoriality, though it
cuts off his stipend ?

Let me instance some of our Diversions when all the members
of the Legation take part in the dramatic performance :

With wild demonstrations, after the manner of Orientals,
except the Ottoman, a Greek fisherman seeks reclamation, in
money, for the destruction of his nets upon the Bosporus, into
which the screw-propeller of our launch had made havoc. It was
quite a comfort to know that, irrespective of rank, it was possible
to plead the relation of a Foreign Minister to a claim founded in
the wrong-doing of the claimant himself; for was not the Bosporus
our easement, our own waters, under the law of nations? And
when the fisherman gave us his infernal jabber, had we not two
native Moslem guards to protect our sacred person? It was not
Greek meeting Greek about our tug, but Greek and Turk contending. Thus, in our subordinates, we find safety and succor,
and, at the same time, one of the pleasantries of the Legation.

Another pleasantry is occasioned by a call from an American
citizen of Greek descent. Whether he is descended from Leoni-
das or Themistocles I do not inquire; probably the latter, as he
has much to do with fighting the marine elements. He presents
himself and his case. He is a diver. He has been at Chios, old
Homer's isle. While diving to raise a vessel in the harbor, he is
arrested by the authorities for illegally diving for sponges. He
has no license. He is jailed. He appeals to the American Cæsar,
i. e., the Legation. It hears his case in full council. As he
speaks no English, little French, some Turkish and much modern
Greek, we call in all our aids to assist the dragoman to interpret.

"Have I not seen you before," I ask him, after his complaints
are understood, and the talk takes a social air.

After much explanation he says:

"Oui; I was in America."

" Which America ? "

" Nord! "

" Bien! "

" Ever in New York or Washington ?"

" Oh! oui, oui," he promptly rejoins.

" Do you ever smoke?" I blandly ask, tendering him a
cigarette. He smiles a fishy smile and illumines the weed.

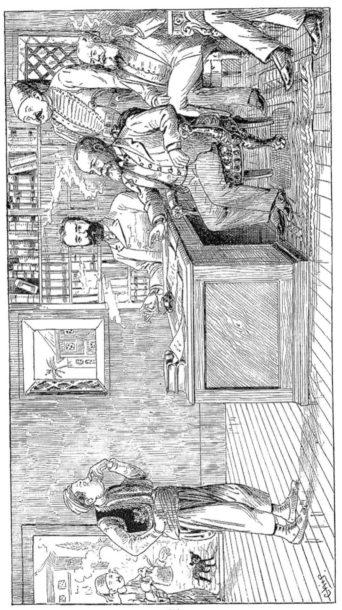

THE SPONGE DIVER AT THE LEGATION.

I know him by that smile.   Dressed in spangled tights, and in an embroidered Greek jacket, I had myself seen him in a tank, under water, smoking.

" You are Kippapaporos, the famous diver, are you not? "

He looks surprised and pleased at the recognition.

" You are the  man who drank  schnapps under water?   How are you, Kippapaporos ? "

He becomes at once genial, and in his muddled style tells his troubles in the Homeric isle—all over again.

I ask him how long he can stay  under water.   He shows us how  to  do  it.   He clutches his  nose  by his thumb and index finger, and  gathers into his capacious chest a surplus revenue of atmosphere.   His wheezy  noise  makes the Legation tremble. The dragoman is astounded, the capouji alarmed and the Kavass confounded.

When his  performance  is  over, I  ask  for  his  passport, as evidence of citizenship and as warrant for our protection.   But it is not  handy; so that the American Cæsar cannot intervene, just now, in the local laws as to  the classic sponges; not even for a descendant of Themistocles.   Besides, he complains that he is impecunious.   He must have help or starve.

I suggest *divers* modes of accumulation, a pun  he never suspects.

" Why not work in the clear waters of the Bosporus, raise boats and thus raise money ?"

He acquiesces and leaves.

Afterward he returns to say that he has had a job; had dived for a sunken vessel in the  Bosporus, but could  not  make more than twenty piastres (a dollar) a day, and  he  had a family to support.

He could stay under water nearly as  long as a porpoise, without a blow.   What became of him I never knew, but he is a sample which diplomats will  recognize as  a class of  citizens who belong to  all  flags  and are really, by their vagabond life, under none.

What singular offices diplomacy has sometimes to perform! Sitting in the Legation chambers upon a beautiful day in October, 1885, I receive from the Assistant Secretary of State a cablegram, which requires me to  look up Professor Sterrit.   He has been lost somewhere in Asia Minor.   He is an archæologist, and his friends have received no tidings of him for six months. He had been permitted to explore the valley of the Tigris and Euphrates and of the rivers adjacent. This the records of the Legation show; but, becoming sick, he drops out of his company, and is left behind at his own request. How to find this gentleman is the question.

First, I inquire at the Bible-house, or of the missionaries. I strike the right trail; for they know more about the interior of Asia Minor than the Turkish officials, and are willing to impart what they know. Following one clue after another, I happen to remember Mr. Haynes, an American, who has been in the company of Professor Sterrit. He had called upon us. He was the photographer of the expedition; and, welcome news! he had just received a letter from Professor Sterrit himself. That gentleman is on his way from Smyrna to Athens. The anxiety of his friends is soon relieved.

I mention this, not so much to show the functions of the Legation, which are various and multiform, but to refer to some strange information about Asia Minor which the incident indirectly furnished. Mr. Haynes spent a day with us at Therapia. He had a grip-sack full of photographs, and the most interesting of his package were those from the ruins of ancient Cappadocia. I venture to say that these are among the most interesting archæological remains of that country, if not of the world. They are the pictures of two rock-hewn cities. Descriptions have been given of them in some of the itineraries of Asia Minor. These ruins are in a valley, like our cañon. They are upon the perpendicular sides of the mountains. They are excavated into a great number of chambers, grottoes, houses, tombs and chapels of the Byzantine age. There are also in these cañons remarkable conical-pointed hills. They follow the valley so closely that they are almost wedged together. They are not hills ; and whether they are natural or artifical has not been determined. Most probably they are natural, worn by the rains and shaken by the earthquake. Mr. Haynes, who visited them, says that he was almost lost in their cones and pillars of rock. There are miles on miles of these rocky cones; many of them only fifteen feet high, others a hundred, and some three hundred. Some are crowned with boulders, which would indicate that time had eaten away most of the foundations upon which they rested. In the interminable confusion, they seemed like some great and ancient city which had been deserted, and had been so carved by time that their strange, fantastic shapes, like the rocks I have seen in the mountains of Corsica, suggested every animal known to the *fauna* of science. In our day, when traveling has become so easy, lukewarm, and almost idle, there have been no ample descriptions written of these remarkable ruins. Mr. Haynes has promised to supply the deficiency.

Many of these ruins are grottoes. They were once Greek chapels. In them were found paintings of Christ, the Virgin and the apostles, and of Bible scenes. The pictures are well preserved, and some of them well done. In some of the pictures the saints have beautiful scrolls in their hands; each scroll with a verse of Scripture, well written in Greek. Some of these ruins were used as mortuary chapels. Evidently there was in the midst of these outré towns a communistic style of living. This is indicated by large dining-halls. The passages to some of these chambers are through narrow holes, so small as to lead to the belief that they were like the Zuni caves of Arizona—fortifications as well as homes; for in the upper stories, dedicated to the women, there was evidence that no ingress was possible from below.

*       *       *       *       *       *       *

Travelers who have been in Kurdistan, and who have traversed its high, wild land, do not speak with much fervor about the magnanimity and glory of its inhabitants; nor is its cultivation a matter of eulogy. If a man became rich in that country by raising handsome crops, it was the custom of the government to lay on him the heavy hand of taxation. When the Pasha finds that the granary of the farmer is full of stores he exclaims :

" Mashallah ! I must have him. Inshallah ! I will force him to pay well for his misdeeds."

Industry has no hope of reward; and, therefore, there is not much content in Kurdistan; and yet its people are brave and courageous.

That reminds me of a little divertissement. It illustrates the marauding and excursive life of the Kurds. When I took charge of the Legation, I found a case pending there against one Moussa Bey. *Moussa* is Moses. But he was not a law-giver, but a lawbreaker. He had robbed some American missionaries, and the stolen property was traced to him. He had done worse: he had

MOUSSA BEY BUYS A BIBLE.

attempted to outrage some of the women who were missionaries in a remote district, where benevolence had been bringing forth its fruits in vain for his regeneration. Before I had reached my post, General Wallace had tried his pious and diplomatic skill to bring Moussa to punishment. Many promises had been made, but the case had never been brought up or determined. No indemnity could be had against him, and although the case was amply proven, he had escaped punishment. I happened to learn, during my prosecution of the matter, that Moussa had been actually promoted from a lieutenant or lower magistrate to the higher post of *mudir*, the governor of a *kaza*, which is a subdivision of a *sanjak ;* a *sanjak* being a subdivision of *vilayet*, or province. I laid this new matter before the Porte—especially before the Minister of Foreign Affairs, who himself was a Kurd. How Moussa knew that the American people, through its new Minister, were again in pursuit of him, I do not know; but word came to me soon afterward from the missionaries in that neighborhood, that Moussa Bey had purchased a Bible! He was behaving himself with wonderful exemplariness—so much so, that the missionaries asked that he might not be pursued any further at present, as everything was serene in his district. The matter of the robbery still hangs over him. His hypocrisy has enured to the benefit of the missionaries. An Irishman would exclaim about him, " Holy Moses! "—for he affects the Christian virtues, if he has them not !

\*    \*    \*    \*    \*    \*    \*

Some of the Diversions of the Legation were *quasi* official. Among them was one occasioned by a letter written from Minnesota. In this the writer, a most religious reader of the Bible, seriously desired to know whether the reports were true, that the Ark had been found imbedded in some of the glaciers on Mount Ararat. He premised his inquiry by stating that Armenia had been divided between Turkey, Russia and Persia, but that Mount Ararat, the monumental frontier of these empires, was within my jurisdiction as Minister. He hoped, if I could not answer the question which he propounded, so as to confirm the Biblical account of the Ark, that I would make proper inquiries at Ararat and give him the details in connection with the animals and other paraphernalia of that remarkable vessel. The truth is, that Mount Ararat is now strictly comprised in Russian territory.

However, it is still a great object of reverence among the smartest people of the Orient—I mean the Armenians.

There have been many volcanic and other excitations, political and social, upheaving and disturbing this Armenian country. In fact, the whole country between and near the Euxine and the Caspian shows signs of volcanic action, as well as of petroleum. It is a table-land of great elevation. It has its sublime mountains. Its temperature is lower than that of other regions of the same parallel. These elements give to it a peculiar aspect and interest. They fit it for the exhibition of some wondrous phenomena like that of the Deluge and the Ark, or the preservation of its timbers and *fauna* amid the glaciers of the mountain.

I have no report to make as to this request of the pious American citizen. I made no inquiry as to the Ark. It was not within my function. I never happened to meet a tourist who had visited the highlands there in search of nature or of the remnant of Noah's navy. But it is a significant fact that the land is besieged by sportsmen and naturalists, for the various kinds of birds which feed on the great plain of Erzeroum. The flocks are so prodigious as almost to cover the earth in certain seasons. They give to the ground the color of their plumes. Surely, here is an illustration, if not a proof, of a variety of one class of animals somewhat confirmatory of the scriptural account of the Deluge.

*     *     *     *     *     *     *

Another Diversion, which comes near home. The names of the *dramatis personæ* are omitted:

One of our leading generals, and a man who had been high in office in America, had been presented with several horses by the Sultan. They were Arab steeds of the finest breed. There were four of them. The dragoman was not a little disconcerted, when calling at His Majesty's stables to look at the present, to observe that one of the steeds—a fine black Arab—was incurably and chronically lame. Here was a dilemma. Could he send a lame horse to the General? He will not disturb the *amour propre* of the Sultan, or look his gift horse in the mouth or in the heel. What does he do? He has a confabulation with the Chief Chamberlain, who is the medium of communication between the Legations and the Sultan. After expressions of thanks for the gift, he confidentially mentions that the gift of a black horse is looked upon in America as ominous. Disaster always follows its presentation. Although nothing would be said about it, of course, on the reception of the horse in America, still, would it not be considered sinister to present a horse around whose color hung such associations? It is needless to say that, in the outcome, the black horse is turned out to pasture and a splendid white horse presented in its place.

There are many diverting stories which only the reserve of diplomacy prevents the outside world from enjoying. One, which I have recently seen in print, has reference to the dragoman of Lord Ponsonby, some time ago British Minister at the Porte. He desires to make a presentation to the Sultan, but being a man of leisurely habits, he requests his dragoman to translate a supposed speech, which he is too lazy to compose and deliver. The humor consists in this:

That the Minister, to save his own labor, is solemnly to repeat in English the arithmetical numbers from one up to sixty, with a grave and dignified air. The dragoman is then to deliver the speech in Turkish, which he himself should commit to memory. The affair goes off to the satisfaction of the Porte. The Sultan responds in the most amiable manner. The labor of the head of the Legation is thus considerably lightened.

During my incumbency as Minister, I am happy to chronicle that no such performance as that of my Lord Ponsonby was ever enacted or needed.

# CHAPTER XXX.

## THE LOWER BOSPORUS—THE COSMOPOLITAN AND KALEIDOSCOPIC CITY—SCENES AT THE BRIDGE.

LVGDVNI BATAVORVM,
Ex officina Elzeviriana. Anno 1632.

CONSTANTINOPLE IN A. D. 1632.

It matters not from what point of view you regard this city, it has no peer. Is it history? It is the rival of Rome. Is it art? There are Greek remains here and hereabouts which thrice pulverize the classic dust of Athens. Is it physical scenery? From the Semplegades near the open mouth of the Euxine to the Dardanelles, there are perpetual and happy surprises. Is it architecture? St. Sophia has the spoil of all temples, the strata of all geology, and the graces of all the arts of Greece. Is it climate? Dr. Henry Bennet, of Mentone—the arbiter on health resorts—regards the Bosporus as the place of all others for salubrity. Was it not here that Medea threw away her poisonous drugs and grew wild in heartiness upon ozone? Is it not here that Therapia—which is philologically cousin-german to Therapeutics—gives her breezes to cool the summer heats, and her moisture to make the magnolia and rose bloom and the creeper cling? Is it the population? Was there ever such a composite? Literally, here are Romans from Roumania, Scythians from Europe and Asia, Africans from the Soudan, Arabs of the desert from Damascus to Mount Sinai, Tartars from the steppes, Circassians from the mountains, Greeks from the isles, Turks from the interior, Italians, French, Dutch, Austrians, English, Germans, Russians, and, in fact, all peoples from the mountains and plains of Hungary, and the " swamp lands " of the lower Danube, Bessarabia and the Dobrudcha to " silken Samarcand and cedared Lebanon."

Constantinople is not a new city. From the time the Greek merchants from Megara chose this spot as the seat of rule and commerce, she has been a factor in the influences for good or evil which follow our race on this planet. For over six hundred years before Christ, she was a political capital, an entrépôt of commerce, and a strategical point in the conflicts of men for empire and glory.

The leading quality which determines this prominence is the geographical situation. Whether this situation be the result of internal fires, volcanic upheavals, or shrinkage of the earth's crust, the wonderful Strait is the grand effect. It connects two continents and two seas. It is this which gives unity and supremacy. It is empire. It is commerce. It is locomotion and transportation—both made easy by waters wonderfully related to lands, and the genius of people adapted to both. By the Bosporus the Black Sea is bound to the Mediterranean. The great rivers of Russia, the Caspian and Azof seas, as well as all the coasts which connect with them, pour their tributary values into this unexampled emporium. It was said by "Eothen," a half century ago, that England had then planted one foot on Egypt and the other upon India—a vast span of the insular Colossus. It is truer now than it was then ; but the nation that will stand here to overlook these forming elements of advancement and power has a score of Egypts and an India of unrivaled resources. Two continents furnish a pediment for such a Colossus. Whether it be Russian or Greek, Austrian or German ; whether it remain Ottoman or become a " free town"—here the image stands, with its emblems of authority. It dominates Asia, Africa, and almost Europe, and with a power to move armies or goods, or block the transportation of both, at its own supreme pleasure. The situation is such that a little dynamite, conveniently handled and placed—not the thousandth part of that which blew up Hell Gate—can guard it from perilous intrusion against the nations of the world.

The city has an unparalleled harbor. It is tideless, but it is in perpetual motion. Its beauty enamours the eye, and its resorts give tonic and comfort. Its history from B. C. 667—almost coeval with the foundation of Rome—to this year of the Eastern Roumelian revolution, has all the vicissitudes of the strangest romance, but the climacteric of its fascination lies in the eminence and glory of its situation, which is the procreant cause of all its marvels.

Is it a wonder, therefore, that Persian, Genoese, Venetian, Greek, Roman and Ottoman have contended for and held these places of interest, opulence and power, and have made and resisted sieges, to be " masters of the situation "? Do you wonder that Constantine saw here a greater than Rome, and sought to realize his ideal upon yonder Seraglio Point, where the Golden Horn, with its cornucopia of wealth kisses the Sea of Marmora, with its archipelago of loveliness and its transport of azure water ? Few relics of this early reign remain to tell of the splendor of old Byzantium. The brazen column of triple serpents from Delphos, some aqueducts, cyclopean walls of massive strength, and castles of later erection, catch and detain the eye, ever here on the outlook for archæological wonders. But this city lives, moves and has its being in the active present. It is not of the dead past altogether.

Constantinople, like Rome, is situated upon seven hills ; but opposite Constantinople proper, or Stamboul, there are plenty of hills. They almost rise to the dignity of mountains. The traveler who lands from one of the Black Sea or Mediterranean steamers, or the tourist who finds himself upon the Golden Horn, or the bridge which crosses it, seeking the hotels at Pera, will find a steep ascent to overcome.

When I visited Constantinople in A. D. 1851, that ascent was never overcome by means of carriages, much less by a railway.

For, to a Turk of the old time, encumbered with his baggy breeches, heavy turban, and immense sash, there is a great deal of specific gravity to be worked off before he rises to those heights of Pera where the Europeans dwell.

The *hamals*, whom we meet at all hours of the day bearing their great burdens up these steeps, and the donkeys and horses with their creels upon their backs, bearing by various methods their loads of stone, timber and merchandise, have no easy ascent, especially in mid-summer.

The *hamal* is generally an Armenian. He works with a view to a release from hard labor after a few years. The Turk does not work on this line. He leaves that to the animal and to the Armenian. He prefers his pipe, or his black coffee, to cultivating that levity which overcomes altitude. When it is known that the streets leading from the Golden Horn to the heights of Pera are crooked, ill-paved, narrow and filthy, many blessings should be showered on the French engineer who built the tunnel by which, with the aid of a stationary engine, a train every five or ten minutes pulls and pushes up and down in the dark, to overcome, by the aid of steam, the imminent disadvantages of Pera.

One of the disillusions of the stranger in Constantinople comes upon him in the very streets, before he crosses the bridge of the Golden Horn. If he has heard that the Mahometan is ignorant as well as bigoted, and that he does not read, he will be corrected. The cries of the newspaper venders, morning and evening, are as common as in New York. At the leisure hour, in all the shops, which are always open, you should see how many are engaged in reading the newspaper. There is scarcely any man of the empire who cannot read and write. Schools are as common as the mosques. The very disposition of the Turk leads him to be a reflective reader. Some of the best scholars of the world are those with large Arabic libraries, who pass their lives in their literary harems.

Before you enter upon the bridge, sometimes called " the Sultana Validé," which connects Galata with Stamboul, you have to pass through a surging crowd. There you are likely to be stranded if you are not well guarded. Vehicles and beasts of burden; men on foot and on horseback; people rushing to the ferry-boats and to the steamers ; pedlers screaming out their wares; stock-brokers excited, from the Exchange, which is near

by—these are the preliminaries to that struggle, before you reach
the man who takes your toll when you are fairly upon the edge of
the rugged and ricketty bridge.

It is not uncommon for writers who are dazed with Constantinople and its variety, to stand on the Stamboul bridge and look
and look, and wonder and wonder. All this dual city passes there.
I suggested to a friend to have a photographer who takes pictures
*instante*, to stand on the Stamboul bridge and master the procession by his sunlight and his machine. Of course I did not include
color in the programme. But the human currents had already
been caught in the endless eddy of this bridge. Before my
suggestion the Italian traveler, De Amicis, had already made a
pen picture of the scene. It is more print-worthy than my own
effort:

" The crowd passes in great waves, each one of which is of a
hundred colors, and every group of persons represents a new type
of people. Whatever can be imagined that is most extravagant
in type, costume, and social class, may there be seen within the
space of twenty paces and ten minutes of time. Behind a throng
of Turkish porters, who pass running and bending under enormous burdens, advances a sedan-chair, inlaid with ivory and
mother of pearl, and bearing an Armenian lady; and at either side
of it a Bedouin wrapped in a white mantle and a Turk in muslin
turban and sky-blue caftan, beside whom canters a young Greek
gentleman followed by his dragoman in embroidered vest, and a
dervish with his tall, conical hat and tunic of camel's hair, who
makes way for the carriage of a European ambassador, preceded
by his running footman in gorgeous livery. All this is only seen
in a glimpse, and the next moment you find yourself in the midst
of a crowd of Persians, in pyramidal bonnets of Astrakhan fur,
who are followed by a Hebrew in a long yellow coat open at the
sides; a frowsy-headed gypsy woman with her child in a bag at
her back; a Catholic priest with breviary staff; while in the midst
of a confused throng of Greeks, Turks and Armenians comes a
big eunuch on horseback, crying out *Larya!* (make way), and
preceding a Turkish carriage painted with flowers and birds, and
filled with the ladies of a harem, dressed in green and violet, and
wrapped in large white veils; behind, a Sister of Charity from the
hospital at Pera, an African slave carrying a monkey, and a professional story-teller in a necromancer's habit; and what is quite

natural, but appears strange to the new-comer, all these diverse people pass one another without a look, like a crowd in London; and not one single countenance wears a smile. The Albanian in his white petticoat and with pistols in his sash, beside the Tartar dressed in sheepskins; the Turk, aside of his caparisoned ass, threads pompously two long strings of camels; behind the adjutant of an imperial prince, mounted upon his Arab steed, clatters a cart filled with all the odd domestic rubbish of a Turkish household; the Mahometan woman afoot, the veiled slave woman, the Greek with her red cap, and her hair on her shoulders, the Maltese hooded in her black *faldetta*, the Hebrew woman dressed in the antique costume of India, the negress wrapped in a many-colored shawl from Cairo, the Armenian from Trebizond, all veiled in black like a funeral apparition, are seen in single file, as if placed there on purpose to be contrasted.

It is a changing mosaic of races and religions, that is composed and scattered continually with a rapidity that the eye can scarcely follow. It is amusing only to look at the passing feet and see all the foot-coverings in the world go by, from that of Adam up to the last fashion in Parisian boots—yellow Turkish babouches, red Armenian, blue Greek, and black Jewish shoes; sandals, great boots from Turkestan, Albanian gaiters, low-cut slippers, leg pieces of many colors, belonging to horsemen from Asia Minor, gold embroidered shoes, Spanish *alporgatos*, shoes of satin, of twine, of rags, of wood, so many, that while you look at one you catch a glimpse of a hundred more. One must be on the alert not to be jostled and overthrown at every step. Now it is a water-carrier with a colored jar upon his back; now a Russian lady on horseback; now a squad of imperial soldiers in zouave dress, and stepping as if to an assault; now a crew of Armenian porters, two and two, carrying on their shoulders immense bars, from which are suspended great bales of merchandise; and now a throng of Turks, who dart from left to right of the bridge to embark in the steamers that lie there. There is a tread of many feet, a murmuring, a sound of voices, guttural notes, aspirations interjectional, incomprehensible and strange, among which the few French or Italian words that reach the ear seem like luminous points upon a black darkness. The figures that most attract the eye in all this crowd are the Circassians, who go in groups of three and five together, with slow steps; big bearded men of a terrible countenance, wearing bear-skin caps like the old Napoleonic guard, long black caftans, daggers at their girdles, and silver cartridge-boxes on their breasts; real figures of banditti, who look as if they had come to Constantinople to sell a daughter or a sister—with their hands embrued in Russian blood. Then the Syrians, with robes' in the form of Byzantine dalmatic, and their heads enveloped in gold-striped handkerchiefs ; Bulgarians, dressed in coarse serge, and caps encircled with fur; Georgians, in hats of varnished leather, their tunics bound round the waist with metal girdles; Greeks from the Archipelago, covered from head to foot with embroidery, tassels, and shining buttons.

From time to time the crowd slackens a little, but instantly other groups advance, waving with red caps and white turbans, amid which the cylindrical hats, umbrellas, and pyramidal head-dresses of Europeans, male and female, seem to float, borne onward by that Mussulman torrent. It is amazing even to note the variety of religions.

The shining bald head of the Capuchin friar, the towering Janizary turban of an Ulema, alternate with the black veil of an Armenian priest; imaums with white tunics, veiled nuns; chaplains of the Turkish army, dressed in green, with sabres at their sides; Dominican friars, pilgrims returned from Mecca with a talisman hanging at their necks, Jesuits, dervishes; and this is very strange. Dervishes that tear their own flesh in expiation of their sins, and cross the bridge under a sun-umbrella, all pass by. If you are attentive, you may notice in the throng a thousand amusing incidents. Here it is a eunuch, showing the white of his eye at a Christian exquisite, who has glanced too curiously into the carriage of his mistress; there is a French *cocotte*, dressed after the last fashion-plate, leading by the hand the beloved and bejeweled son of a pasha; or a lady of Stamboul, feigning to adjust her veil, that she may peer more easily at the train of a lady of Pera; or a sergeant of cavalry in full uniform, stopping in the middle of the bridge to blow his nose with his fingers in a way to give one a cold chill; or a quack, taking his last sous from some poor devil, and making a cabalistic gesture over his face to cure him of sore eyes; or a family of travelers arrived that day, and lost in the midst of a throng of Asiatic ruffians, while the mother searches for her crying children, and the men make way for them by dint of squaring their shoulders. Camels, horses, sedan-chairs, oxen, carts, casks on wheels, bleeding donkeys, mangy dogs, form a long file that divides the crowd in half.

Sometimes there passes a mighty pasha with three tails, lounging in a splendid carriage, followed by his pipe-bearer on foot, his guard and one black slave, and then all the Turks salute, touching the forehead and breast, and the mendicant women, horrible witches, with muffled faces and naked breasts, run after the carriage crying for charity. Eunuchs not on service, pass in twos and threes and fives together, cigarette in mouth, and are recognized by their corpulence, their long arms and their black habits. Little Turkish girls dressed like boys, in green full trousers and rose or yellow vests, run and jump with feline agility, making way for themselves with their henna-tinted hands. Boot-blacks with gilded boxes, barbers with bench and basin in hand, sellers of water and sweetmeats, cleave the press in every direction, screaming in Greek and Turkish. At every step comes glittering a military division, officers in fez and scarlet trousers, their breasts constellated with medals; grooms from the seraglio, looking like generals of the army, gendarmes, with a whole arsenal at their belts; zebecks, or free soldiers, with those enormous baggy trousers that make them resemble in profile the Hottentot Venus; imperial guards with long white plumes upon their casques and gold-bedizened breasts; city guards of Constantinople, as one might say, required to keep back the waves of the Atlantic Ocean. The contrasts between all this gold and all those rags, between people loaded down with garments, looking like walking bazaars, and people almost naked, are most extraordinary. The spectacle of so much nudity is alone a wonder. Here are to be seen all shades of skin-colors, from the milky-whiteness of Albania to the crow-blackness of central Africa and the bluish-blackness of Darfur; chests that if you struck upon them would resound like a huge bass or rattle like pottery; backs, oily, stony, full of wrinkles, and hairy like the back of a wild boar; arms embossed with red and blue, and decorated with designs of flowers and in-scriptions from the Koran. But it is not possible to observe all this in one's first passage over the bridge. While you are examining the tattoo on an arm, your guide warns you that a Wal-lachian, a Servian, a Montenegrin, a Cossack of the Don, a Cossack of Ukraine, an Egyptian, a native of Tunis, a prince of Imerezia, is passing by. It seems that Constantinople is the same

TART-SELLER.

ARAB FROM MECCA.

RUG PEDLER.

TURCOMAN.

as it always was—the capital of three continents and the queen of twenty vice-realms. But even this idea is insufficient to account for the spectacle, and one fancies a tide of emigration produced by some enormous cataclysm that has overturned the antique continent.

An experienced eye discerns still among the waves of that great sea the faces and costumes of Caramania and Anatolia, of Cyprus and Candia, of Damascus and Jerusalem, the Druse, the Kurd, the Maronite, the Croat, and others—innumerable varieties of all the anarchical confederations which extend from the Nile to the Danube, and from the Euphrates to the Adriatic. Seekers after the beautiful or the horrible will here find their most audacious desires fulfilled; Raphael would be in ecstasies, and Rembrandt would tear his hair. The purest types of Greek and Caucasian beauty are mingled with flat noses and woolly heads; queens and fairies pass beside you; lovely faces, and faces deformed by disease and wounds; monstrous feet, and tiny Circassian feet no longer than your hand; gigantic porters, enormously corpulent Turks, and black sticks of skeleton shadows of men that fill you with pity and disgust—every strangest aspect in which can be presented the ascetic life, the abuse of pleasure, extreme fatigue, the excess of opulence and the misery that kills. Who loves colors may here have his fill. No two figures are dressed alike. Here are shawls twisted around the heads, savage fillets, coronets of rags, skirts and under-vests in stripes and squares like harlequins, girdles stuck full of knives that reach to the arm-pits. Mameluke trousers, short drawers, skirts, togas, trailing sheets, coats trimmed with ermine, vests like golden cuirasses, sleeves puffed and slashed, habits monkish and habits covered with gold lace, men dressed like women, and women that look like men; beggars with the port of princes, a ragged elegance, a profusion of colors, of fringes, tags, and fluttering ends of childish and theatrical decorations, that remind one of a masquerade in a madhouse, for which all the old-clothes dealers in the universe have emptied their stores. Above the hollow murmur that comes from this multitude are heard the shrill cries of the sellers of newspapers in every tongue; the stentorian shout of the porters, the giggling laugh of Turkish women, the squeaking voices of eunuchs, the falsetto trill of blind men chanting verses of the Koran, the noise of the bridge as it moves upon the water, the whistles and

TURKISH WOMAN FROM MECCA.

ARMENIAN FAMILY

TURKISH WOMAN AND SLAVE FROM SAARIT.

KURDISH WOMAN FROM INTERIOR.

bells of a hundred steamers, whose dense smoke is often beaten down by the wind so that you can see nothing at all. All this masquerade of people embarks in the small steamboats that leave every moment for Scutari, for the villages of the Bosporus, and the suburbs of the Golden Horn; they spread through Stamboul, in the bazaars, in the mosques, in the suburbs of Fanar and Galata, to the most distant quarters on the Sea of Marmora; they swarm upon the Frankish shore, to the right toward the Sultan's palace, to the left toward the higher quarters of Pera, whence they fall again upon the bridge by the innumerable lanes that wind about the sides of the hills; and thus they bind together Asia and Europe, ten cities and a hundred suburbs in one mighty net of labor, intrigue and mystery, before which the mind becomes bewildered."

\*      \*      \*      \*      \*      \*      \*

But I must resume to say :

If you leave the bridge and go up the hill to Pera you are saluted by the same cosmopolitan noises and groups. A Turkish porter cries out :

"Get out of the way of the street-car! "

A donkey driver halloos, " Barada !"

Newspapers in Greek, Turkish, French, English, Armenian, and some of several tongues in one pentecostal edition, make that end of the bridge noisy with their cries and trade.

The grand bazaar is also a medley and motley microcosm. Indian, Syrian, Arabian and Egyptian goods of every grade of value, beauty and style are sold by polyglotical merchants of unconscionable modes. This city, in fine, is the epitome of the whole Orient, and the bazaar is a sample of the city. If the latter be a camp—a fair—a bewildering variety of transient edifices, with kiosks, lattices, tombs, palaces, balconies, churches, mosques, trees, façades, arches, bridges, and fragments and bits of form and hue, the bazaar itself is an artful combination of all that selfish skill can put together to gratify the taste, passions and comforts of men of Eastern mold.

What a cosmos has this strange government of suzerainty made out of the chaos of defunct and changing dynasties and empires! Do you want to study institutions? Here is your ground of vantage. Not only is the Sultan here the lord and master, doing all things absolutely, but he allows a clever company of Arab scholars to interpret the law according to Mahomet and the Koran. But that interpretation is subject to the old rule of his grandfather, Mahmoud II., and that is:

If the Ulemas do not interpret the law according to the Sultanic will, they are to be pounded to death in a (metaphorical) mortar.

Things are greatly changed since the Janizaries were massacred. With some exceptions toleration is the rule at the capital. Still, some brutal bey or pestiferous pasha in the remote interior makes havoc of an indiscreet American peripatetic teacher or preacher. When such things happen, the American bird tries to scream, but she is so far away from home that she is literally a cowardly fowl, and cannot even rise to the dignity of a vociferous and protesting crow.

It is impossible to tell, except by iterative intensity, the weird and wonderful genius of the sky, seas and soil of this old capital and its environs. That which makes it most interesting, and which makes and determines its troubles and trials—social, ethnographical, religious, military and political—is its unparalleled situation. I have compared it with New York, but it is far more superb in picturesque scenery and commercial advantages. Compared with old Jerusalem, it is more active and varied, if not more pliant and potent, in its religious teachings. Compared with London, its throngs of people that swarm in, around and over the bridges of the Golden Horn, between Pera and Scutari, and the city of Stamboul proper, who come and go on steam ferries up and down the Straits and across into Asia and along the shores of Marmora, it is, at least, more interesting, if not so populous. Compared with ancient Athens, it cannot be said to be a teacher in art or philosophy, but in early and mediæval history, as the Greek Byzantium, Constantinople appreciated, preserved and circulated what Greece had provided for the instruction and delight of our kind. Compared with Paris, there is no luxury —from a bouffé song and dance in a *café chantant* to the Italian opera on the Grand rue, from the wild music of the Mediterranean, as old in its monotone as the pyramids, to the thunder of the old epic upon classic and rocky shores—which this unique and composite city has not. Here absolute power lives with its many wives, eunuchs and odalisques. Private liberty is without much restraint under the shadow of autocratic power.

If it be said that the Sultan enacts over again the rôle of an ancient Persian king, I can only point to the proprieties of his court and the reserve of his domesticities. These do not occasion any of the scandals of the London divorce courts or the ostentatious libertinism of the French and German capitals. If it be said that polygamy is practised, may it not be well to scrutinize the laws and customs of Mohametan marriage? If it be said that Mahomet was an impostor and that Christianity is its foe, would it not be well to study more carefully the kinds of Christianity which obtain in the East? Certainly, one great virtue shines in the Moslem faith. It tolerates no imagery made in the likeness of saint or God. It consults the rituals of every faith, and I doubt if the reader will find so spiritual a recognition of the Unity and greatness of the Deity as that revealed in the prayers of the Moslem.

I have heard in the chapel of the British Embassy prayers quite as fervent and sincere as those of the Moslem to Allah; and among the rest, one which is printed in the English Episcopal Prayer-book, which beseeches the Christians' God—for the safety, preservation and succor of the Sultan, who is the Caliph of the Mahometan religion.

Let me not be drawn from my present object. I was endeavoring to describe the bridge over the Golden Horn. Its aspect is awkward. It rests on iron buoys, and although not as graceful as the Rialto, it is a significant structure, for it is a bridge between two civilizations. It is really a bridge between Asia and Europe; between twenty years of Europe and a cycle of Asia. If it were not an anachronism, I would wonder if Addison took his "Vision of Mirza" from this bridge. What motley groups stand and what individual oddities pass between noisy, busy, bustling Pera and the stately, serious and silent Stamboul! Every nation and every tribe are represented: Soldiers that are of every uniform; Persians from Astrakhan going to the Persian Embassy, where Mochsin Khan, the minister of Persia, rules as if in his own territory for his own Shah; Frankish diplomats and adventurers, passing carriages in which are beauties of henna-stained fingers and painted eye-lashes and brows, veiled to give the eye its glance of danger; Jews in black dress and solemn turban, more Oriental than the Turk himself; Armenian priests with dark robes and square caps, repeating as

ZEBECK FROM INTERIOR.

CIRCASSIAN.

ARAB FROM BAGDAD.

SYRIAN NOMAD.

they walk their orisons over sandalwood rosaries; a dervish nearly as naked as Adam before the fall, looking as if in hopeless chaos, with limbs lank for lack of food; gesturing Italians; screaming people from the Greek isles ; grim and lofty Arabs ; pistoled and yataghaned Nubians, black as a starless night, some of whom are tall, slim, long-armed and long-legged eunuchs and slaves; and to crown all, the Turkish pasha in tasseled fez, and frock coat as collarless as that of a Methodist presiding elder, and as clean as the razor can shave him, except the fine moustache; water-carriers, and firemen on a run with unearthly shrieks ; all in bustle and confusion, and all intent and active as a crowd in old Broadway.

The soldiers here make the bravest aspect of themselves and their uniforms. This is one reason why the Turks seem most numerous, and why, being sent to the wars, they are not growing in population as the Christians, who do not go to war. The description given during the Crimean War of the Turkish soldier is true to-day. Though ill-fed, and worse paid, he is ever devout upon his prayer-carpet as it is turned Mecca-ward. He is powerful in physique, high of feature and brawny of limb. He is sprung from generations of warriors which once threatened to overwhelm the whole Western world in a tide that has long since been at its ebb. Patient of hardship, devoted to the Sultan and to duty, with a fierce and dogged resolution and childish obedience and simplicity, he is the model of a soldier, and, so far as I have observed, of courtesy and gentleness. If Greece or any other nation presumes to try the wager of battle with him, as he is now armed, it will go hard with the Turkish enemy. The Turkish soldier is a peasant at home; and when soldiering, he is not always a Bashi-bazouk, or the swaggering rowdy, as he is often described.

"Some kind casuists are pleased to say," once remarked a Mahometan to me, "that I have no devotion ; but set those persons down with me to pray, and you shall see who has the properest notion."

Substitute "motion," and the Turk will outdo the Christian ten to one. Some one has calculated the motions of his body *per diem*. It gives him healthy exercise and grace of manner, besides a good conscience.

I am not aware of any hostility existing now between cer-

ICE CREAM SELLER.

A CANDY MAN.

WATER PEDLER.

PLATE MERCHANT.

tain sects of Christians and the Mahometan. If any, it has been fostered by influences outside of this city. The Mahdi's campaign in Egypt is an illustration of the olden power of faith and the sword. The enmity, to which I have adverted, to the extension of Protestant and Catholic schools, churches and influences is not of such bitter hostility as that of the anti-Semitic Germans, Austrians and Russians against the Jews. Its bitterness has not risen to the dignity of religious bigotry. It is not a demonstration of unthrifty envy *versus* industrial providence. Nor does it spring so much from fear of Moslem apostacy or proselytism by other religionists. There is no fear of that in Turkey. The Turk smiles —he does not laugh—at all attempts at propagandism. Not fifty Moslem converts have appeared in as many years. But with the spread of education, through American and other auspices, he fears, almost without the courage to tell it, that a new political state or social order may arise within some parts of his empire, having its seat either in Judea or Syria, Beirut or Jerusalem.

Upon this clear morning in mid-winter, upon a May-like day, from my balcony I can see the snow-topped heights of the Mysean Olympus. From yonder melting snows the Sangarius flows to the Euxine. Upon its banks a few hundred nomads, a few hundred years ago, from central Asia, bivouacked. From a few hundred, and with the aid of a force now potential among two hundred millions of people—a religion with a cimeter—they conquered, four hundred and thirty-four years ago, the finest spot for capitalizing commerce and energizing empire, existing upon this planet. Without the arts of Greece or the eagles of Rome, this Seljukian family of Turks mastered many of the ways and means which enable dynasties to hold what is taken. This sway was crystallized as well by the personal qualities of Osman, the Romulus of the empire, as by acts of toleration and moderation in matters of tax, conscription, land-tenure, citizenship and religion. The institutions of this empire were greater than the *personnel* of the Ottoman.

Broussa, which now sits like an Eastern queen in her silken array at the foot of Mount Olympus, became the first capital of these Turkish rulers. But Broussa was the threshold only to this superb throne of Constantinople. Forty years before Columbus found the new hemisphere, the Greek empire fell before this remarkable power. It fell without much contest for its sustentation.

It was not so much the Moslem faith nor the standing army of Janizaries, trained with skill, recruited with Christian youth, and uniformed compactly, nor the personal attachment of this race to its rulers, that enabled this new power to sweep from the Euphrates to the Adriatic and from the Nile to the Pillars of Hercules. The solution is found in the division of power and employment. The local government with its cadi (or mayor) and council of notables, was never lost sight of, even in the ambitions of foreign conquest. The lands which were conquered were saved for tillage and grazing. All who came to the mosque received mercy. Slaves were freed and goods restored. The rule was one of law, and in the clangor of arms its voice was not hushed.

The Christian people of the conquered territory were as much the devotees of superstition and rites as were the heathen who worshipped the sun or fire. Byzantium was a pagan place before Mahometanism destroyed its images and razed its temples. It is thought that the fall of Byzantium was a calamity to the world. Its existence certainly was not a blessing.

There never was a time when Mahometanism could have conquered and held Europe. Its lodgment even in Spain was disputed for seven hundred years. There was a perpetual barrier against it, as well by Alpine ranges as by chivalric courage.

It is doubtful if Turkey is now advancing. Her doctrine of "Kismet" is applicable to her condition. The Christian people of her empire are gaining upon the Turkish. War, plague and contention in and out of Europe—in Africa as well as in Europe —have limited her boundaries and undermined her old and hardy constitution.

Why this unique empire, with its relics of polygamy and slavery, should decay, is not so difficult a problem as why it has grown in four centuries to be such a power that the great land animal, Russia, pauses before it lays its claws upon this capital.

# CHAPTER XXXI.

## THE CAÏQUES OF THE BOSPORUS.

My countrymen who visit the National Museum at Washington will perceive a strange boat from the Orient. It is known in the waters of the Bosporus as a caïque, and in the Turkish tongue, from which it is derived, as a câik. The Yankee boatmen laughed at its Oriental workmanship, with its hull of tulip wood, battened on the inside with small blocks of wood and deluged with pitch; but he could not understand its utility or was not enamored of its beauty. For its size—thirty-five feet long, with only a weight of 340 pounds—it was a marvel among boats when I rode in it upon the Bosporus. May I not say something further about its utilities and graces?

The boat belonged to the American Legation. It was purchased many years ago with United States money. It has often been repaired since. It has served the purpose of a Legation boat before steam became a motor upon the Bosporus. It was only used in good weather, when the Legation was situated up the Straits, and for purposes which the launch granted by Congress now supplies.

There are pleasing associations with it enjoyed by my predecessors, as well as by myself. Upon one occasion, I rigged up this six-oared caïque, to cross the Bosporus, with a view to penetrating into the interior, a mile or so along the "Sweet Waters of Asia." One of the incidents of this trip into Asia was a visit to the various potteries on the shore of the sweet little stream. Halting our boat before one of the potteries, we are attracted by a low musical chant. Having along our Dalmatian servitor, Pedro, we halt to examine the potteries and listen to the chant. The chanteur is intoning from the Koran. He shrewdly keeps one eye upon us, as we are strangers. Not being his prayer time, he is not quite so ceremonious as usual. Directly he stops his intoning, I ask with respect, through Pedro, that I

may see his Koran. It is an old volume, badly worn. It once
had signs of gilt on the outside. It had a cover of morocco, once
beautiful. Inside, it was ornamented with bits of gold leaf for
periods, or pauses in prayers. It had many illustrations, all giving quite a picturesque quality to the book. In the frontispiece,
which, Celtic-like, is at the end, there is the Crescent and the Star.
The first page—where we have our "Finis"—is like an illuminated missal in purple, and with various exquisite arrangements
of line and script. These show that the book had once been of
value. I ask the owner:

"Will you sell the book?"

This is in derogation of law and custom. The owner shrinks
from the negotiation. However, after much talk, I obtain his
confidence. With a little persuasion on the part of his brother
workmen, who are unbelieving Greeks, and who gather about
him, he gives a hesitating acquiescence and remarks:

"I would like to know how much you will give for it?"

I ask, Yankee-fashion, "How much will you take?"

He ponders long. He looks within the cover, as if loth to
part with his consoling companion and says:

"It is worth two mejidiés, is it not?"

That is about two dollars. I leap for the book. I have the
silver ready, jingling it under the potter's eye. Am I too quick?
He turns to his companions, and as Pedro interprets it, he says:

"I fear that these people are spying on me. They are detect-
ives, perhaps. They may arrest me for the sale."

It requires some diplomacy to mollify and conciliate him. But
I had set my heart on the acquisition, and I feared, like the classic
female, Cassandra, that he might raise the price at each refusal to
clinch the bargain. I ask:

"Where are you from?"

"From the city of Scutari in Albania."

"Will you be kind enough to write your name in the
book?"

This he does with a pencil at the end of the book. His name
is Baïram. Whether named after the festive season or not, I do
not inquire. He is not a jolly person, although he bears a
happy name.

He then commences again, intoning piously some of the verses,
to which he longingly opens. Then casting his eyes on the

*mejidiés*, he delivers over the precious volume to my wife. This was on the 23d of October, 1885, on the Moslem Sunday, which is on Friday. I still retain the volume, as one of the curious souvenirs of my religious invasion of Asia, of my visit to the "Sweet Waters" and of the elegant caïque, now naturalized in America. Besides, there is the association with Bairam, the gentle child of Mahomet. His shrewd piety will not be forgotten.

What singular attachments these religionists—even from the shores of the Adriatic, and almost beyond the borders of Greece—still retain for the Islam of their fathers! Perhaps this man had in him the blood of those Moslems of the mountains of Albania, so celebrated for prowess and endurance in the time of Scanderbeg, or of those noted in the Suliote war under Ali Pasha.

When I first saw Constantinople, thirty-six years ago, there were eighty thousand caïques constantly plying between the European and Asiatic sides, and up and down the waters which make Constantinople such an alluring resort and such a commercial capital. The gondola has almost been replaced in Venice by the little steam *mouches* which fly over its limpid avenues. What the gondola was once, and is, to the Venetian and the tourist, the caïque was, and is yet, to the Turk and his Oriental guests. There have been great changes upon the Bosporus by the introduction of steam. The number of the caïques has been reduced. There are perhaps not more than twenty-five thousand now. The larger number of these may be hired like cabs in New York. These are called *kirlangich*, or "swallow boats." There is another bird peculiar to the Bosporus which is suggested by these boats, even more appositely than the swallow. I mean the bird called, from its restless habits, "the condemned soul." These birds fly in flocks constantly. They are never seen upon the wave, but always upon the wing. They are in perpetual unrest. Going down to the city from the upper Bosporus, I have encountered flocks of them by the hundred. They fly just above the surface. Where they nestle, how they live and what they do, are among the questions which the tourist puts in vain to the native, and which only a treatise on ornithology may answer. They suggest the caïque, because of their continually coming and going. Turn which way you will upon the Bosporus, even when the ferry-boats ply every ten minutes, up, down and about, you will see these birds. They fly straight ahead, as if intent on business. They do

not play around upon the waves and become domesticated, glut-
tonous and noisy in the harbor, as the sea-gulls do. For be it
known that the birds of the Bosporus are as multitudinous as the
dogs of Stamboul; and they are as much protected by the Turk
as the dog and other animals.

The Yankee who laughed at our boat has not described it
accurately. It is generally made of thin planks of beachwood,
with a neat finish and elaborate carving. It is sharply pointed at
both ends. The elegance of its construction, the levity of its
materials, the singular shape of the oars—being very thin, wide,
and light at the feather end, and bulbous at the handle—and the
dexterity and picturesqueness of the boatmen, give to it a rapidity of movement and a grace of form exquisite, unique and
Oriental.

The boat, besides having long borne our starred ensign, is one
of the most graceful of its kind. It is six-oared, three oars on
each side, and guided by a rudder.

These boats can always be had for hire at the landing-stages.
The larger ones are used for parties of pleasure, families on a
picnic, and for passengers on business. As the waters of the Bosporus are very deep and are always running, and in some places
with a swift current, much caution is required, not only in entering the caïque, but in trimming it after you are in. It is easily
overset. Two members of the brass band of the *Kearsarge*
the past summer, on the visit of that vessel to the Bosporus, lost
their lives because of their awkwardness in the caïque. The passengers must sit in the bottom, upon a Turkish rug or crimson
cushion. The caïques are like our canoes in one respect. They
are long and very narrow, and sensitive to every motion of the
passenger. Nervous people should never enter them. But the
Turkish lady has a cautious step, and an immobility when seated,
which exactly suit the humor of the caïque.

The water-men of the boats are dressed in white cotton-crêpe
shirts. They wear on their heads a small scarlet skull cap. It is
no protection from the sun; and the amazement is, that such a
head-dress, which is no shade over the eye or the face, should be
acceptable in a country so thoroughly drenched with sunbeams.
There was some sense in the old turban, which absorbed the rays
of the sun and cooled the head, but now you will see nearly every
Turkish subject with a fez cap, worn somewhat on the back of

the head, so that the eye must meet the glare of the pavement and
stream, or the blaze of the sun, and the forehead must be of
perpetual bronze. The idea of the brimless fez is, however, a
religious one. With a rim to the fez, or to a hat, how could the
pious Mussulman touch the earth with his forehead in his
prayers?

The *caïquejis* are a muscular race of men. They are mostly
of the Greek race. Some of them have a disagreeable grunt as
they ply their oars, owing to inordinate exertion when young,
which affected their lungs. These caïquejis are not garrulous. They are mute and reserved. They are machines, in the
regularity with which they keep time with the oars. They neither
look to the right nor to the left, except now and then a rapid glance
to see that their onward way is clear. And yet the Greek boatman, like the gondolier, will sometimes break into song, and the
song will keep measure with the plunge of the oar. The dissonance of the singer may be somewhat drowned, if not harmonized,
with the delightful, dreamy charm of the motion and plash of the
oar. The songs are not only inharmonious but monotonous. They
require distance to mellow them.

When visits were to be made by the Legation, the caïquejis
are arrayed in cleanly white apparel, not unlike that of an ancient
Roman senator. Their bosoms and arms are bare. There is a
rhythmic music in their movement. This adds to the pleasure of
the trip and enhances the beauty of the boat, making it a living
picture upon a mobile element of lucent lymph.

The harbor of Constantinople is not only celebrated for its
natural advantages, but the immense and heavy shipping in the
harbor presents a striking contrast with these beautiful caïques.
Amid the ferry-boats, as large as those that ply between New
York and Jersey City, and the Austrian, French, Russian and
English steamers which crowd the harbor, these faerie boats, with
their arrowy points and precious burden of *hanoums*, are continually darting with graceful rapidity hither and yon among the
heavier craft of a new civilization. They illustrate the fact that
the spell of delight and the dream of enchantment have not yet
entirely departed from the city of the Sultan. Amid the grand
scenery of the Bosporus the little caïque still holds its own.
Within the splendid harbor it still plays its petite part. Crowded
as is the harbor with its myriads of boats, it is yet deep and large

THE MOSQUE OF ORTAKEUI AND THE CAÏQUES.

enough to hold twelve hundred sail, and give hospitality to iron-clads, which moor in its tideless waters even up to the lintels of the houses, as well as to the craft of every rig and nation—the feluccas, xebecs and bragozzi of the neighboring isles, and great ships of iron flying the red Crescent of the Sultan. Still the caïque, amidst them all, is a living beauty and an active utility. Not merely the pasha in his fez, and his wives in their veils of tulle, but the hundred nationalities which here assemble have their story and experience with this fanciful caïque. What tales it could tell, if it were only sentient and voiceful! Would it not speak of the "rage of the vulture, the love of the turtle," the melodious voice of the nightingale, and of "the virgins as soft as the roses they twine"? Would it not sigh over the stories of the Selims and Zuliekas of the fateful Orient?

Upon Friday, which is a day of recreation as well as of religion, when the crowds of the capital turn out on a pleasant afternoon to visit the "Sweet Waters of Asia" opposite the Towers of Europe, or the "Sweet Waters of Europe" at the head of the Golden Horn, every caïque is in requisition. In fact, every kind of boat upon the Bosporus is then active. The vast and varied population of the city and the suburbs of Pera and Constantinople, and of the Golden Horn, are continually embarking or returning on these and other festal days in these frail boats. Although steam ferries run every ten minutes up and down the whole length of the Straits, from Cavak to Seraglio Point, yet a considerable body of the people go to and from the city and their homes by this old, fami-liar method. The caïque is, therefore, by no means obsolete. Now you will see in it a bevy of Turkish women, dressed in silks of every hue, seated upon a rug or cushion smoking their cigarettes, in full glee over their gossip from the bath. Or peradventure, you will notice a company of Persians in their pointed caps, or of Mollahs with white turbans and green, in tinted pelisses, or of Nubian boatmen, with rose-colored jackets, and faces that shine and eyes that sparkle. In the sunshine or in the shadow, dart-ing under the arches of the palaces and houses, under the helm of some eunuch, who is in charge of a household, or between the boats which form the pontoon bridges of the Golden Horn, you see these boats perpetually skimming the clear blue water as if propelled through the air like some fantastic, dreamy creation of the Thousand and One Nights.

These boats are still affected by the pashas who can afford to keep them. You may tell the boat of a rich Turk by the silken gauze sleeves of the caïquejis, or boatmen. Their sleeves wave in unison with the stroke of the oar upon the water. On festive days, and especially among the Greek population, these boats are filled with musicians and revelers, who use the liberty of the occasion to do much shouting, and make what they denominate music, if not melody. The songs may be discordant, but the singers or musicians do not know it. It is quite picturesque and exhilarat-

CAÏQUE AT SWEET WATERS OF EUROPE.

ing to the Occidental taste to look down from the ferry-boat, or, as I used to do, from the deck of our launch, upon the turban, the fez, the caftan, the feridji and the yashmak, and other gear such as the curly, black sheepskin hat of the Circassian, the felt hat of the dervish, and the dark cap of the Montenegrin, dashed with crimson and gold; or slyly peer beneath the gauzy veil of some lady of large, liquid, dark and dangerous eyes, under a red parasol, who is by no means unwilling to be observed. These little incidents of navigation give grace, as well as piquancy, to the scenes of the Bosporus.

Sometimes the caïque is so ornamented as to have all the hues of the prism. But generally it is varnished and has a golden-yellow hue. It is fretted and pointed with elegant tracery. There are seldom any accidents to the caïque upon the Bosporus, although there seems, to a stranger, to be danger and confusion in its movements. You would think that it was about to be run down by some heavier vessel, or by the steam ferry or big steamer; but the caïqueji has a quick glance and a cunning oar, and his slender craft is out of the way in a twinkling.

The grand caïque of the Sultan is now almost out of use. I have seen it but once upon the Bosporus. It is as skillful in its graceful construction as it is gorgeous in its splendors. Nay ; call it not gorgeous ! Its beauty is rather that of simplicity. It is immaculate, except that it is broidered with pink and gold. It has twelve pair of oars. These touch the water as if they were feathered. The twenty-six rowers are dressed in white silk shirts, loose, white, baggy trousers and the scarlet fez. They make a stroke every thirty seconds. There is a crimson velvet canopy over the stern. It is embroidered with gold, upheld by four gilded columns. Under this canopy is a sofa of velvet for His Majesty. Near by are benches for his *aides*. The tiller is held by an Arab dressed in scarlet and gold. At the stern is a big gilded bird. It is not the American eagle ; for our bird is of another beak and shape. Still, it has a resemblance to the eagle in the outspread wings. It is not a bird of prey ; only a peacock !

This description gives a dim idea only of the exquisite beauty of this boat. That beauty is duplicated, by reflection, in the mirroring Bosporus. It is enhanced by the retinue of caïques, which dance after its royal eminence.

This leads to the remark that our own caïque had upon its bow what was supposed to be the American eagle. When I took charge of the Legation, the eagle had lost the main part of its beak. It had been denuded of several of its fierce tail feathers. Its wings did not show the energy of an American spread. After several amendments in the first and second degree to that eagle, I had moved a substitute and had the original bird placed over the Legation, in the alleyway which the American Congress generously allows its Minister to furnish as headquarters. That bird indicates to the American tourist the survival of our nation in the East, in spite of the lamentable lack of appropriations.

When, as Wordsworth sings, Venice, the Maiden City, bright
and free, took unto herself a mate, and espoused the Everlasting
Sea, did not Venice copy her custom from the gorgeous East,
which she once "held in fee"? It was about the time of the
third Crusade, while Dandolo was Ambassador at the Porte, and
before he wore the ducal bonnet made in the similitude of a horn—
from the Golden Horn, its prototype in the East—a few years before
the old hero led the way to the conquest of Constantinople, and
when Venice was full of republican pride and prosperity—that
the espousal of the Adriatic originated. The Pope, being grateful
for the services of Venice, presented the Doge with a gold ring. It
was a pledge of Venetian sovereignty over the sea. " Every year,"
said the Pope, "renew with this ring your marriage with the sea, that
all posterity may know that the Adriatic owes to you the obedience
of a wife to her husband." For six hundred years this ceremony
was observed. The famous *Bucintoro*, or great state galley, leads
the way, with a dazzling retinue of craft, and amid the thunder of
cannon, toward the Lido. When they enter the open sea the
Doge unlocks his private chamber in the vessel, a priest sprinkles
holy water into the sea, and the ring is dropped on the sacred
waves, while the Doge utters in Latinity this sentence :

" We wed thee, O Sea ! in token of true and perpetual
sovereignty."

There is a model of the *Bucintoro* in the arsenal at Venice. The
original was stripped of its gilt ornaments and partly burned by
the vandalic French in A. D. 1797. Still, the hull survived as a gun-
boat until A. D. 1824. The boat was a hundred feet long. It had two
stories and forty-two oars ; four men to an oar. It was profusely
ornamented, inside and outside, with gilt flowers and fruits, shells
and syrens, fish and tritons. It had a double prow, representing
rule over sea and land. Nymphs and caryatides upheld the
canopy of scarlet satin which covered the great saloon. The nobles
and ambassadors occupied the stern about the Doge, who sat on
a gilded throne. Behind this throne were the winged lions and
the gonfalon of St. Mark. These emblems betoken a most gorgeous display. These symbols, like the " properties " in St.
Marks, were stolen from the Constantinople of the Greeks by the
wily Venetian. The Doges who glided in such stately style out
of the lagoons into the blue sea, emulated but never surpassed
the splendor of the contemporary emperors of Byzantium

when, upon their festal days, they passed up and down the Bosporus.

Cleopatra in all her pageantry upon the Nile, with her boat of curiously shaped prow, rigged, like Southey's ship of heaven, with rainbows, never made a more elegant or royal figure than the Selims, Amuraths, and Mahomets of the past when they crossed the Bosporus to make their devotions in the mosques of the old city of Stamboul, or in grand procession paid their devoirs to their harems upon the Isles of the Princes. The royal caïque was a mass of gilding and glitter. It fairly gleamed in the sunshine. It was more than a caïque : it was a painted splendor—a poetic creation which was etherealized by the elements, the water and the air, and the exquisite lustre and shadow which it cast upon the one element, and the graceful rise and fall of its movement through the other.

No wonder our Legation boat, so fragile and so dainty, should receive damage in crossing the vexed Atlantic upon the exposed deck of a Cunarder. Generally these boats give the impression of a light, buoyant, glittering image, hardly substantial. The crimson drapery, fringed with gold, which hangs over its sides, almost dipping into the water, and under the sweet light which has its peculiar properties upon the Bosporus, by the richness and variety of its color, gives a superb costume to the boat. This is in harmony with the costumes of the people who grace it with their languid and decorous dignity.

The boat is an evidence of progress. If you would know how the world has moved, study the galleys of ancient history ; or even the thousand-year-old Norse vessels which, after dis-interment, I saw on exhibition, in Christiania, Norway. I have made a description of the latter in a volume called " Arctic Sun-beams," and instituted the comparison between them and the boats of the Bosporus. There is much similarity ; but the poetic and beateous levity is not a part of the Norse *Yecht*. During the past summer I mixed much with the Greek sailors at Prinkipo. I saw many curious caïques ; for I was eager to know what was the shape, tonnage and size, the utilities and beauties of the old galley—if you please, the Turkish galley—the galley in which Barbarossa and Kairid-Ali won their splendid victories in the Mediterranean. I find a description of this galley in Creasy. It must have been the same kind of boat which the Turks used when they dragged their vessels overland from Dolma-Bagtché to the Golden Horn, at the taking of Constantinople.

The galley was a long boat, provided with a main and fore mast, which might be raised and strung as required. She carried large latteen sails, which could only be trusted under way in light winds and smooth seas, while her great length must have exposed her to foundering in a rough sea. In fact, the galley seems to me to be an enlarged *caïque*, swift to move, and yet uncomfortable and dangerous.

Among the isles of the Archipelago known as the "Princes Isles," where we sojourned in the summer of 1886, the chants of the fishermen as they draw in their nets were quite as common as they were musical—when remote. Summer before last, our experience was not as pleasant with the fishermen of the upper Bosporus. These latter toilers of the sea are of Italian descent. They are quite independent of all national, Turkish or international rules or laws concerning this greatest and grandest of water-ways. Late at night, in their caïques, they set their surface-nets. These nets are buoyed up by gourds or corks, and when the Legations are making their nocturnal visits to one another between Buyukdere and Therapia, or returning home from fêtes or dances—they use their steam launches. Woe to the Russian, German, French, English or Italian "mouche," whose screw makes an entangling alliance (*enchevêtrement*) with these nets upon the "fishy Bosporus." Oh, the wail which rises over the dark blue water and penetrates to lacerate the heart of the unfortunate diplomat or launchman! That wail still rings in my ears —a rasping, howling plaint of agony, long drawn out—echoing from shore to shore, and caught up in a succession of cries, as if each one of the crafty "moonlighters" upon the public preserves would warn his fellow-trespasser of the impending danger. It is a cry of protest, piteous, indignant and despairing; and as long as the bill which the unlucky fisherman presents the next day at the Legation with grimace and lament for the loss of his only means of living—his precious net.

These troubles, however, had their compensations. When we resided at Therapia, many a love-song floated on the evening air, in the gloaming or in the moonlight, from some caïque, as it darted up and down the stream, or was moored idly in the shadow of a palace wall. The music is sometimes accompanied by a rude guitar, a small drum or tambourine. It is hardly a song which is sung. It has no festive ring. It is a melancholy chant, always in the minor mode. It is a recitation rather than a song or a chant. If there be any heroic lay sung upon the Bosporus, as Byron intimated about the songs of the degenerate Grecian isles, " it is tuneless now "—not more tuneless than the effigies of the caïquéjis, whose boat clothes have been imported along with our Legation caïque, and which are hereafter to be filled by the plastic, waxen art of Professor Baird or his Museum employees.

I have frequently asked for the meaning of these songs, and have received for answer that most of them have reference to some heart that was breaking or some beauty to be won. Their burden may be of some fair one who is about to leave her swain for foreign parts ; and the wind blows, the sea is rough, the sails are filled, and like the plumes of a little pigeon she is about to spread her wings for that distant clime. "I weep not for the boat, I weep not for the sails, but I weep for the fair one who is going away." And as the singer intones the sentiment, the tears are in his voice, if not in his eyes.

Again to our balcony near the quay, from the Asiatic shore comes this lugubrious lay:

" Three months elapsed before I saw thee, Ma-ri-a-me-ne ! Ma-ri-a-me-ne ! I thought they were three years. Three sharp knives into my heart did enter, Ma-ri-a-me-ne ! Ma-ri-a-me-ne !"

Then there is another strain, still more lachrymose, seeming to float out of the shadow of Jason's mountain:

" As many as are the stars in the skies, as many as are the windows in Stamboul; so many are the damsels I have kissed on the eye-brows and on the eyes !"

Not a very sad experience, but sung ever so triste ! Then out of the quiet bay of Buyukdere comes drawling this tender bar-carolle :

" Let us make our vows under the columns; and if I do not love thee, Fatima, let them all fall and crush me. So, then, let my lips say that I love you; that the rose leaves of my heart may become conserves of sweetness !"

In the National Museum at Washington, there is a collection, not of these conserved sweet-hearts, but of the unstranded boats of various nations, from Labrador to New Zealand. The time will come when it will contain every variety of boat, from the catamaran of Ceylon to the coracle of ancient Egypt and modern Wales ; from the caboose of the modern merchantman to the galley of the ancient Roman; from the thousand-year-old yacht of the Norseman to the skiff of the Buckeye raftsman of my early days on the Muskingum.

In such a medley, where junks, pinnaces, punts, yawls, tillers, rowlocks and gondolas may illustrate the variety and history of national navigation, I resolve that the caïque of Constantinople should have its well-won prominence. Whereupon, after the Department of State had directed me to dispose of the Lega-

ANCIENT GALLEY.

tion caïque, as no longer necessary for the economic trans- portation of the Minister and his suite, and as ·it required a burden on the Federal Treasury of nearly three mejediés a quar- ter, or $12 a year, and as our six-oared boat was obsolete and could not be sold for the price of its keeping for a quarter—it occurs to me that it would make a useful if not a beautiful exhibit amid the strange and curious boats collected in our Federal capital.

Mr. Bayard cheerfully acquiesced in my wish. As the boat was difficult to ship and could not well be boxed, and as there was no expense to the United States Treasury for its transportation, it again occurs to me to make it the companion of two emigrants which I sent from Egypt, one of whom has now an isolated residence in the National Museum. It did not irk, but it amused somewhat that the enterprising American press had discovered that my mummies, which were presented by a friend—Mehemet Ali—at Luxor, were dead-headed home at the expense of the United States Government. This was one of the many mistakes which my remoteness from home did not enable me to correct. However, it is a solace for my absence that I have been enabled, both by the mummy and the caïque, to add something of interest to the national collection. Certainly, for myself, whenever I enter the Museum, I shall be reminded of the days which were rounded out of the Crescent into the fullness of beauty, not only amid the temples and tombs of old Egypt, but on the waters and amid the scenes which make my memory of the Orient a joy forever!

# CHAPTER XXXII.

## DOGS OF CONSTANTINOPLE—A CANINE REPUBLIC—FIGHTS.

DOGS IN THE STREETS OF CONSTANTINOPLE.

WOULD there be so many cases of hydrophobia if it were not for Pasteur? This was the question of a clever "medicine man" here who has compassed the world in a scientific way. No doubt Pasteur's remedy has called unusual attention to the subject of rabies. Whether his theory of the microbe be correct or his practice uniformly salutary, a layman like myself cannot presume to discuss. Owing to my relation at this capital (of Constantinople), and the presumption that a Minister does or ought to know "all things and some others" in and around his post, I have received many letters about the dogs of Constantinople. I have not studied their statistics ; only their habits. I may say that they do not number 500 dogs to the acre. Yet this is not such an exaggeration as some would suppose. In the old Turkish quarters of Stamboul, where they are petted by the population, they are as

thick as leaves in fall.   They do not seem to lessen in number.
Puppies of every degree, size and age are being constantly turned
out.    There is, therefore, no better place than Constantinople to
study one type at least of the canine family in its relation to the
*genus homo.*

A correspondent from Wisconsin was anxious to know, from
some scientific standpoint, whether rabies prevailed among these
Turkish dogs.   He had heard that they were ownerless and neglected.   His inference naturally was that, being famished and
uncared for, they were therefore likely to become mad   I consulted Dr. John Patterson on these points.   He is at the head of
the English hospital here, and well known in the East as a most
accomplished physician.   He addressed me a letter, in which he
rehearsed his opinions, formed in Labrador among the sled-dogs,
in Egypt among the shepherd dogs, and in Turkey among the
vagrant dogs.   It was that *rabies* was much exaggerated.   He
premised that in Constantinople, Asiatic Turkey and Egypt, where
pariah dogs abound, *rabies* was rare.   The doctor was thirteen
years in Egypt and has been eighteen years in Turkey, and in
each country in full practice.   He never saw a case of *rabies.*
He had treated many dog-bites, and was anxious to see an un-
doubted case of madness.   During these periods he had only
heard of three or four cases.   He states further, that since Pasteur's alleged discovery of a preventive, there has been reported
such an enormous increase of cases of hydrophobia in every
country of Europe as naturally to create doubt of the correctness
of the statements.

The only reasonable explanation of the comparative freedom
from *rabies* in these countries, where dogs abound and exist under
conditions presumably favorable to the development of the disease,
is that the animals live nearly in their natural state—i. e., in the
open air and sunshine—and are not over-fed and pampered.   That
this may be the true reason, is probable from the fact that in
extremely cold countries, as Greenland and other Arctic regions,
*rabies* is also scarce amongst dogs, though they are exposed to
much hardship and privation.   This is the report of the Danish
inspectors and intelligent natives.   No one of them had seen or
heard of a case of hydrophobia.   Against these statements is the
fact that an allied species, the wolf and fox (especially the
former), are in their natural state very liable to become rabid.

Without discussing the paradox as to the wolf and fox, or entering upon the Pasteur theory, I may state that we moved to the Isle of Prinkipo for the summer of 1886. It is in the Sea of Marmora, a dozen miles below the city. There are several ferries running there every day. Doubtless the number of dogs on the island is owing to the easy communication. Most of them are used as watch-dogs and hunters ; but many of them are vagrant, and of the same kind as at Constantinople. It was one of these dogs which gripped my wrist in our garden at Prinkipo. It was a watch-dog. It is of a different breed from that of the vagrant dog. He bit me in the line of his duty, as he supposed. He had been guarding the premises from intruders before we moved into the house, and having returned to his kennel and his vigilance in the garden, he considered us to be interlopers. The snap of his ugly jaw still makes my bone shiver. Luckily, the grip was on the thick and polished shirt cuff. His teeth slipped off the cuff and made but a slight abrasion of the skin. Any fear of rabies ? Not at all ; for there is nothing of the kind here.

However, my bite got into the papers. It was just before the Sultan gave us a dinner at Yildiz palace. My companion at the table was Dr. S. S. Mavroyéni. Whether it was because his initials were sweetly silbilant, like my own S. S.; or because he was unusually accomplished; or because he was the Sultan's chief physician—for that monarch has twelve other doctors under the Mavroyéni Pasha—or whether the Doctor was able to talk in some other tongue than his vernacular Greek, his adopted Turkish, or his favorite German, we became colloquial over the wine; for be it known that the Sultan gives his guests all the wine they desire, whether it be according to the Koran or not. He abstains himself, and thus keeps the law. Well, my dog-bite came up for discussion. I found the doctor to be partial to dogs. He explained that the vagrants were not watch-dogs, but by training, could be made faithful and fierce.

The other day I received from the excellent Doctor a brochure, in French, entitled, " *Les Chiens Errants de Constantinople—Etude de Mœurs.*"

That my scratch could lead to such a learned discussion, should engender a feeling of national pride. When, in its perusal, I found the doctor to be a democratic-republican of the American type, I was patriotically elated. In speaking of these errant dogs, he says that they have an autonomy and are free ; they have no wish to impose their will on any, but delegate different services and functions to each dog, according to his capacity. They have, I suppose, a sort of civil-service. What examination they undergo for selection or preferment we are not told by the Doctor. He finds their government comparable with a confederative republic, and not unlike that of " la grande Republique de l'Amerique du Nord." These dogs are confederate under mutual obligations. Each division governs itself in an independent manner.

It is the custom of travelers and authors always to mention these dogs. Compared with the indolent and inconsequential curs upon the streets and docks of Naples, and other places among the lazzaroni, which have not yet attained to the dignity of a literary and scientific study, they are honorably mentioned.

From Miss Pardoe down to Edmondo de Amicis, I find reference to these dogs. In A. D. 1835, Miss Pardoe found them on the threshold of her entrance into the city. She honors them in the first chapter of her " City of the Sultan " by this mention:

" I could not avoid remarking the little straw huts built at intervals along the streets for the accommodation and comfort of the otherwise homeless dogs that throng every avenue of the town. There they lay, crouched down snugly, too much chilled to welcome us with the chorus of barking that they usually bestow on travelers. In addition to this shelter, food is every day dispensed by the inhabitants to the vagrant animals, who, having no specific owners, are, to use the approved phraseology of genteel almsasking, 'wholly dependent on the charitable for support.' And it is a singular fact that these self-constituted scavengers exercise a kind of internal economy which exceeds the boundaries of mere instinct; they have their defined "walks," or haunts, and woe betide the strange cur who intrudes on the privileges of his neighbors; he is hunted, upbraided with growls and barks, beset on all sides, even bitten in cases of obstinate contumacy, and universally obliged to retreat within his own limits."

Thirty-five years ago I wrote a book entitled " Buckeye Abroad," in which several chapters were given to the " Heart of Mahometanism." That was in A. D. 1851—before the Crimean War had decimated the dogs. I can recall my first timid step as we threaded the then, and still, "dirty, splashy, badly paved, narrow, doggy, donkeyfied, carriageless, up-and-down streets, in traversing which you cannot look at anything for fear of having your head cracked against the burden of some donkey or the load of some head-shouldered carrier, or for fear of treading upon one of the many thousand brindled dogs who act the part of scavengers by day and play that of howling dervishes by night."

At that time the dogs were in the hey-day of Abdul Medjid's reign, to whom all now refer as the Arab does to the good Haroun Al-Raschid, of Bagdad. Little did I then think of coming hither, after thirty-five years, for a long stay, or that some day a bite of one of these "brindles" would give rise to a learned study on errant dogs by the "Hekim-bashi," or head of the medical profession of the empire, and chief physician of the son and successor of Abdul Medjid, of happy memory.

These dogs are of a peculiar race. They are a cross between the jackal and the wolf, but without being as wild, cruel or mischievous as either. They are very intelligent and industrious. They are sweet toward the natives ; they are hostile to strangers, whom they recognize at once as such. This is most observable in the retired quarters, inhabited by Mussulmans. They are numerous, tumultuous and independent. They encumber the streets. This has been so immemorially.

Constantinople has had twenty-four sieges. It has been taken six times. Alcibiades, Constantine, Dandolo, Paleologos and Mahmoud II. severally succeeded in entering its harbors and gates, but the dogs have survived all these captures. Grecian commanders and Roman emperors, Persian chosroes, Arabian caliphs, Venetian doges and French counts, Bulgarian krales and Avarian chakars, Slavonian despots and Ottoman sultans have come and gone, have besieged and been repulsed, or have captured and held the city; but the dogs go on for ever! No balance of power, no Eastern imbroglio, has disturbed their republican autonomy. Their "Home Rule" upsets no administration. It disturbs no dynasty; but it remains stable for ever.

A veritable colony has been acquired by them in their encroachments. They have the right of domicile, which publicists and architects have not contested. Whether or not, *bon gré, mal gré,* the savants are forced to tolerate the colony. They do not know what else to do. Besides, the dogs are so sugary and wheedling, they so insinuate and flatter, that their work, patriotism and services make them acceptable as the guardians of their quarter of the city against robbers and malefactors. They make the streets healthy by disinfecting them, not by the method of the learned doctors Pettenkofer and Koch, but by devouring the carrion and garbage, which is their fare. They do this without salary from the municipality, and are thus an economical and sanitary police.

I am not equal to understanding the methods of the learned Pettenkofer, or his medical brother. Doubtless these men are some of Doctor Mavroyéni's German friends, for he studied when young at a German university. But I can understand that when the terrific howls are raised, about sunrise, around the Hotel Royal, at Pera, by the score of dogs which surround that hostelry with their republican outcries, there is a contest going on between the incursive garbage gatherers and the autonomous dogs, as to which shall have the first examination of the piles thrown out by the cooks at the early dawn. All Acheraunta seems then to be aroused on these festive occasions. Sleep flies from weary mortals. The sleeve of care remains raveled out in a feverish agony of wakefulness. I often wish then that the dogs were more economical—of noise.

The Doctor refers to the incident recorded of Mahmoud II., whom he properly calls the reformer of Turkey. He commends him as the courageous exterminator of the savage horde of Janizaries. His biography is written on the headless gravestones of those enemies of the State whom he slaughtered mercilessly upon the classic square of Stamboul; for these gravestones were by his order made ignominious by being made turbanless. He tried by his iradé to extirpate another race—the boisterous enemy of the European—the dogs. He banished them to the deserted isles of Oxia and Prati, whose rocks leap out of the Marmora, within five miles of our villa and home at Prinkipo. But the dogs were in sight of the Seraskier tower of Stamboul, the Genoese tower of Galata and the graceful minarets of Sophia and Achmed. They soon, by instinct, patriotism or hunger, found themselves *en route* by sea to their old haunts.

The people murmured against the decree of banishment. They received the dogs on their return with huzzas! This happened, notwithstanding the Koran holds—like our Bible—that the dog is an unclean animal. Is this a pious reason why these dogs are masterless? Is this the reason why they are republicans of the

United States type—nameless, homeless and only bound by laws of their own local domicile ? Is this the reason why the Turk never thinks of disturbing them, whether howling by night or sleeping in mid-street by day ? Why, donkey and dervish, horse and hamal, passenger and carriage, invariably turn out to avoid the all-dominating cur ?

When the dogs returned from the isles, the Sultan was not so cruel as to make a massacre of these innocents, as he had of the Janizaries. Besides, was he not preoccupied with the coming war, which the Emperor Nicholas, of Russia, had just declared ? So that the dogs were left out in the streets to work out their own autonomy, regardless of Czar or Sultan.

Doubtless much may be said in favor of these animals, of their docility and their training to charettes, or little wagons, and barrows. They become useful in hunting, from their exquisite scent. Their ratiocinative faculty is shown in their division of quarters—following the divisions of the city. It is the same in the suburbs and surrounding villages—in fact, in all the provinces of the empire. When they were sentenced to the isles, they showed sagacity by swimming to the mainland or introducing themselves furtively on board vessels which touched at the Isles. They become not only attached to their locality, but to one another by reason of friendship and family ties. They love and aid one another. They do not fight with those of other quarters that let them alone. Those who invade them meet a bloody reception or hospitable graves. Each group or little state elects a chief. He is always the most valorous. He is generally calm, haughty and grave ! His gravity changes in a fight. He becomes unbridled when pursuing the enemy which invades the territory. In this case the chief manages and acts as a military leader. Besides, he exposes himself first and prodigally, which a general does not always do. It is body *versus* body. *Corps à corps.* He is followed by the whole tribe. One of the odd and comical performances in these clamorous fights is the attitude of the conquered at the end of the struggle ; for the whipped dog lies humbly on the ground, his tail between his legs, stuck close to his belly, his rear drawn aside and bent, his head cast down and his tongue protruding from his lips. This is the white flag. It is the sign of absolute submission. Upon these conditions the conqueror gives him freedom to depart to his own quarter, or to inscribe himself among the citizens of the conquering commonwealth. They do not impose ransom.

Those who are familiar with the dogs of Pera have noticed certain peculiarities that belong to those in the precincts between Karakany and Tophane. This precinct includes Galata, where the dogs are numerous and various. Here they are best nourished, or at least some of them ; for, strange to say, beside the clean and strong dog, with sharp fang, bright eye and martial air—ready for the fray—is another who is as thin as a jackknife, dirty and cowardly, and cowardly because dirty. His tail is between his legs. He quivers in a corner at the approach of everything. How is this accounted for ? Some of these dogs are favorites with the population. The butchers and the fishmongers give them food. Being well fed, they are more belligerent. They actually make themselves the champion of the rights of their human protectors. If any other dog approaches or any harm menaces the shop, they yelp an infernal chorus of protestation. This shows gratitude, but it is not comfortable. If they are well fed and muffled in their thick and oily hair—*cave canem !* Let those beware who intrude upon their demesne. Around the butcher shops of this neighborhood, they understand their relation to the butcher. They never touch any of his meats, except by permission. Although the butcher sometimes treats them roughly, using his boot and knife freely, when there is a bad day's sale, or when the Ramazan season makes a poor profit ; nevertheless, his dogs live like aristocrats on sheep and beef, and even pork, turkey, goose and game. But the poor, miserable, maimed, bleareyed members of the canine community, draw from the stranger more pity than contempt. They are the pariahs of the race.

The reader of Eastern poetry and history remembers how full of contentions is the land of the Orient. Not to speak of the Trojan war ; not to recall the terrific strife of the frogs and mice, attributed to the author of the Iliad ; not forgetting the Crusades and the Tartar scourges—it would seem as if all animated nature in the Orient had caught the belligerent infection. You pick up Mitford's " Greece " or Gibbon's " Decline and Fall," and the very scenes of battles between Greek and Turk, Slav (or Scythian), Tartar and Persian, are repeated at certain strategetic points in Thessaly, Epirus, in the Balkans, in Syria, or in Anatolia. This part of the East is the chronic theatre of war. My bailiwick has been, and is yet, in perpetual unrest. In Albania and other provinces, the domestic animals copy the heroics of Pergamos.

The donkey is of the Orient. Biblical, classic and Arabic literature praises him, as well for his industry as for his prowess. In another volume—"the Pleasures of Prinkipo"—I have re-counted his deeds of daring. In California he fights successfully the grizzly bear. In the East he has seldom to do more than his daily labor. Being sure-footed and plucky, he is my choice rather than the horse, for a ride over the rough streets of the city. Disguised in a white English helmet, I have mounted this "meek child of misery," to thread the dark and narrow avenues, and have felt safe, in his company, from all canine attacks.

DONKEY RIDING IN THE ORIENT.

Our word "goose" in the Slav language, and, indeed, in all lan-guages, has as its forerunner and root the word "gus." That bird has an ethnological and warlike history, only surpassed by the Homeric mice and frogs. The Eastern goose is a belligerent. Famous as it is for its sanguinary character, I have been informed that the duck is quite plucky in a main. Those who attend these duck and goose fights, as I have pictured them, insist that a duck has the most pluck.

Upon the lake at Scutari, in Albania, the Skodari ducks are bred in great numbers. The skins of their heads and necks are made into linings of cloaks for the Pashas of that country. The plu-mage gives them loveliness as well as costliness ; but before their heads are off and their plumage plucked there is many a fight between these heroic birds. The mountaineers catch from the very duck the courage to contend.

How tame are these heroic conflicts of man and beast compared to those of the dogs of Pera! Galata is their seat of war. Not an hour passes without the miserable rout raising a quarrel with a strange dog; or, if some one happens to pass swinging a cane, or on horseback, or who is dressed in an odd garb—which is not so rare, either, in that part of the city—the quarrel which thus starts rages along the whole line from Galata to Tophane. It is terrible. From every side the dogs rush upon the battle-field! Large dogs, small dogs, strong dogs, weak dogs, nimble dogs, lame dogs, hairless dogs, tailless dogs, wheezy dogs, skin-and-bone dogs, eyeless dogs—all come at the call of their canine captain and the sound of battle, and prepare for its consequences. Can the passenger pursue his way on such occasions in these narrow streets ? No : he is blockaded. The broil which results is enough to give the nightmare to any one unaccustomed to the tumult. It can be heard for miles around. The battle never ceases until some man of courage ends the strife with a cudgel. The passer-by, when one of the fights occurs, escapes well if he is not detained more than half an hour. If he happens to be a tourist, he is sure to be bespattered with dirt while making a note of these performances in his memorandum-book.

In a Canadian city an instruction was issued, that the police when they heard dogs barking at night should wake up the owner and stop the racket. What a splendid opportunity such a police would have in Constantinople; for of all the noises permitted by a serene Providence, those of the canine population are the worst. When, in addition, you hear in the night the noises made by the amiable beckdjié, it is beyond human patience; yet this beckdjié is the policeman himself. He carries a loaded oaken staff shod with iron at the end. It is heavy. I made friends of the beckdjié of our neighborhood to test its heft. Through the night you are waked up by the ringing, metallic defiance of the stone against the beating of this staff. It is this staff which arouses the dogs; it is this staff which evokes their yells of dissonance; it is this staff, symbol of vigilance and quietude, which makes the dogs the masters of the city.

In some parts of the Ottoman territory the dog seems to be

A DOG FIGHT IN CONSTANTINOPLE.

the chief occupant of the country.  He makes his occupation known by his noise.  Classical people call these dogs Molossian, but there is reason to believe that that famous race is as extinct as the old Irish grey-hound.  The dogs which I saw in Egypt are bold, determined animals.  They are unlike the race which inhabits the cities.  There is a class of Albanian dogs that is good for hunting purposes.  The moment you are at a disadvantage in meeting these dogs of the country, they have no hesitation in flying at you.  If you stoop for a stone, or even make a motion, you may disperse them, even if they are quite a company.  These beasts are not as a general thing beautiful.  They have a dun color.  They are often used on guard at sheep-folds.  They are of the same type that prevails over Turkey, Greece and Egypt.

Is there nothing to be said in their favor?  They have an advocate in Doctor Mavroyéni.  They are faithful guardians of their quarter.  They become attached to its inhabitants.  The females are tender mothers.  When their little puppies die they are loath to separate from them.  They try to warm them; they lick them and cry bitterly during many days, because they cannot reanimate them.  The males are comparatively indifferent.  To be sure, they love the family.  They are susceptible of strong attachments to the females.

"I possess," says the Doctor, "a dog of this race.  He was born in my garden.  He is of this stock, even to the fourth generation.  He becomes a watch-dog—superb, grand and vigorous.  He is never maltreated.  He is as proud as a Spanish hidalgo, without having the sixteen quarterings.  He is courageous.  He carries his tail well furnished with tawny hair, with crest exalted!  He chooses two females of the yellow robe.  He likes the golden shade.  For them he cultivates the toilet.  He is neat and clean.  He nourishes them well.  He brings them the tidbits from the kitchen, which he frequents.  His wives owe and pay him obedience.  They are obliged to remain upon the steps of the gateway of the mansion—upon a straw mat that he has dragged thither and placed at their disposition.  If they wish to take the air, they must be gallanted by none other than himself; while he, on the contrary, may philander alone, make court to other females of the quarter, and give sanguinary battles to his rivals."

What does this prove?  That dogs are as adventurous and egotistic as men? Yes: and more happy. They are not consumed by unbridled ambition. They are not mad for riches and luxury. They content themselves with little. They love without reserve, and even criticise the man who is familiar with them, and who bestows his sympathy upon them. They devote their lives to the master. They become his slave. They do even mean actions for the master. They allow themselves to be badly treated and even beaten, without a yelp or murmur when on his behalf.

But when the dog sees the person whom he has elected as his patron—somewhat as the plebeian elected the patrician at Rome—discontented and vexed, he lowers his tail and ears; he conceals himself all abashed, and that too without being angry. A moment after, he returns to humiliate himself anew before the master, by lying on his back. He almost weeps in sympathy, and then strives to coax his master, by his caresses, to forget all disappointments and anxieties.

Besides this passionate affection for man, the dog of these streets feels a friendship for his own race. One meets dogs often who are constant friends, and who aid each other all through their lives and until death do them part.

These dogs do not live as savages, without faith or law. They have certain laws which are neither written nor dictated by man, but which are innate, instinctive and graven in their hearts by the Creator. Thus, they make war only against those who transgress adventurously—those who are impelled by bad instincts and love of pillage. In the quarter which, like Pera, is only inhabited by Europeans, the dog is almost always hostile to them; above all when the foreigners walk with a haughty gait! He is equally hostile to cats, to camels, to bears, and to the Bohemians who show the bears, as well as to all heterogeneous animals who adventure into the city. In acting thus he executes the martial law which governs him. These laws are, it appears, inexorable and Draconian, though not established by a Lycurgus.

These dogs lead a Bohemian life without being altogether wanderers. They are very joyous, finding abundance to live upon; for, outside the carrion and the filth in which they delight, and which serves them as a side-dish of condiments of highest taste, they live on public charity, which provides liberally for all their needs without humiliating them. They are true Oriental beggars. One makes you think of the other. In the Orient, as in some cities of Italy, the beggar's occupation is not a degrading nor debasing one. Beggars—all of them—are proud enough. They extend the hand with a certain air of dignity, without any embarrassment. They sing prayers or canticles, more or less harmonious, addressed to God for the happiness and prosperity of charitable souls, whom they assure that all they do for poverty they do for God, who will recompense them for it a hundred-fold in this world and in the next!

Among the beggars wandering from one quarter to another, in the city and in the country, there are some who are rich. They are established in comfortable houses in certain out-of-the-way districts. They are recognized as a special community, with franchises. They form a body. They are a junta, recognized by the state and directed by a superior officer, whom they call, in Turkish, Dilendjiler Kazassker. This chief has a little ministry under his orders. He charges regularly certain dues, fixed by law, which the beggars pay without murmuring. Of all these, the most impertinent are the Greek beggars. They are very numerous. They have their general. The present chief is a lame fellow, large and very strong. He is regarded with respect. They elect a general from time to time, according to events, by a majority of votes taken in their regular meetings, which take place twice every year, at the commencement or end of the two leading seasons, summer and winter. These beggars are very bold, and it often happens that they insult or revile any one who refuses them a trifle. They have a saint as a patron, whom they celebrate every year with great pomp, having a pontifical mass performed in the orthodox Church of St. Constantine, at Pera, near their general quarter. On the anniversary of the death of their saint, all the beggars dress themselves in their new fine clothes of glittering cloth, put on the fez furnished with a large tuft, gravely assemble and lend to the circumstance a proud deportment, carrying their sticks, as emblems of the noble profession of which they are proud to be members.

Beggary is a profession. It is recognized by the state. It is valued by that part of the population who, bound to ancient uses and customs, are unwilling to understand the ideas of modern civilization, pretending that civilization by no means tends to render happy the people whom it has led away and rendered subject to its laws.

*Eh bien!* Putting aside these festivals and solemnities, we find a great resemblance between the beggars and the dogs of the streets of the Orient.

Public charity, which provides for the needs of both, takes especial care of such of those dogs as have puppies.

The absolute freedom between the sexes, and the possibility of always finding nourishment and water in sufficient quantity, which the inhabitants take care to furnish them daily—these are the causes why madness among dogs is so rare in Turkey. It is the absolute liberty which the dogs enjoy, the extreme facility with which they accomplish their physical needs, and the absence of the muzzle, which are in all probability the principal if not the only causes of the relative rarity of madness among the wandering dogs of the cities of the East.

I should like to leave the question to Mr. Bergh, who is the head of the society in New York for the prevention of cruelty to animals, whether, in spite of the good qualities of these animals, their presence should be allowed in the heart of a great city, where their howlings by night, and their lazy, lounging presence in the way of the public by day, render them an intolerable nuisance.

How would our philanthropist abate it? By deporting them to the isles, or reducing their numbers by death? Would he raise a rebellion in their model republic? It is almost impossible to disturb them, even when a carriage is roaring over the unevenly paved streets. They rise barely in time to save their bones and lives. They lie in groups, in lines, or in rings, sometimes a dozen together. The elements disturb them not, no more than man or donkey. Let it rain or snow, they lie there still. Some, I notice, dig into the earth where it is possible, and make a snug hole; others climb up on benches or on window-sills, and in a pretty circle, tail to head, sleep on. In the old city of Stamboul they board out. The Mussulman shares his meals with them. In Pera and Galata they have to forage about, and hence the intolerable din. When their sentinels on the advanced posts make report that a strange dog has passed the frontier, and has seized a bone that is contraband, the fury begins. If it be dry and hot weather, such a dust is raised that neither the dead nor living are discernible. In the Levantine quarters, as at Galata and Pera, there is a good deal of violence showered on them from passers-by, shop-boys and others.  The least kindly caress, notice or token of good-will toward them will, at times, bring the whole canine state about you with symptoms of delight, eyes shining with pleasure, tails on the wag and the body curving into a circle about your legs, as if to detain you for their own special delight.  It is hard to resist these ways. Two families have been raised in the alleyway under our American escutcheon.  They know all our people, from the Minister down to the capoudji, who is our messenger.  After two months' absence in Egypt last winter, on my return I was accorded a reception by them worthy of the great republic whose autonomy is copied after theirs.

In addition to their troubles in maintaining their right of domicile, the agonies of famine sometimes drive them to eat what a buzzard or a hog would disdain.  Some good Turks leave legacies for the dogs in their vicinity.  More frequently they distribute meat to them.  In some of the places there is a dole of bread for them, in compensation for their playing police upon the streets.  They certainly keep the *beckdjie*, or policeman, alive. When he comes round rattling his long, heavy oak club upon the resonant pavements, the dogs herald his presence by such long howls as Campbell's poetic wolf made on Onalaska's shore.

Sometimes they commit suicide by beating their heads out against the walls.  Now and then, some people who are anxious for quiet in their vicinity, or whose friends are ill, kindly pitch little pellets of bread and poison to the dogs.  Strychnine does the work of destruction only temporarily.  The quarter is soon filled up from the fecundity of other portions of the city.

The shepherd and watch dogs, even if of the same breed, are trained to be fierce to strangers.  We experienced their resentment in Upper Egypt.  In the little mud villages they would rush out furiously.  Although we were mounted on donkeys, we were not safe from their onslaughts.  Our kavasses and guides had to be on the alert.  While in Cairo I bought a cane which, when you swish it, out flies a dirk a foot long.  It was for the dogs of the city; but when I was attacked by a dog in Prinkipo—of course, the cane was innocently reposing in the rack.  Sir Edward Thornton, the British Minister here, was riding out in the suburbs of Pera last spring, when a shepherd dog of fierce aspect flew at him.  The horse shied suddenly, and the Minister was thrown and seriously injured.  His collar bone was broken.  This led to much discussion about the dogs of the city, but this incident was not pertinent to them. They are not aggressive. There are other reasons for their expulsion or decapitation.

As the final appeal on the other side of the question, it should not be forgotten that the East, in Homer's grand epic, has glorified " Argus," the dog of Ulysses, as faithful among the faithless—a fit associate of the patient and beloved Penelope, while Ulysses wandered afar. After twenty years he knew his lord ; and by all the dallying affection of his nature, strove to crawl, kiss his feet, and, by tail and eye, to express his joy. " He takes a last look, and having seen him, dies."

The American Indian joins with Homer in praising the dog ; for he hopes to have his faithful dog bear him company to the happy hunting-grounds.

# CHAPTER XXXIII

## DIVERSIONS IN PERA.

DURING the fall of 1885 and the winter of 1885–86 we sojourn in Pera, at the Hotel Royal. The hotel is near the offices of the Legation. The question is often asked : " How do you pass the time ? " I answer that we never tire of the endless and dramatic transformation scenes of the street; I mean so far as the population is concerned. There is interesting employment for leisure hours in watching the contrasts in the daily observances of life. A street-railway jostles the sedan-chair; a steamship wheels about a vessel as ancient in style as the Roman galleys; a carriage rumbles into a flock of goats and sheep, whose shepherd has on a veritable sheep-skin; and so on.

In our neighborhood in Pera everything is sold. Much quarreling goes on, but no fighting. The wrangles grow out of the prices and the conditions of the bargain. The sugar-dealer and confectioner are generally Persians. Children on their way to school stop and open their gold-embroidered school-bags to get their *para* to buy their candy. Albanians compete with the Persian, and the Osmanli, too, when it comes to the cold jelly or ground rice and milk and clotted cream. All this traffic goes on in the street. There is nothing in Constantinople that is hid except the harem.

You turn to look in another direction. Some one is crying out:

" Oh, ye merciful! Six oranges and five lemons! Soul of my lamb! Lamb of my soul! Who will take the rest of my provender ? "

Then the vinegar-man comes. He is by no means a man of sour aspect. He and the chimney-sweep join purses and buy out the orange-man; and yet in one moment, without a premonition, the call of the Muezzin comes shrilly up the valley and from many minarets beyond and around. At once traffic ceases and devotions begin. Even the Christian population, copying from the Turk, become reverent. The prayer said, the traffic is resumed. I am arrested by some cry that sounds like "Americanico!" What does it mean? It is from a Jew. He carries a heavy bale. It is the product of Lowell. It is unbleached calico! America forever! Furnishing the Orient with fabrics!

At every corner you meet those who sell all kinds of sweets. These sweets are in every imaginable shape, from fig-paste and bonbons to the fine fruits, such as pomegranates and oranges, with nuts, cooked and raw. There is a large market upon the streets near the English Legation. It is odorous with fish; for these are not the enchanted fish so much worshipped in the Greek Church. Still there is a great variety, from the mackerel, turbot, red mullet and soles, to the unknown shining and many-hued finny creatures. Here, too, are sold the *pilaf*, made of rice, and the yahoort, or sour milk, as well as snails in abundance, which are eaten by the Greeks. The oysters sold in the market are of a coppery quality, and too inferior to be for a moment regarded by the American palate.

The striking peculiarity of Pera, as well as of Stamboul, is the freedom with which food is consumed by all classes in the street. The meals are taken on the wing. The coffee-houses, cooking establishments and restaurants are not only open all the time, but they are almost upon the street itself. It is not unusual to see respectable families, even in their vehicles, stop upon the street, quaff their glass of water from an itinerant vender, carve their long loaves of bread, or eat their " simits," or circular pretzels, or their flat, unleavened cakes.

It is not unusual within the city and suburbs, wherever groups are gathered, to see beggars. They are not pretty to see, but they are pictures of the East, from which Constantinople is not exempt. The Moslem used to believe in keeping beggars around, to improve his charitable intent. If the beggar be a lunatic, or a weak brother, he is regarded as specially favored by Allah, and to be favored by men. His body may be on earth—his intellect elsewhere. Some of these beggars are quite popular. There is an old habitué of Pera, Loto Giorgi. He walks about, talking, for lack of better society, with himself. He gesticulates, to give emphasis to his jabber. He has a habit of frightening women and children by a sudden appearance, and howling in their ears. He is not so great a fool but that he knows when the government

employees are paid off.   If he receives a rebuff when he demands
money, he gives a comic response :

"*Aï bashi—aï bashi!*  At the beginning of the month, ha! ha!"

Off he goes, humming and whistling.   He used to be about
the municipal garden gate—until he became a nuisance.   He is
abated by sending him to the asylum.   This is an evidence of
reform.

There is a mendicant who is also a member of the begging

A TURKOMAN AND HIS BEARS.

corporate body, for there is such a system, well organized.   Hur-
pani is his name.   He dances slow steps in a circle to a silly
song, until he tumbles over exhausted upon one of the spectators.
He makes money out of his lazy music and idiotic dance.   He
has provided for his old age, and is less frequently seen than formerly.

The beggars are not so attractive as some other animals.
From the forests of Mount Ida, in Bithynia, there come bears,

generally two in a company, to gladden the *gamins* of Constantinople. They have a Kurd for master. They compete with each other to gratify an admiring circle. The servants of the neighborhood, with their small coins, surround them and their Asiatic hairy master. It is the only menagerie which the city furnishes for the delight of its grocery-boys and Greek maidens; but is it not classic? Does not Mount Ida rise to the swelling of the voiceful Epic? The bears dance to the tabor's sound, sometimes in the street, but more frequently over the graves and amidst the tumbling and broken tombstones which mark the cemetery of the Turk. The animals pass round a contribution-box. When they do not get a "surplus" they growl. In this they are human. This performance is not a fair show of what Pera can do in a histrionic way.

Theatrical amusements are not neglected. There were rival troupes here all the winter of 1885–86. The Petits Champs Opera-House came out ahead. It was led by Mrs. Byron, a Bostonese. The other troupe, an Italian, was led by Lenora Monte. Both were managers and *prime donne.* The Italian left, with her wardrobe, between two days. Mrs. Byron has had the satisfaction of giving a benefit for the impecunious and deserted troupe of her unsuccessful rival.

Mrs. Byron has sung for the Sultan at the Yildiz palace. He and all of his are fond of music, and thrice she has been summoned to please the royal ear and taste. When she sings there, all the ladies of the harem peep out of their rooms to hear, for they are not only musicians themselves, but fond of dulcet things, including the confectionery of sweet Italian sounds. The Sultan calls Mrs. Byron "La petite Americaine," and has bestowed upon her some nice largesses. The new Opera-House which Señora Monte left is now rejoicing in a French vaudeville company from Paris. "Mme. Boniface" was represented to a full house. Good loges cost each two *liras Turque,* or about $9. The prices are about the same as at the Casino in New York.

The instrumental music with which the people are regaled in summer is well done at the *Petits Champs* Garden. This garden occupies the spot of an ancient Turkish cemetery, and there must be many a Moslem dry-bone rattling by no means harmonious with the cadences of the brass band of European composition. The music inside of the Opera-House within the garden is above the average. It makes one forget the shabby scenery, the vexing chorus, the screaming prima donna and the terrible tenor.

Have the Greeks and Turks no theatres? Yes: there is a Turkish theatre in Stamboul, but the plays are modeled on the Chinese pattern. The plot runs through several æons, and the actors are, therefore, long-winded. I was invited to go and see a play there, as it was intended to be a benefit for the Turkish " High School."

Alas, for the degeneracy of the human ear! If the everlasting drawl and tom-tom of the Turkish cafés furnish real music, relegate me to the *Petits Champs* at night, when a rag-picker or a stray dog invades the sacred precinct of the naturalized canine habitants.

The Greeks have an excellent theatre in Pera. The actors know their business. They are graceful elocutionists, and the plays are superbly set. The old Greek dramatic art comes out, and the fine intonations, quick wit or sublime pathos are not wanting. " How do I know? " Well, I took along with me a Greek. He prompted me with a quickness of translation that left nothing to be desired.

" Do the Mahometan women attend the theatres? " Of that I cannot fully speak. They are not backward in being forward, in pleasant weather, when they go to the " Sweet Waters." There they coquette in a simple, child-like way with Ottoman and other dudes. But as a general rule, the Turkish ladies do not stay up late o' nights. They are domesticated. This is a proof and a sign of their virtue. I read in an old Mahometan book the other day that, while its author would not say that all Mahometan ladies were virtuous, for he held that virtue and vice are two sisters, " still," said he, "the former is fair and the latter is otherwise." No nation has ever been uninfluenced by the two sisters. But the Mahometan law, by its restraints in domestic affairs, prevents increase in vice and decrease in virtue. " The Mahometan ladies," he says, " are occupied in needlework, in religious duties five times a day, and in household affairs. They have no leisure to think of admirers. Their marriages are arranged by their parents, who are their best friends. The bride may see her future lord from a loop-hole before she is wedded, but her marriage is free from contamination or the dread of it. In short, seclusion secures the Moslem women from those delusions which irritate the mind with fleeting joys and leave behind the sting of remorse. The triumphs of beauty not being theirs, the pang of lost charms is not added to the sensation of fading power."

Is this not a clever plea from the Salem-lik for the Harem-lik? It is the best plea possible.

The male Turk is, however, not averse to the opera. The fez caps are plentiful when Mrs. Byron sings in " Trovatore " or as *Margaret*. This was seen in a patriotic way the other night. A special performance was given under the auspices of the Legations of all the countries, and of a committee to aid the Turkish soldiers now in the winter "field" on the borders of Greece, Bulgaria and Servia. The " Ballo in Maschera," with parts of "Lucia" and " Faust," were given by the company. The performance was a fête. Even the Russian Ambassador cheered Donizetti and the "Sultan's March." The Minister of Foreign Affairs, Saïd Pasha, made himself at home in the American Envoy's loge, and won all hearts by his sympathies for his hearthless and homeless countrymen in their sad winter quarters. On this occasion, the Opera-House was half full of Turkish Pashas, Beys and Effendis.

" What effect did this music produce upon their sense and sensibilities?" I know the Turk is pervious to the charm of melody. He makes a good musician, whether in a Dervish séance or in a brass band. I was curious to watch the effect of our fair American's tones upon the so-called Unspeakable One! Once I read an unsophisticated narrative given by a Moslem of his first adventure into a London opera-house. After describing the boxes in their semicircular fashion, and the hundreds of lights, at one time reduced to the dimness of night, and at another made to shine like daylight, he was astonished to see the curtain pulled up and two very handsome ladies appear very indecently dressed. An old man, their supposed father, appears on the stage! " They sing," he said, " some historical ballad, and dance expertly. They then tantalize the assembly, but we could not understand it at all. It was not music."

It may not be uninteresting, now that Pera is brought by the aid of steam within a fortnight of America, to bring Oriental humors, amusements and manners within the purview of our American eye. The query always returns :

How do these multifarious people amuse themselves? Do they drink and gamble? Have they music and parties? Yes, and no. To understand the writer's environment and this remark, it must be remembered that Europeans—Rayahs, Christians or Franks, so called—live at Pera. Pera is the residence of D. D.'s (Dreadful Dragomans) diplomats with diplomas, learned in the *lex gentium*, and others of the Greek, Italian, Armenian, English and Slavonic races. Pera is really a Western city. It is equipped with tramways. Each nation, under the "Capitulations," is supposed to be ruled and judged here by the laws of its own nationality. Pera sits upon a summit. Its streets may not be as full of folks as those of Stamboul, the bigger city across the Golden Horn, but on a sunny afternoon its "Grand Rue" is crowded like Broadway used to be and as Fourteenth Street, New York, is now. The palaces here are the embassies. The suburb is Greek and Italian, with a Greek name meaning "The Beyond." Artillery barracks and burial-places make it a place for soldiers and funerals.

Upon its western declivity—upon which I look every morning, and often in the stilly night—are the old Turkish cemeteries. Some of the cypresses are growing sere by the filling from the refuse of the town. The westering orb may gild the remaining trees, which sadly wave over the broken tombstones, only now half-turbaned. The natives and Franks may wander amid these relics with the goats and dogs, and now and then a clump of big-tailed black and white sheep. But all that is left of these cemeteries is the Great and the Little Field for the dead! Upon warm evenings the population—as mercurial as that of Paris—go within the gates of the Petits Champs. There bands play, and a restaurant is handy for your orders, as you sit beneath the foliage. There also is the opera-house. It makes its music above the graves of the Turk. From my window in the hotel I can almost touch the graceful cypress as it sways under the Marmora breeze from the soft southwest. Whenever the sun goes down, we see it making a golden canopy over the domes and minarets of Stamboul, and sometimes a purple lake of the Golden Horn!

But this does not answer the question: How do these people amuse themselves? First, the Turk himself does not drink. But is he not the cause of drink in others? He will sometimes take champagne. That is not prohibited in the Koran. It is like the railroad—a modern and useful invention. Its inventor has long since been apotheosized ! But when the Turk does take to a violation of the edict of Mahomet, he runs to great excess. He does not drink once or twice a day, nor limit himself to wine or mastic, but all liquors are the same to him. He soaks all day.

It is so in his gambling. There have not hitherto been many opportunities to gamble here, but some Spaniards have recently come hither from Monaco. That festive principality is supported by the " little game." Either because the business has become perilous there, by reason of the protests of the purists of Nice, or because it is too much of a monopoly in the royal house of Monaco—immigrants from that maritime Eden are here established. They have a suite of rooms near the new Italian theatre. At any hour of the night, rouge-et-noir, roulette and baccarat are played. The Greeks of Pera are the most numerous of those who patronize the games, but they do not play for high stakes. They venture even so low as a *mejidié*—nearly our dollar. But if a Turk takes to the "green," he gambles like a New York Wall Street lamb—for all that he is worth, and more too!

There are other places, if we are to credit rumor, where money may be wagered. I heard of a young Mussulman who lost a thousand dollars the other night at a gaming-table attached to a *café chantant*. The roulette rattles in the presence of the sirens who present the refreshments which lead the novice to his ruin. Gambling does not, however, run very far before its hells are suppressed by the authorities.

In Pera there is a good situation for a *Place d' Armes*. There is no great open place in Stamboul proper for military reviews. In Pera—near the Taxim, just beyond the Legations, or, rather, between the northern wall of the park of Yildiz and the model farm of the Sultan, there is an excellent site. Here will be the future allotment for military evolution. Battalions are working at it now, in order to make it feasible and convenient. As there is an elegant garden, with music in summer, near the Taxim, there is quite a promenade of the fashionable people in this direction during the warm afternoons.

"*Destoor! Yanghen Var!*" "Make way ! A fire—there is !" When these Turkish words, thus literally translated, are sounded in the streets of Stamboul or Pera, the unaccustomed auditor looks out for a sensation. He will not look in vain. It is the warning of a fire; and when from the towers of Seraskier, or from the top of the tower of Galata, the vivid crimson light throws its beacon over the cities on either side of the Golden Horn, strange sounds are emitted from the firemen. Talk about your Indian war-whoop of the "Wild West," or that of the Yahoos of interior Africa! All comparison fails before the long, wild shriek that goes up from the half-naked firemen, who with bare heads, hairy bosoms and sweating bodies rush through the streets of these cities, bearing upon their shoulders the pump or syringe which is to play its baby part upon the fire, and play, alas! in vain; for it only provokes and does not extinguish. *Yanghen Var!* Far off that shriek is heard. It approaches nearer and nearer. Then come other pompiers, bearing long poles with hooks to them, and coils of rope, and then the axe-men; and every man of them on a yell, and all giving the cry "*Yanghen Var!* Allah! Allah!" with a lamentable length of syllabic agony for which there is no expression in the human lexicon.

There was a conflagration at Pera in 1870. It was accomplished with neatness and despatch. In six hours two-thirds of the town was destroyed; nine thousand houses were burned; two thousand people killed. On such an occasion, all the leading pashas and other men of note, including the Sultan, are required to be present. At this conflagration the Sultan Abdul Aziz appeared; but he failed utterly with all the aid which these firemen brought to stay the catastrophe. But was it a catastrophe? No: Pera to-day, by reason of the fire, has wide and decent streets, and in some places elegant streets, not to speak of her street-railways and other facilities of comfortable locomotion.

In the aforetime, when a fire broke out in Constantinople it was the privilege of any one of the odalisques of the harem to put on a fiery, crimson dress, and panoplied thus from head to heel, push herself into the presence of the Sultan, regardless of where he was or what he was doing. This incident has in it an element of the drama. It might be utilized in some play where the Greek fire and the Turkish firemen play a conspicuous part.

Judging by the terrible disaster at Scutari—of which we hear as the proof of this chapter is being corrected—there has been, as yet, no adequate provision against fires. Firemen, with their puny pumps, rush over the Bosporus to Scutari, a mile of waterway from one continent to the other, and through long distances and bad streets. They climb the hills into the Turkish quarter on the south and the Armenian on the north. The church-bells ring. It is Sunday. The wind blows furiously from the Euxine. The air is dry and the houses are tinder. How can these engines fight the fire in the narrow alleys contracted with latticed balconies? What can the firemen do? Tear down the ricketty, dry houses? No. Pump water on the flames? There is no water.

A steam fire-engine from Pera is sent over; but still no water. Plenty of perilous northern wind and much expenditure of wrath by the Christians of the place, while the Turk sits serenely watching the devouring element! The next morning the churches, schools and dwellings, from the hills to the water's edge, are ashes and a cemetery of chimneys! God wills!

The fire companies established under the superintendency of Count Szechenyi are the results of the great fire of 1870, to which I have referred, but they seem thus far to be of no avail : certainly, without water, all their exercises and machinery are of no moment. The Count is a military man of fine presence. He drills his men as if they were a military *corps*. This is a reform ; as much so as the displacement of the old volunteer fire companies of our American cities by the steam fire-engines. In Constantinople yet, there are rival companies of firemen of the old sort. They go rushing madly through the streets, half naked, with their terrible screams. They not infrequently have a regular set-to at a cross street ; after depositing their little painted pumps in the streets, they fight, regardless of the fire which may be raging in the neighborhood.

But why should there be this lack of water in a city which has no peer in the East or West for its enormous and well-made water-works?

I had some experience with a fire in the Hotel Royal in one of my rooms, owing to the burning of the curtains by a servant; but the firemen happily did not come until I myself had put out the fire, which was consuming the bed-clothes, curtains, window sills and furniture. When they did come in with the police, I had more trouble to put them out than the fire. They hung around, and hung around, so suspiciously that I had to keep my eye on all the unconsumed property. As there were some half-dozen languages spoken by the servants, porters and others—during the blaze, it was a most comical scene. All the women of the hotel—Armenian, Greek, Slav, Italian and Turk—join in the insane hullabaloo. Their persistence in keeping up their noisy presence long after the fire is out, compels me finally to read a sort of riot act, and to explain to the chief of the police, who had to be sent for, that the inter-territoriality belonging to a Foreign Minister is indispensable for the occasion ; and thus I get rid of them, after much unintelligible jabber, during which an official endeavors to make an inventory of all the hotel properties—with a view to a reclamation !

It has been said that the whole of Constantinople is burned down every twenty years ; but I doubt if this be true. Many of the houses look venerable, and the more so because of the lack of paint. Being wooden, they look rusty and tired. When a fire succeeds, the Turk looks calmly at the ashes of his home. Although he may have lost his all, he does not go around shedding tears ; "Mashallah ! What God wills ! God is merciful, and will provide." Besides, Turks are kind to one another. This relieves from much of that which they call fate.

The population of Constantinople is more or less divided into quarters. There is one quarter where the majority of the population is Bulgarian ; but it is mixed with Turk, Greek, Circassian and Gypsy ; in another quarter Albanians prevail, still mixing with others. Each of these races uses its own language, religion and costume. Therefore, they are more difficult to govern. Great credit is due to the government for managing these distinctive nationalities and evoking harmony out of their differences.

There is a great diversity of people in Pera, even among the small trades, street venders and laborers. Few of these are Turks, though Turkish subjects. Most of them are Armenians. Those you see who carry water, and those who are watchmen at the banks and counting-houses, and even the household drudges, and especially the *hamals*, make up quite a feature in Pera. When you ask the names of these Armenian *hamals*, how proudly they dilate ! The humblest does not stagger under a load more weighty than his own high-sounding name. I once said to an Armenian :

"Your name, please you ? "

" Tighrannes, Excellency."

" And yours ? "  to another.

" Argashens "—that is, Artaxerxes.

I ask the porter of the sedan-chair that carries my wife to the ball of the Dutch Embassy, the names of his aids.

He answers : " This man in front is Arisdaghes ; my name, Excellency, is Belschazzar. The man who helped you yesterday is my cousin ; his name is Mithridates."

We have already seen one of this class in a picture, bearing the Tenth American Census to the palace, and we know his burden; we have remarked on the enormous weight of the burdens that they bear; but no such jocund folk keep a festive day as the *hamal* guild. Half full of mastic, and with his immense muscular energy devoted to a dance over the rough, stony paves, and a rude kind of accompanying music—the Armenian makes the fête of this craft a serio-comic Diversion, as elephantine as it is uproarious. Perhaps this is the rebound of their unburdened body and resilient soul. To these men the Bible promises are full of meaning. The promise to relieve another of his yoke, and to bestow " a yoke that is easy and a burden that is light," is so restful that it could come to none other with such emphasis as to the heavy-laden *hamal*. The metaphor takes hold of the Americo-African imagination, for the African is Oriental in many ways besides his superstitious ecstasy:

" Lucretia Culpepper," said a colored girl in Georgia, giving her religious experience. " She done tole me howt' lay my heavy loads onto Jesuses' great big waggins. I han't seed 'um anywhas, but I feel 'um, an' de moh I pray, de moh I seem foh to hear um rumblin' way wid all my heaps o' tiredness on um."

Next in number to the Armenians in Pera are the Albanians. They sell trunks, honey and groceries. The small grocers and workers in iron come from Cæsarea. Janina and Salonica furnish the carpenters; Turks from Trebizond, the wood-cutters; Greece and Bulgaria, the vegetable venders; the milkmen and the gardeners are of every nationality; but the Persian commands the donkey brigade. Owing to the lack of vehicles, the donkey does the main work. Laden with building materials and furniture, he heaves up the high hill with huge loads, while the Montenegrin and the Croat, without much rivalry, do the digging with spade and pick-axe. The Kurds are the longshoremen on the quays.

Now the reader may have some idea of the Pentacostial feast

of languages when he reaches Pera. This is only a feeble description. What with the Maltese goats, who go tingling by to their pasturage, each " with two fair crescents of translucent horn "; what with the vocal seller of bread in the early morning; the mournful cry of the milkman, which wakes you all too early, and, sad to say, wakes the dogs of your neighborhood; the snail-seller, who howls out in some terrible jargon that he has fat, juicy snails, all alive and kicking; and that other genius who peals the Turkish words for vegetables from morning until night—these sounds are only to be heard in all their multifarious howling in Pera. I except one vegetable from my denunciation. What is there about asparagus that makes one kindly disposed toward its raiser and seller? Ah, I have it: his cry, as it is interpreted to me from the Turkish words, is:

"Little lambs, home-raised, just from their milk; little lambs ! "

You do not see any little lambs in his basket, neither alive nor dead. No; the lambs are the asparagus heads. They are plucked out of the very mud of the walls that once defended Constantinople through its historic crises. Why does he call them home-grown? Because they have not come from a distance, and therefore they are fresh ! Another man cries:

" Here are the true sucking-lambs."

He is an artichoke seller. Was there ever anything so Oriental ? Why does he call his vegetables lambs ? Is it a sign of the early history of this Ottoman shepherd race? No: lamb is the choicest term of endearment among the Orientals. Our Bible shows this. If you should go so far as to have an affectionate word with a *hanoum,* she would call you a lamb if you did not anticipate her.

Along comes a man with a bundle of green weeds of some kind. What does he say ?

" Birds don't light on it; birds don't light on it."

I ask, in my simplicity, Why does he thus advertise this ornithological fact ? Birds don't light—on what ?

Oh, he too is selling asparagus ! The name suggests such a fairy, delicate leaf of green sprays, that the tiniest bird would break it down if it should alight upon its little stalk. This is a part of the vendible poetry of every-day life in Pera.

Going down the streets of Pera every day *en route* to the Porte,

I find a narrow street. Its odors of salted fish and every kind of wet-goods indicate the Maltese. Our big carriage tumbles down these bad roads, which are only twelve feet wide, putting in peril all the stock in trade, yet never a word, save in courtesy, from these Maltese, though it seemed as if we endangered some one at every step of the horse and every wabble of the wheels. The greatest peril, however, is to our Kavass, whose adipose rotundity by the

THE MEAT-SELLER AND THE HUNGRY PACKS.

side of the driver has a tendency to be unseated. Ah! if the Comptroller of the Treasury, and the Secretary of State, could have seen Mehmet's countenance, in his agony down this Maltese quarter, they would have hesitated before cutting off our Arabian steeds.

The butchers have something to do with enlivening the city. They have their peculiar noises. They go through the streets dangling their meats on long poles, which they carry upon their shoulders. They awake the carnivorous rapacity of the dogs. I arise early, sometimes, and look out of my window on a vacant plaza. I see the butcher bearing his pole covered with lights and livers. I am familiar with the canine prefecturate, or king-dog, of my neighborhood; for he frequently wraps himself affectionately around my legs. That dog is hungry this morning; it is dawn, and he has light enough to go for a liver. The tawny, cunning brute arouses his tribe. He moves quietly and indifferently. What does he care for the butcher or the liver! He carelessly stands on a little mound of dirt under our hotel window, so as to make a closer inspection as the butcher goes by. He sniffs the morsels. A drop of blood falls upon his cold nose. Now who, if he were a dog, could resist such a temptation? He forgets his loyalty to royalty. He is an enemy—a belligerent. His dignity descends; but he ascends. In one irrepressible moment he strips from the pole a sheep's liver. It is a game of polo; but two play at it. In vain the butcher goes to the rescue of his liver. Still, he believes in Kismet? He does not even swear. I nearly did, from my tower of observation. The butcher is bankrupt. The dog and his followers are his assignees. They have the whole concern. The members of the canine community lick their chops, after a contented meal. There was no battle that morning. The dogs in the neighborhood slept well. They even allowed several strange puppies to stray within their autonomous boundaries and to retire unscathed.

Generally speaking, the dogs which stay around the butcher shops restrain their appetites. There is a dainty dish which you will see in all the restaurants of Constantinople, where the furnaces for cooking protrude almost upon the narrow street, and the fire flushes and warms your face day and night as you go by. This dainty dish is called "kebab." It consists of morsels of mutton with the fat on them. They are pierced with a skewer and roasted hot. They are due on demand, and never protested. It is a succulent dish. It is eaten off the skewer hot, in the dining-saloon or on the street. It constitutes a great temptation to the tawny quadruped of the quarter. He seems to be a part proprietor of the establishment, by the interest which he takes in its cooking. From the time the kebab is placed upon the spit, until consumed by the customer, the dog never takes his eye off of it. He has the oppor-

tunity, after waiting all day—the dog, I mean, not the customer—
of picking up many a stray bit of kebab. The kebab is generally
served with a large, flappy, round unleavened cake, and pepper,
salt and herbs. It looks like a tempting dish, except this, that it
is too greasy. "Put these on the spit and roast them like
kebabs." This was said by a famous Aga of the Janizaries
when he ordered the impalement and roasting of some succulent
Bulgarians, whom he dearly loved—I suppose.

In the city, if seriously inclined, you have funerals at every
church and a cypress grove at every glance. You are not forbidden to join in the cortège—at least in that of a Greek funeral.
Its train generally consists of thirty or forty men in their ordinary
attire. These are headed by a priest. He is arrayed in his long dark
robe, with a colored surplice and yellow fringe to it. He wears a
high, big cap or hat, hung with crape. He bears in one hand a
small brass crucifix, and in the other a prayer-book. Then a boy
follows in a surplice. He carries a cross ten feet in length, and
is followed by other youths, each with a lighted taper. Two
other lads follow ; one with a censer-dish, from which is swung
clouds of incense, and the other with a holy-water basin. As they
move, they intone a drawling, unmusical chant. The face of the
deceased is exposed openly in the coffin. The body is partly
covered with flowers. The coffin is of plain wood. Ten minutes
suffice for the ceremony at the grave. The coffin is then lowered.
A little earth is placed in the priest's hands. He flins it into
the grave. Another prayer, a loud Amen! and one more inhabitant joins his mother Earth, and is added to the elements. Each
of the cortège throws a little of the soil upon the coffin and the
grave is filled up.

There is not much difference in the ritual and burial ceremonies connected with the Turkish, Greek or Armenian people.
When a Turkish official dies, if he has done the state some service, his interment is celebrated with pomp. The army and the
police are represented. The dervishes and the sheiks are on
hand to chant the prayers. Grand people, friends and acquaintances, follow him to his resting-place. Oftentimes this resting-
place has been carefully prepared in advance. It is localized,
generally, in and around the precincts of some mosque, where
it is more sacred than the ordinary cemeteries of the environs.

Pera is a part of Galata, or Galata a part of Pera. Taken

together, they furnish the most polyglotical people in the world. Each foreign community lives under its own laws; literally its own fig-tree, for the fig is often seen shooting over and out of the little yards and walls, as dusty as the street.    There are six different post-offices in Pera.    Each nation works under its own system.    It is, of course, a figure of speech, although nearly a fact, but each has its own church, house, furniture and serv-ants.    A Dutchman lives on his own, canal in Pera.    A Swede here is in Stockholm with its fresh running water, and his little tug for an omnibus.    A German looks up at every window, expect-ing to have a bow from a kaiser.    The American—well, we will pass him by.

When the Sabbath comes round, you hear the bell calling the Christian to worship.    The Greek seems to be dominant; and if this be the case, where is the sense of his everlasting jealousy of the Latin Catholic and Presbyterian Protestant, Lutheran Ger-man or of the parrot cry of Moslem fanaticism.    Almost within sight of the mosque there is as much freedom for Christian wor-ship and religious liberty as is to be found in any part of the world, except perhaps America or France.    Who is it says that the Sultan is intolerant?    Has a charitable building or a church been erected in Pera to which he has not given from his own purse?    How many hundred prescripts have I not signed as Minister, entitling the American missionaries throughout Turkey in Europe and Asia, to the entry of their goods, groceries, medi-cines, furniture and altars—free of all customs duties, if imported for the use of the Christian missions?    When has the time been, within the last fifty years, for we will go back no further, when the Turk has not kept the peace between Christian priests, even at the gate of the Holy Sepulchre, quieting their indecorum and making Latin and Greek respect the sacred ground?    I have seen, in the very manger of Bethlehem, the Turkish soldier with an American Martini rifle, keeping the wrangling religionists asunder. This was Moslem intervention to prevent Christian murder.    The commentary upon this relation of the sects of the East is made by the small boy of the Sunday-school.    The superintendent says:

"Now, children, tell me what heathens are?"

A boy responds, with more truth than grammar:

" Heathens is folks what don't fight over religion."

What a curious reflection the Mahometan guard must have at the door of Christ's sepulchre!

> "The race of Mussulman
> Not oft betrays to standers-by
> The mind within, well skilled to hide
> All but unconquerable pride."

So that we may not record exactly his reflections upon the belligerency of Christians.

# CHAPTER XXXIV.

THE city of Stamboul is, in its term, an Ottoman abbreviation for the word "Constantinople." The reader should consult the map to ascertain how Stamboul is related to Pera. The marked peculiarity of each city is one of the vivacities, as buoyant as the atmosphere of this locality. Diversion is easily had in visiting and revisiting the scenes of each—once, and now, so full of interest and empire.

To what point of interest shall I direct my all too familiar steps ? There are plenty of living pictures in Stamboul. It is a hive of humming activities. Let us not be too eager to find its ruins. Wherever you turn, they are visible.

The stranger who wanders around in the old Grecian paths, in or out of the city, will be struck with the immense quantity of columns which are scattered everywhere. They have been taken alike by the Turk and Greek architects to piece out modern erections. How often have I seen a stony tablet—a dedication to pagan deities or a memorial to a Greek athlete, philosopher or hero imbedded in the walls of a garden, house, mosque or church! It came in so luckily for the builder.

After crossing the bridge and going past the old Seraglio, the Khan Valídé, the mosques of Suleïmanyeh and Bajazet II., across to the New Gate, the Sand Gate, the Cleft Gate and Stable Gate, or, turning from the pleasant breezes of the Marmora, skirt the walls which shut in the Seraglio Point and the Porte ; or linger under the old plane-trees and sycamores by the way— wherever you walk, you cannot indulge in the associations of five hundred years, without noticing the decayed condition of wall, house and temple. The brickwork still shows that it was once exquisitely ornamented, and the stone pillars, in their fragments, are tasteful and classic. The battlemented towers of the Se- raglio are still beautiful, because festooned with creepers and draped in tufts of vegetation, while fig-trees, foxglove and terebinth fill the gaps of the stones. Here and there a marble fountain peeps forth—smirched, dusty and broken—with a Turkish legend about water and sanitation. All this reminds one of a day of industry and art, the glory of whose apogee has long since departed.

There are some new houses building in Constantinople. They are built on the ashes of former buildings, for the people seem too indifferent to remove the ashes or make new foundations. Is this a reason why so few of the monuments of the early Byzantine, Roman and Greek eras ever come to light? Are they buried beneath the débris? Doubtless; for it is only when cutting for a railway or some structure of paramount importance, that the venerable masonry and statuary are seen.

In a land so rich in history, art and classics, and having the sign of so many rare and wonderful adventures by sea and land— where history records "the decline and fall" of the greatest empire of the world—is it not to be regretted that so little interest is taken in the antiquities which must yet remain here, either above or below the earth, as well as in the colonies where the Greek and Roman power was once paramount? There is, however, a law concerning antiquities now in existence. It has recently been promulgated. The museum which is regulated by it has been in existence for some time. Compared with the Boulak Museum at Cairo, or the Greek Museum at Athens, it does not attract much attention or receive much encouragement. The author of the law, Hamdi-Bey, is the director of the museum. He is the painter of fair repute and talent to whom I have referred. The purpose of the law was to increase the collection of antiquities. This is done by the appropriation of all antiquities found in Turkey. It was intended to foster archæology, to protect ancient monuments, and to prevent clandestine excavations. Not only has little been done to encourage proper researches and protect monuments —in other words, to pursue the law—but many fraudulent manufactures have been started, and many fictitious groups, especially in *terra cotta*, have been fabricated. These are sold to the uninitiated at fabulous prices. They are as secret as they are spurious. In other parts of the ancient Byzantine empire, there is more energy in archæology. The Czar patronizes such efforts whenever the imperial armies open up new fields. We know what has been done in Cyprus by one of our own gallant consuls, General Di Cesnola. The same is being accomplished at Tashkend, where *terra cotta* vases, silver-gilt ornaments, and little statuettes have extended our knowledge of the boundaries of the old empire many hundred miles to the northeast. All Central Asia, under Russian research, may yield precious results from these ancient

BURNT COLUMN OF CONSTANTINE.

mines of historic evidences. Of these colonial and distant realms, Constantinople was the nucleus; and here should be achieved the greatest results.

A stranger may well spend a day at the Museum. It is within the confines of the Porte. As to the Museum, as I have had occasion to know while making a rude sketch, there is considerable supererogatory vigilance. The policeman did not like even my poor penciled imagery. He was an iconoclast.

Nevertheless, Constantinople can boast of the most interesting of ancient monuments. It is that of the brazen serpents of Apollo—taken from the temple whence came the Oracles. It is now in the Hippodrome. One of the heads of this triple wonder was struck off by Mahomed II. at the taking of the city. The head is preserved in the Museum.

The seven hills of Stamboul are crowned even yet with edifices which have their foundations in romantic and terrible events. Start from the first hill at the Seraglio Point, and you will find monuments enough on that hill alone for the annals of two empires. It was the Byzantine Acropolis before it was the Seraglio. It had been the temple of Jove. At Meidan is the ancient Hippodrome. It had avenues of marble and bronze imagery fit for gods and heroes. Here the golden chariots flew in the race, amidst the shouts of the populace and the splendors of unbridled luxury and power. The columns and eagles of the early day were flooded in after years by the blood of the Janizaries. What remains? a silent quarter, covered with dust and ruins ; all the ancient glories gone. Pass on—! What is it that strikes a stranger on the second hill ? Not the marble mosque of Osmanli ; for mosques are common. It is the burned column of Constantine. It was once tipped by a bronze Apollo with the head of the Emperor. What porticoes, arches and statues surrounded it ! Now it is charred, ribbed with iron rings, and lifts itself up in a crazy way, as if to warn mankind of the vicissitudes, crookedness and perils of prominence and power.

It is no time now to pursue the other hills ; they belong more to the present than the past, and yet they speak of dead dynasties and sanguinary conflicts.

As to the architecture of Constantinople, no one can speak *ex cathedra*. The domestic Turk has been building only transitory habitations, out of wood. When he builds a palace of marble he seems to build for immortality ; but no one can tell exactly the order of architecture to which it belongs. Still, his palace has the gorgeous and complicated luxury of the Orient; and his mosque, with its graceful minarets, betrays an elaboration not far removed from poetic luxury. The religion of the Turk pervades all the severe Greek and Roman architecture. It is so abstract that he prefers the meaningless Arabesque and the quotation from the Koran, to the imagery of fruit, flower and animal, in which Greek art reveled. In the Turkish work there are no griffins to scare you ; no dolphins to make your head swim ; no birds, butterflies or sphinxes ; few flowers and no nymphs. There are no heraldic or mythical monsters. The living world is forbidden. Nothing shall, as nothing can, in their art and faith, aggrandize the everlasting and sublime unity of Allah !

In these Diversions, it is not to be expected that scenes so often described should be repictured. There is the temple of Sophia, dedicated by Justinian to the Divine Wisdom : no description can do justice to its magnificent dome and its original splendors. It is well known that it has been changed since the Turks have transformed it into a mosque. The four Christian seraphim under the dome, executed in grand mosaic, remain ; but the names of the archangels of the Moslem faith are written underneath them. The bronze doors, the pillars and the galleries are the same. The peculiarities of the Byzantine style are the same, except that four minarets have been added to give their heavenly gesture to its marble poetry. Ancient art furnished the eight shafts of green marble from the Temple of Diana at Ephesus ; and eight of porphyry came from the Temple of the Sun at Baalbec. Egypt gave her granite from the shrines of Isis and Osiris. The Acropolis at Athens furnished much of its Pentelic marble to glorify its interior. This interior was once covered with gilding. Time has faded it. Small pieces of mosaic lie loosely around the building, yet millions of these tiny gems of art still adorn the walls. Around the centre of the dome is inscribed, in golden Arabic text, this sublime verse :

"God is the light of the Heavens and the Earth ! His wisdom is a light on the wall, in which burns a lamp covered with glass. The glass shines like a star ; the lamp is lit with the oil of a blessed tree. No Eastern, no Western oil, it shines for whoever wills."

I confess to a little of the prevalent American irreverence. As I read this inscription, my mind had a Diversion. It concerned Western petroleum, about which as Minister I had considerable to do. Might not a little more of its "blessed oil" add to the glory of the occasions when this Temple is being used upon the fête days? From this idea, my mind leaped, as does that of my reader, like lightning to a brighter light for the Divine Wisdom. Why should not this and the other mosques of Stamboul become radiant with the electric light? If oil, why not electricity? The motto in gold would have a new and subtle meaning, and the splendid edifice take on new splendor in all the angles and curves of its structural sublimity.

The mosques of Stamboul do not impress me as being so beautiful as those at Cairo, nor are the minarets so tastefully carved or decorated. The mosque of Sophia is the largest in Stamboul; it can accommodate twenty-five thousand people. It is on the western declivity of one of the seven hills. Its history and original form, its length, width and dome, have been minutely described. But no pen or pencil, even of Divine Light, can give an adequate conception of the massive arches, gigantic columns and superb dome, including the eighteen smaller domes of this harmonious and magnificent structure. It has fourteen minarets, each of which has been erected by a different Sultan. It is said to be a rule that each Sultan shall erect a minaret for some one of the larger mosques. There is a good deal of patchwork outside the building. This is not so graceful as the minaret. There are other mosques with more prominent minarets than Sophia, especially that of Achmet, which has six minarets. Externally there are several more strikingly grand. It is surprising how very inferior in its aspect is the outside. St. Paul's, in London, is shut in by surrounding buildings. This will, no doubt, some day be relieved, but it is not, like St. Sophia, desecrated with shops and all sorts of fungi fastened to its walls and ignobly dishonoring its shadow. Would that it were like Westminster Abbey, or St. Peter's in Rome! Then its columns, from the temples of Ephesus and elsewhere, would, like a good spirit, have more attraction by reason of its exquisite outside.

The pigeons may be heard to murmur their affectionate cooing all through the Ottoman mosques. There is one mosque, with its *verde-antique*, jasper and porphyry columns supporting a gallery, especially dedicated for pigeons. They are fed by means drawn from the legacies of benevolent people. Those at this mosque are said to be wild pigeons, and lineally descended from a pair of birds which the famous Sultan, Bajazet, purchased of a poor widow who once asked his aid. Every stone in the Turkish calendar is white with a story about charity.

There is one portion of the old city of Stamboul to which I could never get accustomed. It is underground. The city is honey-combed. If you will look at a plat of the city you will find cisterns of immense extent under its most important portions. The royal cistern of Constantine the Great, which receives its water supply from no one knows whither; the cisterns of Theodosius, Arcadius, Phocus, Valens and others, which rest on splendid Corinthian pillars of graceful architecture—furnish evidence of the immense sums expended in providing for the city water of a pure quality from the hills which surround it, so as to stand the inhabitants in stead, in case of siege.

There is an old cistern that comes down from the Greek times in Stamboul, almost as magical in interest as the Brazen Column. It is said to have one thousand and one columns supporting its substantial roof, although two hundred and thirty-four is the real number. It has withstood all the ruthlessness of human endeavor to destroy it, not to speak of earthquakes. It was three hundred and thirty-six feet in length and one hundred and eighty-two in width. It was intended as a reservoir of water in case of a siege. When I visited it in 1881, it was utilized as a factory for silk winding, on account of its damp coolness; for even when the thermometer is up in the nineties on the outside, its interior gives its happy effect to the silken and gold thread. The work done is handiwork. No machinery is used. Those who prepare these threads for the embroidery of the superb fabrics of the East tell me that it is cheaper without than with machinery; the machines when they get disordered take so much time to repair. I surmise it to be pure laziness. It is droning in the old hive.

In festal seasons the city of Stamboul is full of people. The narrow streets are jammed. No quarreling is heard ; no rowdy-ism is permitted. The coffee-houses are crowded with turbaned people. There is not so much fez. They drink black coffee and smoke—and smoke. The Arab music gives its drowsy drawl to the general quiescence. The ideal of an Ottoman vocal artist is one who yells all through the part in a nasal tone. The heart-breaking strain of an Oriental lyrist is very disagreeable. When accompanied by the continual tum-tum of the instrument, within a compass of three or four notes, no melody, only agony, is the consequence. Still, the people like this sort of music. It is time, if not tune. The slow-moving population outside the cafés stop to listen with delighted ear.

In former times there were guilds, or companies, in Constantinople. They each had a saint for tutelary protection. There is something humorous in the fact that Adam and Eve, even Cain and all the personages who figure in the Old Testament, from which Mahomet derived the body of his law and narrative, acted in this patronizing relation. For instance, Adam was considered as the first tutelar. It was alleged that he was taught by the swallows; and doubtless our swallow-tailed coats, after the fig leaf and the fall, are an emanation of his early genius. Sometimes Adam was considered as having been instructed by the beaver; for as the head of his race he had much to do, and was a good worker. Therefore, he was the chief of the guild of builders and sawyers. Hawa, or Eve, patronized bathwomen. She used to go in swimming amid the water-fowls in the Garden of Eden. She started early as a patroness of the bath. Cain was the head of the grave-diggers. He was instructed early by wrens; while Abel, being the protector of sheep, led the grand army of shepherds. And what of Noah? Shipwright! There are fifty different trades which made Constantinople the nucleus of the artisans of the East. It had more than five hundred minor trades. The elements of industry were militant. The first Knights of Labor here had their processions. Before the middle of the seventeenth century they had emblems, ornaments and specimens of their workmanship, which glorified their craft, and would make the great meetings in London, Paris and New York pale their ineffectual fires. Is the world indeed retrogressing? Two hundred and fifty years ago, Sultan Murad III. was about to leave his palace and his harem, upon that beautiful point of the Seraglio. His chief kiosk bore the name of the "Pavilion of the Processions." He invoked a pageant on his departure for the wars. It has not had its equal since. In it are the guilds of Constantinople. In a continuous torrent of human energy, each trade bears its embroidered emblem and specimens of work. Every man is dressed in his best. Two hundred thousand men pass before this fairy-like kiosk, to gratify the ladies of the harem, and to give the Sultan a farewell before he leaves for the siege of Bagdad.

The bazaars do not show the guilds or handicraftsmen, as we would imagine. I was never very much attracted to the bazaars

of Stamboul.   Perhaps it was because of the everlasting wrangle
with the merchants about purchases, or because of the narrowness
of the streets and cross streets of the miniature village.   There
is something about its lighting and ventilation which detracts
from its Orientalism.   In comparing it with the bazaar at Damascus, the latter takes the palm for the display of goods, for chaste
designs and the richness of its fabrics.   Damascus has the suf-

BAZAAR SCENE.

frage of our American tourists.   The merchant of the bazaar in
Stamboul is an Armenian, a Jew or a Greek.   He does not squat
so orientally as the trader of Damascus.   He has not so much
Oriental dignity and reserve.   Many of the traders in Stamboul
walk about and anticipate your coming.   They dilate upon the
goodness and cheapness of their wares, while others keep the
European style by having the luxury of a counter.

It is an old maxim, ‘‘Give a man of Cologne one half of

what he asks in buying." You can do better than that in the bazaars, for sometimes these merchants have been known to drop from thousands to hundreds and from pounds to piastres. I never traded much in these bazaars, but generally left that to another and brighter member of the family, with more experience. In fact, I have been afraid to do it, from a certain warning which the accomplished wife of my predecessor, Mrs. General Wallace, has given in her book on the "Storied Sea." I have no compunction in inserting here her experience:

It is with a Moor from the bazaars of Cairo. He has Mecca scarfs to sell. He appears at the *Hotel de l'Orient.* He is clad in the rich vestments of the gorgeous East. He reminds our lady of Cambyses, Sesostris, Cyrus and other barbaric magnificos, including Othello. He is strikingly handsome and thoroughly polite. He unrolls his bale and spreads out his rugs. Then he lights his cigarette, makes his pose and begins. First, he unfolds a scarf with careless nonchalance. It is from the great city of the Prophet. It has a striped gilt border and gold fringe at the ends. He names a sum equal to forty-five dollars. He dilates on the mode by which he obtained it from the harem of a princess, a niece of the Khedive. Then he displays a green scarf. This proves unattractive. Then he shows his *piece de resistance;* he spreads out some rare towels from Damascus, embroidered in gold.

"Will they wash?" the lady inquires.

"For ever," he responds; "the silk is the best of Syria, and the embroidery is laid on in the delightful gardens of the flowery banks of the Pharpar. It will be shining ten thousand years hence as now. The Bey of Tunis has ordered fifteen dozen as a present to Abdul Hamid, the Beloved."

Thus dilating, he gives fictitious values to each piece of merchandise. The golden embroidery of the last piece displayed is copied from the mystic hieroglyph along the edges of the Holy Flag. But I will let the lady, in her own graphic style, tell the story. Rejecting the last tender, she says:

"'It is too dear. I may look at the towels again.' He lifts one and throws it on the near divan.

"'This is from Bagdad,' said he—'from Bagdad, the land of Aladdin, of Sinbad and Zobeide, Scheherezade, the rose and the nightingale, of ivory and amber, spicery and richest merchandise.'

" The tempter saw my wavering. Those keen eyes lost nothing, and marked every shade of chance, without seeming to see anything.

" ' Beware of the neglected opportunity,' said the born-and-bred fatalist, beguilingly. ' God, the merciful, ordains all things, and only once in a lifetime come the great chances, according as Kismet has prepared them. *Allah kerim!* '

" By this time the servants of the hotel, and several idlers and travelers had come round to watch the trade. They formed a ring, of which the Moor, the interpreter and your correspondent were the centre. Not a word was uttered nor a sign made. They looked on intently, apparently anxious, as though the fate of thousands was in the venture. I sent an appealing glance at the interpreter, who pretended not to see. I could not spend the whole day in bargaining. The delay was tedious; the situation embarrassing to a woman not used to Eastern ways.

" ' What for the towel ?'

" ' The towel from Bagdad ? Twelve dollars.'

" ' Too much.'

" ' Then will madam make an offer ? Americanas are princesses. Their money comes easy and goes fast. Offer ! '

" ' Six dollars,' I said hastily, for I wanted to get rid of the man, and he had stayed so long I felt obliged to buy something, and ' Jewing ' is not my forte. It was the Moor's turn to shake his head now, which he did in melancholy and decorous fashion, not tending to unsettle the turban folded with graceful coils above the olive forehead, which it nearly concealed. The neglected opportunity—was I missing it ? A towel from Bagdad is not in market every day and it would be a nice souvenir. The chance was passing, the supreme moment, the neglected opportunity.

" ' Six dollars,' I said, recklessly.

" ' I lose money,' said the melancholy man, imploring by mournful accent and wistful gesture.

" ' I cannot help it,' I retorted, warming with the day. ' You need not sell if you don't want to.'

" ' A man hard pressed must take what he can get. It is Kismet. The towel is yours. It will please madama's friends across the sea beyond the Straits. May it be like the enchanted carpet of Boudressein, which brought a fresh good fortune to its owner every morning !'

" 'Have I seen all your stock of goods ?'

" 'You have,' he replied, much as to say 'the world is at your feet; what more can mortal ask?' The interpreter counted the money, the crowd broke away smiling, and jabbering in half a dozen languages, and one Neapolitan remarked in French: 'A runner from Sadullah Bey's; a man not pleasant to meet, if one has anything to lose.' The noble Othello alone preserved his calm dignity, and in silence made his courteous, profound salaam. When his few goods were gathered, he leaned his back against the wall, after the manner of people who love repose, looking little like one to mount horse and draw sabre for Islam, willing every hour to die for his faith. Somehow, the noble Othello's bearing made me feel like a robber, and, with a sense of guilt, I turned to the stairs with the spoil. My heart sank. My feminine reader will weep with me when I tell her the first unfolding of the Persian towel revealed several stout coffee stains, which added dirt to the yellow tint, which dulled its beauty and freshness. What a forlorn purchase I had made! Had I been cheated by a strolling pedler, after all the warning fingers lifted at me on both sides of the sea? I? *I?*

" ' Ah!' said my friend, who had listened to the confabulation, ' I see your rage for antiquities again. This towel has arrived at the antique, without becoming a gem, hasn't it?'

" She held it up to the light, which it slightly obstructed, showing a ' body' like the sleazy stuff our grandmothers used to make milk-strainers out of.

" ' Don't you think it's rather—rather thin?' she continued, the dimples deepening in her cheeks. 'And, dear me! what *did* you pay for a fly-speck?' She broke into the gayest laugh in the world.

" I reddened with vexation, but was dumb. She took the Bagdad towel in her two little hands, gave a slight jerk, and the rotten old thing split from one end to the other.

" 'Really, now, this is too bad! I bought this as a souvenir for you, a sample of Oriental magnificence, and you have gone and ruined it.'

" ' Thank you, kindly,' said the spoilt beauty, burying her laughter in the pillows; 'but I always prefer *my* dish-rags without tinsel.' "

\*        \*        \*        \*        \*        \*        \*

Let not my reader confound this Moorish Mahometan with the Turk. I have a much better report to make of the latter:

He is certainly honest, and although the rule is to bargain over an article down to its fair value, commencing very high, the Turk will not always descend to this device. You are an American, and go into the bazaar. You ask the price of an embroidered handkerchief. The merchant is a Turk.

"What is the price?" you ask.

"Seventy-five piastres," responds the merchant. Knowing that among traders it is best to offer less than the first price, you say :

"That is too much. I will give you seventy."

The dealer seems to nod acquiescence. The money is counted out. The surprise, however, is great, when the Turk pushes you back twenty piastres, observing :

"This is more than the just price ; fifty piastres is proper ; these twenty are yours, sir."

A few such instances should redeem the trading Orient, and mantle with blushes the haggling shop-keepers of Paris and the Moorish pedlers of Cairo.

The bazaars of Constantinople are not as interesting as those of Damascus, and, I was about to say, those of Egypt. The besetting which one meets with from the "Touters" disenchants one of this vicinity. The oil of roses, the bracelets, the carpets, the rugs, the boxes, the towels—everything is there ; but, after all, human nature is the same, and does not like to be "Toutered" overmuch.

European fashion is killing the bazaar. Where now is the slipper festooned so daintily, ornamented and cased in glass to allure the stranger, giving a new glory to the bazaar? The slipper is almost obsolete. The leathern black-boot takes its place. Why linger lazily around the market of old clothes in a dirty alley? Why saunter toward the stalls of the seal-engravers, once so renowned? Why marvel at the spoon-makers, and other handicraftsmen? Rest awhile, to glance at the refectory of the pigeons that roost in the cypresses and in the precincts of the mosque of the Sultan Bajazet. Here in the courtyard of this mosque you will see the tempting wares of the East—from Bokara, India and China. They are picturesque and rare—worthy of the columns which support the roof of the mosque of the sacred pigeon. Some of the stalls of these bazaars are highly spiced with the Orient. Dates, pistachio nuts, bananas, fig paste, honey, almonds, and the sweetmeats of the East fill you with such an odor that you are ready to die in aromatic pain. Then there is the China cup and bowl bazaar, with a thousand exquisite charms, amulets, beads, chaplets and precious stones. These are not more precious than the contents of the gallery of the Indian merchant in yonder corner. There are found the toys of China and Japan, and the matting, so common in the houses of Constantinople. If you have literary inclinations, you will find quite a display of Arabic, Persian, and Turkish literature, and you may read there all day without the owner asking you to buy.

Why make a catalogue of this immense variety of goods and traffic. Let us to the open air ! The attraction of the bazaar is too Oriental. It is a castle of Indolence; but a castle full of rare exhibits of human fabrication from every craft and clime:

> " Richly furnished with plate and gold,
> Basins and ewers;
> My hangings all of Tyrian tapestry;
> In ivory coffers I have stuffed my crowns—
> In cypress chests my arras counterpanes,
> Costly apparel, tents and canopies,
> Fine linen, Turkey cushions, bost with pearl,
> Valance of Venice, gold in needle-work,
> Pewter and brass —— "

Let us not forget the brass. You cannot ignore it if you would, for the " Touters " and emissaries of trade are *prima facie* guilty of brazen effrontery. The metallic hardness of feature and voice show its triple quantity and durable quality.

There is a portion of Stamboul which is a Persian colony. It is in the neighborhood of the Persian Embassy. The peculiar customs of the Persian are here observable. In fact, the Persian Ambassador is a civil ruler over the Shah's subjects in Turkey. He executes if he does not make law for the Persians of the vicinage. One law surely ought to be made by this time, and that is to stop the rites which are celebrated at Validé Khan, in Stamboul. This is an exclusive resort for the Persians. These rites take place on the anniversary of the death of Hassan and Hussein, who were the Saints of the murdered Ali, well known in Mahometan history. These rites take place at the Muherrem, or beginning of the Moslem year. Europeans are curious to see them, because of their horrible cruelties. They have a sort of weird attraction. They smell of blood, like the bull-ring. They are fascinating, like tragedy. The Khan is a square court. It is decorated with carpets, cloths and candelabra. All the *personnel* of the Embassy are present on this occasion. The ceremony begins at 7 o'clock in the morning, by the chanting of funereal hymns by the Persian Ulemas. These priests recite the story of the death of the two martyrs, Hassan and Hussein. They anathematize their murderer Yezid. Then a procession of Nezirs appears. They are bareheaded. They wear long, flowing white robes, and in their hands they have large knives. They march into the middle of the court and form a circle. Meanwhile they sing mournful ditties, striking their breasts with the flat of their hands, or making cuts into their heads with their knives. The blood flows. It shows upon the white garment. Dangerous wounds are inflicted even by lads in the novitiate of their penitential ecstasy. On the occasion of this exhibition a year ago, these self-inflictions were practised by a boy of eleven years of age. He had to be restrained by the bystanders. Sometimes, as I have seen at the bull-fights in Spain, those unaccustomed to such scenes faint. The ceremony is too horrible to be allowed, even in a semi-civilized country. The word *Nezir* means, one consecrated to God; so that the religious enthusiasm has much to do with protecting these strange devotees in their curious sanguinary rites.

Do not be too quick to condemn such atrocious penitences. They are not peculiar to the East, nor to Persia. A lady-cousin writes to my wife from New Mexico, and thus pictures a similar scene:

"Many of the natives belong to the Order of Penitents, a class who inflict the most cruel punishments upon themselves in atonement for sin—such as putting pebbles and pieces of glass in their shoes, and then walking on them for half a day or more; sticking the body full of cactus burrs; having three gashes cut down each side of the spine, and then being lashed over the raw and bleeding cuts with a scourge made of soap-wood, which you know is thickly covered with little points sharp as needles. The clothing of the penitents consists only of a pair of white muslin trousers and a cloth tied tightly over the face. I have seen the ignorant creatures lashed with the scourge until their little clothing looked as if it had been dipped in blood, and the scourge would be so thoroughly saturated, that at every stroke the blood would fly in all directions. Until this last year, no Christian work had ever been undertaken at San Rafael, and upon our arrival among them, the people all held back, seeming to fear we were there to do them harm. Children would run screaming to their homes if they chanced to see us on the street, evidently having as much fear of us as we have of Geronimo and his band of scalpers."

No one should omit, if he can possibly get a firman from the palace through the aid of his Minister, an inside view of the Imperial Treasury in Stamboul. It is not all that we would expect in variety and opulence. I am sorry to say, after all my inquiry, that it is not rich in manuscripts, as we had fondly hoped. It is extraordinary for its precious stones, jeweled swords, daggers, aigrettes and figured brocades. A writer in the *London Times*, Mr. Robinson, an expert in matters of this kind, made a revelation of its contents. He removes the impression, of which I had long since been disenchanted, that there were any Byzantine spoils in the Treasury. It is well known that in A. D. 1574, many old Ottoman heirlooms were burned, but there must have been given to the Sultans, by tributary and vanquished kings and princes, some most remarkable objects of art and beauty, if not of Greek, Saracenic or Arabic art; for in wood, jewels and metals no people could then be compared with the artisans of Damascus and other parts of the ancient empire. The contents of the glass cases of the Treasury have never been exaggerated. Do you want emeralds? You will find them there as big as peaches. Diamonds? There are large table ornaments of that jewel innumerable. Cimeters? Fortunes in emeralds as large as a hen's egg are in their hilts, and their sheaths are encrusted with turquoises, opals, rubies and what not, of jewelry. Here, too, are the Sultanic figures in their ancient robes of state. The robes are genuine ; but the waxen faces of the Sultans can hardly be *fac-similes*. The robes are costly in silk, aigrettes and daggers. The colors of the fabrics are faded, but there is no doubt about the fadeless color of the precious stones.

There is a good collection of coins in this Treasury. It is said by Gibbon, that you may learn the history of a nation from its coins; but unless a better arrangement be made, no one will ever read history here in that way, for the coins are so placed in their cases that it is impossible to decipher them.

It is a pity that some one learned in numismatic lore should not have the opportunity of making a catalogue and a commentary upon these thousands of coins. Some of the coins are Roman, some Byzantine, and a large number are Arabian coins of the first century of the Hegira.

There are twenty or thirty custodians of this Treasury. They are of various rank. They are lynx-eyed. The building in which the Treasury is situated is a part of the old Seraglio. It was founded by Mahomed the Second, on the site of the palace of the Palæologi. The Treasury was once supposed to be used as a library. It was thought to hold many of the treasures of ancient literature, among others the missing books of Livy.

I have visited the Treasury on several occasions with Americans, having procured the firman. I think we were favored greatly in this regard, although our company was generally too great for the rules and the guards.

Going from the Treasury, the company is conducted to the Bagdad kiosk. It was built by one of the Sultans—Murad the Fourth—from a model in Bagdad. The tiles are Persian, though some are of the blue sort common in Cairo ; but no country was ever more famous for its exquisite tiles than Turkey.

This kiosk is lined with tiles. Its doors are inlaid and its ceilings are painted. The attendants expect the usual *backsheesh,* and they render a fair equivalent, for they give us coffee in dainty cups set in silver *fingans* of filigree ; and to those who do not affect the black, uncreamed coffee of Arabia, they give cool water or sherbet, and with both conserve of roses. Seated upon the veranda, at this most famous spot of all the earth—Seraglio Point —you have the best view of the Bosporus, with all its loveliness and activities, and of the bridge, with all its picturesque and many colored forms, going and coming. Where in 1851 I wandered amidst the most beautiful of gardens, I regret to say that the lawns and shrubs have departed with the palace. Its veiled beauties are now on the other side of the Bosporus. From this Seraglio Point you can see far up the Straits. Your eye may follow their windings, past Beylerbey on one side, and Orta Këui on the other. Surely, never was a mistake so flagrant as when the Sultans, after the conflagration, gave up this point for a railroad, and left its lovely seclusion and fairy parterres, its glorious view and its grand point of vantage, even to live at Yildiz, in the Mansion of the Star.

Alas for the old Seraglio! Its splendor was consumed. Even before the fire, it was made a sort of old ladies' home. There the widows of dead Sultans, and their elderly friends, received hospitality. There are some out-buildings that speak of the old palace—a mosque, a bath-house and a kiosk. These were saved from the conflagration. When in its prime, this lofty point or peninsula jutted out into the sea, and was washed by the dividing currents of the Bosporus, and by the blue, musical waves of the Marmora. What with minaret, cypress and turret upon this eminent place, it is even yet worthy of palatial honor. A Vanderbilt or an Astor—seeking a terrestrial paradise—if he would unload his bonds and stocks, he could find it here, seven times exalted by the natural beauties of sky, water and land, and by the associations of three thousand years of historic vicissitudes.

After visiting the Treasury and the Kiosk of Bagdad, a plain Corinthian shaft attracts your attention. It is the column of Theodosius. It is fifty feet high, and, like the Delphian tripod in the Hippodrome, it is of great classical interest. Scattered about are many ancient altars and fragments of pillars in these courts of the old Seraglio. Many of them have been collected and placed in the Museum. Not the least interesting portion of these grounds is the ancient Throne-room. With a little *backsheesh*, you visit it as part of the spectacle. The throne is immense. It is in the form of a four-post bedstead. The posts are thickly encrusted with rubies, sapphires, emeralds, and turquoises. It was not altogether a Diversion to be a diplomat in the early days here, for the Greek emperors were accustomed to put out the optics of ambassadors, as witness the blinding of Dandolo; and even since, and within the century, the Foreign Ambassador was ordered to the Seven Towers, or to an execution from this neighborhood. It was within this Throne-room that the Foreign Ambassadors were presented. They had to be bathed first, and then fed. They were clothed in a rich mantle before presentation. They were lifted almost bodily into the august presence of the Vicegerent of Allah on earth. In order that they might not show any sign of breaking down under the awful burden of the Imperial presence, they were supported on either side by officials. I do not see the reason of this rule ; inasmuch as when introduced into the presence before the curtain of the high-posted and jeweled bedstead, the Ambassador did not look upon the august Majesty; only on his jeweled finger, which was thrust out between the curtains to be kissed by the Ambassador.

The Hippodrome remains to-day among the most interesting relics in Stamboul. It is monumental. Upon the open space in front of the mosque of Achmet, there is a museum of Ottoman costumes. It is called Gebecei-Atika. Let us visit this museum! It has pleasant surroundings. It has quietude and shade. These make it the asylum which it was intended to be, for the ancient Ottoman, whose effigies in most singular figure and dress are here exhibited. It strikes one as strange that the Mahometans, who dislike all imagery, who are iconoclasts if they are anything, should themselves have instituted this museum. At the very entrance of the staircase you encounter the figure of a Janizary. He is dead, of course, but quite vital to those who read his history. Enter! Lo! Some four hundred representations of the human form! They are most remarkable personages. A few of their images are pictured in our Chapter IX. on the Janizaries. You think they are caricatures? They are everything else. The old costumes are here with all their voluminousness and ferocity. The belt is at once an arsenal and a pocket, into which everything is gathered, from a tobacco pouch to a yataghan.

The Eden Musée and Madame Tussaud may strive, but they can never rival this exhibition! What motionless and strange visions they have collected, fantastic and weird ! but there is nothing so strange and fantastic to be found in human similitude, as these turbaned Turks of a dead age. A century has not yet gone by ; and yet we find men who can gaze upon this scene, pictured in this museum, and say that Turkey still remains as she was fourscore years ago. This museum teaches that the national habits have been thoroughly broken up. The costumes have become curious antiquities. These strange, bearded visages, with their glass eyes, that mock the very light, have in them something of the wonderful, such as the "Thousand and One Nights" produce upon the imagination. They are not illusions. They are rouged and fierce visages, not unlike the painted bodies of the dead as they appear in their coffins on their way to the grave in this Oriental country. Most of these strange effigies are those of artisans ; but the most remarkable are the functionaries of the Seraglio, and among them the most wonderful of the wondrous is the master of the eunuchs—the *Kisslar Agassi !* He is splendidly clothed. His clothes are embroidered with flowers. What enormous trousers ! half hidden beneath a tunic of silk. A Cashmere shawl of richest rarity is the sash. The turban is of red muslin ; and the boots are of yellow morocco. Look again ! It is the Grand Vizier, the Sheik-Ul-Islam, and the Captain Pasha. These are similarly dressed. Turn your eye, and you see tissues of the richest fabric, massive gold clasps, weapons enough to fill an arsenal, caps in crescent form, and fantastic head-dresses, worthy of the kings of Egypt. The chief scullion carries upon his shoulder a gigantic ladle. It is the emblem of his rank and authority. This ladle terminates in a blade. It is thought to represent the butchery of the brute preceding the cooking. Others bear kitchen utensils used in the old harem. Here on one side you find the candle-lighter in his dress ; there the bearer of the cat-o'-nine tails in a peculiar toilette ; and yonder the servant with the wooden bowl. There are some specimens of the soldiers of other corps than the Janizaries. Their dresses are not unlike those which I have seen in Algiers. Then the Albanian, the Armenian and the Greek come in on their lines, and assist in this wonderful congress of the phantoms of a past era.

Who originated this remarkable museum ? It must have been some Turk, with a cunning malice against the Janizary *corps* and a knack for caricature ; or, perhaps, some descendant of the old Janizary or harem officers, proud and conservative of the ancient nationality. Who could have done it ? I summon this curious congregation of the past actors upon the Bosporus, as well for the delectation as for the instruction of my readers.

Amid all the mountains and waters, and the strange forms of architecture and odd costumes of men, one cannot help but ponder and wonder what the future of this magnificent land may be a half century hence. Who will control it ? The style and stateliness of the old time may not be present in Constantinople now. The throng which once received the Sultan may not be here. What in outward show the Grand Vizier was once, the Sultan hardly is to-day. The horse covered with steel and gold, the files of superbly attired soldiers, the grooms of the harems leading their Arab and Persian horses, and the grand cortège, with its blatant music of drum and trumpet—these have gone to the abysm. The King of kings, with all the titles that belonged to him as Caliph, Conqueror and Ruler, may remain to close the nineteenth century ; for who else will be allowed to take his place ? He moves before us still, in spite of augury. It is a solemn and a curious procession. To understand its meaning and the luxury and costlinesses of its decorations, you must visit Gebecei-Atika.

# CHAPTER XXXV.

SCENES AND DIVERSIONS AROUND THE CITY OF STAMBOUL.

THERE are some days during the summer and in the beautiful fall weather when the time can be fully occupied in making visits to the rare historic and monumental scenes around the city. No city has extant such magnificent remains. Supreme above all I select the triple walls. From the Seven Towers they follow the sides of a triangle, two sides of which are on the shores, and the smaller side by land. There is constant occupation for the observer to read up, with actual inspection, the history of the many sieges which Constantinople has experienced. Or, if he should feel lugubriously inclined and should tire of the sights of the city, if the sameness of the mosque or the variety of the people and streets of Stamboul grow monotonous, there is the magnificent tomb of Mahmoud, who was the grandfather of the present Sultan. That is to be seen and admired. It is a masterpiece of Italian architecture. It is built of parti-colored and highly polished marble. Within is a divan, rich shawls, gilt rails, rare volumes of the Koran, each and all in harmony with the best taste which Turkey could bestow or buy for one of her great Sultans. Or, if time hang heavy, there is a drive through the splendid woods known as the Belgrade Forest, which I visited in the chestnut season, when the poachers were busy, the woods full of Gypsies and the officers of the government were vainly striving to collect the revenue which came from the harvest. Upon the fine roads which penetrate the woods, you may approach the springs and aqueducts of the city's water supply. Superior to the supply of Damascus is the arrangement of Constantinople. In every mosque and at every corner are fine fountains, not only the gift of individuals, but erected by the providence of the ruler. In fact, water is an institution of the Turk.

The fountains of the city are attractive by reason of their designs. Many of them are quite ornamental, and adorned with texts from the Koran. They always look shabby, sloppy and dirty, notwithstanding the handy cleansing element of water. Some of these texts have been translated to me. They are devotional. The water is not carried into the house by pipes. The people supply themselves from the fountains. Water-carriers, *hamals*, loaded like donkies, with their barrels decorated with green leaves, move around the streets distributing it through the city. Bath-houses are common. There are not less than one hundred and thirty for public use in the city. The water comes from reservoirs in the wooded neighborhood of Belgrade, a village fifteen miles north of the capital. To reach it you go through the forest made famous by Lady Mary Wortley Montague. Its shaded roads and paths are by no means free from brigands. For one thing the Turk deserves credit : he endeavors to utilize every trickle of water. He justifies this heed and care by one of his favorite maxims:

" Do good and throw it into the sea! If the fishes do not know it, God will!"

Midway between the Black Sea and the Golden Horn stand the most picturesque castles known to the world, one on each side of the Straits, Anatolio and Roumelia. They were the old defenses of Constantinople, or, rather, the means by which the Turks commanded the Bosporus before the fall of the city.

There are high points of view in Asia—eighteen hundred feet high—from the peaks of which a magnificent and peerless panorama is exhibited.

One never tires of the verdure-clad hills and the gardens, the lovely views, the picturesque landscape, the princely residences, the palaces by the Straits, and the magic power by which on a little fairy pinnace you may dance over the swift, translucent waters, and so speed your craft that you may light your cigar in Europe and shake off the ashes in Asia.

During the summer of 1886 we lived among the " Isles of the Princes," and every day, on our way from Prinkipo—one of these fairy isles—we pass near the enchanting Chrysopolis on the Asiatic shore. It is a mile and a half off the Seraglio Point. It has half a hundred thousand inhabitants. They are generally people of cultivation. The situation is romantic. It is on an elevation. It is the rendezvous of many merchants, whose caravans of camels make it a terminus as they travel from Persia and Armenia to the capital. It is a place of historic celebrity. Constantine the Great here fought and conquered Licinius. It is chiefly notable for its English cemetery, where are buried the heroes of the Crimea, and where many superb monuments may be seen, which are quite in contrast with those of the Turkish, Hebrew and other cemeteries.

Scutari is more the home of the dead than the living. When you land upon its shore you are but a few yards from its cemeteries. There the acacia blossoms in beauty; there its withered flowers fall upon the graves; there the Armenian and the Turkish cemeteries have fellowship in a common mortality.

My description now has to do with the Turkish cemetery. It stretches along the hill under its thickly planted cypresses. Beneath their shadows are the ghostly headstones. Foot-paths lead you into green glades flecked here and there with sunshine. It is indeed a " City of the Dead." The various columns and stones lie heavily on the earth, as if tired of bearing the burden of their eulogies. Here the Moslem sleeps beside his wife or wives. The turban surmounts his headstone; a rose defines hers. From the turban you may learn his profession, like that of the soldier who reposes a few yards off, or of the priest in the same vicinage. Some of the turbans lie upon the ground, struck off by the bâton of the retainers of Mahmoud II. They mark the graves of the Janizaries. The mutilated turbans half buried in the grass testify to their disgrace. You observe terraces which are raised and fenced in with taste. Within their precincts are columns and tombstones with the fez crowning them. The fez is painted in bright scarlet. It is an emblem of a conspicuous Effendi or Bey. As to this cemetery the Turks have a strange idea. They think that on particular times sparks of fire arise from the graves, and flicker and lose themselves among the boughs of the cypresses. They are the supposed souls of the departed. When I was a child I had the same feeling about the graveyards of Ohio. But science soon taught me that the decaying bones made phosphorus, and that the phosphorus was the *ignis-fatuus* of the superstitious. This is chemistry.

Constantinople should take more heed of the degradation of some of the cemeteries on the European side ; for I am no believer in the statement that the reason why the cemetery of Scutari is preferred and guarded is, that the Turk seeks to be buried there because he expects to be expelled from Europe.

These cemeteries are so great in number that the tombstones around the city outnumber the living in the city. They are not altogether cheerless, except those that have been deserted. They are often decorated with colors, and the white sandstone more or less bespangled with gold. They are in strange contrast with the dark cypresses which enshroud them.

THE TURKISH CEMETERY AT SCUTARI.

I have elsewhere written of the mysterious birds which fly restlessly up and down the Bosporus. These birds, in their never-pausing unrest, seem never to be wooed to the earth. Still, they are compelled to be above the water. I am told that there is one exception: when the tempest rages over Marmora or sweeps down the valley of the Bosporus, these birds shriek and fly in wild flocks to the cypress forests of Scutari. There they find shelter. This begets a superstition quite natural in the Orient; for the Turk believes them to be the souls of the damned who have found sepulchre beneath the cypress boughs. They believe that these souls are permitted, during wild convulsions of nature, to return to the spots where the body is buried.

The practice of burial among the Turks is not unlike that of other people in the Orient, but it is very unlike our own. On the death of a Mussulman, the body is first washed with warm water. It is then enveloped in a shroud of white cotton cloth and placed in a coffin made of plain unpolished wood. The lid, of a raised form, is then screwed down and covered with a Persian shawl, of value according to the circumstances of the deceased. The coffin is borne to the mosque on the shoulders of friends of the deceased. When it arrives, it is placed on a marble table. Prayers are recited by the parish Imam. After this it is taken to the cemetery and buried without other ceremonial. Over the grave are afterward placed upright, two stones, one at the head and the other at the feet. Upon these, verses of the Koran are inscribed. The same grave cannot be re-opened at any time for the reception of another body, even if belonging to the same family. The Sultans and members of the Imperial family are always buried in the mosques or mausoleums which they have had constructed during their lifetime. Large wax candles are placed round the tomb, which is also covered with Persian shawls of great value, and on which are embroidered in gold letters the name of the deceased Sultan and appropriate quotations from the Koran.

"Kismet" compels the Turk to abstain from demonstration of sorrow. He regards it as unmanly as well as irreligious to weep. The corpse is buried soon after death. Few accompany it to the grave. The grave of the Turk is shallower than that in our country. His coffin is plain. There is a quiet prayer, and the body is deposited. Then the grave is filled up. Water, which is always his symbol of purity, is sprinkled over the grave by the nearest relative. The idea of water upon the grave is from the Arabic. It is symbolic and poetic. It indicates that, like a plant well watered, the soul will rise to immortality. The cemeteries around Constantinople, and especially the cemetery in which I was in the habit of walking, and which was constantly under my eye in Pera, is almost fantastic. It looks abandoned. The turbans are chopped off by some iconoclast. The very emblem of the

Turk has disappeared. One thing is observed: that, on every gravestone that can be deciphered, the trade of the dead man is symbolized by the anvil, the adze, the lancet or the inkstand. They represent the occupation of the occupant in life. The graves of the Turkish women, of course, have no turban. There is no lying panegyric. One singular thing belongs to all the tombstones: in their upper corner are some little cavities; these are filled with water. What does this mean? It invites the birds to take a drink, and entices them to give their carol and their cheer to the graveyard and the dead. This is an Oriental custom not limited to the Turk. Moses taught similar hospitality to the feathered race. Mahomet copied his code from Moses.

After all, I end this chapter as I began, with the walls. The most interesting monument left by the Byzantine empire is, beyond doubt, the walls. These once formed one triple wall. They were built by Justinian in the sixth century. The highest was thirty feet high. Each line was crenelated on top and flanked at intervals by towers. There was a broad, deep moat with dams at intervals. The moat is now dry, except when watered for the vegetable gardens, for which it is used. The stones of the walls have proved a godsend in two ways: first, they furnished a revenue to the mother of the Sultan. That is now abrogated. Secondly, they furnished the cheap raw material for the buildings of the city. That is now in disuse. Their best use is as a monumental lesson of the vicissitudes of empire and the fragility of power. Outside them are the cemeteries, whose tenants have no census—and, in fact, neither have the living— and whose tenure is much more assured than that of the living, who fill these fields of mortality upon every festive occasion.

There is one gate of the walls called the Top Kapu. Through it the Turks penetrated to the city on its fall; for through this gate the first fifty Turks entered the city. It is now known as the gate of St. Romanus. Another *alias* is that of the Gate of the Big Gun, for here, as is alleged, the monstrous gun, made by Orban, was brought by the aid of fifty oxen, four hundred men and a corps of carpenters to repair the bridges and roads over which it was moved. It required two months to make the usual march of two days from Adrianople, seven hundred men to serve it and two hours to load it. In the end, after battering the gate and tower, it hoisted into eternity its engineer. But who mourns

for Orban now, and, for the matter of that, how few mourn for
Krupp, whose guns are lazing their time away upon the Plaza of
Tophane !

Another gate is called the Silivri. It is within a mile of the
Sea of Marmora. It is upon the edge of a cemetery. In that

TOMB OF ALI.

cemetery, dark with cypresses, is the grave of one Ali Pasha of
Janina. He is the hero of the Albanian conflict. Over his grave
is written :

"He rendered himself independent for more than thirty years.
Here lies his head. No prayers are requested."

Who was Ali ? Why was he headless —or bodiless ?

Ali was born in upper Epirus, of an Albanian-Mahometan family. His father was a brigand. He returned to the bosom of his family in order to exterminate them, and so as to swell the fruits of his pillage. Strange to tell, he was attached to his mother, Khanco. She was a brigand. She had been captured, outraged and freed. Ali promised her, when she was dying, to exterminate the people of the town where she was outraged. This he did afterward, when he became Pasha of Janina, with a vengeance. He became master of the Pashalic by becoming a devoted servant of the Porte. He destroyed the brigands in order to be chief of the country. He distributed the booty where it would do the most good—in Constantinople. From time to time he was promoted by the Porte, until its officials became suspicious of him and of his rich presents to members of the Divan. He was authorized by an order from the Sultan to destroy the Suliotes. This was the sensation at the beginning of this century. The Suliotes had planted the Cross over their mountains as a signal of liberty. They challenged the Mahometans, and Ali as their chief. He became invested with a title only next to that of grand vizier.

This being the character and conduct of Ali Pasha, it was not difficult to find the clue to his life and death. The most interesting statement is in a volume entitled, "The Eastern Shores of the Adriatic in A. D. 1883," by the Viscountess Strangford. I may remark, in a prefatory way, that this lady is the author of some other Oriental books. She had much trouble in her travels from Russian authorities, and as I write these lines I find in the current journals that she has just died. She was a wonderful woman in her prime.

In the volume there is a description of Janina. It is the capital of southern Albania. It was a part of my enthusiasm, never realized, to go there with my Dalmatian servant, Pedro, who was born near by. It is a city which is set upon a mountain and cannot be hid, but the lady to whom I have referred accomplished the journey and stood before the city with all its lovely tenderness of scenery. It was a land with the glory of Greece and the beauty of Italy. The city is above the clouds. Upon its eminence can be seen higher distant mountains, snow clad, and a lake as blue as the Ægean itself. Within the lake is an island. On the island is a fortification. The city itself, with its white houses with red roofs, is a picture in a romance. It is rarely visited by the tourist.

The meadows are only equaled by the gardens which surround the lake, down upon which look the grand groups of the blanched Pindus, with all the classic sanctity of purity. There are, however, in the neighborhood some dirty, dull brown mountains, with a little appearance of rock breaking through their uncrisped slopes. This last dainty sentence is that of the Viscountess. The lake is about three-fourths of a mile wide. It reflects the mountains of Mitzikéli. Upon the island lies the headless body of Ali, whose head is supposed to be in the cemetery near the walls of Constantinople. The lake is seven miles long and three miles wide. It is not supplied from the mountain, but from its own springs. The only historic incident about Janina is that which appertains to our Ali Pasha. Why should the Turks any more than the Greeks bear him honor? That will be developed by a short synopsis of his career. That career is distinguished by the fact that he was in constant, and in the end successful, rebellion. He was the exterminator of the Suliotes, who desired of all things to be independent in their mountains. When Mahmoud the Second, who killed off the Janizaries, undertook to control this distant Albania as a part of his empire, he found Ali in possession. Ali mistook the sagacity and quietude of the Sultan for weakness. Ali defied him. This was in A. D. 1820. The Sultan deprived him of his rule at this mountain capital, and sent an army to enforce the degradation. The Suliotes had been exiled to Corfu, but at the Sultan's command they re-entered their old country of Albania. In the last of the year A. D. 1820, they made a junction with the Mussulman Albanians, who were devoted to Ali. Then the Greek revolution—so celebrated in the speeches of Webster and Clay, and the poetry of Byron and Halleck—broke out in the Morea. Among the many mixtures of race in this Albanian country, the Suliotes stood prominent for their sturdy pluck. Many of them enrolled themselves under Lord Byron.

The name of the Suliote is almost forgotten; but that of the despot, Ali Pasha, lives on, not by his own virtue, but by virtue of the strange tomb near Constantinople.

The Viscountess to whom I have referred, states that the body of Ali, together with the body of his wife Emine, whom he shot down with his own hand, in his fury because she favored the Suliotes, is beneath a turban-topped headstone in Janina. If it ever was buried there, it has been removed since.

I must tell the story of Ali's death.  He is under the Sultan's ban.  On the 29th of January, A. D. 1822, he is assured of forgiveness.  He is induced to leave his citadel in the lake and cross over to a monastery.  Here he settles himself in a room next to that of his favorite wife, Vassiliki.  He is visited, in good faith as he supposes, by Mehmet Pasha, the Sultan's general in Epiros.  Mehmet enters the room; he fires a pistol at Ali.  The shot misses.  Ali fires back.  *His* shot misses.  Ali, however, is wounded in the hand by a shot from an *aide-de-camp* of Mehmet.  Then the old tiger prepares to fight, with his fangs keen and his claws unvelveted.  His wife binds up his bleeding hand.  His enemies beneath his room shoot at him through the floor.  A shot takes mortal effect, and he dies.  Mehmet then breaks into the room and chops off Ali's head with a cimeter.  It is sent, along with the wife, across the lake.  Thence they are despatched to Constantinople.

Now here arises my difficulty.  The question is : Whether the head of this man was sent to Constantinople, or his body without the head ?  Is Ali buried here—a headless body or a bodiless head ?  It does not matter much in these times; but the best impression is, that the tomb at Constantinople makes a decent request when it asks the traveler not to make superfluous prayers, as the head is not there.

The treasures of this wonderful Ali Pasha, like those of Captain Kidd, are still sought after in the country which he ruled so despotically and cruelly.  He is an illustration of a class of Oriental heroes, like that which includes Mehemet Ali, of Egypt, who was an Albanian.  This last hero conquered not only Egypt, and left it to his descendants, but overcame Syria as well.  He would have taken Constantinople, even as against Mahmoud the Second, but for the union against him of the European forces.  The Albanian may be a murderous, vindictive and terrific race— or perhaps they were so in the past—but they have made great struggles for independence, and are worthy of many illuminated pages in the history of freedom among the mountains of our globe.

A visit to the "Sweet Waters" of Europe and Asia on Friday reveals more of the old Turkish enchantment, such as we associate with the extravagance of an Eastern story-teller, than any other incident.  I ought not to undertake to describe visits to these "Sweet Waters" upon their gala-days, for that is beyond my

"SWEET WATERS" OF ASIA.

unfacile pen.   May I make the attempt, however,  to picture the
"Sweet Waters" of Asia?

The valley of Jeuiuksuy, when thronged, is essentially Oriental.
There is a grateful coolness which tempers the noontide sunshine,
a fresh breeze from the Bosporus, and an inviting turf upon which
the ladies spread their carpets.   Screened from the dust by the trees,
and separated from the men who resort to these bossy shades, the
women enjoy their cigarettes and  chibouques, their sherbets and

GROUP OF TURKISH WOMEN AT THE "SWEET WATERS."

melons.   Here the wives of the Pashas and  Beys, Effendis and
Emirs, indulge in the luxury of the *"kadeun chibouque"* or
women's pipe.   Here slaves wait upon their mistresses.   Here
is the vender of sweetmeats, with his wooden platter upon his head,
and the vender of ice-cream, with his yoke upon his shoulder.
Here are seen sometimes, gratifying the children, the dancing
bears and monkeys.   Here is the water-carrier, with his large
turban, his graceful classic jar, and his crystal goblet.   Here are

the negroes—the eunuchs of the upper ten thousand—moving around with carpets, pipes and refreshments for their mistresses If it be in the fruit season, here are venders of peaches, plums, nectarines, apricots, *tchoussi* grapes, pistachio nuts, and filberts, all decorated with fresh green leaves about them, not to speak of the melon merchants, selling their delicious fruit for a very small sum. If your eyes be not surfeited, and your ear loves music, here is the rattle of the tambourine, the wiry sound of the zebec, and the shrill, high voices of the Greeks, who for a few piastres complete this Oriental picture and make the valley, with its trees, its *personnel*, its shadows, and its domesticities, a perpetual reminder of the stories of the East. In fine, here is, indeed—

> " A glowing scene of water, leaves and light,
>     And white-veiled dames and turban'd men are here ;
>   And all around, the earth and sea are bright
>     And beautiful in the sunshiny air."

When evening draws the curtain over the distant city and sea, the *arabis* and carriages are hailed by the slaves, and quietly "wind o'er the lea" for their homes in Asia, and the caïques are called to bear their freight over the blue waves of the pellucid waters. Thus endeth the Friday's outing of the harem at the Asian " Sweet Waters." The European waters are like unto them, only there are a thousand people at the latter for a hundred at the former. Besides, the style and rank of the habitués of the "Sweet Waters" of Europe outvie those of Asia.

When the Turkish woman leaves the harem, in company with her co-wives and slaves and children, she seeks the most delightful natural resorts. It is not for the woman of the West, with the elaborate dissipation of the ball, the waltz, and the champagne supper in the gilded salon, to find fault with the Osmanli *hanoum*, who seeks the breeze, the heath and the wooded valley, where nature displays her rarest charms, and where the sweetness and freshness of the air, enhance the pleasure far beyond the gas-lighted halls of Occidental luxury.

# CHAPTER XXXVI.

## DEMOCRATIC—REPUBLICAN FEATURES IN TURKEY.

ONE phase of the advancement of the Turkish people has been in the direction of simplicity. We have read the grand titles in which the earlier Sultans rejoiced. We have seen their curtailment in recent years. The Capitulations and Articles of Peace between Great Britain and Turkey, confirmed at the Dardanelles in A. D. 1809, in the preface displays how glorious was once, among the nations of the earth, the ascription of all praise and honor to His Majesty. It was thus:

"SULTAN MEHEMED, MAY HE LIVE FOREVER !

" Let everything be observed in conformity to these Capitulations, and contrary thereto, let nothing be done.

" The command, under the sublime and lofty Signet, which imparts sublimity to every place, and under the imperial and noble Cypher, whose glory is renowned throughout all the world, by the Emperor and Conqueror of the earth, achieved with the assistance of the Omnipotent, and by the special grace of God, is this :

" We, who by Divine grace, assistance, will and benevolence now are the King of Kings of the world, the Prince of Emperors of every age, the dispenser of Crowns to Monarchs, and the Champion Sultan Mehemed, Son of Sultan Ibrahim Chan, Son of Sultan Ahmed Chan, Son of Sultan Mahommet Chan, Son of Sultan Murad Chan, Son of Sultan Selim Chan, Son of Sultan Solyman Chan, Son of Sultan Selim Chan."

This rigmarole is no longer customary, even in treaties. The very orthography is changed. The Ottoman is a contradiction in many ways. He loves to abase himself, in order to be exalted. His teaching and his ideal hero are Christian in this regard. The lives of the Prophet himself, and of the greatest of the Sultans, Othman, remind him of the grandeur of those who died in poverty. Sometimes he carries his humility to excess. He practises the pride which apes humility. Let me illustrate by a fable which I found in one of the odd volumes that I happened upon in some literary explorations. The time of the story is in the third century of the Prophet. The place is Egypt. The person is a cadi of Cairo. He is named Mansúr bin Músia. He cannot stand this grandiose name. It had once an original meaning. Was it not compounded from some parental prescription? It literally meant Victor, son of Moses! He divides it into five syllables. Thus: Man-Súr-Bin-Mú-Sia. The old volume I refer to has a diagram of the name as humiliated, thus:

| Syllables of the original name. | Meaning of original. | Substitute. | Meaning of Substitute. |
| --- | --- | --- | --- |
| Man.............. .... | Name of a heavy weight of 40 lbs. | Ratal........ | Pound. |
| Súr............... | A large trumpet .... | Búk......... | Small bugle. |
| Bin ............. | The son............ | Abd-al ...... | Slave. |
| Mú.. ............. | Hair   ........... | Pashm....... | Wool. |
| Sia  ............. | Thirty, in Persian... | Panzdah | Fifteen. |

The third column forms his new name, "Ratal Búk Abd-al Pashm Panzdah," whose humble synonym is "Small-weight-Penny-whistle-Slave-of-Wool-Fifteen," instead of "Heavy-weight-Trumpet-Son-of-Hair-Thirty!"

The title of the Sultan was once by no means to be despised as a heavy-weighted son of Hair. It used to be a mile or more long, but the good sense of the new rulers here has clipped off much of the superfluous title. His name is now as simple as his head-gear. The gear of the head is always, and under all circumstances, the simple red fez. The Turk is a democrat, without guile or ostentation, and, as will appear in the sequel, he never rides fine horses when he can walk, honestly!

I have said that Turkey has a kind of democratic-republican society and government. This is true in many respects. It is a constitutional monarchy under the constitution of December 23, A. D. 1876. This the *Almanach de Gotha* recognizes, but the Constitution is a dead letter and the *Almanach* is a bundle of ignorance, in this as in other regards. The absence of a hereditary nobility—in fact, the lack of any nobility—makes it free from one of the worst taints of the European order. It has its system of government, made up of Ministers and Senators, a Council of State, police regulations, and administrative divisions, of which the Sultan is nominally—and really, when he pleases—the absolute head. He bears the simple title of Padishah. It is a title of honor. It comes down through many generations of heroes. Other countries retain what Turkey discards. The universal Turkish nation, which is given much to gravity, would, for instance, be humorously inclined if a gentleman was introduced to them bearing the name of Prince Charles Frédéric-Karafft-Ernest-Notger, prince et Seigneur d' Oettingen-Oettingen et d' Oettingen-Wallerstein, Compte de Baldern, Scigneur de Sœtern, etc.; and yet this is a veritable habitant between the leaves of the absurd *Gotha Almanach.*

Suppose one of our Western orators should introduce this gentleman by all his titles to an American audience, say in the town of Kalamazoo, Michigan, or Oshkosh, Wisconsin, would he be received with that respect which is due to a son of royalty, or would he be met with universal guffaws? Alas! for the irreverent audacity of the American gamin and his unvenerated parent —this query is easily answered for both the original tree and its scion!

And yet, even in America we have prefixes to our names not established by law, and only allowed by custom. "Esq." and "Hon." are quite sufficient illustrations that we are not altogether free from this anti-republican taint. Compared with other countries, we are, like Turkey, comparatively untainted. Russia is very unlike Turkey in this matter. Titles prevail there to an extravagant extent. The salutations are profound and elaborate. It is so especially in the army. The soldier never addresses an officer without standing at "Attention"! with his hand at his cap during the whole conversation. He does not answer a question categorically with a "yes, sir," or "no, sir," but with a circumlocution, "quite so," or "not exactly so." He addresses a general as "Your Excellency," princes and counts are Illustriousnesses, and a field-officer "Your High Nobility." A company officer, "Your Nobility." If he has occasion to speak to the Emperor himself, and desires to say, "We are glad to serve you," he says this: "*Otchen radom, Vass Imperatorsky veleetches-too.*" One would think that a Russian name was sesquipedalian enough, without adding to it an elongated sneeze and a super-abundance of titular caudle-appendages. An American, not long ago, stated that a Russian nobleman who recently died had a name so long that it could not be sent by cable, and that he could shell an ear of corn with it and have enough left over for a barbed wire fence, a nail cloth and springs for a mattress. This is too exaggerative.

In France, when it was a monarchy, the King was always called *Sire;* in England he was addressed as *Sir;* the Queens were called *Madame,* and the Imperial Princes in France were called Monseigneur. The German sovereigns of both sexes are called " Majesty," and the Princes " Hohheit." The Pope is styled " His Holiness," like the Patriarch of Constantinople, and the cardinals are called " Eminences." In Persia, the Shah is called " the Asylum of the Universe." In the European countries there is, or was, a title, as a prefix, generally recognized. But Turkey had, and has, no nobility. It is only of late years, I think, that some of these prefixes, like " Excellency " for a Minister, have become common, *ad nauseam.* This custom is referable to the Legations and others besides the Ottoman people. Of one thing here I became weary—I may say of two things; *first,* of being so much waited on ; *second,* of being dubbed " Son Excellence !" upon the slightest provocation by everybody, even by American tourists, who fall into the absurd custom. If the Ottoman would only adopt some of the names belonging to the Slav or Greek, he would have no need of any prefix or affix. Taking the former Greek Minister of the Interior, for instance, Mr. Pappamichalopoulos, or even the name of the Greek Minister to Constantinople, Monsieur Coun-douriotti, and you have enough in the surname without any aristocratic appendages. Queen Victoria might herself take a lesson from this simplicity of the Osmanli in the matter of titles, and thereby save much to her scriveners now and hereafter. It has pleased Her Majesty to order, of her royal pleasure, that the sons and daughters born of the marriage of His Highness, Prince Henry Maurice of Battenberg, with Her Royal Highness, Princess Beatrice Maria Victoria Theodora, shall at all times hold and enjoy the style of " Highness." Let us draw a long breath in anticipation of such high distinctions of the unborn Hessians and Guelphs.

It may or may not be a matter of interest to state that one of my Diversions to overcome one of the difficulties of the position of Minister, was in remembering the remarkable names of those with whom it was my duty and pleasure to meet socially and diplomatically. How did I accomplish it ? By a system of mnemonics not peculiar to myself. I tried, with discreet and laudatory rhyme, to arrange the several cards so as to associate the names with euphonious sounds. How the names rise now in my memory ! Dear Kaiserlich Deutscher Botschafts Prediger—whose function was so much more extensive than his name : for he was only the good German pastor, Suhle ! There was Jarasynski and Blankeregg : the one a Pole and the other a Hungarian ; the Roumanian Consul Ecsarho, Mavroyéni and Constantindini ; Grouitch and Bakitch, Servian and Montenegrin, genial and just representatives ; Ghica, the princeliest of princes, and Svétchine, the suave Secretary ; Wallenberg and d' Ehrenhoff, kindest of Norse gentlemen ; the Belgian Borchgrave and Gödel-Lannoy, of Austria ; Ivanow and Smirnow, Ortiz de Zugasti and Coella de Portugal, Canzuch and Metaxas ! These are names upon whose circle we weave many flowers of pleasant memories. But what a relief when we struck such plain patronymics as Woods Pasha, Hobart Pasha, Bax Ironside, Bruce, Lowther, De Gratz, Towers, Fane, Fawcett, Wrench and Potter ; not to omit Blacque Bey and Sir William White, Sir Drummond Wolff and the Rev. George Washington !

It is not a very great Diversion ; nevertheless, when one becomes reminiscent, it becomes amusing to recognize that so much depends, in Europe and elsewhere, upon the name, the title, the decoration, or the rank of people who come and go, both as officers, diplomats, and otherwise. Let me give an illustration.

For many years the office of Minister to Turkey from the United States was simply that of Minister Resident. That made him third in the list of diplomatic personages at the various courts: the first being an Ambassador ; the second being an Envoy Extraordinary and Minister Plenipotentiary ; the third being Minister Resident ; and the fourth being Chargé d' Affaires. When General Wallace began his services in Turkey in 1881, he was simply a Minister Resident. Perhaps it irked the author of " Ben Hur" greatly to know that while he could soar, as few men of genius can, into the hierarchy of literature, and dwell among the princes of the earth, or revel in the Valhalla, with the great ones of the Elder Day—while in gorgeous and glowing imagery he could depict Oriental scenes with rarest skill, learning and dramatic power ; still, as Minister, he had to wait, upon every official occasion, and in all the various phases of Oriental etiquette, while some ignoramus of an Envoy from a little state, or some swell of an Ambassador from an effete dynasty, took precedence of the representative of many millions of progressive and free people. I will not say that he ever complained of this inversion of official and personal dignity, although when I was in Constantinople in 1881, he did use some democratic-republican forms of speech which I thought proper and pertinent. To these I have added some of my own vehemence since, growing out of my own experience. I happened to be one of the Legislators who helped to raise General Wallace's rank from Minister Resident to that of Envoy Extraordinary and Minister Plenipotentiary. It was done to add one step to his rank ; but it was not enough, as the sequel will show.

Now, one would suppose that a man who is entitled to such magnificent and unabridged-dictionary titles as Envoy Extraordinary and Minister Plenipotentiary, ought to take precedence of certain representatives at the court of the Sultan who were representing inferior states. I have occasion to feel this one sultry afternoon in the month of August, 1886. Along with the dragoman, Mr. Gargiulo, I call on the Minister of Foreign Affairs, Saïd Pasha, at the Porte. It is on Monday, when all the various diplomats are received. We are accustomed to record our names on our *entrée* to the reception-room. My arrival is timely; my name is first on the list, as an Envoy Extraordinary and Minister Plenipotentiary! It is 2 o'clock in the afternoon, and the thermometer is 90°. I mop the perspiration from my brow, and am about to be ushered into the presence of the Foreign Minister when, lo! Monsieur Nellidoff, the Russian Ambassador, appears all aglow with heat and all a-growl, like the Bear of the North. By virtue of his being an Ambassador, he makes his courtesy, takes precedence, and goes in. Then comes a Minister Resident from Greece. I have precedence of him, of course, as being an Envoy, but as he has some distance to go this afternoon up the Bosporus, I politely yield my place to him. Thus passes away about an hour, the thermometer trembling at 91° and the perspiration running in canals from my corrugated brow. I am about to congratulate myself that my time has come, when a polite and facile gentleman, the French Minister, Count de Montholon—a connection of Lafayette—with partialities toward our country, and representing a republic, appears. He is registered ; he passes in; and the Envoy from America, a republic which antedates his, still remains outside. The thermometer is still rising somewhere among the nineties. The four thousand pores to the square inch on the cuticle of the Envoy pour forth their beaded drops. The Count, who is very polite when he arrives, remarks :

"I am quite in a hurry, Excellence! you will be detained but a few moments."

He stays about an hour. As I have to go to the island of Prinkipo this afternoon, and am rather loath to test the sultriness which sometimes brings storms over the old Propontis, I become quite uneasy, and begin to perspire freely at 92°, and to go over in my mind the advantage of being an Ambassador, when Herr Radowitz, the German Ambassador, with his pleasant smile and shining spectacles, peeps in after making his registry and the courtesies, and "sorry to take precedence of the American Minister," he enters in. The thermometer begins to rage fiercely at 93°, and the perspiration is as fluent as the Bosporus. I knew that he would not stay long. The representative of "The Honest Broker," as Germany has been called, soon despatches his business, to my great relief. Five o'clock is shown upon the clock, with the thermometer still rising and the sweat still falling ; when—but I cannot swear—when, lo! the deaf-mute, who still hovers around Oriental courts and Portes, appears. He makes his signs, and gives his orders as an "unspeakable Turk" in his ineffable way, smiling over the prospect of my now being reached in order, and over the *backsheesh* at the end of my long experience with the thermometer and the ambassadors, when lo ! the Ambassador from Persia is announced ! Mashallah! He takes precedence, of course. Is he not known as His Excellency Marshal Mirza Mohsin Khan ? CAN is the way to spell it, with capital letters; for he goes in ! He is accompanied by his cousin, who is also quite a dignitary of the Legation; and without saying "by your leave," or looking at the list, the thermometer or the clock, or making apology or inquiry as to my forbearance, they, too, have entered into the penetralia ! The thermometer by this time is near bursting. As he passes in he remarks coolly:

"I will be only five minutes, Excellence!" I know the Marshal Mirza Mohsin Khan well. He is a good Mahometan, and he has many relations with the Porte which do not belong to the outside world. I anticipate his long conversation with the Minister.

After waiting until about 6 o'clock, the shades of evening begin to fall, and the thermometer with them. I gaze into the big black eyes of the dragoman, give one sigh for my far-off country, cast one long look out of the window over the old Seraglio Point, think over its sanguinary scenes, and, while wiping my anxious brow, I indicate to that patient interpreter that if the Ambassador of a little, miserable, half-fed dependency of Russia, known as the Khanate of Persia, may take precedence of an Envoy Extraordinary and Minister Plenipotentiary, representing a nation of sixty million of independent freemen, I wanted to go home. I went. I made a solemn resolution that if I ever entered the American Congress again, I would move to strike out the grand six-footed words by which our Minister is accredited to the Porte, and insert the simple word ambassador, which means "one sent." It is the open sesame to the jewels and gold of Oriental diplomacy.

But can a republic have an ambassador? That is the momentous question. It was settled at the treaty of Paris by the Holy Alliance, and some other Powers confederating, that only monarchical governments could have ambassadors. Republics were then forbidden to have other than Ministers or Envoys. This is a solemn treaty among the Powers, but at that meeting we were not present and not consulted; and then, too, France was a monarchy. She is now a republic. She holds on to the ambassador, with all its advantages. Why should we not have the same? If titles have any value, let us use the best in the lexicon.

There is room for reform in the diplomatic service. In fact, it might be abolished altogether where the telegraph can play its part for special embassies and emergent occasions. What a solemn farce it is, after all, for an American Minister to pretend to any style or rank, when he cannot do as other Ministers—conclude any treaty, or anything, so as to bind any one ! The making and confirming of conventions by our Constitution, depends on the Executive or his Secretary of State, and then absolutely upon the Senate. The Minister is powerless for good, except in a few remote countries, like China, Japan and Turkey ; and in certain cases like the very ones I was waiting to conclude when the other Powers stepped before me into the agitated pool at the Porte. What I mean is this : that for over ten years two treaties accomplished by this country with Turkey have been suspended at the Porte. They had been made by Mr. Minister Boker, signed and already confirmed by the Senate. Our country was anxious for them. They were in accord with the American doctrines of expatriation and naturalization. They were a triumph of the right of locomotion and the liberalities of our time. By the special *Iradé* of the Sultan, and after great trouble, vexation, patience and delay, the ex-Minister—who writes this chapter—succeeded in securing, by the Sultan's favorable interposition, the acquiescence of the Porte with these treaties. It was supposed to be a finality. Have they been consummated now by our chief Executive or his Secretary of State ? No ; and inasmuch as they illustrate a line of honorable progress in diplomacy, secured by a subordinate and remote official, they are now regarded—since their acceptance by Turkey—as of little or no moment ! We prize little that which we obtain, after it is obtained, or which others have secured—even though secured under specific instructions. Of this hereafter, and in another forum than the republic of letters.

If this be the end of such labors under such favorable circumstances, better make an end of all such fruitless and salaried diplomatic intercourse!

The world will not always be moved by mere titles. Much may be expected in the European future from the overturning of these pretensions. It may be remembered that in 1874 the Lord Mayor of London, perhaps in one sense the most comical of all the empty and ostentatious functionaries known to civilization, issued a prescript for a lunch at Guildhall. The foreign Envoys below the rank of Ambassador were relegated to a table by themselves. They left the hall in a body and in a huff. They made a protest to the Foreign Office. The Foreign Office had no jurisdiction over such a corporation. The Ministers who remember this nonsensical slight, based on rank, have never since put their foot in Guildhall, and the stupid corporation has never yet made an apology.

From the revelations which have transpired in relation to the reception of General Grant at the court of Queen Victoria, and the insulting discriminations at that court against the American women who desire presentation, it would seem but a very small matter to be "relegated" to a lower rank when bearing such a magnificent title as Envoy Extraordinary and Minister Plenipotentiary, but it is otherwise when such illustrious titular personages as Ambassadors have such extraordinary privileges. Perhaps some day there will be reformatory movements in respect to certain grades connected with the public service, and such movements will certainly comprehend merit as the main element by which facilities and courtesies in office shall be accorded.

This is aside from the observations pertinent to this chapter.

Is the Turk an arrogant or an humble personality? Do the Mahometan faith and Eastern institutions tend to promote egotism and vanity? These queries, if truly answered, give the key to unlock many of the historic, individual and social points in Oriental experience.

The Psalmist refers to a class of men of old who laid out towns which they named after themselves. It is said in the Old Testament that there were no "Smiths" in all Israel, but the class of which the anonymous Smith is the type existed then. Smith of Smithville, and Boggs of Boggsville, and their congenitors, like Shakespeare, are for all time. But it is one of the anomalies of the East, wherever the Koran is the rule of conduct, that the names of people are of the simplest kind. In fact, in the Turkish empire, and in its highest official roster, the names are of the simplest. With repetitious inconvenience, the Mehmets, Achmeds, Alis, Suleïmans, Osmans, Saïds, Abdullahs, Emins, Mustaphas, Selims, Moussas and Tewfiks have such "damnable iteration" as to confuse the native as well as the foreigner.

The lists of titles in the books of heraldry of Western nations have little to compare with the humble nomenclature of the East. The religion of Mahomet makes all equal before the Supreme Spiritual Allah. In fact, when an Oriental, by the partiality of parents, is endowed with a grandiose name, the child, when of discreet age, assumes the virtue, if he has it not, of reducing his appellation.

In the East, or in Turkey, all names, as well of localities as of persons, have an interior and sometimes a poetic meaning. The names of the valleys and hills, as well as of the very castles and palaces on the Bosporus, signify something substantial. Take the names along the Straits. For instance, Dolma Bagtché, the rarest of palaces, signifies a ravine, once a garden and now filled

up! Pilav Kaïa means a rock of rice ; it is white.   Fil Bournou
means the nose of an elephant ; Buyukdere is a great valley ;
Yéni Mahallé is a new quarter ; Madjar Kalessi is a Hungarian
fort ; Therapia is Greek for health ; Beycos is the place where
Beys did congregate ; Yeni Keui is a new village ; Kandilli, an
illuminated spot ; Kouroutchesmé, a dry fountain ; Ortakeui is
literally Middletown; Bechïktash is a stone cradle; and Kadikeui
is the village of the judge.   When there was a bad judge, they used
to send him there out of the way.   Every town or stream, as
Emerson said of Irish scenery, is full of poetry, and the names
have ideal significance !

It may strike the superficial observer of Oriental usages as
peculiar that, in the Ottoman dominion, there are no titles of
nobility, no aristocracy or inherited titles.   The Sultan himself
is no more, in the light of the Koran, than his meanest *serviteur !*
Another democratic element here comes out of the Oriental land
of religion, where every soul is equal before its Maker.   It is this:
that every Mussulman, however high his rank, from the Sultan
down to the lowest Dervish, is compelled to have a trade.   The
grandfather of the present Sultan was a tooth-pick maker.   I do
not know to what trade the present Sultan was apprenticed ; but
certainly he is a good machinist, judging by the skill with which
he investigates all the contrivances of enginery tendered him for
the protection of the Bosporus and the capital.

The boatman, porter, slave or groom may not only be eligible
to be called Pasha, but there is no exclusive clique or caste to
render them ineligible to any office in Turkey.   " The butcher of
to-day," says some one, " may be the generalissimo of to-morrow;
and the barber who takes an Effendi by the nose on Monday, may
on Tuesday be called by the throne to take him by the hand."
The lowest slave to-day may become Grand Vizier to-morrow.   In
fact, many of the present Ministers have arisen from the humblest
walks and avocations to their exalted positions.   " Our poets of
the East," said Saladin to the Lion-Hearted King Richard, " say
that a valiant camel-driver is worthy to kiss the lip of a fair queen,
when a cowardly prince is not worthy to salute the hem of her
garment."

Where in all this Oriental wealth of imagery and incident may
one find an humble pearl to string for my readers?   Well, I find
it in a little verse of Beaumont and Fletcher.   I call it the humil-

ity of the Oriental. The self-abnegation of "the best of men that e'er wore earth about him" was that of

> " A soft, meek, patient, humble, tranquil spirit ;
> The first true gentleman that ever breathed."

I may conclude, therefore, with a tribute to the humility of the Oriental, whence came this gentlest of "gentle-men."

# CHAPTER XXXVII.

### TURKISH TIME—FASTING AND FESTAL DAYS.

THE time of day and night in Constantinople needs to be heeded. It is a great puzzle to those who are not initiated. It requires that the stranger should buy a journal every day, in order to be certain of the time when the steamers and the cars leave. The hotels are compelled to keep two clocks. Sometimes 1 in the morning, Turkish time, means 6 o'clock in our time; and sometimes it means 9 o'clock. Besides, owing to the numerous races and religions in the Orient, there are various days for the Sabbath, Christmas, New Year and Easter. They make inextricable confusion, while the old time of the Russians and Greeks still more confounds us—as to the fêtes and Saints' days. It is a pity, if only on the argument *ab convenienti,* that Saint Gregory, with his calendar, is not unanimously acceptable to these diverse peoples.

There are many periodical returns of festive or religious days among the Mahometans. On the 28th of September, A. D. 622, the prophet left Mecca for Medina. The last city was more faithful to him than Mecca. From this event comes the first day and year of the Hegira. Hegira literally means "emigrate." It is from an Arab word called *Heudjret.* Seventeen years after the Hegira, Caliph Omar, brother-in-law of the Prophet, felt the necessity of having a chronological system, and as the Arabs were learned in such matters at that time, they called a grand council of the Mussulman notables and arranged a system. By common accord, the era of two hundred millions of people upon our planet begins on the first of Muherrem, or the 28th of September, in the year of our Lord, 622.

The Mussulman's year is eleven days shorter than our own. There is no equivalent for the months of his calendar. The month which corresponds to January in one year will, sixteen years afterward, correspond with July.

The Turkish month takes its name and its season from the moon, and the Turkish Ramazan fast runs through every season in the course of thirty-three years. It is hard on the poor work-man and boatman in summer; but they stand fast by their prin-ciples, despite thirst and fatigue. When Ramazan ends, do these Faithful rush for their *kebabs* and *pilafs?* No: they have their pipes filled and the match in hand. Tobacco has a prior attach-ment to food.

This *Muherrem*, or the first day of the month of that title, is celebrated by all Moslems, from the highest to the lowest. The Hegira, which occurred in A. D. 1886, was the thirteen hundred and fourth. As an anniversary, it has not so much significance among the Arabs as among the Turks; nor has it had, until lately, so much among the Moslems of Turkey. The Turks are beginning to keep the Western custom of New Year's Day. There is a recep-tion at the palace of Yildiz. It begins at 9 o'clock in the morn-ing, by our time; when the functionaries—civil, military and religious—repair to the palace to pay their homage to the Sultan and Caliph. The two leading chamberlains receive the visitors for His Majesty. Many formalities are exchanged. One inter-esting custom is the presentation of money to those who call. This money is literally a New Year's gift—a *Monharremic*. Presents with the Turk symbolize happiness. They indicate a wish for the prosperity of the recipient. Last year there were a number of Turkish gold pieces specially minted for this purpose. To Osman Pasha, the hero of Plevna, was confided the function of distributing these coins to the various functionaries and the members of the household. They are considered as talismans. They bring blessings. The upper ten thousand of the Mahometans follow this example in their own households. So that New Year is really a day of gifts as well as of felicitations. Are the Foreign Ministers included in this precious ceremony? I regret to say, only so far as the Dragoman, or interpreter, of the Legation is concerned. He goes to the palace for the pur-pose of presenting the congratulations of his chief, the Minis-ter. I wish it had fallen to my lot to bear away one of the small purses. They make a pretty souvenir—made as they are of white tulle, containing some of the fresh golden mint drops, which glisten with pleasant associations. But I have a more enduring and tasteful souvenir of the Sultan. It pleases me to remember the decoration of the first class of the Order of the Medjidié, made a still more precious memorial, not only by the privilege accorded of dedicating this volume to His Majesty, but by the fact that, after I had resigned my post, and could no longer in any way, except as a good friend in a distant country, be accounted in any relation to the Sultan, he tendered me the order established to honor his father, Abdul Medjid, whom I saw in A. D. 1851, on my first visit to the capital. Such gifts in our little life, which is " rounded with a sleep," seem like dreams of faïrie land; so remote are they from our ordinary experiences.

In order to usher in the New Year, a rocket is fired from the heights of Kandilli. It is the best ground of vantage for observation to be found on the Straits. The rocket is a signal for the precise moment of the New Year. It is regulated, as it is said, by the southing of Sirius, which occurs three-fourths of a minute before midnight. Responsive signals in the shape of blue and Bengal fires flash back from the hills of Hissar, Bebek and Scutari. Then the city knows that its Mahometan New Year has begun.

On the first day of the year the Gregorian Armenians, through their Patriarch, Monsieur Vehabédian, make their prayers for the preservation of the precious life of the Sultan. The Greek churches may do the same. The English do.

The Meolond is another fête day. It is the anniversary of the birth of the Prophet. To announce it, a sunset gun is fired at Tophane and from the men-of-war in the Golden Horn. The day begins at sunset. The mosques, public buildings and ships are illuminated. The streets are filled with people. It is celebrated with pomp at the palace. An assemblage gathers to see the Sultan go to the mosque. Carriages throng the palace gates with officers of high rank; some in simple morning dress and others ablaze with decorations. Illustrious strangers appear at the *Corps de Garde.* The troops are there, as if it were Salemlik. The Sultan appears with the usual company; sometimes on horseback, sometimes in a magnificent phaeton and a pair of white barbs, which he drives. The ceremony inside of the mosque is according to ancient usage. It consists of special prayers for the festival, and the reading, by the almoners of the palace, of passages from the biography of the Prophet. Refreshments are offered, sweetmeats being the prevailing delicacy. Pounds and pounds of bonbons are distributed among the spectators. The dignitaries are admitted to the Throne-room, and pay their respects to the Sultan.

The 10th of March, old style, comes around. It is the anni-

versary of the birth of the Emperor of Russia. That must be
celebrated, also, by the good Slavs. Constantinople is not so
bigoted but that a *Te Deum* is possible in the Russian Embassy
at Pera. At this ceremony all the *personnel* of the embassy
and all the Russian boats and folks which are in and around the
harbor assist. They know how to assist, and sing too. Then
follows the customary salutations to the Russian Minister from
the Russian colony. Then there is a grand dinner in the evening, and all the Slavs secretly rejoice in some dim future connected
with her orthodox religion in St. Sophia, and her rule in the olden
home of its prelates and rulers.

The Greek Church signalizes its felicity upon the first day of
the year in the old style. The Russian Embassy, at that time,
has mass said and the *Te Deum* sung in their chapel, in the presence of their embassy, including its male and female heads. They
are all in full uniform. The Montenegrin Minister is there, along
with the Servian, and many Bulgarians attend. It is a Slavonic
occasion. Delegates from the Patriarchs often attend. After
the religious services are over, the Russian Minister receives a
deputation from the colony in grand state, for it is a welcome to
the Greek, Russian and other orthodox residents of Constantinople. It may be more. It is meant as a significant sign of the
coming time when Mahometanism and the Sultan shall give place
to the Czar and orthodoxy.

Whenever a prince becomes of age, as in the case of the Prince
Royal of Greece, last year, or a birthday of some princeling, king
or emperor happens, there is much made of it in the Legations and
churches. On the Greek occasion, in the Church of St. Maria,
the Minister, Monsieur Coundouriotti, and the members of the
consular and diplomatic bodies, were present, and a reception was
held afterward.

Whenever a Minister leaves Constantinople for another post,
as when Count Corti left for England or Monsieur Grouich for
Russia, there is much to-do about giving him a gallant send-off.
My impression is that they deserve and appreciate the good-will
which is loth to part with them; for while in service here most of
their life seems to consist in the perpetual recognition of courtesies, which they return with ceaseless and exemplary reiteration.

The Ramazan and Bairam fêtes have often been described.
The first is like our Lent; the second, our Easter. The Rama-

zan lasts a month or more.   It is during this fast, on the twenty-
fourth night, that the decrees of Mahometan fate are taken
from the preserved table by God's throne and settled for ever.
They are turned over to the angels to be executed.   As it was on
this night that Mahomet received his first revelation, it is called
*Kadir gejesy* or "night of power."

During Ramazan the good Moslem neither eats, drinks nor
smokes from sunrise to sunset.   He makes up for it after sunset.
Still, he is not physically happy by day or night.   Hence Bairam
is welcomed; not only because it terminates Ramazan, but it is
the beginning of joyance, with its receptions and congratulations.
Of these receptions, that of the Sultan is supreme for its splendor.
It is both religious and civil, and all the dignitaries, including the
diplomats, are on hand at the palace to partake in and enjoy the
spectacle.

The Bairam is always hailed as no other gala season.   To the
faithful, the salvo at sunset which ushers in Bairam is a cheerful
sound.   Annoyances, dyspepsia and wrongs disappear.   All that
is associated with hospitality, fun, frolic, good temper and congratulations are ushered in with noisy exhilaration.   All the gay
colors and rich silks and satins of the higher class, and all the
bright wardrobes of the lower class, are worn in scrupulous neatness upon the streets.   The Turk then puts on his best suit of
store clothes.   The muslin of his turban is as unflecked as polar
snow. The fez is no longer soiled.  The metropolis is dressed in holiday attire.   Music pervades the streets, plays at the doors of the
houses, and is rewarded with gifts of charity, not in money altogether, but in articles of all kinds, so that the musicians go home
from their *charavari* with laden baskets.   Neighbors and friends
make the Turkish salute and salaam.   They kiss their fingers across
squares.   From early morning there is an animated scene on the
water and in the streets.   The vessels are decorated from boom to
truck.   Gilded boats have their finest tapestries and are manned
by their best oarsmen.   The very gulls and other sea birds fly
around screaming their joy at the vanishing of Ramazan and the
advent of Bairam.

But the grand pageant at the palace is not now what it was
before the burning down of the Seraglio.   Then the officers of the
government, civil and ecclesiastical, thronged to this spot. Strangers were allowed, as they are to-day, to visit the grand kiosk—the

charming pavilion which overlooks the lovely scene. In the olden time, when the gates of the Seraglio were opened, it was a gay throng that passed through the court and lingered under the immense plane-trees, some of which remain to this day. In its general features the Bairam at the palace now is the same as that of the olden time. There is some marked change, especially in the dress of the people and officials. The Ministers and others are clad in straight, methodistical frock coats. Where now are the flowing robe, the big round turban and the enormous breeches? The coats are covered with embroidery and decorations, but the tarbouch, or fez, is not very grandiose and impressive. No one, unless he has seen it, can imagine the splendid appearance of the soldiers and officers on these occasions. Embroidery, in which the Turks excel, silver and gold embroidery, and swords damascened and gilded, in which they also excel, give their tasteful richness to the scene. The housings of the horses, the very playfulness of the horses, and the ornamentation of the carriages indicate that the joyful time has come. On these occasions we have an idea of the wealth of "Ormus and of Ind," in all their gorgeousness of apparel and luxury of power.

At first, the way in which the Ottoman measures his time seems odd to us. His day commences at sunset, and the hours of the day swing around in that cycle to sunset again. But the most curious performance for a nation which has drawn so much from the first astronomers of Arabia, is that by which the recurrence of the festive day of Bairam is regulated. On one occasion the Ramazan lasted only twenty-eight days. This was not because the moon failed in punctuality; but probably the Astronomer Royal, and not the moon, was at fault, or grew tired of fasting. On another occasion the feast of Ramazan was prolonged for thirty-one days. This was owing to the negligence of a judge. He lost his head for his *laches*. Is it not somewhat comical that, in a land where there is ample mathematical and astronomical knowledge, its civil and ecclesiastical rulers do not rely upon exact science for the appearance of the moon or the setting of fasts and feasts? There must be no conjuring with Arabic numerals or zodiacal signs in these matters. The moon must be seen actually and optically by some one or more persons, and these must be credible witnesses. They must give their testimony that they saw the moon; mark you, one moon only.  If they saw two or more moons, it would go to their credibility.  These witnesses must present themselves before the cadi of Constantinople, and prove the fact circumstantially.  The cadi is sometimes an ecclesiastical judge; one of the canons, as it were.  He weighs the testimony religiously.  If the evidence is reliable and the circumstances of the case are satisfactorily proven, Bairam is fixed for the next morning ; very early in the morning, as we know to our sorrow.  The first witness of the moon receives a gift of ten thousand piastres ($450).  A piastre is nearly four and one-half cents.  The second witness receives a gift of five thousand piastres, and the third of twenty-five hundred. The witnesses selected to catch the first glimpse of the moon are special functionaries of the Sheik-ul-Islam.  There is great competition among them.

The witnesses of the appearance of her lunar majesty seek the highest point in the neighborhood from which the moon can first be seen ; and from which, reckoning very closely, they can bring the authentic news to the cadi in the city, before her majesty announces herself.  Last year Mount Olympus was selected as the point of observation of some of the witnesses.  Others selected certain Daghts, in Asia, nearer by, but not so high as Mount Olympus.  From these watch-towers what a race takes place !  At Modana, small steamers are kept puffing, to bear the news from Olympus to the city.  No pen of mine can describe the trial of speed which these witnesses make for the specific reward. May I draw on the pencil of fancy ?  One of the witnesses is on foot, another is upon a donkey, and a third on a dromedary; and a fourth, who was rather slow in getting up the mountain, is very fast in coming down.  He is mounted on a fleet horse.  Others in various ways seek to be the first with the glad tidings of great joy.

The Bairam which occurred the 2d of July, 1886, was a rare one in our experience.  The United States ship of war *Kearsarge* was in the Bosporus.  I was, in all hospitality, bound to look after her officers.  The Fourth of July was approaching.  The Commencements of the American College and the American Female Home School in Scutari were also on hand; all within two or three days, and Bairam was expected every moment!  We had been deprived of the privilege of Bairam the year before, owing to the breaking out of hostilities in Bulgaria; therefore, we were more than usually anxious to be on hand at the Palace of

MOON-GAZERS RUNNING FOR THEIR REWARD AT BAIRAM.

Dolma Bagtché when the artillery should announce that Bairam
had begun.  We were on the tiptoe of expectation.  Would it be
the 1st of July?  We were all fearful of it.  In that case
some of our engagements would be spoiled.  Is it to be the
2d?  We will not know until the guns are fired on the 1st.
We are at Prinkipo, fifteen miles from Constantinople.  In order
to reach Dolma Bagtché, we must voyage for two hours and a half
over the sea of Marmora in our launch.  Would we have good
weather and a smooth sea?  Besides, we have to make our toilet.
All will be hurry and confusion.  Luckily, the night before we
are advised.  A telegram comes from the First Chamberlain.
Translated it reads as follows:

" To His Excellency the American Minister, Prinkipo :

" In order to be present at the ceremony to-morrow, you will come in the
morning to the Palace of Dolma Bagtché, between one and half-past, time *à la
Turque*, in company with Madame Cox and Monsieur the first dragoman.

"Munir."

It will be noted that the time is half-past one, Turkish time.
That means six or seven hours after our time, according to
native reckoning ; so that, in order to be present at the 7 o'clock
reception at Dolma Bagtché, we have to sail over the ancient
Propontis by the light of the morning stars.

We arrive on time.  We meet our friends at the Hotel Royal.
There are several tourists from America to go with us.  Among
them is a bevy of "sweet girl graduates" from Chicago.  They
are alive to the grand occasion.

From the palace gates at Yildiz, mounted on a splendid white
Arab steed, the Sultan rides forth!  He rides down the declivity from the heights of Yildiz to the mosque of Dolma
Bagtché for prayers.  Lines of soldiers from all the regiments
guard his way.  The procession which follows him is brilliant.
There is the Sheik-ul-Islam, the spiritual head of the faith !
Behind him are the Grand Vizier, the Ministers, and all the dignitaries of the household—military, civil and domestic.  The crowds
on the streets are enormous.  Excitement and enthusiasm fill every
avenue.  Is this Turkey in decrepitude?  The fervor of the
reception accorded to the Sultan does not indicate the " Sick man.'
The weather is perfect.  The morning is fresh.  The scene is
charming.  The Sultan dismounts from his charger before the

mosque and enters. There is a hush in all the streets. The air seems full of the solemnity of prayer. At the end of a half hour the bugles sound. The artillery thunders. Its echoes resound from hill to hill. This is the signal that His Majesty has ended his devotions ! He is about to enter the palace ! The grand

INTERIOR STAIRCASE OF DOLMA-BAGTCHÉ PALACE.

reception ensues ! This is the jocund occasion of the year. The vociferous greetings of the troops and people are wildly joyous !

The deference shown to this Ruler and Father of the Faithful is beyond comprehension to the Western mind. We are accustomed to regard Turkey as almost dying, if not dead. Far from this being the case here, all is active loyalty and patriotic enthusiasm.

It is impossible to give a description of this palace of Dolma Bagtché. The eye alone can appreciate its grandeur and beauties. Its general view we have pictured in another chapter. Its gates, like fairy handicraft, "twined in many a freakish knot," and wrought into marble under the spell of Oriental Magi, have also been presented. Its staircase is now before us. It is only equaled in exquisite and beautiful proportion by the hall of reception. This is a splendid chamber.

The great hall is prepared for the ceremony before we arrive. After much kindly courtesy on the part of the Sultan's aids, who come to greet us at the gates of the palace, we are shown to the gallery of state. It overlooks the scene. Rich carpets of the Orient are laid over the marble pavements. They are arranged to indicate the stations for the throng of officials who come to pay festive homage. There is a throne in the midst of the chamber. It is covered by a cloth of gold. There is a band in an alcove, which discourses operatic music. There is a buffet near, where those who arose early may indulge in the refreshments of coffee and sandwiches. At 7 o'clock we are all prepared for the entrée. There is a hush in the vast chamber! From one corner of the hall emerges the Sultan! The cloth of gold is removed from the throne. Three young princes take their station near His Majesty; two are his nephews, one his son. The officers of the household are aligned near his person. Thus ushered by the grand master of ceremonies, this autocrat of forty millions of people is enthroned. The band plays the Imperial march. The assembled multitude shout, "Long live the Sultan!" The princely salutation is taken up by the crowds without. It rolls in patriotic outbursts through all the streets. The hand-kissing follows. First come the civil functionaries, from the Grand Vizier down. They approach on His Majesty's right. They make the regulation salute. It is a most singular performance. They press reverently to their forehead a broad scarf attached to the right arm of the throne, which is held during the ceremony by the First Chamberlain. Then they withdraw to their places. The naval and military officers now come to the front. They repeat the ceremony. Then the religious personages with great grace and dignity approach. They are upon

another line of carpets. They touch with lip and forehead the
Sultan's vestment. This is their especial privilege. It is sacred.
One is utterly dazed at the rich, ornate confusion of color and
costume which belong to this gracious Oriental proceeding.

We lean over the balcony to see what comes next. An *aide* is
near. We whisper to him :

" Who is that," we inquire, " in white robes, followed by officers in green ? "

" It is the Sheik-ul-Islam," responds the *aide*. " Those in green
are the Cazaskiers."

"What ! Are the orders known by their colors ? "

" Yes. Note two other orders ; one in green, one in violet—
and still another in dark blue. The last are the Stamboul
priesthood."

The Sheik-ul-Islam is the most conspicuous of those who
attend upon this ceremony. He is dressed in his white caftan ;
his turban of white is crossed in front by a band of gold. He is
next to the Sultan in religious rank, and when he undertakes to
make the salutation which is usual, the Sultan prevents the performance of the homage and meets him half way. All this goes
on while the band plays airs from some delightful opera and the
cannon thunders from fort to fort, and amid shouts of " Long live
the Sultan ! "

How long this ceremony occupies, it is impossible to recall ;
perhaps two hours. The music stops. The fifth act is ended—
without a tragedy. The members of the Imperial family retire to
the private room of the palace. There they receive the remainder of their Bairam felicitations.

We are particular in describing this ceremony, because it has
in it much of Oriental style. It is redolent of the days of the
early Sultans and Caliphs, who received at Bairam, in the Seraglio,
before its conflagration. Besides, at this ceremony we see the
high officials of the religious, civil, military and naval establishments. It does not entirely exclude the Foreign Ministers. We
are permitted to pay our special respects after the ceremony,
through our dragomans, at the palace of Yildiz.

There are two Bairam seasons. Seventy days after the one
just described is the festival of *Kurban Bairam.* It is the
feast of sacrifice. It is doubtless taken from the Jewish system.
It is a sacrifice of sheep and oxen, and lasts four days. Artil-

lery announces the beginning of this latter fête at 5 in the morning. At once the true Mussulman leaves his bed and begins the sacrifice. In every house at least one sheep must be sacrificed. It is a family offering. The meat is distributed to the poor, and a portion kept for the family. At the palace this sacrifice is on a grand scale. In the cemeteries the priests are busy making their sacrificial offerings upon the graves of departed relatives. A ram is killed for every member of the Imperial family at the palace. Where do these animals come from ? At the beginning of this Bairam, you see men and boys leading them around the streets gaily decorated. They are for sale. Sometimes, if the ram, by his good keeping, has grown beyond ordinary size, you will see a *hamal*, or slave, carrying him about the streets for the owner. Some of these sheep are of enormous bulk; the tail is no exception to the exaggeration. The rams sacrificed at the palace number about two hundred.

Before they are displayed or sacrificed, they are led into a Turkish bath, where they are soaked and washed. The wool being thus made immaculate, is carefully combed. Their horns are covered with thin golden leaves and adorned with artificial flowers and ribbons of gay hue. A mirror is attached to their foreheads, which are tinted with henna. This toilet of the royal rams is made in the park of the old Seraglio, after which they are conducted to Yildiz. It is quite a procession. Each ram is led by two men. The men wear an ancient costume. It is a long coat of green, adorned with gold lace. The heads of the men are shaven ; they wear a long green hat.

Along with this sacrificial ceremony there is a custom called the Bairam Namazi. This year it is performed at the mosque of Bechïktash, with much military and civic demonstration. The Sultan rides a magnificent white palfrey. It is from Bagdad. He is accompanied and followed by the court marshals and the high functionaries, civil and military; Osman Pasha, being Grand Marshal of the court, is on the right ; and Namyk Pasha, the Senior Marshal of the court, on the left. As the Sultan approaches each regiment in turn, the troops cheer and each band plays the Imperial March. When he reaches the mosque he is received with tremendous cheers. The devotions last a short time. The outsider cannot see ; he only hears the melodious chanting of the Arab Ulemas from Mecca. When the prayers are over, the troops form a line on either side to the Dolma Bagtché palace. Then are brought out the magnificent horses of the Imperial stud, harnessed and caparisoned. The saddle-cloths are of violet velvet, covered with rich embroideries of gold and pearls. They are distinguishable even amidst the decorations and lace of the Pashas, who mount the horses and follow His Majesty. The Sultan's suite is composed not only of the high dignitaries of his court, but all the superior officers of the realm on foot. Then the court carriages follow, surrounded by eunuchs on foot in their uniforms ; but their vigilance is not so keen as to prevent a bright eye and beauteous form, arrayed in diamonds and other jewelry, from making itself seen in the carriage and felt outside ; nor can the black guard prevent the eyes of the odalisque from shining like stars in a heaven of beauty.

Arriving at the palace, four rams are sacrificed at once. The Great Almoner recites prayers for the preservation of His Majesty. Then follows the ceremony inside the palace, which is not unlike that of the other Bairam, of which we had personal observation. Considering the condition of the Turkish realm at the last preceding Bairam; observing the intense loyalty now displayed on both these occasions, in this year of grace, 1886; and knowing the amiable and moderate qualities of the Sultan—the present is truly a season for gladness. No doubt the dignitaries of state so consider it. Turkey survives the dangers which the agitation in the Balkan Peninsula engenders. One reason why the ministry was dismissed at the Bairam season of 1885 was, that they advised instant war to suppress the insurrection in East Roumelia. The Sultan was wiser than his counselors. He called in a new ministry, and by self-restraint sheathed the sword that was half-drawn. His political foresight discerns that a war in Bulgaria about East Roumelia would involve Servia, Greece, Macedonia and Crete. Such a belligerency would involve Europe. The Powers observe the sagacity of this forbearance on the part of the Sultan. They recognize that in his wisdom lies the strength of the Ottoman power. Therefore, this last Bairam is a time of national and universal rejoicing, not only for the Sultan and his Ottomans, but for those who love peace and forbearance rather than war and passion. Long may this wise Sultan remain as father of the Faithful ! Long may he enjoy the recurrence of the feasts of Bairam!

# CHAPTER XXXVIII.

### THE HAREM—INNOVATIONS, DRESSES AND INCIDENTS.

THOSE who say that Constantinople is permanent, and likely to remain as she was a half century ago, are not competent judges, unless they have seen the city inside and outside within this period.

It is thirty-five years since I saw the city first. Five years after that time the Crimean War came. It changed nearly every phase of life. A different condition of men and things existed before that war. For example: never was there such a cascade of rough-hewn stones as the street, which yet remains, known as Step Street. It was the main thoroughfare between Galata and Pera. Now a railway brings you and your merchandise up the high hill of Pera and back to its foot at Galata. The old walls, towers and the moat have been modernized. The moat is a vegetable garden. What with the aid of conflagrations and reasonable police, the streets of Pera, which were so narrow that you could almost shake hands with your neighbor across them, are a memory. In 1851 they were unlighted. They had no names or numbers. Now it is different, at least in Pera. Now there is a local post. I will not avouch for its promptitude. They have a telegraph, and it is well administered. It is under the government control. They have railway lines and a tramway. Here and there, even in old Stamboul, may be seen some stray cabs, called *talikas*. The dogs still remain in all their howling perversity, and so do the dervishes. In 1851 it was dangerous to go through the streets of Pera and Galata after sundown. Practical improvements have certainly grown apace.

Since leaving Constantinople, the rumors have been rife of various innovations, not merely in the world of Islam, but inside the harem and seraglio. It is said that the ladies of the harem have heretofore occupied particular apartments, which have only been known to the Sultan and the Chief of the Eunuchs. The innovation consists in sharing this knowledge with the physicians attached to the household. Certainly, if this be the case, no more worthy selection could be made than that of Doctor Mavroyéni, who is the chief physician. He is the father of the present Turkish Minister to the United States. It is said that each Sultana now enjoys the luxury of a visiting card, which she affixes on the outer door of her apartment. Where there is much visiting to

A TURKISH LADY OF 1851.

and from room to room, doubtless many facilities are given by this new mode of communication.

The story is told that one hundred and fifty of the women of the seraglio have been recently vaccinated. This was done in a large hall, under the superintendence of four eunuchs, by an Italian surgeon—but not without some innovation? The surgeon is stationed in front of a huge screen, behind which are the women. A hole is made in the screen, large enough to allow the female arm to pass through. The surgeon does not see the face of his fair patient. But in order to avoid the possibility of seeing it, two of the eunuchs stand over the operator, and the instant the operation is concluded, cover his face with a shawl.

Whether this be true or not, and I am inclined to doubt it, there has been much change in the sanitary regulations of the harem. Hereby hangs a little story, whose locality is farther east than Stamboul. It is told of a young Oriental houri. She is anxious to be cured of some temporary illness, but has no faith in the native physician. She wants a European doctor. She arranges cunningly to be rumored for a time as a famous male saint, one who had accomplished the great pilgrimage to Mecca. She dresses herself in saintly robes. She is quite reserved and learned. Had not the saint achieved a great reputation ? In fact, she is one of the household, if not a wife, of the saint she represents. She plays a shrewd trick; for when the doctor, who was ostensibly summoned by this saint, arrives at the harem, he is led, not without tremor, by the eunuch through many an empty room without carpet or seat. He wearies with his long trudging through the many seatless chambers. At last he reposes upon a raised window-ledge. The guide disappears. There is a dead silence, only broken by the hum of a wasp or a blue-bottle. Time hangs heavily; the hours pass; the doctor becomes impatient. Thinking that he is imprisoned, or that he is played upon, he shouts at the full pitch of his voice. The servant returns hurriedly; his manner is changed. He conducts the doctor to the holy man's apartment. The saint remains reserved. He does not rise on the doctor's entrance, nor offer the doctor a cushion. The doctor has "to take the floor in his own right," as they say in Congress. Then the holy man pretends to regret the want of civility; it had not been intentional. The doctor sees his patient—that is, a piece of *her*, for it was the odalisque. She thrusts a plump arm from out of a large veil, and takes care that naught but her lips should be visible; she puts out her tongue; the prescription is written on a cigarette paper, and the doctor retires amidst roars of laughter from a crowd of veiled women, who form the saint's seraglio.

There is much objurgation from the old Turk against the changes that are going on within the harem. The innovations have begun, not merely in the dress of its inmates, but in the very furniture. The divan is being crowded out by chairs. Girandolas of Austrian manufacture, portières and curtains of rich crimson silk velvet, with borderings of gold, beautiful beyond expression, still remain to give their gorgeous orientalism.

It is a pity that the rascals in Anatolia should have been allowed to drive a prosperous trade by forging ancient coins; for this counterfeiting has detracted from the handsome bracelets and necklaces which Turkish ladies wear, and which are composed of these ancient golden coins. As they were once very scarce, they were highly appreciated as a superb style of ornament. Their disuse is an innovation, but is it reform?

What is the boy selling yonder? Let us ask. Orris root for tooth-brushes and tooth-picks. His business is brisk, for the tooth-brush, in spite of the prejudice of the Koran against the hair of the hog, has become a part of the furniture of the harem. Is this also a sign of reform? A little! Even the *henna* no longer stains the fingers of the houri. That custom, at least, has been in great part abolished. Is not this reform?

I sometimes wish that Spanish almonds had never been invented or imported into Turkey. The beautiful Turkish woman, whether the effeminate Circassian or the brilliant Georgian, oftentimes, previous to the great event of her life, plucks out every hair of her eyebrows; then she replaces them by two stripes of black dye from the burnt almond. These stripes are raised about an inch high upon the forehead. Does this fashion indicate a Tartar or Turkish relation with the Chinese? It used to be more of a habit with the Turkish women, on great occasions, than it is at present. If this custom is a matter of coquetry, do they not mistake human nature? In many ways they exercise good taste in dressing, but this fantastic eyebrow is atrocious. Sometimes they paint the eyebrows to meet across the nose; sometimes they raise them at the outer point to the temple. These caprices of the harem are barbaric. They are falling into deserved desuetude. Here is room for—reform. Indeed, although there is much the same general costume among the Turkish women now as in 1851, there are differences, apparent even in the sketches here presented.

I have the best authority—no less than that of Mrs. Walker, an artist who has been frequently called upon to paint portraits of princesses and other ladies of quality in the harems—that time has written wonderful changes in its inner life. It is no longer the lustreless and lazy Ottoman life, where education and employment are forbidden, and where nothing is to be heard except the tinkle of the zebec, the notes of the fiddle, the rattle of the tambourine, and a chorus of female voices, which require immense distances to mellow into harmony.

The police orders are frequent as to the rearrangement of the

A TURKISH LADY OF 1887.

costume, as if the Turkish women were endeavoring to assimilate their habits and difficulties to the freer life of the Frank. Still, there is great reserve as to the harem, and the recent innovations by which European doctors have been called in to vaccinate and otherwise care for the physical well-being of its inmates is an accomplished and significant fact. There is, therefore, great improvement in the care of women and children under the new conditions of medical progress.

It is by no means easy to have the entrée to the inner life of Turkey. Sometimes necessity is the password, even to the doors of the seraglio. Sometimes the vanity of its inmates touches the magic spring. Mrs. Walker, to whom I refer, is the author of an interesting book on Eastern life and scenery. She entered the harem because she was an artist and a teacher, and the inmates desired her to paint the portrait of a Sultana ! The account of her preliminary and other visits and of her attempt to tame some of the inmates, and especially of the Sultana's contumacy about the portrait, are humorous. It seems that the Sultana · was determined to be painted in the newest style, and not in the old Ottoman costume. Hence many tears and groans from the artist, for the Sultana had to be gratified. The innovations which are beginning to make their way into the Turkish harem, especially in matters of dress, seem to have made it impossible for the artist to secure either a natural position or the ordinary habit and habitudes of the regal lady. The artist was compelled, therefore, to contemplate the conclusion of her work without approving it, but which seemed to content her model.

Before leaving Constantinople my wife had presented to her a couple of large French dolls dressed up in the latest style of the harem. They represent the wardrobe of a lady of rank, with her *antarys*, *schalvas*, and *feridjies*, slippers, boots, and clothes, gloves, head-dress, and all. The material is rich in color and costly, and is made to harmonize inside of the harem with the furniture. The very dust-pans of the seraglio are generally of solid silver, the coffee *zarfs*, *chibouque* rings, and even the bathing wooden clogs are incrusted with jewelry. But my inartistic pen is not equal to the task of a man-milliner. I delegate the description of these dresses, for the benefit of my lady readers, to one of their sex. I present my wife's account :

"The costume of the Turkish lady for the street is very simple. The *feridjie* is a large overwrap, much like our ulster or waterproof. It has the additional large cape, which would correspond to our dolman, worn over the ulster or *feridjie*, forming in part the sleeves, though often the sleeves are made separately —full and flowing. The garment is generally made of rich silks, very long. It fastens up all the way in front, concealing entirely the in-door costume beneath. The dark shades of silk are preferred for ordinary wear, while the brightest colors are none too

TURKISH LADY AND SLAVE IN THE HAREM,

gay for gala days. The *yashmak* is the head-covering It is of
thin white mull and covers the head entirely. A band or fold
passes across the forehead, just above the eyes. Another and
similar band passes just below the eyes, both being fastened at
the back with pins and falling beneath the *feridjie*. Thus only
the eyes are seen, save now and then, when the features are dimly
revealed if the veil be not too thick. When this revelation becomes
too common, an edict is issued from the palace to correct the
custom, and thick veils are again commanded. The gay silk parasol completes this out-door costume.

"As to the house costume, it has greatly changed since the
earlier days. Now we hear it is the height of a Turkish lady's
ambition to wear a French costume—I mean the ambition of
those who are called the more advanced in their midst. Of
the old style, the full trousers were always worn. They are
known as *schalvas*, of yellow silk. They were fastened by a
sash, and embroidered elegantly. Over these were worn long
flowing robes, cut in three separate trains, each sweeping about a
half yard on the floor. The train at the back is longer and more
flowing than the two in front. The stuffs of which they are made
were Oriental, with many woven threads of silver or gold. A fancy
head-dress, and diamonds on neck and hair, complete the attire.
In later times the front trains gave way to shortened robes, until
now they are almost abandoned. Of course, when the street wrap
was assumed, these trains were pinned up and entirely hidden
beneath the *feridjie*. On festive days the banks of the "Sweet
Waters" are lined with bevies of Turkish ladies, reclining on
their Turkish rugs, in groups or by families. Now and then
they vary this rest by a promenade along the stream, and then it
is observed that they are quite as fond as their European sisters
of the silk-embroidered hose and slipper which adorn the feet of
civilized communities. Only among the latter they are reserved
for in-door wear and not for out-door promenade. The little
stream is thronged with the picturesque caïques, with their gilded
prows and crimson velvet draperies. The children are not so
romantic-looking. They resemble rather, in their quaint robes,
little old men and women, owing to the style of making their garments touch the ankles.

"Sweets, ices, lemonade, and cold water are handed around by
the carriers on these crowded festal days. It is thought that this

mode of celebrating a festal day cannot be wildly exciting; yet there are slanderous tongues that assert that there is much mischief done with the dark eyes of these houris coquetting with the gay and dashing "uniforms" which fill the promenade."

\*　　\*　　\*　　\*　　\*　　\*　　\*

The afternoon drive to the "Sweet Waters" is, after all, a part of the seclusion of the Turkish women. They are in the outer world, but not of it, except in fancy. Observe that elegant turnout at the door of the haremlik! It is a pretty brougham. The horses are from the steppes of Russia or the prairies of Hungary. They are neat, long-tailed, spirited animals. Two females appear, and are carefully helped by the slave into the vehicle. The coachman does not get a glimpse of the ladies. They are screened with their sunshades. The brown satin cushions receive their forms; the hand-mirror is brightened, and to its reflection they commit their glances. They are then ready for their confectionery and their drive. Their lips are of carnation; their faces are of a rich, creamy delicacy. Whether on the Gezireh drive at Cairo, on the Bois at Paris, or the Row in London, in the Park at New York, or on the way to the "Sweet Waters" of Europe, these fair ones are not disposed to be too much concealed from the world.

Only a few of the rich garments which fill the wardrobes of the harem are ever worn. They are too heavy. They are only for display. They are presents from the head of the house, and bestowed with great ceremony. As in all the harems, so even in the seraglio, the visitors, whom the master of the house does not see unveiled, drive him from the penetralia of his home to seek a refuge in the Salemlik. The porter never allows ingress without some testimonial. This requires the countersign of the black *aga*, who keeps the key to the cage. But why call it a cage? Nothing can be more delightful, especially in warm summer weather, than a *konak* on the hills or a palace on the shores of the Straits. At midday the inmates take their siesta. There is a lullaby in the laughing ripple of the current almost at their feet. There is an occasional measured plash of passing boats; the regular rattle of the oar-locks; the murmuring of music in other chambers; besides a drowsiness and a lack of garish light, which reminds one of the Cave of Sleep in Spenser's "Faërie Queen."

When a stranger is admitted to such a palace, she is compelled to wait awhile. Slaves appear from time to time, with the expression, "Sheimdy!" "Sheimdy!" This means that after a little—directly—the lady of the house will appear. Then comes a stately Circassian dame. She is authorized to conduct the visitor up the staircase across the salon into the presence of the mistress, the chief *hanoum*. If she be a Sultana, her highness, observing Frankish ways, is seated in an arm-chair near the trellised window overlooking the Bosporus. She is arranging her toilet, even to her silk antary, in French style, for the skirt has not put in a general appearance within these sacred precincts.

Most of the stately dames of the richer harems are Circassian, of fair skin, with blonde or rather chestnut hair, gray or grayish-blue eyes, a charming mouth and a seraphic smile. The Sultana who is to be portrayed by our artist, and to whom reference has been made, is only nineteen. She is bright and well informed as to the current news. She cultivates those harsh, guttural sounds which are the sign of the Arabic, Persian, or aristocratic utterance of the Turk. She is a daughter of Abdul Medjid. She marries for political considerations. Being indoctrinated with the reform movement, which at that time was making many a heart flutter in the dovecotes of the East, she is determined to be painted, if not altogether, yet in part, as wearing a European lady's ball dress. Of course, the diamonds are abundant on the dress. They are worth a satrapy, and, in numbers and abundance, uncounted.

Her harem consists of about one hundred women and girls. They are variously bestowed in the palace. As a sign of their belonging to this special harem they wear a *toque* of red cloth, with a small blue tassel hanging from it at the back of the head. It is a symbol of subjection, like the fez of an Ottoman. From the observation made of this harem, it is certain that its inmates are kindly cared for, not merely in the every-day repasts, but in the amusements which they improvise.

The visitor at Constantinople who goes on Friday to see the Sultan enter the mosque at prayers, may, if he keeps his eyes alert, notice many servants bearing circular wooden trays going to or coming from the palace of Yildiz. These trays are covered by a thick leather cap, and the whole tied up in a woolen cloth. They are borne upon the head of the stout servitor whom I have pictured in Chapter VI. From them are furnished the meals of those who depend upon the Sultan, or are connected with him by blood. The viands are delicate, and the Sultana whose portrait is to be taken by our artist receives her share of them from the Imperial kitchen at Dolma Bagtché.

Another observation about this *quasi*-imperial harem: the pasha who married this Sultana is never allowed to see the younger females of the harem. They scatter when he comes, like a covey of quail on the appearance of a hunter. So, too, when the Sultana's brothers arrive. When the Sultan himself comes, no concealment is necessary. He has the supreme right of gazing at any of his subjects. He can order the veil to be removed!

There is much teaching going on in the palace of this Sultana, most of the teachers being native. What they learn is Arabic, Turkish, reading, writing, and sometimes arithmetic. Some of the instruction is religious, and some of the girls of the harem say their prayers. There are classes in music and dancing, and lessons on the string instruments which are peculiar to the East. In the afternoon, if it be favorable, the garden opens for these houri. Every Thursday they may veil themselves, and, with their gala-colored *feridjies*, and under the guard of a eunuch, disport themselves outside. They make excursions to some favorite place, returning before the sun goes down. The Sultana generally remains at home, taking her exercise within her grounds. Here she has a little lake, with a little boat. She has a horse with a side-saddle, and here she rides! She has a carriage, and drives about within her own petty domain. When some unusual attraction allures her from her seclusion, she carries her harem with her, and under the command of a black *aga* she takes her walk or ride either to the "Sweet Waters" of Asia or of Europe.

Our artistic friend, in making a picture of this palace and its inmates, gives a very strange lesson as to their endeavors to be amused. The Sultana has a military band. They are Georgians and Circassians. One lady plays the flute, another the horn, and a moon-faced beauty the trombone; while another fair one, Yildiz by name—meaning the star of the harem—crouches pensively at the feet of a blue-eyed, dark-haired girl of the Orient, who could not sit down because she must saw a monstrous double-bass viol. The double-bass is a Chaldean. Her cheek is olive, her eyes immense, and the fringes of her eyelids astounding. Being of mountain growth, she has a wildness of temper and aspect

THE MUCHOIR-DANCE IN THE HAREM.

which nothing but the big double-bass can tame. They are dressed after the manner of musicians. They wear a tunic and pantaloons of white woolen stuff, faced with blue, and little shakos to match. They are quite martial in their appearance. Perhaps they furnish the hint for many of the fine displays upon our melodramatic stage.

How are they taught music? Some of the masters in the theatres of Constantinople are called in to give lessons. While practising with the masters, the women use a strip of muslin over the head and shoulders, not always a successful veiling of their charms.

Not satisfied with the band without utilizing it, the Sultana must have a comic dance, then a Turkish dance and a pantomime. A bright girl plays the young hero, who is a Claude Melnotte, except that he is a house-painter and not a gardener. There is a heroine and a porter, each of whom has a heavy father, and there is a Harlequin and a Columbine. As lawyers say—this arrangement is bad on demurrer for multifariousness. To crown the whole, a ballet is led by the "Antelope"—a beautiful girl of that name. The pantomime is a rendition of European life, but the ball which follows is more bizarre than the pantomime is fantastic. It is painfully unrealistic. Our artist assists them in the preparation. One of her instructions is, that if a lady drops her handkerchief her partner should pick it up and restore it, with a bow. All the ladies of the ball provide themselves with gay bandanas, and while dancing the mazurka, the galop or the polka, and especially in the quadrille, the floor is inconveniently strewn with handkerchiefs. The ball becomes farcically European by this extraordinary politeness. I do not claim any royalty for any performance which may be suggested by these revelations of the harem, but doubtless many of the most interesting of our light and spectacular dramas have their source in the contrasts, gayeties, oddities, simplicity and splendor of these Oriental homes.

The life which every day passes in the ordinary harem is not unlike that which I have described as prevalent in this palace. In the harem of a well-to-do Turk there is a leading lady called the *buyuk hanoum.* She is the principal of the establishment—the only wife, perhaps, of the pasha. Her home may be full of female relatives, for the Turk is nothing if not hospitable. Now and then a buffoon is on good terms with the family, and especially with the children. One thing, however, is to be remarked : the very young girls do not wear the yashmak or the *feridjie*, but otherwise their costume is almost the same as their mother's, while that of the boy is very comical. Almost before they are weaned they are dressed up in the full uniform of a pasha or military officer— sword, belt, fez and epaulets. Imagine such a child, when tired of his uniform, rushing to his milk-mother for his natural refreshment.

Generally a harem is made up of the women of various nationalities. Sometimes it is difficult to harmonize them. I should imagine that in the winter season, owing to the peculiar structure of the houses and the insufficient caloric of the charcoal pans, there would not be very much visiting, and probably not as much contentment, as in spring or summer.

There is something inside the harem which reminds one of the nomadic ancestors of these people. The very beds lie around as if about to be picked up, packed and carried off. Great wicker trunks and camel's-hair sacks are handy, in which the rich stuffs, apparel and furniture may be stowed away in a hurry; so that at the shortest notice the domestic paraphernalia of a family may either be packed in these round wicker trunks, ready for the caïque or the back of a donkey, or in these camel-hair sacks, which suggest the wandering Seljukians of six centuries ago. Besides, as fires are common, it is convenient to pounce upon the dresses and furniture, when in portable shape, and save them from the flames. In the larger houses there is a watchman, kept going her or his rounds about the building, so as to prevent and extinguish conflagrations.

The slaves of the household are paid very little in money. They save nothing; for what they receive goes for the trinkets sold by the itinerant Jewesses who come along the quay or hills, or hang about the harems. Still, the slaves are never harshly treated, and if they are sent out or given away in marriage, they are always cared for when their proprietors are people of reasonable opulence. In the Ramazan season this life of the harem is much modified. It is an error to suppose that the women are regarded, either in the teachings of the Koran or otherwise, as soulless persons.

When these inmates take the opportunity of their freedom to move around the city with their peerless beauty half displayed, either upon foot or in the slow progress of their carriages at the grand promenades, there may be chances for some flirtation. A forward girl may make mischief for a whole harem or family. She may not mean it ; but she may be so childish as to smile inadvertently on strangers. Her signs and coquetry really go for nothing; but the vanity of the other sex is inflamed, and trouble ensues. Existence inside the harem is too vapid for some constitutions. Some of the harsh objurgations about these beauties may have a piquant foundation. Doubtless there is more smoke than fire in these stories. When we read in an American paper of the improper, fascinating and mysterious beauties of Constantinople, and their harem life, I fail to find the facts to bear out the romancing.

I have been told by a gentleman, now a leading lawyer of New York, and formerly a teacher of mathematics in the American (Robert) College, upon the hills of Roumeli-Hissar, that he and the students were accustomed to promenade along the stony quays, even as far down as Bechïktash. In the time of Abdul Aziz, the palace, was full of the wives and odalisques of this amorous Sultan. They could be seen only in dim profile, by our professor and the students, behind the lattices. Were they heard ? They knew who the young men were and where from. They were in the habit of hailing them without fear of the eunuch, the times being troublous and the ebony people full of intrigue. What do you think these houri call our innocent peripatetics of the quay ? In sweet notes they cry out:

"*Kuzu Amerikànji !*"    Lamb of America!

Sometimes they add:

"*Sheker*," which is the Arab root of our word sugar. It must have been provoking to hear their salutation:

"*Sherifiniz haïr ola èng ghyuzèl chok kuzu*," or, to translate freely:

"Good evening, most pretty and much confectionated lamb."

These students still live to make autonomy in Bulgaria, preach the gospel in Armenia, and practice law in New York. They were not made into lamb chops by the headsman of Aziz. These young men were as innocent as the lambs to which they were likened; and the young women equally so. Still, they were playful. Are not lambs playful by nature ?

The most beautiful of the women of the capital have a way, in the presence of the sterner sex, of revealing, coquettishly, the contour of the face, and the exquisite complexion which their incessant bathing bestows. I have in my mind an article in an American paper purporting to have been written last May from Constantinople. It pretends to give a sensational account of the conduct of these beauties in their promenades by the "Sweet Waters." While their husbands are devoutly smiting their breasts in the mosques, the Turkish ladies, it is hinted, are driving in their carriages, enveloped in clouds of gauze and decked with jewelry. Where is the eunuch? it is asked. He sits by the coachman. How can he prevent or eclipse the flashing of the black, swimming, languid eye? The thin yashmak has not the courage to conceal such eyes! A voluptuous form, delicately small milk-white hands, blonde locks, or perhaps now and then raven hair, features not at all coarse—these are all hidden. The eye alone must bear all the odium of an intriguante.

These stories are born of the sensual pen. Some writer desires to get his penny-a-line, and he represents the *hanoum*, not as giving her numerous lovers the sack, in our homely phrase, but as actually killing them for self-safety. And thus a story goes, that a beautiful houri of a pasha's harem in Cairo actually killed one hundred and twenty beautiful Greek gentlemen, whom she had induced by her flirtations to enter her siren home—and all within three brief years! And thus, too, the old story about the sacks filled with such degenerate beauties being sunk in the river where it was deepest. These are the illusions of the romancist. The Moslem cares more than is represented about the defection in his harem. But is he not a Moslem? What is writ is writ, and he can divorce and wed again!

Among the fables which are related by the amateur tourist for the open-eyed wonder of his fair cousins at home, is the description of the magnificent buildings and romantic adventures upon the superb streets through which he has the pleasure to pass in surveying these lands of old renown. I have read an account of a young writer who said that as he passed through some of the streets they seemed deserted. He could fancy himself walking through the streets of Pompeii, when, hark! a light laugh is heard! He looks up. Voilà! A pair of sparkling black eyes dance at him for a moment behind the jalousie, and then disappear. He advances a little farther; he hears a gentle cough, then a flower from an upper casement drops at his feet from a tiny jeweled hand, and the romance ends. These mysterious revelations are made more entrancing by the sound of a soft Turkish love-song, but no stenographer is possible, and the susceptible young traveler cudgels his head to know whether he is living in the resplendent afternoon of the nineteenth century or has been transported back to the golden days of Haroun Al-Raschid.

One of these houris is upon the streets of Pera. She drops her fan. Her jeweled hand is reluctant to reach for it; the eunuch is not prompt enough; the carriage stops; the fan is picked up by a handsome giaour; the eunuch is sent to a restaurant for a glass of sherbet; she writes a little note on a cigarette tablet, with her dainty diamonded pencil, and, making a ball with the small leaf, drops the billet, which the youthful admirer picks up with rapture. Thus a rendezvous is said to be arranged, generally in some fashionable millinery establishment on the Grand Rue or in some other resort in Stamboul. It is a pity to emasculate such pretty tales. They are from the inner consciousness of the writer. I venture to say that no one knows of any such extraordinary practices.

Nothing is more dangerous, especially for a Christian man, than thus to dally. One case is always cited, and only one. It is so exceptional as to prove the rule otherwise. That is the case of the mother of Izzet Bey. The latter is a noted exquisite of the capital. She was married to a son of Fuad Pasha, the Grand Vizier, some few years ago. She was a rare woman, with all the accomplishments of the East and West. She received Christians at her house. She eloped with a Belgian secretary of Legation. In three days the pair were in Paris. Of course she was married, and yet lives, as it is said, a happy life. This case is one among ten thousand, and not altogether unlovely.

It is no wonder that something of intrigue which borders on the humorous, is used for the purpose of receiving proper medical attendance. The day of incantation is being supplanted by medical science, and the diseases which too partial mothers sometimes create, by cramming their infants with indigestible food, are yielding to better sense and medical skill.

The Turkish woman is neither so bad nor so good as she is painted. If I should pick out one prevailing quality, I should say that she is a good eater. Elsewhere I have described a Turkish meal. But nothing can describe the amount of confectionery and tobacco consumed in the harem, and outside, at the picnics of its inmates. The *hanoum* is inordinately fond of jewelry, and has just enough vanity to be interesting. Her coquetry is not of the perilous kind. She obeys her lord and master passively. Her peculiar affections, judging by her associations, are with her children, her slaves and friends. No one can justly say that the Turkish mother, notwithstand ng much slander about the premature destruction of the infant, has not great maternal love. Unless educated after the European method, she is but a grown child, and her time is passed in much frivolity. When her lord appears, she makes a seemly acquiescence and her gossip stops.

The literature which pretends to describe the East is permeated with stories of Turkish intrigue. The subject commands the attention, especially of the ardent and young. But he who writes of these matters should understand the domestic economy of the Turkish system, its inveterate usage and its progressive amelioration. From the information which I have received—and especially from the accounts of trustworthy women who have been admitted into the harem, such as I have endeavored to describe—I am sure that there is almost as much freedom given to the Turkish women as there is to the English or American. Although they have not as much choice in the selection of their husbands as other women, nevertheless they do resist temptations that are thrown about them, notwithstanding the small number of amusements by which their *ennui* is sought to be mitigated. What with their needlework, their studies, their housework, the reception of visitors and their wifely duties, not to speak of the constant and loving care of their clustering children, the great body of those who make the harem their home do so from conscientious and affectionate motives. Their love of nature and their pious thoughts, their visits, their baths, the cultivation of their love of jewelry, flowers, and toilet—these furnish much restraint on their naturally passionate natures, and for the practice of that restraint they are entitled to at least the good-will of other women who are born under more favoring stars. Besides, it is not by any means to be forgotten that the tendency at the present time is against polygamy in Turkey, and that but very few of the better families have more than one wife within the harem.

# CHAPTER XXXIX.

## THE EUNUCH AND OTHER INCIDENTS OF THE HAREM.

THE EUNUCH OF 1887.

WHY should there be so much discussion about the Turkish harem and the numerous wives of the Sultan? Is not Turkey a country where, from time immemorial, the polygamous custom has existed? If she be so bad, why have a Minister there? Or, to go further, why cultivate the good-will of the Chinese Emperor, whose palace holds some five thousand male slaves, who act as guards upon the harem of the Emperor, who has as many young beauties in his seraglio? The Emperor of China is named Kuang Hsu. That signifies "Succession of Glory." He is seventeen years of age, and is about to take a wife. She has been chosen from the family of Duke Choa, a Manchou nobleman. Kuang does not have any choice himself. His mother, the Empress Dowager, makes the match. But if Kuang does not affect the duke's daughter, he may solace himself—as Solomon did—by numerous secondary wives. At present the Mahometan law seems to be the legal limit allowed by the Dowager, viz., four. There is quite a rivalry among the Manchou officials, as to which family shall furnish the remaining three wives. These officers delight in having the prettiest of their daughters in the Imperial harem. They are the rounds upon the ladder of their preferment. The young ladies of China begin at fourteen years of age, and remain inside the harem until they are twenty-five; but woe be to them if they fail to bring forth children. In that case, they are sent home to their illustrious parents to wed some local Mandarin. The Emperor of China also has his eunuchs. This custom is handed down to him from the early Mogul sovereigns; and these sovereigns obtained their customs from what is known as the Assyrian and Turkish empires. The defense of this institution of polygamy, in its extent and that of the eunuch as its guardian, is based upon one idea, and one only: China, like Turkey, will not allow the nation to be disappointed by the failure of an heir to the throne.

I have hinted that in Constantinople there is not what we call "society" among the Turkish people. Women are indispensable to society, but they form no part of the general society of the Orient. All their amusements they must find for themselves. They interchange much comfort, gossip and pleasure; but in their harems, at their picnics and in their baths, they are isolated from all the world except themselves. Upon the street, no husband dare appear with his wife.

The head female of a family may be seen sitting under a sycamore upon the green grass, or, rather, upon a Smyrna carpet. Within twenty paces is her husband, who has his own male coterie. Custom forbids them to turn their eyes toward one another. The women, with a freedom humorous beyond expression, make their fun at the expense of the men, and with a language too, as it is said, as astonishing as it is sometimes indelicate.

The home life of the Turk is bound up with the harem. Any information concerning it must be, at best, second hand, unless some trustworthy woman has the privilege of entering the establishment.

Do you ask whether they lament their condition? A few of them who have come in contact with the outer world have a natural ambition to travel, and to see more and mix with those whose influences and habits are so novel to them. The body of them, however, do not care for other society than their female friends, their children and husbands. No man addresses them except the shop-keeper. I have to repeat in this connection, that the universal head-dress is a white handkerchief. A plain cloak of cloth or silk covers the whole person, and is fastened with a common clasp. The silk *feridjie* is used for the better class. They wear no gloves, but their fingers have a stain with which the reader is no doubt familiar. This henna stain is growing obsolete. Their complexions are somewhat sallow, and their gait is listless ; but their eyes—!

The visitor to Turkey is at first surprised at seeing so many females roaming about the city, apparently aimless. He wonders that so much freedom should be allowed. This wonder comes from his ignorance of their relation. The wife can go and come at her pleasure. She has no reproach from her husband. He may, to be sure, enter her apartment when he pleases and at all hours; but he never avails himself of this privilege. He rarely summons his wife or his family to his own room in the Salemlik. There is one sight for him always, as a reminder. If he sees a slipper at the door of the harem, it is a sign that he is not wanted. The truth is that the Turkish woman is more free than almost any other woman. If she wishes to drive or promenade or call upon a friend, she summons her slave, who carries her little bundle, adjusts her veil, covers her toilet with her *feridjie*, and goes. She can spend several days with her friend without exciting any alarm or suspicion on the part of her husband.

The black eunuch known as the *aga*, or *lala*—which are synonymous terms with guardian—is of a class of slaves found in the houses of rank and wealth. They are kept, just as a family in

New York would keep a carriage, to denote the social position. This eunuch is haughty. He is defiant of public opinion. He resents smiles and sarcasm at his expense, when in public; but when in charge of the women in the harem he is quite good-natured. There is much exaggeration about his acting as a messenger in intrigues. His office consists in caring for the children when walking out or driving, and he has much to bear from the willful whims of the little Beys and *petites hanoums.* There is always a porter or a guardian of the harem on hand at the door of the harem. He allows nobody to come in or go out without inquisition. He is the engineer or the waiter by which matters and things are passed in and out of the harem. He is by no means a dumb-waiter, either; for the women of the harem keep him continually on the go. Without repose or *kef*, he must fulfill every possible commission. This provokes a good deal of Moslem profanity. Invention has, however, come to relieve this guardian somewhat; for there is in the Salemlik wall a wheel. It is like the baby-basket at the door of the foundling asylum. The wheel operates as a sort of horizontal dumb-waiter. It facilitates the service between the harem and the Salemlik, without permitting the women to be seen.

Excepting the husband, no other man is allowed to enter the harem. It is a cardinal sin for a woman to appear with her face uncovered before a stranger. If she happens to be about the house or in the garden when a stranger, be it Mussulman or foreigner, unexpectedly enters, she rushes for anything handy— a handkerchief, a pillow or even a dish, with which to hide her face. The Sultan alone enjoys the privilege of free access to every harem; and then all the women in that harem have to stand before His Majesty with their faces uncovered.

When the eunuchs accompany the ladies on their expeditions, the latter drive always in closed carriages, the eunuchs following on foot or horseback, with a lash in their hand, which comes down like lightning on any foreigner who approaches too near. Turkish ladies are, however, no less artful than their European sisters; and eunuchs nowadays, are not hopelessly incorruptible.

The office of Chief Eunuch of the Imperial palace is a very important one, and the holder of it ranks equally with the Grand Vizier and Ministers of state. He is often admitted to the privy councils of the Sultan. His title has a grandiose sound. He is styled " His Highness the Guardian of the Gate of the Imperial Felicity and Repose." He is the head of the household of the Sultan. Of him and his functions, which are many, I may add that he is considered almost as much of an attraction, and is saluted with as much consideration, as a first-class bull-fighter in Spain. He is often the object of lyric poetry! Why? Because he has an influence upon the Sultan and thus upon politics. This influence he exerts, often, through the women of the harem. When he is inaugurated at the palace there is much display. He rides to the palace on a fine horse. His decorations glitter on his breast. He is received by the *aides* of the Sultan. Lambs are slaughtered as a token of welcome; and servants look up to him as to a demi-god. The emblem of his office is a silver pastoral staff. Why pastoral? Does he not care for the lambs? He becomes "Aga of the Sublime House of Othman," by which title he is designated in his commission.

The Chief of the Eunuchs has just died. The sad news is wafted to our hemisphere as I correct the proof of this chapter. His name was Hafiz Behram Aga. He is now among the angels— or the houris. Those who speak French at the palace called him *l'Altesse Noire*—literally, His Black Highness! He was nearly fourscore years of age and quite black, of pure Nubian descent. I recall his burly, gigantic form. He had an imperial air; and when he bore the keys about him he was sublime. He was a moss-back Moslem of the old type. He had no love for the innovations of the harem or the persons of Europeans. The appointment of a successor has given rise to much surmise, and, it is said, great excitement in and around the palace. An Armenian, it is rumored, has carried off the prize. The people of that race are never backward where power is attainable. No sacrifice is too great for its acquisition. He is a white man, but, as the "insert" shows, it is nothing new to have a white Chief of the Eunuchs. The illustration represents these twain, in company with a favorite dwarf. They are all of the time of Mahmoud II., the grandfather of the present Sultan. They are faithful portraits—dress, color and features. The eunuch of our time is not so gorgeously appareled.

Next to the *hamal* who labors under burdens, or, perhaps, to the dogs of Constantinople, who excite so much pity, I think the Eunuch should have the most compassion. He is an incarnation of a degradation too infamous for the ordinary human nature which has inflicted it. He does not belong alone to Turkish civilization. This the Bible shows us. There were great men among the eunuchs in the time of the Greek empire. Because of his mutilation, which has its hidden and physiological or other reason, the eunuch who walks with slow step and swinging arms, upon the quay of the Bosporus, is a pitiable object. He is the policeman of a system of which he is the victim. It is his figure drawn against the sweet and beautiful Oriental sky which is the most revolting. He is not an invalid in one sense. He has survived the knife; but it was not the knife of a sanitary and religious ceremony, like circumcision.

Some of these sad-eyed creatures, as I have seen them at the restaurants in the city and along the quays, are garrulous to a degree. Most of them are tall and long-legged. Some are fat, but their flesh has an unnatural flabbiness. Even when young their faces are often withered. Even when manly looking they are beardless. To one who has been familiar with the presiding elder of a Methodist church, their long, dark, straight-cut frock-coat, with pantaloons *à la Franka*, there is a curious and comical resemblance. Their coat has no collar which turns over. It has a famous row of buttons which suggest the good brother of the camp-meeting. In vain would we seek in the hand of that brother the whip of hippopotamus-hide which the eunuch carries as the symbol of his office. They have a quiet, long stride, like that of the gods whose feet were shod with wool, or like that of the burglar, who goes to his prey with a soft and sinister step. They are not now so common in Constantinople as they were in times past, but still they are seen everywhere. Their looks indicate no special expression, until some giaour casts a too curious look at the object of their vigilance; then the jealous ferocity of their temper is quickly displayed.

The men of this class do not take much interest in human conduct around them, except in the line of their daily duty. I have watched them in-doors and out. They have no social jocundity among men, whether white or black. Their clothes are always of glossy and fine broadcloth. They have an air of the inner circle of the harem. They are perfumed with all the essential vanities, from the attar of roses down to the latest importation of cologne.

That man who derides them is only a little less than a brute.

It is heartless to greet them with a laugh. It is a mistake to suppose that they do not know and feel their isolation and misfortune. They are called the custodians of a felicity, the barriers of jealousy, the bolts on the door, and the rags to hide the treasure existing among the glories of youth, with all its sweetness of passion and gladness of living. They are nameless, loveless, almost outside the pale of humanity. Is it strange, therefore, that they become the instruments of intrigue for, as well as the jailors of, those who tempt them? It is said that even the cruel coquetries of the harem pursue them, and that some of them, who have sensual passion left, even in a very small degree, are crazed by their peculiar situation.

Some of these men have been mutilated in their African home, at the head-waters of the Nile, and some in Syria. When they are made the servants of the Pasha's harem they are decorated in a thousand ways with a cruel mockery of phrases. They are called the "possessors of the lily," "keepers of the rose," and "tillers in the garden of the hyacinth"! They take their revenge, however, upon mankind, and although they are not Tartars, who are worst when caught, they are something worse in their debasement. Who shall blame them? Their condition is not of their own seeking.

I cannot refrain from quoting a paragraph which bears the evidences of veri-similitude. It is from De Amicis:

"One evening," the doctor said to me, "I was coming out of a rich Mussulman's house, where I had gone for the third time to visit one of his wives, who had disease of the heart. At my departure, as at my arrival, I was accompanied by a eunuch, calling out in the customary way, 'Women, withdraw!' in order to warn ladies and slaves that a stranger is in the harem, and that they must not be seen. In the courtyard the eunuch left me to find my own way to the gate. Just as I was about to open it, I felt a touch upon my arm, and turning, saw before me in the twilight another eunuch, a young man of eighteen or twenty years of age, who looked fixedly at me, with eyes swimming in tears. I asked him what he wished. He hesitated a moment to reply, and then seizing my hand in both of his, and pressing it convulsively, he said in a trembling voice, full of despairing grief, 'Doctor! you who know the remedy for every ill, do you know of none for mine?' I cannot tell you how those simple words affected me ; I tried to answer, but my voice failed me, and hastily opening the door, I took to flight. But all that evening, and for many days after, the figure of the youth stood before me, and I heard his words, and my eyes moistened."

How could it be otherwise ? A good man would be painfully struck with the appearance and emotions of the eunuch.

He has a part not only in the history of the Orient, but in its present condition. Gibbon has said that the higher the price of the eunuch, the more corrupt was the empire. He spoke this in reference to the Greek empire and its white eunuchs.

I cannot picture to my mind a more humble situation than that of these God-forsaken images of their maker. They are of our kind, or, rather, among their kind, but not of them. They are the most striking examples of "man's inhumanity to man," and of that selfish sensuality for which there is no name in any language.

The common families, the groups of whom you may see strolling around the high places of the hills, and the green, shady spots of the meadows, are not guarded by the eunuch. Only families of rank or wealth are thus accompanied.

The women of the East, the Turkish women at least, remind me of the peacocks. They seek the high places, where at least they can be admired. They are quite gregarious among themselves. You always see them in groups of four, six and eight, and uniformly clad in their long mantles. Those of the poorer class are generally clad in white cotton mantles. Thus clad they look like troops of phantoms. Moreover, it is a mistake to suppose that these groups of veiled women are in all respects good examples of the housewifery of the Moslem. These have more or less broken away from the old customs. The class of women who really give tone to the social order in Constantinople are those who are seldom seen in public. They have never passed the threshold of the harem. Their lives are engrossed with home duties. Their visits are rare. Their outside occupations consist in the inspection of the wares of female pedlers, an occasional jaunt in the country, and a picnic upon the shore; still, they are always superintending the larder, as other women do in other countries. They make pickles and preserves ; look after the clothes of their children and the raiment of their slaves ; distribute alms to those who call, buy provisions and clothes, and in other respects fulfill the obligations of a good Mahometan, the chief among which is alms-giving. Of course, a woman of this class is always ready to receive visitors. Oftentimes, if she be a woman of means, she has a lady-superintendent, who relieves her of much of this duty. This assistant greets the visitor at the door of the harem. The visitor is supported by the elbow up the stairs ; then the veil and the *feridjie* are removed. If the visitor retain a band of muslin across the forehead, it is understood that she will not stay long ; still, the practice prevails of removing the yashmak to be ironed, and the *feridjie* to be carefully folded away. The same toilet is resumed, preliminary to the departure of the guest. In these calls there is much smoking, coffee-drinking and talking, but nothing excessive. The young ladies of the family always quietly defer to the elders. I am bound to say, from reliable information, that their conversation is not, as represented, of the malodorous quality. The house is scrupulously clean. It ought to be so, as the floor, or the matting on the floor, is used for spreading out their fabrics when they would cut out or fold garments. They do not permit a stain on the prayer-carpet, and hence no one enters who does not leave the out-door shoes at the door.

If you ask me to what particular spots the Turkish women resort in their recreations, I can only answer by another question: "In what place are they not to be found before the going down of the sun?" They always arise early. They are always in the bazaars. They crowd the steamers going up and down the Bosporus. They visit the "Sweet Waters" of Europe and Asia. If you cross the bridge between Galata and Stamboul, lo! at all hours the veiled mystery is there in grand procession. Ascend the tower of Galata, and lo ! she is there. You hear that she cannot attend the mosque; but she does. Friday evening prayer-meetings draw her out in Ramazan season, for have I not seen her as coy and débonnaire there as upon the hills of Prinkipo ? She may be a slave inside of beautiful gardens, grottoes and chambers, surrounded by slaves, smoking her *chibouque* and drinking her sherbet, but she is about as free and lively a slave as you can find in many a day's travel. No one interrupts her. No policeman and no one of the inhabitants of this composite city offer her discourtesy, much less indignity. Her veil is as sacred as that of a nun. She may be served at a shop kept by an Armenian, or waited on at a millinery store by a Hebrew, or be shown to a bath by a Nubian, or be rowed in a caïque by a Greek ; she may buy her grapes from a Syrian, and her fish from a Maltese; or be sailing in a steamer commanded by a Dalmatian, or be driven by a Bulgarian coachman, and be doctored by the English physician, whose prescription is filled by a French druggist; and her elegant teeth, albeit inclined to confectionery, may be filled by an American dentist, and her rounded arm be vaccinated by an Italian doctor; but not one word of insult or gesture of interruption are ever shown by these varied populations, even in their high carnival, toward the *rara avis* of the pashalic cage.

Writers upon the Turkish empire attribute most of the disasters and all of the decadence of that empire to the mischievous creed of Mahometanism. They hold that creed, and especially the sensualism which is taught by it, to be a hindrance to progress. Indeed, all the prophecies which have been rife for two hundred years as to the inspiration of the Turkish race have been founded upon the alleged sensual character of their religion. Doubtless it is true that the antipathy of the Christian to the Turk is due to those passions which mock the best precepts of the Moslem, Christian and Hebrew religions : but as Dr. Hamlin well remarks, while approaching the worst attribute of Moslemism—its sensualism—"this feature is found rather in tradition than in the Koran." It is almost impossible to reconcile the stories told about the conversation and the conduct of the women of the harem with other reports which are made upon that subject by some of our best women.

It is a mistake to suppose that the Turks deny to the woman the possession of a soul. The Moslem has his own Eden. He may have his own particular houri to crown with flowers his noble brow, or give him those sensuous delights which belong to the Orient of the seventh heaven. But there is no enjoyment in the future, after death, in which the inhabitants of the harem, in some wondrous mystery, may not join in the destiny of their lord. The women are not debarred from the pious ceremonies of the mosque, like the women of other countries, except that they are restricted to the latticed galleries, like those for women in the House of Commons. Therefore, intuitively they are religious. In the seclusion of their homes, and in the humility of their lives, from beneath the veil with which they conceal themselves, they pass with prayer into the presence of Allah.

Outside of that seclusion, they are the worshippers of Nature. In this they copy their husbands with enthusiasm. "Born," says Lamartine, "in the mountains and valleys of Asia—the sons of shepherds—they bring with them into their very palaces the memory, the images, the passions, of rural nature ; they love her too much to bedeck her. A woman, a horse, a weapon, a fountain, a tree—such are the five paradises of the children of Othman !"

How can it be possible that so many kindly compliments are paid to the Turkish gentlewomen by those of her own sex for her courtesy, which is almost intuitive, and her simplicity of feeling and sincerity of good-nature, which give a double charm to this courtesy, if indeed it be true that the harem is not a home, but only a resort of sensuality ?

There are some cases recorded in the Turkish annals where the vanity of the male has been quite conspicuous. In fact, the system of polygamy is of such a peculiar kind that it may persuade the superior sex to believe that he is more or less like a game fowl in a barnyard surrounded by his pullets. Much fun has been made of George the Fourth for his exquisite vanity in dress and manner. It is said that Mahmoud the Second, the grandfather of the present Sultan, made perpetual sacrifices before the altar of self-adornment. He even painted himself white and red with costly cosmetics, to enjoy the admiration of the ladies of the seraglio; and yet this was the man who immolated the Janizaries to reform the empire !

Considering the many changes and reforms in this empire, what may we not expect next, in a realm where there is so much room for advancement in the social virtues and the economies of the state !

# CHAPTER XL.

THE slave market at Constantinople has gone to the rear. If it exist at all, it exists in the mind of some libelant. It is hidden from human sight in the city. But suppose it were open, so that all could understand it ! It is not, in comparison with the old slave mart of America, that with which we should reproach the Turks. There is no cruelty—no insult to the slave. When the slaves become members of the family into which they are inducted, they are sure to rise if they are worthy. The negroes in the old slave markets of Stamboul sat on one side in groups. The Circassians are, or were, brought to Constantinople by their parents at their own voluntary request; and they had close apartments. They were not exposed to the gaze of the idler or the curious. The Turk himself never made sport of the relation of slavery, and always mitigated its severity.

It is very doubtful whether the Circassian beauties, of which there has been so much boast, are all our fancies picture them. Those whom I have met, and I have seen many, freshly brought by steam to Constantinople from Circassia at so much a head, have been degraded by likening them to a drove of cattle. They are called Circassians, but since the Russian conquest of that country the greater part of these recruits are derived from inferior tribes; and therefore their charms are not what we expect. In fact, a captain of a Black Sea steamer has insisted that out of a thousand girls and women whom he had carried to the capital, the great majority were ugly, most of them half famished, and all of them dirty. Is it thus that we are robbed of our illusions ?

There is scarcely a family in Turkey which has the means, that does not possess a number of women and girl slaves, black and white. The black are from Central Africa and Nubia; the white are Circassians sold by their parents. The Circassian traffic has greatly or apparently ceased. Many families moved to Constantinople to rear their girls for this condition.    I do not believe that there is now any public market for slaves.    There is no selling at the bazaars, as there used to be.    Still they are bought and sold, and the authorities very likely know how and where, and regulate the traffic.    The price varies with the beauty. The ungainly are used for domestic work.    The beauties are educated.    Besides, they learn to sing and dance and to become agreeable.    Each wife of the Sultan is a slave.    When she becomes a mother she is raised to the rank of *cadina;* but never to the rank of wife.    Those who are not cadinas or wives in the Turkish harem, are known as *odalisques.*    When they are favorites, they are called *ikbal.*    The slave men do the cooking; the slave women the housework.    The Sultan, properly, has no wife or wives. His dignity is too great to allow him to enter into any matrimonial relation.    He has a numerous harem; and among them are gradations of rank.    From four to seven of the more favored take the title of *kadin*, or lady.    These have a separate establishment and some precedence.

In the Imperial family the princesses choose their own husbands, or the Sultan does for them.    They generally choose some one about the palace, or a young bey of good repute. Whether the young bey likes it or not, he is not permitted to show his displeasure.    If he does, he is exiled.    It is said that the princesses like the soldiers best; and the soldier-husbands must behave with prudence; otherwise they will be discarded.    These husbands are more enslaved, in fact, than the actual slaves.

Most of the harems, and especially those of the Sultan, are shut in by high walls.    The doors are never locked.    The bed, with some exceptions, where European habits have been introduced, consists of a small mattress, laid on the floor—sometimes several mattresses.    In the morning early—for the Turk rises early—these are taken out and placed in the closet.    There is not much to relieve the eye or the fancy in the harem.    The sons of prominent Pashas and others when they reach fourteen years, demand an odalisque.    She is generally selected from the harem of the father.    She is then freed with honor, and the moment a child is born she becomes a *hanoum.*

The slave has not a hard lot.    The child of the slave has a part of the inheritance of the father.    More than half of the marriages in Turkey are with the slaves.

There is much criticism as to the condition of things in the harem. It is supposed to be the great obstacle to Turkish advancement. This statement is to be taken not without stint. What I desire to make clear is, that the slave trade is not what it was, and slavery is not what it is represented to be. When slaves are purchased, it is generally through intermediaries. They are generally Arab brokers. They have a rendezvous in a certain quarter of some of the narrow streets of Pera and Stamboul, the entrance to which is prohibited to all save the Mussulman.

You ask : "What are slaves worth ?" A white boy may cost two hundred dollars, depending upon his acquirements ; a girl under ten, one hundred dollars ; a maiden between twelve and sixteen, if she be attractive and can play on the zither, brings from thirty-five hundred to five thousand dollars. If the young woman be a blonde, with black eyes and rare beauty otherwise, she may bring from four to six thousand dollars. An amateur will pay double that for a choice specimen, well educated in French and other graces. This tariff by no means applies to the slaves from Africa, the dépôts for whom are in Scutari and in the villages on the Bosporus. The black slave will bring ninety dollars, the black maiden seventy or seventy-five, and a eunuch from three hundred and fifty to four hundred dollars. In buying the slave there are not such harrowing details as we used to read in Uncle Tom's Cabin. All that has passed away—if it ever existed.

The fact is that slavery in Turkey is but a name. It is actually forbidden by law, and although it still goes on, the slaves have nothing to complain of in Turkey. The white slaves rush to slavery as an alternative from something else and worse ; the black slaves, however, who are brought from Africa, have undergone all the tortures which belong to the traditional slave trade. The slave of the family may be looked down upon as one of under-condition, but is nevertheless treated from infancy, when received, to old age, as one of the family. After the female slave has worked for awhile faithfully, say seven years, she is nearly always freed voluntarily by the mistress or master of the household. This clement element illustrates what I have endeavored to picture—the fidelity of the Turkish character to old ties and associations. Many touching stories are related of the demeanor and goodness of the Turkish women toward those who are regarded as their slaves.

The slave trade in Africa supplies a certain portion of the

market in Constantinople. Its methods are violent. No one in our day can defend the slave trade. The relief which slavery gives after the trade is over, may be a compensation for the cruel barbarism which makes slavery possible within the domain of Africa. If the truth were known, the insurrection of the Soudan was an insurrection of the slave-dealers. The attempt to suppress slavery in Africa was like the attempt to prohibit commerce. Even Gordon desisted from the policy of its suppression. In fact, he asked that his former Bey, Zebehr, who was king of the slave-traders, might be appointed Governor-General of the Soudan. The truth is : that in these Oriental countries slavery has not the same meaning that it had in Brazil, Cuba or America. The ideal of the African, if he has any, is immunity from all sorts of labor ; and if he be thrown on his own resources, he falls into a bottomless pit.

In the Orient the slave prefers always to remain with his master, if his master be a Mahometan ; for he is placed upon an equal social footing sometimes with the family. Sometimes a slave is sold from hand to hand, and from Timbuctoo to Algiers, Zanzibar or Arabia, until he reaches the Constantinople market through many journeys, after which slavery is a positive blessing.

# CHAPTER XLI.

THE Turk is fond of water from his very birth. He is at no time a bibber of wine. He is positively fond of his bath. He begins when young to take his ablutions many times a day and under every circumstance, especially before prayer and before he enters the mosque.

As with the usage of the bath, the mode of dressing the infant Turk follows it into childhood. It curves its tiny extremities in youth and at maturity, and until old age. Carlyle has shown what everlasting things depend upon the dressing of a human being. How then are the infantry of Turkey dressed? It is enough to say that the legs and hands—in fact, the entire child—is enwrapped. A portion of the wrapping-cloth exceeds the length of the babe. The little creature is folded, and enfolded, and re-enfolded, and sometimes so tightly that the circulation of the blood is stopped and the baby's face turns blue! If the mother be loving, or the nurse kind, this dressing is changed frequently. The little one is refreshed by this renewal. A change twice a day of three long strips of cloth is reckoned suitable relief in ordinary families; it is only in a well-to-do family that the encasement is less painful. This swathing process is so peculiar as to tend to shape the legs of the mature Turk to resemble the crescent, which is the emblem of growth and of Turkey. Moreover, the tiny baby Turk wears a bonnet. It is of a gay color, generally the Prophet's favorite hue—green. This bonnet is worn by both sexes. Upon it is set sometimes a blue gem, say a turquoise. Sometimes a piece of garlic is hung upon it, to keep off the evil eye of jealous visitors. Thus accoutred, the little Turk passes the boundary of the "professional" who presides at its birth, into the grand domain where the nurse rules supreme.

Among the Christians in the East, the nurse is not so important as with the Mahometans. With the latter, she is sacred. She ranks after the mother.    She is like the old African "Aunty" of the South.    If the nurse have children of her own, they are styled the "milk brothers and sisters" of her adopted nursling.    Even at the palace of the Sultan, the nurse who nourishes a prince or princess has golden opportunities of advancement.    She secures her own and her children's welfare for life.    She is loaded with presents.    These presents differ in value, according to the means of the master, and are given on every possible occasion.    When the child says "baba!" or "father;" when it has its first tooth ; when its birthday comes round; and when it makes its first step— the nurse has presents.    It is the same at Bairam, the festal Mahometan season; and thus upon every slight occasion presents rain down from father, mother, grandparents, uncles and aunts.

If the parents are wealthy, the nurse's duty is limited.    It consists simply in feeding the baby; for an odalisque—one of the women of the harem—performs the duty of caring for the child. After the fatigues of nursing, she regales herself with a narghile; for smoking is by no means confined to the ruder sex in Turkey.

In addition to these two aids of Turkish babyhood, in every well-regulated home a servant or two have charge of the washing and cleaning of the nursery and linen.

As soon as the child is old enough to be able to take ordinary nourishment, it is taken from the nurse and put into the hands of the oldest male servant.    If the child be a boy, this servant is to be the tutor until the boy is sent to school.    The boy remains in his hands for about five years.    It is here that he obtains his first moral impressions.

As a general rule, these servants or slaves to whom Mussulman children are entrusted are not the most cultivated or liberal among the Moslems.    No wonder, then, that the little Turk becomes imbued with the prejudices of this guardian, who has not learned to leaven his faith with toleration, as do the more enlightened of his race.    No wonder if the child be taught to despise those not of his race or of the creed of the Prophet.    So far as my observation goes, this hatred of other than Mahometans has died out considerably since I visited here in A. D. 1851; and even since I was here in A. D. 1881.    It is said that the first time the child sees a Christian or a Jew passing by, he is taught to spit or throw water on him, as a sign that he repels the contact with such an unbeliever.    It is said that he is thus early taught to hate all "giaours" or infidels. This may be the case among the lowest classes of Moslems; and where the windows of the houses which are covered with Venetian blinds or screens may hide the servant and child, it may be done with impunity, and as a sort of sport for the ignorant attachés of the household.

My observation does not, however, lie in this direction. Last Friday I visited the "Sweet Waters of Asia," across the Bosporus. The *hanoums* bring their families—odalisques, children, servants and slaves, black and white. Children by the score play around upon the green under the plane-trees near the "Sweet Waters" —called sweet, because not brackish. Yellow maize on the cob, smoking hot, is sold by itinerant venders to the groups of families, who eat it off the ear. Confections and cakes in every shape are sold, along with all the toys that ever Caleb Plummer fancied.

No one complains that we giaours gaze upon this Moslem holiday. The women peep out from under their cambric wraps, quite pleased to be gazed upon. They move around on the greensward in their silken *feridjies*. They no longer wear the slipshod yellow slipper as of old. Even with the high-heeled French shoe they do not walk gracefully. Now and then you find one in superb costume, perhaps a golden-haired blonde, and with a style of walking as elegant as that of the belles of Belgrade or Bucharest.

But the children; well—I happened to look earnestly at a handsome boy of about five years and a little girl of the same age. Their portraits I cannot get; but I present, nearly as may be, pictures representing their dresses. They were in a bevy of children, near a large group of women, seated, as usual, upon the ground. The boy was handsomely attired in fancy garments, in which silk braid and gold play a part. He exhibited no distrust or dislike, but with elegant grace he gave me the salaam of the East, or, rather, of the dervishes of the East. The higher person in rank receives the lowest obeisance. The boy who saluted us touched the earth with his right hand, brought it up to his mouth, and then tipped his forehead. It is a courtesy which, from a child, says:

" From the earth our mother, I gave you my heart, and with my hand to my brow, intelligently I salute you ! "

I was surprised and pleased with the young gentleman's exquisite taste. His female relatives almost dropped their yashmaks, and gave a laughing salutation to my wife—but not to me of the debarred sex. They were pleased with the delight afforded by their children.

Wandering about the grounds, I found seated by some provender a little hunchback boy whose family had wandered off on a promenade by these "Sweet Waters" of Asia. Was he distrustful? Not a whit. Our kavass—the Mahomedan guard of the Legation—asked him to sing his prayers for us; and he raised his "*La-Il-Allah!*" with a plaintive and sweet voice. He seemed happy in his effort to please.

So that I doubt the universal application of the statement, that the Turkish children are all trained to show signs of hatred to those of other faiths. I have yet to see one unruly movement or ugly grimace from a Moslem child. Near our Legation at Therapia there are barracks. Several families live near by— families of soldiers. The soldiers as well as the children salute the Minister every day, and if I meet one of them in the city, the courtesy I describe is made with smiling recognition.

It may be noticed, from some of the illustrations, that the Turk is not subject to the standard or to the fancies of Europeans. He has his own tests in his ways of dressing, as well as in the colors and the pattern of the material which he uses for that purpose; so much so that in Germany, Austria, France and England there are factories where articles are made specially for consumption in the Orient. The Turk buys colored calico of bright yellowish or pink color, or with such a combination of colors that Joseph's coat only can rival, and that no European would use, except for window curtains. He prefers wide stripes to any other pattern. He never imitates the Christian mode of dressing, so long as he can help it. It irked the Turkish soldier at first to wear the French uniform. Thus, long dresses are worn by young girls, and short ones by babies, whereas it is usual among Christians to dress the baby, up to the time he steps about, with long dresses; and as soon as he is able to walk, with short ones. The little Turkish girl, when *en promenade*, has the aspect of a little old lady, except in her infantile features. The only article of dress which the Turk adopts from the Christian—and that is of recent occurrence—is the shoe or boot. This they adopt as more comfortable in locomotion; though that is a matter of doubt.

The shape and the style which have prevailed in manufacturing the clothes to be seen in these illustrations, indicate something different from that which is commonly known everywhere outside of Moslem countries. Some Turks consider it a religious obligation to differ thus as to their modes of dress. They never put a hat on their heads. Even the women have their "*bashliks*," approaching to what one may call a hat, but it is a different thing. It is called by another name. A hat would be a "*shapka;*" and the name given to this head-covering means a bonnet, or, rather, a cap.

These characteristics of the Turk—and of his chief, the Sultan himself, who wears, like all his subjects, the fez cap—go to show that they are misjudged greatly from childhood up. If indeed, as is said, the child is taught by the servant some naughty words, and incited to hurl them at the infidel as a part of his "fun," or that of his nurse or servant, I am, as I said before, in ignorance of the fact. There is much written, and truly, about the irreverent audacity of Young America. He will cry out, "Go up, Bald-Head!" and add defiantly, "Now, bring on your Bears!" Compared with the "bad boy" of other lands—of which the American boy is a representative, as I myself from experience know—the young Turk is as a cooing dove to a malicious sparrow, or to a loquacious jackdaw.

Of course all children must have amusement. If it be not tendered, they will break out into mischief. They must also have variety in their entertainment. They must be petted. The philology of the word "*pet*" signifies it. A child soon tires of one kind of diversion. He must find something else. The Turkish child is no exception. Whether running about, as I see him here, in his little baggy clothes, over which is a sort of dressing-gown padded with cotton made out of cheap prints, highly colored, generally red ; or munching sweetmeats in his satins and silks, tassels and gold laces, with his little cane, strutting by the side of his veiled mother, over the green at the "Sweet Waters" near the Palace of Ghiocksouyee ; whether he be rich or poor, of crockery or porcelain—he is of the same "earth earthy" as the American bad or good boy.

He is, perhaps, more plastic in the hands of servant or slave. This personage is often put to the use of all his wits to make up stories wonderful enough to fill the imagination of these inchoate Sinbads and Haroun Al-Raschids—these children of Bajazet and Suleïman. Generally such stories refer to a boy or girl of their own age as the hero or heroine. Perhaps the hero is some Arab cowboy of the desert or plain ! In these narratives, there are battles with the enemies of the Faith, in which millions of Christians are slain by a handful of Moslems. The hero has slaughtered most of them. Robberies, incendiarisms, murders and piracies are committed by the enemy of the heroic Mussulman, who cuts them down with his crescent-shaped cimeter. In these stories the bad Unbeliever is punished ultimately by the good Moslem. The tale winds up with the immunity of the true believer ; nay, with a reward in proportion to the number of enemies killed ; a reward in a paradise of rare beauty and delight !

With such stories, we do not wonder that the Turkish child should grow into a bigoted man. We do wonder that in his contact with other nationalities, and the constant encroachment on Turkish domain in Africa and Europe, that when he comes to man's estate his early training so little affects his natural tolerance and urbanity.

There is one occasion on which the Turkish children are taught to be respectful and obedient ; that is when they are brought in presence of their father and mother. They learn to approach their parents in the same humble attitude as the servants ; for instance, as soon as the child is brought in he must approach them with his hands upon his stomach. On coming nearer, he must take their hands and kiss them. After this, he must withdraw some three or four steps and stand with his hands on the stomach and not seat himself until he is permitted. On this account the little Turk likes better to be with the servants than with his parents.

So far as the outward show may be proof, there is no lack of love from the father to the child. The father cares sedulously for the child when it is sick   He plays with it when it is well. He carries his love of children so far as to be constantly adopting the children of others. These are called " the children of the soul." They are reared with the same tenderness as the children of the household. On their marriage they are apportioned with the same munificence as if it were a natural instead of a voluntary claim. The regard for the parents is imperishable in the Turkish mind. The Turk will say to himself :

" My wife or wives may die ; they can be replaced. My

children may perish ; others may be born ; but who shall restore
to me my mother ; for when she goes, she is seen no more ? "

If the " child be father of the man," then the Turkish child
is not so bad after all, considering the provocation and allurements to be otherwise. In places where the Turk does not mingle with those of other creeds and nations, he may, if ignorant, be
haughty. He may, as child and man, beat or abuse with facile
stick or tongue the children who are alien to the commonwealth
of Islam. He sees the servants about him subdued to the son of
their master, and as he has no communications outside, the only
surprise is that he does not become more absolute and arrogant.
Upon the whole, I am yet to meet a Turk who is not gentle. He
is more polite than the French, and more sincere in his politeness. The Turkish peasant is a good sample of the uncorrupted
stock ; and he is a sober and simple person. Daughters marry
young, and their housekeeping is a model of cleanliness compared
with the squalor and dirt of other Oriental races and homes.
Their vices are from alien sources ; their virtues are from the
teaching of the Koran ; and their hospitality and courtesy are
among these virtues.

It may be interesting to follow the Turkish child from its birth
to its nurse, and from its nurse to its attendant, when it reaches
the third and most interesting epoch in its plastic life; but it is
more interesting to solve the question: " How, and how much, is
the child educated; and what are the ceremonies of its introduction to the schools of Turkey ? "

Not until the child reaches its sixth year does this question
agitate the household. The father and mother, in a preparatory
way, then commence petting him more than usual. Small presents
are given him. Among other things, there is given a bag with a
strap. This is to be hung on his shoulder. The bag is square-
shaped. It is large enough to contain his primary book. This is
ordered for the occasion.

The bag and book are covered with elaborate embroideries.
Arrangements are made with the teacher of the school to which the
child is to go.

The day on which to begin school is decided upon. It is a
day marked with the whitest stone. It is a day of ceremony. No
such ponies are to be found like the spirited yet gentle iron-gray
ponies of the East. One of these is gorgeously caparisoned. The

TURKISH SCHOOL CHILDREN.

cloths are covered with gold embroideries of rarest skill. The pupils of the school are advised of the great event, and of the advent of the new comer. These pupils are arrayed in their "store clothes."

Our photographs represent some children in this holiday attire. These children are taken to the house of the budding scholar. A priest makes a short prayer. The child is placed on the pony; and the pupils, male and female, are formed in double line. The procession moves. It sings hymns as it moves. The little horse, with the little hero of the day, follows. The pony feels the importance of the occasion. The photograph shows also how the child is dressed in a costume especially made for the occasion. If it be a boy, the costume is that of a Turkish colonel of the army or a commodore of the navy; or sometimes in the costume of an Ulema or law interpreter.

The Spanish nation has many traits of an Oriental kind. Perhaps they were transmitted by contact with their Moorish neighbors in the earlier years of the peninsular history. It was only the other day that the son of Alfonso XII., a little over one year of age, was presented by the Tailor's Guild of Madrid with a uniform of a titular grade in the army. The gold lace of the suit, the miniature chapeau, the plume, the aigrette of diamonds and the tiny sword made the little one a droll doll. Such is royalty.

In Turkey, if the costume be for a little girl, it is a fancy one, which is neither Turkish nor European. She wears a great profusion of artificial flowers and gay feathers. Thus the child makes its entry into the school, or, rather, into its new world.

It may be understood from the preceding that among Mussulmans, in the primary schools both girls and boys study together. The teachers are taken from the priesthood and from the graduates of the theological universities. They must have learned to read the Koran, which is written in Arabic, and which all good Mussulmans learn. This class of teachers are consequently stringent religionists. Some are quite fanatical. If the pupil does not acquire much discipline or information pertaining to modern material progress, it is because the twig is not bent in that direction.

Pertinent to this, let me say, that never does our Legation steam launch stop at any of the wharves between Constantinople

TURKISH SCHOOL TEACHERS.

and Cavak, near the Bosporus mouth, that it is not observed by the children. They gather about it in crowds. They quit their fishing to look at it. They scarcely give its passengers a glance or smile. They care not for the flag of our beloved land. They, however, peep down into the engine-room, not exactly with surprise, for a Turk is not supposed, even in youth, to show surprise. The boy scrutinizes its stern, to see the play of the screw propeller, which the clear water of the Bosporus displays. Thereupon, there follows much sapient discussion. Are these urchins of the quay inglorious Newtons, Fitches and Fultons, Morses, Edisons and Ericsons, that they take such a sedate interest in the mysteries of physical science, when harnessed as forces, upon this element, so constantly dedicated here to the oar?

I have said that the Turk never shows surprise, even if he feels it. Dr. Washburn, president of the Robert (American) College, illustrates this point by an anecdote. He brought here from America one of Edison's phonographs. He exhibited it to a company of Turks. He vociferates into its orifice. The machine grinds out of its vocal tin-foil much talk in English, in its squeaky way. It is no marvel to the company. There is not an eyebrow raised in wonder; not a question asked. When it talks Turkish, ah! Then, how they marvel! How could it learn the Turkish language so soon!

In one of my calls the other day upon a leading Turkish gentleman of education and refinement, I had a conversation as to Eastern and Western modes of thought and tuition. He said to me:

"Excellency! I think there are modes of good-nature, by which the ends of discipline and justice are attained."

I asked him to explain his remark; he replies:

"Oh, Excellency! you are accounted a man of good-humor, and evidently it is a part of your education."

I rejoin, giving him back—for he was a Minister and a Pasha —the usual courtesy:

"Excellency! the forum in which my good-nature has been tried has no counterpart in the East. A parliamentary body has its gravity, ever drawing one to itself as to an arena of wrangle and not of good-humor, and yet—," I added, "good-humor has its uses even in deliberative bodies."

As the Turks are proud of being accounted just, I add:

" You know that the root of the English word 'justice' or 'juice,' is the word from the Greek which means 'moisture' or 'humor.'"

Here he exhibited unwonted surprise. He was of Kurd descent. He had the warm blood of Saladin the Saracen. I resume:

" Justice is like rain—or *jus*, i. e., juice. It falls upon all alike—the just and unjust. This idea and its philology are of the Orient. Almost all moral humor, like the fable, parable or story, comes from the East."

" Ah," he responds quietly, " the West gives us steam, telegraph, telephone and a hundred other evidences of growth in experimental science; and thus it compensates us for what we give to them in moral and religious truths. The East and West are necessary to each other."

This man, as I say, was a Kurd. He was a descendant of the tribe from and through which Xenophon made his celebrated retreat of the ten thousand. He is now the able and courteous Foreign Minister—Saïd Pasha.

I have yet to see the Turkish man or child here—for I am not speaking of the Turkish woman—who did not seem pervious to good-humor.

It is a mistake that the Turk is always too grave for a laugh. The children especially are full of sportive ways. The men are not devoid of that simplicity which is easily amused. Is it because they are fond of children? At every turn, we see here the father playing with his young ones, or petting them. He makes them his companions. Indeed, the father seems to be devotedly attached to the little ones, whose " flitcherin naise and glee" is the echo of his own hilarity.

The schools here do not afford the opportunities for mischief which are recorded in English novels about English boys, and which make so many paragraphs in American journals.

The studies in the primary schools are not very complicated. On the contrary, they are primitive.

A primary school is composed of one or two rooms or " holes in the wall," round which there are large divans against three of the sides of the room. The seat of the teacher is against the fourth side. The pupils sit cross-legged in a line on the divans. They hold their books on their knees, and recite all at the same time, in a loud, shrill voice, so as to form a sort of monotone, producing an indescribable cacophony, not unlike the horrid music of these shores. They learn grammar, and the four rules of arithmetic. After they are able to read from the Koran a little, they take up writing. There being no writing-tables or desks, they hold their copy-books in their hands. This is all the education they receive in the primary schools.

As the Arab gave us numeration—in fact, arithmetic, as well as kindred modes of calculation—Young America may not be averse to doing one of the sums I copy from a primer in the

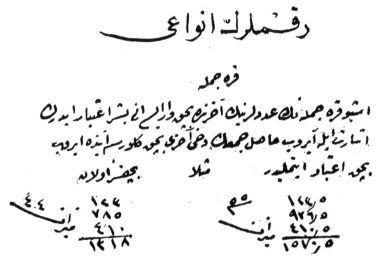

A SUM IN TURKISH ARITHMETIC.

Turkish script. At least, it is a curious "sum" to look at, if it cannot be "done."

A few years ago the Sultan gave the matter of education his serious attention. Much progress has been made toward putting the primary schools on a better footing. Besides the primary, there are few superior schools, except the military and naval schools and the school of medicine, established in A. D. 1830. These "high schools" were established some forty years ago; so that, outside of these government and primary schools, there is no other education to be had. Wealthy men hire European teachers to assist their children in the study of languages and modern science. But the common people, not being pecuniarily able, satisfy themselves with what is obtained at the primary schools. If one is astonished that the governing class here generally speak French, and often English, Greek, Italian and German, it may be stated that the Turk, like the Russian, has an aptitude for tongues. He makes his necessity the mother of his—study.

The distribution of the prizes at the model preparatory school of Bechïktash has just taken place, in the presence of a grand concourse of people. The audience was principally composed of the best society of Moslems. This splendid establishment was instituted by the present Sultan. It is under his patronage. It has justified the hopes that were conceived at its creation. About thirty of the pupils received certificates of scholarship. These permit them to enter higher schools. The school of Bechïktash thus gives proof of the progress accomplished within a few years in primary instruction.

During the reign of Sultan Abdul Medjid, some thirty-five years ago, an effort was made to extend the normal school system throughout the empire, but without success. It is only during the reign of the present Sultan that the matter of education has been earnestly taken up. In the course of eight or nine years, the administration of public instruction has established throughout the empire, in Europe, Asia and Africa, 388 primary and normal schools. There were in this year, A. D. 1886, 20,093 students. Besides these, there are 80 primary and normal schools in Constantinople, in which there are 5,401 students, out of which 275 are in the gratuitous school—the only one in existence in the empire—and 634 are in private schools. In all, I should say that there are some 30,000 pupils in Turkish schools being gratuitously educated. The number is increasing every day.

The instruction in these schools differs little from that which was formerly given. The programme of the studies, divided into four years, indicates the course of studies for each year or class.

Here is the course of studies in primary schools :

*First class, or year :* Alphabet, Turkish, six times a week; Koran, six times a week and prayers; and Turkish lectures, five times a week; and moral stories.

*Second class, or year :* Koran, six times a week, and memorizing it; religious precepts, twice a week and the reading of a primer; addition, once a week; and writing.

*Third class, or year :* Koran, six times a week, and explanations; Turkish grammar, twice a week; four rules of arithmetic and proofs, twice a week; and different kinds of writing.

*Fourth class, or year :* Koran, six times a week; geography, once a week; and Ottoman history, once, and general history twice a week; orthography, once a week; and writing, as well as memorization of lessons.

It may be a surprise, but it is nevertheless true, that there is compulsory education in Turkey. Every citizen or father is compelled to enter his son's name for schooling on reaching the age of six years. If they can afford the means, their children are educated at home. Why should a citizen of Berlin, London or New York think that he monopolizes the business of education? Why should he look down upon the Turk in that regard? Even in the old temples of Cairo, while wandering around, winter before last, I heard the hum, hum, hum of the schools. It sounded like a swarm of bees. In following the murmurous noise, I have wandered into some scattered nook of some temple of Rameses or Osiris, where the infantile voices are heard in chorus almost any hour of the day. They sit cross-legged with their *vakeer,* or schoolmaster. Each child has a board on which his lesson is written. This lesson he screams to the top of his compass. The hubbub is anything but agreeable; but the moment a stranger enters the noise becomes that of boisterous hilarity. The pupils must recite by heart, out loud, besides writing down the lessons.

The programme of studies of the Imperial Lyceum includes the Turkish language, composition and translation, Turkish history and literature, Arabic language and literature, the Persian language, religious instruction, mathematics, philosophy, physics, history, design, French, geography, book-keeping, the Greek language, French caligraphy, gymnastics and the German, English and Italian languages.

There are two schools in Constantinople for professions and arts. These are for boys as well as for girls. These are of course separate. In the boys' school there are three hundred students, and in the girls' one hundred and fifty-nine. There they learn handicraft and trades of all kinds. There is also a superior school in prospect, but it is not yet in operation.

The Lycée Imperial has eight hundred students, for which the annual pay for boarding students is $240 a year, while the day students pay about $55. The course of studies in this is copied from the French schools.

There has also been an administrative school in operation for four or five years. The curriculum of this school has a wide range. It includes the study of sanitation, agriculture, literature, composition and translation, geography, history, French, chemistry, mining, cosmography, zoölogy, government, finance and economy, legislation, commercial and international law, Turkish law, bookkeeping, Arabic, Persian, engineering and algebra. This administrative school has five hundred students. By administrative, is meant the knowledge of the modes of administering governmental affairs. In this regard America might take a lesson from Turkey. With the exception of this last class of students—who are supposed to be sufficiently posted to take a position in the government at once after they leave the school—these scholars, as soon as they finish their studies, are placed in some bureau of information, but without pay. Their only occupation is to copy old letters which are of no use. They do this to form their handwriting. Their literary exercises, and principally their orthography, after three or four years of exercise are supposed to be good. When there is a vacancy in the government, they get in by some hierarchical order or civil-service reform movement, and advance little by little, according to the vacancies which occur. It happens often that men thus trained become Foreign Ministers, Governor-Generals and even Cabinet Ministers.

In Turkey, any one, even a slave, can become a Marshal of the empire, or Grand Vizier. There are no hereditary or other titles of nobility. The names of the great and small folk are as simple as can be. The titles of Aga, Effendi and Pasha are as common as our "colonels" were after the civil war. They are handles, like our Mister. Some of these scholars enter upon a military career. Then they must go through the military school. Some enter the navy. They have to go through the naval school. The fact is, that every boy who goes to school has one object in view: it is to enter into the employ of the government.

The real education of the Turkish child commences with his babyhood. It follows him up until he is a man, with his principles and conduct more or less molded by ignorant servants. These habits are more or less refined away at school, and by contact with other boys, who have something new to teach one another. I am bound and glad to say that, with all the disadvantages, the Turk is naturally good-natured and good-hearted. When he enters upon public affairs, he is the most generous, the most polite, and the most patient official to be found anywhere. He does not lack either in natural faculties or in acquired intelligence. He may be cunning, and, as a general rule, although slow, he is well equipped for his business.

# CHAPTER XLII.

AFTER some Diversions in my library, in glancing over the marvels of the thousand and one adventures of princesses and *hanoums*, recorded by the story-tellers of Bagdad, and minutely observing the illustrations of the famous volume, I take down the heavy tome of Mahometan law, which the East Indian judges have collated out of the Koran and customs of Mahometan countries. As the constant question about the Orient is that of the relation of the sexes, I resolved to make a serious "diversion" into the domain of matrimony.

The institution of marriage, whether with one or more wives, is at the base of human society. Upon it rests social stability and order, and domestic felicity and virtue. Under its wing are the "little ones" gathered, upon whom depend so much of present comfort for parents and future safety for state and people. Perhaps the greatest anomaly connected with human advancement is the fact that Christian nations have formed their institutions upon models of the Old Testament, with its patriarchs and tribal system, and its Jewish kings and their Oriental households, and yet have so eliminated the primal feature of ancient Judean life as to have ignored Abraham and Solomon in their practice of the plurality of wives. Only the Mormon, that thrifty branch of a dead stump, preserves this practice and peculiarity. Like the Chinese artist, he faithfully copies the ugly flaw of the vase, along with its elegant shape and proportion.

Whether, or when, our "twin relic," which now flutters as if wounded in a vital part, shall be abolished from the domain of America, is a problem almost as insoluble as that which now, owing to the presence of the Ottoman in Europe, vexes the nations over the conditions of Turkish civilization.

Why is it that polygamy, as practiced in the Orient, and especially in Turkey, and which, as most argue, saps the foundation of social vigor and home content, remains to this day? What is there in its secluded and strange methods, copied from the customs of those whom we daily commend for their faith, devotion and wisdom, which has given it strength to defy our Federal government for thirty years and more? To respond to these queries involves an examination of the force of sensual allurements and religious enthusiasm. Nowhere can the many curious and peculiar features of the system be better studied than in Mussulman countries. Polygamy is the chief one of these features. It has never been thoroughly investigated, save in India and other Eastern countries, by the Western jurist, although it constitutes the basis of manifold social relations.

What, then, is a Mahometan marriage? It is well known that in the Orient polygamy is legally and religiously sanctioned. It is regulated by an elaborate code.

Before entering upon the subject, let us understand the points which make such a code a necessity. Without such a code the followers of Islam could not be extricated from the innumerable difficulties in which they are involved by reason of polygamy.

In order to make this statement clear, it must be premised that the Mahometan, like the Christian religion, has its schisms. The principal and best defined divisions are those of the Sheeahs and the Soonnees. Both of these sects recognize the same fundamental principles and laws of Islam. They worship in the same mosques, and perform the same ceremonies. Still, there is a difference in their marriage code, to say nothing of the hatred existing between them.

The Soonnees are Turks and Arabs. Of these, there are great numbers in India, China, Central Asia, and on the African continent. The Sheeahs are Persians. In A. D. 1499 they proclaimed the Sheeah faith to be the national religion of the country. Quite a number professing this creed are to be found in India. Sheeah means a troop or sect. It is the distinct appellation of the followers of Ali, or of all those who maintain that he was the legitimate Khalif or successor of Mahomet.

Marriage with Mussulmans is merely a civil transaction. It has attached to it no religious ceremony especially obligatory. Contracts of marriage cannot be made, except by those authorized by the code, which enacts six prohibitions. These are consanguinity, fosterage, affinity, completion of number, imprecation and infidelity.   Another and peculiar marriage is that of slaves, either by contract or by right of property.

It is customary among the Mahometan people to betroth their children in their infancy.   The right to contract belongs to the father, the paternal grandfather, the master, the executor, or the judge.   Contracts made by either of these are binding on the children, even if the marriage has not been effected up to the time they attain their majority.   In case the grandfather and the father contract with two different persons, the choice of the grandfather prevails.   But if, by the time the child attain its majority, no contract has been entered into by any of the persons intrusted with the power to do so, then their authority on the subject is at an end.   The consent of an adult is thereupon necessary for her or his marriage, unless insanity exists.   As to the slaves, a master may contract his female slave in marriage.   Whether young or mature, sane or insane, she has no option in the matter.   The same rule prevails in the case of a male slave.

Let us now consider the formalities with regard to the marriage of free men and women, and limit the statement to mature marriages, or those not contracted for those in infancy.

As soon as the boy attains the marriageable age, his father and mother cast about to find him a wife.   The mother visits her acquaintances.   She makes quiet quest into their harems; for, as I have said, the Turkish houses have rooms exclusively reserved for the women.

The mother may not allow the object of her search to transpire among her friends and neighbors ; but still she is indefatigable and subtle in her search of a suitable bride for her son.   At length, and after much maternal anxiety, she finds what seems to be the actual of her ideal.

She reports the fact to her husband.   She details to him the particular graces of her choice.   Then, if the family to which the elect belongs suits the husband, and the " bill of particulars " is satisfactory, and if the accomplishments of the girl are approved, the "managing" mother arranges a party to the Turkish bath— for the bath is an institution in Oriental realms, and almost a part of the devotion of the faithful.   There the future bride is to be the principal object of attention.   There her future mother-in-law is to ascertain whether or not the girl has any constitutional defects.

Sir Thomas More, before composing his "Utopia," must have studied this custom of the Orient ; for he wrote that it seemed strange to the Utopians that in other countries great caution was displayed in buying a horse or other animal, so as to ascertain whether it were sound and healthy, and yet, when it came to a solemn contract for good or ill, and for life, no such painstaking was exercised. The Utopians thought such remissness most culpable.

The day is appointed for the bath. Great preparations are made. It is tacitly understood, though not expressed, what the bath party means. The cooks of both parties are kept busy for several days. They prepare dainty dishes and sweetmeats of every description and flavor. The Turkish women, not unlike the "children of the azure sheen," are very fond of confectionery. The greatest attention is paid, also, in procuring the rarest and most elegant suits for the bath. A competitive but friendly excitement arises between the families ; for the Turks are as particular about their bathing clothes as the fashionable belle at Schevningen or Newport.

The bride, or the nominee for that function, is arrayed in her most elegant dress. She is escorted to the bath in her best bravery of silk and satin, *feridjie* and parasol. She is accompanied by her mother and all the women of her house. The servants and slaves are summoned for this service ; and the more numerous these are, the more the display of luxury is enhanced. As soon as the parties meet, there is a series of endless compliments. In this the Turkish people excel. Coffee and sherbet are served around to the company, which is seated on the divans. Amidst clouds of smoke from narghile, pipe and cigarette, and with gossip and laughter which "make old wrinkles come," the future mother-in-law adroitly seats herself by the nominee. She persuades her to talk. Unconscious of the object, the girl undergoes a skillful cross-examination. Her intellectual and moral character is thoroughly scrutinized. Her life, with its tastes and qualities, is winnowed. When the smoking terminates, there is the disrobing in order to go into the interior of the bath. Then follows the robing for the bath. The bath being intensely hot, the robing is not cumbrous or extensive. It consists simply of a big towel around the waist covering the person down to the knees, and a second towel which is thrown over the shoulders like a sash.

This last towel is taken off as soon as the interior of the bath is entered, as the heat and consequent perspiration make it intolerable. Gibbon says that Zenobia, when led in triumph by Aurelian, almost fainted under the intolerable burden of jewelry. Not so with our candidate for the bridal office. Her decorations are reserved for her triumphal procession and entry into her new household.

The hair is unloosened and hangs over the shoulders. Each lady is taken care of by one or two servants ; but the future mother-in-law never quits the nominee. She makes thorough investigation until the bath is over. If, like the sisters of the Gorgons—the Graeæ—who had but one eye and one tooth among the entire sisterhood with which to go out and make their calls, our nominee should be found wanting in these or any other pre-requisites to healthy and beautiful womanhood, is it not reasonable to believe that the future mother-in-law would discover the flaw and announce the fact to her lord and husband ?

The place and mode of bathing are quite different from those of the European or American. The bath is a large square room. It is paved with marble or stones. It is air-tight. In it there are fountains attached to the walls. They furnish cold and hot water. Under these fountains there are small basins about fifteen inches wide and ten inches deep. These are fixed at about half a yard above the floor. The basins are filled with water, the degree of whose heat is regulated at will. The bather seats herself on the floor by the basin and the servant washes her, soaping and lathering her head and then her body, pouring the water from the basin over the head and rinsing off the snowy suds. If in a festive mood, the younger females play the Naïad, and, not infrequently, throw water about, over themselves and others, with a hilarity belonging to youth in its sportive morning. Sometimes these nymphs thus dally with the elements for hours. Sometimes the more lethargic lie in soak or undergo the process of maceration, but not often on these betrothal occasions.

After this, dry clothes are brought. Neither are these "voluminous and vast," for they consist of two towels, with a third one to crown the head, like a turban. Before leaving the interior of the bath, all the party, including the damsel, dye their nails and the palms of the hands with henna. Then they hie in a group to the cooling-room. Then the banquet begins. Rugs are spread upon the floor. A stool is placed in the middle of the room. On this is placed a large salver. The company seat themselves, cross-legged, on the rugs and around the stool and salver. The former is covered with a gorgeous table-cloth. A long strip of finest linen, bordered and broidered with golden or silken figures, say one yard wide and nine yards long, is passed around to the guests. What for ? To be used as a napkin, in common. It gives unity to the sentiment and the festivity. Then the servants bring in the delicacies. Each dish is placed in the middle of the salver. The "leading lady," with dainty finger and thumb, takes up the acceptable tidbit, and accomplishes the first responsible bite. Then the others follow ; plunging their henna-tinted fingers into the single dish. Bite after bite follows, with lively and glee-ful procession. This interesting process—if one could only see it—would reproduce one of the pictures of Spenser in his " Faërie Queen." It is that enchanted vision where Sir Callidore, in going through the Bower of Bliss, is saluted by bevies of beauteous damosels, who pluck luscious clusters of grapes from the over-hanging vines, and press the nectar into golden goblets with fairy fingers. "So fair a wine press makes the wine more sweet." With a little changing of Spenser's fancy, may it not be said, " So fair a group of banqueters makes the banquet more tasteful." There is no enchanted viand before the happy company. No drink is allowed to stimulate or drown the senses. The only drink is pure water and lemonade! The mother-in-law has no chance to get at the incautious truth, on the maxim—*in vino veritas.*

The artist, when called upon to paint the grief of Iphigenia over the death of Agamemnon, dropped the curtain. We do not follow this gruesome example ; for the subject is not sad. But we have not the artistic skill to create, in the reader's imagination, such imagery of this bath and banquet as to do justice to the scene.

The banquet may last three or four hours. Generally, the bride does not know or seem to know its object. Sometimes even the mother of the bride ignores it ; although she may suspect it. After the dinner, the coffee and smoking are finished, the parties separate with earnest promises to renew the entertainment.

The mother of the boy goes home. There she is expected with anxiety by her husband. He waits eagerly to hear her impressions. She gives him such a detailed account of her investigations as only a female and a mother can give. If the report be satisfactory, the next step is to rally for the election of the nominee. A day or two after, the mother of the boy pays a visit to the family of the girl. There she reveals her object. As a matter of course, the mother of "the nominee" is surprised! She dodges the proposal by postponing an answer until she consults her husband, who happens to be absent; but she promises to speak to him about it. In returning the visit, the girl's mother bears the answer of her husband. If the proposition be agreeable, the mother manages a meeting of the husbands, in order to arrange the terms of the contract and dower, as well as to fix the time for the marriage.

Perhaps one disadvantage connected with the marital relation in this polygamous country is that there is no courting. The amusement, comfort and delight implied in this term are not altogether unknown; but if done at all, it is so surreptitious that the satisfaction is limited. The marriage, in fact, is a lottery. Sometimes the betrothal takes place when the bride and groom are but children. They have never seen each other. Of course, he is attracted by the wonderful poetry and eulogium which the go-between gives in extravagant phrase of the girl's beauty. Is she not fair? What is the lily at the dawn? Is she not slender and graceful as the doe; as mild and radiant as the full moon? The "old aunty" thus arouses the imagination of the boy who would wed.

To the expected bride she will say: "Is he not as brave as the sword of Selim? Is not his hand open to charity, even as that of the Sultan? Will he not give you children as radiant and as fair as the dewy rose?"

But they seldom have a chance in advance to test these extravagant expressions. However, there is one consolation if it be a lottery, for if, when the bridegroom sees the bride, he is not pleased, divorce is easy, even though it be expensive.

The betrothal of a young Turkish girl calls for a grand party. How this betrothal is accomplished; how the young girl may possibly have a peep at her husband through some lattice or chink in the door—has often been described. It is generally believed that the bridegroom does not see the bride until many days after the betrothal. The betrothal consists in a marriage contract. The bride may then take a new name. She becomes a *hanoum*. When she is brought home to the bridegroom, another festival is inaugurated, with furniture and other gifts for the housekeeper, and a throne for the bride. A prayer-carpet is also given, and at last a peaceful and happy home is almost invariably the finality.

There has been much difficulty in establishing Turkish schools for girls. Mrs. Walker, in her book about Turkey, was employed in one of these schools to teach drawing. Her picture of the school is a humorous one :

She has charge of some forty girls; some of them are matured women. They are all eager to be educated, just as our young Africans were after the war ; but a cigarette was more attractive to them than a slate and pencil, and the promenade more alluring than even making pictures in oil or water. Their minds ran more on matrimony than in depicting ruined temples and spoiled kiosks. An incident in connection with her school in a Turkish village of the Bosporus, illustrates the mode by which sometimes the young women are selected as wives. When the girls are assembled in the school, a strange, weird, old woman enters. She produces a flutter in the dove-cote. The teacher makes inquiry:

"Who is she ? "

" Oh! she comes to look at the girls."

" For what purpose ? " asks the artist-teacher.

" You will see soon," reply the giggling beauties.

The old woman settles down to a special stare at two of the houris, and then leaves. Then the explanation comes. She is picking out a wife for some one. The school then becomes a sort of marital market. After such a scene, those selected for matrimony begin to dress with extraordinary attire and fantastic splendor. The girls wear all their jewelry and their head-dresses, with a " twittering " sort of consciousness and a general airiness of manner.

In case the children have no father or grandfather, the consummation of the contract depends on their guardian. He assumes the same authority in the premises as if he were the father himself.

In the perfection of a marriage contract, and in order to make it valid, care must be taken to avoid the legal prohibitions. They are as follows : A man cannot marry his mother or grandmother,

AN OLD WOMAN LOOKING FOR BRIDES IN THE SCHOOLROOM.

nor his daughter nor their daughters, nor the daughters of his sons and sisters, nor the daughters of these and the daughters of their children, nor his aunts and the sisters of his grandfathers, maternal or paternal. The like classes are prohibited to the women. Consanguinity is attributed where there are valid marriages or the semblance of them. Still, marriage with a natural child is prohibited both to father and mother. Fosterage, which is established by the milk, is another impediment ; but it has reference to the quantity of the lacteal fluid, and it must be such as gives increase to the flesh and strength to the bones. According to the " Sheeahs," no effect is attributed to anything less than fifteen acts of suckling, or continued suckling for a day and a night. These fifteen acts must be consecutive from one woman ; and if another woman intervenes before the completion of this magic number—like Rip Van Winkle's drink of schnapps, after he swore off—they do not count. The nurse does not become the foster-mother of the child, unless she complete the nursing. She does not obtain the benefactions and gifts which ensue, unless she perfect the work. All these conditions have reference to an infant under two years old.

The milk must be drawn from the breast. Any " deludation," or tainting of the milk, or any artificial nursing, does not incur prohibition in marrying. The nurse should be of the Mussulman faith, chaste and pure. No infidel is allowed, except under great necessity. She must be restrained from drinking wine or eating pork. It is an old traditionary rule that she must not be a fire-worshipper. The children nursed by the same woman cannot intermarry. Their fathers and mothers cannot marry any of the children nursed by the same woman who nursed their child. The husband must be of the Mussulman faith ; that is to say, a Mussulman can marry a Christian or Jewish woman, but a Muslimah (Mussulman woman) cannot marry with a Christian or Jew. Marriage with fire-worshippers is utterly prohibited. No marriage is permitted with a repudiated woman, unless six months have elapsed since she has been repudiated. A thrice-repudiated woman cannot remarry with her husband, unless she has been intermediately married to another man, and the marriage has been actually consummated. If the man has taken the legal number to wife—i. e., four—he cannot contract any new marriage, unless he repudiate one of his wives.

All these impediments being taken into consideration, the contract is signed.   The dower is payable, half in advance ; the other half remains to be paid to the wife in case of repudiation.   This reservation is prudence itself.   It enables her to support herself during the time she is forbidden to contract a new marriage.

The marriage service in Turkey is very simple.   Every marriage is substantially based upon this formula :

*The man to his intended wife :*  "It is my right to love several women, and your right only to love me!   Attend to your duty, and I will look out for my rights! "

This is concise, and somewhat after the teachings of the Koran ; but if she chose to make trouble in the family it is costly, for divorce means dower ; and dower to some people in the Orient means death.

It is the custom, in most of the places in the Ottoman empire, that the marriage festivities should last four days.   They generally commence on Mondays.   Invitations are sent out for the first day, to the high dignitaries of the place ; on the second day to officers of the army and navy, as well as to magistrates ; and on the third day, to civil functionaries and to financial folk and tradesmen.   The fourth day, the doors are open.   All friends and acquaintances may then enter in and tender congratulations. This tender must be made late in the afternoon.   The bridegroom is then associated with relatives and friends.   The same ceremonial is followed on the part of the bride.

On Monday morning, one or two bands of Turkish music are on hand.   A Turkish band is composed of a kind of banjo, some tambourines, and sometimes the clarinet and violin.   The men who play the banjo and tambourine also sing.   Games are made and plays performed.   Juggling is common.   Dancing and gymnastics are not neglected in the fête.   As the men and women do not mingle, and as the Turks never dance, professional dancers are engaged.   They don a sort of petticoat for the purpose. Sometimes Gypsy women are hired, who dance after certain methods hardly in vogue in fastidious communities.   It is quite proper that only the men are present to enjoy these sensuous diversions. There are buffoons, dwarfs, story-tellers and wrestlers, who contribute to the amusement of the men ; for amusement seems to be the sole object of their gathering, in which, however, are not wanting eating and drinking, sherbet and syrups, and then talking loosely, after the manner of gregarious men on such assemblages.

Upon occasions of this kind, the wedding parties generally go to some watering-place near the city or town, to spend part of the day. There the wrestlers and other genii perform. Among other amusements, there is a separate party to the bath for both sexes. This takes place on Thursday. The bridegroom goes with his friends, and the bride goes with her friends. It is a singular feature of the wedding, that every amusement at the bridegroom's house is repeated at the bride's house.

On the afternoon of Thursday, the two parties gather under the one roof of the house which is to be the abode of the newly married couple. The women meet in the *haremlik* and the men in the *salemlik*. Not among the least of the delights upon this occasion, is the display by the bride of her diamonds and other jewelry. The custom is not, as we know, peculiar to the Orient. The presents she receives, her trousseau and toilet, are viewed with the optics of critical and admiring female friends. These are arranged in one or two rooms, so as to display their symmetric and lustrous beauty, and so that the guests may felicitate the happy possessors. After having admired the bride herself and the wealth wherewith she is adorned and endowed, and wherewithal she is arrayed—even to the trimmings of her dress and the adornments of her hair—the company themselves begin to share the happiness of the pair.

The writer, being of the ruder sex, has never been admitted as yet to admire any bride in Turkey but—his own. He is unable to say how the Turkish bride looks or acts in her elegant toilet; but, on veracious hearsay, he undertakes to reproduce something of the graphic and vivacious hilarities and scenes of the " home coming " of the wedded in this Oriental land.

Let the reader, therefore, enter in fancy into the haremlik, where the writer cannot go. The room to which the bride is taken is decorated with flowers hung on the walls and on the ceiling. These are intermingled with silk stuffs of bright and variegated color. The divan is covered with a richly embroidered cloth. In one corner there is a special seat for the bride. It has the appearance of a throne. Why not? Is not the bride to be a queen here —until dethroned? Next to this room is the bridal chamber. It is shown to the visitors. The bed is magnificently made up with embroidered silk hangings and velvet coverlets, that would make the old home-made quilts of our grandmothers in America "crazy." Every convenience to begin comfortable housekeeping appears. On one side of the couch are the "night gowns" of the bride and the bridegroom. On the divan is the morning gown of each. On the table there are two small vases. They contain Oriental perfumes. These are the usual objects in the Oriental bridal chamber. As to the general furnishing of the bedroom, it depends on the pecuniary and social position of families.

There is a third room shown to visitors. Here are elegant dresses and toilets, mirrors, table services, linen, tables, chairs, etc., down to the most menial kitchen utensil. The Turks do not make much use of stoves; but there are braziers for warmth by charcoal, called *mangals*. They are of metal—silver, bronze or copper. They give their shining beauty to the room.

The crowd is immense in the haremlik on Thursday, when the bride makes her entrance into her new home. So great is the throng that a mistress of ceremonies is a *desideratum.* She prevents overcrowding, and endeavors to make the guests comfortable. The room in which the bride is to be received is kept free from the mass. The visitors are seated in the surrounding rooms and in their nooks and angles. As there are no men allowed in the haremlik, the women rush in there with absolute freedom. Nearly all of them uncover their faces. Mischief fairly dances in their large black eyes!

Now comes the very acme and the heyday of this unique entertainment! Upon the forenoon of this eventful day, a long procession of carriages, loaded with elegant toilets, moves toward the house of the bridegroom. In its midst there is one carriage specially honored. It may not compare with the bridal chariot described in the Bible, whose wood was of cedar, its pillars of silver, its bottom of gold, its covering of purple, and the midst thereof paved with love for the daughters of Jerusalem. It may, at least for the poorer class, be only the ordinary arabi or wagon, gilded outside, and furnished within with yellow silk, or for the richer, such as one may see going from Stamboul over the bridge to Pera in a coach of French or German manufacture, with an elegant high-stepping team of bays. But, for rich or poor, there is a favored vehicle, in which, as yet in maiden meditation, sits the central figure of the procession! She is dressed in faultless array; her artist has prepared the eye with a pencil, quite worthy of Meissonier. Her face is shrouded under a thick veil of gold threads, which floats down to her waist. As soon as the procession approaches the house, notice is given to the bridegroom. He hurries to the door of the haremlik, to receive the bride; for, be it known, as to this day of days, the bridegroom is made an exception, and is graciously allowed to enter the sacred precincts where the group of women awaits him. He tenders his arm to the bride. He conducts her through the crowd of women to the throne room. He seats her on the throne. He speaks to her some honeyed words, full of Oriental metaphor and loving ardor. Perhaps he recites a verse from Hafiz, about the love of the bulbul and the rose; or, perhaps he compares his beloved, after Solomon's ornate style, with all the fragrance of the gardens and the glory of the morning. Perhaps he calls her a bundle of myrrh, a cluster of camphire in the vineyards of En-ghadi, the rose of Sharon, the lily of the valley; or like unto a young hart upon the mountains of spices! Perhaps he tells her that she is as fair as the moon and clear as the sun; or something, if not so grandiose, more appropriate and gentle for the occasion.

In passing amidst the women, he bows low and hangs his head modestly downward. Nevertheless, the women affect surprise and indignation at his intrusion within their precinct. They begin a general howling. They cover their faces with fluttering haste; for is not this apparition a horrid monster? Regardless of feet or hands, the Turkish women must cover their faces. Then they are indeed secluded. No reck for any other part of the body. As is generally the case on such occasions, if their yashmaks are not near, they take hold of their skirts and with them hide their blushes. The bridegroom continues his compliments to the bride. She continues to enshroud her face. He retires bent like an interrogation point, and looking sheepishly absorbed in æsthetic study of the figures and hues of the rug upon the floor. While retiring, he scatters among the crowd small coin by the handful— gold, silver or copper, according to his wealth and position. The women still keep their faces under cover; and, from under cover, as from the chorus in a Greek drama, there comes a murmur of approbation for the happy match, and sometimes of disapprobation, if, in the opinion of the chorus, it is a bad match. The bride then takes refreshments, and rests a little. The gold-thread veil covering her face is taken off. She is ready to show herself to the visitors; but only, of course, to the female portion.

To give a description of the attire of the bride demands a dainty pen and a nicer sense than belongs to the sterner sex. The writer essays to do it with apprehension. First : She wears wide trousers, not unlike a petticoat, tied at the ankle on each leg. The fabric is of red, blue or yellow silk, embroidered with gold. Then there is a robe of silk or velvet, and a long train, glittering with gold embroideries and precious stones and surrounded with gold trimmings and lace. Her boots or shoes are adorned in the same mode. The dressing of her head is remarkable, and her face is painted in the most exaggerated manner, in white and red, and her eyes, her eyebrows, and eyelashes are delicately penciled. These elegancies of the toilet rob something of grace from her naturalness by defacing her maiden beauty. Upon her cheeks are stuck two jewels, each as large as half a dollar. In the middle of each cheek there is a big diamond. Over the cheek and on the forehead are affixed small gold stars, mounted with precious stones. This completes the costly disfigurement of the face. Over the forehead, a tuft is mounted with an extremely large diamond ; if the family be well off, this gem is something less than a walnut. Another diamond, oblong in shape, is fixed on one side of the head. From the crown of the head down to the ear, diamonds are scattered over and through the hair. Kid gloves cover her hands, over which a large number of rings are worn. A beautiful fan completes the picture of the bride *en toilette.* It is disenchanting to know that the tuft, the oblong diamond, and the wedding dresses are often hired for the ceremony. That is not unreasonable, because it is economical ; for these portions of the regalia cannot be used on any other than a wedding occasion, or by any one else than a bride.

The bride being refreshed, the congratulations of the visitors commence. The mistress of ceremonies shows the ladies into the bride's room. In groups of eight or ten they approach the bride, examine her with the greatest curiosity, and address her a "Mashallah! Mashallah!" which means, "May Allah guard you!" They then retire. All the visitors make this round of ceremonious piety.

Meanwhile, the amusements, on both sides of the house, haremlik and salemlik, continue. After sunset, the bridegroom, who is supposed not to know his bride—never having seen the face of his wife—is expected to make a call upon her by the inside door which communicates with the harem. This is the effort of his life. It requires exquisite diplomacy and stalwart courage; for has he not to escape from his own hilarious friends and relatives, who are ready to play every prank known to human mischief, and who make every exertion to detain him from the society of his beloved? This is the culminating pleasantry of the occasion. It commences smoothly enough, and the bridegroom takes it with good temper and vivacity; but the more he tries to avoid, deceive and flee from them, the more teasing and vigilant they become. Finally, in despair, he tries to elude them by sheer force. In some instances he fails in this. He is sometimes thrashed soundly; but no question of assault and battery is ever raised.

When the bridegroom at last reaches his bride, he finds her still with face covered, as when she came into the house. Usage requires that, after he gives her a present, he should uncover her face. They then exchange compliments. From that moment her face is to be veiled to every one of the other sex, except to him.

This is marriage in its most simple and ordinary ceremony. The husband, as it is his right, may want to marry a second wife, and after the second he may want a third and a fourth one. These are in addition to the odalisques, which he may have *ad libitum*. Here is where the entanglement and trouble begins in the household.

The first wife has no right to oppose her husband's marrying a second, third and fourth time. He is not compelled even to ask her opinion about the matter. He is free in the premises, so long as he does not exceed four wives. The only instance where the consent of the wife is required is in case the husband wants to marry a cousin or an aunt of hers. She may oppose and prevent such an alliance. If he insist, in spite of her opposition, he must repudiate the wife and pay her dower. This sometimes is a difficult thing to do.

The dower is obligatory, though it is not necessary that it should be a part of the contract. Its amount is fixed by agreement. As a rule, it varies according to the social condition of the woman. Thus, in case no dower has been allowed, as often happens, the judge fixes it under the law; and although the law has fixed some limits to it, still it is left to the discretion of the judge.

He may make it sufficient for the kind of living to which the woman has been accustomed.

In making the dower obligatory, the code has in view principally a provision for the repudiated wife. Dower is intended also as a shield against too frequent repudiations. It happens often, that though the husband is desirous of repudiating his wife, he finds it impossible to pay her dower ; so he abstains from repudiating her. The law fixes the dower to five hundred *drams* of silver, or sixty-five ounces of silver. This is but a pittance nowadays; but it was fixed by the Prophet. This is the amount which he assessed for his own wives. It must have been adequate for the few necessities required by a woman among the Arab tribes at Mecca and Medina thirteen hundred years ago. Besides, it was fixed at an epoch when silver was scarcer than it is now, and before bonanzas of the white metal had leaped out of the sunless temples of the earth.

Moreover, anything which is capable of being legally acquired may be made in payment of dower, except wine and hogs! One of the odd forms of dower is the teaching of a chapter of the Koran by the husband to the wife. It is a pious, though a pecuniary equivalent! Dower also may be a slave, or a house, or anything of value. If the husband is not able to furnish them, he is liable for their value. The dower may also be agreed upon after the marriage. The wife may exonerate the husband from the dower, or she may commute it for something else. She becomes the proprietor of the dower, and may legally dispose of it ; but should the husband divorce her before the marriage is consummated, the half of it reverts to him. Should she forgive him that which belongs to her, the whole would be his. If a slave be assigned as dower, and she should emancipate the slave, and she is divorced before the consummation of the marriage, she is liable for half the value of the slave. In case of dispute with regard to the amount of the dower, the word of the husband is preferred until the contrary is proved ; whereas, if he acknowledge the amount stated as the dower, and alleges its delivery, but fails to prove it, credit is given to the word and oath of the woman.

The code provides as to the time to be devoted by the husband to each one of his wives, in case he has more than one. This rule of law has its initiative in the organic law that each man has a right to four wives, and that a man has the absolute disposal of all the hours of the day for himself. The law allows no right to the wife to claim the attention of her husband during the daytime. It creates an obligation upon the husband to divide the rest of his time equally between his wives, or, at least, he is not bound to make his court, or to be with one wife, more than once in every four days, and this, whether he has one wife or more. If among his wives there is a slave, she has the right only to receive half the time allotted to the free wife. This does not include slaves or odalisques who are not lawfully married.

The temporary marriages being admitted only by the Sheeahs, and these temporary contracts not being under general Mahometan law, it may suffice to state that such marriages can be legally made for one month or one year. They are allowed by the religious rules of that sect.

The harshness of the marriage contract toward the women of the Mahometan countries is greatly exaggerated, if not entirely fanciful. Marriage is, as we have said, a civil contract. It gives no preference or right to either of the contracting parties over the property of the other party. The wife retains her power of disposing of her estate. She can be sued or sue. In suing, she has no need of a " next friend " or trustee. She may summon her own husband into court. Nor is he liable for any debts of her contracting. He does not vulgarly, as was once the custom in America, advertise her absence from bed or board to avoid the payment of her debts. True, he must maintain her and pay her dower, as we have stated, in case of separation.

So that, in many respects, if Western nations may not learn something of utility and equity from the Mahometan code, in the matter of marriage, they may at least refuse to credit the wild and unfounded statements that the woman of the East is a slave to her husband, and compelled to serve him, as if he had the ring of the Arabian story, upon which the genii were accustomed to wait.

In the second chapter of the Koran, there are several paragraphs in relation to wives and divorce. From these the law of Turkey, in these respects, is drawn :

" The women ought also to behave toward their husbands in like manner as their husbands should behave toward them, according to what is just."

The family relation is so often discussed in connection with Turkey, that full justice cannot be done unless there is emphasized the doctrine of adoption. That doctrine is a part of the Oriental religion. It is sacred to the Turk. During the time of the grandfather of the present Sultan, there had been adopted by the princess, the Sultana Asme, a beautiful girl called Nazip Hanoum. The Sultan desired to wed her; but she defied him. The Sultan, with all his autocratic power, rich gifts and imperial prestige, could not obtain his wish or move the adopted girl to enter his seraglio, for was she not adopted by a princess, and free to judge as to her own domestic life?

Every Pasha, whatever may be his domestic predilection, is compelled to have one principal wife. She is called the *Buyuk* Hanoum. She is always attended by two slaves, and has often privileges which the other wives do not possess.

From wrong impressions as to the domestic life of women in Turkey, as in all Moslem countries, it is often inferred that there is no home in Turkey; and the question is asked, How can a man with more than one wife, and with his household separated into two parts—the Haremlik and Salemlik—and with his children and wives so thoroughly screened from the outer world, contribute to the incomparable happiness of the hearthstone? But I dare avouch that no people are more fond of their homes than the Turks, and toward their children they are inordinately partial. So far as I have observed, their courtesy to the other sex is unfailing. The Turk treats his wife at home, as I have understood, with the same inbred courtesy which he displays toward the gentler sex away from home. Outside of his own *zenana*, the accomplished Turk, who is connected with the governing power of his country, while making no reckless display of knightly courtesy, is always chivalric and gentle.

A race of men which has been so tolerant as the Turk toward other religionists—which finds it so pleasant to be neighborly and honest toward strangers, and which always treats animals with kindness, cannot, unless spoiled by contact with other races, be other than kind. Considering their history as peasants and soldiers, and their dominant Tartar blood, and the fact that they are descended from the same race as those saintly heroes who, like Ghengis Khan and Tamerlane, ravaged the very earth itself, it should be said, to their credit, that they have, perhaps, by means of the teachings of the Koran and Arabic literature, cultivated and practiced the knightly graces toward the female sex.

# CHAPTER XLIII.

It is a busy week for the Legation which brings together the Ramazan and Bairam fêtes, the honors and dinners to the officers and men of the *Kearsarge* and the Commencements of the American College and Home School. Besides, does it not include the Fourth of July, which happens on Sunday? Our political Sabbath is not celebrated with that hilarity which the day should inspire, because it was a *dies Dominicus.* This day and its glories, however, do furnish the climax of all the honors to the *Kearsarge*, in which the Minister had his Diversion. The Sultan determines that nothing shall be omitted to make his hospitality to the United States complete. He gives the naval officers and their diplomatic representative a grand entertainment at the Arsenal Palace. Among Turkish officials present are Hassan Pasha, Minister of Marine, who presides; the Commodore commanding the *Mahmoudie;* Munir Pasha, First Chamberlain to the Sultan; Ibrahim Bey, Hakki Pasha and others.

The dinner begins at eight. The Turkish band, which is famous for its rare music, entertains the company. The quay and the Golden Horn in front of the palace are illuminated, and with the lights on the stream and from the Bairam illuminations, and the moon, there is displayed a scene for a weird picture by Turner. Munir Pasha, is the bearer of many choice compliments from the Sultan. At the conclusion of the feast, the Minister of Marine makes an address in Turkish. In this he expresses the kindest wishes of the Sultan and the pleasant impression which the visit of the *Kearsarge* has made upon his people. A warmer welcome could not have been tendered. The Minister responds. Among other things, he remarks that "America, like Turkey, is a composite nation. In the United States, many peoples of divers races and religions make a mosaic of all qualities, united in one character.

Among these qualities, how much had been given, not only to America, but to the world, by the Oriental mind ? Has it not transmuted astrology into astronomy, and alchemy into chemistry ? The Department of Marine, with its explosives and forces for war and peace, knew what the West had given to the East of practical science, in return for the Oriental abstractions of mathematics. The West," continued the writer, or, rather, speaker, " shakes hands in many ways with the East to-night. As we go west around our planet, we meet the East; and as we go east we meet the West; and thus we merge into one at this happy board, knit together by that boundless hospitality which only the Orient can bestow." Evidently, the wine at this feast had made the round of the table with a magic rapidity, only equaled by that of Puck around the earth!

The Minister closes by wishing long life and a happy reign to His Majesty; and compliments the Minister of Marine and the courteous company who honor his country.

His Majesty also tendered to the crew of the *Kearsarge* a dinner; but as only a select number, fifty, could be spared from the ship, that number partook of a dinner in the adjoining rooms. The American Minister appeared before them and made a little more rhetoric. Rousing cheers are given for the Sultan. The remaining sailors on the *Kearsarge* are not forgotten by the amiable sovereign; for he orders for them a dinner of the same kind to be sent to the vessel.

As the sailors leave the Arsenal quay with the *Kearsarge* band, they sing our national song. The Bosporus rings with unwonted acclamations.

Following this dinner, the day after, Prince Mehmet, the eldest son of the Sultan, and his companions, the nephews of the Sultan, are received on board the *Kearsarge* by the Admiral and his officers, the Minister, and by that most admirable of all courteous gentlemen, Mr. Gwynne Harris Heap, the Consul-General. The son delivers, as His Majesty afterward told me, his second public speech. He is a young man about seventeen years of age. He is exceedingly modest and well-behaved. He is already married ; and we are told that he is devoted to his wife.

Following this reception, on the next day, is the Salemlik. It has already been described. After that the Sultan gives an audience to the Admiral and the Minister. This passes off in the most

agreeable manner. These hospitalities surprise the other Legations. They do not consider the fact that America has no
designs upon either the dynasty or the territory of Turkey. Why
should not the Sultan be partial to our country?

In connection with this visit of the *Kearsarge* to the Bosporus,
it becomes a part of the duty and pleasure of the Minister's wife
to give an entertainment to our officers. The Hotel Royal is
thrown open for the occasion, with such adornments of flags and
such a presence of the Ministers of all nationalities as to make the
festivity one long to be remembered, not merely because the dance
is kept up until late in the morning, but because, with the aid of
the band of the *Kearsarge* and the skill and grace of the officers
in dancing, the young people of all the Legations, of both sexes,
have mutual and cordial Diversion.

To conclude this series of entertainments, this week of continuous enjoyment, by the renewal of old acquaintances and the
making of new—the consummation is reached when, from the
State Department, I receive a friendly, semi-official letter that its
Head is interested in these performances, which are *quasi* national,
and that the Secretary is happy to know that "old friends,
even when staggering under diplomatic burdens, do manage to
have a reasonably good time and enjoy fresh air in the 'Islands
of the Blest' and along the historic shores of the Bosporus."
This is hardly official phraseology, but it will not be disowned
by Mr. Secretary Bayard.

There is a better design than this festive quotation suggests.
The presence of the *Kearsarge* at Constantinople has its uses. It
gives prestige to the American government and people, and thereby
enhances the interest of American benevolence. That benevolence
has taken here the practical form of education. In this, the
American colleges and schools are without a parallel, either at
home or abroad, for their endowments and advantages.

I have referred, in other connections, to Dr. Cyrus Hamlin,
who was the first president of Robert College. The delays and
impediments to its establishment were overcome by his patient,
strenuous and indefatigable efforts. His volume of personal reminiscence connected with his life in Turkey illustrates that personal
pluck and persistent energy which might be expected from a typical American. He stopped at no experiment to make his success
sure; and even under protest from his colleagues at home and

DR. CYRUS HAMLIN, FIRST PRESIDENT OF ROBERT COLLEGE.

abroad he started, during the Crimean War, a bread factory, where a good article was made, and much reputation, if not cash, manufactured. Dr. Hamlin is a double cousin of the ex-Vice-President of the United States. His grandfather, Colonel Francis Faulkner, was of staunch Revolutionary stock, and his uncle, Francis Faulkner, has an honorable record in the Battle of Lexington. These ancestors had a Yankee knack for a trade; for it is recorded of one of them that for the sum of six pounds and a red coat, he purchased of the red man the town site of Andover. If we read, "twenty gallons of rum and a red coat," we have, according to the family tradition, a better knowledge of the barter! The tribe from which Dr. Hamlin is descended was Puritanic to a high degree; but like others of that persuasion, they were not averse to a thrifty bargain.

One of the daughters of Dr. Hamlin is Mrs. Washburn, whose husband is the able and learned president of the college. Another daughter is at the head of the " Home " in Scutari, so that, although the good doctor has returned to America, his influence remains, along with his strength of body and length of years. Truly, "the glory of children are their fathers," and *vice versa*.

There are other pioneers in the work of founding the American College. Next after Mr. Robert, the benevolent New York merchant, we should honor Doctors Dwight, Goodell, Schaufler and the elder Dr. Riggs. The first and last survive. The rest are gone to the better land. Dr. Riggs is the member who supervised the Bible House. He returned to America last year. He has worked for half a century in translating the Scriptures into the Turkish and Bulgarian languages. He made himself gracious to the Moslem, for he did not proselyte. He simply elevated. They looked upon him as one of the chief men of " The Book." Therefore they honored him. He is regarded with universal respect by the younger missionaries, among whom the most active and far-sighted is a son of Dr. Dwight. The business of the Bible House and of the " Home " Female Seminary is well conducted. The grounds of the latter are ample, upon a commanding situation, and the building and rooms are beyond all praise for neatness and commodiousness.

In these institutions there is every facility for the education of both sexes. These schools are the offspring of American generosity. They are the co-adjutors in the work of teaching, printing and preaching throughout the Turkish empire; and although they are constantly demanding the supervision of the American Minister, and the protection of our flag, yet never were these instrumentalities of civilization put to nobler use, and never was there more need of a diplomatic service than in this relation.

These schools, however, are but the sample, if not the symbol, of that which is done elsewhere throughout the Turkish empire. At Aintab, Harpoot, and Beirut, there are institutions of superior grade. The two former are situated in the interior of Asiatic Turkey. The number of missionaries scattered throughout the empire speak of many trials and troubles, but the " peace that passeth understanding," the missionary does not have, except in his dreams, or in his last sleep.

I have been told by Doctor Hamlin, who served as a missionary and teacher for forty years at Constantinople, that the presence of Admiral Farragut at the Porte with his vessels some years ago—before Robert College received its charter and its permit to build—had a wonderful effect in consummating that business. This effect was skillfully seconded by the diplomacy of my lamented friend, Edward Joy Morris, who was then the American Minister. When the Admiral was visiting the konaks of the Pashas and was feted by the Sultan and his Ministers, he was reserved about the object of his visit. Upon one occasion the question was asked him :

"What, Excellency, do you think about Turkey ? "

He gave at once a response which started every one upon inquiry. It was a quiet request or question about the college. He had no diplomatic function ; but he was suspected of being ready, by his ships and guns, to take advantage of the situation. He was only observing, as he said, "strange countries." As at that time the island of Crete was in insurrection, and as the Turks were considerably annoyed by the fact that these gallant Greeks were demanding a legislative assembly, and a government somewhat like that of our States, and as the Turkish Ministers did not understand the relation of our country to other countries, namely, the policy of non-intervention—they thought it best to conciliate America and placate Admiral Farragut. By an unexpected dénouement, the permit to build the college was signed, and the *Iradé* by which Robert College was instituted was delivered.

It is not necessary to say here, how much good this college has accomplished for the Orient. In another chapter, and in connection with Bulgaria, I may refer to it. The presence of the *Kearsarge*, with its chivalric history, in the waters of the Porte during the summer of 1886, enabled the American Minister to produce a proper emphasis upon the Turkish mind in relation both to Robert College and the Home School. Admiral Franklin—ever gallant and ever American—and Captain Sigsbee, of the *Kearsarge*, and of the "Deep Sea Soundings," placed the band of the old fighting ship at the call of the Minister. The Admiral never failed when the music of the gun lit up the fires of battle ; and the Captain never failed when called to sound the chromatic scale of nature beneath the surface of the seas.

When Commencement season came, the officers of the vessel, in uniform, together with its band, were present. In fact, the English-speaking community on both sides of the Bosporus were in attendance. The most remarkable aspect of the occasion was the composite character of the assemblage and scholars. Many of the scholars were of the Armenian race. Their names are known by the termination "an." Those that end in *'itch, 'off,* and otherwise, are either of the Bulgarian or Slavonic race.

The occasion is one of unusual interest. Dr. Washburn, the President of the College, assists the Minister to preside, because, as he says, the Minister is not able, with his short acquaintance with the various tongues of the country, to pronounce the names of the graduates. Oratory finds facile though polyglotical utterance from the young men of these races. Much applause and many bouquets mark the appreciation of the audience. After the speaking, diplomas and prizes are presented to the several members of the various classes. Rounds of applause punctuate these marks of merit. Of course, the Minister is compelled to air his rhetoric. He is not a little disconcerted by the strange tongues which he hears, not so much the English or the French, as the others. "There was much discussion," remarks the Minister, "as to what language was spoken in the Garden of Eden. Paradise was situated in Armenia. I think the Low Dutch or the Basque contestants must give way, for Adam spoke to Eve in the soft, sweet language of Armenia. This was before the fall. After the fall, they talked Bulgarian ! I do not depreciate the language of the latter race, for it reminds me of the ragged, jagged and tough Teutonic tongue, which I have in a feeble way the honor to speak." This sally was received with various interpolations, as the French phrase it. After allusions to the College, which, for certain reasons of the censor, were not fully reported by the journals, the Minister referred to the peculiar environment of the College :

" But it is not alone the romantic and historic associations of the Bosporus and of Roumeli-Hissar ; not alone these tombs and mosques and towers, which mark a great period in human annals; not alone the strange creed and race which yet hover about these hills ; not alone the sight of Olympus, nor the nearness of Ilion, with its plain, mounds and woes ; not the witchery of water, sky and mountain: these enchant the vision and animate the spirit, and make an aureole around the beautiful brow of your eminence ; but it is the fact that this spot is consecrated to the noblest of purposes. Is it not the home of education and learning? the fountain of benevolence and the author of piety ? These objects lift your eminence into a loftier and serener height than yonder classic mountain. They give amenities more charming than the picturesque prospect of the Bosporus. They celebrate an *annus mirabilis* more wonderful than the historic year which marks the erection of those towers and the fall of yonder superb city. Here you are taught to master your spirit; and that is education. He who taketh a city, is not greater ; for, as it is said by Bulwer of *Rienzi :* 'So great may be the power, so mighty the eloquence, so formidable the genius of one man, without arms, without rank, without sword or ermine, that nothing can withstand him.'

" But to those of us who are American, there is a patriotic attraction growing out of the fact that this College is the offspring of American benefaction. It grew under the planting and thrives under the watering of our fellow-countrymen. It grows with the consent of a government and ruler whose virtues of charity and toleration demand honorable recognition. While the beneficiaries of the institution are of another race and clime, the large, roundabout humanities, symboled as well by the classics as by the American flag, enfold them. I may be pardoned, as the Fourth of July is nigh, for referring to the flag. Its roseate stripes blush modestly for the backwardness of our countrymen, or, rather, for the modest republic ' farther west.' Spangled with thirty-eight stars, every star a State, and every State a star, it kisses the breezes coming to it, from Bithynia or the Balkans, from Alexandria, Athens and Jerusalem. It is said by Gibbon, 'that whatever rude commodities were collected in the forests of Germany and Scythia, and far as the sources of the Tanais and Borysthenes ; whatsoever was manufactured by the skill of Europe and Asia ; the corn of Egypt and the gems and spices of the farthest India —were brought by the varying winds into the port of Constantinople, which for many ages attracted the commerce of the ancient world.' But in all the facts of the historian, or even in the dreams of poetry, no importation comparable with this College from America, has ever hitherto reached this Oriental capital! The means, the teachers, the flag, being given, what else was needed ? The gracious consent and sanction of the just and tolerant ruler of this realm ; and that is accorded. Next, the medium of teaching is the English language, which never syllabled the idea of servility, and which has been honorably represented in many nations, including our own, by the distinguished Minister, Sir Edward Thornton—who honors us by his presence. Given these elements of success, what an arena have we here, whose beneficent result, whose blessing, no one can measure in its far-reaching influences upon the Oriental mind !

" As the olive-trees of the academy furnished oil for the victors of the Grecian festivals, so this institution furnishes no crude article like that from Baku, wherewith to strengthen the wrestlers in the intellectual arena of these elder lands. It is a pleasure to know that your lamps are not like those of the foolish virgins ; but that, under the direction of your energetic President and his associates, they are filled and burning with the white light of the refined American article."

The following is a list of the graduating class and their residences. What a commentary they furnish upon the diffusion of American instruction:

Constantin Apostoloff, of Yambol; Michaïl G. Arnaoutoff, of Sliven; Nigoghos H. Boyadjian, of Constantinople; Todor Dimitrieff, of Shtip; Hovsep A. Djedjizian, of Adabazar; Zlatan A. Draganoff, of Sistov; Gullabi S. Gulbenkian, of Talas; Ivan J. Kardjieff, of Shumla; Arshag Kevorkian, of Constantinople; Jordan Kousseff, of Prilip; Parnag H. Minassian, of Constantinople; Simeon D. Mishaïcoff, of Monastir; Hovhannes S. Missirian, of

Panderma; Levon Muggerditchian, of Constantinople; Anastase Petcoff, of Shumla; Karekin M. Shiririan, of Galatz; Dimo P. Smedoffsky, of Shumla ; Georgey P. Stamatoff, of Calofer; Peter Thomoff, of Kotel ; and Dimiter S. Velcheff, of Eski-Zaghra.

More interesting than names and homes, are the themes of their discourses.  Moral Forces were discussed ; then the Preservation of Nationalities, significantly, by an Armenian ; then the Power of Motion over Nature, and the Destiny of Nations ; the Power of Circumstances ; the Spirit of Adventure ; Despotic and Constitutional Government and Public Opinion.  These addresses indicate, as they leap fresh from these young Oriental scholars, how they intend to shape their lives and to influence the society in which their fortunes may be cast.

The American quality of the exercises was accented by the presence of our flag and music.  It is our sentiment that so permeated the Balkan peninsula and Asia Minor, as to give the hope of its resurrection into a better condition if not into free and federative states.  " Joseph," said the patriarch, " is a fruitful bough," and, in this respect, Robert College is not unlike the favorite son of the patriarch.

It may not be generally known, but for the young orators who copy Demosthenes, it should be stated that after the Persians had conquered Byzantium and other Greek cities of the neighborhood, it became a conspicuous practice of the Athenian to thunder his anathemas in this direction until the Persian power was overthrown.  In the days of Philip of Macedon, Byzantium was an ally of Athens.  It stood a great siege from Philip.  The happy issue of the siege was due to the philippics of the orator. In one of his eloquent passages does he not, fearful of its yielding, urge the Athenians to send succor to Byzantium ?  During the siege so consecrated to oratory, was there not seen a luminous crescent in the sky?  It was not the moon, but a light, perhaps, from a comet.  Still it was accepted by the Byzantines as a pledge of deliverance !  When Philip was repulsed, the crescent became the device of this Greek city.  It continued to be so until the Turkish Conquest in A. D. 1453.  Whether the Turks had used the crescent before the Conquest, or whether, as has been alleged, they borrowed it from the Chinese, or whether its legend came from this luminous crescent of the sky ; whether the symbol came from one point of the compass and sky, or another—certainly it is a beautiful emblem for an ensign or a nation.

The castle of Roumeli-Hissar, every stone of which is sentient with sermons, and into whose eyrie I have penetrated, to the disturbing of its birds of prey—was once the prison in which the rebellious characters of the Janizaries were chastened. An embrasure on the lower part of the rampart is still filled by a large gun. This gun was always fired so as to advise the authorities at the Porte that the criminal whom they had condemned

THE AMERICAN ROBERT COLLEGE.

had been executed. This castle is the gentle neighbor of our American college; but it is not dominant, as of old, on the Bosporus. By a happy combination of some sketches, I am enabled to present the College upon its lofty site between these renowned and conspicuous towers.

Another of our recreations is that in connection with the Home School at Scutari. Its Commencement takes place during the same busy week. It is also honored by the presence of our naval officers, the professors of the College, the female teachers, and others interested in its success. Never have I seen, at home, an institution more thoroughly American in all its appointments, unless we except the foreign languages in which many of the compositions and speeches are made. At the conclusion of the Minister's remarks upon this occasion, many gentlemen of various nationalities speak, in Turkish, Greek, Armenian and Bulgarian. The exercises conclude with diplomas, music, bouquets and applause. A collation is provided. Our American launch bears many of the guests across the Bosporus, out of Asia and its refinements, into Europe, and its selfishness and grossness.

How this American school at Scutari performs its duty as the educator of other races, will be seen by the names of those who graduated, and the titles of their graduating compositions. Some of the names are as follows:

Aroosiag G. Serapian, Fota V. Dugmedjieva, Anka T. Naidenova, Genka N. Tapchileshtova, Heranoosh Aghlaganian, Manooshag H. Besharian, Paris M. Kiatibian, Stefanka J. Beleva, Tomnie P. Yazmadjian and Yevkine Balukdjia.

These euphoniously named young ladies discussed Emblems; Circumstances making the Man, which included the Woman; La Liberté; Elbows—a very droll composition; the Life of a Word; True Greatness; The Heir of Nineteen Centuries, etc. Most of the subjects had reference to the Orient. They were admirably presented. The young ladies were dressed in white ; each, like Una, making sunshine in a shady place; only that their great, black Armenian, Bulgarian and Grecian eyes gave the light of a " night set thick with stars."

The exercises conclude with a class song. It still lingers in my memory; for it spoke of prophetic peace and the heavenly hills, and of the angels, who joined in the chorus !

There is much trouble brewing about closing the American schools of Asia Minor. Constant complaints come up to the Legation from the consulates on that head. The American Protestant schools are not alone in suffering from the recent intolerance of the Mahometans, in certain localities where they predominate over the Christians, and where they are aloof from the central authority. Shortly after the closing of the Protestant schools in Syria, an official order was sent out by the Minister of Public Instruction to the provinces, to close all the Jesuit schools established without official permission, and to refuse thenceforth permission for the foundation of new schools by this Society. The same order was issued about our American schools. This, however, under our energetic remonstrance, has been remedied to a great extent. If the United States had more power to its naval elbow, there would be less occasion for the constant protests of the American Consuls and Minister. The secret incentives for these anti-educational vexations I have not fathomed. I suspect the Greek or the Armenian; and not without reason. Still, the allegation is—Mahometan bigotry.

There are five millions of Greeks in Turkey. They compete with all other races in their educational systems. They are not disturbed by the government. Why should other Christians be disturbed? I am proud to publish the encomium in the language of an intelligent English official in Turkey, upon "the moral influence that America is exercising in the East, through the quiet but dignified and determined policy of its Legation at Constantinople, free from political intrigues and rivalry."

"That policy," to quote again, "would guard with a jealous care the rights and safety of the missionaries, who are loved and respected wherever they settle. Their influence is felt for the welfare of all, in the remotest corners of Turkey. It is America that will be entitled to the gratitude of all Christians, for her ready aid in elevating the masses to the dignity of civilized beings."

But on the educational question, I fear the Greeks and their bearing. Have they not pre-empted the Oriental land for the Christian faith? How dare Yankees like Dr. Hamlin, Dr. Long or President Washburn invade their prescriptive, orthodox and apostolic premises?

Still, I did not fail to note that Western Asia is undergoing its periodic, if not spasmodic, Moslem struggle for sustentation against alien education and other advancing influences. How far the firmans of the Ministers agree with the Sultan's idea, and how far the latter is influenced by the improgressive hierarchic element in Stamboul—it is certain that quietly, and in remote sections like the Taurus and Nusaireyeh mountains, where the intense Mahometan zealot lives—afar from the centres of diplomatic and governmental influences—there is a concerted effort to destroy the influence of the Catholic and Protestant teachers. Recently the telegraph is used by the Turk; better roads are being built by him; and the best repeating rifles arm the soldiers; and, as a consequence, the jealousy of foreign education takes the forceful form of suppressing the foreign schools. The schools near the sea are not harmed or harassed. When menaced, they are able to counteract the effort.

Along with these efforts the old mosques and holy places are restored. The Exchequer of the Porte is not plethoric, but it disburses freely in behalf of new Moslem establishments. It aids, by its meagre means, the regeneration of the Moslem faith and its structures. Even the little shrines, or *wileys*—the tombs of saints, covered with the votive threads and rags of pious devotees—are rounding into new proportions. Or, rather, the dead saints are all alive again, to inspire the Moslem. There is an earnestness about this revival of the Ottoman religion, that indicates an apprehension of a coming conflict, in which the banner of the Prophet may be flung to the breeze; if not in Europe, then in Asia. It means a consolidated Ottoman empire. It means a further lease of power for the Sultans. It means—well, it means business. I trust that my successor, with the aid of our dragoman, may be able to cope with this new phase of the Islamic or Eastern problem.

Here I beg to tender to the good men of the American missions my acknowledgments for their testimonial to the President, in eulogy of my feeble efforts in their behalf.

The spirit of civilization may sometimes be tested by progress in reading, writing and arithmetic—the three "r's." The schoolmaster has been abroad, even in Turkey. In spite of adverse administration, education is thriving. It has even invaded the harem. I have a note written by a Sultana to a commissioner, who was ordered to do some shopping for her. It shows the remarkable advancement of the East in our English tongue. I insert it here, *verbatim*, and for the edification of those who are striving for a better cult!

It is a note from Adile Sultana, the betrothed of Abbas Pasha, to her commissioner. It is dated at Constantinople:

"MY NOBLE FRIEND:

"Here are the featherses sent. My soul, my noble friend, are there no other featherses leaved in the shop besides these featherses? & these featherses remains, & these featherses are ukly. They are very dear; who byses deses? And, my noble friend, we want a noat from yourself: those you brot last tim, those, you sees, were very beautiful; we had searched; my soul, I want featherses again, of those featherses. In Kalada there is plenty of feather. Whatever bees, I only want beautiful featherses : I want featherses of every desolation to-morrow."

This specimen of improvement in English is not a fair sample of what the Oriental can do. I had a servant whose name was founded on a rock—*Peter ;* Pedro or Pierre. Although Pedro had been with our Consul-General, Eugene Schuyler, in Constantinople, he had lost all that he had gained in English by this scholarly association. He came to me with good testimonials of his ability as steward, linguist, accountant and purveyor. He had the fidelity of a Slav. He was born on the Adriatic. He was a Dalmatian. Once, when I happened to remark that he was a *Dalmatian*—good serviteur—he never appreciated the subtle profanity of the observation. Two years, through sickness and health, at Therapia, in Constantinople and on the isle of Prinkipo, he was literally my body-guard. He spoke French admirably; modern Greek like an Athenian; Turkish like an Effendi; and Italian like a tenor. Russian, Servian and Bulgarian, as connate with his own difficult Dalmatian tongue, he had easily conquered. He had been with an engineering company, as commissary upon the heights of the classic Greek Olympus. He was fitted for all the emergencies of the lower world, except that he did not know the English language. But this ignorance, for me, was his best qualification. Why? Because I wanted him to talk French, so that I could learn of him.

One day, the genial Minister of Foreign Affairs, Saïd Pasha, said to me:

" Excellency, why do you not practise your French on your servant? When I was Minister at Berlin, no one knows the eloquence of the domestic rhetoric which I first tried on my servants, before the Chancellor, Prince Bismarck, or the Kaiser listened to my Teutonic efforts."

So I reckoned upon Pedro for my French. If he had spoken English, where, in that case, was the *quid* for the *quo*, in his service and its compensation? While at Prinkipo, he began to creep stealthily upon my caution. I had learned English in Congress. It was not good English; but it was all I had. Pedro longed for it. He began to pick up my English words while waiting on the table and elsewhere. This would not do. I was not his employee;

he was mine. I could not correct this tendency, until one day—
happy thought!—as we are walking over the piney mountain to the
Monastery of St. George in Prinkipo. I commend his polyglotical acquisitions, and especially his essays in English. He is
pleased, and smiles. I say to him :

"Pierre, tell Madame, when she inquires, about our delightful
walk."

He said that he would. I add :

"Say to her, good Pierre: 'We have had a d——d good
promenade.' She will be pleased to know of your acquisition of
elegant English, and of our nice time."

He said that he would. I train him carefully *en route*. He
said it ! In fact, he repeated it several times.

The consequences, when the Madame hears his remarks,
were never entirely obliterated. The Madame, being Puritanic,
is simply stunned. Pierre insists that "His Excellence had
instructed him." He insists in vain. He comes to me for explication and consolation. I explain :

"*Damnus*, good Pierre, means, in Latin, a loss. It is a familiar word. It is easily naturalized by the English. It is handy
in emergencies." I continue:

"Pierre, you have heard the Baron, whom you accompanied to
Mount Olympus, speak of Amster-*dam ?*" He had.

"You have heard of Rotter-*dam ?*" He had.

I enumerated other like profane Dutch haunts; adding a
hydrostatic disquisition upon mill and other dams. He swallows
all; but he cannot make out what His "Excellence" meant by
the exceptional expression, until I mention that "Dalmatian" is
only another but intenser form of the same liquid linguistic
accomplishment.

Strange to say, I could never get him to learn English of me
any more. He taught me French after that with great assiduity.
The Madame had demoralized my tuition in English.

Poor Pedro! He followed us from Varna, and left us when
within seven days from America! America—his hope and goal !
The last I saw of him, he was using his handkerchief with eye
and hand, to weep and to wave, as he stood at the end of the
dock at Havre to bid us "godspeed," when the *Champagne*
began to breast the Atlantic billows.

What trouble he had, by flood and field, to reach his subsequent post at Teheran—he wrote to me in pure and perfect French; but after some time with Mr. Pratt, under the American Legation at Teheran, I received a remarkable letter, which is a sign and proof of his progress in the only language which he does not understand; to wit, American-English.

It reads literally as follows:

" My inestimably Excellency, mon premier devoir est de vous demander de votre bonne santé. I suppose, Excellency, your very well in America, and your not bad at Prinkipo. I suppose mit chants 'Pepini,' for moment."

He used to hear me sing a little Greek air at Prinkipo: " When we are all happy on that Isle of the Blest." I used to call him Alexis Delatour, from a French fable about a lazy servant, and thus he writes about Alexis and Pharaoh (Rameses II.), whom we saw in pictures throughout Egypt, and whose mummied form we looked at in the Boulak Museum at Cairo.

"Excellency, I am not Alexis, in Persian capital. I suppose Alexis stope in Constantinople, mit Mehmed and Compagnie. Remeses stope in Egypt mit Hassan Hassan. I am yours wraith every Excellency, and your wraith my plaise—tanks for our peper, for my it is very great—and very great *souvenir* of your Excellency.

"Excellency, I am wraith naou passably Inglisch. Je prie toujours pour votre santé, esperant que je vous reverai encore une fois. I am of health your bon garçon, bad boy.                                                            *Pierre.*

" Excuse my plaise, Excellency, my liberty of dis leter. Votre trés reconnaissant serviteur,                                                         " _____."

Mehmet is our Kavass; the Hassan to whom Pedro refers is the dragoman of our Consulate in Egypt, who accompanied us to Nubia. From him, also improving in English, I have received an "epistle to be known and read of all men." Let M. Maspero endeavor to decipher this sacred glyph :

" Excellency : I am very happy to write these few lines which could recognize my longings to you, and, I believe, that it is about you. We hope that your Excellency and Mrs. Cox are well, our health is good and wish you the same forever; we shall be very happy if we could have the chance of receiving a letter from your Excellency again, of which we can learn that your Excellency are well; waiting patiently to see your Excellency here again in Cairo, do I send herewith three portraits of my new suit."

Need I apologize to my readers for these interesting scripts from the republic of letters, as illustrative of educational progress under adverse circumstances ; or, rather, should not my apologies be tendered to the authors of the epistles?

# CHAPTER XLIV.

## CONTRARIETY OF OPINION ABOUT THE FATE OF TURKEY.

THERE is in the Orient a halo of mysticism. There never was a country as to which there is so much contrariety of opinion, as to its condition and destiny. One can say with Shakespeare's Juliet, with every recurrence of the Oriental question, "What storm is this which blows so contrary?" When Juliet heard of the death of Tybalt, supposing it was Romeo, her sad and ambiguous fancy suggested such contradictions as the fate of Turkey seems to occasion: "A serpent heart, with a flowering face, a dragon in a cave of beauty, a beautiful tyrant and an angelical fiend, a dove-feathered raven, a wolfish-ravening lamb, a damned saint and an honorable villain."

A few years ago a distinguished countryman prophesied that the Turkish empire was coming to an end, and that its four hundred years were being wound up in a catastrophe. But the end did not come. It does not hasten to come. Has the imperturbable Turk retired upon Asia? Is he degenerate or regenerate— or what? Are these contrary winds to have harmonious vent and gentle cadence? When such dispassionate and unimaginative observers thus fail in prophecy, what is to be said of the statements of others less intelligent and calm?

I pick up a volume about Constantinople. It is by De Amicis. It is the seventh edition. It has had a wonderful success. Its success is owing to its poetic extravagance and its equivocal voice. While there are many contrary winds fluttering its leaves, the facts and the outcome are not in harmony. For example: Within ten pages I find two chapters about the theatre. In them, all the worst possible is said about the songs, the highly spiced jokes and the impudent gestures of the Turk. They are presented to dislodge the Turk from his dignity and to betray the grossness of his sensual life. Yet in the proximate paragraph is it not said that the Turk hides his sensuality, that he is rarely accompanied in the streets by a woman, that he rarely looks at one, and still more rarely speaks to one? You cannot ask after the health of his wife. By appearances he is reckoned austere and chaste, and yet this Turk, who blushes when asked about his wife, will send his children, says the writer, to witness the filthy obscenities of the theatre. This is a contradiction altogether too grotesque. The stories about the Turk, "foul-mouthed as a fish-wife and wanton as a satyr," are perversions. It is the exaggeration of one who could not, or would not, see the difference between the modern Alhambra of London and the ancient Alhambra of Grenada.

The same writer indulges in comment as to the tendency of the Turk toward intoxication. It is impossible for one who has lived in Constantinople to believe this. The Koran is not set aside. This writer may select many men of history, even the Sultans and the wives of Sultans, who reveled in Tokay, Cyprus and Sherry wines. He may recall to our mind Suleïman the First, who burned in the harbor all the vessels which were loaded with wine, and who died while drunk, from an arrow by one of his own soldiers. All these pictures of the Turk as a ferocious hypocrite, staggering about the streets or the harem, are a libel which is only to be accounted for because of the wild imagination of the author.

It has been written, by the same pen, that the Osmanli were scandalizing the Koran by debauchery, and that the fruit so carefully forbidden is rendered more tempting by the "prohibition;" and yet, upon another page, we have the information that, in the Ramazan season, the same writer had endeavored to bribe the boatman of his caïque upon the Golden Horn to eat before the lawful moment. He confesses that the Turk always answered "Yok, yok, yok!" "No, no, no!" and invariably pointed to the sun, waiting for that luminary to descend before breaking his fast, under the law of the Koran.

As it is not fair to judge Turkey by Constantinople, so it is not fair to judge the qualities of the Turk by what is said of him at the capital; for here there are intense pro and anti Turkish proclivities and prejudices.

Mr. James Baker, in writing about Turkey, where he had been a visitor, asks about the integrity of a certain Pasha, who is a government officer. He receives for answer a glowing eulogy from the friends of the old Turk. He thereupon instinctively raises his eyes to the shoulders of the Pasha, expecting to see the budding of angelic wings; but on turning to another old inhabitant, and putting the same question, he receives such a reply as makes him turn his inspection to the Pasha's slippers in search of the cloven foot. The truth, in these matters, lies between the extreme opinions. Doubtless, that Pasha had done many just acts. Doubtless, he had been more or less influenced, if not corrupted, by *backsheesh.* And thus, this mixture of poison with the pure fluid creates a divergence of opinion very common and very unjust to the people of this country.

If the Custom-house be a sign of civilization, and its rigors mark refinement, then the Turk, by the facilities that he grants, is not entitled to the honor of a civilized nation. What is his custom tax on commerce? A small per cent.—say half per cent. on exports. On all articles imported the tax is uniform. It is eight per cent. *ad valorem.* As things go in civilized lands, this is a sign of barbarism.

An American friend coming through a Custom-house in Turkey, indulges in a diatribe against the government. He has some Custom-house trouble. His baggage is searched. The only disturbance made is when the officers spy a big red apple! This he has brought from America. He protests against its seizure; but in vain. He demands, in his unknown tongue, the reason why the paradisaical fruit is contraband. The case, as it transpires, is comical. The officers seem finally to understand my friend. They give him, as the explanation of the cruel seizure of his big red, tempting apple, that they are executing the law against phylloxera—a disease of grapes! No doubt, the tempting apple, which is lost to my friend, is a gain to the Custom-house officers. Doubtless they were consumers. Besides, is it not an illustration of the worst feature of the Turkish customs system, of which no American will complain when he looks first at home and then remembers that, while our tariff is over forty per cent., for the articles of our American missionaries there is in Turkey a free entry?

There is much said about the Turk being a spoiler. There is some evidence of the iconoclasm of the Mahometan, whether Arab or Turk. Did he not deface the tombs and temples in Egypt? Has he not destroyed the ruins of Greek art and empire, so that he is to be regarded as an Oriental vandal?

Let the tourist visit Baalbec, whose massive masonry has defied time and earthquake, storm and battle. By whom and why has such Cyclopean architecture been mutilated? He will be told that the work of destruction was performed by Christians; for were not the temples of Baalbec dedicated to another religion? Because the Sun was here worshipped—the innocent Christians endeavored to eclipse the radiance of the glorious orb!

For many years it was the fashion to prefer the Greek to the Turk, and *á fortiori*, the Christian, to the Moslem. This partiality depended on the political vicissitudes growing out of the selfish interests of nations in the East. After a while, the Greek was loathed and the Turk was liked; and to-day, as recent events in East Roumelia have shown, the Turk has received more sympathy from the Christian world than the Greek, who declaimed so ineptly and bitterly about the progress which Bulgaria was permitted to make by the *coup d'etat* of Prince Alexander, and which the Greek, by the treaty of Berlin, was not permitted to share.

After the battle of Navarino the Turk was regarded by Europe with more or less contempt; but when afterward he contested with the Giant of the North, alone, and began to reform his government, in the interests of social and political order, the Turk then was another person.

If we would regard simply the transient observations which the press of Europe make about Turkey, it would seem that the Turkish empire reeks with corruption; and yet, in order to prove to the contrary, the next gush of the observer is that of partiality for this unspeakable and corrupt being. He is regarded as a man whose traditional honesty remains, although surrounded by mercenary self-seekers and worshippers of the "golden image." For the Turk himself, take him in general, he has a large-hearted hospitality, which does not seek its own aggrandizement. He is to be considered, not at the capital, but as diffused throughout the realm, of which the Sultan is the best representative.

The Turk is regarded as a man who has risen to power by means of brutal force. That alone is regarded as the lever of his political and religious strength; but in another breath, which blows contrary, he is regarded as one who trusts to his corruptness for his success.

To some extent both views are right. Surrounded by enemies

who seek to despoil him, he is wary and diplomatic. He plays one Power against another, and, while entirely honest, he may seem otherwise when in contact with or instructed by the Christians who surround him.

It has been said, again, that he has no religion; only a ritual and a forgery. If that be said of him who prays five or seven times a day, and regards the unity of Allah as worthy of perpetual devotion by orison and alms, what can be said of the other religionists, who live by Turkish toleration, and who, if not agnostic or hypocritical, do not show that devotion of which the Turk is an ensample.

Again, it is said that the Turks hate the Christians with such bitterness that they cannot do justice to them. But is it true, when we regard the "Capitulations," which pronounced for religious freedom and Christian rights, and which were made in the eras of Ottoman strength and empire—made even before Roger Williams or Lord Baltimore recognized soul-liberty, or before our Bills of Right were engrafted on the American Constitutions.

One of my friends, in writing recently about Turkey, has spoken of Abdul Hamid II., the present Sultan, as the last of the Sultans. On what proofs does he thus speak? For the last one hundred years the same parrot-phrases have issued from the lips of those who long to have Turkey, or portions of it, as their own. Many decades may still roll around before the Russian, the Greek, the English, or the Austrian will unfurl their flag on the dome of St. Sophia, or on the tower of the Seraskierate.

It is said that if the Turk had less of the Koran he would have less badness in his nature; and then, again, that in so far as he copies Christian precept and practice, and departs from the Koran, he degenerates. The tourist often repeats the trite idea that the Turk is strong by reason of his fanaticism, and yet, that his system is that of religious weakness. It is the old trick. Give the dog a bad name in order to hang him. If we could get rid of the European prejudices, which come to us through books and newspapers, we would read a better horoscope out of Turkish character and history, and there might be other nations who would be regarded as unspeakable. The nation which repelled Russia at Kars, and which held Plevna against the attack of the Slav, is not a nation to be despised when the great conflict shall come in the Orient.

TURKEY AND THE "POWERS" READY TO CARVE.

Turkey is forever called the "sick man," or the "dying man." If he be sick, he is a long time in dying. It would be very difficult for any one to give the death-rate. The ordinary impression in America, taken from foreign sources, is that the Turk is the foot-ball of European diplomacy, and as lacking in all liberal and reformatory elements. Such ideas are regardless of his early and recent liberalities. It forgets that within sight of the Palace of Yildiz, the American Robert College dominates the landscape and Bosporus! Why should Turkey be counted so illiberal in her polity? Did she not, at Kataya, shelter the Hungarian patriots against Russian and Austrian vengeance? Who are the people that call the Turk so sick, so improgressive and so bad? Are they of the number who are waiting for his decease? By what right do they expect to share in the general spoliation? Have they any better right to Turkey in Europe, or Turkey in Asia, than the Turk himself? It is said that the Turk is only encamped in Europe; that he speaks of himself as apart from Europe; that the cypress-trees in Scutari, across the Bosporus, are his chosen "shades;" that his caïques are ever ready to bear him to Asia when the grand rising shall take place that dethrones him in Europe ; and that his traditions, religion and tendencies point toward Asia as his future home. This is the merest trifling and trash. I am yet to hear the first Turk intimate that he expects, on this account, to be buried at Scutari. Besides, is he not replacing the eighty thousand caïques, which I saw upon the Bosporus thirty-five years ago, with steam-vessels, which run up and down, and zig-zag between two continents?

The Turk is not what he was in the reign of Suleïman the Magnificent. True; but has he not grown stronger in the last few decades? The more he is pressed on every side by those who would divide his territory for their own benefit, the more compact is his government and the more permanent his rule.

It is often said, as a sign of reproach, that millions of other races are governed by a handful of Turks at Constantinople, either directly from the Porte or through its vilayets. If this be the case, is it a sign of decadence? If we take the word of the Levantine, the Greek, or the Armenian, we might infer that the Turk was a perpetual laggard, and yet we know that he has made wonderful advancement. He is being for ever bullied and encroached upon; but in spite of his stubborn nature, he has not been unmindful to make efforts for more liberal institutions. Do you point to Cyprus as being transferred to England, and Egypt as practically gone from the Ottoman? Say what we may, Cyprus is no longer a hindrance to Turkey, and Crete has an autonomy which some of our own States may copy. Her legislature is of a composite quality, but the autonomy of the island is preserved, and contentment is the lot of the mixed population, in spite of the efforts of the Greek consuls and emissaries to disturb i . As for Egypt, she is—under the present arrangement, which seems temporary—less a source of weakness and menace to Turkey than she was in the time of Mehemet Ali, who threatened Constantinople.

Is it said that the earthquake is an enemy to Turkish progress? There may be two sides to this question, judging by Greece in her elder glory, and Spain under Charles V. and Philip II. Besides, the United States are becoming somewhat familiar with earthquakes. After many shocks, the fear which they engender departs. I have heard our late Consul-General (Mr. Heap) say that when, in, his early youth, he was with Commodore Porter at San Stefano, the earthquake was regarded with great *sang froid* by the inhabitants of that neighborhood. A gentleman mentioned to me, upon one occasion, that he was in a house which was violently shaken, with much creaking and cracking. When he asked, with great consternation, the cause, " Oh," said his host, lighting his cigarette coolly, " it is only an earthquake !" In fact, the Bosporus itself, with all its rare beauty and advantages, is the result of the earthquake. There is nothing like an earthquake—unless it be war—to stir some populations into energy ; and even earthquakes are insufficient to arouse them into discontent and advancement. Whether earthquakes aid or retard civilization, I leave Buckle to determine. In his volume on Civilization, he makes the comparison between Scotland and Spain, to the disadvantage of the latter. I am not prepared to accept all of his conclusions.

In representing these contrary winds, how can we cast the horoscope of Turkey? How reconcile these contrarieties ?

Shall we do it by flippantly repeating the common phrase applied to the Turk, as " unspeakable "? It was applied by Carlyle. If he meant by it, as I suppose he did, an incomprehensible person, hard to be understood—he had better have cared for his own glass house, before stoning that of the Turk; for of all the incomprehensibilities incarnate, Thomas Carlyle was, and is, the most unspeakable.

The Ottoman power ascended to its zenith with as much rapidity as it has declined to the nadir. This fact makes its rise and progress an interesting subject of philosophy. Under Suleï-man the Magnificent—the most cultivated of all the Ottoman rulers—the empire achieved its greatest glory. It was—if not the very first—among the first nations of the earth in power and prestige. A few years later, it began to wane. In spite of all attempts to stay its eclipse, it is declining yet. It did not decline because it lacked skill in governing, so much as the ability to keep step with the advancing progress of the world in physical and other sciences.

Much has been said, and will continue to be said, about the contentment which the peculiar religion of the Turk inspires; as if that contentment were the foil to enterprise. It is thought that the black coffee and solacing chibouque, the cross-legged posi-tion, and the seeming leisure, laziness and obesity of the Turk, are signs of that contentment which can only be found in the fatalistic East. I do not doubt this, as a rule ; but there are so many exceptions that the rule is almost made contrariwise by the exceptions. There is an easy quietude, gentlemanly polish, and a spoken smoothness in the manners of the Osmanli, which seem to have no anxieties for the future and an abundant serenity in the present. Under the Turkish dominion there is no hereditary influence except that of the Sultan's family. " Wealth is a highly volatile blessing, and not always transmissible." The officers for the time being are the aristocracy. These may or may not be humbly born and bred ; for any one may rise in the state.

Many years ago I laughed over the account which Eöthen gave of his first meeting with a Turkish Pasha, in the province of Servia. He had crossed the border of the new into the elder world, and through the aid of a dragoman he held a most comi-cal and complimentary colloquy. The Pasha was led to regard the Englishman as a grandiose personage—Lord of London, scorner of Ireland and suppressor of France—who had quitted his government and left his enemies to breathe for a moment. He had crossed the broad waters in strict disguise, with a small but eternally faithful retinue, in order that he might look upon the bright countenance of the Pasha of Pashas of the everlasting Pashalic of Karagholookoldour!

This wonderful introduction led to much conversation, in which the traveler pledged England to preserve the integrity of the Sultan's dominions.

To the remarks upon physical progress and steam enginery the Pasha responded :

"Wonderful magic! Whirr! All by wheels ; whiz, whiz ! all by steam ! Wonderful people! Whirr, whirr ! all by steam ; whiz, whiz ! all by steam!"

The Pasha seemed to have found out that the English talk more through their machinery than with their lips. It was only yesterday that I picked up a Persian paper, in which the editor strongly urges upon that ancient realm that it is not by force and arms that its people are to be cultivated and elevated, but by adopting the arts, the mechanism, the sciences, the education, and the civilization of the West.

Eöthen was proud to know that the Pasha similarly, fifty years ago, regarded the manufacturing energy and commerce of England. In order to aggrandize the English, the Pasha gently and diplomatically suggested that the Russians are only drilled swine; the Germans, sleeping babes ; the Italians, the servants of song; the French, the sons of newspapers; and the Greeks, the weavers of lies ; but that England and the Osmanli are one, and always together in righteousness. The Pasha wound up his interesting colloquy by exclaiming :

" Proud are the sires, blessed are the dams of the horses which shall carry Your Excellency to the end of a prosperous journey ! May the saddle beneath you glide down to the gates of the happy city, like a boat swinging on the third river of Paradise! May your eyes flame red through the darkness—more red than the eyes of ten tigers! Farewell! "

Less of this high-flown persiflage, and more heed of markets, machinery and transportation, and Turkey would realize some of her dreams of avarice and visions of magnificence.

The Turks are the ruling class; but other races assist in the functions of the State. In Constantinople the masses are Greeks, Armenians, Italians, French and Levantine. The cultivated Turk, when discovered, becomes a Cadi, Ulema or Pasha. In fact, it is held generally that the Turks themselves are decreasing, and that their race and religion are dying out. For one, I do not believe a word of it. The families of children seen in public do not look that way. New and more elegant mosques are being built on the European side of the Bosporus. The most superb of mosques is now being erected almost within a stone's throw of the Sultan's palace at Yildiz. In fact, within the last few years, since the Seraglio was burned down, the Sultan has preferred to live in Europe. It is not true that Europe keeps the Turk in his place by preventing the existing arrangements from being disturbed. It is the Turk, rather, which keeps Europe in its place. The armies of the Sultan are said to be composed of others than Turks. But what does it matter? The Albanians, Circassians and Kurds, and even the blacks from the Soudan, which make up the majority of the Army, are Mahometans. Many of the sailors are Greeks, though very good care is taken, since the Greek revolt, that the officers shall be Turks.

The religions of the world, which determine the conduct of human society, are not so unlike one another as the world is apt to suppose. The Koran is not so unlike the New Testament as people think. There is taught in its pages sobriety and contentment. There is, as a result of its lessons, an absence of crime among the masses, greatly to the credit of the Turk. A graphic writer, Major Johnson, in his volume, "On the track of the Crescent," just published in London, has had the courage to do justice to this race, and to encounter prejudice by his sincere tribute. He says that "those who have lived among the Turks say that they are very conscientious and honorable, far more pleasant to do business with than a good many so-called Christians in the East. They are very kind to dumb animals, and are hospitable to the friendless and outcast. As Turkey received the Armenians in the fourteenth century, so in 1849 she received the Hungarian and Polish refugees; and in 1869, the Circassians. These latter have, however, but scantily rewarded their benefactor, for they have been as a thorn in her side ever since."

Such hospitalities are not the sign of an ungenerous people. In comparison with other nations, and as a sign of good-will and permanence, they are significant.

# CHAPTER XLV.

THE empire of Turkey is rich in many resources. Its natural advantages, especially in producing the great staples of food and manufacture, have no parallel. Its cotton exports were once more important than they are to-day, but still the cotton lands are exceptionally fine. Turkey has always been celebrated for her fleeces of wool. Her best sheep come from the ancient stock, *ovis aries*. Their relatives may still be found in a wild state in the mountains of Asia Minor. Mohair, the fleece of the Angora goat, with its staple of five inches in length, its silky texture, and its white color has no superior of its kind. It is to be regretted that the Turkish government, while allowing the hair to be exported, forbids the exportation of the goat itself. Its hair enters largely into the material for ladies' dresses and tailors' trimmings, and for gentlemen's summer clothing. It has its place in the more elegant shawls, velvets and a great variety of articles of utility. The silk-worm is extensively reared in Syria. Broussa is the great emporium of silk. The finer fabrics, if not woven in the loom, are made by the hand-shuttles of the skillful Turk and Armenian. The Turkish tobacco is plentiful. It flourishes in both European and Asiatic Turkey. Its aroma is delicate and peculiar. The finest is perhaps that of Latakia. It is called the "Father of Perfume." Madder is also raised. It is easily propagated, and is exported in the root. It is quite prolific and profitable. The acorn-cups of the oak furnish another article for dyeing. Opium is raised, but is used less than formerly in Asia Minor and Turkey in Europe. The soil within the domain of Turkey produces from twenty-five to one hundred fold. Thus in some respects Nature tries to compensate for the taxes imposed by the government and the discouragement of every industry.

As for the agriculture of Turkey in Europe, it is not what might be called scientific. The plains are unfenced and level, and attempts made to introduce agricultural implements have failed. Some winnowing machines were bought by the best farmers, but they were destroyed. The farms occupied by the Bulgarian and Turkish farmers are too large—more than can be profitably managed. The farmers use no manures. The old wooden plow, with oxen, and sometimes with camels, is very superficial in its work, as no harrows are used.

The mode of threshing by the Turks is upon the old threshing floor: sometimes by horses, who tread out the grain; sometimes with a flail; sometimes with cattle drawing a hurdle on which a man is standing. There is a difference between the humors of the Greek and Turk while threshing. It is said that the Turk performs the threshing with dignified solemnity, while the Greek, like the Celt, is always jocular and enjoys the business.

Wax, raisins, olive oil, morocco, saddlery, swords of rare quality, shawls, carpets, dye-stuffs, embroidery, essential oils, attar of roses, meerchaum-clay, honey, sponges, drugs, gall-nuts, resin and wine, are to be added to the catalogue of products and exports in which Turkey ought to rejoice. These show the great fertility of her soil and the variety of her climate. But how feebly this catalogue represents the elegance and comforts enjoyed two thousand years ago in Thrace and Macedonia, Elyricum, Moesia, Thessaly and Epirus, with their many villages and teeming people.

As in Judea, so in Asia Minor, the very terraces of the mountain-sides are evidence that they once rivaled the fertile valleys at the foot of the mountains. These terraces are a protest in favor of a just Providence against the improvidence of man.

Among the other changes which are noticeable, in this " Land of the Sun and of the Orient,'' is the failure of that artistic work in sculpture, painting, in the metals, in precious stones, in rich fabrics, which once found their highest refinement around Byzantium.

What room there is for improvement in Asia Minor alone ! How many millions of acres of arable land are running to waste ! How could it be otherwise in a country where every donkey and tree, every bushel of grain and crop of figs, every olive grove and vineyard have been taxed almost out of existence, and the very animals massacred to avoid the oppressive taxation.

Not to speak of wheat, barley, maize and dried fruits in abun-

dance, and especially the fig from Smyrna, there is one resource
of Turkey outside of the agricultural product which would
furnish a sure presage of a splendid and prosperous future
for this country, but for the neglect, abandonment and miserable
codes by which the production of her minerals is impeded.
The coal-mines in the ranges of Asia Minor forming
the southern coast of the Black Sea, and the copper of the
Taurus range, only lack steam, skill, enterprise and capital to
bring their hidden wealth to the surface. When Turkey shall have
worked her unworked mines and untilled plains; when her magnificent
mountain slopes, her rivers flowing to the sea through
beautiful valleys, her forests of oaks spreading boll upon boll, in
infinite richness—shall have been thoroughly developed by enginery
and energy, Turkey may take a new position in the world of
commerce.

There is a demonstrative centralization in the Turkish economies,
which is not apparent in the governments and their administration.
This is a bane, and not a blessing. When that is
liberalized, as it is being liberalized by a liberal Sultan; when
taxes are levied upon an intelligent and rational plan; when the old
modes of working by hand shall have ceased to exist, and the
spinning-jenny, the power-loom and the blast-furnace appear upon
every eligible spot; and when by the vigilant care of advanced
statesmen, these elements are developed and their product sent
into the markets of the world—this marvelous country will have
a fresh impulse to greatness, and resume among the Powers of the
earth its ancient prosperity.

The mineral resources of Turkey must some time come to a
rich result. There seems to be an impression that mineral wealth,
undeveloped, is like a hoarded treasure, already minted and
ready for use. This was the Chinese idea, but even China is
burrowing beneath the surface, and is doing its best to realize
this hidden wealth. Some one will penetrate the sunless caves of
Turkey, and bring these natural values to the light and the
market. A new system, as to mines, is being inaugurated in
Turkey. It may interfere with many existing contracts. The few
mines which are in working order are leased by the government
to the Greeks. These mines are in Asia Minor. They are of
copper, argentiferous lead, silver ore and pure silver, not to speak
of iron ore and coal in abundance on the shores of the Black Sea.

These call for much capital and enterprise on the part of the Western nations, but produce little result as yet, owing to the jealousy of the Turk, who regards treasure-delving as a species of lottery, in which he reserves for the state all the prizes, and allows all the blanks to the contractor.

The student will remember that in the early era, in the sands of many of the rivers of Asia Minor, and in Macedonia and elsewhere, there was gold dust, but these surface diggings have long since been exhausted.

The mineral resources of this country have never been thoroughly understood. The Sultan has studied, as I have intimated, the American mode of mining. He will probably derive all the advantages from the latest scientific skill on this subject. Extended intercourse and mechanical skill will bring forth these resources of the East.

There is a Department of Mines in Turkey. It has much to do with concessions to those who would work them. Sometimes, in these concessions there was allowed the right of exportation abroad, paying the customary six per cent., according to the quality of the mineral. That used to be the rule. Now, the discoverer of a mine is obliged to lose five, eight or ten years in waiting, after the acceptance of the first sample. These delays ruin the mining business of Turkey. It is a loss to those who seek concessions, and a loss to the Treasury. Besides, so much red tape is required, that to pay for the tape alone, not to speak of its incidents, requires the time of a generation in order to have a benefaction. But this system is about to be improved.

Like the Russian peasant, the farmers generally live in villages, and not upon their farms. This is a matter of safety. They have to pay a tithe to the tax-gatherer. The government police is on hand to make the farmer pay, if he be derelict. The *zaptieh*, or policeman, has been the greatest annoyance and burden to the farming population. How the tithe is estimated, sometimes on the crops in advance, without any allowance for a bad season ; how the levy of tax is made without appeal to any authority above the policeman; how a good deal more is levied than goes to the government exchequer—all this has been written about. Many remedies have been proposed. When to taxation is added the destruction of barns and houses, by a war of races and of religion, as in A. D. 1877–78, it may well be inferred that

European Turkey is fenceless, treeless, and almost cropless. The Bulgarian or Turkish farmer exclaims, "It could not be worse under any other rule." But very likely it might be worse, for the rule in Greece is not better, and somewhat worse; and the rule under Russia would be incomparably bad. Certainly, if there be a scintilla of truth in the account of this Thracian land—such as Dr. Bird recounts in his drama of the gladiator *Spartacus*—the Roman legions and mercenaries were even worse still; and compared to their ravage, the rule of the Greek or Turk is moderation itself.

It is a curious commentary on the mode of levying taxes in Turkey, that when a petition for relief is sent in from some quarters, it has to be inscribed in the shape of a "round-robin," so that no special person shall be held responsible for the memorial.

It is a mistake to suppose that there is any element of personal permanency in the Turkish administration. The Sultan changes his Ministers as frequently as he changes his Governors. This is done for a purpose; for he is determined that no opportunity shall occur to his officials, by a long stay in one position, to absorb and detract from its resources.

As an illustration of this "home rule," or economy, which obtains even in distant provinces, and which still renders its proper accountability to the capital, it is a fact that the oppressed people of the Vilayet of Mecca, where the religious and loyal enthusiasm is the most pronounced, used that element of progressive physics —the telegraph—to present charges against the Governor, Osman Pasha, for his spoliation of the province. These despatches bore the signatures of the first men connected with the Mahometan church and state. They charged upon the Governor the wrongful taking of two hundred thousand dollars, the property of the public, to swell his purse and that of his friends. These charges were not made in vain. As did the officials of the Greek empire, so do the Turkish officials. By their autocratic control they create a rule for the special circumstances of each case, thus displaying in every corner of their realm a subtle, practical common sense.

The best illustration of the tax upon the peasants of the Orient, and which is as old as the earliest Assyrian dynasties, is the mode by which certain articles on which taxes are levied is farmed out. There is in Turkey a tobacco Régie. Its officers are called *coldjis.* They are the servitors of an Austrian company, which undertakes to collect this tax. As everybody of both sexes smokes in Turkey, the tax is a matter of great importance. Smuggling is as common here as upon our Canadian border. There are as many romantic stories told about tobacco smuggling, as there was about smuggling on the coast of Ireland in earlier times. A convoy of contrabandists—in Asia Minor —fifteen in number, meet the *coldjis.* A fight ensues. Firearms on such occasions are lively. The smuggler generally gets the worst of it. He flies, and the Régie goes on with its inquisitorial arrangements. The company which farms this business have made many demands to stimulate the authorities to assist in the collection of this revenue, but as it is a foreign monopoly, it would be better to do with the tax as they do in Austria, Italy, France and America—collect it directly by the state. The Turkish government may not want to offend the bulk of its people, who are consumers; the Régie, controlled by foreign capitalists, is unpopular; the three millions and a half collected by the company may represent a very imperfect system of taxation; but, after all, the government cannot well protect the company where additional fragrance is given to the " virtuous weed " by the fact of its being contraband. One of the difficulties connected with its collection, is that advances are made to growers, and this does not lead to a perfect product. Much improvement was instituted of late in its collection, and I began to think that this farming out of the revenue was the best mode; but when I read about the attack upon a man near Broussa, who had in his sash an empty tobacco box, and when the *coldjis,* by the aid of their noses, determined that the very smell of the tobacco in the box was contraband, and that a grand fight was a consequence of these discoveries—I reconsidered; and concluded that the best way, after all, was for the government to do its own business and not contract it out to others, especially to aliens. Moreover, it is by no means an easy matter to collect taxes from a population which has within its bosom the nomadic instinct. Their sense of freedom rebels against such exactions; and if they cannot pay—they resort to rebellion or brigandage.

The word " Tartar " is simply the duplication of a word signifying "to move." Tar means " to move," and Tar-tar means "to move—move ;" and as the nomadic Tartars were always on the move, their name fixes their distinguishing peculiarity. Do not let this derivation be confounded with the word Tartarus ; for that, if a good old pun, is philologically erroneous. It, however, came from a king and a saint. Saint Louis, of France, in speaking of the Mongols of A. D. 1241, remarked that " either we must thrust back those whom we call Tartars into their own place in Tartarus, whence they come, or they will send us all to heaven."

The word " Tur " is supposed to mean the same thing, and in connection with the word Koman, which means an arrow, it signifies that the original Turks, or Tur-comans, were bowmen. That this is an established fact, may be seen from the weapons of Turkish warfare on exhibition in the Treasury at the Porte.

Is it this nomadic quality which tends to prevent tax-gathering and to encourage brigandage ? If the brigand were confined to the Turk, this might be accepted. The worst of the brigands are Circassian, and next to them are the Greeks. Accounts of their outrages, and the consequent death or ransom of their captives, are not common only because publicity is not allowed. However, many stories slip through the censor's fingers.

About the time I left Constantinople, at the town of Zilé, on the shores of the Black Sea, there was a Circassian brigand named Lofitcha. He was a terror; but he was promptly retired from public life. I do not know what has become of any portion of his human body, but I trust that the many gentlemen of his *suite* have found that, when his head was off and the brains were out, the man, if not his tribe, would cease. The Turkish brigand has not much to brag of. Give me some redoubtable Greek captain who demands twenty-five thousand dollars *per capita*, and who can be right in the midst of a town to receive the ransom—from the authorities ! On my trip to Egypt, I had the pleasure of having the company of Mr. Whithall. He is an Eastern merchant well known in New York. He has a house not far from Smyrna, behind which the brigands had a rendezvous. This was within a few minutes' walk of the police-house in the village. These brigands were hunted over the mountains, when they were in the town. There is nothing very humorous about this business, but if you happen to be a merchant traveling through Macedonia, trying to sell your goods at one of the fairs, and on your return meet several highwaymen, who relieve you of your profits, and you happen to be no linguist, would you not consider the deafness and dumbness of your situation to be almost as great a misfortune as the brigands ? They care little for your infirmity, when you do not give the indemnity.

It has been to me amazing, ever since I landed in Smyrna in A. D. 1851, and was warned against going to the castle on the top of the mountain—that Smyrna, of all places, should be the spot where the brigands are most prosperous. They take the disguise of police ; they play the part of *Fra Diavolo,* except that they lack his politeness. Their cruelty toward their captives is horrible. Still, they survive all the attempts of the authorities to obliterate them.

It is no new literature to write the facts connected with the highwaymen of Albania, or the connection between such brigands of the Kanniots and the powerful Turkish rulers of the neighborhood. Fine looking mountaineers are these Kanniots. They have a touch of Gypsy blood in them. They are romantic enough for a drama. They are fiery, revengeful and reckless. In vain the Turkish government has endeavored to suppress them. This it is that makes the life of the tourist a doubtful one at best in these countries of the Orient.

There is only one advantage in taking a company of Turkish soldiers or policemen along with you in traveling through the country; and that is, though the guard may run away at the first appearance of a brigand, and fail to give you protection, yet if you fail to demand or have an escort, you have no claim for compensation upon the authorities; and, to a Minister who has been prosecuting such claims, this indeed seems a most comical condition.

I do not know that it belongs to America, with its train-robbers and Chinese-raids, to criticise very closely the police or conduct of this city and country. In cities which are poorly lighted, there must be many lamentable cases of the municipal foot-pad and of the military rascal. The worst cases are those given in the reports of the out-lying provinces. According to one of these reports, from October, 1885, to December, 1886, in the Smyrna district, no fewer than three hundred and four brigands have been taken alive, twenty-nine more were killed, and eight others wounded. The Smyrniotes were disappointed at these meagre returns, and they have some right to complain.

Six policemen, or *zaptiehs,* are escorting some money in the eastern part of the empire. A band of Albanian brigands kill the

BASHI-BAZOUKS.

sergeant, the *zaptiehs* receive wounds, the ruffians get the money and escape. In Macedonia the same thing happens, except this : that a Monseigneur of the Greek Church is captured, and refusing to pay any ransom, his corpse is found. In vain the Ottoman troops pursue the brigands. In the district around Trebizond such outrages are common. The soldiers and police often fail to capture the bandits. Around the Trebizond neighborhood, no fewer than fifty-three persons were killed by bandits recently. Rich traders are preferred by them—for capture. They pay dearly for their release. Villages are pillaged and women dishonored. No bayonets appear to stop these extraordinary performances.

During the Crimean War, and at its end, there was great complaint about the ruthless bands of roystering, devil-may-care land pirates and *quasi* soldiers, known as the Bashi-Bazouks. They were a "rakehelly rout of ragged rascals"—both a terror and a scourge. They still exist in certain parts of the empire, and occasionally they are to be seen upon the Bridge of the Golden Horn, arrayed in all the hideousness of their attire. My readers doubtless prefer to see their counterfeit presentment in the pictured page to meeting them on a lonely plain or in a mountain fastness.

I have not heard that any such plagues followed the recent recruits on their disbanding.

To those who speak lugubriously about the condition and destiny of the Turks, a few facts may disturb their pessimistic view. These are facts that come red-hot out of the caldron which was simmering during the fall of 1885, and the years 1886–87. It was during the last days of September, 1885, that the insurrection of Prince Alexander took place. It looked to the overthrow, really, of the Sultan's Suzerainty and power in East Roumelia and Bulgaria. It was accomplished in a night. It had been the general opinion that, some ten years before, Turkey was utterly crushed by the Northern Bear. Russia dictated peace within a few miles of the Golden Gate of Constantinople. Turkey was deprived of rich and populous provinces. She was adjudged to pay an indemnity, which she was utterly powerless to discharge. The treaty of Berlin, which had the good effect of modifying the treaty of San Stefano, nevertheless was more rigorously carried out against Turkey than in her favor. Indeed, it was said that

Turkey simply lived, as it were, from hand to mouth on the sufferance of other Powers, and that the first popular movement in the Bulgarian provinces would demonstrate her weakness, bankruptcy and disorganization.

When, therefore, the revolution occurred in East Roumelia, although Turkey had some six to seven thousand troops on the border, near Phillipopolis, she seemed to the outside world utterly helpless ; but to those of us who were looking from the inside, it was not so. It was not much concern to her that her Governor-General had been expelled from East Roumelia, and that Prince Alexander had been placed over the united provinces. There seemed to be little or no military force to protect the border, either on the Grecian boundary or in the Roumelian country. Then began a series of orders which energized the Turkish empire. The reserves, or *redifs*, were called out. They came with loyal huzzas and promptitude. The equipments were ready. The ships which were chartered to convey them from the Asiatic to the European provinces were also ready, though it required much push, skill and diplomacy to accomplish these results.

At Salonica alone, before the end of the year 1885, seventy thousand troops were landed. Right under my eye, at Therapia, the garrisons of the Bosporus were reinforced. The wild tribes of Albania, where rebellious fighting had been going on for centuries, were held in check. The army on the Greek frontier could have crushed any movement of the Greeks against Turkey. It is unnecessary to say that the Turk did not want to fight, for it might have involved consequences that were as unforeseen as they were perilous. It is also due to truth to say that he was ready upon the frontier of Eastern Roumelia with a sufficient force. Two hundred thousand soldiers is not too great an estimate for the human defenses, which were in a most effective state at the end of the year 1885. Scarcely three months had flitted away before this immense force was mobilized. Compared with England in the Crimean War, or the third Napoleon in the Prussian war, or the Czar himself in the Russo-Turkish War, the military readiness and resources of Turkey are immensely to her credit.

This could not have occurred without a financial prop beneath her military strength. As Turkey has been always considered in the light of a pauper, or bankrupt, before the bourses of the world and in the eye of nations, it may be as well to say that not more loyal to her integrity were her reserves and her army than her bankers and her merchants in the financial stress. It was to me a special marvel that Turkey should have met the extraordinary costly military expenditure with so much facility and readiness. For, be it known that the present mode of carrying on war is by no means to be likened to that of the age of the bow and arrow, or even to that of the old musket or the smooth-bore gun.

The Sultan had called his reserves to the probable point of attack. He had transferred them from his Asiatic provinces. He had collected vast materials of war. Was the money for these purposes borrowed? No; unless it be a half a million sterling, by an arrangement with a Smyrna railway company. There were negotiations for money with a prominent Austrian banker, and with the Imperial Ottoman Bank, but the Turk was able to refuse the terms, as too onerous, although they were as nothing compared with the old usury rates which he had formerly been compelled to pay. There was no urgent need of money, apparently, in the Turkish exchequer, and this was the astonishing element. It was more unexpected than her military strength. A decade before, she had compromised with her creditors. She had almost repudiated a portion of her debt; but she kept her compromise and paid the reduced interest. That interest amounted to two millions of sterling a year. She kept her faith, notwithstanding the great demand for her military expenses.

The financial history of Turkey for twelve months before the end of the last year shows that the external debt was provided for, and the floating debt reduced to little or nothing. The revenue met the expenditures, with a probable increase of the revenue and a decrease of the expenditures. If the new commercial treaties which were then inaugurated, are concluded, it will increase the revenue by a larger general tariff against foreign nations. There may be more revenue, if not so much liberty to trade. A new Minister of Finance was named at the end of the year 1886. His reforms bid fair to make some improvements in taxation, so as to make the vast, rich and virgin land smile with a better cultivation.

So that, based on the inchoate enterprises of Turkey, which the Porte seems to keep in its grasp, there are resources beyond the computation of any fiscal officer of the Turkish government. If the Turk himself abhors the influx of foreign capital, he commits fiscal suicide, for no nation, and certainly not our own, ever prohibited the influx of capital which would develop industry without sacrificing something of future prominence and glory.

If I should make a résumé of the financial and political condition of Turkey and compare it with a year and a half ago, I should say that it is less critical now than it was then. It improves. It advances toward a sounder system. Abuses are melting away. There is a closer system of accountability, and although the impediments of 1886 were happily tided over, as I have undertaken to explain, the operations of 1887 indicate a steady pursuit upon stable ground, after an economic system which will give to Turkey a new hold upon the sympathies and business of mankind.

Is it said: That she does not pay her army; that she is yet in arrears; and that her contracts are yet to be complied with? This may be so; but beyond the annuity which she pays to her public creditors, she has had her secret resources. These were found in the splendid railways which are possible, even probable, and the mines, which are richer than the dreams of avarice. These were, and can be, hypothecated, in the emergencies of her future.

Do you ask whether she has mitigated her taxing system? I need not repeat here that her tariff is a sign of liberality beyond that of more boastful nations, but that her direct tithe-tax has not yet been mitigated. Its mode of collection is mischievous and harassing; but it has been ameliorated.

From all these statements there is a corollary more important than the conclusions. While as a formidable antagonist with Russia in former wars, she suffered enormously by reason of the poor officering of her army, she has improved in that regard. The patient, dogged, almost fanatical courage of her soldiery made up in former wars for lack of commanders. Because Turkey speaks with a small, still voice, displaying caution and practicing prudence, neither provoking that Power which is ready to leap upon her splendid capital at the first provocation, nor offending the German and Austro-Hungarian, French and English Powers in her own natural desire to assert her authority in her own vassal provinces—it does not follow that that still, small voice may not be as potential as that of the Prophet of old.

# CHAPTER XLVI.

It is not just to deny credit for what the Turkish government has done. No doubt there are many wrong-doings and short-comings, in administration, which should be corrected. This I have been made officially to understand. But certainly, in comparison with the Christian, the Turkish population has nothing to fear. If it be said that assassinations are frequent in Turkey, and that Sultans have been dethroned by poison and poniard, it must not be forgotten that two Presidents of the United States have been assassinated, and that Russia has also been the scene, and is yet the scene, of crimes of this nature. As to venality, there may be much apathy in the Turkish administration. My observation is that her sins of omission are greater than those of commission.

The charge alleged to have been made by the Russian Ambassador, M. Nellidoff, that England secured the assent of Turkey to the recent Egyptian convention by the payment of £600,000, was indignantly denied. To those who know Sir William White, the present Grand Vizier—Kiamil Pasha—and the Sultan himself, there was no need of any vehemence by way of denial. If the English government were as generous as the sum represents, the objects to be attained by the treaty were of such little practical consequence that they fell by their own insignificance. Had the amount named passed into the Turkish Treasury for railroad concessions, we could understand the value of the grants and the integrity of the transaction.

I agree with those who believe that the Turkish government does not need any betterment of the laws. The laws are admirable; the machinery is made on a perfect plan. It is the administration, if anything, that is wanting. Besides, there is always some other nation ready to pounce upon every possible *peccadillo* of the

Turkish administration, and hold it up to scorn as a sign of
Turkish improgressiveness and decay.

Do you ask if there has been any liberality in Turkey; any
experiment on the line of improvement and freedom? I cannot
say that there has been much. There was a Constitution and a
Congress in the reign of Abdul Aziz. Both were failures. They
happened in the stress of a general upturning. Midhat Pasha
was the Grand Vizier, and the genius of this reformatory endeavor. He was regarded as an enlightened statesman. He
was educated in France, while it was under the sway of the third
Napoleon. Like John Locke, he could elaborate an organic law,
which seemed logical, but his polity was not practical. He was fond
of the illusions of politics, and must have been delighted with everything in France, except the conclusion of Napoleon's reign. He
had no difficulty in adopting advanced theories, even when he
alarmed the old Turkish party. Having afterward been complicated with the assassination of Abdul Aziz, he was sent into
coventry. He has never been heard of since. Considering the
condition of the ruling powers in other countries; considering the
absolute tyranny and ambition of the Czar; considering the bigotry which Russia exercises, not merely toward the Hebrews, but
toward Lutherans and other Protestants, of which the world knows
but little—the present liberal conditions of Turkish rule, in spite
of her anomalous position, deserve unstinted commendation.

There have been many reforms dictated to Turkey by the
European Powers. Her constitution is not yet formally abrogated. It surpasses in liberality the provisions of other European
states. Among its valuable features is a proclamation of the
equality of Moslem and Christian before the law. Was this a
novelty? No: not even in Turkey. The celebrated Hatti-Scherif,
by which Abdul Medjid glorified his reign, had three provisions:
*First,* Guarantees to his own subjects as to the perfect security of
life, honor and fortune; *Second,* A regular system of taxation;
and *Third,* An equally regular system of military levies and duration of service. There never was a decree promulgated and sanctioned with so much ceremony as this celebrated "Hatti." If
it has not been carried out in practice, it is only because Turkey
has been too much occupied in defending the integrity of her
territory and the existence of her government. Scarcely a day
passes over the Bosporus that Turkey has not been compelled,

if not to do battle in this behalf, upon fields of carnage, at least to contend upon the less sanguinary fields of diplomacy.

I confess that such a reformer as Midhat Pasha has not come fully up to my ideal; for facts jut out prominently in his career to indicate more selfishness than patriotism. He was neither a Madison, a Cavour, a Thiers, or a Gambetta, much less a Bismarck, a Derby, or a Gladstone. Besides, it is said, that the order for the Bulgarian outrages, for which so much reproach was fixed upon the Turkish government, is attributable to him. If that be the case, his banishment into southwestern Arabia, for aiding in the accomplishment of the death of Abdul Aziz, was neither unjust nor regrettable. But his schemes and fate, however, mark an era in Turkish movements looking to the regeneration of the state.

Lately, Turkey has had no statesman who has energized any great movement for the betterment of her fundamental government. She has had, and has needed, astute diplomatists and capable financiers. She has concentrated her energies for self-existence upon diplomacy and her fiscal system. She has been weak—she is yet weak ; and has thereby invited encroachment, as well as because she has been and is poor. When her credit is re-established she will be rich, because she has the means of being so in her mines and lands. There is a vigorous life in her empire which only needs arousal. Enterprise and money would develop it. Turkey has not failed in military achievements. Why should she be smitten with languor, when rivalry with her old Slav enemy seems to be imminent ! All the evanescent glories of her past are nothing, unless in this nineteenth century she cultivates physical enterprise, and that mechanical ingenuity which shortens time, develops industry, and makes even of such little nations as Belgium powerful factors among the nations of the earth.

The railroads in Turkey proper are a mere bagatelle, compared with those of Germany, France, or our own country. In this we are not counting the railways of Egypt—the mileage of which is considerable for its area and population. There are but five railways in Turkey proper.

The *first* runs, and with many possible and probable connections with the European system, to Adrianople from Constantinople. It is otherwise of great utility, although it is not submerged under encomiums on account of its conduct.

The *second* is in Cilicia. It runs from Mersina to Tarsus, and thence to Adana. This railroad is not of great length, but it makes up for its brevity by the richness and produce of the soil, and its historic and religious associations. Notwithstanding these attractions, the country has suffered the past year by a drought, which has impoverished the people, even unto starvation. If you would visit Tarsus now, for lack of other provender, you might feast your eyes on a castle, alleged to be built by Bajazet, the traditional tomb of Sardanapalus, who founded the city, and the supposed church in which St. Paul baptized his converts, and the imaginary tree which the apostle of the Gentiles planted with his own hands ! The city is but half the size it was when it claimed Paul as a student and a citizen. Still, it is no "mean city " now; for a place which had such a founder as the Assyrian monarch, such a university in the old eras, that it rivaled Athens and Alexandria, and such Grecian grandeur as Alexander, and such Roman pride as Mark Antony and Julius Cæsar contributed—can never be truly called a "mean city."

The *third* is the railroad from Scutari, opposite Constantinople to Ismid. The western terminus at Chalcedon is known as the entrepôt of the caravan commerce of fifty years ago ; and its eastern terminus at Ismid marks the place of ancient Nicomedia. It is near Nicæa—where the creed of Christendom was established by the Fathers in the fourth century. Around Ismid there is a swamp, through which hunters in high India-rubber boots take their weary way after snipe, woodcock and an occasional wild-boar. The American missionaries in the vicinity are endeavoring to make the swamp blossom as the rose, by discreet cultivation of the indigenous population.

The *fourth* is the Aïdin railroad ; it runs out of Smyrna toward and beyond Ephesus, into the richest fig and raisin country of the world. It is a paying road, and is under English control. The product of the soil and the industry of the people give to its trade extensive circulation, and to Smyrna a commercial importance only equaled by the beauty of its women and the bigoted arrogance of its Greek population.

The *fifth* is known as the Turco-Servian junction railways. They are beginning to take on force, and are almost ready to reach their destination at Salonica, and thence to all the world. In fact, the new prince of Bulgaria and the sovereign of Servia have been junketing with their people at Pirot over the opening of the section from Nisch to that place. Under the convention between "the four Powers of 1883," the Nisch-Vranja Salonica junction line should long since have been opened to the Ægean Sea. Turkey is said to be the obstacle. When the agreement is carried out, then will a rich country be made accessible, either to the Danube or to the sea.

This is at best but a poor showing for the railroad enterprise of a land like Turkey. Since she is so rich in mines, arable land, and resources of all kinds, why is she not more prosperous? Simply because of the lamentable lack of transportation and enterprise. She must reach out into the old haunts of Mongolia, as Russia is doing by her Trans-Caspian railway system. Asia Minor and the lands and waters of the Balkan Peninsula are still hers; and with them, could she not command a better civilization? By joining the Mediterranean and the Persian Gulf, could she not create a better system of transportation than the canal which joins the Mediterranean with the Red Sea?

The project of a canal for such *termini* has been started. It begins on the mainland nearly opposite and east of Cyprus, follows the Auràuntes, and proceeds thence to the Euphrates. Thence the route is by steamers to the Persian Gulf. It would thus save fully six days, or two thousand miles, between London and Bombay. This canal is only a project. In our time, the railroad supersedes the canal.

No one can consider this matter of a railway system in the Orient, without taking into account the Russian Central Asian system. If there were not so much antagonism between Russia and England, there might be a Turkish connection made with the Russian and the Indian railway system. There are political and dynastic objections to this arrangement. A line which would follow the railway from London to Dover, and from Calais to Brussels, Cologne, Berlin, Warsaw, Kief, Khartoff, and Vlaid Kafkas at the foot of the Caucasus, would soon reach the Caspian Sea, on a plan already projected, if not accomplished; so that London and the Caspian Sea would be bound together by an iron chain, without a break. Then crossing the Caspian Sea to the new port of Usunada, it meets the terminus of the Russian Central Asia railroad. This railroad, reaching from Merv to Afghanistan by way of Herat, would land you at Quetta. There it is allied with the

Indian railway system. Thus Asia in its centre and south would be connected with the farthest and most potential realms of Europe. All this and more, if the great Powers were not jealous of one another.

Once talking with the Sultan, he remarked : " I have thought of sending my son Selim in a naval vessel around the world. How far is it to New York from here ? "

I said : " Your Majesty, I have just received a letter, only thirteen days old, from New York."

He was astonished ; I presumed to add this platitude :

" Much of the way through Europe is upon land, and as the locomotive has less resistance from the air than the vessel upon the water ; and whereas the latter can only go twenty miles an hour, while the other makes sixty—there is great utility in having as much railroading around our star as is consistent with the safety, intercourse and comfort of its peoples."

Then I asked him the question :

" How long, Your Majesty, does it take your messengers to go from Constantinople to Bagdad ? "

He replied, smilingly, " You could go to America and return, and go home again from here, before my mail messengers could reach the Tigris or the Euphrates."

This conversation was leading somewhat in the direction of railroad building. I had no scheme. There were no Americans then pushing any enterprises in that direction. The Sultan had evidently been impressed with the necessity of railroads through his unsettled territory ; so that the population might follow the locomotive, and the lands be made valuable by facile modes of carrying freight. It is no new project—that of making a railroad to the Euphrates, and down its valley to the Persian Gulf. Perhaps for that purpose the English leased Cyprus. It would not be hard, at one bound, to connect that island with the corner of the Mediterranean and the Gulf of Iskanderoon ; and then, making water-stations of Antioch and Aleppo, follow the valley of the Euphrates, with all its wealth of soil and immensity of interest, to the head of the Persian Gulf. Between that valley and that of the Tigris, lies old Mesopotamia, and further on, the East Indies. Constantinople would then become the distributing centre of Europe and Asia.

Besides, a railroad from Constantinople should reach out

toward Armenia. It has progressed only so far as the end of the Gulf of Ismid. A few more propulsions, and it will be in the opulent country around Angora ; and then it is not so very difficult, following the fortieth parallel, to reach the plains of Erzeroum and the upper Euphrates.

Disregarding the Suez canal as on one side, the two hundred millions of people in Europe might shake hands with three hundred millions in Asia. London would be as near to Bombay as New York is to Liverpool, and the lines of empire, if not of dynasty and boundary, together with the stir and marts of commerce, would be changed with the changing of the routes of transportation.

As this volume goes to press, rumors quite authentic—much more authentic than the ordinary statements from the Orient—are current that, through the aid of Sir William White, the British Minister, an Imperial *Iradé* has been issued by the Sultan to a syndicate of British financiers, granting them the right to construct a grand trunk line over the great central plateau of Asia Minor. Its termini will be Constantinople and Bagdad. If this be true, it probably ends a long contest for supremacy among the rival speculators for concessions applied for by the citizens of different nationalities.

The French are vexed at this decision of the Sultan. As a consequence, Russia is, if possible, more irate than France. Protests are filed against it ; but the Sultan answers them by saying that, as a railway in Turkey affects no frontier of Russia or France, it is not a question which concerns any other government than that of the Ottoman.

The line which is proposed to be run, starts out from Scutari, and pursues the present line as far as Ismid. It touches at many prominent towns in Asia Minor, and, among the rest, at Angora, Sivas, Harpoot and Diarbekir, until it reaches Bagdad, the grand old romantic capital of Mesopotamia. This should interest America, whose missionaries, as I can avouch, are very hard to reach at their distant stations in Armenia and Kurdistan. The running of this road will not only develop a line rich in minerals and agricultural wealth, but revolutionize the social condition of the people along the route. The condition of the country upon the Persian and Russian border is lamentable. By Article 61 of the Berlin treaty, Turkey agreed to " carry out, without further delay, the ameliorations and reforms demanded by local requirements in the provinces occupied by the Armenians, and to guarantee their security against the Circassians and Kurds." It also agreed, " periodically to make known the steps taken to this effect to the Powers, who will superintend their application." Notwithstanding the presence of numerous Russian and English Consuls, and one American Consul recently established at Sivas, nothing has been done to effectuate these guarantees. The old foes of Xenophon on his retreat—the Kurds—harry the Armenians. The brigands roam at will over the rich lands east of Erzeroum. They pursue parties even to the old Georgia capital—Tiflis—and kindly relieve the armed Muscovite convoys of the collected taxes and cash wherewithal the Russian government is wont to pay its officers. When pursued, these brigands dash over the borders into Persia, and are safe from pursuit.

A railroad through this harassed land will be a godsend. It is now in a fairer way of being constructed than at any time since it was projected, sixteen years ago, by Mr. Charles Waring.

It is within my knowledge that Governor Stanford, of California, was tendered the concession for this road, while on a visit to Constantinople. Reasons of pre-occupation in such matters prevented his acceptance. Some Americans subsequently endeavored to get a foothold, so as to apply the American system, as they called it, of a subvention of lands and mines for the building of the road. As these adventurers had no substantial backing, they naturally failed. When they failed, they indulged in much objurgation upon the writer for not promoting, as Minister, their sinister designs. Besides, they made reclamations, as I feared they would, upon the Ottoman Treasury, for alleged promises. These claims have been rejected by the honest indignation of my successor, Mr. Straus.

When it is understood that Constantinople depends upon other countries for her supply of food, and spends nearly ten million dollars a year for that object, when she might be supported at home, with a proper transportation, from the plains of Angora and Adarbazar; and when it is considered that a large surplus of grain for exportation might be a consequence of this railroad—the project assumes even a grander proportion than that of mere military strategy. Why may not this splendid enterprise restore to Constantinople her ancient advantage as a commercial centre? Joining the Roumelian and Servian lines from the

west with this railroad to the East, would she not stand prominently on a route more direct to India than the Suez canal?   She
becomes at once and again the capital of Asia Minor—in fact as
well as in form, in commerce as well as in civism.   In that case,
Persia would depend more upon Turkey than upon Russia; England would be nearer by many days to India; and the vast plateau
of Armenia would be better defended from the Czar than by any
other possible mode.   It would enable Turkey speedily to command the gorges of the Taurus mountains, and to occupy them
in force whenever menaced.

Leaving Ismid, the projected railroad pursues a course toward
Angora, to which point it will be completed in four years; and in
four years more to Bagdad.   It is to be thirteen hundred miles
long.   The main line is to cost not less than one hundred millions
of dollars.   The engineering difficulties, though considerable, are
more easily surmounted than those of other railroads which have
been built within the past few years.

It must be patent to the reader that this project could not have
been secured without great diplomatic tact and exertion—I will
not say great expenditure.   It is no new project; for in the time
of Abdul Medjid, during the Crimean War, the question came up
as one of military strategy.   It was an anxious question to
England in the time of the Indian mutiny.   The Sultan of that
day, and his Grand Vizier, blew hot and blew cold; and though
surveys were made, blue-books published, maps fabricated, and
public discussions held everywhere—the interests of France in
Syria dominated, and the project fell through.   Again and again,
the Minister of Public Works at the Porte, together with commissions made up of Armenians, Greeks and Turks, with now
and then a Frenchman or a German, presented the matter.   But
the successor of Abdul Medjid—Abdul Aziz—threw cold water
upon the movement.   Then Mr. Cazalet, a London merchant,
formed a syndicate for this object.   This too failed.   So it has
come down to the present time, which may see its consummation
by the English, assisted by those of other nationalities, probably
German and Austrian capitalists.

There have been various plans to reach Bagdad from the
Bosporus, and various branches were projected from the main
branch; for instance, one to Aleppo, and on to Urfah and Mardin, and so by the Tigris valley to Bagdad.   Another was *via*

Koniah and Adana, with a branch to Diarbekir, and so on to the Euphrates and the Tigris.

If the Turkish empire holds together; if Austria will adhere to her policy of trading by sea and land, east and west; if the need of military strategy remains the same as it is to-day for the Powers which are seeking prosperity and influence by roaming over land and sea to annex loose territories—then there is every likelihood of the construction of this line to the Indian frontier. Nay, of two lines: for if this one be made, there will be constructed two fast routes to the far East; one under Austrian auspices, through Salonica by sea to Alexandretta, and by rail to Bagdad, perhaps there to meet an Anglo-Indian line through Persia and Beluchistan to Kurrachee. The other will avoid all sea passage, save the mere ferry across the Bosporus, and run by Constantinople, Scutari, Diarbekir to Mosul and Bagdad. It is thought that Bombay will thus be brought within eleven and Calcutta twelve days of London. But letters and passengers from Bombay already reach London in nineteen days, on a route three-fourths of which is in England's own hands; so that the expenditure of $100,000,000, which is the lowest estimate, may not seem, in the eyes of English capitalists, to be very well laid out.

But it is no fanciful scheme, so long as the railway can beat the water-way in fleetness and cheapness; and although the local travel and freightage may not be great, nor the prospect of travel through Mesopotamian, Persian and Beluchi deserts transporting, in a sentimental sense; still, capital is likely to pocket fair dividends by a land route which brings the ends of our star so near to each other as this project contemplates.

The sums which have been expended by syndicates in procuring these advantages from the Porte, are as fabulous in statement as they are fictitious in fact. The present Sultan took hold of the matter with an honest intention. This was evidenced by his selection of Mouktar Pasha—now the Commissioner of Turkey to Egypt—to examine the projects. Never has a breath of scandal been uttered against his name. I know whereof I speak ; for he is a warm friend of the writer. He reported in favor of several lines from Constantinople, to open up the country of Asia Minor. His fellow commissioners only recommended routes, but did not lay down absolute conditions. Still, nothing was done in pursuance of their recommendation. The German influence seemed then to prevail in disparagement of the enterprise thus recommended. It is supposed now, by those who are initiated, that the German influence, along with that of Austria, has more or less to do with the recent firman. The present Grand Vizier also takes an interest in the matter, and it is fair to presume that the long conflict upon which so much depends for the vitalizing energy of this empire will have a successful termination.

# CHAPTER XLVII.

## ORIENTAL PROBLEMS— PRINCE ALEXANDER AND THE INSURRECTION IN BULGARIA.

In the mutations of European politics and the phases of the Oriental question, it is difficult to fix for a long time the boundaries of the Ottoman empire. Changes have taken place, not only in its European provinces, but in its African and Asiatic dependencies. It is a constantly recurring problem, and has been for the last hundred years: What shall be the outcome of these Oriental movements? how are they affected by the movements of trade, railroads and the aggressions of other Powers?

First, it may be well to ascertain, up to this present writing, what are the various bonds, according to their strength or weakness, by which this empire, once so great and strong, is now held together. Are they ropes of sand? The Ottoman empire has not, in the usual sense of the term, any colonial possessions, but it includes certain provinces in Europe and Africa which are more or less dependencies, or provinces, of the central power at Constantinople. Some of these are held by the frailest tenure. This tenure is known, and has been known for centuries, as that of "Suzerainty." The "immediate possessions" of Turkey in Europe contain only about 4,500,000 population, of the 8,650,-000 of the whole population of Turkey in Europe. The other possessions of Turkey in Europe are Bosnia and Herzegovina, and the Sandjak, or sub-province of Novibazar. These are "occupied" by Austro-Hungary, under treaty stipulations. They are now only nominally a part of the Ottoman empire.

Bulgaria is in nearly the same predicament. By the terms of the Berlin treaty, it should be ruled by a prince with a popular parliament. Events loosened the ties of "Suzerainty" between Sultan and prince. They are now nearly severed. Prince Alexander of Battenberg was selected as prince. On the 18th of September, A. D. 1885, he moved his army upon Phillipopolis, the capital of East Roumelia, to unite the two Bulgarias, so-called. East Roumelia, in A. D. 1880, had a population of 411,601. It is still a Turkish province in Europe. It was, and is, more nearly connected with the Porte than its kindred province of Bulgaria. It is, and has been, for two years nearly *in transitu.* It awaits either the wager of war or that of diplomacy, to ascertain its status and establish its contentment and government. Its present condition under its representative assembly, the Sobranjé, a responsible ministry and a new prince, elected outside the treaty of Berlin —is quite anomalous.

In Asia the Turkish possessions have a population of 16,173,000. In Africa the same remarks may be applied as those in reference to the Balkan provinces, except that Tunis may as well be altogether omitted. France has that province irrevocably. Tunis, by the treaty of the 12th of May, A. D. 1881, was placed under the protectorate of France, the Bey remaining as a *quasi* sovereign. The relations between Tunis and the Porte have little or no substance. If any, it is that of the Mahometan faith and a semblance of suzerainty, kept up in the ancient palace of the Bey by the blowing of a trumpet by a soldier of loyalty to the Sultan. Egypt is now in the joint possession of England and Turkey ; but the acknowledged supremacy belongs to Turkey, whatever may be its treaty condition. The total population of Egypt is 5,500,000. That of Tripoli is 1,000,000. Tripoli is still a part of the Turkish empire; but it hangs by a hair.

This statement comprehends all that is left of Turkey ; but it leaves her still a grand empire.

Without discussing the vigor of that faith by which the Caliph of the Moslem world exercises so much religious and moral control, is it not enough to say that he is at the head of two hundred millions of Moslems? Although that control may be more or less weakened, according to the remoteness of the people ruled, yet the Father of the Faithful exercises other and more than a political control, in distant countries which are under other dynasties.

No census has yet been taken of the Mahometan people. It is impossible to ascertain their number. Some authorities fix the number at 122,000,000; others at 160,000,000. The nearest approach to a correct estimate has been made by an Englishman, who wrote his results for the *Fortnightly Review,* some six years ago. He stationed himself at Yeddah, the seaport town leading to Mecca. There, by inquiries of pilgrims from all parts of the Moslem world—Russia, India, Borneo, Northern and Central Africa, including the Ottoman empire—he was enabled to approxi mate the immense numbers which make up this still vital religion. He fixed them at 200,000,000. This means an army of 5,000,000 to be arrayed, in a crisis, under one flag and commander. Hence, when the sickly condition of the Turkish empire and the weakness of the rule of its Sultan is depicted, we should not forget its enormous elemental religious power. It was the foundation of its early dominion. It is its strongest prop to-day, among the nations which would despoil its empire.

The Saracen who overran the Mediterranean upon all its shores, did not menace Europe so truculently as the Turk who, in following him, led the forces of Central Asia across the Dardanelles into the European continent. The Saracen is dead, or, rather, dormant. He may be energized into new life by the banner of the Prophet. When led by the Turk, with new arms of precision and new motors of explosion and enginery—it is not well to surmise too emphatically that the Moslem devotees will be vanquished in their contest with the Muscovite, even though that race be aided by Republican France. Besides, there are other alliant factors to be considered in the problem.

*       *       *       *       *       *       *

It has been customary for the Sultan, at the end of Ramazan —the season of religious fasting—to begin a season of festivity. This is a religious observance. This festive season, as we have described it, is Bairam. At this time the pious Mahometan not only makes sacrifice on the graves of his friends and relatives, but he indulges in much congratulation. We have seen, at the beginning of this occasion, the Sultan holding high court in the palace of Dolma Bagtché. At this time he receives the high dignitaries of the Army, Navy and state, including the ecclesiastical priesthood, from the Sheik-Ul-Islam down to the lowliest Mufti, or head of a dervish organization.

How the time is fixed for this peculiar welcome to all the leading people of his capital and surroundings has been pictured.

At the last Bairam feast in A. D. 1886, there was much doubt, owing to the quality of the weather, as to when the grand court should be held; for the moon was quite as uncertain as Shakespeare himself could have desired. Being at the isle of Prinkipo, we depend upon a telegram for our time to start. As the court is held at the first day-break after the discovery of the moon, the anxiety is increased.

In the year before, 1885, no such difficulty happens. Then we are invited to come from Therapia, down the Bosporus with the other Legations, to observe the grand ceremony. When halfway down, our launch is met by that of the Sultan. It bears the Crescent and the Star. It has on board an adjutant from the palace. He hails us to say that the usual Bairam demonstrations are postponed.

On making inquiry, I ascertain that an astonishing *emeute* has occurred in Bulgaria. Prince Alexander has committed a *coup d'état.* He has, in a night, annexed East Roumelia to his principality of Bulgaria. As East Roumelia is a part of the empire, and is not by any treaty a part of Bulgaria, this audacious step of the Prince excites the wildest commotion, especially among the government people, who are principally Ottoman. I determine, however, to pursue my journey. If I cannot enter the palace, I can at least see the Sultan coming from the mosque, and observe the excitement which is predominating around the Imperial quarters.

After the Sultan had mounted his white charger to ride up the hill, through the narrow streets to the highway which leads to his palace, there is a bold dash; and a crush of officials, civil and religious, military and naval, in carriages and on horseback, follow, and vie in excited vigor with each other for the lead. The gold lace shimmers upon their uniforms. The long burnous of the priest trembles and wavers as if with the spirit of a new prophecy. What is the cause of all this apparent commotion? Does it presage the distraction of the empire? Is it a new phase of the old imbroglio? Is it a new move on the part of Russia? What does it mean?

It becomes necessary for the American Minister—in pursuing his instructions from Washington—"to transmit information concerning the policy of that country to which he is accredited."

A study of this Bulgarian question, therefore, becomes a duty. I endeavor to make an impartial observation. As the burden of Ministerial correspondence, so far as it affects the United States is concerned, relates mostly to capitulations and treaties by which American interests are protected in the East, the writer has a natural bias toward keeping the faith of treaties. His despatches are colored with this peculiar idea of faith-keeping.

It has been stated that the principality of Bulgaria is the creation of the Berlin treaty in A. D. 1878. When, therefore, the Bulgarian people—like an overflowing stream—dash beyond the proper channel by an unexpected freshet from the Balkan mountains, is it to be wondered that consternation falls upon the Porte and the palace?

It is regarded as strange that the Turk does not at once declare war, and send the seven or eight thousand troops on the Balkan border to Phillipopolis, the capital of East Roumelia. Thus he can at once rescue East Roumelia from the clutch of this Hessian prince, and his then possible ally, the Czar.

But it should be remembered that it is because the Sultan is patient, moderate and forbearing that this resort to violence is not had. Although Turkey has the treaty-right to protect East Roumelia from this revolt and annexation—wiser counsels prevail in the mind of the Sultan. He at once dismisses the old Cabinet for its heedlessness in not making closer observation of the events which were preliminary to the outbreak. A new Grand Vizier is called to the head of the Ministry. I knew him very well before that time, not only by his reputation as a Governor in Syria, but by his ministerial office in Stamboul. This man is Kiamil Pasha, who is still Grand Vizier.

When this sudden uprising in Bulgaria takes place, the Prince expects to be met by a Turkish array. He is not altogether unprepared. When he arrives at Phillipopolis he finds a supply of arms. He calls out every male inhabitant between the ages of eighteen and forty. He has an array of thirty-five thousand men. These he divides into lots of a thousand each. He then begins telegraphing to the Powers. He summons all the tailors of the town to make military clothes. The tailors rebel—bodkin in hand. Most of them are Greeks. They do not like the situation. If East Roumelia be freed from Turkish rule, why not Macedonia? They are, however, starved into manufacturing gray overcoats. Then, behold an army in which each soldier has, not only a uniform, but an opauk sandal and a sheepskin hat. Foreign consuls remonstrate in vain. Then the Prince mixes these soldiers up, gives them officers, and they are in tolerably good fighting trim.

If the Turks had met them then, what a Bulgarian Bull Run would have resulted!

Such a revolution attracts the attention of the Powers which were "signatory" to the Treaty of Berlin. At once they enter into *pour parlers.* As nearly all the Ministers then resided upon the upper waters of the Bosporus, either at Therapia or Buyukdere, I notice that my neighbors are in a flurry. Their launches fly around and over the Strait, under an extra pressure of steam. Out of this discord in the Balkans comes the "European concert!" The refrain is: Shall the *status quo ante* be restored? This is a phrase to signify that Prince Alexander should be relegated and limited to his own dominions, as designated by the treaty of Berlin.

It may be said generally, that wars always come, when they come at all, upon frontiers. It is here that there is found the close collision, local irritation and jealousy of dominion. The question arises: Where is the proper border within which the Battenberg Prince should be confined? Shall his border reach below the Balkan range? If so, in case the Prince be, as was then apprehended, in concert with Russia—would not the taking of East Roumelia enable Russia, through her Slavonic influence and her ecclesiastical polity, to overcome that old historic mountain frontier which bears, among its lofty honors, such names as Plevna and Shumla? A good map shows the line of military occupation at that time, between the Turkish and Bulgarian forces. It runs from Adrianople along the railroad to Phillipopolis.

This is the situation as it appears on September 18, A. D. 1885: The town of Moustafa-Pasha is the centre of Turkish operations. There troops are gathering as a nucleus. The railroad is not interrupted to a great extent—a dozen English miles, perhaps. The insurgent forces are ranged *en échelon,* between Adrianople and Phillipopolis, on the railway. They have some artillery. Of these troops, more than half are at Khaskeim. The map will show how near the contending troops are to each other.

Turkey is acting with forbearance; as well because her Mahometan population is in peril among hostile people, as because of the insurrection. She is conscious of being in the right; and is, perhaps, advised thus to act by the Powers or by some of them. Perhaps she expects the rising to die out from inanition. The insurgents are spending $125,000 a day in the expenses of the militia and volunteers. Can they keep this up very long?

With this question, involving the breach of the Berlin treaty, arises another which tends to help the Turk: Roumania—another child of the Berlin treaty, with a king—represents by her Ministers, at home and abroad, that the contemplated union between East Roumelia and Bulgaria diminishes Roumania's importance as the accepted leader of the Danubian provinces.

Where is Greece in these movements? Are Greece and her kindred population in Macedonia to remain under Slav domination? There is a "cry from Macedonia;" and much excitement in Athens and Albania.

So that it will be perceived that this is not altogether a war of religions, nor of races. It is an endeavor, rather, to increase the local importance of certain "asteroids" in the Eastern sky. It is my belief now, that the Turkish Army could temporarily have settled the trouble, if it had not been that the Sultan disliked to use force, fearing it might involve a general war.

There are other relations to be considered. Bosnia and Servia are occupied by Austria under the conditions of the Berlin treaty. Servia has a king, Milan, the creature of Austria. Austria desires access to the Mediterranean at Salonica, through Turkish provinces. It is a splendid commercial ambition. The map will show how nearly it encroaches on Turkey—in her susceptibility and dignity, as well as in her rights and domain. Turkey reserves her fire—if war comes—for the guardianship of these rights and domain. In this emergency, her hereditary foe, Greece, may be her ally; or may not. That depends on the share of the spoil.

The Eastern question relates not only to the religious creeds—Greek, Armenian, Mahometan, Latin, etc.—but to the states wherein Bulgarian, Wallachian, Greek, Slav, Roumanian, Servian, Bosnian, Herzegovian, Montenegrin and Turk have been mixed for centuries in the most heterogeneous manner, with flexible boundaries and changeful domination. As to this question, the great Powers are in perpetual unrest, despite the obligation of treaties and the conscience of mankind.

The signatory Powers hold a prompt conference at the house of the Italian Minister, Count Corti. He lives in our neighborhood at Therapia. He is the Dean of the Ministers, by longest service;

but whether any conclusion is arrived at, it is impossible to ascertain. The Ambassadors are reticent as to their action. In fact, they are awaiting with much impatience—which is intensely shared by the Sultan and his Ministers and Army—the reply of the Powers to the Sultan's circular upon the situation.

As my duty calls me to see the new Foreign Minister, Saïd Pasha, I take occasion to impress him with our own friendly American regard in the present unexpected embarrassment. As the interests of America depend on the faith of the treaties or capitulations, I make all the emphasis possible, consistent with non-intervention, about the disregard of the Berlin treaty which these events display.

These events happen nine years after the Berlin Congress concluded its labors. Its president, Prince Bismarck, congratulated the nations on the lasting quality of their work. Disraeli, on his return to London, said, "I bring peace with honor." But how long is this pacific work to last? How many breaches must be made before that treaty is utterly riddled?

What is the tenor of this treaty? Its first article provides for an autonomous and tributary principality for Bulgaria. Bulgaria was to have "a Christian government and a national militia." It was to contribute to the Ottoman revenue. Nothing of the revenue has ever been paid to Turkey, and there is a breach on the part of Bulgaria in that regard. Whether she has an autonomous government, is a matter which these concluding chapters will elucidate. She has a national militia, but it turns out to be rather a standing army, in defiance of both the spirit and the wording of the treaty.

Its second article provides that the Sultan shall defend the Balkan frontiers of Eastern Roumelia. But when Eastern Roumelia joins with Bulgaria, is not the treaty defied? Does it not radically change the relation of that region? Where is the defensible frontier against Russia held by Turkey, if Eastern Roumelia becomes a part of Bulgaria; and where is Russia in her attitude toward Turkey in case Russia holds Bulgaria?

Article ten provides for the completion and connection of certain railways through Servia to Constantinople and Salonica. The Varna-Rustchuk line being already in working order, Bulgaria has no difficulty on that score. But, as we have seen in chapter XLVI., other railways are yet in embryo, or in progress.

Article second provides that the local government should demolish and raze the old fortresses within one year, or sooner, if possible, and that they should not be allowed to construct fresh ones. This has not been done; hence another breach of the treaty.

Article seventeen declares that the Governor-General of Eastern Roumelia should be named by the Porte, with the assent of the Powers, for the term of five years. Twice in eight years has this article been violated. Bulgaria, by absorbing Eastern Roumelia, violates its own organic law, which affixed the boundaries of Bulgaria.

Article thirty-three concerns Montenegro, and article forty-two Servia. They were to pay a portion of the Ottoman debt. This has never been done. But the monetary consideration is nothing in comparison with the reckless disregard of the provisions of this much vaunted treaty. It is likely to be torn to atoms, and consumed in some general conflagration, by the Powers which concerted its celebration.

Already the first sounds of the conflict are heard all through the Balkan peninsula. A thousand memories of past terrible conflicts are awakened. Europe stands tip-toe, eager to catch every note of preparation. Even from far-off America telegrams are sent to me, as to the probable outcome of these events. Is it war—or peace? The markets of New York sympathize with the Bourse of Paris, the Börse of Berlin and the Exchange of London.

# CHAPTER XLVIII.

BALKAN PENINSULA ; ROUMANIA ; SERVIA ; PREPARATIONS FOR
FIGHTING; GREECE—ITS KING AND QUEEN.

THE plains below the Balkans are not unlike Belgium in one
respect. They have been called the bloodiest cock-pit of
Europe. The beautiful valley of the Maritza—the ancient Heb-
rus—has been deluged with blood. From the earliest days of
ancient Thrace, when Philip and Alexander subdued its tribes, or
from the time the Romans, under Trajan and Adrian, made their
conquests, even up to and beyond the Danube, down to the time
when the Bulgarians laid the foundation of a kingdom upon the
worn out empire of the Romans—wars have been the rule, and
peace the exception. Since that time, Christian and Turk,
through many centuries, have had here many bitter and fanatical
conflicts. Looking at the battles of Shipka and Plevna, we find in
them a repetition of former contests at old points of strategy.
In these conflicts the Danubian principalities have always figured.
Their people gained independence by their own courage. Strictly
speaking, Roumania is not a Balkan province; and just now she
is aloof from its entanglements and trials.

The capital of Roumania is Bucharest. It deserves special
mention. It is not merely the capital of an interesting kingdom,
but it has the fine touch and color of Western civilization. It
is half Orient and half Occident. You may see the Turk there,
and yet you are away from the Turk. The Roumanians are
by no means home-bodies. They travel a good deal. They
return with the customs and costumes of the French capital.
They are fond of music and shows. Nothing pleases them more
than a theatre, unless it be a circus. They love the latter with
the affection of the old Romans, of which they esteem themselves to be the legitimate heirs. I noticed their fine horses, and
the rattling pace with which the Jehus drive. They are unexampled for the gayety of their equipages.

Roumania played a chivalric part in the war by which she was freed and organized. She was carved out of Turkey by the union of Moldavia and Wallachia. The treaty of Berlin called her into being as a state whose suzerain was the Sultan. Some tribute was to be paid, but it has not been paid. She sits at the foot of the Carpathians with her King and Queen, with all the felicities of her autonomy, as ready for the arts of peace as the honors of war.

There are many reasons why Roumania is interesting. The houses of her capital, although never more than one or two stories, are shapely and elegant. Her streets are well paved and cleanly, and the people are penetrated with the old Roman *esprit.* Many interesting ruins show that Roumania was a prominent Roman province at an early date. The relics of her greatness still remain in the character, gallantry and pride of her citizens.

If the reader would know something about Turkey in Europe, and how much even recent wars have limited its domain, let him turn to a map and glance at the country between the Black Sea, the Ægean, the Adriatic and under the Balkans. Or, let him stand in the south of Turkey in Europe, on classic Mount Olympus, or its neighbor Ossa, and observe, in fancy, old Thessalonica and the beautiful city of Janina, with its mountain lake; or stand upon Pindus and survey the lands of the Eastern Adriatic, or look down from the Black Mountain on Montenegro, or glance at the distant snow-covered mountains of Herzegovina ; or let him traverse the rugged country around Sophia, or take the railroad from Phillipopolis through Adrianople to the Bosporus—he will observe that its scenery and cultivation have not improved by any measure of self-government or of relief from the Ottoman rule.

This land was once in better trim and culture than it is at present. It is now almost a treeless, fenceless and arid waste. There are portions of it capable of being redeemed. Much of it in the valleys at the foot of the Balkans is already redeemed in a most attractive way. I do not mean that its redemption came through glorious war, or from the influence of the fortresses of the Oriental quadrilateral amid the mountains of the Balkans.

Let the reader follow the Russian army, as it passed in 1878, not without struggle, over the Balkans, driving before it the Turkish armies. Although the paths which he may follow over these mountains and vales are Alpine, yet he will soon come upon a plain where for miles the atmosphere is lovely with roseate tints; for is not this the land of Eskizagra, where the sweetest roses of the earth bloom in prodigality, and the precious *attar* is manufactured in its purity ?

This country under the Balkans is so beautiful, and at the same time so fruitful, that it is called the " Basin of Roses." It is in the Kasenlyk district. Its Turkish name is Ghyulteknâsy and its chirography in Turkish looks like our shorthand caligraphy. It has a poetic significance deeper than the typography. The distillation of the rose in the Sanjak of Phillipopolis is immensely productive, but it depends, like all other crops, upon a state of peace.

The word *attar*, or *otar*, in the Turkish tongue means perfume; but there can be no bloom or perfume upon the rose when the thieving Cossacks are around, or the bugles of war are resounding in the vales. This paradise has not been spared. Perhaps some of the color of the rich red rose may remind the reader of those realms of which Tom Moore sang, and of which Cashmere, in the still farther Orient, at the foot of the Himalayas, is another and lovely example.

The southern base of the Balkan range does not depend on the attar of roses altogether for its fragrance or its prosperity. It has an exuberance of vegetation and production, as all Piedmontese countries have. It is redolent and rich in the jasmine and the wall-lilac, and in vineyards and forests of fruit trees. These give to the plains a fragrance and beauty only equal to that which blooms in and is distilled from its roses. Is this fair land to be the sanguinary battle-ground of the dynasties?

Since there has been so much said and printed in relation to the Balkan peninsula, and the collisions growing out of the ambitions of its various provinces, it is as well to correct—as I have endeavored to do—the apocryphal, exaggerated and misleading views which have been entertained about this arena of conflict.

After the events which have been narrated, there were various meetings of the Signatory Powers at the house of the Italian Ambassador. Out of these meetings there was formulated a note. It maintained the Berlin treaty, which had been flagrantly and unexpectedly violated by the action of Prince Alexander. This note was understood as allowing the Sultan to carry out, without any intervention or obstacle from the Signatory Powers, his authority over East Roumelia, under the Berlin treaty. It was hoped, however, that no breach of the peace, and no bloodshed, would result. Whether Turkey was or was not ready to take the initiative thus accorded her by these then neutral Powers, by using force over her Balkan dependency, had not then been ascertained absolutely.

What is known is that which all who were near saw: recruits and conscripts from all parts of the empire, and soldiers and munitions from the capital, moving with expedition to the border. Intense activity is seen in all departments of the Ottoman government. At any moment, a spark may enkindle a blaze which will involve the whole peninsula, reaching unto the Adriatic in its consequences, including Greece, and, in fact, engrossing all the warlike courage and resources of the countries whose fate is affected by the Berlin treaty.

The position of Russia is constantly referred to as equivocal. Russia, as the *soi disant* guardian of the Bulgar or Slav—for reasons which are apparent in this narrative—dislikes the mode adopted by Prince Alexander; but why should she dislike the union of the "two Bulgarias"? Does not this union enhance her greatness, as the leader of the Slavonic race? Does it not, in fact, macadamize her road to Constantinople?

It is rumored, and it is *a priori* probable, that Servia and the other small Powers affected, are ready to aid Turkey in the contest for the integrity of the Berlin treaty. It is apparent that Greece especially, is madly jealous of the growth of the Slav element. An immense public assemblage to demonstrate this object is expected on Sunday, the 18th of October, A. D. 1885, at its capital, Athens. Even Austria is regarded as jealous of Slav encroachment. There is jealousy everywhere in relation to this Bulgarian *emeute*. Each one of the Powers interested desires to have some word in the matter, or share in the partition of Turkey, if any is to be made. Servia seems to be the most ravenous. She bases her demand on her ancient dignity, when indeed she was a Power of imperial magnitude.

The position of Great Britain I cannot exactly understand. Her Premier, Lord Salisbury, has just spoken, upon the hustings, rather in favor of maintaining the *status quo*. He seems to oppose the disturbance of the union of the Bulgarias. In Constantinople it is understood that all the Powers, including Great Britain, are to unite upon a proposition for the *status quo.* Great Britain is represented in Constantinople by Sir Henry Drummond Wolff, but he is intent only on Egyptian matters. She must be either friendly to Turkey and join the Powers in their efforts, or fail in her diplomacy as to Egypt. Her position is not without embarrassment and ambiguity. Besides, England has a memory of the Crimean War and its unsatisfactory conclusion. That war cost England twenty-four thousand lives; and, reduced to dollars, about two hundred millions. Along with her allies, England succeeded in crippling Russia temporarily. Turkey was restored to many of her privileges. Certainly, the allies received from Turkey many promises and some performances as to justice and reform. Still, England has posed as the friend of liberty in the provinces; and now that a Battenberg—connected with Queen Victoria—is aggrandizing himself and family in the Balkans, is it for England to oppose the union of the Bulgarias? We will see.

For some days, the telegraph from Adrianople has been cut. Much excitement and gloom exist in government circles at the indefinite nature of the news. On the 16th of October, A. D. 1885, His Excellency Saïd Pasha, the Minister of Foreign Affairs, makes his calls of courtesy. He honors our Legation at Therapia. He expresses himself as more cheerful over the situation than he has been hitherto. He more than intimates that the action of the six Powers has aided to dispel the gloom and brighten the hopes of peace and the re-establishment of the *status quo ante bellum.*

It is understood that a deputation from the Prince, or from the Bulgarians, has visited the Czar at Copenhagen, so as, if possible, to have his good-will, which is that of Russia, in the controversy. The treatment of the deputation by the Czar is reported in various ways. It seems, however, that Russia, by its Minister, M. Nellidoff, in Constantinople, is acting with the other Signatory Powers. The best impression here is that war will be averted, owing to the stand taken by the six Powers.

In the early days, when Turkey rose potentially in the East, France seemed to be most dominant. In fact, the French language is the prevailing language yet, outside of the languages of the country. "Capitulations" from the early Sultans to the French, fixed the status of the Christian world with respect to the Orient. But, for reasons not requiring dilation, the French have not retained their old standing in the East, when Napoleon the Great was represented here by Sebastiani.

As the controversy appears, about the last of October, A. D. 1885 : the Prince has given his complete submission to the Powers, and has left Phillipopolis. Again, it is said that he is only gone to inspect certain portions of the interior of East Roumelia, and will soon return to Sophia to preside over a council of Ministers; and again that he will withdraw his army, upon a promise given him to sanction some assimilation of the institutions of East Roumelia and Bulgaria.

As I had prophesied in my despatches home, trade is hampered. Even America is to be affected by these semi-belligerent conditions. The Bulgarian authorities, for the second time, prohibit the export of maize and wheat from Bourgas, an East Roumelian port. The Powers protest. We have no protest to make, as to any restriction which tends to enlarge our own grain market. In fact, we have nothing at all to do or say in these matters. For the present, it is ours to observe.

At the beginning of the complication I wrote a despatch to my government that I feared the American (Robert) College, most of whose students are Bulgars, might be embarrassed in consequence of the nationality of these students; and especially so in case the students should leave, or endeavor to leave, for their homes to take part in the insurrection. This fear was founded on the fact that Dr. Washburn, the President, had just returned from a tour through Bulgaria. There he had received a triumphal reception from his former pupils.

I called at the College and saw Dr. Washburn. He said that but one Bulgarian student had left, and that he had returned. The College was full. There were nearly two hundred students. Their good conduct was admirable. I ask the President:

"What is your judgment as to these recent events." He replies:

"I believe that the uprising is spontaneous with the people of the two provinces. It is a surprise to all the Powers. It is such a surprise that Russia suspects Austria, and Austria suspects Russia. Even the Russian Ambassador, M. Nellidoff, was puzzled at first. As Russia sometimes works in these provinces in a mysterious way, and without the knowledge of her own Minister—his protestations, like those of Austria, are sincere."

" But, Doctor, what of Germany; what of the Chancellor ? "

" I understand," he rejoins, "that the astute Chancellor is not unwilling to see Austria and Russia divide up the Balkans and other parts of Turkey in Europe, and thus close up these ever-recurring controversies."

" But what Power will get Constantinople ? Who will allow Russia to control these splendid commercial waters ? "

This is not, as he confesses, so easily answered. He can only say:

" That is a puzzle ! "

" Besides," I presume to add, " Turkey is not now a ' sick man. Turkey generally lacks money; but then her tithes are now coming in, and a loan of over three millions of dollars is being made upon certain chartered railway guarantees in Asia. Her soldiers care little for their pay, so that they are well housed, fed and clothed. Besides, is not the Sultan the Chief of Islam, at the head of two hundred millions of Mahometans in Asia, Africa and the isles ? Is she to be despised where the Faithful pray toward Mecca, either by Russia in Asia; or by England in Asia and Africa ; or by Germany, Spain, England, Portugal, Belgium, France or Italy—in Europe or Africa; or by any or all of the Powers which are moving over the earth and seas, seeking what remote realms they may—rescue from barbarism?"

The part which Germany may play in this drama, it is difficult to foretell. Her Minister is highly honored by the Sultan. Germans here are supplanting the English and other nationalities in the service of the Porte. The new Minister of Foreign Affairs, Saïd Pasha, has recently been Minister at Berlin, and was, before he left, decorated by the Emperor of Germany and honored by Chancellor Bismarck. Germany, in fact, has the sword of Brennus. Will she throw it into the doubtful scale? I presume, from her reserve, that she favors the *status quo ante bellum*, and then a conference. Time will show.

It is generally believed that, at the meeting of the three Emperors at Cremsier, this insurrection was arranged. As each of the Powers—whatever their secret wish or bias might have been—disclaimed any part in the uprising, so each of them seems to be horrified at the audacious breach of the Berlin treaty; and all, unless now we except Great Britain, pretend to desire the *status quo ante bellum*. If so, why are they so slow to compel the *amende* to Turkey? Delay works in two ways: it helps, at one view, to establish the union of the provinces; and in another, it costs the Bulgarians immensely for troops, munitions and provisions. The impatient Bulgar expects ready sympathy and aid from the Powers, especially Russia. He is already discouraged. Time is dispiriting the people of the two provinces and disintegrating their forces. The exchequer of the Prince is not large, and results have not been realized. The volunteers of Bulgaria are said to be hiding in the mountains, and many are on half rations; while many more are fearful of a Servian as well as of a Turkish attack.

Events are likely soon to produce a new settlement of the Balkan question. The conditions may differ from those of the Berlin treaty. This result, it seems, the Porte is willing to hazard; for the Porte, as I hear, has sent to its representatives accredited to the great Powers, a circular proposing a conference of Ambassadors in Constantinople, to settle definitely the Roumelian question; to consider that question only.

The situation before the Servian attack on Bulgaria is nearly this: the three great Powers—Austria, Russia and Germany—are agreed; England hesitates; France and Italy are reluctant, but are supposed to be in accord about the conference. The Porte desires to prevent bloodshed, but insists upon the Berlin treaty being preserved in its entirety and in good faith. The Porte does not fear Bulgaria so much as Servia and Greece. It would be a great relief to the Powers and people—who are apprehensive of a great war, involving every race and nation, from the Adriatic to the Black Sea—should these apprehensions be allayed.

The Ambassadors of the six Powers had several meetings. It would seem, from this, that nothing had been concluded absolutely. Several days ago they met to discuss the reply of the Porte to the so-called "Identic note" of the Powers. It is said, and truly, that they are still united upon the Berlin treaty, and the rights of the Sultan under it. A further conference is called to settle what seems to have been already agreed upon.

These vicissitudes, with their rumors and apprehensions, indicate to the reader who is unacquainted with the Eastern question and the modes for its settlement or suppression, one of the Diversions of an American Minister at the Porte, whose anxiety, if he indulges in any, is that freedom should prevail, and that his own country, if war comes, may not be harmed, but helped, in the controversy.

Meanwhile, arming and mobilization go on. Servia has 100,000 men ready. Her whole population is only 1,865,000. She is eager for a fray, either with Bulgaria, or any Power which presumes to lead the Balkan peninsula, or grow in domain or power without her consent or her own aggrandizement! Russia has 80,000 troops in Bessarabia, on the Roumanian frontier; and still her battalions come! Servia, however, is giving Bulgaria more apprehension than she gives Turkey. Greece is having an excitement worthy of her early historic and rhetorical activity upon these shores; but she has not yet, owing to restraining influences outside, broken from her moorings. Servia is about to launch herself upon "a sea of trouble."

A modern Turk may not imitate his ancestry so far as energy is concerned. He may temporize. He says: "I will do nothing to-day; to-morrow, *Bacaloum*, we shall see." And yet, he is wary as well as patient. He is gathering upon the frontier for this emergency a fine army, well ordered and equipped. He has already there 40,000 good, trained soldiers, and cannon of the best make. His notes trumpet along the Bosporus with no uncertain sound, from morning till evening. His conscripts are coming into the city by the thousand. Drilling goes on every hour upon the barrack-grounds and on the shores of the Straits. Many of his soldiers are going to Salonica, as if the point of danger were in Macedonia. The Austrian Lloyd Company is employed continually in carrying troops to that important point. Turkish vessels are constantly passing up and down the Straits, or coming in from the Black Sea, or from Syria, loaded with troops. The vessels have a roseate tinge, from the multitude of red fez caps which crowd their decks.

These grand movements indicate a question more important than Prince Alexander and his insurrection. The greater question is one which neither diplomacy, treaty nor arms can readily reconcile or settle. In its most comprehensive expression, it is a question of race and nationality. It is :

"Shall this or that race dominate within certain natural or artificial boundaries ?"

There is much uncertainty as to these Balkan races and their mixture with one another. Even the proud Greek strain is chal-

lenged as being more or less Slav. From Herzegovina to the
Dobrodcha, from the Gulf of Corinth to the Danube, there is a
strange composite of many races, so interchangeably mixed by
blood, tradition, history, war, exodus and social and domestic
relations that no one can aver where one race begins and another
ends, or which dominates in any one locality.

The distinct races in these provinces are the Gypsy, Ottoman,
Jew, Slav and Greek. They appear each with their peculiar
prejudices and traditions. Neither of these races constitutes distinctively any one of the lesser provincial luminaries. Neither
of these shines with a lustre altogether peculiar to itself, or with a
magnitude great enough to be other than a satellite moving around
stars of superior orbit and destiny.

It will not do to trust to the ordinary observer, be he ever so
clever, for our knowledge of the political situation of the East, and
especially in the Balkan peninsula. The contradictory reports of
the outrages of Bulgaria, and the number of people who were massacred there some years ago, should lead one to be cautious. The
English Minister, Layard, once said, " The Orient is given to men-
dacity." It will not do to trust to the estimates of those connected
with one nationality, who may be partial or interested in covering
the facts. As well seek to rely upon a three months' visit to Turkey,
with the time spent socially among its hospitable people at the
hotels of Pera or the *konaks* of the pashas, for the mode and manner of life of the various races who make up the capital of Turkey.
There is a great dearth of reliable information as to the Orient,
and but for certain volumes like that edited by "A Consul's
Daughter," who had two decades of experience, we would not be
able to do justice either to Greek, Turk or Slav, in their relations
to the Porte or to the Oriental problem.

Before any one can, therefore, arrange the dynasties and
boundaries of southeastern Europe, reliable facts are indispensable. If we rely upon the volumes which have been written
about Turkey since the Russian or the Crimean war, we would
suppose that the Bulgarian was deeply attached to Russia as her
savior. From another quarter, since the hostility developed in
Bulgaria against Russia, we would think that the Bulgarian was
attached to the Porte. For many years of this perpetual contention, with very little reliance upon the sources of information,
and especially as to those questions into which religion and race

enter, it is well to have an informant who has had personal observation.

I have before me a volume on the "Balkan Peninsula," by Emile de Laveleye. He is a voluminous writer on economic and social questions, a member of all the academies and institutes, a learned linguist and a worthy gentleman. His book is introduced to the public by Mr. Gladstone, who commends M. Laveleye for his prudence, energy and ability, and who regards the accomplished author as a champion of "the well-being, tranquillity and liberty of that region which has come to be of more critical importance than ever, to the interests of Europe." It must be remembered that Mr. Gladstone is a Russophile. He is by no means kind to the Turk; and making much allowance for a certain classic and sentimental partiality toward the Greek and Slav, in this volume of M. Laveleye, nevertheless, it is to be regarded as a tolerably fair and full presentation of the events which are but briefly hinted at in these concluding chapters.

Much has been said and written in favor of a confederation of the Balkan states. Such a confederation, now that Turkey has been somewhat eliminated from that section of the European world, would include the two great Christian races in Turkey— the Greek and the Slav. Can these two bodies sympathize? If they could only act as one, they would be stronger ; if they could have a Zolverein, so as to trade with each other, as Germany had, and as our States have, it would be to their advantage. It would enhance their strength as an economic and political community. But the Greek is not a Slav, and the Slav is not a Greek. They are rivals. The Bulgarian *coup d'état* displayed that relation at once. There is to be no regeneration by their joint action, under the Balkans. It would take a heroic man— somebody greater than the Battenberg, or any other princeling, to solve, in this light, the problem of Bulgaria and the Balkans. The Bulgarian may recognize the intellectual eminence of the Greek, but the ecclesiastical independence of Bulgaria shows that when it comes to the emotional nature, which takes hold upon the unseen world, the Bulgarian accepts no domineering from any quarter.

Along with the Bulgarian, and nearer perhaps than the Greeks imagine, or the Powers of Europe dream, are the Servians, Bosniacs, Montenegrins and other Slavonic races. These have some

Slavonic links, ethnologically if not nationally. They have a temperament that defies control. They are likely to act together, as they have acted. But between them and the Greek there is a wide chasm which no diplomacy can bridge. I have had some opportunity of observing the Slav. My servant Pedro is of that race. He is a good illustration of its superstitious weaknesses, stability and fidelity. He is, like his kindred, determined and independent. The Greek is subtle, impulsive, and egotistic. There are not many Greek communities north of the classic Olympus and its parallel ; and the Greeks upon the Princes Islands, and in the insular dependencies of Turkey, are but few, comparatively, in number. They are not disposed to be revolutionary. If the Greeks were not so whimsical ; if Greece, since A. D. 1833, had not had over thirty-odd ministerial changes to illustrate her impulses ; if the Russians were once more at San Stefano, and the question came before the great tribunal of the Powers of Europe, who hold the destiny of three continents in their control, as to what Power should have Constantinople—what country could they name ? England ? No. Russia, France, Austria and Italy would all protest! France ? No. Her day in the East is past. Italy ? She too has long since lost her domination at Galata, or at the other marts of her ancient commerce. Austria ? She has too much traffic to make her the disinterested ruler at its great centre. But her interests are most tenacious, because those of trade. Would it be Russia ? "Never," is the chorus of all the Powers. Might it not become, under general control, a free port, and not be left in the hands of any one people? Perhaps then all the Powers and all the interests would be harmonized. The interests centring at Belgrade on the Danube, at Salonica on the Ægean, and at Ragusa on the Adriatic, would contribute, along with the railroad schemes, when completed through Asia Minor eastward to India—to elevate Constantinople into her early commercial supremacy and imperial magnificence.

Ah, there is Greece ! Has she the *stamina* to organize her old empire ? If the contest should be between the Slav and the Greek alone, the Slav being assisted by Russia, and the Greek by the Latin races, including those of Germany and England, the result—if I may indulge in the best *a priori* prophecy—would be, if these were the only alternatives, that Constantinople would be controlled by the Greeks. But there is no such alternative.

There are from five to seven millions of the Greek race in Turkey. They are a buoyant and active business people; and, notwithstanding their apparent devotion to the Sultan, quite ready, if aided, to welcome their vaunted palingenesis. If it depended on the personal qualities of the king of Greece, this result, under such a leader, would not be so improbable. But he is not the power in his state. Greece is a monarchy, tempered with a fickle legislature and a versatile ministry.

\*    \*    \*    \*    \*    \*    \*

It is nothing to the discredit of King George that he " reigns, but does not govern." He was married to the Princess Olga, a daughter of the Grand Duke Constantine. He may, therefore, have a bias toward Russia, as well royally as ecclesiastically. But the queen is averse to the intrigues of politics, and the king holds his limited state with a steady hand. The moving spirit of all the charities of Athens—the queen—is worshipped by the Greek people. Her blue eyes and brilliant complexion have yet to be saddened or eclipsed by the dark shadow of the Oriental problem. Her husband, whose likeness is presented along with that of the queen, is a worthy mate of an estimable woman.

I have had the pleasure of seeing Queen Olga, but only in a frame, in the palace at Athens. As I passed through the antechamber to meet the king, I doffed my hat to her portrait, instinctively, as to a good woman. I cannot fail to recall the pleasure of this palatial Diversion. We had just returned from Egypt, and were *en route* to the Bosporus. We were " busy as bees when the buckwheat blows," finishing our investigation of the Acropolis, and from its elevation making a survey of the classic mountains and plains, and the city, which had grown greatly in size and elegance since we saw it in 1851.

After a breakfast with Dr. Schliemann and his scholastic wife, at their splendid home, from which we had retired replete with enthusiasm and archæology, we follow the guidance of an American Hellenic scholar, who had been making studious researches into the marvels of the Acropolis. We are forgetting our massive Egyptian wonders, as well as the warlike enterprises which are stirring the very stones of the temples of the Acropolis into classic rage at the conduct of Bulgaria—when we are summoned to an ovation in a little shanty of a museum, just below the Temple of Minerva. And for what? The archæologist who reads this

THE KING AND QUEEN OF GREECE.

page anticipates me; for it was in February, 1886, and there had been discovered here certain rare treasures of Archaic art. We had seen the workmen, with pick and spade, sweating among the *debris* between the Erechtheum and the spot where the bronze Athena stood. Many attempts had been made before to burrow here, below the rubbish of marble and stone. They had failed; but these last efforts did not fail. They were rewarded by a collection of pre-Phidian statues of Parian marble, of rare interest and peerless loveliness. One of these had glass eyes; others were painted, and the colors preserved in their primitive lustre; some are colossal in proportion, and they all bespeak an antique age of art, from which the modern world were long expecting opulent results. These art treasures were rescued in three hours from their graves. They are ready to delight a great circle of scholars and artists. It is the especial pride and glory of King George that he has been summoned to brush the dust of ages from these sculptures, preliminary to the—photograph.

I am watching this photographing process, when a messenger appears in the little museum. He summons me to the palace. What had I been doing? A note from the king's secretary— signed Botzarris—explains the hidden inspiration of this royal mandamus. Our Minister, Mr. Fearn, is reciprocating his presentation to the Sultan. I leave the Archaic statues to the photographer and all Acropolitan associations to the past—to answer the summons. We meet on the threshold a descendant of the Botzarris family, who inducts us within the palace. We receive a cordial greeting and welcome, and spend an hour in the company of one of the most charming and elegant gentlemen whom it is possible to meet abroad.

It would be a matter of regret if he, as the king, should be distracted from his life as a moderate and wise ruler, to be launched upon the stormy waves of Eastern conflict; now, at this equinoctial season, as wild and unruly as the seas which lash the isles of his domain.

Greece, however, will not be called to lead her compatriots in the conflicts of the East.

After all, surmise and ratiocination are vain. We come to the same old conclusion as that of the past century: that so long as no two Powers agree as to what race, system, or government shall occupy Constantinople—that city will remain most content with her present possessors, until some social or religious cataclysm occurs, to change the tide of human passion and the ambition of human nature.

# CHAPTER XLIX.

THE Bulgarians are of the Turanian stock. They came from the Volga in the fifth century and mixed with the Slavs, with whom they coalesced. They besieged Constantinople in A. D. 559. Along with the Slavs they became such a Power as to levy tribute upon Byzantium. They have fought with the Magyars in the north, with the Greeks in the south, and with the Turks ever since the latter crossed into Europe. Ravaged by Tartars and scourged by her neighbors, still, Bulgaria in the Middle Ages had so far advanced that she had a refinement of civilization, comparable then with that of Germany, Hungary, France and England.

The language of Bulgaria shows its Slav relationship. In fact, before it was corrupted by the Turkish conquest, and by admixture with the other Danubian tongues, it was a pure, and, therefore, the ecclesiastical, medium of expression. It has a literature, although it is limited to national songs. Since Robert College has aroused its dormant intellect, Bulgaria has been stimulated to resume her elder glory.

With all the relations of Church and state associating Bulgaria with the Greeks, and with the question constantly propounded through the centuries, " Will you be Slav or Greek ? " she has refused to be Hellenized, just as to-day she is ready to make armed protest against being Muscovized. God grant that she may stand fast and upright in the light of that dawning liberty which she has deserved by patience, persistence and patriotism.

The Bulgarian people as a body are peasants. Their social order should dictate their political character. As in Norway, Kansas, Switzerland and Texas, the rural democracy control; so in Bulgaria, the institutions should be a government fitting the simple quality of the people.

The attempt to create Russian dictation by army officers

failed. The attempt to shake off the Liberal Ministries formed since 1880, also failed. Leaders like Zankoff and Karaveloff voiced the popular opinion for some years, despite a *coup d'état* in May, 1881, two years after the Tirnova constitution—which failed after much anxiety among the people, and despotic rule from pro-Russian conservatism. Prince Alexander himself, irritated beyond expression by the meddling arrogance of the Russian Generals, Skobeleff and Kaulbars, at last compelled these generals to resign from the Ministry and retire from the country. Home coalition ministries against alien domination followed, until at last, after six years of exasperations, Bulgaria rose to the need and height of self-government. At last, Karaveloff—accomplished in political economy and learned in the logic and practice of statesmanship, became the responsible head of the sentiment, "Bulgaria for the Bulgarians," and of the surprising revolt of September, 1885, out of which has flowed unnumbered woes and a glorious prospect of relief and independence.

The scene of these events so intimately associated with the action of Turkey was at Sophia. It is the capital of Bulgaria. It is a city—having a population of fifty thousand. It is as nearly as possible at the centre of the Balkan peninsula, and in the southwest corner of Bulgaria, not far from the Servian and Roumelian frontier. It is near the north foot of the Balkan mountains, upon a little stream which contributes to the Asker, which is itself a tributary of the Danube. Sophia is on the highway between Constantinople and Belgrade, over which, for thousands of years, many armies—Greek, Hungarian, Slav and Turk—have moved. It is situated on a vast plain, cultivated not unlike the Hungarian and Russian prairies, by tillers and graziers, who live in little villages or hide in the mountains, having no farm-buildings and houses. The traveler, as he winds his way up the mountains, will see few men, but many women, going to work. The latter wear a black apron, red belt and a long white tunic. A red handkerchief decorates the frizzly hair, and a baby slung in a bag ornaments the back. The carts and ploughs are primitive, but they are beautified by being attached to cross-looking buffaloes.

This is a sample of the land which has been uptorn for a dozen centuries by the ploughshare of war. The only object of taste and utility to be seen on these routes to the Bulgarian capital, is

here and there a Turkish fountain shaded by a magnificent tree—
"gracious monuments," says M. de Laveleye, "offering their
beneficent waters to the animals and people thirsty from the heat,
and to the Faithful in their ablutions."

Upon ascending to the summit of the pass, the traveler reaches
the elevated table-land. It is flat, barren, almost grassless. The
prospect is brown except a conspicuous white spot in the centre
of the plain. That is Sophia. It is situated in the midst of a
waterless lake. The streets of the city are narrow and crooked.
The houses are indifferent. There are churches and mosques,
baths and bazaars and other relics—like the Khan—of Oriental
memory. It is an ecclesiastical see, both of the Greek and Latin
Churches. It was founded by Justinian, but ever since A. D. 1382,
when the Turks conquered it, the city has been held under many
vicissitudes. Not the least interesting of these are the more
recent events; and since the Berlin treaty gave Bulgaria
autonomy and a prince. The outward signs of these blessings
are the palace and the parliament house, which the artist has
pictured for the reader. The exciting incidents which have
inflamed the Powers of the world, have occurred here on this
border, where Pirot and Slivnitza, are surrounded by a martial
halo.

It is fashionable for Americans to praise Russia. The sympathy of our country with Russia was strengthened by the reforms
projected and carried out under Alexander II. It is by no means
certain that the present Czar sympathizes with these reforms or
takes much pride even in the emancipation of the serfs accomplished by his predecessor. He believes in the policy of Nicholas.
The clergy are still to be enfranchised, instead of being used as
they are, for police duty and other than spiritual purposes. If
there be any freedom of speech or of the press in Russia ; if the
corruption of the courts of justice, of which I had proof in my
travels through that country nearly ten years ago, has been corrected ; if intelligence has been awakened by education ; if the
fiscal system has been improved ; or if there has been any
progress in the liberalities of politics, domestic or foreign, of recent
years—the world is yet to know it.

It will not do to dilate upon her vast landed area, as the proof
of her strength ; for the larger the territory the more difficult to
suppress the constantly smoldering revolution which threatens

PALACE AT SOPHIA, BULGARIA.

PARLIAMENT BUILDING AT SOPHIA, BULGARIA.

the life of the system, and of the occupant of the throne himself. True, the Czar is the father of his people! But he is their despot also. He is at the head of a hundred and three millions of subjects! True again, that he has his immense armies in Europe and in Asia. But the money wherewithal to pay them is scarce, and what of it is current is an irredeemable paper currency. We in America know what that means. It is worth now only about half its face. In case of a general conflagration in Europe, it will be worth little or nothing.

What, then, is this overshadowing strength of Russia? It is the compact Slavonic element of sixty millions, not so much on the boundaries as in the heart of the empire. It is moved by one sentiment, and this sentiment is founded on the superstitions, emotions and ceremonies of the orthodox Church.

Russia has many alien nations in her midst. They would be her weakness rather than her strength in an emergency. She may for a time intrigue upon the Danube and be allied with the French. She may trample upon and over the Balkans, and her Minister may dictate terms of peace in Constantinople; but unless her own government be radically reformed, and the Slavonic element in the Balkan peninsula be more closely united with a similar element in her own country, her Slavonic enthusiasm will end in vapor.

Whether or not Russia has pursued, since the time of Peter the Great, the movement upon Constantinople with as much vigor as she would have done without the intervention of the other Powers, it is a fact that her greatest sovereign, Catherine II.—the murderess of her husband, and of Ivan, the presumptive heir to the throne—fixed over the gates of Kherson this inscription: " This is the road to Byzantium!" This was a perfidious violation of the treaty of Rustchuk, signed on the 10th day of July, A. D. 1774.

Is it asked: " What are the intentions of Russia? Will she be content with the effectual closing of the Straits, so as to give her guarantees of their inviolability? Is she only anxious to be an ally of Turkey for its security? What are her real designs? Has she any in connection with the partition of the Ottoman empire?"

The answer may be found in the conversation of the greatest of the Czars, Nicholas, with the English Ambassador in A. D. 1853. After coolly offering Egypt to England for her acquiescence, he desires the Danubian principalities for himself. He disposes also of Servia and Bulgaria with the same frosty breath. But he takes pains to forbid the reconstruction of the Byzantine empire, having his own eye upon St. Sophia. Nor would he make out of Turkey little republics, asylums for the Kossuths, Mazzinis and other radicals of Europe. " Rather fight," is his remark, " as long as I have a man or a musket." It is on this occasion and from this Czar that the expression of his belief creeps unawares upon his caution : " We have on our hands a sick man, and he may suddenly die on our hands!"

Is Russia preparing a hospital for the sick man, that she organizes new railways and new orthodox convents—to Russify the wild tribes on the eastern border of Turkey in Asia, and the Christian youth of Armenia ? Has she in view no secular militance along with her monastic crusade ? What is her motive in stirring up bad blood and revolt by the means adopted by her Kaulbars, Zankoffs and others in the Balkans ? What means the Rustchuk rebellion last March—1887 ? Why is she so bitter toward the regency, the Sobranjé, and toward every prince named for the succession, except her own creatures ? Has not the regency carried on Bulgarian affairs without anarchy and with order, firmness and dignity ? Russia has been called the Bear, and Bulgaria the Hive. The bear, in trying to turn over the hive for the honey, finds more bees than honey, and bees that have a skill in piercing even the hide of a bear.

The generalship which distinguished Osman Pasha and his officers and men in the Russian war of 1877–78 has never been sufficiently praised. It is said that at Shipka Pass the contest was unequal. The Turks may have had the advantage of numbers and position. At Plevna, where fully twenty thousand men died fighting on the vine-clad hills that surround the town, and sixty thousand were wounded—the contest was greatly to the disadvantage of the Turks so far as numbers were concerned. Whether in open assault or artillery duel, attacking or repelling, the Turks under Osman Pasha there won undying fame. In this conflict, just north of the Balkans, and on which depended the taking of the Balkans itself, and, in fact, the taking of Constantinople—ninety thousand Russians gathered in front of the Krishin parapet, and fought in vain to overcome it. The assaults were commanded by the best generals of the Russian army. The Czar himself was present. The Grand Duke

Nicholas was in command, Such soldiers as Todleben, King Charles of Roumania, and Skobeleff were in command. They were assisted by such officers as Gourko. Nevertheless, the final assault, upon the Emperor's name-day, with a terrific bombardment of four days, failed to conquer the Turk. Only starvation drove him from his entrenchment. On the 10th of December Plevna fell. It fell because Osman Pasha found his provisions reduced, but it was no tame surrender. He massed his troops during the night, pierced the Russian lines on the west, and endeavored to escape to the Balkans—a hopeless onslaught, but it had all the fierceness of the early Turk, for it was like a whirlwind. The truth is, the war was one of religious fanaticism. The Russian knows nothing else in any war than God and the Czar. He is like the Turk, who, when embattled, recks of nothing but Allah, Mahomet and the Caliph!

The war did not end at once, as many supposed it would. A winter campaign followed, pushing into spring. During its continuance, seven hundred thousand Mahometans abandoned their possessions; most of them, as refugees, sought a new Asiatic home. Three hundred thousand Bulgarians also left their homes when the reflux wave of Gourko's retreat took place in July.

When this war is renewed, the Balkans will not be so easily surmounted. Nor will the chivalry of Carpathia, nor the hussars of Austria-Hungary, nor the intrepid Slavs of the Peninsula, be there to aid the Muscovite. If they take part, they will probably side with the Ottoman, from whom they have had more privileges in the faith and more liberties in the state than other races have had under Muscovite control. If Russia's road to the East, as it is said, lies through Vienna, with or without the consent of Germany, the Muscovite will never travel that way so as to achieve domination over the Bosporus.

Whenever Turkey is *in extremis*, and when the Christian nations, so-called, begin to think that the Alexanders and the Gortchakoffs are the especial vicegerents of God, to conquer or suppress Turkey, or to drive its race out of Europe into Asia, in order that the Muscovite, with his peculiar love of liberty may be paramount —when that threatens, there is one desperate resort. It is like taking a lighted match into a magazine and blowing up the citadel. It is only for the Sultan to do as he did when once before Russia menaced his capital. He can go to his army, raise the standard of the Caliphate and of the Sultanate, and, with the help of Allah, maintain the independence of the Osmanli, and sacrifice, if necessary, his life to the honor and independence of his country.

It is difficult to discriminate between the various Sultans who ruled beneficently. Those who had the best intentions, like Selim the Third, were short-lived. Many of his successors endeavored to carry out his reforms. They found it impossible. But whatever may be said as to these rulers and the characteristics of their subjects, nothing can equal the atrocities of the Russian in Poland, even as late as the year 1863, in Central Asia as late as 1875–76, in Siberia at all times, and in the domain of the White Czar, in which, at this moment, these barbarities are oppressive and infamous.

So that, as between Muscovite and Ottoman, if there be a choice, well-evidenced by tradition and history, for the calamities it has brought, the Muscovite bears the palm. Our sympathies in America are misplaced, if they regard the relation of Russia to civilization as better than that of the Turk.

Take one element of social order—that of religious toleration and liberty: compare the religious toleration of the Turk with the cruel persecutions of the Hebrews in Russia ! If it be said that the Hebrew is justly obnoxious in Russia, and in many nations besides Russia—which may be denied—let me state that in traveling through the Danubian principalities, I met Protestant and Lutheran ministers and teachers who gave such accounts of the bigoted Russian atrocities in Poland and elsewhere as to make the darkest year of the Middle Ages bright in comparison. From one case, learn all. Take the case at Revel, in Russia, recently: There were some ten thousand dollars revenue from a certain ecclesiastical property. It was held by trustees for the benefit of the pastor of the Lutheran church, and the expenses of Protestant worship. The council was compelled by the Russian government to disgorge this money. It was forbidden to give any more help to the Lutheran people. What benefit do the Protestant pastors receive by granting them the empty privilege of their posts with such self-sacrifice. They only contribute, along with other poor people, to the common suffering.

As between the Muscovite and Ottoman, on the vital issues of civil and soul liberty there can be but one verdict among liberal minds. In Russia, it is said that her philosophers are theologians, and her theologians are Cossacks. In Turkey the philosophy of toleration is as just and as venerable as that of her first great Emperor, Othman, and her civil functions are much less hampered and corrupt than are those of the Northern Autocrat.

# CHAPTER L.

BEFORE the autumn of 1885 had ended, the war cloud which hung over the Balkan provinces seemed to vanish under the controlling influence of the Grand Conference. This body was sitting from day to day and week to week. But the excitement in Servia and in Greece grew more intense as it appeared that Bulgaria would likely acquire the accession of East Roumelia. When, therefore, in the middle of November, a fourth meeting of the Conference of the six Powers was held, although secrecy was enjoined, much transpired to show that the broken faith, under the Berlin treaty, had not been altogether healed. The Conference seemed to have had no definite result. There were wide differences among the Powers. These differences had reference to the conditions of restoring the *status quo ante*. Russia, of course, did not want the Balkan barrier between her and a southern progress toward the capital of Turkey to continue. But she disliked Prince Alexander for his infidelity to the Czar, who had been vaunted as the savior of Bulgaria from the Turk, and the leader of the Slav element. She would protect and patronize the Bulgarians and the Roumelians, but not the prince. She had her own latent purposes.

What then was the prospect before the war which sprang up between Servia and Bulgaria?

To speak in the present tense, it is nearly as follows:

Germany, as it seems, takes part with Austria and Russia. What England means, would be better expressed if her elections were over. Italy seems satisfied to be with France. Both lean toward English ideas. These relations may change at any moment, and because of new movements, diplomatic or martial. Meanwhile—as Mr. Fearn, the United States Minister, who has been sojourning at Bucharest and Belgrave, and is *en route* to Athens, informs me—Servia is not quite ready for a conflict with

Bulgaria. Still, she is controlled with difficulty. Prince Milan is not so eager as his people to leap over the border and take the Sandjaks of Widdin and Sophia, which Servia claims for ethnographical and historic reasons.

Greece, like Turkey, is still arming. Both are borrowing money. Bankruptcy impends; but out of these embarrassments come concessions for railroads, so that enterprises may eventually spring out of these evils. At present, I am a pessimist. Matters seem clouded, and the silver lining is hardly visible.

Immediately preceding the declaration of hostilities between Servia and Bulgaria, or, I may say, just before the battle of Slevnitza, which occurred on the 17th of November, and while making calls upon the Ministers of Servia, Roumania and Greece, along with Mr. Fearn—our Minister to these countries—Mr. Grouitch, the Servian Minister informs us that hostilities have begun on Servian soil. An attack is made by the troops of Bulgaria upon those of Servia on the banks of the Timok. We do not hear further news until the middle of November, when this information is reversed. Then telegrams are plentiful from Belgrave, Sophia and Nisch. The Servians declare war against the principality. The Servian forces at once enter Bulgarian territory. They march upon Vratanitza. The king of Servia and the prince of Bulgaria command their respective armies. The scene is on and near the frontier, amid mountains. The passes are defended by soldiers of both nations. These petty conflicts appear small in the light of larger events; but they are the beginning of a conflict by no means small in its consequences.

Diplomacy is staggered by the declaration of war and the hostile movements. I call to congratulate Rustem Pasha, who has just been appointed Minister to England. He is well known in the East as the excellent ex-Governor of the Lebanon. While dining with the Sultan the evening before, as he relates, a telegram comes from the prince of Bulgaria. It asks Ottoman aid.

The king of Servia also telegraphs to the Porte, asking the Sultan's support against Bulgaria. The Sultan does not respond to the first telegram; and what his answer is to the last, has not transpired.

The Balkan question is swelling beyond its banks rapidly. These telegrams show how peculiar is the contest. Two Slav provinces seize each other by the throat, and for what ? Because the one has broken a treaty in order to aggrandize itself; while the other, by keeping faith, as she alleges, does not come by her own ! As the quarrel now stands, the interests of Turkey are not in jeopardy.

The Bourses of Europe show a heavy fall in certain stocks, especially Turkish and Greek. Their fall is " marked by spurts," as these financial vicissitudes demonstrate. The sound of the cannon upon these belligerent frontiers reverberates throughout Europe. Was it not Disraeli, in " Vivian Grey," who said that " there is nothing like a fall in consols to bring the blood of the English people into cool order ? It is your grand state medicine," said he, " your veritable Dr. Sangrado." He limits his remark to the people of England. What effect this fall of securities will have upon the more excitable people of the southeast of Europe, time will develop.

It is not until the first day of winter that authentic news comes of the result of the battle between Servia and Bulgaria. The Bulgarian troops under the prince, after a struggle, capture Pirot, on Servian territory. It is thought that he will enter that town on that day. It is also said that he will demand the Pirot district. Better news soon arrives: an armistice is agreed upon, and peace is possible ! Germany, Austria, Russia and Turkey have coerced the armistice.

The Powers then have their last conference on the Roumelian question. All outside of that question is *dehors*. There may be another meeting of the Conference under another call, but upon other and more comprehensive questions. The Porte has been under constant anxiety. As soon as the smoke of the battle blows away, Lehib Effendi, accompanied by Gadban Effendi, in accordance with a decision of the Conference, starts for Phillipopolis. They are to investigate the condition of affairs in East Roumelia, and to prepare the ground for the arrival of an Imperial commissioner.

The province of East Roumelia is again an autonomous province of its Suzerain. Djevet Pasha is the president of the commission. The Conference has not been, after all, so influential in determining matters. It was rather obstructive, owing to the attitude of England. It was the war which brought events to a climax.

There is nothing during these two months of anxiety which

has disastrously affected American citizens. The trouble we have apprehended for Robert College, where so many of the students are Bulgarian, owing to the prudence of its president, is averted. Nothing happens to jeopard its interests. The Minister of Instruction informs us that he hears that the Bulgarian students are drilling, preparatory to joining the army of the prince. This he subsequently discovers to be an error, and so the Minister of Instruction is content.

Greece is likely to be as much disappointed as Servia, but she is not humiliated by disasters in the field, and will not be, unless she begins hostilities. Turkey is still massing troops and sending munitions and supplies to the Greek border.

One of the incidents of this Roumelian movement is the support given to Turkey by the Christian population of the Ottoman empire. This fact negatives a good deal of the current belief as to the hostility of race and religion within the Turkish empire.

The winter of 1885–86 is not passed without discontent and apprehension. As spring begins to dawn, I note that great anxiety prevails as to what may be done at the end of the armistice. This is fixed for March 1, 1886. Everywhere, as in all these complicated troubles in the Orient, there seems to be a threatening lack of confidence.

In observing the significant political movements connected with Turkey, I do not fail to observe that since the armistice began, and until March 1, 1886, there is also a threatening lack of confidence between the great Powers themselves, between Turkey and the Powers, and between Servia and Bulgaria. Mass-meetings, the press, broils and collision of troops are evidence of the ill-feeling between the small Powers. Servia has been vanquished. Her *amour propre* is keenly touched, as if by caustic. No commissions, military or civil, no lines of demarcation for the armies of occupation at Pirot or Widdin, and no constraint from Russia, Austria, Germany or the other Powers, are of avail to quiet the unrest or dispel the distrust. No decision is reached as to peace; or as to the place where future conferences to settle the vexed questions are to be held. Bulgaria insists on a large war indemnity. About this Servia is unwilling to treat. The relations of suzerain and vassal are quite faint in parts of the Peninsula, and the responsibility as to negotiations is therefore either divided or ignored with impunity. The Porte urges upon the Powers an immediate reassembling of the Conference. The Porte would stop this dubious and expensive condition. The armistice only temporarily chloroforms the sensibilities of the late belligerents. The Balkan peninsula is quiescent under its snows and ills, but it is "on compulsion." The armistice is only a protraction of the crisis. No demobilization of Ottoman or other troops is as yet possible. In fact, mobilization is going on, with a special view to the Greek frontier. A strong line of defensive works has been completed from Catherina to Metzova, in case of Greek invasion into Macedonia or Epirus. Salonica seems now "as in the aforetime," a point of strategetical as well as of commercial importance.

Against these movements and discouragements, there exists a general feeling that war is no cure of wrongs and no safeguard of rights ; and that if once entered upon, it would induce a general conflagration, involving the pre-eminent Powers, and causing endless calamities. After all, there is in this conflict thus opened, and the union of the Bulgarian provinces and people, some compensation for the outlay and anxiety. It is this : that the cause of human nature and of popular liberty receives in East Roumelia and Bulgaria a grand impulse. That impulse is not bounded by the Danube or the Balkans, by the Adriatic or Black seas. Russia may not retard, and cannot control it. By perusing the history of Bulgaria, this is hardly to be expected, as by tradition, race and faith, Bulgaria is akin to the Slav and to Russia.

Owing to the munificence of Mr. Robert, a New York merchant, an educational edifice arises above the towers of Roumeli-Hissar, on the Bosporus. As an orator said on its dedication, "It rises upon higher ground than these Towers, dominating them spiritually and eternally." It becomes the home of scholarship, under American auspices and energy. More than one-half of its scholars have been and are Bulgarians. As their education progresses, the graces of cultivation and of democratic-republican sympathy ennoble their patriotic devotion ; so that many of the officials of Bulgaria, by reason of superior qualifications, were and are of and from this American institution. The East Roumelian revolution—though an infraction of the Berlin treaty, it must be confessed—is the leaven which American teaching has infused into the lump of Bulgarian liberty.

Looking at the delays in diplomacy since the 18th of September, 1885, when the insurrection began, and the failure to restore the *status quo ante*, and considering the other dynastic, national, provincial, commercial and race complications since that time, it seems impossible that the former condition of things should be reinstated.

It is not necessary, for the purposes of this volume—intended as a Diversion from diplomatic and other sedate employment—that I should rehearse the events which followed the annexation of East Roumelia to Bulgaria, under Prince Alexander. What harassments he encountered, and especially from Russia, after his peace with Servia ; what obstacles, notwithstanding the favor of the Sobranjé or Congress, and the good-will of the people—these are graphically summed up in the account of his seizure, within his own palace at Sophia, by Russian emissaries, and his deportation over the border, with every mark of indignity. In a letter to his sister, the Countess Erbach, written before his last tour through East Roumelia, he pictures his situation as that of a stag hunted on all sides.

" The Bulgarians," he says, " have little heart, and to satisfy them seems impossible. To be threatened again, after all I have done, with being driven away, is hard and unmerited. Everything is attributed to foreign intrigues, but the Bulgarians are old enough to distinguish between true and false friends. Ninety-nine per cent. of the Bulgarians are on my side ; the remaining 1 per cent. may, however, succeed, with the help of Russia, in getting rid of me. Until the revision of the Organic Statute—that is, till autumn—my throne will be like a dynamite bomb. In any case, I shall fall fighting ; but should the Bulgarians prefer foreign rule to an honest prince, that will be their affair."

What estimate the present or the future may place upon the services of Prince Alexander on behalf of Bulgaria, it is difficult to determine. There is, as will be seen, a contrariety of opinion about his qualities as a man and qualifications as a ruler. In fact, even his skill in war, which was manifested, as we all thought, with singular tact and courage, is somewhat questioned. Already his experiences in Bulgaria are coming from the press, with various comment. The best impression is, that he was a better soldier than civilian. His worst fault is that he tried, but failed to placate the Czar. This will not be treasured against him by any liberal and thoughtful mind. Along with the portrait, which graphically shows an honest and handsome face, I present a pen-picture of the prince from Dr. Roy's volume, just published at Paris. This description was written at the moment of the battle of Slivnitza. I translate it thus :

" He is thirty years of age; a man of high stature, strongly defined and somewhat stout. The head is regular in shape, the nose large and straight. His brown beard is cut *à la* Henry IV., while his hair is of a darker shade. His eyes are of medium size, brown and languishing. They reveal no special vivacity. His speech is engaging, and he easily gains the sympathy of his interlocutor. He impresses one favorably by the manliness of his countenance and the amiability of his presence.

" But the prince is of a versatile humor. He has not the frankness nor the precision of a soldier. He is a diplomat who never entangles himself, and if by chance he has been carried away or excited about anything, he preserves a loop-hole of escape. His politics are uncertain, variable and full of reservations.

" It appears, from the most accurate information, that if he gained the battle of Slivnitza, it is because he had—a good horse. Believing that all was lost, he had quitted his army in order to return to Sophia, and it was during this absence that the Bulgarian troops gained the victory !"

The court chaplain, Mr. Koch, has published his reminiscences of the reign of the prince. He begins by berating the supporters of the prince. Herr Koch does not even allude to the military success of the prince at Slivnitza; nor does he exalt the ex-prince unduly.

It seems, from these chronicles, that the prince was advised of the advent of the revolution in East Roumelia. He endeavored to dissuade the committees who called upon him from embarking in the revolt. He was surprised at his farm near Varna by the event. Karaveloff, his Minister, was not to be found when the affair happened. All of which goes to show how easily the Turk could have suppressed the rising.

The burden of this book of the chaplain is the attachment and fidelity of the prince to Russia, which, if true, has a tendency among true Bulgarians, to destroy the very niche in which this hero poses so statuesquely. He had a difficult rôle to play, between the devil of a Czar and the deep sea of diplomacy.

What renders the character of the prince still more ambiguous is his own declaration, as revealed by this intimate friend, that Prince Milan's revengeful policy was justifiable—"not undeserved by Bulgaria."

Doubtless he had the good-will and enthusiasm of his troops, and a fair appreciation of the absurd attitude of these two little Powers clutching at each other, when under the shadow of the great throne of the Czar.

How the prince was abducted by the Russians—and, owing to the perfidy of his own troops, successfully abducted—it is well to quote Prince Alexander's own vivid words :

"On August 21 I had been working far into the night, and had scarcely fallen asleep when I was awakened by a noise that reached me from my passage before my bedroom. It might have been 1:30. The next moment Dimitri, my Bulgarian servant, burst into the room, trembling and quaking in every limb. He cried, 'You are betrayed; they mean to murder you. Fly before it is too late!' I sprang out of bed and seized my revolver. Then I heard the military word of command, and breathed more easily. I said to Dimitri, 'I am saved; the military is there.' But he, still trembling, ejaculated, 'No, fly; it is the soldiers, who mean to kill you.' Then I rushed, in my shirt, to the door leading into the garden, but as I opened it I was met by firing. Immediately after, I heard shots on all sides. I went from here through the dark corridor toward the servants' wing, and up the first story into the winter garden, to obtain a bird's-eye view, and see if it were still possible to escape. Up there it was so dark that I could not see my hand before my eyes, but from the line of fire of the soldiers shooting below, I found that the whole palace was surrounded, and it was useless to think of escape. The shower of bullets permitted no doubt as to the serious nature of the situation."

That he persisted in refusing to return to the throne from which he was forcibly ousted, and which he had been urgently invited to resume, is not surprising. As a consequence of this gap in the government, and the failure to find a prince, under and according to the Berlin treaty, the regency began to accomplish what they could to allay excitement and preserve order. This they have done admirably.

The facts in reference to the revolt and annexation have, as revealed in the latest and best lights, from German, Austrian, Russian and Turkish sources, are these :

*First :* Prince Alexander was not present at Sophia, but on his farm near Varna, on the 18th of September, when the rising took place, and when he was advised by Karaveloff of the fact.

*Second :* He was not in favor of the rising. He gave it no encouragement. It was not his work. It was a surprise to him. He acquiesced in it ; and why ?

*Third :* Because he was caught in a dilemma. He had to choose between accepting the new situation, or leave Bulgaria under its indignation.

*Fourth :* This dilemma was prepared as a trap for him by Russian emissaries. The Czar disliked him, and thought to force his exit by presenting him the alternative of favoring the union with East Roumelia, and thus allow Russian influences below the Balkans, or of abdicating. He disappointed Russia by remaining, and becoming the popular and military idol.

*Fifth :* Russia—being disappointed—made a merit of vindicating the Berlin treaty, which the revolution that she had fostered had flagrantly repudiated.

*Sixth :* By these complications and indignities, Russia—being herself entrapped—was compelled to resort to all the devices, intrigues and protests of her diplomacy, by which, covertly and openly, she has foiled Prince Alexander, harassed the regency, rejected the Sobranjé and its election of Prince Ferdinand, and menaced his tenure of office, and the peace and order of the united provinces.

During the existence of the recent struggle, there has been no bloodshed laid at the door of Turkey. The drain on her exchequer has been met. There has been no interruption of commerce. Scarcely can we record one act leading to a change in boundary or rule; and no convulsion either on account of religion or politics. Turkey sits serenely, yet not without observation, upon the old ways of international intercourse and national conquest—as yet under the control of no other Power, while discreetly and diplomatically deferring to all. She preserves her independence, and is regarded as a part of that Concert whose dread responsibilities are not unknown even in the interior of Asia, and in the wilds of Africa, as well as in Western Europe.

# CHAPTER LI.

RESIGNATION AS MINISTER—RETURN HOME—PRINCE FERDINAND
—FRESH EVENTS—HOROSCOPE OF THE EAST—CONCLUSION.

DURING the summer of 1887 the writer enjoyed a recreative
sojourn upon one of the Princes Isles. At Prinkipo he was not
distant from the sphere of active diplomacy, which had no sur-
cease during the summer and fall. Circumstances, partly domestic
and partly political, led him to resign his office as Minister, and
to return home to resume his former position as a Member of
Congress from the city of New York. Why he made this change,
it may not be entirely uninteresting to state. It was not because of
any dissatisfaction with the service, nor from any derogative
treatment by the officers of the Porte or the Sultan, nor because
of any disenchantment of the Orient, as this volume, and another
upon the "Pleasures of Prinkipo," enthusiastically demonstrate.
The heart has no reason; or, rather, it has reasons of its own.
Call it home-sickness, or patriotism, or an inclination after old
and fixed parliamentary habits, or the ineradicable desire to be
near one's own—and you have the best explanation that can be
made for my premeditated and unprecipitate return. I had done
all that a Minister of my ability could do, to place the Legation
and the American interests in excellent condition. The treaties
pending during the service of my predecessors—Messrs. Boker,
McVeigh, Longstreet, Maynard and Wallace—I had the honor to
consummate with the approbation of all these Ministers, except
that of Mr. Maynard, who had died; and under the instructions
and, as I supposed, to the satisfaction of the President and the
Department of State. What more was there for me to do in
Turkey, unless I gave up the *animus revertendi* altogether? What
remained could easily be accomplished by others of tact, probity and vigilance.

With the consent of the President, kindly accorded, I returned
to America in the fall of 1887, and re-entered upon my old career

PRINCE ALEXANDER OF BATTENBERG.    PRINCE FERDINAND OF COBURG.
CZAR OF RUSSIA.

as a Member of the Forty-Ninth Congress, from which I had resigned to go abroad; and as the Member-elect of the Fiftieth Congress, to which I had been returned at the same election.

These duties, distant from the scenes and Diversions which I have endeavored herein to portray, did not withdraw nor blind my mind from the observation of the exciting events of the Orient, and the vital problems still agitating the Powers and vehemently pressing for solution. The regency in Bulgaria held its own with remarkable and patriotic tenacity. The Russian efforts to create trouble and rebellion in Bulgaria, through the arrogant intervention of General Kaulbars; the complete abdication of Prince Alexander; the struggles of the province and of the Powers to place an eligible prince on the throne—these are fresh incidents of current history. The tremulousness of the Continental equilibrium occasioned by the jarring interests of England, Austria and Russia, and the designs of the other "signatories," have, contrary to expectation, left Bulgaria in a *quasi* unity with her annexed neighbor, which Turkey did not seek to break, and free from the open and active attacks, either by diplomacy or arms, of any policy of compulsion from other potential quarters.

Various events have contributed to keep the peace and preserve the autonomy of the united provinces. Servia has not forgotten the lesson which Slivnitza and the bayonet taught. Her Prince Milan and his beautiful Queen Nathalie have been almost divorced, as well by domestic infelicity as by the partiality of the former for Austria, and the latter for Russia. Servia therefore still remains neutralized, if not Austrianized.

Greece, where the flame of Hellenic pride swept the classic blue sky with lurid glare, has, under the new ministry of Tricoupis, given her sedate and solid energies to the relief of her exchequer and her taxed people, and to the arts of good neighborhood and prosperity. Her king, who is at once affable and sage, has not been remiss in cultivating these amicable relations, which betoken a wise successor of the historic names of her splendid history.

Albania, Epirus and Macedonia have been learning how much better it is to be reliant on their own resources and rule, rather than by reaching out after the illusory nebulæ of ethnographical conditions, which cultivate no olives and grain, pay off no mortgages, and support no families.

England has endeavored, with one foot on Egypt and the

other on India, to fix by treaty the right, in case she evacuates the Nile, to re-occupy it when there shall occur certain emergencies affecting the canalization of the Isthmus of Suez, and the material prosperity and political order of Egypt. Failing to make such conditions with Turkey, she makes a neutralization convention with France; but she continues to occupy Egypt. She will so continue, so long as Russia threatens to compete with her in the struggle for Asiatic dominion.

Russia constructs her trans-Caspian railways upon strategetic lines, to concentrate, in some near future, her military strength upon Herat, or by water to transport her armies and supplies to those mountainous frontiers which open their sublime gorges through Hindu-Kush into the heart of India. Water has been drawn from the desert around Merv, and fuel from the oil wells of Baku; pipes, naphtha, canals and the very vegetation of the far-off and far-famed hive of Central Asia, have been harnessed into locomotive forces to finish her 1,000 miles of railroad wherewith to bind the Caspian with the Oxus, and re-establish the ancient Capital of Tamerlane—" Silken Samarcand." Russia is already thundering at the outer gates of the British empire. Her inimitable thunder is not heard so much by the Western Powers as by the Ameers and other rulers of Asia; but England knows what it means, and may well tremble for her supremacy in the East.

This remote contest has never obliterated from Russia the ambitious visions of Peter the Great, Catharine and Nicholas. These visions can only find full realization by making Old Byzantium the ecclesiastical and secular capital of her continental and imperial magnificence. As Constantine conquered by the sign of the Cross in the sky, so Russia expects dominion by the obscuration of the Crescent of her ancient Ottoman enemy.

This programme finds many obstacles to its accomplishment. The alliance between Germany, Austria and Russia no longer exists, so as to aid in the performance of this rôle. Austria— whether allowed by Germany or not—now begins to assert herself as against Russian schemes. Her sagacious emperor and his able counselors consult the material interests of his diverse peoples. They especially regard the trade and commerce of those who live along the Danube and the Adriatic, and who are reaching out for markets and enterprises, as well by her Lloyds and other steamers as by the system of railroads projected in the Balkan peninsula, and whose termini are at Varna and Salonica. The traditional mission of the Austro-Hungarian people lies in these directions of potential commerce and dynastic rule.

The Berlin treaty allowed Austria to occupy Herzegovina and Bosnia. Servia is almost ripe for annexation to her double crown without protest from the Kaiser or his Chancellor. Germany, to-day, holds the balance, or, rather, she places the jeweled and victorious sabre in the scales to determine these grave eventualities.

"Why, then," you ask "did she not protect Prince Alexander on his throne?" Perhaps, because he was not entirely suited to the situation; or because his military feather was rather too pretentious, and the enmity of the Czar too pronounced and bitter toward this prince, for the continuance of the harmony at that time prevalent between Germany and Russia.

After a long hiatus—after scouring the world from the Rhine to the Caucasus—Bulgaria, in defiance of the Berlin treaty, selects a prince. It is Prince Ferdinand. Whence comes this prince? Is he of faëry-land? What supernal spirit supplies the audacity thus to accept a battered crown in derogation and defiance of the Great Bear?

If it comes to a prodigious pedigree and royal blood, this prince combines enough to double the size of the Gotha Almanach. His genealogical ramification reaches deep into the nadir and mounts high into the zenith. It is English, German, Portuguese, French, Belgian, Danish, Brazilian and Austrian. Since he has grown in our esteem by his prudence and pluck, may I be allowed to place his portrait in this volume between the antagonistic Alexanders—the ex-Prince of Bulgaria and the Emperor of Russia? Besides, since he is to play such an eminent part—until it please the Powers to issue a prescript otherwise—let us ponder, in behalf of the harassed and infant principality, the consanguinity which Ferdinand bears to all the royalties.

Prince Ferdinand, born in 1861, is the son of the late Prince Augustus of Coburg-Kohary, and the grandson of Prince Ferdinand, uncle of the reigning Duke of Saxe-Coburg-Gotha, Ernest II. His grandfather's brother, Leopold, ascended the throne of Belgium in 1831, and was succeeded on it in 1865 by his son Leopold II., the reigning king. Ernest II.'s brother, Albert, married Queen Victoria in 1840, and in 1841 became father of the Prince of Wales, the heir apparent to the throne of Great Britain. Prince Augustus's brother, Ferdinand, married in 1836 Maria da Gloria, Queen of Portugal, daughter of the Emperor of Brazil, Pedro I., and in 1837 became father of the late King of Portugal, Pedro V., and in 1838 of the present King, Dom Luis. Prince Ferdinand's mother, Princess Clementina, is the daughter of Louis Philippe, king of the French in 1830–48, and the aunt of the Comte de Paris, who now unites in his person the pretensions to the throne of France of both the elder and younger (or Orleans) branch of the House of Bourbon. Clementina's sister, Louise of Orleans, was the consort of Leopold I. of Belgium. Clementina's brother, the Duc de Montpensier, is the husband of the Infanta Louisa, sister of the ex-Queen Isabella II. of Spain, and aunt of the late King Alfonso XII., father of the present infant King Alfonso XIII. Clementina's nephew, Gaston of Orleans, Comte d'Eu, son of her brother, the Duc de Nemours, married in 1864 Isabella, daughter of Pedro II. of Brazil, and, as his only living child, heiress apparent to the throne. Another son of the Duc de Nemours, the Duc d'Alençon, married in 1868 the Bavarian Princess Sophia, sister of the Empress of Austria. The Comte de Paris's daughter, Amélie, was in 1886 married to the Duke of Braganza, Crown-Prince of Portugal. Princess Marie, daughter of Duc de Chartres, brother of the Comte de Paris, was married in 1885 to Prince Waldemar, son of the King of Denmark, brother of the King of Greece, and brother-in-law of the Czar of Russia and of the Prince of Wales. Of Prince Ferdinand's two brothers, one married a daughter of Leopold II. of Belgium, and the other a daughter, now deceased, of Pedro II. of Brazil. Of his two sisters, one was married to Archduke Joseph, a second-cousin of the Emperor of Austria, and the other to Duke Maximilian, brother of the Empress of Austria.

Notwithstanding all this confusing array of the bluest-blooded royalty, Ferdinand does not please Russia *Non constat,* but that he may please Germany, England and Italy; and certainly Austria. If not avowedly, yet covertly, Austria props his romantic though doubtful establishment. Bulgaria seems content.

Why not? Already, out of his own full purse the Prince is generously aiding in the completion of the railways of Bulgaria, to which that government is pledged. The election in October, 1887, shows only twenty-seven Russophiles to 200 patriotic Bulgars elected to the Sobranjé; and as Bulgaria is pleased with the prince, and does not yet seek to be an independent republic, whose business is it to interfere?

France seeks alliance with Russia, and has tendered to the Porte guaranties against further English encroachments and permanency in Egypt. In this, the republic of M. Grévy has the sympathy of the emperor Alexander. Russia returns the cordiality of France; and Germany, ever alert, makes a threatening note of the strange *entente cordiale* between Cossack and republican. Russia, therefore, receives a counterblast in Berlin on the Böerse, and in Bulgaria from Bismarck. Turkey is thereby encouraged, as she always is, by the jealousies and collisions of the great Powers; and resolves to stand loyally by the Berlin treaty. To stand? Yes; but to make a move? No. Without a move, what avails the impossible *coup de théâtre* called "the restoration of the *status quo ante*"?

These events look to the retention of Prince Ferdinand. The purchase of 200,000 repeating rifles by the plucky little Power gives much meaning to the situation. Prince Alexander abdicated because the Czar was inimical to him personally, if not otherwise. Prince Ferdinand holds on, despite the frowns of Russia and the hostility of France.

With her other and vast schemes, how can Russia make war upon Bulgaria or upon Ferdinand? If she does, the war will not be of that insidious insolence and domestic limitation which Kaulbars attempted to provoke. Will Abdul Hamid, with his views of a *juste milieu*, veto the election of this prince to gratify the old enemy of Turkey? Will Russia seek compensation for its failure on the Balkans by taking the remnant of Armenia from the Sultan? Dare Russia, in the face of her bankrupt treasury and her dynamitic Nihilists, strike down the little principality which is struggling to be autonomous and free?

However these questions may be answered—which one of the six Powers is to be aggrandized or humiliated by the result, whenever any change takes place—Turkey is to be the victim. She is dressed with ribbons and flowers for the sacrifice. The Balkans are the pawns on the board to be moved for the gratification of dynastic ambition. Why should this be so? Is there disorder in Bulgaria or East Roumelia? No! Is there a lack of firmness at the palace of Yildiz or at the Porte? If so, it is not

shown.   Is Turkey to be partitioned and Bulgaria to be Russian-
ized, in our day and generation, without a struggle ?   Are there
no factors to countervail these schemes and safeguard the people
of the smaller states ?   Yes : the united Balkan states, Austro-
Hungary, and the Sultan as the Caliph of Mahometanism—these
three elements of strength, along with the regenerated humanities and liberties of our age, can master the situation without the
active alliance of England, Italy and Germany.

The step taken by Prince Ferdinand must have been coun-
tenanced by Austria.   It seem to have received the acquiescent
regard of Germany.   No armed intervention by Russia will be
brooked.   The great danger is from that Machiavelism in which
the Muscovite excels, and as to the practices of which there is,
on her part, no fluttering impatience or cessation.

Last month—October, 1387--Russia prepared to foment disturbances in Bulgaria by renewing the Kaulbars tactics.   She
sought Turkish assistance in favor of her General Ernoth as a
commissioner to regulate the recent elections.   The Porte fought
shy of the device.   It failed.   By its failure Ferdinand becomes
more securely seated upon his throne.   He is no longer called
the "reckless, foolish Ferdinand."   He seems to-day to be surrounded by a devoted nation, which, if not great in numbers and
area, is courageous in action, and may in the outcome succeed in its
aspirations for self-government, despite the wiles of diplomacy
and the forces of autocracy.

The present position of the matter at Constantinople was
considered less than a month ago, at a special cabinet council.
Its *mazbata* was certified to the Imperial Chancellery in the form
of a reply to Germany.   Its tenor was that—Russia excepted—
none of the Powers had formulated a solution of the Bulgarian
imbroglio, and that the Russian proposition of intervention along
with Turkey, was not approved by the Porte. It was only submitted
to Germany with a view to the intervention of the latter, *à titre
facultatif*.   Germany was sought by the Porte as the medium to
reach all the Powers for a solution ; the Porte still adhering to
its idea maintained since September, 1885, that the Berlin treaty
should be maintained in its integrity.   The Porte, however,
promises adhesion to the decision of the Powers.   This means
delay, discussion and disagreement.   Meanwhile Russia is foiled,
and Ferdinand becomes every day more and more "a fixed fact."

What the Powers may do, by sheer force and by selfish negotiations, when they next meet in conference, is not clear. All prophecies may fail. The ulterior motive of Russia to control or capture Constantinople, with its prosperous commerce and dominating position, surely cannot receive encouragement. It is an impossibility. Turkey has shown extraordinary force of arms and activity of movement, sufficient self-confidence and opposition to self-effacement, to make her position respected, and, so far, sufficient for the maintenance of the peace.

What will be the finality of these complications with such far-reaching results, is indicated by the events every day transpiring. Whether the pivot be in Persia, Armenia, Egypt, Bulgaria, Macedonia, Afghanistan or India, the most momentous crisis known since the fall of Constantinople in A. D. 1453, or certainly since the fall of Sebastopol, impends imminently over the great ruling Powers and peoples of three continents.

What may be the horoscope of the Orient, cannot be read in its serene stars or by its astrological professors. Indeed, it puzzles the best rational prescience of the Occident—quickened by the sense of self-interest and the sensibility of ambition. But the world has progressed too far on lines of light and liberty, to resign itself to the control of a Power like that of Russia—a Power loaded at home with debt and goaded by despair, and everywhere, at home and abroad, challenged by protests against its conduct and continuance.

On the contrary, the Padishah of the Ottoman state—the Pontiff of the Mahometan faith—is emerging from the eclipse of the last few decades. By energizing and elevating his people; by the revival of education and religion; by advancing his subjects in the arts of a new civilization—he prepares the very elements that are tempestuously raging around his throne and capital, to become the allies of his personal strength for the durability of his rule. In the words of his father, Abdul Medjid, he would "make the political, civil and religious conditions so equal between Mussulman and Christians of every denomination throughout the empire, that there no longer would be, under the laws of the Sultan, but one and the same people under different races and religions. In a word, to nationalize all the fragments of nations that cover the soil of Turkey by so much impartiality, amenity, equality and toleration, that each of these populations should find its honor, its conscience, its security, interested in concurring toward the maintenance of the empire in a species of monarchical confederation under the auspices of the Sultan."

In endeavoring to realize this ideal of his father, the present Padishah excites the admiration and subserves the interests of mankind. His people will shake off the incubus of "destiny." As Lamartine once said to Abdul Medjid, when he was the guest of that Sultan at the beautiful kiosk of Fhlamour:

"The fatalism of your race and religion will become the fatalism of heroes—which determines its own destiny."

**THE END.**